Cases on Metaverse and Consumer Experiences

Maria Antónia Gonçalves Rodrigues
CEOS.PP, ISCAP, Polytechnic of Porto, Portugal

Maria Amélia Carvalho
CEOS.PP, ISCAP, Polytechnic of Porto, Portugal

Joaquim Fernando Monteiro Pratas
CEOS.PP, ISCAP, Polytechnic of Porto, Portugal

IGI Global
Scientific Publishing
Publishing Tomorrow's Research Today

Published in the United States of America by
IGI Global Scientific Publishing
701 East Chocolate Avenue
Hershey, PA, 17033, USA
Tel: 717-533-8845
Fax: 717-533-8661
Website: https://www.igi-global.com E-mail: cust@igi-global.com

Library of Congress Cataloging-in-Publication Data

Names: Rodrigues, Maria Antonia, 1977- editor. | Carvalho, Maria Amélia Machado, 1989- editor. | Pratas, Joaquim Monteiro, 1980- editor.
Title: Cases on Metaverse and consumer experiences / edited by: Maria Rodrigues, Maria Amélia Machado Carvalho, Joaquim Pratas.
Description: Hershey, PA : IGI Global Scientific Publishing, [2025] | Includes bibliographical references and index. | Summary: "This book aims to present a set of real cases, methodologically based on academic perspectives, that exemplify the use of the Metaverse in companies' marketing, in the development of new businesses, or the creation of new consumer experiences"-- Provided by publisher.
Identifiers: LCCN 2024054538 (print) | LCCN 2024054539 (ebook) | ISBN 9798369372456 (hardcover) | ISBN 9798369372463 (paperback) | ISBN 9798369372470 (ebook)
Subjects: LCSH: Internet marketing--Case studies. | Consumer behavior--Case studies. | Metaverse--Case studies.
Classification: LCC HF5415.1265 .C379 2025 (print) | LCC HF5415.1265 (ebook) | DDC 658.8/72--dc23/eng/20250212
LC record available at https://lccn.loc.gov/2024054538
LC ebook record available at https://lccn.loc.gov/2024054539

British Cataloguing in Publication Data
A Cataloguing in Publication record for this book is available from the British Library.

Table of Contents

Detailed Table of Contents

This chapter explores the growing impact of the metaverse on customer experiences in today's digital landscape. The metaverse is defined as a persistent, immersive, virtual environment that blends physical and digital realities through the use of technologies like virtual reality (VR), augmented reality (AR), artificial intelligence (AI), and blockchain. It highlights the importance of these technologies in transforming various sectors, including retail, education, entertainment, and professional training. The metaverse enables rich, interactive experiences that enhance user engagement by providing personalized, customizable, real-time interactions within digital spaces. Furthermore, the economic potential of the metaverse is discussed, emphasizing opportunities such as virtual real estate and NFTs, which create new avenues for businesses to monetize digital assets. The chapter also addresses the role of AI and machine learning in providing adaptive and intelligent user experiences, while blockchain ensures secure ownership and transactions of digital goods.

This chapter examines Accenture's implementation of the Nth Floor, a pioneering enterprise metaverse platform that has transformed corporate training and onboarding processes. Through detailed analysis of quantitative and qualitative outcomes, the chapter explores how Accenture successfully deployed virtual reality technology across its global workforce of 700,000 employees, resulting in the onboarding of 150,000 new hires and deployment of 60,000 VR headsets. The study investigates the strategic planning, technical architecture, and change management approaches that contributed to achieving a 33% improvement in learning retention and a 4.7/5 employee satisfaction rating. The chapter provides comprehensive insights into implementation challenges, success factors, and best practices for organizations considering similar digital transformation initiatives. Additionally, the research examines the platform's impact on global collaboration, organizational culture, and operational efficiency, while identifying future implications and research directions for enterprise metaverse adoption.

The chapter explores the rise of virtual influencers within the Metaverse and their significant impact on marketing's future. The Metaverse, blending augmented and virtual reality with the real world, is a new frontier for brands to engage the digital generation innovatively. Virtual influencers, created through CGI with scripted personalities, have gained immense popularity and influence. The research examines the concept, origins, and psychological factors driving these digital avatars' impact on consumers. It looks at how they reshape marketing strategies through sponsored content, product placements, and brand collaborations, driving consumer engagement and purchase behaviour. The study also highlights their impact on traditional advertising and potential for hyper-personalized experiences using data analytics and AI. Finally, it addresses ethical considerations, including transparency, authenticity, potential exploitation of vulnerable consumers, and the need for responsible practices in this emerging field.

E-business is changing quickly, pushed by artificial intelligence (AI) and machine learning (ML), enabling new efficiencies and growth. With this evolution, however, comes lingering ethical and legal vulnerabilities specifically at the level of consumer privacy and security. As personalised experiences are developed, AI and ML algorithms must focus on breaking down silos, which will inadvertently expose greater amounts of sensitive information that is susceptible to cyberattacks or pathway into a data breach or fraud. This chapter comprehensively explores the concerns of consumer privacy-security in era of digital disruption with AI and ML in the ethical and legal implications of e-business transformation.

Preface

With the evolution of the internet and the expansion of the digital world, the metaverse has emerged. The term "metaverse" combines "meta" (implying transcendence) and "universe," describing a hypothetical synthetic environment linked to the physical world (Lee et al., 2022). The metaverse can also be defined as a new plane of existence (Knox, 2022), where the physical and virtual worlds blend (Riva & Wiederhold, 2022). The technology behind the metaverse has evolved significantly with the use of virtual reality (VR), augmented reality (AR), extended reality (XR), holograms, headsets, and haptic gloves, enabling immersive experiences with high levels of interaction (Dwivedi, 2022). Although the term is now well-established and widely recognized, the concept was first introduced in the novel Snow Crash by Neal Stephenson, published in 1992. In the novel, Stephenson defines the metaverse as a virtual environment of VR and AR parallel to the physical world, in which users interact through avatars (Joshua, 2017; Lee et al., 2021).

While the initial applications of the metaverse were primarily in computer games featuring virtual worlds where gaming companies competed to provide unique experiences, the recognition of the metaverse as the future of the internet has drawn interest from various sectors (Narin, 2021). The metaverse presents enormous potential for companies to reinvent or adapt their business models and engage with consumers. From education to healthcare, from leisure to tourism, hospitality, and retail, the metaverse is being actively studied and holds significant potential for further development (see, for example, Chanda et al., 2024; Dhingra & Abhishek, 2024; Donvito et al., 2024; Kılıçarslan et al., 2024; Nguyen & Voznak, 2024; Pratas, 2023; Wu et al., 2024). The metaverse market is projected to reach a value of US$74.4 billion in 2024 and US$507.8 billion by 2030 (Statista, 2024). By 2030, the number of users in the metaverse market is expected to reach 2.63 billion (Statista, 2023).

In the field of marketing, the metaverse offers managers numerous opportunities related to new business models, market research, the creation of novel experiences, fresh value propositions, innovative communication strategies, and new ways to interact with consumers. Additionally, it poses challenges in understanding consumer behavior (Diogo & Veiga, 2022; Yadav et al., 2024). Once a strategy is defined, it is equally crucial to measure the return on investment (ROI) in the metaverse.

As a cutting-edge topic, several challenges remain in producing knowledge and gaining a deeper understanding of the metaverse in its many dimensions, particularly in marketing and consumer behavior (Crespo-Pereira, 2023; Rosário et al., 2023). As Petit et al. (2022) note, "Younger generations, more interested in experiences and virtual possessions than physical ones, are driving the adoption of the metaverse. The emergence of the metaverse will transform consumer behavior and policy-making."

The book, *Cases on Metaverse and Consumer Experiences*, aims to present a collection of real-world cases, methodologically grounded in academic perspectives, that illustrate the use of the metaverse in companies' marketing strategies, the development of new businesses, and the creation of new consumer experiences. This publication is ideal for managers, students, and researchers interested in the metaverse. The content of this book will enable readers to understand and discuss real cases of metaverse applications in marketing, business model development, and consumer experience design.

ORGANIZATION OF THE BOOK

This book is organized into 12 chapters, each providing an in-depth exploration of a different aspect of the metaverse. Below is a brief description of each chapter:

Chapter 1 was written by Joana Neves from the University of Porto and CEOS PP, Coimbra, Portugal, and is titled "The Impact of the Metaverse on the Gaming Industry: A Case Study of Epic Games". The gaming industry has been a pioneer in metaverse adoption. This chapter examines how Epic Games, through Fortnite and the Unreal Engine, has expanded its business model by embracing virtual economies, user-generated content, and branded entertainment experiences. Beyond gaming, it also explores the Unreal Engine's broader applications in industries such as healthcare, architecture, and film.

Chapter 2, titled "The Metaverse in Education: A Case Study", was written by Ana Catarina Monteiro, from ISCAP, Polytechnic of Porto and Maria Antónia Rodrigues, from CEOS.PP, ISCAP, Polytechnic of Porto, both from Portugal. The education sector is adopting the metaverse to develop three-dimensional learning environments. This chapter presents a case study on how educational institutions are using metaverse technologies to create more engaging and inclusive learning experiences. It also highlights key strategic and technological factors necessary for successful implementation.

Chapter 3 was written by Manpreet K Riyat, Amit Kakkar and Ruchi Kakkar, from Lovely Professional University, India and is titled "The Metaverse: Redefining Learning Spaces and Educational Experiences". Building on the previous chapter's topic, this chapter explores virtual classrooms, digital twins, and immersive learning experiences. It discusses how educators, researchers, and policymakers are shaping the future of metaverse-based education, along with the challenges of making these experiences inclusive and effective.

Chapter 4, titled "Wine Tourism Meets the Metaverse: A Case Study", was written by Belém Barbosa from the University of Porto, Portugal, Shalini Singh from the Rovira i Virgili University, Spain, Tuğçe Yetik, from the Sabanci University, Turkey and Camila Carvalho from the University of Porto, Portugal. Tourism is beginning to integrate metaverse technologies to enhance customer experiences. This chapter focuses on wine tourism, using the Portuguese winery Sandeman as a case study. It explores how digital platforms can enrich tourist experiences by blending physical and virtual elements.

Velmurugan R. and Sudarvel J., from the Karpagam Academy of Higher Education, Coimbatore, India, Jothi K. from the KPR College of Arts Science and Research, India and Ravi Thirumalaisamy from the Modern College of Business and Science, Oman, wrote Chapter 5, "Use of Metaverse in Tourism and Hospitality Services". The way people travel is being redefined by the metaverse. This chapter explores the use of virtual reality (VR) and augmented reality (AR) for virtual tours of global landmarks, personalized hotel previews, and immersive digital events. While these technologies offer exciting new possibilities, the chapter also discusses challenges such as data security and digital accessibility.

Chapter 6, "Analysis of the Impact of Metaverse on the Retailer's Brand Perceptions: The Example of Nike with Nikeland", was written by Joaquim Monteiro Pratas from the Instituto Superior de Contabilidade e Administração, Instituto Politécnico do Porto, Portugal, Gabriel Dias Moreira, João Guilherme Garcez, Ivan Simões, Leonardo Roberto Neves Andrade and João Miguel Da Silva Martins, all from the University of Maia, Portugal. The metaverse is transforming brand perception and consumer engagement. This chapter analyzes Nike's Nikeland, a virtual store experience, and its impact on brand loyalty, consumer expectations, and product perception. The findings highlight how companies can leverage digital spaces to strengthen their brand image.

Muhammad Usman Tariq, from the Abu Dhabi University, United Arab Emirates and University College Cork, Ireland, wrote Chapter 7, "Revolutionizing Retail-Enhancing Customer Experiences With the Metaverse". Beyond Nike, many retailers are embracing the metaverse to create interactive shopping experiences. This chapter explores virtual stores, personalized environments, and evolving consumer behaviors in digital commerce. It also examines ROI considerations, ethical concerns, and privacy challenges in metaverse-driven retail.

Chapter 8, titled "Metaverse Healthcare: Advancing Patient Care Through Digital Realms" was written by Rajaprabakaran Rajendran and Yavana Rani S, both from CMS Business School, Jain (Deemed-to-be University), Bengaluru, India and Senthilnathan Dhanasekaran, from JP Morgan, Unites States of America. The intersection of the metaverse and healthcare opens up new possibilities for telemedicine, medical training, and professional collaboration. This chapter examines how emerging technologies—such as AI, blockchain, and the Internet of Medical Devices (IoMT)—are being integrated to improve patient outcomes and accessibility to care.

Sekarini S., and Selvabaskar S., both from SASTRA University, India, wrote Chapter 9, "Metaverse Mastery: Elevating Consumer Experience in the Digital Era". The metaverse is impacting industries beyond gaming and retail. This chapter explores its economic potential, discussing virtual real estate, NFTs, and new revenue streams. It also covers the role of AI and blockchain in enhancing user experience and ensuring secure transactions.

Chapter 10 was written by Sahil Kohli, from Chandigarh University, India, and is titled "Corporate Metaverse Adoption: A Case Study of Accenture's Nth Floor Virtual Onboarding and Training Platform". Global corporations are using the metaverse to enhance employee onboarding and training. This chapter presents the case of Accenture's Nth Floor, a corporate metaverse platform that has significantly improved knowledge retention and employee satisfaction. The analysis details the strategic planning, technological challenges, and lessons learned from its implementation.

Chapter 11, titled "Metaverse Marketing: Unleashing the Potential of Virtual Influencers", was written by Anadi Trikha and Madhu Bala Kaushik, both from Manipal University Jaipur, India. Marketing strategies are evolving with the rise of virtual influcncers—CGI and AI-generated personas that engage audiences like real human influencers. This chapter examines how brands are leveraging these digital figures for advertising campaigns, sponsored content, and hyper-personalized interactions. It also discusses ethical concerns regarding transparency and authenticity in digital influence.

Bhupinder Singh, from Sharda University, India, Kittisak Jermsittiparsert, from Shinawatra University, Thailand and Saurabh Chandra, from Bennett University, India concludes the book with Chapter 12, titled "Artificial Intelligence and Machine Learning: Ethical and Legal Challenges in E-Business Transformation". As AI and machine learning (ML) drive the evolution of e-commerce, they also introduce ethical and legal risks. This chapter explores the challenges surrounding consumer privacy, data security, and digital rights, particularly in an era where vast amounts of personal data are collected and monetized.

Through these 12 chapters, this book provides a detailed exploration of how the metaverse is transforming key business sectors and management practices. Whether in gaming, education, retail or healthcare, the metaverse presents tremendous opportunities and complex challenges that must be carefully managed.

This book serves as an essential guide for professionals, researchers, and students, offering valuable insights into the impact and potential of this emerging digital environment. As we move toward a future that is increasingly interconnected and immersive, understanding and leveraging the metaverse will be crucial for success in marketing and management.

REFERENCES

Chanda, R. S., Pabalkar, V., & Sharma, S. (2024). Attitude and behavioral intention for using metaverse in education: Learner's perspective. *Journal of Applied Research in Higher Education*, 16(5), 2168–2184. Advance online publication. DOI: 10.1108/JARHE-07-2023-0307

Crespo-Pereira, V., Sánchez-Amboage, E., & Membiela-Pollán, M. (2023). Facing the challenges of metaverse: a systematic literature review from Social Sciences and Marketing and Communication. Profesional de la información/Information Professional, 32(1). DOI: 10.3145/epi.2023.ene.02

Diogo, J., & Veiga, P. M. (2022). Metaverse applications in business: A systematic literature review and integrative framework. Implementing Automation Initiatives in Companies to Create Better-Connected Experiences, 110-136. DOI: 10.4018/978-1-6684-5538-8.ch006

Donvito, R., Acuti, D., & Song, S. (2024). Fashion and the metaverse: Implications for consumers and firms. *Journal of Global Fashion Marketing*, 15(1), 1–5. DOI: 10.1080/20932685.2023.2293290

Dwivedi, Y. K., Hughes, L., Baabdullah, A. M., Ribeiro-Navarrete, S., Giannakis, M., Al-Debei, M. M., Dennehy, D., Metri, B., Buhalis, D., Cheung, C. M. K., Conboy, K., Doyle, R., Dubey, R., Dutot, V., Felix, R., Goyal, D. P., Gustafsson, A., Hinsch, C., Jebabli, I., & Wamba, S. F. (2022). Metaverse beyond the hype: Multidisciplinary perspectives on emerging challenges, opportunities, and agenda for research, practice, and policy. *International Journal of Information Management*, 66, 102542. DOI: 10.1016/j.ijinfomgt.2022.102542

Joshua, J. (2017). Information Bodies: Computational Anxiety in Neal Stephenson's Snow Crash. *Interdisciplinary Literary Studies*, 19(1), 17–47. DOI: 10.5325/intelitestud.19.1.0017

Kılıçarslan, Ö., & Yozukmaz, N. Albayrak, T. & Buhalis, D. (2024). The impacts of Metaverse on tourist behavior and marketing implications. *Current Issues in Tourism*. Advance online publication. DOI: 10.1080/13683500.2024.2326989

Knox, J. (2022). The metaverse, or the serious business of tech frontiers. Postdigital Science and Education, 4(2), 207-215. DOI: 10.1007/s42438-022-00300-9

Lee, L.-H., Braud, T., Zhou, P., Wang, L., Xu, D., Lin, Z., Kumar, A., Bermejo, C., & Hui, P. (2021). All One Needs to Know about Metaverse: A Complete Survey on Technological Singularity, Virtual Ecosystem, and Research Agenda, 14(8), 1–66. http://arxiv.org/abs/2110.05352

Narin, N. G. (2021). A content analysis of the metaverse articles. *Journal of Metaverse*, 1(1), 17–24.

Nguyen, H., & Voznak, M. (2024). A Bibliometric Analysis of Technology in Digital Health: Exploring Health Metaverse and Visualizing Emerging Healthcare Management Trends, in IEEE Access, 12, 23887-23913. DOI: 10.3389/fpsyg.2022.851753

Pratas, J. M. (2023). Metaverse and Digital Twins: An Opportunity to Increase Retailers' Profitability? An Exploratory Research Using Nike Case Study and Retail Managers' In-Depth Interviews. In *Management and Marketing for Improved Retail Competitiveness and Performance* (pp. 217–235). IGI Global., DOI: 10.4018/978-1-6684-8574-3.ch011

Riva, G., & Wiederhold, B. K. (2022). What the metaverse is (really) and why we need to know about it. *Cyberpsychology, Behavior, and Social Networking*, 25(6), 355–359. DOI: 10.1089/cyber.2022.0124 PMID: 35696299

Rosário, A., Lopes, P., & Rosário, F. (2023). Metaverse in Marketing: Challenges and Opportunities. In IGI Global Handbook of Research on AI-Based Technologies and Applications in the Era of the Metaverse. DOI: 10.4018/978-1-6684-8851-5.ch003

Statista Market Insights. (2024). Metaverse – Worldwide. Accessed through https://www.statista.com/outlook/amo/metaverse/worldwide#market-size

Wu, P., Chen, D., & Zhang, R. (2024). Topic prevalence and trends of metaverse in healthcare: A bibliometric analysis. *Data Science and Management*, 7(2), 129–143. DOI: 10.1016/j.dsm.2023.12.003

Yadav, S., Pandey, S.K. & Sharma, D. (2024). Marketing beyond reality: a systematic literature review on metaverse, Management Research Review. DOI: 10.1108/MRR-06-2023-0456

Acknowledgment

The editors would like to acknowledge the support of the researchers and the IGI Global editorial team involved in this project. Among the editors, authors, and reviewers, more than fifty researchers participated and committed to the book.

Twenty-six authors from diverse countries and continents—namely India, Ireland, Oman, Portugal, Spain, Turkey, Thailand, the United Arab Emirates, and the United States of America—contributed to the book. The editors would like to thank each of the authors for their contributions.

All chapters were reviewed by three or more reviewers, whose valuable work helped enrich and improve the final result of the book. Therefore, we are grateful for the support of the researchers who contributed to the review process of each chapter, including the collaboration of Ana Monteiro (ISCAP, Polytechnic of Porto), Ana Nunes (ISCAP, Polytechnic of Porto),Anabela Ribeiro (ISCAP, Polytechnic of Porto), Anadi Trikha (Manipal University), Angelo Gomes (ISCAP, Polytechnic of Porto), Belém Barbosa (University of Porto), Bhupinder Singh (Sharda University), Cristina Torres (ISCAP, Polytechnic of Porto), Devaraj E (CMR University), Jessy Michla J R (Kalasalingam University), Joana Neves (University of Porto), Jorge Alves (ISCAP, Polytechnic of Porto), Jorge Remondes (ISCAP, Polytechnic of Porto), José Duarte Santos (ISCAP, Polytechnic of Porto), Luis Matosas-López (Rey Juan Carlos University), Madhu Kaushik (Manipal University Jaipur), Muhammad Usman Tariq (Abu Dhabi University), Rajaprabakaran Rajendran (CMS Business School), Saurabh Chandra (Bennett University), Sekarini S. (SASTRA University), Susana Bernardino (ISCAP, Polytechnic of Porto), Susana Pinto (ISCAP, Polytechnic of Porto), Vera Castanheira (ISCAP, Polytechnic of Porto) and Zaíla Oliveira (ISCAP, Polytechnic of Porto).

The editors also appreciate IGI Global's support throughout the process.

This work is financed by portuguese national funds through FCT - Fundação para a Ciência e Tecnologia, under the project UID/05422: Centre for organisational and Social Studies of Polytechnic of Porto.

Chapter 1
The Impact of the Metaverse on the Gaming Industry:
A Case Study of Epic Games

Joana Neves
https://orcid.org/0000-0001-9675-5683
CEF.UP, University of Porto, Portugal, & CEOS.PP, Polytechnic University of Coimbra, Portugal

EXECUTIVE SUMMARY

This chapter explores the idea of metaverse in the context of the gaming industry using the case of Epic Games. Concentrating on Fortnite and Unreal Engine, the case study describes how Epic Games has expanded its business model, leaving behind the conventional types of revenue generation and focusing on event-based virtual economies, user-generated content, and branded entertainment experiences. The research also looks at broader applications of the Unreal Engine, especially when used for industries outside of video gaming like healthcare, architecture, and film industries. Moreover, the current chapter investigates the emerging issues regarding regulation, possession of virtual assets, and essential ethical issues of the metaverse. The conclusions present ideas useful for practitioners and researchers when exploring the nature of innovations that may appear in the new environment.

DOI: 10.4018/979-8-3693-7245-6.ch001

1. INTRODUCTION

The gaming sector has experienced continuous growth since the mid-20th century, with notable advancements occurring from the 1960s onward. For example, "Tennis for Two" (1958) and "Spacewar!" (1962) were among the earliest interactive games, employing available technology to provide users with amusement. The launch of the first home video game console, Magnavox Odyssey, in 1972 marked a pivotal moment by popularizing home entertainment and paving the way for the future console market (Metuarau, 2023).

During the late 1970s and early 1980s, several arcade games, such as Atari's Pong, released in 1972, and Space Invaders in 1978, thrilled the public, contributing to the arcade's golden age (Kalning, 2008). During this period, Japanese companies like Nintendo and Sega entered the market, establishing their prominence with the launch of the Nintendo Entertainment System in 1983 and iconic games such as Donkey Kong and Super Mario Bros. These innovations solidified home consoles as a mainstay in the gaming industry (Jones, 2008; Kalning, 2008).

The 1990s and early 2000s transitioned towards more sophisticated gaming experiences, with 3D graphics and CD-ROM technology enabling richer narratives and complex gameplay mechanics (Jones, 2008). Sony's launch of the PlayStation in 1994 exemplified this shift, offering advanced hardware at an accessible price point. Simultaneously, the rise of internet connectivity facilitated the emergence of online multiplayer games, such as World of Warcraft and Halo 2 in 2004, introducing social dimensions to gaming (Metuarau, 2023).

More recently, mobile gaming and cloud gaming platforms, including Google Stadia and Microsoft xCloud, have further democratized gaming by enabling play across various devices without requiring specialized hardware. The growth of eSports, driven by popular titles like League of Legends and Counter-Strike, has transformed gaming into a spectator sport and fostered professional gaming communities (Feng et al., 2007; Jones, 2008).

More recently, new technologies like virtual reality (VR) and augmented reality (AR), interconnected with the creation of Metaverse, brought a new perspective to the gaming sector. Metaverse is a shared virtual environment connected with VR, AR, Mixed Reality (MR), and Extended Reality (XR). This space also enables users to casually meet actual face-to-face and other avatars in the physical and digital hybrid environment. This environment came from science fiction, and Neal Stephenson was the first to introduce it in his Snow Crash novel, published in 1992. The current evolution of technology has made it plausible for various industries, such as gaming, social networks, and commerce. For the gaming industry, the metaverse means an approach to engaging players, as it rewards users with vast virtual environments where they can socialize, play against rivals, and even make transactions. Even today's popular games, such as Roblox and Fortnite, are examples where millions of their users spend their time daily with other commitments that go beyond the basic game in a specific metaverse-type environment, such as socializing, buying and selling virtual objects and attending concerts. Because of this interest, more technologies in the technology industry have been directed at trying to extend the capabilities of the Metaverse (Metuarau, 2021).

Notably, the metaverse can relate to gaming because of the combination of Artificial Intelligence (AI), blockchain, and XR. AI is important in at least three aspects of user experiences, including, avatars customization, automatic content generation, and improving the realism of worlds. For example, lifelike avatars and brilliant Non-Playable Characters (NPCs) that can adapt to the changing dynamic of the game can be used by AI. Additionally, more technologies help exchange virtual goods, such as game assets or non-fungible tokens (NFTs), in the metaverse to address ownership and economic exchange queries.

As the metaverse concept grows, it is expected to go beyond the traditional games industry and impact other areas, including education, medicine, and interpersonal communications, by linking different virtual worlds. However, there are still aspects that need to be improved in these realities, such as user privacy, dealing with the psychological effects of long stays in virtual worlds, and tackling the technical issues that can prevent the widespread use of virtual worlds.

Virtual worlds have been important for users, mainly since the COVID-19 pandemic. The metaverse has also acquired significant importance in games, with some brands standing out in this market, such as Epic Games.

Epic Games was established in 1991 and is involved in the gaming industry. It is well-known for Unreal Engine, a cross-platform game development that supports gaming and XR applications. This paired gaming is the core of Epic Games's conception of the metaverse, a real-world and virtual space merged harmoniously (Jungherr & Schlarb, 2022). Epic Games has gone further in its metaverse strategy by announcing in 2022 that it has raised $2 billion to develop social and interactive experiences in games such as Fortnite or Rocket League. Long-term metaverse objectives are also maintained through its strategic partnerships, most notably with Sony (EpicGames, 2022).

The following research question arises from this market perspective: How has the metaverse impacted Epic Games? This study aims to understand how the metaverse has impacted the gaming world and how it has favored the biggest gaming companies, such as Epic Games. In addition, it aims to understand how this path can impact the daily work of professionals and academics, not only in this sector but in all areas that are somehow impacted by this dynamic environment.

This chapter is divided into a literature review, showing the importance of Metaverse and Gaming industry in this virtual world. Next, the case study of Epic Games will be presented since the growth of Metaverse and its impact, competitors, and characteristics affect user engagement and dynamics in this virtual world. It will discuss the case, leading to the conclusion of the chapter with the implications for practitioners and academics with future research directions.

2. LITERATURE REVIEW

2.1. Metaverse

The metaverse has evolved into a transformative paradigm in digital spatial computing, driven by the convergence of immersive technologies, virtual economies, and interactive games (Taçgın & Dalgarno, 2021). At its core are immersive realities, such as VR, AR, and mixed reality (MR), each playing a pivotal role in shaping the user experience within virtual environments. Through immersive realities, individuals can enter virtual worlds created by computers and transcend physical boundaries, opening doors to new realms. VR technology spans a spectrum of experiences, from non-immersive desktop systems to completely immersive settings, encouraging a profound sense of presence and engagement through sophisticated visual and audio stimuli (Harley, 2022). Conversely, AR creates a smooth transition between virtual and physical worlds, enhancing users' settings with interactive digital overlays (Qadir & Alwardat, 2023). Virtual and real-world elements can interact dynamically within the metaverse's dynamic environment thanks to MR, which further improves immersion by fusing features of VR and AR (Neves et al., 2024). These immersive technologies provide users with unmatched chances for engagement and interaction, forming the fundamental foundations of the metaverse. The metaverse blurs the lines between reality and virtuality by seamlessly combining VR, AR, and MR experiences under the general heading of Extended Reality (XR). This allows users to engage with various experiences beyond conventional interaction (Abrash, 2021). Digital markets see a significant metamorphosis inside the complex network of technologies forming the Metaverse, changing conventional trade and value exchange (Bhattacharya et al., 2023). A new era of economic paradigms is being ushered in by this evolving digital world, which is defined by the combination of blockchain, AR, VR, and decentralized technology. At the heart of the Metaverse's economic environment lies Decentralized Ledger Technologies (DLT) and Blockchain, which revolutionize digital asset ownership and exchange (Massaro, 2023). With blockchain technology ensuring transparency and immutability, decentralized markets within the Metaverse provide a secure framework for trading virtual products, digital assets, and

Non-Fungible Tokens (NFTs) (Huynh-The et al., 2023). Smart Contracts, integral to the dynamics of Metaverse markets, automate transaction rules and reduce reliance on intermediaries, fostering efficient and trustless transactions (Wu & Liu, 2023). By streamlining digital asset exchange, these programmable contracts enhance the fluidity of decentralized Metaverse markets, empowering participants with seamless transaction experiences (Koohang et al., 2023). Enabled by blockchain technology, Tokenization of Assets transforms intangible digital assets into marketable tokens, democratizing participation in the digital economy and enhancing asset liquidity (Vidal-Tomás, 2023). Tokenization not only broadens accessibility but also fosters fractional ownership, expanding the scope of digital asset ownership within Metaverse ecosystems (Lee et al., 2023). Non-fungible tokens (NFTs) serve as the cornerstone of individualized value in the Metaverse, redefining ownership and scarcity in a transparent, decentralized framework (Wu & Liu, 2023). By empowering creators and collectors alike, NFTs drive a paradigm shift in Metaverse markets, encompassing diverse digital assets such as art, virtual real estate, and technological objects (Sung et al., 2023). Dynamic virtual economies thrive within the Metaverse, supported by digital currencies exclusive to virtual environments (Vidal-Tomás, 2023). Digital exchange platforms serve as market intermediaries, integrating liquidity pools and decentralized finance (DeFi) components to enhance market liquidity and efficacy (Koohang et al., 2023). As these technologies converge and evolve, the Metaverse's marketplaces become complex ecosystems, revolutionizing digital commerce and shaping a new era of economic interactions. Within this emerging digital frontier, traditional boundaries dissolve, and the digitization of value becomes integral to economic exchanges. In this dynamic environment, brands have unprecedented opportunities to create immersive brand experiences that resonate with consumers in virtual environments (Bonetti et al., 2018). From virtual product demonstrations to interactive storytelling experiences, immersive realities empower brands to forge deeper connections with their audience in the digital realm, fostering engagement and loyalty in an increasingly interconnected world. As brands navigate the complexities of the metaverse, understanding the interplay between immersive technologies and consumer behavior is essential. By strategically leveraging VR, AR, and MR experiences, brands can create immersive activations and virtual environments that captivate audiences and drive meaningful interactions. Additionally, embracing XR as a holistic approach to immersive experiences allows brands to explore new brand engagement and storytelling frontiers, establishing a competitive edge in the evolving digital landscape.

2.2. Importance of Metaverse in Gaming

The Metaverse represents a fundamental transformation in the gaming industry, reshaping user experiences and unveiling new opportunities for technological and economic innovation. The most important elements that metaverse is changing gaming experiences are immersive and persistent worlds, interactivity and community-building, MR, and digital economies. Another important aspect of the metaverse is that players are placed in a constantly evolving persistent world where the game is played in real-time and connected to others. In contrast to conventional games that take place in virtual worlds during actual gameplay, the Metaverse offers users infinite world exploration even when they are not participating. Games like Epic Games' Fortnite have already embraced this model by hosting virtual events and integrating social experiences within the game (Hasan et al., 2024). That is why social interaction forms the foundation of the metaverse gaming experience, in which individuals are no longer passive participants, but are actively contributing members of a global virtual society. Players are not gamers anymore; they become active members of a global community where they can interact, cooperate, and produce user-created content. Games serve as platforms for creativity and interaction, further increasing player engagement (Yasar et al., 2023). The concept of MR is important to conduct these environments. The integration of AR and VR creates a blend of physical and digital worlds, offering new forms of gameplay. This kind of experience changes how players approach their environment, thus opening the doors to renewed interaction in a game (Fegert, 2023). Furthermore, the metaverse presents new opportunities to use the game economy business model where players can buy and sell virtual goods, assets, and currencies within the blockchain environment. It can include actions like collecting, producing, and trading NFTs or any other virtual assets that have a potential market value via blockchain platforms (Hasan et al., 2024). The growth of Metaverse brings new opportunities. From virtual goods and assets to digital real estate, companies can explore novel revenue streams. For example, players can purchase in-game items, attend virtual concerts, or engage in in-game commerce (Shukla & Taneja, 2024). The success of virtual economies also opens opportunities for brand integration and advertising. Conversely, the Metaverse´s interconnected nature encourages collaboration between gaming companies and other industries such as fashion, music, and education. Epic Games has demonstrated this through partnerships with music artists for virtual concerts, merging entertainment and gaming experiences (Healy & Standiford, 2023). Another aspect of opportunity is the rise of blockchain and NFTs, where players gain ownership of digital assets, which can be transferred across different games and platforms. This decentralization reduces reliance on traditional power structures and fosters a player-driven ecosystem (Joshi et al., 2024). Although the metaverse is rich in opportunities, it brings numerous issues associated with modern innovations and virtual worlds. Controversial questions, including the regulation's role, the destiny of IP rights, and the protection of privacy and security, must be solved as the future of the metaverse develops (Yasar et al., 2023). Regarding legal and regulatory aspects, it is still possible to observe that virtual economies, NFTs, and digital assets are still unregulated. Issues related to copyright infringement and ownership of digital goods can pose challenges, especially when assets are traded across different metaverse platforms (Yasar et al., 2023). Another issue is that the player´s data is collected and analyzed on a massive scale, raising concerns over the misuse of personal information. Additionally, the risk of cyberattacks in virtual environments poses a challenge to ensuring secure transactions and interactions (Fegert, 2023). These vats of technology and information require vast computing resources, advanced hardware, and seamless intent connectivity to function effectively. These technical limitations may hinder widespread adoption, especially in regions with poor infrastructure or limited access to high-end VR/AR devices (Al-Ghaili et al., 2022). In the end, is important to note some challenges in ethical and social issues. The Metaverse could intensify social injustices because only individuals with the right technologies can engage in it. Approaching this issue more critically, there is concern regarding addiction and the psychological effects of spending a significant amount of time in the virtual space of a metaverse, as well as the questions about digital welfare that such a focus on the metaverse brings up (Deavours, 2023). As a result, the metaverse can potentially reinvent the gameplay and the overall concept of gaming as a shared environment for entertainment, socialization, and trading.

The Metaverse gaming market is expected to reach US$20.9 billion in 2024, and the key player in this market is the United States, which is US$7.5 billion. The number of users in the gaming market is estimated to grow to 0.9 billion of users in 2030 (Statista, 2024). However, as this potential opens, the industry must face significant questions about regulation, security, and ethically sound management if the risks and benefits of such developments are to be distributed fairly. As it has the potential for introducing new types of revenues, cross-industry collaborations, and users' emancipation, it faces problems such as regulation issues, privacy and security concerns, and technology limitations.

2.3. Policy Framework in the Gaming Sector and Metaverse

Consequently, policy frameworks have an essential role in addressing emerging challenges in the gaming industry, given the innovations of metaverse technologies. Here, the policy context implies the legal standards, industry rules, and regulations that shape the functioning of firms, including Epic Games, in digital spaces. These frameworks are supposed to protect users, maintain fair competition, and encourage innovation with the help of addressing possible risks, including privacy violations, economic abuse, and piracy.

2.3.1. Regulatory Policies

Some of the prominent issues related to the policy framework within the context of the gaming sector include provisions that deal with data and information privacy and security. Since data collection by metaverse platform amounts to personal information ownership, fundamental response to laws such as the General Data Protection Regulation (GDPR) governing the European Union and the California Consumer Privacy Act (CCPA) in the United States of America should be complied with (Sebastian, 2023). European regulations require those who collect and process personal information to be open about it, and they give users ways to protect their data and enforce penalties.

Another significant regulatory concern is intellectual property (IP) rights. Users often create content in metaverse environments, such as avatars, virtual buildings, and digital art. Protecting these creations while ensuring that companies do not infringe on user rights is an ongoing challenge. According to Kalyvaki (2023), platforms like Fortnite have adopted user agreements that grant limited rights to user-generated content, balancing creator autonomy with corporate control.

Moreover, policies around digital asset ownership and trade are gaining prominence. Blockchain technology enables players to buy, sell, and trade virtual goods, raising questions about the legal status of such transactions. Türkmen and Sürmeli (2024) argue that existing financial regulations may need to be updated to accommodate these novel economic models, ensuring that virtual economies remain transparent and fair.

2.3.2. Economic Policies

As an integral part of digital business, in-game economies, and virtual currency require sound economic policies. Virtual currencies such as Fortnite V-Bucks are usually tied to virtual items, leaving questions regarding taxation and consumer protection unanswered. According to Yuan and Yang (2022), international guidelines on taxing virtual transactions are still evolving, highlighting the need for consistent global policies. Some frameworks being considered at the policy level relate to the nature of virtual goods and currencies so governments can generate revenue from the growing digital economy without dampening innovation.

Besides taxation issues, anti-money laundering (AML) rules are becoming more important. Thus, since virtual economies can be used for abuse for general purposes, the platforms apply measures to counteract the sphere of AML. Egliston et al. (2024) emphasize the need for collaboration between gaming companies and financial regulators to establish robust systems that detect and deter illegal activities.

2.3.3. Industry Standards and Self-Regulation

Apart from regulations imposed by the government, industry standards are instrumental in determining the policy environment within the country. Many organizations, such as Epic Games, work closely with industry associations to create ethical codes to avoid inappropriate and safe customer conduct. Mosco (2023) argues that industry-driven governance is essential for ensuring user trust and platform sustainability.

Furthermore, content moderation and community management are essential components of self-regulation. Given the social nature of metaverse platforms, ensuring a safe and inclusive environment is a top priority. Lee and Min (2022) highlight AI-driven moderation tools as a key strategy for maintaining community standards.

2.3.4. Ethical Considerations

Ethical concerns also form a vital part of the policy framework. Issues such as digital addiction, psychological well-being, and digital inequality are gaining attention from both policymakers and industry leaders. Basyoni et al. (2024) state that guidelines on healthy digital engagement and privacy-enhancing technologies are critical for safeguarding user welfare.

Additionally, ensuring equal access to metaverse technologies is crucial. High-end devices required for fully immersive experiences may not be accessible to all users, potentially exacerbating digital inequality. Policies that promote affordable access to technology can help bridge this gap, fostering a more inclusive digital future.

3. CASE STUDY: EPIC GAMES

The analyzed object, Epic Games, is one of the leaders in utilizing metaverse technologies, thus, it can be used for this analysis. Along similar lines, many concept voices of the metaverse can be derived from the company and its experience in creating appealing virtual worlds, encouraging UGC, and producing value streams through different monetization schemes. This section explains why Epic Games has been chosen as the subject of the study, describes its advantages and disadvantages, the data that can be obtained, and positions the investigation within the works that have been previously conducted.

Epic Games has been pivotal in transforming traditional gaming models, broadening the scope of what the metaverse can achieve. Two of its products, Fortnite and Unreal Engine, discharge model examples of how businesses can approach the complex digital terrain. For instance, Fortnite is a social metaverse that enables communication, virtual events purchasing, and possession of virtual commodities while the unreal engine is a sophistical tool to produce vivid Virtual Reality in gaming as well as in architecture, films, and health sectors, among others (Ball, 2022). This case study explicitly targets Epic Games to explore all possibilities in which companies can bring new Opportunities to increase revenue for informational purposes and to bring new value for users using cross-sector applications of Virtual environments.

Several factors make Epic Games an intense case study. First, the company exemplifies how to diversify revenue streams beyond traditional models of game sales and microtransactions. Fortnite has pioneered event-driven revenue models by hosting virtual concerts, branded events, and other interactive experiences that generate income through in-game purchases and sponsorships (Ferrari & McKelvey, 2023). Such events show that new types of virtual platforms can be launched that will generate both economic and social value and open new ways to monetize content.

Second, the Unreal Engine provides Epic Games with a versatile technological foundation that extends beyond gaming, positioning it as a cross-industry tool. Its use in creating virtual training environments, digital twins, and immersive experiences across sectors like architecture and healthcare exemplifies its broader impact on business models that extend into the metaverse (Chen & Cheng, 2022).

This case study draws on secondary data sources to comprehensively analyze Epic Games' role in the metaverse. First, it includes financial reports, and official announcements from Epic Games, which provide direct insights into their strategy. Secondary sources include academic papers, industry reports, and case studies that offer a broader context. Relevant research highlights critical elements of virtual economies, UGC, and the integration of immersive technologies across sectors. For instance, Hardy et al. (2022) provide a detailed analysis of how companies like Roblox and Epic Games monetize user-generated content, while Ferrari and McKelvey (2023) discuss the potential for event-driven revenue within metaverse platforms.

3.1. Epic Games in the Metaverse

Epic Games, which allows Fortnite and Unreal Engine, was able to advance in the metaverse development. In recent years, Epic Games has gone beyond just games and begun developing rich and connected virtual worlds, standing up for the future of online interaction, where entertainment, social networking, and commerce converge in immersive 3D spaces (Ball, 2022). The company's involvement and contributions to the emerging metaverse are visible in key areas. First, Fortnite was launched as a Battle Royale game, evolving into a social platform that supports user interaction, concerts, and virtual experiences. From being just a game that players competed in, Fortnite has gradually turned into a Metaverse that hosts users in gameplay, events, and social interactions. Ferrari and McKelvey (2023) argue that Fortnite is a preparation ground for the Metaverse given that it is flexible enough to allow for things such as concerts, events, and collaboration between major brands such as Nike and Balenciaga with the creation of new and unique digital economies and cultures. The most famous virtual events have been hosted on this platform, for example, the Travis Scott concert in 2020, where more than 12 million players participated, and generated over $20 million from related in-game sales; such examples show that virtual spaces can act as places for entertainment and communication. Fortnite´s cross-platform compatibility with different devices (computers, consoles, and mobile phones) supports the importance of Metaverse platforms. Fortnite has over 500 million registered players in 2023, with a revenue of US$20 billion in 2022, making it one of the largest virtual platforms globally (Clement, 2024). Epic Games leverages Fortnite to enable users to participate in more than the game, socializing, events, and purchasing digital assets. Change from Fortnite as a bubble to a game and a part of the social environment contributes to Epic Games's bigger agenda of participating in the metaverse.

On the other hand, Epic Games with its Unreal Engine, is the other player that has played an enormous role in building the metaverse. Furthermore, Wang et al. (2023) have pointed out that Unreal Engine is the basic platform, based on which it is possible to create photorealistic and open integrated virtual environments. In other words, The Unreal Engine, Epic Games´s game engine development tool, is instrumental in creating high-quality 3D environments that grow Metaverse (Wang et al., 2023). This steam engine is widely used beyond games, including in sectors such as architecture, film production, and virtual training, contributing to the metaverse's vision of an interconnected virtual ecosystem. The Unreal Engine is a platform for creating scalable virtual experiences. The versatility allows developers to build interconnected, scalable virtual environments that align with the core vision of the Metaverse—making Epic Games a major player in shaping its technological infrastructure. Unreal Engine is widely adopted across industries beyond gaming, where in 2022 the engine was used in 153 projects, just in film and TV-related projects, meaning an increase of 44% (UnrealEngine, 2023). The monthly active users grew 23% across all geographical locations in the same year compared with other years (UnrealEngine, 2023).

According to Ferrari and McKelvey (2023), it is a significant facilitator of interoperability, an essential feature of the metaverse that allows various virtual environments to communicate and connect, a vision adopted by Epic Games. Furthermore, it is also worth mentioning that Epic Games pioneered virtual economies. In Fortnite, players can purchase virtual goods such as skins, emotes, and other items that exist only in the digital world. These digital goods form the basis of what could evolve into digital property in the metaverse (Chen & Cheng, 2022). With the future possibilities of NFTs, Epic Games's virtual economy is laying the foundations for the functioning of economic exchanges in the metaverse. This is closely related to Epic Games' acquisition of platforms such as Sketchfab, a 3D content platform, to enable the creation of user-generated virtual assets that can be exchanged or sold.

3.1.1. Impact on Business Models

Implementing the metaverse, as an aspect of a game universe, has completely changed the approach of Epic Games to its business shifting from the linear model of revenues and offering new opportunities to engage users. In front of these ideas, most gaming companies solely relied on selling games and additional bucks for the gaming features, typically called microtransactions. However, through affiliation with the metaverse, Epic Games found a reasonable extra revenue source for virtual events, brands, and, more importantly, now virtual economy profits (Chen & Cheng, 2022).

Epic Games has emerged as a pioneer in event-driven revenue models, leveraging virtual concerts and branded in-game experiences within Fortnite. These events not only generate significant in-game purchases, such as themed skins and items tied to specific events, but they also offer lucrative sponsorship opportunities with global brands such as Nike and Marvel (Ferrari & McKelvey, 2023). For instance, the Fortnite Travis Scott concert in 2020 attracted over 12 million participants, blending entertainment with digital commerce in a new way (Ball, 2022). Moreover, the introduction of NFTs and blockchain technology hints at future avenues for monetization through virtual asset ownership and decentralized economies (Chen & Cheng, 2022).

In addition to these in-game innovations, Unreal Engine, Epic Games' game development platform, represents another significant business opportunity. Licensed to developers across a range of industries, Unreal Engine is increasingly used to create not just games but also virtual training environments, digital twins, and immersive experiences in sectors such as architecture, film production, and healthcare (Chen & Cheng, 2022). This cross-industry adoption exemplifies how Epic Games has expanded its footprint beyond the entertainment sector into other areas aligned with the broader metaverse vision (Hardy et al., 2022).

Unreal Engine is more commonly used outside the gaming sphere in various industries. Architectural firms utilize Unreal Engine to develop virtual walk-throughs of buildings before they are built, enabling clients to engage with the design in real time (Chen & Cheng, 2022). In the same way, the healthcare sector utilizes the platform to create virtual training spaces for healthcare workers, offering lifelike simulations for surgeries and other essential procedures. Digital twins, created with Unreal Engine, are revolutionizing industries such as automotive manufacturing by allowing companies to digitally test and optimize processes before physically implementing them.

Additionally, Epic Games has effectively incorporated a virtual economy in Fortnite, focused on digital items and in-game transactions like V-Bucks (the game's currency). This economy has become a significant source of income for the company, particularly due to partnerships with well-known brands. For instance, virtual assets linked to real-world brand collaborations allow players to personalize their gaming experience while also driving microtransaction revenues (Ferrari & McKelvey, 2023). This virtual marketplace model aligns with a broader trend in the metaverse, where digital goods and services, as well as user-generated content (UGC), contribute to the development of self-sustaining virtual economies (Rostami & Maier, 2022).

In comparison to competitors like Meta and Microsoft, which focus more on virtual reality and enterprise applications, respectively, Epic Games emphasizes user engagement and entertainment-driven experiences. This is, for instance, seen with Meta, which has however invested lots of resources into social VR through apps like Horizon Worlds, and Microsoft, which has focused on business collaboration through the Mesh apps targeting working environments and related solutions (Rostami & Maier, 2022). On the other hand, Unreal Engine has discovered that its use extends beyond gaming and encompasses industries such as digital twins, virtual training simulations, and virtual pipelines for construction, engineers, and health sectors (Chen & Cheng, 2022).

Finally, Epic Games has effectively tapped into the power of UGC as a driver of innovation and monetization. By allowing players to create and share their experiences within Fortnite using the Unreal Engine, Epic has cultivated a thriving ecosystem that rewards creativity, fostering a self-sustaining content economy (Hardy et al., 2022). This approach, alongside large-scale virtual events, positions Epic Games as a leader in the entertainment and social aspects of the metaverse while also pushing the boundaries of digital content creation.

3.1.2. Market Positioning and Competition

Some of the players, in a broad context of the Metaverse, are Epic Games, Roblox, Meta, and Microsoft, and they are making significant contributions (Lbmsolutions, 2024). Each company contributes with unique characteristics to promote the evolution of this virtual world. For this, Table 1 highlights the comparative strengths, core contributions, technological foundations, and key differentiators among these prominent players in the Metaverse ecosystem. This comparative analysis offers valuable insights into how each player positions itself within this rapidly evolving digital frontier.

Table 1. Comparative analysis between key players on Metaverse

Company	Core Contributions in Metaverse	Technological Foundation	Key Differences
Epic Games	Fortnite is a virtual social platform, and Unreal Engine is a cross-industry tool for building scalable, high-quality virtual worlds.	Unreal Engine, Fortnite, partnerships with Sketchfab and MetaHuman.	High-quality 3D experiences, interoperability focus, and event-driven virtual environments (like concerts and social spaces).
Roblox	A UGC-centric platform enabling users to create virtual worlds and games; extensive in-game economy based on Robux currency.	Proprietary game engine, UGC-heavy platform.	Large-scale UGC, highly monetized creator economy, focus on younger audiences and user-driven innovation.
Meta	Horizon Worlds focuses on virtual identity and social interaction through VR, which is the integration of Oculus VR hardware.	Oculus, proprietary VR engines.	VR and social networking investments focus on avatar-based virtual identity and immersive experiences.
Microsoft	Focus on enterprise Metaverse applications (like Microsoft Mesh), Minecraft and Azure for cloud and XR technologies.	Azure Cloud, Mesh, HoloLens.	Focus on enterprise, collaboration tools, strong cloud infrastructure for virtual collaboration, and XR applications.
Apple	Vision Pro aims to introduce immersive experiences through spatial computing, blending AR with digital elements for consumer and enterprise use.	Vision Pro, ARKit, Spatial Audio, M1/ M2 chips.	Focus on spatial computing and AR rather than a purely virtual world - high-end hardware targeting premium consumers for MR experiences.
Google	It focuses on AR and immersive content creation tools through platforms like Google Earth VR and Tilt Brush and explores metaverse initiatives around XR tech.	Google Cloud, ARCore, Google Earth VR, Tilt Brush.	Heavy investment in AR rather than VR. Focus on educational, mapping, and creative applications instead of gaming and entertainment.

continued on following page

Table 1. Continued

Company	Core Contributions in Metaverse	Technological Foundation	Key Differences
The Sandbox	A blockchain-based metaverse with virtual land ownership (LAND) and a strong emphasis on NFTs enables players to create, own, and monetize experiences.	Ethereum blockchain, VoxEdit, Game Maker, NFT-based assets.	Decentralized metaverse with a strong NFT economy. Virtual land ownership and a creator-first economy supported by blockchain technology.
Decentraland	A decentralized virtual world where users can purchase, develop, and trade virtual land and assets using cryptocurrency (MANA).	Ethereum blockchain, decentralized governance (DAO), VR support.	Fully decentralized model governed by a DAO. Focus on virtual real estate and ownership of digital assets, as well as strong NFT and blockchain integration.

Source: Adaption from Lbmsolutions (2024), Rostami and Maier (2022), Cao (2023), Chen and Cheng (2022), and Ferrari and McKelvey (2023).

Epic Games distinguishes itself from competitors like Meta, Roblox, and Microsoft by focusing on high-quality 3D experiences and cross-industry interoperability. While Meta centers its strategy on VR-based social experiences through Horizon Worlds, and Roblox leans heavily on UGC to target a younger demographic, Epic Games' investment in Unreal Engine sets it apart. By integrating cutting-edge tools like MetaHuman and collaborating with platforms like Sketchfab, Epic has enabled creators across multiple sectors to build immersive, cross-platform worlds (Hardy et al., 2022). This versatility allows Epic Games to cater to gaming and non-gaming sectors, fostering stronger market positioning.

Epic Games has three main characteristics: technological foundations and innovation, economic ecosystems, user experience, and target audience. Epic Games stands out for the versatility and cross-sector applications of the Unreal Engine. While Meta focuses mainly on VR experiences through Oculus, Epic Games's engine supports applications in various sectors, from architecture to film production. Roblox, on the other hand, has its engine optimized for UGC, allowing players to create and monetize their virtual experiences, as detailed by Hardy et al. (2022). Microsoft, however, takes a different approach, focusing on business and professional collaboration through its Mesh platform and Azure Cloud. According to Rostami and Maier (2022), Microsoft is not trying to create a metaverse for entertainment or socializing but rather for productivity and collaboration, which makes it unique compared to Epic Games' entertainment-oriented vision. However, Microsoft 2022 changed its vision with the acquisition of Activision Blizzard for $69.7 billion, becoming the third-largest gaming company in the world to do this step, after the Sony and Tencent companies (Cao, 2023).

Similarly, Apple introduces a distinct perspective on the metaverse through its Vision Pro, blending AR with digital environments, focusing on spatial computing rather than the fully immersive virtual worlds seen in Epic Games' or Meta's platforms. This approach targets high-end consumers looking for mixed-reality experiences rather than entertainment-driven applications (Korkmaz, 2023). While not directly competing in the gaming metaverse, Google plays a key role in shaping digital interactions through AR and immersive experiences with tools like Google Earth VR and ARCore. Its focus on educational and creative applications differentiates it from the more socially interactive or entertainment-driven models of Epic Games and Roblox (Google, 2024).

The Sandbox and Decentraland represent decentralized approaches, focusing on user autonomy and virtual land ownership, supported by blockchain technology. In The Sandbox, players can own and monetize virtual real estate using NFTs, creating a strong, creator-driven economy (Chen & Cheng, 2022). Similarly, Decentraland offers users the ability to purchase and trade virtual land governed by decentralized autonomous organizations (DAOs), which further emphasizes community control and decentralization compared to Epic Games' more centralized model (Hardy et al., 2022).

Economic systems in the metaverse are a crucial differentiating factor. Epic Games has established a virtual economy in Fortnite centered on in-game purchases and digital assets. This is a significant part of the evolving economic framework of the metaverse (Chen & Cheng, 2022). Roblox has also monetized UGC with players purchasing experiences and goods using Robux (Hardy et al., 2022). This model has positioned Roblox as an important example of how UGC-based economies can thrive in virtual worlds. Meta continues to invest in virtual goods for avatars and digital identities. At the same time, Microsoft has taken a more business-centric approach, creating tools for virtual collaboration and professional spaces in the metaverse (for example, through Mesh and HoloLens). Sandbox and Decentraland, however, are unique in their NFT-based economies, providing users with direct ownership and control over their assets, which exemplifies the decentralized metaverse model.

Epic Games appeals to a wide audience by organizing large-scale virtual events such as concerts in Fortnite, turning a key metaverse platform, with this integration of entertainment and social interaction (Ferrari & McKelvey, 2023). Meanwhile, Roblox mainly targets a younger demographic, allowing users to create and share virtual experiences. Meta, conversely, focuses on virtual identity and social VR experiences through Oculus, aiming to create an immersive social network within the metaverse (Ball, 2022). Apple's Vision Pro, while still in its early stages, focuses more on AR, positioning itself toward immersive digital experiences rather than large-scale social or gaming events (Korkmaz, 2023). Microsoft is promoting collaborative business applications, positioning itself as a leader in the business metaverse with platforms such as Mesh. Finally, The Sandbox and Decentraland offer decentralized, community-driven platforms where user-generated assets and virtual land are critical, showing the evolution of ownership models in virtual spaces.

In this way, Epic Games represents high-quality 3D environments, cross-platform interoperability, and event-driven experiences. Fortnite is a key player in the metaverse, shaping technological, economic, and social models. The emergence of alternative players like Apple, Google, The Sandbox, and Decentraland illustrates the diverse approaches in the race to shape the future of the metaverse, with each competitor emphasizing different technological and economic foundations.

3.1.3. User Experience and Community Building

The metaverse has significantly transformed the user experience within Epic Games' ecosystem, particularly through its flagship product, Fortnite. Integral to this transformation is the platform's ability to provide both a social presence and a highly interactive virtual environment. Epic Games views the metaverse as a constantly evolving space where users are not only players but active participants in a broader digital ecosystem. This ecosystem allows them to game, attend concerts, or explore various environments. By leveraging tools such as Unreal Engine, Fortnite users can personalize their experience, creating new content and events that enhance participation and communication (Cheremnykh, 2024).

User experience is heavily influenced by the flexibility and creative freedom that the metaverse offers. Players actively reshape the virtual world through UGC, making it dynamic and constantly evolving. Epic Games enhances player engagement and retention through features like challenges, rewards, and collaborative gameplay. Additionally, the ability for players to monetize their creations via virtual goods and assets, supported by decentralized marketplaces, adds an economic incentive that complements their creative engagement. However, this user-driven environment also poses challenges, such as ensuring content quality and addressing intellectual property concerns. Epic tackles these through AI-powered moderation tools (Kaur et al., 2024; Soliman et al., 2024).

Community building is a core element of Epic Games' metaverse strategy, which emphasizes social interaction as essential for enhancing the virtual experience. The platform encourages forming global communities that transcend geographic borders, allowing users to connect through shared experiences like virtual concerts, movie viewings, or collaborative in-game events. These interactions not only enrich gameplay but also extend into cultural and creative expressions, such as digital fashion or virtual real estate, reflecting real-world social dynamics (Latino et al., 2024). Epic Games facilitates cross-platform participation, enabling users from different devices to engage in collective experiences, thereby expanding the boundaries of the metaverse. By incorporating features such as shared events and UGC, the platform fosters new social structures and subcultures, enhancing the overall user experience (Soliman et al., 2024).

In conclusion, the metaverse has profoundly reshaped user experience and community interaction in Epic Games' products. By embracing UGC, seamlessly integrating social interaction, and offering collaborative opportunities, the platform has cultivated a vibrant digital environment that enhances individual engagement and collective creativity. As the metaverse continues to evolve, new opportunities for building communities and digital interactions will emerge, solidifying Epic Games' position as a leader in this growing digital industry.

4. DISCUSSION

Examining Epic Games in the metaverse context identifies valuable lessons on how firms can operate and evolve in emerging digital environments. For this, through its video games Fortnite and Unreal Engine, Epic Games has shown how the video game industry can adopt the metaverse to develop multiple opportunities for revenue generation, improve interaction with the players, and establish dynamic virtual economies. The analyzed case example illustrates that companies' success in the metaverse depends not only on the creation of new technologies but the companies' capacity to adjust strategic decisions and respond to emerging user demand.

The first and one of the most critical influences left by the metaverse on Epic Games is the shift in its business model. Earlier, the flow of revenue in the gaming industry was primarily dependent on sales and micropayments. Nevertheless, the combination of virtual events, branded content collaborations, and Web3 economies has given Epic Games other streams of income. Concerts in Fortnite with artists like Travis Scott and Ariana Grande and other events that millions of players have attended demonstrate how Fortnite can use Metaverse. Not only do these events improve the user experience but they also present marketable occasions for brand integration and products that can be purchased from within the game further proving that the event-driven content in the metaverse is capable of being a primary source of revenue (Ferrari & McKelvey, 2023).

The use of Unreal Engine in industries cuts across from video games, therefore expanding the applicability of Epic Games. The versatility and flexibility of the technology that forms the metaverse are reflected in concurrent use cases as diverse as medical-simulated training environments and architectural and engineering models using digital twins (Chen & Cheng, 2022). This means that the metaverse is not only an item within the gaming industry but a paradigm shift that can potentially redefine many industrial and commercial sectors by offering believable and highly elastic worlds. By licensing Unreal Engine to outside developers within almost every sector, Epic Games has effectively claimed itself as a role model for gaming and non-gaming metaverse domains.

Moreover, since its introduction, UGC has played an enormous part in metaverse engagement and monetization. Users in Fortnite can even customize their experiences unlike any other platform, which is not stagnant it is evolving. Integrating blockchain technology and NFTs further enables players to monetize their creations, offering new economic incentives and promoting a decentralized model of digital asset ownership (Hardy et al., 2022). However, the shift towards UGC also presents challenges, particularly in terms of quality control, intellectual property (IP) management, and the balance between creative freedom and content moderation. Epic Games addresses these challenges using Artificial Intelligence (AI) driven moderation tools. However, relying on user content also means the company must remain vigilant about safeguarding its platform's quality and legal standing (Soliman et al., 2024).

Despite Epic Games' advantages in the metaverse, several limitations and challenges arise from this analysis. First, focusing solely on one company may limit the generalizability of these findings to the broader metaverse landscape. Companies like Meta, Roblox, and Microsoft approach the metaverse differently - whether through VR platforms or enterprise-focused applications (Rostami & Maier, 2022). Meta focuses heavily on social interactions within immersive environments, while Roblox leans more on UGC from a younger demographic. Meanwhile, Microsoft emphasizes productivity and professional collaboration through platforms like Mesh (Cao, 2023). Each of these companies contributes to the evolving dynamics of the metaverse. Yet, their differing strategies indicate that the concept of the metaverse is highly adaptable, and no single company or model dominates the space entirely.

Moreover, as the metaverse evolves, legal and regulatory challenges are expected to grow. Intellectual property rights, data privacy, and security concerns are already areas of concern within virtual environments. The decentralized nature of digital assets and economies, exemplified by Epic Games' potential future use of NFTs, poses significant regulatory questions that must be addressed. While blockchain ensures transparency, it also complicates issues surrounding IP protection and the ownership of digital goods across various platforms (Vidal-Tomás, 2023). Furthermore, the reliance on advanced technologies like XR and AI requires substantial infrastructure and hardware investment, which may limit the metaverse's accessibility, especially in regions with less technological development.

In the case of Epic Games, the use of metaverse via Fortnite and Unreal Engine shows the outstanding prospects that the virtual environment can bring even to change commercial tactics and enhance clients' attitudes towards them including the potential use of the sectors that have not been affected by the innovation before. Nevertheless, the effect of the metaverse expansion on the gaming and non-gaming industries means that innovation, cooperation, or regulation will prove to be a requirement in the future. Though Epic Games has presented good examples of the successful model of the metaverse integration, existing issues, such as regulation, technological constraints, and competition, will define the further development of the digital economy in this context.

4.1. Theoretical and Practical Implications

The theoretical contributions of this study are hence vast and can be applied to numerous areas such as digital innovation, gaming environment, and virtual economy. This study enhances the knowledge base on how metaverse technologies are integrated into Epic Games, focusing on how digital platforms adapt to provide immersive user experiences and decentralized economic systems. First, the findings support the theory that metaverse platforms foster hybridized realities where users can seamlessly navigate digital and physical spaces. This hybridization underscores the theoretical framework of spatial computing, which posits that virtual environments will increasingly blend with real-world contexts to enhance user interaction and engagement. Second, this study reinforces the theoretical perspectives on user-generated content (UGC) as a critical driver of platform growth and innovation. By allowing users to create and monetize virtual experiences, Epic Games demonstrates how companies can cultivate a participatory culture that sustains long-term engagement. This aligns with theories of participatory media, which suggest that digital ecosystems thrive when users are empowered as co-creators. Lastly, the research highlights the potential of blockchain-based virtual economies to redefine traditional economic paradigms. The introduction of NFTs and decentralized assets within games suggests a shift toward new ownership models, supporting emerging theories on digital property rights and the tokenization of assets.

From a practical perspective, the findings of this research provide purposeful strategies that metaverse industries could employ. Epic Games represents how gaming companies can expand revenues by hosting virtual events, including brand experiences, and developing profound virtual economies. The entertainment industry should be targeted, among others, as well as the fashion industry, where practitioners should seek possibilities for cooperation to increase the number of users and receive additional income. Metaverse technologies are not confined to the gaming industry, as Unreal Engine can be used in architecture, education, healthcare, and many other fields. Industry leaders could open their platforms to third-party developers to access new market segments and generate synergies across sectors. Allowing users to create and monetize content fosters a dynamic and evolving platform ecosystem. Companies can adopt similar models to encourage creativity, build community, and enhance retention. However, robust content moderation mechanisms must be implemented to ensure quality and compliance with intellectual property regulations. Due to the uncertainty of the legal requirements governing digital assets and virtual economies, companies need to consult with policymakers on the structure of the law. Meeting all the requirements of data privacy laws, intellectual property rights, and financial regulations will need to remain a priority for future growth. Therefore, the companies that will enter the metaverse need to solve the following ethical issues: the problem of digital addiction, concern about individuals' psychological state in the metaverse, and the digital divide. Developing guidelines for healthy engagement and promoting accessibility will help create a more inclusive and responsible digital environment.

5. CONCLUSION

The use of the metaverse by Epic Games through Fortnite and Unreal Engine demonstrates how organizations can apply new technologies for new strategies of developing business models and engaging with customers. In particular, the company illustrates how one can find new ways of making revenue and connecting people within the metaverse through building virtual economies, driving experiences based on events, or encouraging user-generated content. These observations offer important takeaways for professionals and scholars as the metaverse grows and develops.

For industry professionals, the case of Epic Games offers critical insights into how businesses can diversify revenue streams in digital spaces. Practitioners must consider the importance of event-focused strategies, like virtual concerts and branded experiences, that can involve users and bring valuable sponsorships. Furthermore, businesses could incorporate cross-platform technologies such as Unreal Engine to provide flexible solutions across various sectors, including gaming, architecture, and healthcare. Companies can improve their standing in the competitive online environment by implementing these tactics. Furthermore, companies need to consider the possibilities of blockchain and NFTs in developing fresh economic frameworks in virtual worlds, empowering users to possess digital assets. Nevertheless, professionals should also take note of the legal obstacles related to intellectual property rights and data privacy, as these will be important concerns for companies working on decentralized platforms.

For academics, the study of Epic Games offers several avenues for further exploration. One key area is the study of virtual economies and the impact of decentralized systems on digital asset ownership. Academics can also investigate the role of AI in moderating user-generated content, exploring the ethical and technological challenges posed by large-scale virtual platforms. Another fruitful area for research is the cross-industry application of metaverse technologies. Expanding Unreal Engine into non-gaming sectors, such as healthcare and architecture, opens possibilities for understanding how immersive technologies can enhance productivity and innovation in traditionally non-digital fields. Lastly, the ethical implications of digital welfare, including issues like addiction, psychological impact, and digital inequalities, represent vital topics for future research.

Future research should delve into the evolving role of regulation and governance within the metaverse. As companies like Epic Games continue to push the boundaries of digital economies, researchers need to explore the development of legal frameworks that can govern intellectual property, data privacy, and ethical content creation. Additionally, further studies on blockchain integration in virtual economies and the role of NFTs in defining new ownership models will provide deeper insights into how the digital economy will evolve.

In conclusion, Epic Games is a model for businesses and academics exploring the metaverse. While the company has already revolutionized virtual experiences, ongoing innovation and research will be crucial to addressing the challenges and seizing the opportunities that lie ahead.

REFERENCES

Abrash, M. (2021). Creating the Future: Augmented Reality, the next Human-Machine Interface. *IEEE International Electron Devices Meeting*.

Al-Ghaili, A. M., Kasim, H., Al-Hada, N. M., Hassan, Z. B., Othman, M., Tharik, J. H., Kasmani, R. M., & Shayea, I. (2022). A review of Metaverse's definitions, architecture, applications, challenges, issues, solutions, and future trends. *IEEE Access : Practical Innovations, Open Solutions*, 10, 125835–125866. DOI: 10.1109/ACCESS.2022.3225638

Ball, M. (2022). *The Metaverse: And How it Will Revolutionize Everything*. WW Norton. https://books.google.pt/books?id=fPyqzgEACAAJ

Basyoni, L., Tabassum, A., Shaban, K., Elmahjub, E., Halabi, O., & Qadir, J. (2024). Navigating Privacy Challenges in the Metaverse: A Comprehensive Examination of Current Technologies and Platforms. *IEEE Internet of Things Magazine*, 7(4), 144–152. DOI: 10.1109/IOTM.001.2300197

Bhattacharya, P., Saraswat, D., Savaliya, D., Sanghavi, S., Verma, A., Sakariya, V., Tanwar, S., Sharma, R., Raboaca, M. S., & Manea, D. L. (2023). Towards Future Internet: The Metaverse Perspective for Diverse Industrial Applications. *Mathematics*, 11(4), 941. Advance online publication. DOI: 10.3390/math11040941

Bonetti, F., Warnaby, G., & Quinn, L. (2018). Augmented Reality and Virtual Reality in Physical and Online Retailing: A Review, Synthesis and Research Agenda. In Jung, T., & tom Dieck, M. C. (Eds.), *Augmented Reality and Virtual Reality: Empowering Human, Place and Business* (pp. 119–132). Springer International Publishing. DOI: 10.1007/978-3-319-64027-3_9

Cao, Y. (2023). Microsoft's Layout in the Gaming Industry and Metaverse: Starting from Blizzard. *Advances in Economics. Management and Political Sciences*, 36(1), 99–103. DOI: 10.54254/2754-1169/36/20231791

Chen, Y., & Cheng, H. (2022). *The economics of the metaverse: A comparison with the real economy*. Metaverse.

Cheremnykh, P. (2024). *Gaming the Metaverse: user experience analysis and insights from Fortnite* Metropolia University of Applied Sciences]. https://www.theseus.fi/handle/10024/850495

Clement, J. (2024). *Registered users of Fortnite worldwide from August 2017 to March 2023*. Statista. Retrieved 22 September 2024 from https://www.statista.com/statistics/746230/fortnite-players/

Deavours, D. (2023). Virtual Allies: Why Allyship is Critical to Diversification of Virtual Reality Gaming? *Games and Culture*, 0(0), 15554120231208406. Advance online publication. DOI: 10.1177/15554120231208406

Egliston, B., Carter, M., & Clark, K. (2024). Who will govern the metaverse? Examining governance initiatives for extended reality (XR) technologies. *New Media & Society*. Advance online publication. DOI: 10.1177/14614448231226172

EpicGames. (2022). *Sony and KIRKBI Invest in Epic Games to Build the Future of Digital Entertainment*. Epic Games. Retrieved 10 September 2024 from https://www.epicgames.com/site/en-US/news/sony-and-kirkbi-invest-in-epic-games-to-build-the-future-of-digital-entertainment

Fegert, J. (2023). *Virtual realities, real participation: Challenges and opportunities of public participation in the metaverse*. Project Immersive Democracy. Retrieved 17 September 2024 from https://www.metaverse-forschung.de/en/2023/11/13/virtual-realities-real-participation-challenges-and-opportunities-of-public-participation-in-the-metaverse/

Feng, J., Spence, I., & Pratt, J. (2007). Playing an action video game reduces gender differences in spatial cognition. *Psychological Science*, 18(10), 850–855. DOI: 10.1111/j.1467-9280.2007.01990.x PMID: 17894600

Ferrari, F., & McKelvey, F. (2023). Hyperproduction: A social theory of deep generative models. *Distinktion : Scandinavian Journal of Social Theory*, 24(2), 338–360. DOI: 10.1080/1600910X.2022.2137546

Google. (2024). *Google AR & VR*. Google. Retrieved 23 September 2024 from https://arvr.google.com/

Hardy, W., Paliński, M., & Rożynek, S. (2022). *Roblox and the digital market for virtual experiences* (3). DELab.

Harley, D. (2022). "This would be sweet in VR": On the discursive newness of virtual reality. *New Media & Society*, 17. Advance online publication. DOI: 10.1177/14614448221084655

Hasan, H. R., Madine, M., Musamih, A., Jayaraman, R., Salah, K., Yaqoob, I., & Omar, M. (2024). Non-fungible tokens (NFTs) for digital twins in the industrial metaverse: Overview, use cases, and open challenges. *Computers & Industrial Engineering*, 193, 110315. DOI: 10.1016/j.cie.2024.110315

Healy, P., & Standiford, H. (2023). Enter the Paraverse: Challenging Assumptions of Live Music in the Metaverse. *European Conference on Games Based Learning, 17*, 251-259. https://doi.org/DOI: 10.34190/ecgbl.17.1.1634

Huynh-The, T., Gadekallu, T. R., Wang, W. Z., Yenduri, G., Ranaweera, P., Pham, Q. V., da Costa, D. B., & Liyanage, M. (2023). Blockchain for the metaverse: A Review [Review]. *Future Generation Computer Systems*, 143, 401–419. DOI: 10.1016/j.future.2023.02.008

Jones, S. E. (2008). *The Meaning of Video Games: Gaming and Textual Strategies* (1st ed. ed.). Routledge. https://doi.org/https://doi.org/10.4324/9780203929926

Joshi, R., Pandey, K., & Kumari, S. (2024). A Metaverse: Significance and Dimensions in Various Sectors. 2024 11th International Conference on Computing for Sustainable Global Development (INDIACom). https://doi.org/https://doi.org/10.1177/20563051221107641

Kalning, K. (2008). *The anatomy of the first video game*. NBC News. Retrieved 10 September 2024 from https://www.nbcnews.com/id/wbna27328345

Kalyvaki, M. (2023). Navigating the Metaverse Business and Legal Challenges: Intellectual Property, Privacy, and Jurisdiction. *Journal of Metaverse*. .DOI: 10.57019/jmv.1238344

Kaur, G., Pande, R., Mohan, R., Vij, S., Agrawal, P., Shobhane, P., Pinjarkar, L., Maheshwari, S., & Bagane, P. (2024). A Comprehensive Review of Metaverse: Taxonomy, Impact, and the Hype around It. *Engineering Proceedings*, 62(1).

Koohang, A., Nord, J. H., Ooi, K.-B., Tan, G. W.-H., Al-Emran, M., Aw, E. C.-X., Baabdullah, A. M., Buhalis, D., Cham, T.-H., Dennis, C., Dutot, V., Dwivedi, Y. K., Hughes, L., Mogaji, E., Pandey, N., Phau, I., Raman, R., Sharma, A., Sigala, M., & Wong, L.-W. (2023). Shaping the Metaverse into Reality: A Holistic Multidisciplinary Understanding of Opportunities, Challenges, and Avenues for Future Investigation. *Journal of Computer Information Systems*, 63(3), 735–765. DOI: 10.1080/08874417.2023.2165197

Korkmaz, B. (2023). *Shaping the Future of Spatial Computing with Apple's Vision Pro*. Medium. Retrieved 23 September 2024 from https://barankorkmaz.medium.com/shaping-the-future-of-spatial-computing-with-apples-vision-pro-e70448cb21d9

Latino, M. E., De Lorenzi, M. C., Corallo, A., & Petruzzelli, A. M. (2024). The impact of metaverse for business model innovation: A review, novel insights and research directions. *Technological Forecasting and Social Change*, 206, 123571. DOI: 10.1016/j.techfore.2024.123571

Lbmsolutions, B. (2024). *Who Are the Top Investors in the Metaverse and How Is It Used in Real Life?* Medium. Retrieved 21 September 2024 from https://medium.com/@bhavya21.lbmsolutions/who-are-the-top-investors-in-the-metaverse-and-how-is-it-used-in-real-life-751df6d292ef

Lee, C. T., Ho, T. Y., & Xie, H. H. (2023). Building brand engagement in metaverse commerce: The role of branded non-fungible toekns (BNFTs). *Electronic Commerce Research and Applications*, 58, 101248. Advance online publication. DOI: 10.1016/j.elerap.2023.101248

Lee, J., & Min, H. (2022). *Review of legal protection measures against security threats related to Metaverse*. Korean Association of Public Safety and Criminal Justice. DOI: 10.21181/KJPC.2022.31.3.321

Massaro, M. (2023). Digital transformation in the healthcare sector through blockchain technology. Insights from academic research and business developments. *Technovation*, 120, 102386. Advance online publication. DOI: 10.1016/j.technovation.2021.102386

Metuarau, T. (2023). *A History of Video Games (Version 2)*. Te Herenga Waka—Victoria University of Wellington.

Mosco, V. (2023). Into the Metaverse: Technical Challenges, Social Problems, Utopian Visions, and Policy Principles. *Javnost - The Public*, 30, 161 - 173. .DOI: 10.1080/13183222.2023.2200688

Neves, J., Bacalhau, L. M., & Santos, V. (2024). *A Systematic Review on the Customer Journey Between Two Worlds: Reality and Immersive World*. Marketing and Smart Technologies.

Qadir, A. M.-A., & Alwardat, R. B. Z. (2023). Get Real in the Virtual World: Branding in the Metaverse Demystified. *Tuijin Jishu/Journal of Propulsion Technology, 44*(3), 163-170. https://doi.org/DOI: 10.52783/tjjpt.v44.i3.254

Rostami, S., & Maier, M. (2022). The Metaverse and Beyond: Implementing Advanced Multiverse Realms With Smart Wearables. *IEEE Access : Practical Innovations, Open Solutions*, 10, 110796–110806. DOI: 10.1109/ACCESS.2022.3215736

Sebastian, G. (2023). A Descriptive Study on Metaverse: Cybersecurity Risks, Controls, and Regulatory Framework. *International Journal of Security and Privacy in Pervasive Computing*, 15(1), 1–14. DOI: 10.4018/IJSPPC.315591

Shukla, P., & Taneja, B. (2024). Navigating the Metaverse in Business and Commerce: Opportunities, Challenges, and Ethical Consideration in the Virtual World. *Advances in Social Networking and Online Communities Research, Innovation, and Industry Impacts of the Metaverse*, 183-196. https://doi.org/https://doi.org/10.4018/979-8-3693-2607-7.ch011

Soliman, M. M., Ahmed, E., Darwish, A., & Hassanien, A. E. (2024). Artificial intelligence powered Metaverse: Analysis, challenges and future perspectives. *Artificial Intelligence Review*, 57(2), 36. DOI: 10.1007/s10462-023-10641-x

Statista. (2024). *Metaverse Gaming - Worldwide*. Statista. Retrieved 22 September 2024 from https://www.statista.com/outlook/amo/metaverse/metaverse-gaming/worldwide

Sung, E., Kwon, O., & Sohn, K. (2023). NFT luxury brand marketing in the metaverse: Leveraging blockchain-certified NFTs to drive consumer behavior [Article]. *Psychology and Marketing*, 40(11), 2306–2325. DOI: 10.1002/mar.21854

Taçgın, Z., & Dalgarno, B. (2021). Building an Instructional Design Model for Immersive Virtual Reality Learning Environments. In *Designing* (pp. 20–47). Deploying, and Evaluating Virtual and Augmented Reality in Education. DOI: 10.4018/978-1-7998-5043-4.ch002

Türkmen, N., & Sürmeli, D. (2024). *The Metaverse Virtual Economy: A Comprehensive Overview*. MANAS Sosyal Araştırmalar Dergisi. DOI: 10.33206/mjss.1350087

UnrealEngine. (2023). *Real-Time round-up: the state of interactive 3D*. Epic Games. Retrieved 22 September 2024 from https://www.unrealengine.com/en-US/blog/real-time-round-up-the-state-of-interactive-3d

Vidal-Tomás, D. (2023). The illusion of the metaverse and meta-economy. *International Review of Financial Analysis*, 86, 102560. Advance online publication. DOI: 10.1016/j.irfa.2023.102560

Wang, H., Ning, H., Lin, Y., Wang, W., Dhelim, S., Farha, F., Ding, J., & Daneshmand, M. (2023). A Survey on the Metaverse: The State-of-the-Art, Technologies, Applications, and Challenges. *IEEE Internet of Things Journal*, 10(16), 14671–14688. DOI: 10.1109/JIOT.2023.3278329

Wu, C. H., & Liu, C. Y. (2023). Educational Applications of Non-Fungible Tokens (NFT). *Sustainability (Basel)*, 15(1), 7. Advance online publication. DOI: 10.3390/su15010007

Yasar, A. G., Thomas, A., Barr, K., & Eben, M. (2023). Gaming without Frontiers: Copyright and Competition in the Changing Video Game Sector.

Yuan, Y., & Yang, Y. (2022). *Embracing the Metaverse: Mechanism and logic of a new digital economy*. Metaverse. DOI: 10.54517/met.v3i2.1814

ADDITIONAL READING

Alotaibi, O. (2024). Role of Artificial Intelligence in Enhancing Metaverse Gaming Experience and Human Interaction. *International Journal of Metaverse*. DOI: 10.54536/ijm.v2i1.2933

Bawankule, A. (2024). Metaverse: Advancements, applications, and education. *International Education and Research Journal*, 10(6). Advance online publication. DOI: 10.21276/IERJ24981587561935

Friess, P., & Ruche, A. (2023). The Metaverse, 2030: A Boring Virtual Future Averted by Inspired Entrepreneurs and Artists. *Leonardo*, 56(4), 447–449. DOI: 10.1162/leon_a_02369

Jansen, M., Donkervliet, J., Trivedi, A., & Iosup, A. (2023). Can My WiFi Handle the Metaverse? A Performance Evaluation Of Meta's Flagship Virtual Reality Hardware. *Companion of the 2023 ACM/SPEC International Conference on Performance Engineering*. DOI: 10.1145/3578245.3585022

Mele, C., Spena, T., & Russo, S. (2024). Experimenting on the metaverse to foster innovation. *Spanish Journal of Marketing - ESIC*. Advance online publication. DOI: 10.1108/SJME-05-2023-0117

Sami, H., Hammoud, A., Arafeh, M., Wazzeh, M., Arisdakessian, S., Chahoud, M., Wehbi, O., Ajaj, M., Mourad, A., Otrok, H., Wahab, O., Mizouni, R., Bentahar, J., Talhi, C., Dziong, Z., Damiani, E., & Guizani, M. (2023). The Metaverse: Survey, Trends, Novel Pipeline Ecosystem & Future Directions. DOI: 10.1109/COMST.2024.3392642

Wu, D., Yang, Z., Zhang, P., Wang, R., Yang, B., & Ma, X. (2023). Virtual-Reality Interpromotion Technology for Metaverse: A Survey. *IEEE Internet of Things Journal*, 10(18), 15788–15809. DOI: 10.1109/JIOT.2023.3265848

Yu, H., Shokrnezhad, M., Taleb, T., Li, R., & Song, J. (2023). Toward 6G-Based Metaverse: Supporting Highly-Dynamic Deterministic Multi-User Extended Reality Services. *IEEE Network*, 37(4), 30–38. DOI: 10.1109/MNET.004.2300101

KEY TERMS AND DEFINITIONS

Avatar-Driven Interaction: A mode of communication and engagement in virtual spaces where customizable digital personas represent users.

Cross-Platform Integration: The ability of a virtual platform or game to function across multiple devices and operating systems, enhancing accessibility and user reach.

Experiential Branding: Marketing strategies that leverage immersive environments to create interactive brand experiences, fostering more profound engagement with users.

Immersive Commerce: A computer-based economy in virtual worlds where customers can purchase, sell, and exchange virtual commodities and services.

Platform Monetization: Revenue generation strategies employed by virtual platforms, including in-game purchases, virtual events, and branded experiences.

Spatial Computing: The use of digital technology to interact with and manipulate 3D spaces, forming the backbone of immersive environments.

Synthetic Economy: An entirely virtual economy operating within a digital ecosystem, often governed by platform-specific currencies and market dynamics.

Chapter 2
The Metaverse in Education:
A Case Study

Ana Catarina Monteiro
ISCAP, Polytechnic of Porto, Portugal

Maria Antónia Rodrigues
https://orcid.org/0000-0003-0968-7358
CEOS.PP, ISCAP, Polytechnic of Porto, Portugal

EXECUTIVE SUMMARY

The metaverse, which is still in its infancy, has great potential to transform education, enabling the creation of immersive, three-dimensional virtual environments where students can interact dynamically, carry out simulations, and make teaching more diverse and inclusive. This chapter, through a case study, sought to understand how and why educational institutions are exploiting the metaverse. The results of this research provided a better understanding of the process of creating a metaverse platform for teaching, as well as important variables to consider, highlighting the objectives with the presence in the metaverse, the overall strategy of the educational institution, and the technological infrastructure. The conclusions offer valuable insights for other institutions interested in adopting metaverse in education, helping to guide strategic decisions, and exploring the potential of this emerging technology.

DOI: 10.4018/979-8-3693-7245-6.ch002

INTRODUCTION

In the last few years, advances in digital technologies have brought about profound transformations in the way we interact with the world around us. One of these transformations is the development of the metaverse, an immersive virtual space that combines elements of Augmented Reality, Virtual Reality and other digital technologies to create an interactive environment where people can socialise, learn, play and consume through avatars. In this context, the metaverse has been gaining increasing attention in various areas, including education. The integration of the metaverse into teaching presents itself as a unique opportunity to revolutionise traditional teaching methods, providing more engaging, interactive and personalised learning experiences.

The topic was chosen for a number of reasons that reflect both the current relevance of this phenomenon and its potential impact on the future of education. The metaverse has emerged as one of the most discussed and explored trends in the field of technology, with great potential in the education sector due to its numerous applications.

BACKGROUND

Metaverse Concept

Since the popularisation of the Internet in the 1990s, cyberspace has continued to evolve. Various computer-mediated virtual environments have been created, including social networks, videoconferencing, 3D virtual worlds and Augmented Reality applications. These virtual environments, although not permanent and not connected to each other, have given us various degrees of digital transformation. The term metaverse was coined to further facilitate the digital transition in all aspects of our physical lives. At the centre of the metaverse is the vision of an immersive Internet as one large, unified, persistent and shared realm (Lee et al., 2021).

Although the metaverse is a relatively recent addition to the everyday lexicon of researchers and academics, the term was first used in 1992 in a novel by Neal Stephenson entitled *Snow Crash*. The novel describes the metaverse as a Virtual Reality (VR) space that utilises the Internet and Augmented Reality (AR) through avatars and software agents (Dwivedi et al., 2022).

Figure 1. Metaverse evolution from McKinsey & Company (2022)

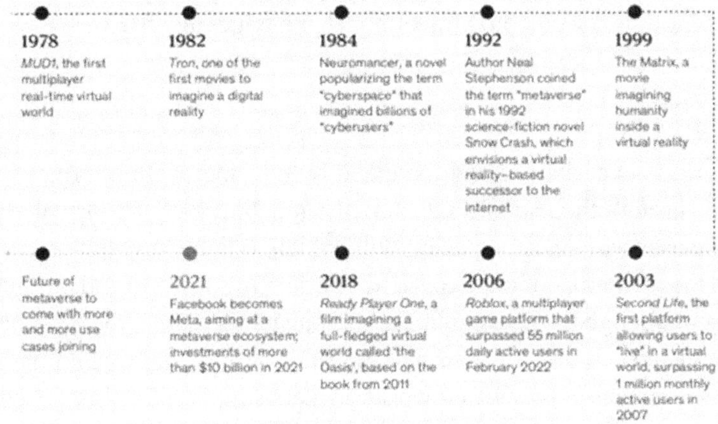

The metaverse is still being defined, both literally and figuratively. However, its potential to trigger the next wave of digital disruption seems increasingly clear, with significant benefits emerging for users and early adopters. Studying its potential effect should be part of strategic discussions, with leaders accelerating their analysis of how the metaverse could lead to a very different world in the next decade (McKinsey & Company, 2022).

The metaverse incorporates Virtual Reality, Augmented Reality and exists in real time, acting as an interface between the real world and virtual worlds. The economy around the metaverse is entirely virtual in nature, fuelled mainly by cryptocurrencies or other digital assets (such as NFTs) (Chowdhury, 2023).

Hardware in the metaverse plays an important role in the immersive experience, but it is also a technically limiting barrier. In the metaverse, hardware is rapidly improved by the effects of technological advancement, but it still needs to be improved compared to the real-world experience. The essential hardware of the Metaverse is a vision-blocking HMD to enable immersive participation (Park & Kim, 2021).

There are currently four different types of hardware available to enhance the user experience in the metaverse. HMDs that show an image through the display and also play sound (they are a basic tool of the metaverse). There are the manual input devices that allow the user to have a tactile sensation of objects. Non-manual input devices such as eye tracking, head tracking and voice input. Finally, there are the motion input devices that provide the physical sensation of space, as well as body tracking (Park & Kim, 2021).

Users of the metaverse can extend their real-life experiences and present themselves in personified avatars to take part in meetings, concerts, parties, art exhibitions, sporting events, sightseeing and travelling (Dwivedi et al., 2022).

Avatar

Any world is experienced and mediated by our bodies. In a virtual world, this is achieved through the use of an avatar (the inhabitant of the virtual world) that provides the user with an active agent with which to interact with the world. These avatars are the mediators of our experience of the virtual world and our interactions with others. Although the user can make their avatar invisible, the presence of each avatar is registered in the system, making their actions observable. By enabling embodied movement in the virtual world, avatars support our sense of presence in a shared space (Girvan, 2018).

The avatar refers to the digital representation of users in the metaverse, where users interact with each other or with computer agents through the avatar. A user can create different avatars in different applications or games. For example, the avatar created can take the form of a human being, imaginary creatures or animals (Lee et al., 2021).

The avatar has a similar meaning to a digital twin and the digital 'I' of the virtual world. A digital twin is a virtual model for predicting behaviour. Digital twins are used to create agents similar to real objects in the virtual world and predict outcomes in advance through situations that may occur in real life (Park & Kim, 2021).

In a first-person view, we don't see the avatar represented, but others see our avatar and its actions, an experience similar to our everyday lives (Girvan, 2018).

Collaboration and communication are important values for the metaverse. User avatars can collaborate and share experiences. They create value through this collaboration and sharing. Unlike in the real world, this collaboration makes it possible to transcend time and space. It also gives users a common goal and allows the metaverse to continue as a society (Dwivedi et al., 2022).

In the expansive universe of the metaverse, the relationship between avatars and virtual worlds is deeply symbiotic. As avatars navigate these digital spaces, they shape and are shaped by the immersive environments they explore.

Virtual Worlds

The metaverse is synonymous with user immersion, which is why virtual reality technology has traditionally been associated with this phenomenon. Virtual worlds seek to create an alternative reality, different from the real world, in which individuals find themselves immersed. For this immersion, the technology is already available: virtual reality glasses or visualisers or HMD (head-mounted display). These devices take presence and immersion to another level thanks to technology that allows high-quality image rendering and freedom of movement in the virtual environment. With them, the boundary between the real and virtual worlds is blurred (Crespo-Pereira, et al., 2023).

Virtual worlds are three-dimensional environments where users have a goal to fulfil. They are called 'game-orientated' virtual worlds (e.g. World of Warcraft), or they are left free, without any specific objective imposed by the virtual world, called 'free-form' or 'social' virtual worlds, such as There and Second Life (Hassouneh et Brengman, 2013).

These 3D environments, which mimic the real world, allow real-time interactions between user avatars and provide unlimited possibilities and experiences. Users can freely create and control their environment. They can create, buy and sell products and services, get married, dance, eat, among other actions. In other words, they can live a complete virtual life (Hassouneh and Brengman, 2013). Universities, political parties, international organisations and even embassies can be found in virtual worlds (Hassouneh et Brengman, 2013). Virtual worlds are not about how they look, but about what is contained within them (Spence, 2010).

According to Oliveira (2023), the founding characteristics of VWs are:

- Interactivity: it exists on a computer, but with the possibility of remote access (i.e. via an Internet connection) and simultaneously by a large number of people, with one person's command inputs influencing the results of other people's commands;
- Physicality: people access the platform via an interface that simulates a physical environment in the first person on their computer screen - the environment is generally by the natural laws of the land and is characterised by the scarcity of resources;
- Persistence: the programme continues to work whether someone uses it or not, and it remembers the location of people and things, as well as the ownership of objects.

In virtual worlds, users encounter countless digital environments that offer immersive and interactive experiences. These digital spaces are not limited to entertainment, but also extend their impact to areas such as education.

Education in the metaverse

Virtual worlds have great potential for education and training. However, it seems that VR applications for education are scarce. The interest of these studies lies in creating training programmes in safe, accessible and affordable environments that would be impossible in real life (Crespo-Pereira, et al, 2023).

Online education is becoming a more viable alternative to learning for a growing number of people who have jobs, families and wish to continue their education in their spare time. Teachers are finding new and innovative uses for web-based 3D environments. Virtual worlds allow students to visit places that cannot be visited, overcome stereotypes, role-play, collaborate in groups, carry out scenario simulations and interact with a global audience. The increase in distance learning enrolments and the use of distance technologies in many major institutions is accompanied by a driving force to search for and identify different synchronous and asynchronous teaching models to meet the demands of students who need a 24/7 service (Spence, 2010).

The metaverse as an educational tool is analysed from the perspective of gamification, classroom teaching, cognitive value, and is also considered an option for people with neurological problems (such as autism) or intellectual disabilities. The monetisation of education is another predicted scenario for the benefits of the metaverse (Crespo-Pereira, et al., 2023).

Over the last two decades, we have seen the transformation of the education sector as digital tools have been integrated into teaching, learning and assessment processes. The use of digital educational platforms (e.g. Moodle, Blackboard, edX, etc.) has enabled students to have asynchronous learning experiences. Virtual meeting platforms (e.g. Zoom, WebEx, etc.) have helped students and educators participate in synchronous learning across spatial boundaries. These tools have revolutionised students'experiences (i.e. learning experiences), educators' teaching approaches and provided new business opportunities for education providers, paving the way for AI-based adaptive learning systems (Dwivedi et al., 2022).

To design metaverse platforms for education, it is important to thoroughly understand the elements of face-to-face learning and identify how to emulate them in the virtual world. Challenges in this regard could include, for example, simulating avatar social interactions in the metaverse that incorporate the gestures and body language of students and educators (Dwivedi et al., 2022).

In the metaverse, with the use of AI and multimodal data analysis, educators will have a broad spectrum of information about students' reactions, teaching materials and approaches at their disposal. For example, they will have information on micro gestures or interactions to see if students are attentive and interested (Dwivedi et al., 2022).

Regarding the potential of the metaverse in the field of education, laboratory simulations (e.g. safety training), the development of procedural skills (e.g. surgery) and the teaching of science, technology, engineering and maths are among the first areas of application with spectacular results in terms of training speed, performance and retention with AR and VR-supported lessons. In addition, new distance learning models driven by the metaverse could emerge to break down the limitations of 2D platforms. Meta-education can enable rich, hybrid formal and informal active learning experiences in perpetual, alternating, online 3D virtual campuses, where students are co-owners of the virtual spaces and co-creators of personalised curricula (Mystakidis, 2021).

Although the use of the metaverse for learning purposes is still in its infancy, it is expected to make great strides in the coming years and become a new paradigm in education (Dwivedi et al., 2022).

METHODOLOGY

This topic discusses the methodology and techniques used to obtain data for analysing the research.

For this case study, a qualitative methodology was adopted, using the structured interview technique, which made it possible to collect data in greater depth, with a view to analysing and understanding it.

The main aim of the research is to understand how the metaverse is being used in teaching, by studying the case of an educational institution that has already adopted it.

Case Study

A case study is an empirical enquiry that investigates a contemporary phenomenon in depth and in a real-life context, especially when the boundaries between the phenomenon and the context are not clearly evident (Yin, 2010).

Thus, the main aim of qualitative methodology is to describe a problem that is not yet widely known and to characterise it, i.e. to explore a concept that leads to the description of an experience or attributes meaning to that experience. It focuses on what, how and why (Silva & Dixie, 2020).

Structured interviews are characterised by fully following an established script, reserving the researcher the role of mere data compiler and the responsibility of creating an environment conducive to the interviewees answering the questions posed (Sá et al, 2021).

According to Yin (2014), the case study is a comprehensive method that encompasses logic, data collection techniques and specific approaches to analysing data. It is a method that focuses on the rigour, validity and reliability of the data.

Triangulation arises from the need to improve validity and credibility, starting from the principle that there is a need to understand the different dimensions of the study and consider them in order to analyse it. It is a multidimensional approach to collecting and analysing data, based on the principle that the phenomenon can and should be analysed in various ways and from various perspectives.

There are four types of triangulation:

a) triangulation of data sources: when we use several sources of data;
b) researcher triangulation: several researchers working as a group;
c) theory triangulation: the emerging theory is analysed by several researchers;
d) methodological triangulation: using various methodologies (Silva & Dixie, 2020).

Case Selection

The case study chosen is related to the research topic, being an example of a national educational institution that has been a pioneer in building a presence in the metaverse.

Based on the following criteria, the case was selected for the study:

1. National educational institution with at least five years of existence;
2. To be an educational institution with notoriety and relevance at national and international level;
3. Presence of the educational institution in the metaverse for at least one year.

Case Study Procedures

Based on the theoretical background, a script was drawn up to collect data through a structured interview. The main aim of the topics covered in the interview is to understand the educational institution's perspective on the metaverse and its approach to entering it, as well as prospects for the future.

The interview is one of the most widely used techniques in scientific work today. It allows the researcher to extract a very large amount of data and information that makes for a very rich piece of work. The interview is certainly the most flexible of all the data collection techniques available to the social sciences (Júnior & Júnior, 2011).

The selection of the interviewee was based mainly on their in-depth knowledge of the educational institution under study and its presence in the metaverse.

The interview followed a structure with the following stages:

- Initial moment of the interview: presentation of the researcher and the research topic, as well as requesting authorisation to record the interview with a view to analysing it later.
- Interview: questions related to the themes explained in the theoretical framework were asked, as well as questions about the educational institution and its presence in the metaverse. Initially, the interviewee answered questions about the metaverse - including its meaning, why they felt it was important to take this step, the objectives with their presence on these platforms and whether they created everything internally. Also included were questions about the educational institution's presence in the metaverse - such as their future prospects, their target and positioning in the metaverse, how they included the metaverse in teaching, the importance of the metaverse in improving the performance of educational institutions, among other questions deemed relevant. The aim was to understand how the metaverse is being used in education, in this specific case, as well as the interviewee's perceptions of the institution's presence in this context.
- Closing the interview: the interview ended with an important question for the research, which aims to understand how the institution's metaverse strategy is linked to the institution's overall strategy, as well as the value that the metaverse represents in terms of investment. The interview ended with thanks for the interviewee's co-operation in the research.

The interview took place on 4 July 2024 and was followed by data processing and analysis.

DATA ANALYSIS

Analysing the Results

The first question aimed to understand the interviewee's perception of the metaverse concept. The answer revealed an optimistic and future-oriented vision, highlighting the transformative potential of this technology in consumer behavior. He identifies the metaverse as the natural next step in the evolution of online shopping, offering a more realistic and immersive experience compared to traditional internet shopping methods. By emphasizing the feeling of immersion and augmented reality, the interviewee suggests that the metaverse could complement current forms of digital consumption. This perspective underlines the importance of the metaverse being seen not just as a technological tool, but as a new paradigm that could profoundly change the way we interact with commerce and other online activities.

Regarding the importance of entering the metaverse, the interviewee highlights a clear commitment to innovation and technological leadership. He emphasizes that the main objective of this educational institution is to be at the forefront. This attitude demonstrates a proactive and ambitious vision, seeking to anticipate trends and prepare the institution for the future.

According to the interviewee, the objectives with its presence in the metaverse are related to its recognized ambition to innovate. The growing relevance of the metaverse is mentioned, especially as technology evolves and the importance of virtual reality and augmented reality grows.

This educational institution aims to provide its students with an immersive experience, simulating what it might be like to be at college. With its fully online portfolio, the metaverse can gain even more value, especially for networking and remote networking events. This point highlights the versatility and potential of the metaverse to improve interactions and connections between students, teachers and the business community, regardless of geographical barriers.

The next question was about how they included metaverse in their teaching. They have incorporated the metaverse into existing programs and also intend to incorporate it into new programs that may be developed. The interviewee emphasizes their commitment to what they see as the future of digital transformation. The institution seeks to show this future by creating avatars and a virtual space, like a classroom, where participants can interact and learn. This approach represents an advanced stage of digitalization, in which the digital transformation cycle is almost complete. The creation of this virtual environment aims to provide an immersive and interactive experience, reflecting the educational institution's vision of the potential of digital technology in teaching.

In response to the question about the role they want to play in the future in the metaverse, the interviewee highlights the institution's ambition to be a reference in teaching within this new digital environment. He emphasizes that this leadership stance extends to both online and offline teaching, indicating a commitment to integrating the metaverse into the institution's educational strategy.

About their target in the metaverse, the interviewee states that there is a correspondence between their target online and their target offline. The programs currently on offer are entirely in Portuguese, which defines the initial target audience as mainly Portugal and the Portuguese-speaking countries. At the same time, the interviewee recognizes that there is a gradual transition towards English, which eventually aims to reach a global audience.

To characterize the students' experience in the metaverse, the interviewee relies on feedback from participants. He divides perceptions into two groups: those without virtual reality glasses, who tend to have a more ordinary and less exciting experience, and those with virtual reality glasses, who engage more immersively and show an interest in repeating the experience.

The interviewee says that the creation of value and the engagement generated in the metaverse is done through the environment and its ability to provide an almost face-to-face experience. The use of augmented reality to modify and interact with digital content is mentioned. In practice, at this institution, this involves recreating past experiences in a classroom, allowing participants to watch previous sessions as if they were students present, with the teacher teaching. In addition, the interviewee mentions the possibility of interacting with bots, creating a "question and answer" dynamic virtually. This approach aims to enrich the educational and informational experience within the metaverse.

In response to the question about the importance of the metaverse in improving the performance of educational institutions, the interviewee recognizes that this technology is still currently seen as something a little unrealistic. He points out that the adoption of virtual reality glasses and the ability to interact intuitively with avatars are limited to a minority. However, he emphasizes that, despite being at an early stage of learning and development, the metaverse has the potential to become a valuable tool. It could become a significant asset for communicating the institution's brand and positioning it at the forefront of innovation.

The results and return on the metaverse presence are evaluated through satisfaction questionnaires, a common practice for gathering feedback from participants. These questionnaires aim to understand the users' experience in the metaverse by assessing various factors such as whether they would like to repeat the experience, how they would like to deepen their involvement, whether the experience was relevant to them and what suggestions they have for improvement.

Regarding how they manage their presence in the metaverse, the interviewee mentions the existence of a Digital Experience Lab, a knowledge center dedicated to the digital area. To manage their presence in the metaverse, they use resources from this Digital Experience Lab, which also collaborates with the institution's IT team. The interviewee emphasizes that the metaverse is not currently an absolute priority for the institution. Although they are developing their presence in this area, the management and allocation of resources is not as intense as in other strategic areas.

The positioning they wish to have in the metaverse coincides with their offline positioning, the interviewee indicating that he believes it is only a matter of time before this alignment takes place. He suggests that in both the physical and digital environments, including the metaverse, the institution intends to achieve the same objectives and targets.

The interviewee's response about the steps they considered important for preparing the metaverse shows a strategic and cautious approach. By highlighting the importance of starting internally, providing employees and students with direct experience of the metaverse, he demonstrates a commitment to familiarizing the institution's own members first. This not only helps to create an environment where everyone is aligned with the goals and benefits of the metaverse, but also empowers everyone involved to contribute ideas and improvements to the implementation process.

On the relationship between the institution's metaverse strategy and its overall strategy, the interviewee compares the metaverse to a "small satellite" in relation to the university's main operation. This suggests that the metaverse, although seen as an area of interest and experimentation, does not yet occupy a central or priority role in the overall strategy. By mentioning that the metaverse is not a priority at the moment and that it is being managed according to the resources and time available, the interviewee shows a gradual and cautious approach to this new technology.

About investment in the metaverse, the interviewee again mentions that, although it is not an absolute priority, the institution considers it important to be present in this emerging environment. He mentions again that they are using internal resources, such as the IT team and the Digital Experience Lab, thus taking advantage of skills that already exist within the institution, without making a significant additional investment. Compared to other strategic investments, such as artificial intelligence, it highlights the allocation of resources in proportion to the priorities perceived by the educational institution.

Discussion

First of all, in relation to the concept of the metaverse, the interviewee recognizes the importance and potential of this technology and characterizes these experiences as realistic and immersive. Compared to the theoretical framework, this coincides with the interviewee's view that the metaverse has the potential to trigger the next wave of digital disruption. As also mentioned in the theoretical framework, it is important for leaders to investigate and include the study of the potential of the metaverse in their strategies, as this institution has done.

Regarding the importance considered and the objectives with their presence in the metaverse, the ambition to be at the forefront and to innovate is highlighted. As in the previous answer, the interviewee mentions the relevance of the metaverse and the growing importance of virtual reality and augmented reality. This view corresponds to a vision explained in the theoretical framework which confirms a relevant competitive advantage for those who are early adopters of metaverse technologies.

In including this institution in the metaverse, the importance of avatars and the immersive environment of a virtual classroom was mentioned. The avatar is recognized as a digital representation of the students and as a mediator of the metaverse experience. Its use to collaborate and share experiences is also recognized. These experiences include a simulation of the university, something very common in metaverse teaching. The response reflects a strategic vision that aims not only to stay ahead of trends, but also to create value for students and participants through immersive, quality learning experiences.

This educational institution aims to be a benchmark in metaverse education. This statement highlights an adaptive strategy of gradual expansion, starting with a specific national and international focus based on the Portuguese language, but with plans for future expansion to reach a wider audience with the availability of programs in English.

The students' experience in the metaverse is characterized differently based on HMD ownership. The interviewee says that those who own this type of hardware tend to have a more immersive and engaging experience, while those who don't tend to have a more ordinary and less exciting experience. Based on what has been covered in the theoretical framework, it is important to note that hardware is both important and limiting when it comes to the user experience in the metaverse, and this is perceived by the interviewee. This technology provides a high degree of immersion in the virtual environment and often ends up blurring the boundary between the physical and the virtual. Virtual worlds are characterized by their interactivity, physicality and persistence, but HMDs make it possible to experience these worlds in a much more impactful way.

The shopping experience in the metaverse is something that has yet to be explored, but the monetization of education is one of the great benefits in this area. Whether through the purchase of training or educational materials, training events, a monthly subscription with access to exclusive content or personalized support. The interviewee's response demonstrates a strategy of using the metaverse not only as an educational environment, but also as a marketing and interaction tool.

The creation of value and the engagement generated in the metaverse are done mainly through sharing and collaboration, with the aim of providing relevant and differentiated educational experiences. They seek to recreate the environment experienced in a classroom, something very common in education in the metaverse. In addition, they also want to create tools that allow students to have a personalized, dynamic accompaniment free of spatial and temporal barriers (for example with interaction with bots).

The metaverse could play a key role in enhancing the performance of educational institutions. According to the interviewee, it is something with significant potential, though, in the current context, somewhat unrealistic. Additionally, only a few users have access to the necessary hardware for a truly immersive experience. This view is supported by the theoretical framework, which describes education in the metaverse as having vast potential due to the endless possibilities within virtual worlds. However, its applications in education are still limited, as is users' access to the required hardware. Furthermore, there are several barriers that must be addressed in relation to the metaverse, including privacy and data protection challenges, training for teachers and support staff, institutional, technical, and financial barriers, accessibility, and digital exclusion.

The metaverse could be extremely useful for exploring simulations in learning environments, such as realistic business scenarios or immersive case studies. Another relevant aspect is the potential for hybrid educational experiences, where students can learn both on campus and online through the metaverse. This flexibility is increasingly valued, especially in specialized programs, training courses, undergraduate and graduate degrees, where students often need to balance their academic pursuits with professional commitments. Another important application relates to inclusivity in education, enabling comprehensive support and learning experiences for students with health challenges, which are sometimes difficult to provide through in-person classes alone.

The perceived importance is related to how they manage their presence in the metaverse. Given that it is not a priority, the allocation of resources for this purpose is not as intense as for other projects (related to Artificial Intelligence, for example). However, it is important to highlight the commitment to monitoring the impact and reception of your initiatives in the metaverse, making continuous adjustments and improvements based on user feedback. This evaluation method also reflects the institution's awareness of the need to adapt to new technologies and ensure that they contribute effectively to its educational and strategic objectives.

The educational institution is adopting a posture of observation and experimentation in relation to the metaverse, aligning its strategy with priorities and available resources, while assessing the potential impact of this emerging technology on its educational and institutional model. Their strategy in the metaverse coincides with their global strategy, since in both channels they intend to be "at the forefront" and make a mark on the national and international scene with the innovation and excellence they are recognized for.

Finally, about the veracity of the answers, a triangulation of data sources was carried out, which made it possible to compare the interviewee's answers with other available sources, mainly news and articles on the subject, thus confirming the veracity of the data.

CONCLUSION

This chapter has analysed the integration and impact of metaverse in one of the main higher education institutions in Portugal. The purpose of the research was to understand how the transition and integration of the metaverse is being carried out in educational institutions by studying a specific case.

The theoretical background to this research was based on four main pillars: the concept of the metaverse, the concept of the avatar, virtual worlds and education in the metaverse. It made it possible to understand various concepts and realise how the metaverse is being applied in education, as well as the potential of this tool.

The metaverse is being recognised as the next step in education, as it can offer an immersive and differentiated experience compared to traditional methods. This phenomenon has the potential to transform education, something that was emphasised by both the theory and the interviewee's perceptions.

The use of avatars in education facilitates personalisation and the creation of immersive learning environments, increasing interaction between students. It is important to emphasise that these avatars must be able to clearly convey their reactions, as this is essential for the trainer to understand how they are feeling about their lesson and the content being taught.

Education in the metaverse has the potential to revolutionise teaching, providing learning experiences that transcend physical and geographical limitations. The possibilities are endless and can include, for example, realistic simulations, collaborative experiences, hybrid learning environments and personalised support for students with special needs. With the significant increase in distance learning enrolments and a growth in the use of synchronous and asynchronous learning tools, it is essential to consider these platforms as an instrument for learning. However, there are still some constraints to the adoption of the metaverse in education, such as limited access to suitable hardware and the early stage of development of this technology.

In these first steps in metaverse education, it is important to include everyone involved in the learning process in order to create something that meets everyone's needs and requirements. Furthermore, before setting up a presence on these platforms, it is crucial to master and understand the learning elements that exist in person in order to identify how to replicate them in the best possible way.

The methodology chosen for this case study was qualitative, using a structured interview. This approach made it possible to gain a detailed insight into the perceptions and strategies of this educational institution in relation to the metaverse. The interview provided valuable insights into how they are integrating the metaverse into their programmes, the perceived importance of this technology and the associated opportunities.

The interview showed that the institution has a proactive and innovative vision of metaverse, recognising its transformative potential. It is integrating metaverse into some of its executive programmes and exploring new ways of providing more enriching experiences for students. Although the metaverse is not currently a top priority, they are using internal resources to develop and manage their presence in this new digital environment.

They intend to align their metaverse strategy with their global strategy, maintaining a commitment to innovation and excellence. The use of avatars and immersive virtual environments is seen as a natural extension of their educational offerings, providing new opportunities for learning and networking.

This case study highlights the importance of exploring new technologies and adapting to changes in the educational and technological landscape. This educational institution is preparing for a future where the metaverse could play a crucial role, not just as an educational tool, but as a new paradigm for digital interaction and consumption.

It is important to note that, although research presents an optimistic view of the metaverse, several barriers need to be overcome. Challenges include digital exclusion, accessibility, data protection and privacy, teacher and trainer training, as well as technical, financial, and institutional barriers. Educational institutions should strive to address these challenges by, for example, seeking partnerships, securing government funding, or even developing low-cost alternatives for immersive learning technologies.

REFERENCES

Abovitz, R., Banerjee, S., Gilliland, G., Liu, C., Sackey, E., Timashkov, A., & Trollinger, R. (2022). How the Metaverse Will Remake Your Strategy. Boston Consulting Group. https://mkt-bcg-com-public-pdfs.s3.amazonaws.com/prod/impact-of-metaverse-on-business.pdf

Ante, L. (2022). The Non-Fungible Token (NFT) Market and Its Relationship with Bitcoin and Ethereum. MDPI. https://www.mdpi.com/2674-1032/1/3/17

Bálint, K. (2024). The Possibility of Creating an NFT (Non-Fungible Token) Based University Diploma. https://ieeexplore.ieee.org/stamp/stamp.jsp?tp=&arnumber=10432827

Bhandari, P. (2023). What Is Qualitative Research? | Methods & Examples. https://www.scribbr.com/methodology/qualitative-research/

Canavarro, A., & Moreira, B. (2024). *Metaverso no Marketing, nas Marcas e nos Negócios*. Grupo LIDEL.

Chandra, Y. (2022). Non-fungible token-enabled entrepreneurship: A conceptual Framework. Elsevier. https://www.sciencedirect.com/science/article/pii/S235267342200021X?via%3Dihub

Chohan, U. W. (2024). Non-Fungible Tokens (NFTs): Early Thoughts & A Research Agenda. *SSRN.*

Chowdhury, R. (2023). The Metaverse Will Transform Existing Brand Marketing Strategies. O https://www.prweb.com/releases/the-metaverse-will-transform-existing-brand-marketing-strategies-raj-chowdhury-894680040.html

Crespo-Pereira, V., Sánchez-Amboage, E., & Membiela-Pollán, M. (2023). Facing the challenges of metaverse: a systematic literature review from Social Sciences and Marketing and Communication. Profesional de la información. https://revista.profesionaldelainformacion.com/index.php/EPI/article/view/87104/63308

Digest, H. (2022). The Metaverse Will Transform Existing Brand Marketing Strategies: Raj Chowdhury. CISION PRWeb. https://www.prweb.com/releases/the-metaverse-will-transform-existing-brand-marketing-strategies-raj-chowdhury-894680040.html

Dionisio, J. D. N., Iii, W. G. B., & Gilbert, R. (2013). 3D virtual worlds and the metaverse: Current status and future possibilities. ACM computing surveys (CSUR), 45(3), 1-38. https://dl.acm.org/doi/abs/10.1145/2480741.2480751

Dixie, M. A. (2020). Investigação Qualitativa. Politécnico de Leiria. https://iconline.ipleiria.pt/bitstream/10400.8/5250/1/Manual%20de%20apoio_Investiga%c3%a7%c3%a3o%20II_Qualitativa_Silvia_silva_FINAL_alunos_29.09.2020.pdf

Dwivedi, Y., Hughes, L., Baabdullah, A., Ribeiro-Navarrete, S., Giannakis, M., Al-Debei, M., Dennehy, D., Metri, B., Buhalis, D., Cheung, C., Conboy, K., Doyle, R., Dubey, R., Dutot, V., Felix, R., Goyal, G., Gustafsson, A., Hinsch, C., Jebabli, I., Janssen, M., Kim, Y., Kim, J., Koos, S., Kreps, D., Kshetri, N., Kumar, V., Ooi, K., Papagiannidis, S., Pappas, I., Polyviou, A., Park, S., Pandey, N., Queiroz, M., Raman, R., Rauschnabek, P., Shirish, A., Sigala, M., Spanaki, K., Tan, G., Tiwari, M., Viglia, G., Wamba, S. (2022). Metaverse beyond the hype: Multidisciplinary perspectives on emerging challenges, opportunities, and agenda for research, practice and policy. International Journal of Information Management

Hollweck, T. (2016). Yin Review. Canadian Journal of Program Evaluation. https://www.researchgate.net/publication/308385754_Robert_K_Yin_2014_Case_Study_Research_Design_and_Methods_5th_ed_Thousand_Oaks_CA_Sage_282_pages

Júnior, A. F. B., & Júnior, N. F. (2011). A utilização da técnica da entrevista em trabalhos científicos. Revista Evidência. https://ojs.uniaraxa.edu.br/index.php/evidencia/article/view/200/186

Lee, L., Braud, T., Zhou, P., Wang, L., Xu, D., Lin, Z., Kumar, A., Bermejo, C., & Hui, P. (2021). All One Needs to Know about Metaverse: A Complete Survey on Technological Singularity, Virtual Ecosystem, and Research Agenda. Journal of Latex Class Files, 14(8).

Martins, H. T. S. (2004). Metodologia Qualitativa de Pesquisa. Universidade de São Paulo. http://educa.fcc.org.br/pdf/ep/v30n02/v30n02a07.pdf

McKinsey & Company. (2022). What is the metaverse? https://www.mckinsey.com/featured-insights/mckinsey-explainers/what-is-the-metaverse

McKinsey & Company. (2022). Value creation in the metaverse. https://www.mckinsey.com/~/media/mckinsey/business%20functions/marketing%20and%20sales/our%20insights/value%20creation%20in%20the%20metaverse/Value-creation-in-the-metaverse.pdf

Mystakidis, S. (2022). Metaverse. Encyclopedia, 2(1), 486-497. https://www.mdpi.com/2673-8392/2/1/31

Oliveira, J. I. V. R. (2022). Gestão da Presença da Marca no Metaverso - O caso da marca de moda Fly London [Unpublished master's thesis]. ISAG.

Parham, A., & Breitinger, C. (2022). Non-fungible Tokens: Promise or Peril? https://arxiv.org/pdf/2202.06354

Pinto-Gutiérrez, C., Gaitán, S., Jaramillo, D., Velasquez, S. (2022) The NFT Hype: What Draws Attention to Non-Fungible Tokens? DOI: 10.3390/math10030335

Regner, F., Urbach, N., & Schweizer, A. (2019). NFTs in Practice – Non-Fungible Tokens as Core Component of a Blockchain-based Event Ticketing Application. *Fortieth International Conference on Information Systems*

Sá, P., Costa, A. P., & Moreira, A. (2021). *Reflexões em torno de Metodologias de Investigação: recolha de dados*. Universidade de Aveiro.

Safian-Demers, E. (2022). The metaverse glossary. Obtido a partir de https://www.vml.com/insight/the-metaverse-glossary

Vieira, C. A. (2023). Case study as a qualitative research methodology. Performance Improvement, 62(4).

Wang, D., Yan, X., & Zhou, Y. (2021). Research on Metaverse: Concept, development and standard system. https://ieeexplore.ieee.org/stamp/stamp.jsp?arnumber=9741935

Wang, Q., Li, R., Wang, Q., & Chen, S. (2021). Non-Fungible Token (NFT): Overview, Evaluation, Opportunities and Challenges. https://arxiv.org/pdf/2105.07447

Wilson, K. B., Karg, A., & Ghaderi, H. (2022). *Prospecting non-fungible tokens in the digital economy: Stakeholders and ecosystem, risk and opportunity*. Elsevier.

Wunderman Thompson Intelligence. (2021). *Into the Metaverse* (2021 Edition). Wunderman Thompson Intelligence.

Wunderman Thompson Intelligence. (2022). *New realities Into the Metaverse and beyond* (2022 Edition). Wunderman Thompson Intelligence.

Yin, R. K. (2009). *Case Study Research: Design and Methods* (4th ed.). Bookman.

Yin, R. K. (2013). Validity and generalization in future case study evaluations. *Evaluation*, 19(3), 321–332. DOI: 10.1177/1356389013497081

Yin, R. K. (n.d.). How to do Better Case Studies (Chapter 8). https://books.google.com.br/books?hl=pt-PT&lr=&id=9_bUtEp-bGUC&oi=fnd&pg=PA254&dq=yin+case+study+research&ots=-xO67LJMXN&sig=IUg2rTfPCO9JPGFeIbIXr7WVwdc#v=onepage&q=yin%20case%20study%20research&f=false

ADDITIONAL READING

Canavarro, A., & Moreira, B. (2024). *Metaverso no Marketing, nas Marcas e nos Negócios*. Grupo LIDEL.

McKinsey & Company. (2022). What is the metaverse? https://www.mckinsey.com/featured-insights/mckinsey-explainers/what-is-the-metaverse

Wunderman Thompson Intelligence. (2022). *New realities Into the Metaverse and beyond* (2022 Edition). Wunderman Thompson Intelligence.

KEY TERMS AND DEFINITIONS

Augmented Reality: Technology that overlays digital content, such as images, sounds, or information, onto the real world, enhancing a user's view of their physical surroundings. It blends the virtual and physical worlds by using devices like smartphones, tablets, or AR glasses.

Avatar: Digital representation or character used by a person to represent themselves in virtual environments, such as video games, social media, or the metaverse. It can be a 2D image, 3D model, or customizable figure that users control to interact with others and the virtual world.

Metaverse: Virtual, interconnected digital space where people can interact with each other and digital environments in real time, often through avatars. It integrates elements of virtual reality (VR), augmented reality (AR), and online social platforms, enabling immersive experiences like gaming, shopping, socializing, and working in a shared virtual world.

NFT (Non-Fungible Token): Unique digital asset stored on a blockchain, representing ownership or proof of authenticity for items like artwork, music, videos, or virtual goods. Unlike cryptocurrencies, NFTs are indivisible and cannot be exchanged on a one-to-one basis because each one has distinct properties.

Virtual Reality: Technology that immerses users in a fully digital, simulated environment, typically experienced through a headset with motion tracking. It allows users to interact with and explore 3D virtual worlds as if they were physically present.

Virtual Worlds: Immersive, computer-generated environments where users can interact with each other and digital objects through avatars. These worlds can simulate real-life or fictional settings and often involve social interaction, gaming, or exploration in a shared, persistent digital space.

Chapter 3
The Metaverse:
Redefining Learning Spaces and Educational Experiences

Manpreet K. Riyat
https://orcid.org/0000-0002-1190-0819
Lovely Professional University, India

Amit Kakkar
Lovely Professional University, India

Ruchi Kakkar
Lovely Professional University, India

EXECUTIVE SUMMARY

This chapter examines the transformative capacity of the Metaverse in education, emphasizing how immersive technologies like virtual reality (VR) and augmented reality (AR) are redefining the traditional education environment. This chapter analyses essential components such as virtual classrooms, digital twins, and immersive learning experiences, illustrating how educators can utilize these innovations to improve student engagement, collaboration, and learning results. It also discusses the used cases of various components of metaverse that are executed in Metaverse-oriented educational settings, providing insights into existing applications, prospective developments, and anticipated progressions. The chapter examines the role of stakeholders in metaverse-based education, researchers, and policymakers, as well as a thorough comprehension of the opportunities and problems associated with developing inclusive and participatory learning experiences within the Metaverse.

DOI: 10.4018/979-8-3693-7245-6.ch003

1. INTRODUCTION TO THE METAVERSE

Metaverse is derived from the combination of the Greek prefix "meta," meaning transcending, and "verse," signifying universe. It is a nearly parallel world linked to the tangible world, the outcome of the development and the amalgamation of many technologies, the subsequent phase of advancements in the internet and a digital living environment with social interaction characteristics (Wang et al., 2023). Neal Stephenson's 1992 science fiction novel Snow Crash introduced the concept of the Metaverse, in which humans, in the form of programmable avatars, engage with software agents and one another in a three-dimensional virtual environment that employs the analogy of the real world (Damar, 2021). The evolution of the Metaverse signifies the advancement of the virtual realm to a degree. Dionisio et al. (2013) outlined five stages in the growth of virtual worlds, ranging from their early existence solely in literature and games to the contemporary immersive 3-D virtual environments where users can independently generate content.

Metaverse is a collective virtual shared space created by the convergence of virtually enhanced physical reality and physically persistent virtual reality. This space is accessible through the internet and can be experienced through virtual reality (VR), augmented reality (AR), and other immersive technologies (Ritterbusch & Teichmann, 2023). VR creates an immersive environment that immerses the sensation of "being there" for users (Bowman & McMahan, 2007; Wohlgenannt et al., 2020) whereas, AR is a digital enhancement of an individual's visual and auditory perceptions (Jingen Liang & Elliot, 2021), commonly accessed by smart glasses, laptops, tablets and mobile phones. It is defined as the application that "augments the physical world with computer-generated virtual entities that seem to exist concurrently within the same environment as the physical world" (Azuma et al., 2001). Another notion used in the chapter is immersion or immersive experience of using these technologies in educational environment, its meaning is previously given by many researchers such as stated that (Zhang, 2020) "immersion means either the system engages us or we are captivated by the system." The concept of immersive technologies are predominantly associated with AR and VR this can support learning paradigm such as experimental learning in technological educational environment permeate mobile learning environment (Baxter & Hainey, 2024). Immersion is a frequently used synonymously with the concepts of presence and involvement (Nilsson et al., 2016). It is multifaceted concept viewed via a technological lens, frequently linked to immersive technologies like virtual reality and digital gaming (Feng et al., 2018).

Initially regarded as a speculative notion in science fiction, the Metaverse has progressed considerably in recent years, propelled by advancements in virtual and augmented reality, artificial intelligence, blockchain, and cloud computing (Yang et al., 2022). As these technologies advance and become more accessible, the prospect of the Metaverse as a concrete reality has approached. Corporations such as Meta (previously Facebook), Microsoft, Roblox, and others have significantly invested in the development of Metaverse platforms, resulting in an increased interest in the use of this emerging domain across several businesses. This chapter seeks to investigate the transformative potential of the Metaverse in education, analysing its progression from conceptual beginnings to practical implementations in contemporary educational settings. Further explores the integration of advanced technologies such as virtual reality and augmented reality in education. It focuses on key elements such as virtual classrooms, digital twins, and immersive learning experiences. The goal is to demonstrate how educators may utilize these technologies to enhance student engagement, promote collaboration, and improve learning outcomes. In addition, the chapter will address the necessary technological infrastructure for conducting educational initiatives based on the Metaverse. Further it intends to give educators, researchers, and policymakers with useful insights on utilising the Metaverse to build inclusive, engaging, and effective educational experiences for learners globally. The Metaverse is redefining the education domain by providing students with immersive, interactive, and novel learning experiences through Immersive Learning Environments that use 3D modeling to improve retention. Global collaboration and accessibility can be improved as Virtual campuses in the Metaverse enable students and educators from around the world to collaborate effortlessly, breaking down geographical constraints. Gamification can help to increase student participation in classes. Interactive games and challenges in the Metaverse increase student interest and participation. The Metaverse promotes ongoing education by providing flexible, self-paced learning modules for professionals and adult learners.

This will be achieved by emphasising present use cases, future directions, and predicted innovations.

2. EVOLUTION OF THE METAVERSE IN EDUCATION

The Metaverse has evolved into a viable technological domain with significant implications for various fields, including education (Alfaisal et al., 2022). Since the pandemic, online learning has become increasingly prevalent, and the education sector is now primarily concentrated on the integration of immersive technologies into academic curricula to enhance the learning experience (Gupta et al., 2022; Kim & Lee, 2021). Educationalists worldwide prioritise the Metaverse as one of their focal points (Alfaisal et al., 2022). It endeavours to engage students in an immersive experience that allows them to engage in enjoyable activities, thereby making the learning process more enjoyable (Garcia & Jung, 2020). The days of students imagining textbook scenarios through the explanations provided by their instructors are long gone. We are currently a part of a digitally connected world in which concepts such as the Metaverse are demonstrated through real-world applications (Alfaisal et al., 2022). It is not difficult to envision the transformative effects that this network of virtual worlds, known as the Metaverse, could have on the global education system in such a scenario. This insight will explore the relationship between the Metaverse and the education system, and it will demonstrate how the Metaverse can transform education.

The Metaverse provides an environment in education where digital simulations can elucidate abstract or complex subjects (Akyürek et al., 2024). It transcends passive knowledge intake, cultivating an atmosphere where learners can actively interact, investigate, and experiment. For example, students could journey to ancient civilizations to observe historical events in real-time, perform scientific experiments in virtual laboratories without physical constraints, or enhance language proficiency in entirely generated cultural environments (Saleh, 2024). These immersive learning experiences can connect theoretical concepts with practical application, providing learners with a more profound and engaging comprehension of the subject matter (Lampropoulos et al., 2024).

The Metaverse has developed from prior digital spaces, including massively multiplayer online role-playing games (MMORPGs) and social media platforms, which established the groundwork for interactive virtual environments (A. Chen et al., 2020). In MMORPGs, players create avatars and engage with others in a continuous online environment, frequently participating in activities such as overcoming obstacles or constructing virtual communities (Ng et al., 2022). Likewise, early virtual environments such as Second Life enabled users to create, socialise, and conduct commercial transactions within a wholly digital realm (Ng, 2022). These antecedents demonstrated the capability of generating collective, immersive experiences in a virtual setting, which the Metaverse now enhances by incorporating educational content. Based on the discussions in the past, there are four key stages of evolution of Metaverse in education are identified in Figure 2:

Figure 1. Classroom in the metaverse environment

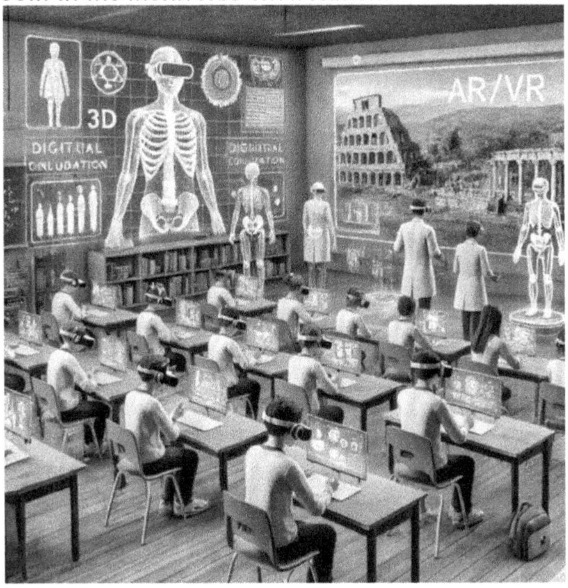

Stage 1: Traditional learning: Traditional learning occurs in physical classrooms where educators utilize textbooks, whiteboards, and direct instruction (Pham et al., 2018). The interactions between students and teachers are confined to face-to-face conversation, resulting in a predominantly passive learning environment where students mainly receive information through lectures. This approach predominantly depends on creativity and memory, offering less chances for experiential learning or practical interaction with the content.
Stage 2: Online learning: The pandemic caused a swift transition to online learning, schooling, rendering digital platforms indispensable for learning. Students engaged in video-based leaning via platforms such as Zoom and Google Classroom, facilitating distant participation (Escueta et al., 2020). This strategy enhanced flexibility and accessibility, although frequently fell short in interactivity and engagement. Notwithstanding its constraints, online learning served as a catalyst for the use of advanced technology into education, paving the way for more immersive methodologies.
Stage 3: Immersive learning technologies (AR/VR integration): As educational institutions adopted immersive technology, AR and VR were integrated into classrooms. These technologies enabled students to engage with 3D models, do virtual experiments, and investigate simulations in a more tactile manner (Garcia & Jung, 2020). These technologies augmented student engagement

and comprehension, introducing novel aspects to conventional pedagogical approaches, and enhancing the memory of intricate knowledge.

Stage 4: Metaverse in education: The Metaverse signifies the advancement in education, wherein virtual realms, interactive avatars, and digital twins establish entirely immersive learning settings (Kaddoura & Al Husseiny, 2023). Students can participate in virtual lectures, engage in global collaboration with peers, and experience real-time simulations of historical events or scientific processes. The Metaverse provides boundless prospects for customised, interactive education using AI-powered technologies, eliminating geographical constraints,

Figure 2. Stages of the evolution of metaverse in education

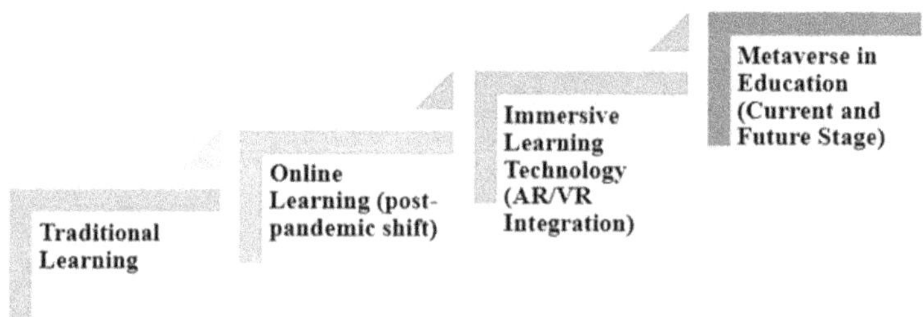

Source: Authors own creation

2.1. Potential Impact of Metaverse on Education

The Metaverse's transformative promise for education resides in its capacity to establish environments that surpass the constraints of conventional learning models (Alfaisal et al., 2022). Traditional education frequently depends on linear approaches such as lectures, textbooks, and examinations that inadequately stimulate students' creativity, critical thinking, or collaborative abilities. Conversely, the Metaverse offers dynamic, interactive environments that enable students to engage more actively in their learning (Akyürek et al., 2024). Engaging in immersive simulations enables learners to encounter authentic events, cultivate problem-solving abilities, and communicate with peers in virtual environments that replicate real classrooms or professional contexts. The detailing about the Potential impact of the Metaverse is constructed from a non-systematic review of the literature. Following is the potential impact of the Metaverse on education:

- **Dynamic, interactive learning environment:** The Metaverse generates immersive settings that surpass conventional educational paradigms such as lectures and textbooks (Sopher & Lescop, 2023). Students participate in experiential learning via real-world simulations, enhancing their problem-solving and critical-thinking abilities (Bartolotta et al., 2023). Virtual environments facilitate collaboration, emulating classroom or professional contexts (Scavarelli et al., 2021).
- **Increased accessibility:** Students from diverse geographical regions or those with physical limitations can engage in identical educational experiences (MİTRA, 2023). Virtual laboratories and simulations provide students with restricted access to advanced resources and equitable learning opportunities. The Metaverse facilitates inclusive education by providing customisable platforms that cater to individual requirements and situations (Lee, 2023; X. Zhang et al., 2022).
- **Self-paced learning:** The Metaverse's versatility enables learners to investigate themes at their own speed. Students possess the autonomy to explore subjects of interest, facilitating unique learning experiences (Yu et al., 2020).
- **Enhanced experiential learning:** The Metaverse conflates formal education with actual experience. Architecture students can conceptualize and examine their designs in real-time (Sinha, 2023). Medical students can engage in realistic virtual simulations to rehearse surgical operations, enhancing their abilities without incurring real-world hazards.
- **Bridging theory and practice:** Immersive simulations provide practical experiences that facilitate the comprehension and application of abstract concepts in real-world contexts (Berndtsson et al., 2020). Virtual environments offer chances for interactive, scenario-driven education that enhances retention and comprehension.
- **Shift in educational delivery:** The incorporation of the Metaverse is transforming the methods of knowledge dissemination and assimilation in educational institutions (Hussain, 2023). This transition signifies a progression towards more interactive, technology-enhanced educational settings that more effectively equip students for the digital era.

3. CORE COMPONENTS OF THE METAVERSE IN EDUCATION AND THEIR BENEFITS

Utilization of technologies in teaching and learning settings has transformed traditional approaches by introducing virtual classrooms and digital twins, which offer immersive and interactive teaching learning experiences (Chen et al., 2023).

Virtual settings are simulator of traditional classroom environments in a digital world, utilizing AR, VR platforms that provide features for lecture delivery, learning and active engagement (Tan et al., 2022). This enables learners to join in lectures, engage in debates, and collaborate on projects regardless of their physical location. Digital twins are virtual replications of real objects that allow students to engage with complex systems, such as functional models for medical students or architectural structures for engineering students. The emergence of the Metaverse in education has profoundly altered tradition teaching and learning methodologies by combining the technology such as virtual classrooms, digital twins, AR and VR, rapid feedback, and gamified learning environments that is rendering education increasingly immersive, interactive, and internationally accessible. These technologies seek to enhance student engagement, cooperation, and learning outcomes by offering practical experience in a virtual context. These technologies aim to get learners more involved, collaborative learning, and achieve better results through hands-on experiences in a virtual world.

Here is a table 1 that lays out the key components of the Metaverse in educational setting along with their application and advantages. The detailing about the core-components and their benefits are constructed from a non-systematic review of the literature:

Table 1. Core components & benefits of the metaverse in education

Components	Technology	Application in Education	Educational Benefits
Virtual classrooms	AR, VR platforms	Virtual classrooms, lecture, discussions, & group projects	Better global collaboration, team works and real time interaction
Digital twins	3D modelling, Internee of Things	Interactive models for learners for medicine, engineering	Safe, risk-free practice with simulations
Augmented reality	AR applications	Overlaying 3D model on real world environment	Makes abstracts, topic tangible enhances learning
Virtual labs	AR, AI, Machine learning	Simulation labs for biology, physics, chemistry etc	Hands-on experience without compromising safety or material constrain
Gamified learning environment	Game design elements	Quests, challenges, rewards, role-playing	Increases learners' engagement, motivation and encourage active learning
Avatars and identity representation	Avatar systems	Student-avatars for role-playing, participation in virtual classes	Foster inclusivity, encourages participation, and overcome social barriers

continued on following page

Table 1. Continued

Components	Technology	Application in Education	Educational Benefits
Haptic technology	Tactile feedback devices	Physical interaction in virtual worlds, for fields like medicine and design	Enhances practice training by providing tactile feedback
AI and personalized Learning	Machine learning, AI	Adaptive learning paths, personalized tutoring	Customized learning experiences improves outcome through individual attention
Collaboration tools	Cloud computing	Virtual workspace for group projects and real-time feedback	Encourages teamwork problem solving, and collaboration

- **Virtual Classrooms:** These virtual classrooms bring school experiences into the virtual world, with AR and VR apps, learners can be together even if they are not. This is due to the tools that these online spaces are accompanied with like virtual whiteboards and real time chat options, one on one sessions through VR (Waquar et al., 2024). It helps learners from all over the world to connect and learn together smoothly (Wang et al., 2022). These virtual classrooms can break barriers between online and offline learning places, that encourages collaborations around the world and encourages teamwork, thus ensuring the students from small towns also get quality education.
- **avtarDigital Twins**: Digital twins are the virtual version of real-world things; they help student learn complex system safely (MİTRA, 2023). In educational settings, digital twins are used a lot in medicine and engineering fields (Arantes, 2024). For instance, medicine students can perform surgery on a virtual body. This tech lets learners practice without any risks, danger that is normally found in real-world situation.
- **Augmented Reality Learning Tools**: AR tools enhance learning by adding digital content to learning activities. This is super helpful for tricky subjects like biology or astronomy. Imagine seeing characters from history come alive or getting 3D models of our body's insides right before your eyes, thus makes tough ideas easier to grasp (Song et al., 2023).
- **Virtual Laboratories:** Virtual labs mimic real science labs but are way safer! Students can run experiments without any risks or costs that come with actual labs. It is super useful for subjects like chemistry and biology were trying things out is crucial for learning (Gonzalez-Romo et al., 2023). These labs let students explore freely without worrying about any risk of accident and boosts their involvement and helps them master concepts better.
- **Gamified Learning Environments:** Gamifying education means adding game-like elements and fun into learning, the Metaverse is approach where

learners can tackle quests or role-play scenarios related to what they are studying, this makes schooling exciting who would not want that (Pakinee & Puritat, 2021). For instance, when learning feels like a game, learners get way more excited about it and this fosters team skills that is useful too

- **Avatars & Identity Representation:** In the Metaverse, most used element is avatar, kind of like digital versions of themselves (Mystakidis, 2022). These playful avatars help people interact easily in virtual spaces a big win for collaborative work. Avatars give everyone an equal chance to participate comfortably, especially those who might feel shy face-to-face.
- **Haptic Technology for Physical Interaction**: Haptic tech adds another layer by making it possible to "feel" things while interacting virtually (Sun et al., 2022). Students can use special gloves or suits to interact with virtual objects as if they were real This tech brings realness into teaching methods especially when it comes to manual skills like surgery or car repairs. This benefits in adaptive learning of individual students needs, ensuring students learn coping up with their strengths and weakness.
- **AI & Personalized Learning**: With AI and machine learning on board, personalized learning becomes possible, AI-driven systems analyse how each student learns best letting them learn at their own pace (Kadaruddin, 2023). Each student gets lessons made just for them leading to much better learning progress, furthermore AI enables virtual tutors or assistance to help students navigate complex topics, ensuring personalised attention in large virtual classrooms.
- **Collaboration Tools in the Cloud:** Cloud-based collaboration solutions enable students and educators to collaborate in real-time, irrespective of their geographical locations. Virtual workspaces within the Metaverse facilitate group projects, debates, and feedback, so fostering a collaborative learning environment (Jovanović & Milosavljević, 2022). Cloud computing facilitates these connections by supplying the requisite infrastructure for real-time data exchange, project oversight, and file storage. Students may engage in collaborative work, exchange resources, and obtain immediate feedback from both classmates and teachers. Cloud tools let students' team up anytime and anywhere this helps in working together on projects online as if you are all at one table how convenient. These tools help build team spirit as they tackle problems together while working across different locations.

The Metaverse is transforming the education by integrating tech like virtual classrooms and customized AI to transform learners experience, enhancing immersive experiences, and improving their engagement in their learning while improving their skills too. Further this section will discuss the application and some used cases of Metaverse in transforming education.

4. APPLICATION AND USE CASES

Virtual laboratories and practical training provide learners with the opportunity to develop and apply their skills in a controlled setting (Navarro et al., 2024). For example, chemistry students can observe reactions and manipulate virtual compounds without any physical hazards, while medical students can get experience by performing virtual procedures. In addition, the Metaverse facilitates experiential learning by offering virtual field visits to otherwise inaccessible destinations, such as the Great Wall of China (Roman et al., 2022). This enhances understanding and memory retention through immersive exploration. Moreover, virtual meeting places and collaborative tools using platforms such as VRChat and Mozilla Hubs encourage social and collaborative learning, promoting social contact, teamwork, and a sense of community among learners. To summarize, the Metaverse offers a flexible and inventive platform for education that integrates hands-on training, immersive learning, and collaborative participation to improve the entire learning process.

- **Environments for Immersion Learning:** Metaverse gives an experience of immersive education. Metaverse can replicate real-world environments in virtual learning spaces (Garcia & Jung, 2020). Rather than reading about something, experiencing that place by visiting there has a long-lasting effect. But visiting every place is very difficult, time and money-consuming Metaverse enable learners to visit historical locations, breathtaking natural formations, and evcn space, without ever leaving the classroom. Learning from the past has become more dynamic and captivating when they are virtually brought to real life. In case of science-based experiments students can securely investigate ideas that might be risky or unfeasible in a physical context by conducting experiments in a virtual lab (Navarro et al., 2024). In the same way in a simulated setting, students can practice comprehending and speaking a foreign language. For instance, students can engage with historical events directly by being virtually immersed in crucial moments, such as traversing Ancient Rome, observing the signing of the Declaration of Independence, or investigating medieval European castles (Boffi et al., 2023). Metaverse facilitate collaborative projects, debates, and feedback, fostering a cooperative learning atmosphere.
- **Collaboration Across Geographies:** Metaverse has made it easy for students worldwide to work together in real-time in shared virtual environments,

which removes geographical restrictions (Dreamson & Park, 2023). Students from many nations can collaborate on a group project in a virtual laboratory in which they can communicate, work with data, and create projects (Chen, Zou, et al., 2023). No matter where they are physically located, students can cooperate on projects, take part in discussions, and work together in real time. Students can collaborate virtually on projects while exchanging ideas and materials. In a virtual scientific laboratory, students globally can collaborate on projects in real time, eliminating geographical constraints. A cohort of students from several nations could collaborate on a climate change simulation. Utilizing virtual laboratory tools, they can examine global databases, conduct environmental impact research, and communicate effortlessly through avatars. This promotes cross-cultural collaboration, improves teamwork, and enables students to exchange information and resources from their different locations, resulting in a more enriched and dynamic learning experience.

- **Personalized Learning:** Metaverse gives the option to create Avatars for individuals. Using adaptive learning pathways, students can design their own avatars. Apart from that personalized learning avatars can serve as virtual teachers, adjusting to the unique needs and learning preferences of each learner (Hassan et al., 2021). They make learning more interesting and immersive, offer immediate feedback, and mentor students through interactive sessions. In virtual learning environments, avatars can also imitate peer interactions, encouraging teamwork and boosting motivation (Zhao et al., 2022). AI-powered virtual tutors can help students with challenging courses by providing personalized, real-time feedback that suits their learning style and speed. So, AI can assist customize the learning process to meet the demands of each individual student.
- **Events and Virtual Campus:** Colleges and universities can create virtual campuses where staff and students can participate virtually in social events, lectures, and seminars (Wang et al., 2022). This has been particularly beneficial in surpassing the constraints of conventional virtual learning. For instance, colleges and universities with virtual campuses provide flexibility by making events and lectures accessible to staff and students from anywhere. They unite varied participants and promote worldwide collaboration. They also save money on travel and physical infrastructure, all the while promoting social engagement through immersive virtual worlds. Stanford University offered virtual lectures in a "Virtual Human Interaction Lab," where students may engage in simulations and 3D model interaction (Reeves & Crippen, 2021).
- **Skill-based Learning**: Metaverse works with the combination of real-world and highly interactive training settings. Before using practical skills in real

life, Metaverse enables them to undergo vocational training in secure virtual environments (Gomathi & Rajamani, 2018). Metaverse has made it possible for medical students to practice surgical treatments in a virtual operating room, using digitized instruments with accurate results dependent on their decisions and actions. With the combination of gamification into the realm of the Metaverse, learning has become more dynamic and captivating. Children can construct and explore while learning with the help of Minecraft Education Edition, which use a simulated environment to teach disciplines like coding, history, and mathematics and many more (Bar-El & Ringland, 2020). In a virtual environment, students can complete assignments and challenges to receive some motivators like tokens, badges, or other prizes.

- **Credentialing and Blockchain**: Sometimes people misplace their certificates and face lots of problems. In the Metaverse, educational credentials and certifications can be safely stored via blockchain technology (Golam et al., 2024). This approach guarantees the tamper-proof and worldwide recognition of diplomas and certificates. Students may keep their degree in a virtual wallet that is confirmed via blockchain, making it simple for prospective employers to confirm their credentials.
- **Customized education:** The requirements of every brain are not the same. A teacher in a class is not able to take about every individual's requirement. Whereas Metaverse may provide tailored information and feedback based on each student's unique learning style and pace (Tlili et al., 2022). Personalized instruction that fits each student's requirements and learning style will increase motivation and engagement. By providing adaptable learning paths that are based on real-time data, it maximizes the effectiveness of learning (Wu et al., 2023). By concentrating on each student's unique strengths and shortcomings and offering tailored feedback and assistance, customized learning promotes deeper comprehension and critical thinking abilities while boosting self-efficacy and confidence in the learner.
- **Simulated Teaching Environments:** Teachers are as a nation builder. But these nation builders must be updated time to time. Trainings and workshops for teachers after a regular interval tends to be very costly. So, to enhance their knowledge and stay current with educational trends at low cost, teachers can participate in virtual workshops and conferences (Kye et al., 2021). By trying out various teaching techniques and getting feedback, educators can hone their craft in an online classroom.

With the ongoing advancements in technology, the Metaverse presents even more fascinating educational opportunities. The Metaverse has the power to revolutionize education by offering individualized, collaborative in nature, and immersive learning experiences (Onu et al., 2024). There are many examples where Metaverse is being successfully used for learning purpose.

Here some used cases of Metaverse in educational frontier: Students can experience historical events firsthand by being virtually transported to significant moments, such as walking through ancient Rome, witnessing the signing of the Declaration of Independence, or exploring medieval European castles (Boffi et al., 2023). This creates a dynamic way to teach history, bringing context and immersion to dates and facts. TimeLooper, a VR app, helps users to explore historical moments, like being in London during the Blitz of World War II or ancient Rome (Crews et al., 2023). Assessing virtual museums and historical sites globally, eliminates geographic and financial barriers. Students can "visit" places like the Louvre, the Pyramids of Giza, or the Colosseum without leaving the classroom (Tamimi & Toth, 2023). The British Museum offers a VR experience where users can explore the Rosetta Stone and ancient Egyptian artifacts (Aziz et al., 2024). Historical narratives can be brought to life with virtual avatars and simulations, offering a more engaging way to understand historical figures and events. This can include interactive discussions with famous historical personalities. Students can perform complex or dangerous experiments in a risk-free environment, enabling them to interact with simulated chemicals, biological systems, or physical phenomena. This can help enhance understanding of scientific processes without physical constraints. Labster, a virtual science lab platform, allows students to conduct experiments like gene editing, chemical reactions, or even quantum physics simulations (Tsirulnikov et al., 2023). The Metaverse offers opportunities for students to explore the universe virtually. They can travel to the International Space Station, explore Mars, or experience celestial phenomena like supernovas up close. NASA's VR experiences allow students to visit Mars, walk on the moon, or experience life as an astronaut aboard the ISS (Holt, 2023). Medical students and biologists can delve into virtual dissections, medical procedures, or even molecular and cellular structures in immersive 3D. This provides deep learning without the need for physical cadavers or costly equipment. Holo Anatomy, developed by Case Western Reserve University, offers a detailed AR experience of human anatomy where students can explore the body layer by layer (Ruthberg et al., 2020). Metaverse can simulate the effects of climate change or environmental degradation, enabling students to visualize and interact with ecosystems and their changes over time. Virtual simulations of rising sea levels or deforestation allow students to see their long-term impacts on the planet. The Metaverse allows students to explore virtual archaeological digs or study fossils in 3D space. They can recreate ancient environments or study extinct species by immersing themselves in accurate, scientifically-constructed simulations. A virtual reenactment of Galileo's telescope experiments, where students can participate and observe the night sky as it was in the 17th century (BOTEZATU & CIUPERCĂ, 2023). Roblox is a well-known Metaverse platform that is frequently utilized in classrooms. Teachers and students may build immersive learning experiences with the help of Roblox Education. Students can use interactive simulations in a virtual environment to learn physics, game design, and coding (Bar-El & Ringland, 2020). Additionally, it has collaborated with academic institutions to create curricula and engaging lessons (J. Han et al., 2023). Microsoft owns Minecraft, and ClassVR has instructional versions of the game. Science, math, engineering, and history are among the subjects taught in classrooms using Minecraft: Education Edition. Students can design and explore buildings, work together on construction projects, and even model historical occurrences like the rise and fall of ancient civilizations or ecosystems in virtual environments. Instructors can choose from a variety of lesson plans and learning resources that are incorporated into the game. The platform is used by educational institutions all around the world to give students immersive experiences like viewing historical sites, walking on Mars, or investigating the human body, which makes learning more dynamic and interesting. A virtual and simulation-based training platform for vocational education is called Skillful Craftsman. In China, a company called Skillful Craftsman leverages the Metaverse to provide interactive, practical instruction in various industries, including engineering, building, and manufacturing (Yang, 2022). Students can apply practical knowledge in a safe and affordable environment by using VR and 3D simulations to practice real-world skills in a virtual setting. Meta (formerly Facebook) offers Horizon Workrooms, a virtual space designed for remote collaboration (Hedrick et al., 2022). Horizon Workrooms are used by universities and institutions to create virtual classrooms where students and teachers can meet, interact, and collaborate in a fully immersive environment. Universities can host discussions, virtual lectures, and workshops with students who can attend from anywhere in the world. Users can create, explore, and trade digital assets in Decentraland, a decentralized virtual environment. The University of Nicosia is investigating the Metaverse through lectures, events, and networking opportunities in Decentraland (Ramezani et al., 2024). The university offers programs in blockchain and decentralised technology. On a completely virtual campus, students can engage with teachers and fellow students as well as attend virtual lectures.

Figure 3. Stakeholders of metaverse ecosystem in education

5. ROLE OF STAKEHOLDERS' IN METAVERSE BASED EDUCATION ECOSYSTEM

Incorporating immersive experiences in education via the Metaverse technologies requires collaboration among a variety of stakeholders, each of which playing a significant unique role in the ecosystem. These stakeholders facilitate the development, executions, and sustainability of Metaverse-based education. Here are some major stakeholders (as shown in figure 3) with their key role in Metaverse based education is discusses in table 2:

Table 2. Stakeholders and their key role in metaverse based education

Stakeholders	Role in Metaverse education	Key Contributions	Examples
Educational Institutions	Curriculum design and infrastructure	Adoption of Metaverse, invest in technological infrastructure	Designing VR-based courses, setting up virtual labs, integrating immersive learning in curriculum
Educator and Instructors	Content creation and delivery	Adapt tech-based teaching methods, create immersive lessons	Developing virtual lessons, guiding students in simulations, creating VR-based assessments
Students and learners	Active engagement	Engage with immersive learning content	Participating in virtual classes using AR/VR simulations for hands-on learning, collaboration in virtual projects
Technology providers	Platform and hardware developers	Create platforms and hardware for Metaverse based education	Developing AR/VR devices, building virtual world, seamless access to virtual environment.
Content Creator and Designers	Develop virtual environment	Design and build virtual world, simulations, and avatars	Creating 3D educational models, building immersive environment for classrooms, design interactive learning space
Edtech companies and startups	Innovators and integrators	Develop Metaverse tools and integrate with learning management system	Creating immersive learning platforms, integrating AI for personalized learning, providing virtual classroom tools.
Government and policy makers	Regulations and funding	Set standards and provide fundings for technology infrastructure	Offering grants for immersive technologies in educational institutes, ensuring data privacy and security in virtual space.
Private sectors and industry partners	Collaborators in vocational training	Provide real-world virtual training experience	Partnering with schools for industry-specific simulations, offering virtual internships or job training.
NGOs and Non-Profits	Digital Equity advocates	Ensure equitable access to Metaverse technologies	Providing VR devices to backward areas, advocating for inclusive educational content, improving access to broadband
Parents and guardians	Advocates for adoption and safety	Support adoption and monitor safe use	Ensure children have safe access to virtual learning environment, regulating screen time
Investors and venture capitalists	Funding innovation	Provide capital for tech startups in education	Investing in edtech startups funding R&D for Metaverse educational tools, supporting tech for scaling efforts

- **Educational Institutions:** including schools, colleges, and universities, are pivotal in integrating the Metaverse into their curricula. They allocate resources to infrastructure, including VR laboratories, and collaborate with developers to execute immersive educational solutions. Institutions additionally equip educators to deliver content in virtual environments (Lin et al., 2022).

- **Educators and Instructors:** They adapt their pedagogical approaches to deliver immersive education in the Metaverse (Han & Noh, 2021). They produce interactive content, facilitate student engagement through virtual simulations, and devise innovative methods for accessing education within virtual environments.
- **Students and Learners:** They actively participate in the Metaverse by attending virtual classrooms, utilising immersive tools for practical experience, and interacting in a virtual environment (Suh & Ahn, 2022). Their engagement with the platforms enhances the efficacy of Metaverse-based teaching.
- **Technology Providers:** Companies that develop Metaverse platforms and gear for AR/VR supply the essential infrastructure for immersive education. Their contribution includes the development of gadgets and programs that facilitate the virtual learning experience (Zabel et al., 2023).
- **Content Creators and Designers:** these experts craft the 3D environments, virtual worlds, and avatars utilized in the Metaverse. Their artistic endeavours guarantee that the virtual environment is captivating, authentic, and congruent with instructional objectives (Radanliev et al., 2024).
- **Edtech Companies and Startups:** innovate by developing new immersive learning platforms and technologies that interact with existing learning management systems (Wang et al., 2022). They also guarantee AI-driven customisation to improve the learning experience.
- **Government and Policymakers:** they play a crucial role in the integration of Metaverse technologies in education; they can allocate cash through annual budgets for technological adoption, establish educational standards, and safeguard the privacy and security of student data (Lnenicka et al., 2024).
- **Private Sectors and Industry Partners:** Industry collaborators engage with educational institutions to deliver virtual training and simulation experiences tailored to practical applications, including healthcare, engineering, or technical skill development.
- **NGOs and Non-profits:** Non-governmental organizations and non-profit entities advocate for digital equity by endeavouring to furnish underprivileged populations with access to Metaverse technologies. They regularly commit funding for hardware and advocate for inclusive content creation.
- **Parents and Guardians:** Parents act as crucial advocates for the adoption of Metaverse educational tools (Han et al., 2023). They ensure that students have secure, monitored access to virtual environments while concurrently addressing concerns related to screen time and data privacy.

- **Investors and Venture Capitalists:** Investors provide crucial funding to startups and technology companies developing Metaverse solutions for education. Their support drives research, product development, and the growth of immersive learning technology.

6. THE IMPORTANCE OF CONTINUOUS PROFESSIONAL DEVELOPMENT FOR EDUCATORS

To remain current, productive, and enthusiastic about their work, educators must engage in continuous professional development, or CPD. It guarantees that they have the most up-to-date information, abilities, and tactics to address the changing demands of both the educational environment and pupils. The following should be considered by educators for their ongoing professional development (Figure. 4-a, b).

Figure 4. Professional growth of the educators a.

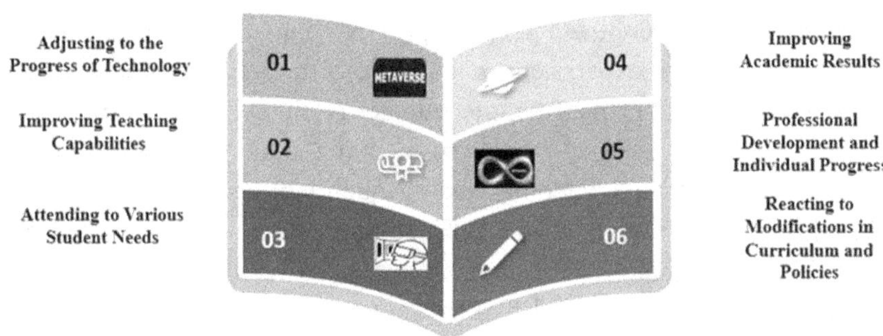

Figure 5. Professional growth of the educators b.

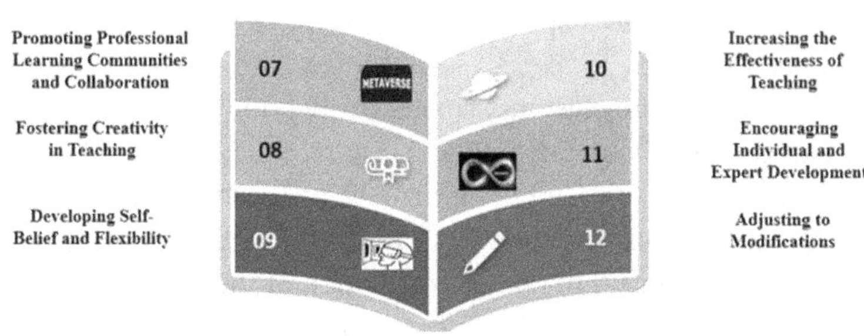

- **Adjusting to the Progress of Technology:** As new technologies emerge, instructors need ongoing professional development (CPD) to stay current and skilled in incorporating them. Through immersive, interactive learning environments that can bring abstract ideas to life, AR and VR are influencing modern classrooms and encouraging a hands-on, engaging approach to teaching for students (Rane et al., 2024). Collaborative learning environments that transcend physical borders are made possible by the Metaverse, a digital shared place that blends AR, VR, and the internet. To fully utilize AR, VR, and the Metaverse, educators must engage in continuing professional development. This will enhance the learning environment and better equip students for a future in which the digital and physical worlds will be increasingly interwoven.
- **Improving Teaching Capabilities**: With the advancement of educational research, incorporating AR, VR, and the Metaverse into CPD (continuous professional development) gives teachers access to state-of-the-art resources to use research-proven strategies such as tailored instruction, active learning, and collaborative learning. In order to promote more engaging and inclusive learning experiences, these technologies provide immersive environments where teachers can experiment in real time with novel teaching methodologies and classroom management techniques (Chiu et al., 2022). By ensuring that teachers are equipped to use these cutting-edge resources successfully, CPD improves student outcomes and the quality of instruction.
- **Attending to Various Student Needs:** By assisting teachers in meeting the varied requirements of their pupils, augmented reality, virtual reality, and the Metaverse play a critical part in Continuous Professional Development (CPD). With the use of these tools, educators may design individualized, fully immersive lessons that meet the needs, styles, and skills of their students (Baden & Burden, 2024). Teachers can create inclusive learning environments and differentiated education using AR and VR through Continuing Professional Development (CPD). This allows teachers to provide specialized support for children with special needs and make sure all students can succeed in the classroom.
- **Improving Academic Results**: Transformative tools like AR, VR, and the Metaverse can greatly improve student results, and professional development guarantees that teachers can fully utilize them. Teachers can improve student motivation and accomplishment by developing more dynamic and engaging learning environments through the integration of these technologies (Tsappi et al., 2024). In addition, CPD exposes teachers to cutting-edge assessment techniques that use AR and VR to provide real-time feedback and individual-

ized training, which eventually improves academic achievement and creates customized learning opportunities for every student.

- **Professional Development and Individual Progress**: using CPD, educators may take advantage of exciting opportunities for professional progression and personal improvement using AR, VR, and the Metaverse. Acquiring proficiency in these state-of-the-art technologies allows educators to focus on topics such as technology integration, which makes them invaluable in leadership or curriculum creation positions (Rane et al., 2024). By utilizing immersive learning resources through CPD, educators can also breathe new life into their methods and avoid teacher burnout by improving the dynamic and fulfilling nature of instruction. By investigating AR, VR, and the Metaverse, educators can broaden their knowledge and acquire new insights, which keeps their work interesting and satisfying.
- **Reacting to Modifications in Curriculum and Policies:** Regardless of their location, educators may stay up to date on curriculum and policy changes in real time with the support of the Metaverse's dynamic CPD platform. Teachers can engage in interactive exploration of new content requirements, assessment approaches, and standards by means of immersive simulations and virtual worlds (Fakhar et al., 2024). In order to ensure that educators are ready to put best practices into practice and protect pupils in accordance with changing educational legislation, the Metaverse can also support collaborative learning spaces where educators can participate in conversations on changes in education law and child protection.
- **Promoting Professional Learning Communities and Collaboration:** By establishing immersive, virtual environments where educators may work with peers, exchange experiences, and learn from one another regardless of physical location, the Metaverse improves continuing professional development (Taghizadeh & Ejtehadi, 2023). By encouraging professional learning groups, it makes knowledge exchange, mentoring, and in-the-moment engagement possible. Teachers with and without experience can collaborate and learn continuously in this virtual environment, sharing best practices and strengthening their pedagogical approaches.
- **Fostering Creativity in Teaching**: By giving teachers a state-of-the-art platform to test out novel teaching strategies like immersive project-based learning and interdisciplinary integration, the Metaverse encourages creativity in continuing professional development (Avara, 2023). Teachers have access to up-to-date educational research, evidence-based practices, and real-time testing of innovative teaching approaches in these virtual environments. By doing this, teachers may continue to be at the forefront of educational innovations and guarantee that their classrooms are dynamic and interesting.

- **Developing Self-Belief and Flexibility:** With immersive, risk-free simulations and virtual worlds, the Metaverse helps instructors develop their confidence and adaptability, which improves continuing professional development (Coulter, 2023). Teachers can develop creativity in their teaching by practicing in real-time managing issues such (Reis et al., 2024)as curricular changes or a variety of student requirements. The Metaverse gives educators the flexibility and resiliency they need to keep ahead of trends and confidently adjust to changing educational environments as the field of education quickly changes, including changes like remote learning.
- **Increasing the Effectiveness of Teaching**: By providing immersive training settings where educators may hone critical skills like classroom management, questioning techniques, and feedback strategies, the Metaverse dramatically increases the effectiveness of teaching (Reis et al., 2024). Teachers can address issues, such behaviour management and student engagement, in a supportive setting by using virtual experiences. With the use of this practical experience in the Metaverse, teachers can improve their methods, which will ultimately benefit students' learning and performance more.
- **Encouraging Individual and Expert Development**: Through the creation of collaborative virtual places where educators may communicate, share best practices, and support one another, the Metaverse promotes educators' personal and professional growth (Chiu et al., 2022). Participating in CPD in these intensive settings gives teachers more self-assurance, empowers them in their positions, and improves their teaching skills. Furthermore, the Metaverse's inventiveness demonstrates a drive to professional growth, putting educators in a favourable position for career progression and highlighting their commitment to lifelong learning.
- **Adjusting to Modifications**: Because the Metaverse offers a dynamic platform for continuing professional development that mimics upcoming opportunities and difficulties in education, it plays a critical role in aiding educators in adapting to change. Teachers can learn new skills and knowledge that improve their resilience and flexibility by participating in immersive scenarios (Alfaisal et al., 2024). This cutting-edge setting equips teachers to successfully meet the varied requirements of their pupils and ensures that they are ready to deal with the rapidly changing nature of education both today and in the future.

7. CHALLENGES IN IMPLEMENTING METAVERSE

Implementing the Metaverse in education offers transformative potential but also comes with a range of challenges and issues. Here are some key issues (table 3):

Table 3. Challenges in implementing metaverse in education space

Challenges	Details of Challenges
Technological Challenges	**Hardware and Infrastructure**: High-end gadgets like AR tools and VR headsets are expensive and need strong internet access, which not all students or institutions can afford. **Interoperability:** It is difficult to ensure interoperability across different Metaverse platforms, technologies, and current Learning Management Systems (LMS).
Accessibility and Equity	**Digital Divide**: There is a gap in participation because certain learners do not have equitable access to the necessary gadgets and the internet. **Physical and Cognitive Barriers**: Unless particular accessibility features are implemented, students with disabilities may have trouble utilizing some VR/AR systems. **Global Disparities**: Organizations in underdeveloped nations might not have the funds to implement Metaverse technology.
Pedagogical Issues	**Content Creation**: It takes a lot of time, money, and skill to create educational experiences that are immersive, captivating, and in line with the curriculum. **Learning Effectiveness**: To make sure that Metaverse experiences enhance learning outcomes and are more than a novelty, their educational worth needs to be thoroughly evaluated. **Teacher Training**: To use Metaverse tools and modify their teaching strategies, educators require specific training.
Social and Psychological Concerns	**Digital Addiction**: Overuse of immersive technologies can result in addiction, a loss of connection to the outside world, or a decrease in in-person social contacts. **Effects on Health**: Extended usage of VR/AR systems may result in problems with posture, eye strain, and motion sickness. **Cultural Sensitivity**: In a global educational system, creating inclusive curriculum that honors various cultural and social norms is essential but difficult.
Ethical Concerns	**Bias in Algorithms**: Metaverse platforms' underlying algorithms may unintentionally perpetuate prejudices or stereotypes. **Manipulation and Influence**: Because the Metaverse is so immersive, pupils may be more susceptible to subtly harmful influences or false information. **Age-Appropriate Content**: It is crucial to make sure that all virtual content is appropriate for both age groups and educational objectives.
Financial Constraints	**High Initial Investment**: Many organizations may find the cost of creating and implementing Metaverse environments to be unaffordable. **Maintenance Costs**: Budgets may be strained by ongoing expenditures for personnel training, hardware repairs, and software updates.

continued on following page

Table 3. Continued

Challenges	Details of Challenges
Regulatory and Governance Issues	**Absence of Standards**: There are currently no widely recognized standards or norms for educational applications in the Metaverse, which is continuously developing. **Legal Difficulties**: In a virtual environment, issues with copyright, intellectual property, and jurisdiction are complicated. **Ethical Oversight**: It can be difficult to define precise moral guidelines for the application of immersive technologies in the classroom.
Health and Well-being	**Motion Sickness**: When utilizing VR/AR technology, some users may feel uneasy or suffer from motion sickness. **Eye strain and fatigue**: Extended use of VR/AR headsets can lead to headaches, eye strain, and exhaustion. **Addiction and Mental Health**: There are worries about the effects of virtual worlds on social interaction and mental health, as well as the possibility of addiction.
Data Privacy and Security	**Sensitive Information**: Concerns regarding privacy and possible misuse are raised by student data acquired in the Metaverse, including biometric data and learning patterns. **Cybersecurity Risks**: Hacking, data breaches, and exposure to hazardous content are just a few of the threats that can occur in virtual environments. **Digital Identity**: It's critical to safeguard student identities and stop cyberbullying and harassment in the Metaverse.
Resistance to Change	**Cultural Resistance**: Because they are unfamiliar with or distrustful of Metaverse technologies, educators, parents, and students may be reluctant to embrace them. **Fear of Over-Commercialization**: Opposition may arise from worries about how corporate interests may shape educational opportunities.

8. CONCLUSION

The Metaverse is at the forefront of educational innovation, poised to revolutionize learning through immersive technologies including virtual reality, augmented reality, and artificial intelligence. The Metaverse offers numerous opportunities to engage students and enhance educational outcomes, including virtual classrooms, digital twins, experiential learning, and personalized educational experiences. We anticipate the continuous advancement of haptic feedback devices, sophisticated VR/AR headsets, and AI-powered learning systems to transform the educational landscape. These innovations possess the capacity to offer enhanced immersive learning experiences, increased accessibility, and equitable educational opportunities globally. The Metaverse has the potential to democratize education by overcoming geographical limitations and fostering diversity, enabling learners from many backgrounds to enjoy superior, interactive educational experiences. Immersive technologies such as virtual reality (VR), augmented reality (AR), and artificial intelligence (AI) are enabling the Metaverse to revolutionize education and provide transformative possibilities. By facilitating virtual classrooms, digital twins, and tailored learning experiences, it has the capacity to engage students in unparalleled manners and markedly improve learning results. The swift progression of haptic feedback devices and VR/AR headsets, along with AI-driven adaptive learning systems, is poised to establish more dynamic, engaging, and inclusive educational settings. This technological transformation may democratize education, disassembly geographical and socio-economic barriers, and cultivating global learning communities where diverse students can obtain high-quality education. Educators, institutions, and stakeholders must comprehend the present applications, prospective advancements, and methods for using Metaverse technologies as they traverse this growing landscape. By harnessing the power of the Metaverse, we can create a more fair, accessible, and engaging educational landscape that equips learners for the challenges and possibilities of the 21st century.

9. FUTURE AGENDA

Prioritizing equal access through reasonably priced devices and enhanced internet infrastructure should be at the top of the future agenda for integrating the Metaverse into education. Creating immersive, curriculum-aligned content and educating teachers about Metaverse technologies should be the main priorities. In order to serve the different requirements of learners, including those with impairments, accessibility elements must be implemented. Strong guidelines for cybersecurity, ethical use, and data protection should be put in place. Governments, organizations, and tech companies must work together to build inclusive and interoperable platforms. The long-term effects on learning results and student welfare should be evaluated in research. Funding approaches that are sustainable must encourage the growth, upkeep, and ongoing innovation of Metaverse-based education.

REFERENCES

Akyürek, S., Genç, G., Çalık, İ., & Şengel, Ü. (2024). Metaverse in tourism education: A mixed method on vision, challenges and extended technology acceptance model. *Journal of Hospitality, Leisure, Sport and Tourism Education, 35*. DOI: 10.1016/j.jhlste.2024.100503

Alfaisal, R., Hashim, H., & Azizan, U. H. (2022). Metaverse system adoption in education: a systematic literature review. In *Journal of Computers in Education* (Issue 0123456789). Springer Berlin Heidelberg. DOI: 10.1007/s40692-022-00256-6

Alfaisal, R., Hashim, H., & Azizan, U. H. (2024). *Empowering the Metaverse in Education: ChatGPT's Role in Transforming Learning Experiences* (pp. 13–31). DOI: 10.1007/978-3-031-65996-6_2

Arantes, J. (2024). Digital twins and the terminology of "personalization" or "personalized learning" in educational policy: A discussion paper. *Policy Futures in Education*, 22(4), 524–543. DOI: 10.1177/14782103231176357

Avara, H. (2023). *The art of teaching English in the 21st century settings.*

Aziz, O., Farooq, M. S., Khelifi, A., & Shoaib, M. (2024). Archaeometa: Leveraging blockchain for secure and scalable virtual museums in the Metaverse. *Heritage Science*, 12(1), 308. DOI: 10.1186/s40494-024-01416-w

Azuma, R., Baillot, Y., Behringer, R., Feiner, S., Julier, S., & MacIntyre, B. (2001). Recent advances in augmented reality. *IEEE Computer Graphics and Applications*, 21(6), 34–47. DOI: 10.1109/38.963459

Bar-El, D., & Ringland, E., K. (2020). Crafting Game-Based Learning: An Analysis of Lessons for Minecraft Education Edition. *International Conference on the Foundations of Digital Games*, 1–4. DOI: 10.1145/3402942.3409788

Bartolotta, S., Gaggioli, A., & Riva, G. (2023). The META-Learning Project: Design and Evaluation of an Experiential-Learning Intervention in the Metaverse for Soft Skills Improvement. *Cyberpsychology, Behavior, and Social Networking*, 26(3), 221–224. DOI: 10.1089/cyber.2023.29268.ceu PMID: 36827312

Baxter, G., & Hainey, T. (2024). Using immersive technologies to enhance the student learning experience. *Interactive Technology and Smart Education*, 21(3), 403–425. DOI: 10.1108/ITSE-05-2023-0078

Berndtsson, I., Dahlborg, E., & Pennbrant, S. (2020). Work-integrated learning as a pedagogical tool to integrate theory and practice in nursing education – An integrative literature review. *Nurse Education in Practice*, 42, 102685. DOI: 10.1016/j.nepr.2019.102685 PMID: 31841809

Boffi, P., Clerici, M., Gallace, A., & Lanzi, P. L. (2023). An educational experience in ancient Rome to evaluate the impact of virtual reality on human learning processes. *Computers & Education: X Reality, 2*, 100014. DOI: 10.1016/j.cexr.2023.100014

Botezatu, U. E., & Ciupercă, E. M. (2023). Expanding the virtual learning horizons: the case of Galileo and Copernicus space-based technologies and services. *Proceedings of the International Conference on Virtual Learning - Virtual Learning - Virtual Reality (18th Edition)*, 27–42. DOI: 10.58503/icvl-v18y202302

Bowman, D. A., & McMahan, R. P. (2007). Virtual Reality: How Much Immersion Is Enough? *Computer*, 40(7), 36–43. DOI: 10.1109/MC.2007.257

Chen, A., Mari, S., Grech, S., & Levitt, J. (2020). What We Know About Massively Multiplayer Online Role-Playing Games. *Harvard Review of Psychiatry*, 28(2), 107–112. DOI: 10.1097/HRP.0000000000000247 PMID: 32134835

Chen, X., Zhong, Z., & Wu, D. (2023). Metaverse for Education: Technical Framework and Design Criteria. *IEEE Transactions on Learning Technologies*, 16(6), 1034–1044. DOI: 10.1109/TLT.2023.3276760

Chen, X., Zou, D., Xie, H., & Wang, F. L. (2023). Metaverse in Education: Contributors, Cooperations, and Research Themes. *IEEE Transactions on Learning Technologies*, 16(6), 1111–1129. DOI: 10.1109/TLT.2023.3277952

Chiu, T. K. F., Sun, J. C.-Y., & Ismailov, M. (2022). Investigating the relationship of technology learning support to digital literacy from the perspective of self-determination theory. *Educational Psychology*, 42(10), 1263–1282. DOI: 10.1080/01443410.2022.2074966

Coulter, J. (2023). Using E-Textiles to Challenge Gender Perceptions in STEM, Design and Career Aspirations of Secondary School Students. *Journal of Textile Design Research and Practice*, 11(1–2), 168–193. DOI: 10.1080/20511787.2023.2209960

Crews, T., Goodwin, C., Rowe, S., & Olmeta-Schult, F. (2023). The Quest to Support Community Resilience in the Face of Coastal Hazards and Natural Disasters. *Current: The Journal of Marine Education*, 37(2), 3–7. DOI: 10.5334/cjme.81

Damar, M. (2021). Metaverse Shape of Your Life for Future: A bibliometric snapshot. *Journal of Metaverse*, 1(1), 1–8.

Dionisio, J. D. N., III, W. G. B., & Gilbert, R. (2013). 3D Virtual worlds and the Metaverse. *ACM Computing Surveys, 45*(3), 1–38. DOI: 10.1145/2480741.2480751

Dreamson, N., & Park, G. (2023). Metaverse-Based Learning Through Children's School Space Design. *International Journal of Art & Design Education*, 42(1), 125–138. DOI: 10.1111/jade.12449

Escueta, M., Nickow, A. J., Oreopoulos, P., & Quan, V. (2020). Upgrading Education with Technology: Insights from Experimental Research. *Journal of Economic Literature*, 58(4), 897–996. DOI: 10.1257/jel.20191507

Fakhar, H., Lamrabet, M., Echantoufi, N., khattabi, K. E., & Ajana, L. (2024). Towards a New Artificial Intelligence-based Framework for Teachers' Online Continuous Professional Development Programs: Systematic Review. *International Journal of Advanced Computer Science and Applications*, 15(4). Advance online publication. DOI: 10.14569/IJACSA.2024.0150450

Feng, Z., González, V. A., Amor, R., Lovreglio, R., & Cabrera-Guerrero, G. (2018). Immersive virtual reality serious games for evacuation training and research: A systematic literature review. *Computers & Education*, 127, 252–266. DOI: 10.1016/j.compedu.2018.09.002

Garcia, G., & Jung, I. (2020). Understanding immersion in 2D platform-based online collaborative learning environments. *Australasian Journal of Educational Technology*, 57–67. DOI: 10.14742/ajet.6106

Golam, M., Ara Tuli, E., Naufal Alief, R., Kim, D.-S., & Lee, J.-M. (2024). Meta-Learning: A Digital Learning Management Framework Using Blockchain for Metaverses. *IEEE Access : Practical Innovations, Open Solutions*, 12, 92774–92786. DOI: 10.1109/ACCESS.2024.3408878

Gomathi, C., & Rajamani, V. (2018). Skill-based education through fuzzy knowledge modeling for e-learning. *Computer Applications in Engineering Education*, 26(2), 393–404. DOI: 10.1002/cae.21892

Gonzalez-Romo, N. I., Mignucci-Jiménez, G., Hanalioglu, S., Gurses, M. E., Bahadir, S., Xu, Y., Koskay, G., Lawton, M. T., & Preul, M. C. (2023). Virtual neurosurgery anatomy laboratory: A collaborative and remote education experience in the Metaverse. *Surgical Neurology International*, 14, 90. DOI: 10.25259/SNI_162_2023 PMID: 37025523

Gupta, R., Aggarwal, A., Sable, D., Chahar, P., Sharma, A., Kumari, A., & Maji, R. (2022). Covid-19 Pandemic and Online Education: Impact on Students, Parents and Teachers. *Journal of Human Behavior in the Social Environment*, 32(4), 426–449. DOI: 10.1080/10911359.2021.1909518

Han, J., Liu, G., & Gao, Y. (2023). Learners in the Metaverse: A Systematic Review on the Use of Roblox in Learning. *Education Sciences*, 13(3), 296. DOI: 10.3390/educsci13030296

Han, S., & Noh, Y. (2021). Analyzing Higher Education Instructors' perception on Metaverse-based Education. *Journal of Digital Contents Society*, 22(11), 1793–1806. DOI: 10.9728/dcs.2021.22.11.1793

Hassan, M. A., Habiba, U., Majeed, F., & Shoaib, M. (2021). Adaptive gamification in e-learning based on students' learning styles. *Interactive Learning Environments*, 29(4), 545–565. DOI: 10.1080/10494820.2019.1588745

Hedrick, E., Harper, M., Oliver, E., & Hatch, D. (2022). Teaching & Learning in Virtual Reality: Metaverse Classroom Exploration. *2022 Intermountain EngineeringTechnology and Computing*, 1–5, 1–5. Advance online publication. DOI: 10.1109/IETC54973.2022.9796765

Holt, S. (2023). Virtual reality, augmented reality and mixed reality: For astronaut mental health; and space tourism, education and outreach. *Acta Astronautica*, 203, 436–446. DOI: 10.1016/j.actaastro.2022.12.016

Hussain, S. (2023). Metaverse for education – Virtual or real? *Frontiers in Education*, 8, 1177429. Advance online publication. DOI: 10.3389/feduc.2023.1177429

Jingen Liang, L., & Elliot, S. (2021). A systematic review of augmented reality tourism research: What is now and what is next? *Tourism and Hospitality Research*, 21(1), 15–30. DOI: 10.1177/1467358420941913

Jovanović, A., & Milosavljević, A. (2022). VoRtex Metaverse Platform for Gamified Collaborative Learning. *Electronics (Basel)*, 11(3), 317. DOI: 10.3390/electronics11030317

Kadaruddin, K. (2023). Empowering Education through Generative AI: Innovative Instructional Strategies for Tomorrow's Learners. *International Journal of Business, Law, and Education*, 4(2), 618–625. DOI: 10.56442/ijble.v4i2.215

Kaddoura, S., & Al Husseiny, F. (2023). The rising trend of Metaverse in education: Challenges, opportunities, and ethical considerations. *PeerJ. Computer Science*, 9, e1252. DOI: 10.7717/peerj-cs.1252 PMID: 37346578

Kim, Y.-J., & Lee, S.-H. (2021). The Relationships among Quality of Online Education, Learning Immersion, Learning Satisfaction, and Academic Achievement in Cooking-Practice Subject. *Sustainability (Basel)*, 13(21), 12152. DOI: 10.3390/su132112152

Kye, B., Han, N., Kim, E., Park, Y., & Jo, S. (2021). Educational applications of Metaverse: Possibilities and limitations. *Journal of Educational Evaluation for Health Professions*, 18, 32. DOI: 10.3352/jeehp.2021.18.32 PMID: 34897242

Lampropoulos, G., Fernández-Arias, P., Antón-Sancho, Á., & Vergara, D. (2024). Affective Computing in Augmented Reality, Virtual Reality, and Immersive Learning Environments. *Electronics (Basel)*, 13(15), 2917. DOI: 10.3390/electronics13152917

Lee, S.-M. (2023). Second Language Learning Through an Emergent Narrative in a Narrative-Rich Customizable Metaverse Platform. *IEEE Transactions on Learning Technologies*, 16(6), 1071–1081. DOI: 10.1109/TLT.2023.3267563

Lin, H., Wan, S., Gan, W., Chen, J., & Chao, H.-C. (2022). Metaverse in Education: Vision, Opportunities, and Challenges. *2022 IEEE International Conference on Big Data (Big Data)*, 2857–2866. DOI: 10.1109/BigData55660.2022.10021004

Lnenicka, M., Rizun, N., Alexopoulos, C., & Janssen, M. (2024). Government in the Metaverse: Requirements and suitability for providing digital public services. *Technological Forecasting and Social Change*, 203, 123346. DOI: 10.1016/j.techfore.2024.123346

Mitra, S. (2023). Metaverse: A Potential Virtual-Physical Ecosystem for Innovative Blended Education and Training. *Journal of Metaverse*, 3(1), 66–72. DOI: 10.57019/jmv.1168056

Mystakidis, S. (2022). Metaverse. *Encyclopedia*, 2(1), 486–497. DOI: 10.3390/encyclopedia2010031

Navarro, C., Arias-Calderón, M., Henríquez, C. A., & Riquelme, P. (2024). Assessment of Student and Teacher Perceptions on the Use of Virtual Simulation in Cell Biology Laboratory Education. *Education Sciences*, 14(3), 243. DOI: 10.3390/educsci14030243

Ng, D. T. K. (2022). What is the Metaverse? Definitions, technologies and the community of inquiry. *Australasian Journal of Educational Technology*, 38(4), 190–205. DOI: 10.14742/ajet.7945

Ng, L. L., & Chew, S. Y. (2022). Factors Influencing ESL Players' Use of Vocabulary Learning Strategies in Massively Multiplayer Online Role-Playing Games (MMORPG). *The Asia-Pacific Education Researcher*, 31(4), 369–381. DOI: 10.1007/s40299-021-00578-6

Nilsson, N. C., Nordahl, R., & Serafin, S. (2016). Immersion Revisited: A review of existing definitions of immersion and their relation to different theories of presence. *Human Technology*, 12(2), 108–134. DOI: 10.17011/ht/urn.201611174652

Onu, P., Pradhan, A., & Mbohwa, C. (2024). Potential to use Metaverse for future teaching and learning. *Education and Information Technologies*, 29(7), 8893–8924. DOI: 10.1007/s10639-023-12167-9

Pakinee, A., & Puritat, K. (2021). Designing a gamified e-learning environment for teaching undergraduate ERP course based on big five personality traits. *Education and Information Technologies*, 26(4), 4049–4067. DOI: 10.1007/s10639-021-10456-9 PMID: 33613080

Pham, L., Williamson, S., & Berry, R. (2018). Student Perceptions of E-Learning Service Quality, E-Satisfaction, and E-Loyalty. *International Journal of Enterprise Information Systems*, 14(3), 19–40. DOI: 10.4018/IJEIS.2018070102

Radanliev, P., De Roure, D., Novitzky, P., & Sluganovic, I. (2024). Accessibility and inclusiveness of new information and communication technologies for disabled users and content creators in the Metaverse. *Disability and Rehabilitation. Assistive Technology*, 19(5), 1849–1863. DOI: 10.1080/17483107.2023.2241882 PMID: 37585705

Ramezani, D., Jaferian, G., & Wagner, M. (2024). An investigation into the educational possibilities of metaverse in the context of educational gaming. *RE:view*, 5120–5129. DOI: 10.21125/inted.2024.1326

Rane, N., Choudhary, S., & Rane, J. (2024). Leading-edge Metaverse in education: Framework, applications, challenges, and future development. *TESOL and Technology Studies*, 5(2). Advance online publication. DOI: 10.48185/tts.v5i2.1002

Reeves, S. M., & Crippen, K. J. (2021). Virtual Laboratories in Undergraduate Science and Engineering Courses: A Systematic Review, 2009–2019. *Journal of Science Education and Technology*, 30(1), 16–30. DOI: 10.1007/s10956-020-09866-0

Reis, I. W., Peruchini, M., Ulbricht, V. R., & Teixeira, J. M. (2024). The Dilemma of Teacher Training for the Use of the Metaverse and Other Immersive Technologies in Teaching and Learning Processes. *Communications in Computer and Information Science*, 2130, 105–123. DOI: 10.1007/978-3-031-63235-8_7

Ritterbusch, G. D., & Teichmann, M. R. (2023). Defining the Metaverse: A Systematic Literature Review. *IEEE Access : Practical Innovations, Open Solutions*, 11(January), 12368–12377. DOI: 10.1109/ACCESS.2023.3241809

Roman, M., Kosiński, R., Bhatta, K., Niedziółka, A., & Krasnodębski, A. (2022). Virtual and Space Tourism as New Trends in Travelling at the Time of the COVID-19 Pandemic. *Sustainability (Basel)*, 14(2), 628. DOI: 10.3390/su14020628

Ruthberg, J. S., Tingle, G., Tan, L., Ulrey, L., Simonson-Shick, S., Enterline, R., Eastman, H., Mlakar, J., Gotschall, R., Henninger, E., Griswold, M. A., & Wish-Baratz, S. (2020). Mixed reality as a time-efficient alternative to cadaveric dissection. *Medical Teacher*, 42(8), 896–901. DOI: 10.1080/0142159X.2020.1762032 PMID: 32401090

Saleh, M. I. (2024). From tourism in the Darkverse to tourism with digital detox: Designing responsible Metaverse tourism experiences. *Current Issues in Tourism*, 1–21. DOI: 10.1080/13683500.2024.2322694

Savin-Baden, M., & Burden, D. (2024). The Metaverse for Learning and Education. In *The Metaverse for Learning and Education* (pp. 4–16). Chapman and Hall/CRC. DOI: 10.1201/9781003413875-2

Scavarelli, A., Arya, A., & Teather, R. J. (2021). Virtual reality and augmented reality in social learning spaces: A literature review. *Virtual Reality (Waltham Cross)*, 25(1), 257–277. DOI: 10.1007/s10055-020-00444-8

Sinha, E. (2023). 'Co-creating' experiential learning in the Metaverse- extending the Kolb's learning cycle and identifying potential challenges. *International Journal of Management Education*, 21(3), 100875. DOI: 10.1016/j.ijme.2023.100875

Song, Y., Cao, J., Wu, K., Yu, P. L. H., & Lee, J. C.-K. (2023). Developing "Learningverse"—A 3-D Metaverse Platform to Support Teaching, Social, and Cognitive Presences. *IEEE Transactions on Learning Technologies*, 16(6), 1165–1178. DOI: 10.1109/TLT.2023.3276574

Sopher, H., & Lescop, L. (2023). Learning in Metaverse: The immersive atelier model of the architecture studio. *Archnet-IJAR: International Journal of Architectural Research*, 17(3), 536–553. DOI: 10.1108/ARCH-10-2022-0213

Suh, W., & Ahn, S. (2022). Utilizing the Metaverse for Learner-Centered Constructivist Education in the Post-Pandemic Era: An Analysis of Elementary School Students. *Journal of Intelligence*, 10(1), 17. DOI: 10.3390/jintelligence10010017 PMID: 35324573

Sun, Z., Zhu, M., Shan, X., & Lee, C. (2022). Augmented tactile-perception and haptic-feedback rings as human-machine interfaces aiming for immersive interactions. *Nature Communications*, 13(1), 5224. DOI: 10.1038/s41467-022-32745-8 PMID: 36064838

Taghizadeh, M., & Ejtehadi, A. (2023). Investigating pre-service EFL teachers' and teacher educators' experience and attitudes towards online interaction tools. *Computer Assisted Language Learning*, 36(8), 1633–1667. DOI: 10.1080/09588221.2021.2011322

Tamimi, R., & Toth, C. (2023). Comparison of iPhone 13 pro's camera and lidar sensor to uas photogrammetric model of the great Pyramid of Giza. *The International Archives of the Photogrammetry, Remote Sensing and Spatial Information Sciences,* 3, 299–306. DOI: 10.5194/isprs-archives-XLVIII-M-3-2023-299-2023

Tan, Y., Xu, W., Li, S., & Chen, K. (2022). Augmented and Virtual Reality (AR/VR) for Education and Training in the AEC Industry: A Systematic Review of Research and Applications. *Buildings (Basel, Switzerland)*, 12(10), 1529. DOI: 10.3390/buildings12101529

Tlili, A., Huang, R., Shehata, B., Liu, D., Zhao, J., Metwally, A. H. S., Wang, H., Denden, M., Bozkurt, A., Lee, L.-H., Beyoglu, D., Altinay, F., Sharma, R. C., Altinay, Z., Li, Z., Liu, J., Ahmad, F., Hu, Y., Salha, S., & Burgos, D. (2022). Is Metaverse in education a blessing or a curse: A combined content and bibliometric analysis. *Smart Learning Environments*, 9(1), 24. DOI: 10.1186/s40561-022-00205-x

Tsappi, E., Deliyannis, I., & Papageorgiou, G. N. (2024). Developing a Performance Evaluation Framework Structural Model for Educational Metaverse. *Technologies*, 12(4), 53. DOI: 10.3390/technologies12040053

Tsirulnikov, D., Suart, C., Abdullah, R., Vulcu, F., & Mullarkey, C. E. (2023). Game on: Immersive virtual laboratory simulation improves student learning outcomes & motivation. *FEBS Open Bio*, 13(3), 396–407. DOI: 10.1002/2211-5463.13567 PMID: 36723273

Wang, H., Ning, H., Lin, Y., Wang, W., Dhelim, S., Farha, F., Ding, J., & Danesh-mand, M. (2023). A Survey on the Metaverse: The State-of-the-Art, Technologies, Applications, and Challenges. *IEEE Internet of Things Journal*, 10(16), 14671–14688. DOI: 10.1109/JIOT.2023.3278329

Wang, M., Yu, H., Bell, Z., & Chu, X. (2022). Constructing an Edu-Metaverse Ecosystem: A New and Innovative Framework. *IEEE Transactions on Learning Technologies*, 15(6), 685–696. DOI: 10.1109/TLT.2022.3210828

Wang, Y., Lee, L.-H., Braud, T., & Hui, P. (2022). Re-shaping Post-COVID-19 Teaching and Learning: A Blueprint of Virtual-Physical Blended Classrooms in the Metaverse Era. *2022 IEEE 42nd International Conference on Distributed Computing Systems Workshops*, 241–247. DOI: 10.1109/ICDCSW56584.2022.00053

Waquar, A., Sujood, , Kareem, S., Yasmeen, N., & Hussain, S. (2024, July 26). Sujood, Kareem, S., Yasmeen, N., & Hussain, S. (2024). From traditional to virtual classrooms: Unravelling themes and shaping the future of Metaverse education. *Interactive Technology and Smart Education*. Advance online publication. DOI: 10.1108/ITSE-02-2024-0032

Wohlgenannt, I., Simons, A., & Stieglitz, S. (2020). Virtual Reality. *Business & Information Systems Engineering*, 62(5), 455–461. DOI: 10.1007/s12599-020-00658-9

Wu, S., Xu, L., Dai, Z., & Pan, Y. (2023). Factors Affecting Avatar Customization Behavior in Virtual Environments. *Electronics (Basel)*, 12(10), 2286. DOI: 10.3390/electronics12102286

Yang, Q., Zhao, Y., Huang, H., Xiong, Z., Kang, J., & Zheng, Z. (2022). Fusing Blockchain and AI With Metaverse: A Survey. *IEEE Open Journal of the Computer Society*, 3, 122–136. DOI: 10.1109/OJCS.2022.3188249

Yang, R. (2022). Multimodal Fusion Blended Teaching Under the New Era of "Internet+. *Lecture Notes of the Institute for Computer Sciences, Social Informatics and Telecommunications Engineering*, 439, 686–698. DOI: 10.1007/978-3-031-04245-4_61

Yu, H., Wen, G., Gan, J., Zheng, W., & Lei, C. (2020). Self-paced Learning for K-means Clustering Algorithm. *Pattern Recognition Letters*, 132, 69–75. DOI: 10.1016/j.patrec.2018.08.028

Zabel, C., O'Brien, D., & Natzel, J. (2023). Sensing the Metaverse: The microfoundations of complementor firms' dynamic sensing capabilities in emerging-technology ecosystems. *Technological Forecasting and Social Change*, 192, 122562. DOI: 10.1016/j.techfore.2023.122562

Zhang, C. (2020). The Why, What, and How of Immersive Experience. *IEEE Access : Practical Innovations, Open Solutions*, 8, 90878–90888. DOI: 10.1109/ACCESS.2020.2993646

Zhang, X., Chen, Y., Hu, L., & Wang, Y. (2022). The Metaverse in education: Definition, framework, features, potential applications, challenges, and future research topics. *Frontiers in Psychology*, 13, 1016300. Advance online publication. DOI: 10.3389/fpsyg.2022.1016300 PMID: 36304866

Zhao, Z., Zhao, B., Ji, Z., & Liang, Z. (2022). On the Personalized Learning Space in Educational Metaverse Based on Heart Rate Signal. *International Journal of Information and Communication Technology Education*, 18(2), 1–12. DOI: 10.4018/ijicte.314565

ADDITIONAL READING

Alfaisal, R., Hashim, H., & Azizan, U. H. (2024). Metaverse system adoption in education: A systematic literature review. *Journal of Computers in Education*, 11(1), 259–303. DOI: 10.1007/s40692-022-00256-6

Alkhwaldi, A. F. (2024). Understanding learners' intention toward Metaverse in higher education institutions from a developing country perspective: UTAUT and ISS integrated model. *Kybernetes*, 53(12), 6008–6035. DOI: 10.1108/K-03-2023-0459

Almarzouqi, A., Aburayya, A., & Salloum, S. A. (2022). Prediction of user's intention to use metaverse system in medical education: A hybrid SEM-ML learning approach. *IEEE Access : Practical Innovations, Open Solutions*, 10, 43421–43434. DOI: 10.1109/ACCESS.2022.3169285

Camilleri, M. A. (2024). Metaverse applications in education: A systematic review and a cost-benefit analysis. *Interactive Technology and Smart Education*, 21(2), 245–269. DOI: 10.1108/ITSE-01-2023-0017

Inceoglu, M. M., & Ciloglugil, B. (2022, July). Use of Metaverse in education. In *International conference on computational science and its applications* (pp. 171-184). Cham: Springer International Publishing.

Nguyen, A. H. D., Le, T. T., Dang, T. Q., & Nguyen, L. T. (2024). Understanding metaverse adoption in education: The extended UTAUMT model. *Heliyon*, 10(19), e38741. DOI: 10.1016/j.heliyon.2024.e38741 PMID: 39416817

Onu, P., Pradhan, A., & Mbohwa, C. (2024). Potential to use metaverse for future teaching and learning. *Education and Information Technologies*, 29(7), 8893–8924. DOI: 10.1007/s10639-023-12167-9

Tlili, A., Huang, R., Shehata, B., Liu, D., Zhao, J., Metwally, A. H. S., Wang, H., Denden, M., Bozkurt, A., Lee, L.-H., Beyoglu, D., Altinay, F., Sharma, R. C., Altinay, Z., Li, Z., Liu, J., Ahmad, F., Hu, Y., Salha, S., & Burgos, D. (2022). Is Metaverse in education a blessing or a curse: A combined content and bibliometric analysis. *Smart Learning Environments*, 9(1), 1–31. DOI: 10.1186/s40561-022-00205-x

Zhang, X., Chen, Y., Hu, L., & Wang, Y. (2022). The metaverse in education: Definition, framework, features, potential applications, challenges, and future research topics. *Frontiers in Psychology*, 13, 1016300. DOI: 10.3389/fpsyg.2022.1016300 PMID: 36304866

KEY TERMS AND DEFINITIONS

Digital Divide: The digital divide in the Metaverse refers to a lack of access to important technology, such as high-speed connectivity, virtual reality/augmented reality devices, and computer competencies. This divide can hinder students' access to immersive, interactive, and personalized virtual educational experiences.

Efficient Teaching: Efficient teaching in the Metaverse utilises VR/AR, AI-driven analytics, and interactive simulations to enhance instructional methods. It enables personalised learning, real-time assessment, and adaptive content delivery, optimising educators' efforts while improving student engagement, knowledge retention, and overall learning outcomes in virtual environments.

Engagement: Actively involving students in interactive, hands-on learning settings that promote deeper understanding, involvement, and emotional ties to metaverse content is called engagement in education.

Gamification: Gamification is the process of adding features to a game, such as challenges, prizes, and points, to work to make them more engaging and enjoyable. It helps people stay engaged and motivated by creating interesting, satisfying and inspiring work or learning.

Personalization: In the Metaverse, personalization refers to customizing learning experiences to meet the requirements, preferences, and learning styles of each individual learner in virtual environments. It promotes a more interesting and successful educational experience by enabling personalized material, flexible learning routes, and immersive interactions.

Self-Paced Learning: Self-paced learning is a method of learning in which students can explore virtual worlds and materials at their own pace. This concept makes personalized learning possible, letting students interact, review, and study content according to their own development.

Virtual Tours: Virtual tours immerse students in digital explorations of real-world sites or simulated environments, providing interactive, experiential learning opportunities that improve comprehension, engagement, and access to distant or worldwide educational events through VR and AR.

Chapter 4
Wine Tourism Meets the Metaverse:
A Case Study

Belem Barbosa
https://orcid.org/0000-0002-4057-360X
University of Porto, Portugal

Shalini Singh
https://orcid.org/0009-0002-8305-4794
Rovira i Virgili University, Spain

Tuğçe Yetik
https://orcid.org/0009-0000-4763-2708
Sabanci University, Turkey

Camila Carvalho
https://orcid.org/0009-0009-4593-4724
University of Porto, Portugal

EXECUTIVE SUMMARY

Technological developments are presenting new ways for companies to organize their businesses and offer new products, services, and experiences to their customers. The Metaverse allows the participation and interaction of individuals in immersive experiences that merge virtual and real worlds. The adoption of metaverse platforms by companies worldwide is growing steadily, with the potential to change business in various industries, including tourism. However, the literature on the Metaverse applied to tourism is very scarce. This chapter addresses this gap by exploring a case study of the implementation of a Metaverse strategy by a Portuguese wine brand, Sandeman, as part of their wine tourism experience offerings. The case study is

DOI: 10.4018/979-8-3693-7245-6.ch004

built on secondary data, observation, and interviews with tourists.

INTRODUCTION

The ever-evolving digital landscape and growing competitiveness present ongoing challenges for the tourism industry. One of the most interesting technological trends is the metaverse, a key component of Web 3.0, the next generation of the Internet, enabled by virtual reality, blockchain, and other technological innovations. Cui and van Esch (2024) define the metaverse as an interactive, immersive environment that allows users to navigate between virtual and physical worlds, interacting with digital content and other users in a shared space. As explained in the literature (e.g., Buhalis et al., 2023; Di Paolo et al., 2025) and industry reports (e.g., Constantin et al., 2023), metaverse tourism enables tourists to virtually engage with destinations and tourism offerings, evaluate them, and participate in showcases and events. Thus, metaverse tourism has the dual potential to facilitate tourist decision-making and to enhance leisure and tourism services and experiences that tourists can acquire and enjoy.

It is estimated that, by 2030, the metaverse could be worth $5 trillion (McKinsey and Company, 2022), driven by strong consumer interest in integrating immersive experiences in their activities, especially in areas such as social interaction, entertainment, gaming, travel, and shopping. A study released by Meta Group and Delloite estimates that the metaverse could contribute between €259 and €489 billion to the European Union's Gross Domestic Product in 2035 (Christensen & Robinson, 2022). Tourism in Europe appears to be one of the areas with the most significant potential for this tool, as it is the region that generates 50% of the sector's global revenue (Gomes, 2024). The metaverse potential is extensive and applicable to any location around the globe. In an article published by the World Economic Forum, Chan (2023) stresses the impressive impacts that the metaverse is expected to have in world economies, mainly because the metaverse is being built on open standards, democratizing technology access.

Overall, the literature unanimously anticipates that the metaverse has the potential to revolutionize several industries, particularly tourism (Ampountolas et al., 2024; Natarajan et al., 2024; Rather, 2023; Sanchez-Amboage et al., 2024).

According to McKinsey, the metaverse's primary impacts on tourism focus on the pre-trip and in-trip stages of the traveler's journey (Constantin et al., 2023). In the pre-trip phase, the metaverse allows potential visitors to virtually explore destinations and make informed decisions before leaving home. During the in-trip phase, the metaverse enhances experiences related to lodging and entertainment, visitor support, and shopping (Constantin et al., 2023). The scientific literature supports these views by suggesting that the metaverse can enhance travel experiences (Buhalis et al., 2023; Natarajan et al., 2024) and also assist tourists in their travel decisions, with potential positive impacts on intentions and physical visits to the experienced destinations (Buhalis et al., 2023; Natarajan et al., 2024; Shin & Kang, 2024).

In line with this, some early adopters have started exploring the potential of the metaverse to engage younger audiences and attract more physical visitors to their sites. One example is Saudi Arabia's Hegra Archaeological Site, the first UNESCO World Heritage site brought to the metaverse (Farrant, 2022). It was launched on Decentraland in 2022, allowing virtual visitors to explore its ancient Nabataean tombs, including the renowned Tomb of Lihyan. This metaverse experience provides a unique opportunity to enter the tomb's interior, which is inaccessible to physical tourists for preservation reasons. Visitors can also experience an immersive hot air balloon ride over Hegra, gaining 360-degree views of the desert landscape. By bringing Hegra into the metaverse, Saudi Arabia intends to engage the young and well-educated population in the country with a growing interest in digital innovations and attract more physical visitors to the site (Farrant, 2022).

Being an emergent technology, literature on the impact of the metaverse on tourism is still scarce, especially concerning wine tourism. One exception is the article by Di Paolo et al. (2025), who adopt a social capital perspective to analyze Enoverse, an Italian rural wine tourism consortium in the metaverse. This study highlights the challenges of implementing a metaverse strategy to offer authentic experiences to tourists, concluding that stakeholder integration facilitates the metaverse's implementation in rural tourism destinations. However, the study focuses on management and implementation perspectives, leaving tourists' experiences and impacts on their behavior unaddressed. Additionally, Monaco and Sacchi (2023) provide an overview of the opportunities and challenges of the metaverse for food and wine tourism. These authors highlight accessibility, sustainability, concept testing for tourism stakeholders, and enhanced decision-making for tourists as the main benefits of metaverse tourism. Accordingly, the main challenges identified by Monaco and Sacchi (2023) are energy costs and consequent impacts on the environment, potential social exclusion due to the digital divide of the global populations, and privacy concerns associated with virtual environments. Despite addressing both the managerial and consumer perspectives, Monaco and Sacchi (2023) adopt an opinion approach to their article and do not provide empirical evidence on the impacts of wine tourism experiences in the metaverse.

The main aim of this chapter is to explore the potential of metaverse experiences in the context of wine tourism. In line with this, the research objectives defined for this chapter were:

- Explore the perceptions of tourists regarding metaverse experiences in wine tourism,

- Analyze metaverse experiences as strategic choices of wine tourism companies,
- Identify the main strategic choices for integrating metaverse experiences in wine tourism offerings.

This chapter adopts a case study approach by analyzing the case of the Sandeman Metaverse Experience. The chapter starts with a theoretical background by contextualizing wine tourism, the experience economy, and the expected outcomes of consumers' experiences in the metaverse. Then, the chapter presents the adopted methodology, followed by the analysis and discussion of the case study. Based on the findings, the chapter also includes recommendations for managers and future research directions.

BACKGROUND

Wine Tourism

Wine tourism refers to travel focused on wine-related experiences, such as visiting vineyards, wineries, wine festivals, and events, with the primary goal of tasting and learning about wine (Hall & Mitchell, 2000). It has evolved into a complex type of tourism, wherein both the wine and the encompassing "winescape" – including the rural environment, landscape, and cultural attractions – are essential to attract visitors (Bruwer & Rueger-Muck, 2019). Since the 1990s, wine tourism has grown exponentially, driven by a growing wine customer demand for unique and authentic experiences. The trend is anticipated to continue, as the size of the wine tourism market is expected to more than double from USD 46.47 billion in 2023 to USD 107 billion in 2030 (Grand View Research, 2024). The growth of the wine tourism industry is driven by the Millennials (Grand View Research, 2024), a generation that is tech-savvy, environmentally conscious, and that values unique and immersive experiences.

Wine tourists are motivated by a combination of push and pull factors, including wine tasting, purchasing, and experiencing the winescape environment (Quintal et al., 2022). Motivations differ across segments, with some tourists seeking education or bonding experiences while others prioritize escapism or new, unique encounters (Gaetjens et al., 2023). Wine tourists can be segmented into groups such as "wine lovers," "wine interested," "curious," and "disinterested tourists" (Charters & Ali-Knight, 2002). These varied motivations and segments highlight the importance of understanding both wine-specific and broader experiential desires within the growing wine tourism market. Overall, and as demonstrated by Gómez-Carmona et al. (2023), wine tourism experiences favor tourists' attitudes and loyalty towards wine, further demonstrating the relevance of wine tourism for wine brands.

Experience in Wine Tourism

Pine and Gilmore (1998) categorize experiences into four realms, depending on the level of customer participation and immersion: entertainment, education, escapism, and esthetics. Entertainment is characterized by passive engagement, where consumers absorb the experience, like watching traditional grape stomping. Education encompasses active engagement where consumers increase their knowledge or skills, such as in a workshop on grape varieties. Escapism is an experience characterized by active participation that immerses consumers in a new reality, like a virtual reality tour of a vineyard. Esthetics is an experience marked by passive immersion in an environment without actively altering it, such as exploring a scenic landscape. Pine and Gilmore (1998) suggest that the "sweet spot" is the ideal blend of the four realms of experience that creates a memorable, immersive experience. The "sweet spot" occurs when a company balances these elements to engage customers fully, providing an experience that is both enjoyable and meaningful. This optimal mix ensures that the experience resonates with customers on multiple levels, enhancing engagement, satisfaction, and lasting impact and creating competitive advantages.

Considering that the wine tourism sector predominantly functions within the service economy, it is essential for organizations to successfully differentiate their offerings, as emphasized by Pine and Gilmore (2011). Wine tourism's definitions have evolved over the years, but experience remains at the core of all forms of tourism, including wine tourism. Thanh and Kirova (2018) performed a netnographic analysis of online reviews on TripAdvisor posted by tourists who visited the French wine tourism region Cognac. They confirmed the four realms of the wine tourism experience but concluded that entertainment and education are the dominant perspectives in the reviews. (Kastenholz et al., 2022) applied Pine and Gilmore's framework to the Bairrada wine region in Portugal and found that aesthetic and educational realms of experience are particularly stressed by visitors, highlighting the importance of the physical environment and landscape to the visitors' experience and to explain satisfaction and loyalty.

In a complementary perspective, Schmitt et al. (2015) adopted the lens of experiential psychology and conceptualized consumer experiences as multidimensional, encompassing sensory, affective, cognitive, and behavioral elements. As such, they consider sensory dimensions composed of experiences that stimulate the senses (e.g., sight, hearing, taste, touch, and smell), creating memorable and engaging experiences. The affective dimension refers to the emotional responses associated with the experience, which trigger loyalty and attachment. Cognitive experience refers to the mental engagement of the consumer as, for instance, a result of intellectual stimulation. The behavioral dimension refers to the physical actions and behaviors associated with the experience. Finally, the social dimension refers to the interpersonal aspects of the experience, such as social interaction. Schmitt et al. (2015) view consumer experiences as a combination of these dimensions, arguing that their combination is needed to provide immersive and holistic experiences that create emotional attachments with the relevant target audiences.

Wine consumption has been described as inherently multisensory, involving visual, olfactory, gustatory, tactile, and auditory elements (Cui & van Esch, 2024). Brochado et al. (2021) analyzed reviews from wine tourists in the Douro region, Portugal. They found that the main themes included in the reviews were associated with vision and taste, followed by audition, while touch and smell were rarely mentioned.

Santos et al. (2022) developed a framework to summarize wine tourism. According to their contribution, the wine tourism experience comprises six components: winescape, attachment, emotions, sensory, storytelling, and involvement. These components explain tourists' intentions and behaviors, particularly satisfaction, loyalty, and word-of-mouth communication. Santos et al. (2022) also stress the importance of innovation to enhance the wine tourism experience, including virtual and augmented reality events such as digital and hybrid wine events.

Overall, integrating multisensory technology within the wine industry through augmented reality, virtual reality, and metaverse is expected to reshape wine tourism experiences. Immersive technologies are acknowledged for their ability to enhance emotional reactions and engagement (Flavián et al., 2021; Martins et al., 2017), so it is expected to trigger escapism.

Immersive Experiences in the Metaverse

The metaverse can assist tourists before, during, and after their travels (Buhalis et al., 2023; Liu & Park, 2024). In fact, metaverse experiences offer tourists the opportunity to prepare for their travels, create realistic expectations, and assist their decision-making (Buhalis et al., 2023; Mahmoud et al., 2024). The metaverse can offer enhanced experiences during travel, including rich information and time travels (Buhalis et al., 2023). After the trip, the metaverse can be used to revisit and share experiences with others (Buhalis et al., 2023).

It may appear challenging to understand how wine and tourism, which are intrinsically linked to sensory experiences, may integrate into the metaverse. Still, various studies have highlighted the seamless transition of these industries into the metaverse. A recent review of the metaverse by Dwivedi et al. (2022) indicates that the food marketing and tourism sectors are the primary domains where companies explore solutions to provide individuals with the chance to engage in a fully operational, immersive metaverse that bridges the virtual and real worlds. Gastronomy in the metaverse may sound paradoxical, as food is strongly linked to sensory and tangible experiences. However, food and wine are much more than simply the act of eating and drinking: they involve connecting with communities, cultures, and different territories. In wine and gastronomy tourism, sharing experiences with friends, family, followers, and peers has emerged as a crucial element of traveling across regions. As such, expanding food and wine-related experiences in the Metaverse may present innovative and unconventional opportunities, like the ability to explore production locations, breweries, or farms across various states or countries and to engage with influencers and chefs (Monaco & Sacchi, 2023).

Martins et al. (2017) proposed a specification for multisensory virtual experiences in wine tourism. Their framework encompasses a combination of virtual experiences (i.e., history, manufacturing process, and winescape) that stimulate primarily visual and auditory senses with mixed realities (i.e., wine tasting) to include taste and olfactory senses and hence provide an immersive, multisensory, and holistic wine tourism experience.

Compared to virtual reality experiences, the metaverse enhances traditional motivations for wine tourism, such as community and sensory engagement, by providing a more interactive and accessible platform (Cui & van Esch, 2024). Recent studies by Sousa et al. (2024a, 2024b) found that wine tourism immersive experiences with VR technology foster intentions to visit the physical location and to recommend both the wine tourism destination and the VR experience. These intentions are explained by the satisfaction with the experience (Sousa et al., 2024a) and the perceived quality of the VR experience (Sousa et al., 2024b). Moreover, immersive experiences like the metaverse are expected to foster fantasy, inspiration, and imagination (Di Paolo et al., 2025) and help tourists with their decision-making (Buhalis et al., 2023; Di Paolo et al., 2025; Dwivedi et al., 2022; Flavián et al., 2021; Monaco & Sacchi, 2023)

In the case of wine tourism, virtual platforms can be used to immerse users in a sensory experience, enabling exploration of vineyards, observation of the winemaking process, and participation in virtual tastings, regardless of geographical location (Spence, 2019). The immersive quality of virtual reality cultivates an in-depth emotional bond with wines and their cultural history, hence increasing wine appreciation (Maumon & Bédé, 2023).

The literature also highlights the challenges and potential negative impacts of metaverse adoption by the tourism industry. Buhalis et al. (2023) note that, despite the disruptive innovation opportunities offered to the tourism industry, the metaverse could also potentially harm both tourists and service providers. The adoption of metaverse strategies by the tourism industry encompasses several types of challenges (Buhalis et al., 2023):

Technological Challenges: Different from the maturity of virtual gaming in the metaverse, the benchmarking in the tourism industry is still very limited, and consequently, it is difficult to identify the best practices and critical success factors to guide strategic decisions. Also, the expense and technical requirements of high-quality experiences limit access to this technology.
Economic Challenges: Metaverse operational platforms and infrastructure remain limited and have high costs. Many tourist destinations, particularly in less wealthy or peripheral areas, may not have the economic resources to invest in metaverse technology. High costs for equipment, like VR or MR headsets, create financial barriers for both users and businesses, potentially increasing inequality and deepening the digital divide.
Consumer Experience Challenges: Even those who can afford this technology may face issues like motion sickness, which can limit their engagement with immersive experiences. Furthermore, the immersive nature of the metaverse can blur the line between reality and virtuality, potentially reducing users' critical thinking and imagination. This virtual-real overlap may also encourage addictive behaviors, with users increasingly relying on the metaverse as an escape.
Ethical and Legal Challenges: Virtual environments in the metaverse can foster unethical or illegal behavior, such as harassment, cyberstalking, and fraud, particularly due to the anonymity of virtual personas. Further, addictive tendencies and excessive digital engagement may lead to mental health issues, as evidenced by the World Health Organization's classification of "gaming disorder.

Therefore, it is recommended that companies adopting the metaverse for their businesses define strategies to mitigate the potential negative impacts for both their business and their customers so that it creates value for all stakeholders and effectively contributes to the differentiation and competitiveness of businesses and to valuable experiences for tourists.

METHOD

This chapter adopts a single case study as a methodological approach. As noted in the reference literature (e.g., Clark et al., 2021; Hartley, 2004; Yin, 2018), case study is not itself a research method. A case study is a research design that focuses on examining the unique features of a specific case rather than seeking generalizable conclusions (Clark et al., 2021; Hartley, 2004; Yin, 2018). The case study provides context-related rich data and, therefore, is particularly valuable to research novel topics (Clark et al., 2021) and address research questions that require a detailed understanding of social processes (Hartley, 2004), as it is the case of metaverse tourism in general. Yin (2018) highlighted the potential of case study approaches to explore contemporary events and address how/why research questions.

Hence, the case study design refers to an intensive and detailed analysis of a case (Hartley, 2004; Yin, 2018), which can be associated with different research methods for data collection (Yin, 2018). In the present study, we adopt a qualitative approach, comprising observation, secondary data analysis, and structured interviews with customers. Traditionally, case studies adopt a combination of research methods (Hartley, 2004), although they tend to prioritize qualitative approaches (Clark et al., 2021; Hartley, 2004; Yin, 2018), often associated with the exploration of new phenomena or innovative strategies adopted by organizations, as is the focus of this chapter.

Case Study Selection

Case studies typically do not aim to represent a broader population or class of cases; instead, they provide in-depth insights into the particularities of a single instance (Clark et al., 2021). The present study adopted a single unit of analysis, aiming to understand it in depth. As suggested by Yin (2003, 2009), the selection of the case was driven by the research objectives as well as by the sufficient accessibility of data.

The main criterion that guided the selection of the case was its relevance to the research objectives. Sandeman is a wine brand established in 1790 and one of the most well-known producers of port wine. The long history of the brand is marked by its innovation, including the early development of a brand identity (in the early 1800s), the creation of one of the oldest and most well-known logos in the wine industry in 1928, and the success of being a pioneer in advertising in the wine industry. Sandeman was also one of the first wine brands to use metaverse technology. In 2023, the Sandeman Metaverse Experience introduced a virtual tour of Quinta do Seixo, addressing the lack of vineyard views at Vila Nova de Gaia, its most visited tourist site. While in the cellars, visitors can interact in real-time as avatars with the Douro vineyards, located 150 km away (a two-hour drive). Wine tourism managers suggest that the metaverse enhances the desire to travel rather than replacing real experiences (Gomes, 2024), and therefore expect the experience to increase the physical visits to Quinta do Seixo. The Sandeman Metaverse Experience was awarded the Portuguese 2024 "National Innovation Prize" in the category of Web 3.0 and Large Company (Gomes, 2024), recognizing the company's innovativeness in a traditional industry.

Data Collection and Analysis

This study used data from three complementary sources:

Secondary data: Information on the company website, corporate reports and press releases, news in the media, and social media posts.
Observation: The researchers participated in the metaverse experience, visited the cellars, interacted with brand representatives, and observed wine tourists visiting the cellars.
Interviews: A structured interview was conducted with three Portuguese citizens after participating in the metaverse experience.

These methods and the qualitative approach were chosen for this study due to their ability to generate rich data and provide a detailed examination of the case. The interview outline was divided into three sections. In the first section, the interviewees were asked to describe their experience. The second section explored the outcomes of the experience, including their intentions to visit. Finally, the third section examined their perceptions regarding the profiles of wine tourists who would be most interested in and satisfied with this experience. The characteristics of the sample are detailed in Table 1. A purposive sample (Clark et al., 2021) was selected for this study,

Table 1. Profiles of the interviewees

Participants	Gender	Age	Education level	Occupation	Prior experience in the metaverse
Participant A	Female	Mid 20s	Bachelor degree	Student	No
Participant M	Female	Mid 20s	Bachelor degree	Full-time worker	No
Participant S	Female	Mid 30s	PhD	Full-time worker	Yes

Source: The Authors

A combination of data-driven and theory-driven content analysis was adopted (Clark et al., 2021), as the themes were initially defined based on the literature review and complemented with new themes that emerged from the data.

CASE STUDY: THE METAVERSE SANDEMAN EXPERIENCE

Sandeman, founded in 1790 by Scottish George Sandeman, is one of the oldest and most iconic producers of Port (Portugal) and Sherry (Spain) wines. Originally established in London, Sandeman quickly grew in reputation for its high-quality wines. By the early 1800s, the company had developed a distinctive brand identity, marked by its famous logo featuring the mysterious "Don" figure—a silhouette in a typical Portuguese student cape and a Spanish wide-brimmed hat—created in 1928 as a symbol of Sandeman's Iberian identity. This figure became the most emblematic symbol in the overall wine industry. As noted on the brand's website, Sandeman is an advertising pioneer, being "one of the first wine brands to label and advertise its wines" (Sandeman, 2024a). In the early 1900s, Sandeman stood out in an industry that only sporadically invested in advertisements by making partnerships with artists and using commissioned paintings in ads, posters, and labels.

In 2002, Sandeman was acquired by a leading player in the wine industry in Portugal, Sogrape, a family-owned fine wine company founded in 1942 and operating globally, with their wines sold in five continents. Sandeman has profited from its know-how, investments, and footprint, namely in the Douro region, where Sogrape owns several vineyards.

Over the centuries, Sandeman has continued to innovate while staying true to its roots, combining traditional winemaking methods with modern approaches. Today, Sandeman is celebrated not only for its Port and Sherry but also for its offering of diverse wine tourism experiences at several iconic locations (Sandeman, 2024b). Visitors can explore the port wine cellars in Vila Nova de Gaia, where guided tours and tastings highlight Sandeman's rich heritage. At this location, Sandeman provides a range of immersive experiences, from traditional tastings of port wines to unique pairings like port wine and chocolate (Sandeman, 2024a). Additionally, at Quinta do Seixo in the Douro Valley, guests can experience vineyard landscapes and traditions associated with port wine production. Quinta do Seixo is perfectly integrated into the Douro landscape, with 70 hectares of vines, where traditional grapes are planted in multi-faced century-old terraces.

The Sandeman & Douro Metaverse Experience is a pioneering initiative, the first of its kind in Portugal's wine industry, and one of the few available worldwide in the wine industry, that allows the virtual exploration of Quinta do Seixo. Through VR technology, visitors can immerse themselves in the vineyard environment. According to the company, "this project is a gateway to bringing the Douro to the world," fulfilling the desire of many visitors who cannot travel to the vineyards (Gomes, 2024). The metaverse experience remains in a preliminary implementation stage, allowing a limited number of visitors to test it and gathering visitors' feedback to improve the experience and sustain future strategies.

Strategic Perspective

The Ansoff matrix is widely used within businesses to make well-informed decisions about strategic expansion (Hussain et al., 2013). Ansoff's Growth Matrix focuses on whether the market and the product/service are existing or new for the company, with four strategic options: market penetration, product development, market development, and diversification (Johnson et al., 2017). Market penetration is about increasing the market share with the current products that the company already has in the current markets, and it is widely used by companies since it does not require significant investments. A product development strategy involves introducing new products to existing markets; however, it carries risks and costs as it requires new resources and capabilities. Market development carries fewer risks as it delivers existing products to new markets, such as reaching new customer segments or expanding into new geographic regions. Lastly, diversification involves offering new products in new markets. It is referred to as related diversification if the expansion is linked to the existing businesses, and as conglomerate diversification if the expansion has no connection to the current businesses (Johnson et al., 2017).

Using the lens of the Ansoff matrix to analyze the Sandeman Metaverse Experience, it can be concluded that Sandeman's metaverse experience fits into a product development strategy. Sandeman produces wines and offers wine tours at selected locations in Portugal and Spain (Sandeman, 2024b). Their recent entry into the metaverse can be positioned as the introduction of an experience distinct from their traditional wine tourism experiences at Sandeman cellars in Vila Nova de Gaia. As in the initial stage, the experience is being sold to the tourists who visit the cellars as an alternative experience they can enjoy during their visit.

However, the metaverse experience has the potential to attract new market segments, especially if, in a second stage of development, in the future, the company decides to make the virtual experience globally accessible online. This approach could target younger generations who are more familiar with technology and interested in immersive experiences and let the brand go beyond their traditional public. In such a case, the initiative would transition into market development, enabling Sandeman to reach new market segments and attract a diverse demographic of users, expanding its brand presence beyond physical limitations.

It is interesting to note that, as a growth strategy, a metaverse experience can be strategically positioned in alternative ways. In fact, it could be designed as a new experience or service to make a brand relevant to the new public, and in that case, it would pertain to diversification.

Consumers' Views

Description of the Experience

During the interviews, the participants provided detailed descriptions of the main components of the experience, which included a tour of the wine cellars before the metaverse experience and was followed by a wine tasting. Here is one of the descriptions:

The experience started with a guided tour of the wine cellars, where the guide showed us the various rooms and the wine barrels and explained how the older and younger wines were managed, how they were preserved, and how all the stages of maintaining the wines' quality worked, including when they would be bottled or become vintage. Then we went to the wine tasting room, where we put on the VR goggles and had the metaverse experience. Here, we were virtually in a part of the Douro estate simulating a wine tasting, with tables featuring virtual cheeses and an outdoor terrace, as well as a 'shop' where we were supposedly able to choose wines and view their labels, but on the day of the visit, this functionality was not working. Afterward, we had a wine tasting outside the metaverse, where we tasted two wines: a white Port wine [designed for mixology and to add, for example, tonic water] and a 10-year-old Tawny, a red Port wine. (Participant A)

These descriptions highlight some of the advantages of having the experience at the cellars, not only due to the complementarities of the atmosphere of the cellars and the opportunity to taste the wines but also regarding the technical support provided by the staff, which is particularly valuable for tourists that are not too familiar with VR technology and the metaverse.

What I liked the most about the experience, in general, was visiting the wine cellars and listening to all the explanations provided by the guide during the visit, learning how the wines are preserved, along with various curiosities and facts. We had the opportunity to ask questions during the visit, which made it much more dynamic than just listening to the explanation. (Participant A)

The support provided by the staff throughout the experience facilitated interactions and helped me understand where I was in the process. (Participant S)

Based on the participants' views in this study, one can infer that offering the experience on Sandeman's premises, specifically at the wine cellar store, provides several advantages to tourists. From a multi-sensory perspective, combining the physical visit to the Vila Nova de Gaia cellars with the virtual visit to Quinta do Seixo enhances overall immersion by engaging multiple senses. As noted by Martins et al. (2017), a truly immersive wine tourism experience benefits from stimulating the visual and auditory senses through virtual components, as well as incorporating taste and olfactory senses in physical wine tasting. The activities before and after the metaverse tour created a more holistic and multisensory experience (Schmitt et al., 2015), allowing visitors to experience the winescape's visual landscape and traditions alongside sensory elements of taste and smell. This blend of sensory stimulation offers a more authentic and immersive wine tourism experience that would not be possible if the metaverse experience were solely virtual.

Tourists' Motivations Regarding Metaverse Experiences

According to the participants in this study, the motivations for engaging in Sandeman's metaverse experience included a desire for unique, immersive encounters and an interest in exploring new technology within a familiar cultural context.

One of the participants stressed the integration of innovation and tradition that the immersive experience enabled, highlighting the combination of history, the sensory-rich environment at the physical wine cellars, and the immersive and novel experience in the metaverse.

> *What I liked the most was the combination of the physical environment of the wine cellars with their historical atmosphere and the immersive experience of the metaverse. In fact, I loved seeing how it is possible to combine such distinct elements, uniting traditional Port wine with something as innovative as the metaverse. (Participant M)*

Another participant stressed the immersive realism and unrestricted exploration of the virtual environment, offering a unique experience in otherwise inaccessible spaces.

> *I didn't know Quinta do Seixo, so the immersive experience was my first contact with the place. I liked the 'realism' of the experience. (...) The fact that we could walk around the estate without any temporal or physical limitations is very interesting, and the ability to visit places that are inaccessible in reality (like the Quinta Chapel) also makes the experience more exclusive. (Participant S)*

Additionally, participants were also motivated by curiosity about the technology itself, as they noted it was their first experience with a VR headset and with the metaverse.

> *I also really liked the possibility of using VR glasses; it was my first experience with VR and the metaverse, and although it was simple, it was interesting to understand how it works. (Participant A)*

Overall, the participants suggest that visitors are motivated both by curiosity and their interest in wine and value innovation and novel experiences. In fact, wine lovers often seek exclusive experiences, enhanced sensory experiences, and additional opportunities to learn more about wine. Besides wine lovers, some participants suggested that this experience may best attract younger, tech-savvy, or novelty-seeking visitors who prioritize unique and innovative experiences in tourism.

The metaverse might attract younger people, as it offers something innovative. Ideally, this would appeal to someone who enjoys both wine and new technologies. (Visitor M)

I would recommend this experience to someone interested in Port wine or who at least appreciates it and is curious about the metaverse and technology. People who are more comfortable with technology would likely enjoy this more. (Participant A)

These findings align with the literature that stresses that tourists are motivated by a combination of push and pull factors (Quintal et al., 2022). Interestingly, these factors encompass both wine-related and technology-related motivations. These results suggest that the metaverse experience may attract "wine lovers" to "curious" tourists (Charters & Ali-Knight, 2002). Furthermore, the findings suggest that the motivations may differ across segments (Gaetjens et al., 2023), as some tourists may be moved by enhancing their wine knowledge, and others favor the uniqueness and novelty of the experience.

Perceived Challenges of Metaverse Tourism

Participant feedback also revealed difficulties felt during the experience, which resonate with challenges highlighted in the literature (Buhalis et al., 2023), namely technological, economic, and consumer experience issues. Technological limitations included incomplete features and the need for realistic images to provide a holistic and immersive experience.

There was a 'shop' where we were supposedly able to choose wines and view their labels, but on the day of the visit, this functionality was not working. (Participant A)

I also missed a greater degree of interactivity, which could be resolved if, for example, I had the option to engage with [my friend who was experiencing it with me]. But the option was not available on the day of my visit. (Participant M)

Additionally, participants mentioned some discomfort, particularly motion sickness and initial disorientation. This could be explained by the fact that, for some participants, this was their first experience with VR equipment.

I felt some dizziness during the first 2–3 minutes of the experience. (Participant S)

Participants also stressed the physical conditions of the experience that could be improved by more relaxing and comfortable conditions when participating in the experience.

The fact of standing throughout the experience was not very pleasant. (...) I think a dedicated room for the experience, with seating and staff to facilitate it, would be ideal. (Participant S)

Finally, some participants may have higher expectations for the experience, desiring full access to various environments within the metaverse location and unrestricted access to all its areas.

The space available was restricted to the tasting room and the surrounding area, limiting the immersion. Having the opportunity to 'walk' through the terraces or explore other parts of the estate, as it seems they plan for the future, would greatly enrich the experience. (Participant A)

Dimensions of the Experience

The descriptions provided by the three participants in this study can also be analyzed through the lenses of the experience realms, as proposed by Pine and Gilmore (1998), depending on the level of customer participation and immersion: entertainment, education, escapism, and aesthetics. The only realm that was not identified in the participants' narratives was entertainment. This might be explained by the fact that the experience was dominantly immersive and participative.

Escapism was one of the main realms of the metaverse experience offered by Sandeman, which immersed participants in a new and rich reality. One of the participants described the experience as follows:

The immersive experience allowed me to explore the Douro landscapes as if I were there, surrounded by the terraces and the characteristic views of the region. It felt like being transported to the Quinta itself, where I could freely walk around and appreciate the beauty of the environment without any physical limitations. (Participant S)

The aesthetic realm was also stressed by participants, who were impressed by the Douro landscape experienced through the metaverse:

The panoramic view offered a sense of immersion in the characteristic scenery of the Douro, with the terraces and the river as a backdrop—an image that reinforces the beauty and uniqueness of the region." (Participant M)

Regarding the educational realm, participants acknowledged that the metaverse experience provided some knowledge about wine traditions. However, the most significant educational component was gained during the short guided tour with the staff before engaging in the metaverse experience.

The guide showed us the various rooms and barrels and explained how the older and younger wines were managed, how they were preserved, and how all the stages of maintaining the wines' quality worked. (Visitor A)

Hence, the fact that the Sandeman Metaverse Experience includes interaction with the staff and a visit to the cellars enables the overall experience to be more holistic, as it provides a relevant contribution to the educational realm of experience. Given the participative and immersive nature of the experience, the entertainment realm was absent for these participants.

Consequently, the experience did not provide the "sweet spot" (Pine & Gilmore, 1998) for these participants. One way to achieve this would be to include some entertainment aspects to either the physical or virtual components of the experience. Some examples would be to enable participants to take pictures during the virtual experience, to interact with other virtual visitors, or to attend any type of game or show within the virtual experience. Interestingly, the physical tours to the cellars are usually conducted by guides dressed as "the Don", and often tourists ask to take photos with them. As such, Sandeman usually considers the entertainment component, which was not highlighted by the two interviewees who participated in this study.

Analyzing the participants' experiences through the multisensory lens proposed by Schmitt et al. (2015), it is noteworthy that the combination of physical and virtual components in the Sandeman Metaverse Experience enabled the stimulation of multiple senses. For instance, the cellar visit stimulated the sense of smell, and the wine tasting following the metaverse experience engaged the sense of taste—two senses that could not be stimulated during the metaverse experience itself.

We were welcomed by the characteristic aroma of the cellars, which gives the space a unique identity. (Participant M)

Afterward, we had a wine tasting outside the metaverse, where we tasted a Port tonic and a 10-year-old Tawny. (Participant A)

Schmitt et al. (2015) also stress the multidimensional nature of experiences, encompassing sensory, affective, cognitive, and behavioral elements. In this case, the most important dimension highlighted by the participants was the sensory. Beyond the olfactory experience in the cellars and the taste experience of the wines, participants particularly emphasized the visual aspects, especially the landscape views of the Douro during the metaverse experience, as noted above. However, the auditory senses were not significantly acknowledged by the participants. Additionally, participants mentioned the affective aspects of the experience, including positive emotions such as joy and pleasure, as well as negative emotions like fear of heights in certain sights within the metaverse. The cognitive dimension was also highlighted, involving learning about both wine and the metaverse technology and equipment. The social dimension, on the other hand, was primarily noted for the lack of interaction during the virtual experience. Finally, regarding the behavioral dimension, much of the participants' narratives revolved around active virtual and physical exploration, which, as mentioned earlier, also included some degree of physical discomfort (e.g., dizziness from VR equipment and tiredness from standing).

These findings are in line with the literature, particularly with (Flavián et al., 2021) and Martins et al. (2017), who stress that immersive technologies enhance emotional reactions and trigger escapism.

Impacts on Loyalty

The visitors who participated in this study considered the experience worthwhile and interesting, and the overall feedback was positive. In line with suggestions by the literature (Di Paolo et al., 2025; Sousa et al., 2024a, 2024b), one of the participants confirmed that the initiative may generate actual visits by creating the desire to travel to the Douro Region and visit Quinta do Seixo.

I didn't know Quinta do Seixo, so the immersive experience was my first contact with the location. Worth visiting! (Participant S)

Another participant stated that she would not recommend the metaverse experience to wine tourists visiting the cellars, as she considered that the added value of the experience was small compared to what was offered to a wine tourist by visiting the cellars:

I would only recommend visiting the cellars. The metaverse experience is undoubtedly innovative and appealing. However, it still does not add much to what the cellars already offer. The visit to the Sandeman cellars provides a highly sensory and complete experience, allowing one to immerse in the history and unique atmosphere of Port wine. Unless there is a strong curiosity to explore the metaverse, the physical experience will certainly be the most enriching. (Participant M)

Another participant provided a complementary view, as she would recommend the metaverse experience only to people interested in technology, as this would increase the enjoyment of the experience.

I would recommend it to someone who is a Port wine lover or at least someone who appreciates it and is interested in learning about the cellars and how the wine is preserved. I would also recommend it to someone interested in the metaverse and who is inclined toward the use of technology, as they would likely find it easier to use the VR equipment and have a greater interest in experimenting with new technologies and understanding how they work. (Participant A)

While many of the visitors who choose to do the metaverse experience may be attracted by the novelty of the initiative, these findings highlight again the challenges faced by visitors without prior experience with VR equipment and how this may limit the expected positive outcomes of the initiative.

SOLUTIONS AND RECOMMENDATIONS

Figure 1 summarizes the findings of this study. As detailed in the previous section and based on data collected from three participants, customer motivations include factors related to the metaverse technology, such as curiosity about the technology and interest in unique and immersive experiences. The findings demonstrate that by combining the metaverse with additional physical experiences, such as wine tasting, Sandeman offers a multi-sensory and holistic experience to customers, potentially encompassing the four realms of experience and reaching a "sweet spot." However, there are challenges associated with the experience. Innovative projects often face technological challenges, particularly in their initial stages, as is the case with the Sandeman Metaverse Experience. Additionally, customers' inexperience with the metaverse may create further challenges, such as physical discomfort, which the staff dedicated to guiding the experience can only partially mitigate.

Figure 1. Summary of findings

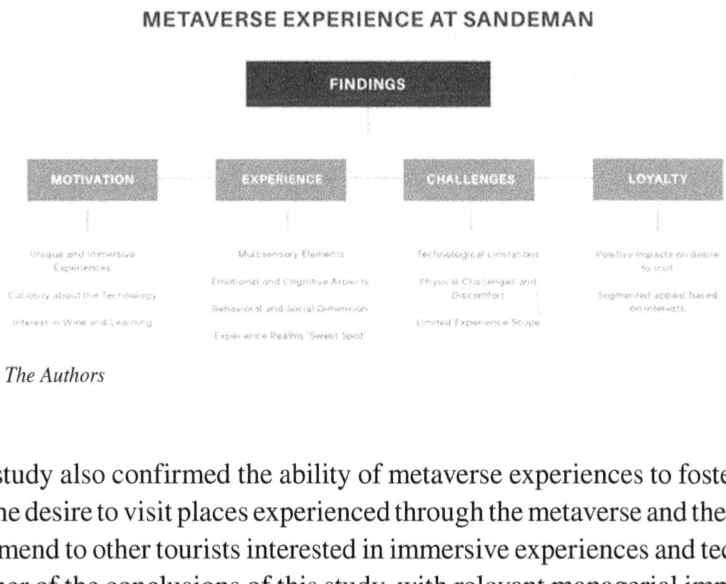

Source: The Authors

This study also confirmed the ability of metaverse experiences to foster loyalty, namely the desire to visit places experienced through the metaverse and the intention to recommend to other tourists interested in immersive experiences and technology.

Another of the conclusions of this study, with relevant managerial implications, is that there are three strategic approaches for introducing metaverse experiences in wine tourism, which are summarized in Figure 2. These strategies—Outreach, Focused, and Phased—offer distinct ways to leverage the metaverse, targeting different customer bases and risk levels to achieve the brand's objectives.

Figure 2. Three alternative strategies to introduce metaverse experiences into a company's offerings

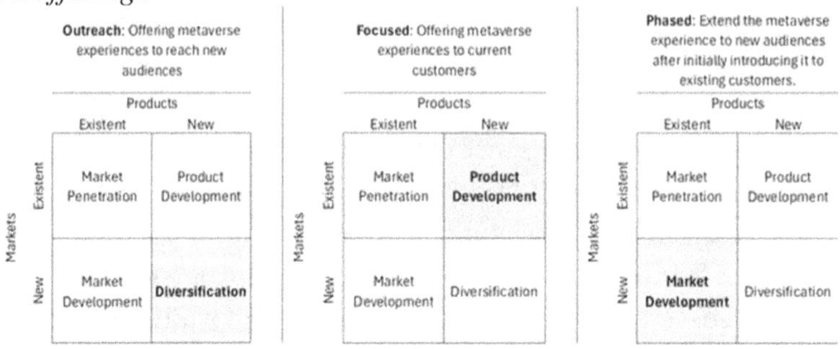

Source: The Authors

The Outreach Strategy aims to attract new audiences to wine tourism, particularly audiences more likely to be interested in innovative, immersive technology—such as young, tech-savvy individuals and international wine enthusiasts who may not otherwise visit in person. By creating virtual vineyard tours, interactive wine tastings, and educational modules in the metaverse, wine tourism businesses can engage with audiences who value cutting-edge experiences and prioritize convenience and accessibility. Some of the advantages of this strategy include:

- Targeted appeal to tech-savvy audiences, as it appeals to demographics with a high interest in virtual and digital experiences, such as Millennials, Gen Z, and early adopters of new technology, who are more likely to appreciate the novelty and convenience of virtual experiences.
- Global accessibility, as it can reach international audiences who may have geographical or travel-related barriers to visiting in person, thereby broadening market reach.

However, this strategy also poses some challenges, particularly the inherent risks of targeting a very different audience with whom the company has no prior experience. This lack of familiarity can make it more difficult to anticipate the target audience's preferences and needs, making the experience's design and success more challenging. Additionally, virtual experiences might not fully capture the sensory richness and authenticity of wine tourism, potentially leaving new audiences with a limited or less compelling impression of the company and its offerings. Therefore, while this strategy offers high potential to tap into new markets and appeal to digitally native audiences, it also carries high levels of risk.

The Focused Strategy targets the metaverse experiences specifically for existing wine tourism customers. Rather than attempting to attract new markets, this strategy aims to add value by creating virtual experiences for those already familiar with the brand, including the ones visiting their premises. By integrating metaverse experiences—such as virtual tours or educational sessions—this approach seeks to deepen customer engagement and loyalty, enhancing the overall experience for current visitors. Its advantages include:

- Lower risk since it targets an already-engaged customer base and potentially gives the company more information and control over the experience.
- Enhanced customer experience, as metaverse components may be used to provide an added layer of engagement and exclusivity, allowing existing customers to connect with the brand in new, innovative ways
- Opportunity for upselling, since these offerings allow for cross-selling and upselling additional products or services, enhancing revenue potential from loyal customers.

However, this strategy may have limited growth potential, as it disregards potential new audiences and relies on only a small portion of current wine tourists being interested in virtual experiences. Traditional profiles of wine lovers and wine tourists often differ significantly from tech-savvy, metaverse-oriented consumers, particularly in terms of age. This limited potential for market expansion could pose profitability challenges and even make metaverse investments unviable for most wine tourism companies.

The Phased Strategy combines elements of both growth and risk management by initially offering metaverse experiences to existing customers before expanding to new audiences. This approach allows the brand to test and refine its virtual offerings with current customers, gathering feedback and optimizing the experience. Once the metaverse product is proven effective and engaging, the brand can then extend it to new markets, gradually expanding its reach while minimizing risk. Hence, the advantages of this strategy are:

- Balanced risk and growth, as in the initial stage, the strategy minimizes risks while retaining the potential for market expansion in later stages.
- Learning experience with ideal customers, as the offering can be developed based on the feedback of wine tourists, improving the likelihood of success when reaching new audiences.

While the phased strategy allows for risk mitigation, it slows the process and risks losing potential competitive advantages to faster second movers. Moreover, this strategy may create some challenges, as, as previously mentioned, the current audience (e.g., wine lovers) and the potential audience (e.g., tech-savvy individuals) may have very different characteristics and expectations for metaverse experiences. This affects not only satisfaction with the experience but also the success of the metaverse as a business strategy.

FUTURE RESEARCH DIRECTIONS

Studies on metaverse applications in the tourism context remain scarce, particularly in the area of wine tourism. Informed decisions by companies in this sector require further research, whether through the analysis of success or failure cases or through studies involving different consumer segments to understand motivations, factors contributing to satisfaction, loyalty, and purchase intentions related to metaverse experiences, as well as intentions to visit physical locations following various types of metaverse experiences.

Therefore, it is recommended that future studies explore innovative use cases of the metaverse in wine tourism, analyzing the critical success factors. Research employing qualitative, quantitative, or mixed-method approaches is also necessary to better understand consumer behavior, particularly regarding loyalty, visiting intentions, and visiting behaviors. The fact that the metaverse experience can be positioned both as a service or as a trial opportunity before physically visiting a location requires clear understanding, as it affects marketing (e.g., pricing) and management (e.g., investment) strategies.

CONCLUSION

The Sandeman Metaverse Experience serves as a relevant case study for understanding the metaverse's impact on wine tourism. By creating an immersive virtual tour of Quinta do Seixo, Sandeman offers a unique digital approach to traditional wine tourism. While at the cellars, visitors can interact in real-time as avatars with the Douro vineyards, located 150 kilometers away (a two-hour drive), experiencing the beautiful landscapes and some traditions associated with wine production.

This case study illustrates the metaverse's ability to provide holistic experiences to wine visitors, particularly when complemented by physical experiences at the company's premises, such as wine tasting. It also highlights the advantages and limitations of adopting a focused strategy (i.e., targeting the company's existing markets). Targeting the cellars' visitors, who are traditionally wine lovers and often from older generations, creates a potential contradiction regarding the ideal audience for metaverse experiences, which tends to be younger, innovative, and tech-savvy consumers. Additionally, the fact that the experience may be purchased by consumers without any prior experience with VR equipment presents a unique challenge.

Sandeman exemplifies a clear case of balancing risk and growth by targeting existing customers while facilitating metaverse experimentation through measures such as providing VR equipment and offering staff support to guide tourists through the metaverse experience.

the overall implications are positive, as evidenced by customer satisfaction, the intention to physically visit locations experienced through the metaverse, and the intention to recommend the metaverse experience. Furthermore, the initiative (and the innovation prize it earned) generated publicity and is expected to have positive impacts on brand awareness and perceived differentiation, contributing to reinforcing the brand's innovative image.

ACKNOWLEDGMENT

The authors would like to thank Sogrape Vinhos, S.A. and Head of Research and Development António Graça, for the information and experience that was essential for this work. And for inspiring us with your passion and knowledge.

This research received no specific grant from any funding agency in the public, commercial, or not-for-profit sectors.

The authors declare no conflicts of interest.

REFERENCES

Ampountolas, A., Menconi, G., & Shaw, G. (2024). Metaverse research propositions: Online intermediaries. *Tourism Economics*, 30(1), 255–261. DOI: 10.1177/13548166231159520

Brochado, A., Stoleriu, O., & Lupu, C. (2021). Wine tourism: A multisensory experience. *Current Issues in Tourism*, 24(5), 597–615. DOI: 10.1080/13683500.2019.1649373

Bruwer, J., & Rueger-Muck, E. (2019). Wine tourism and hedonic experience: A motivation-based experiential view. *Tourism and Hospitality Research*, 19(4), 488–502. DOI: 10.1177/1467358418781444

Buhalis, D., Leung, D., & Lin, M. C. (2023). Metaverse as a disruptive technology revolutionising tourism management and marketing. *Tourism Management*, 97, 104724. Advance online publication. DOI: 10.1016/j.tourman.2023.104724

Chan, K. (2023). *Metaverse: What are the economic benefits?* World Economic Forum. https://www.weforum.org/stories/2023/06/what-will-be-the-economic-benefits-of-the-metaverse/

Charters, S., & Ali-Knight, J. (2002). Who is the wine tourist? *Tourism Management*, 23(3), 311–319. DOI: 10.1016/S0261-5177(01)00079-6

Christensen, L., & Robinson, A. (2022). *The potential global economic impact of the metaverse*. Analysis Group. https://www.analysisgroup.com/globalassets/insights/publishing/2022-the-potential-global-economic-impact-of-the-metaverse.pdf

Clark, T., Foster, L., Bryman, A., & Sloan, L. (2021). *Bryman's social research methods*. Oxford University Press.

Constantin, M., Genovese, G., Munawar, K., & Stone, R. (2023). *Tourism in the metaverse: Can travel go virtual?* McKinsey & Company. https://www.mckinsey.com/industries/travel-logistics-and-infrastructure/our-insights/tourism-in-the-metaverse-can-travel-go-virtual

Cui, Y., & van Esch, P. (2024). A sip in the Metaverse: How to implement a multisensory vineyard. *Journal of Wine Research*, 35(2), 160–178. DOI: 10.1080/09571264.2023.2254248

Di Paolo, F., Bettiga, D., & Lamberti, L. (2025). Leveraging social capital for destination promotion in the metaverse: The Enoverse case. *Tourism Management*, 107, 105072. DOI: 10.1016/j.tourman.2024.105072

Dwivedi, Y. K., Hughes, L., Baabdullah, A. M., Ribeiro-Navarrete, S., Giannakis, M., Al-Debei, M. M., Dennehy, D., Metri, B., Buhalis, D., Cheung, C. M. K., Conboy, K., Doyle, R., Dubey, R., Dutot, V., Felix, R., Goyal, D. P., Gustafsson, A., Hinsch, C., Jebabli, I., & Wamba, S. F. (2022). Metaverse beyond the hype: Multidisciplinary perspectives on emerging challenges, opportunities, and agenda for research, practice and policy. *International Journal of Information Management*, 66, 102542. Advance online publication. DOI: 10.1016/j.ijinfomgt.2022.102542

Farrant, T. (2022). *Fancy a virtual hot air balloon trip over Saudi Arabia's ancient tombs? Now, you can*. Euronews. https://www.euronews.com/culture/2023/02/22/fancy-a-virtual-hot-air-balloon-trip-over-saudi-arabias-ancient-tombs-now-you-can

Flavián, C., Ibáñez-Sánchez, S., & Orús, C. (2021). Impacts of technological embodiment through virtual reality on potential guests' emotions and engagement. *Journal of Hospitality Marketing & Management*, 30(1), 1–20. DOI: 10.1080/19368623.2020.1770146

Gaetjens, A., Corsi, A. M., & Plewa, C. (2023). Customer engagement in domestic wine tourism: The role of motivations. *Journal of Destination Marketing & Management*, 27, 100761. DOI: 10.1016/j.jdmm.2022.100761

Gomes, R. S. (2024). *Portugal dá passos tímidos no metaverso*. Jornal Expresso. https://expresso.pt/premio-nacional-turismo/2024-04-18-portugal-da-passos-timidos-no-metaverso-babd3116

Gómez-Carmona, D., Paramio, A., Cruces-Montes, S., Marín-Dueñas, P. P., Montero, A. A., & Romero-Moreno, A. (2023). The effect of the wine tourism experience. *Journal of Destination Marketing & Management*, 29, 100793. Advance online publication. DOI: 10.1016/j.jdmm.2023.100793

Grand View Research. (2024). *Wine tourism market size & trends*. Grand View Research. https://www.grandviewresearch.com/industry-analysis/wine-tourism-market-report

Hall, C. M., & Mitchell, R. (2000). Wine tourism in the Mediterranean: A tool for restructuring and development. *Thunderbird International Business Review*, 42(4), 445–465. DOI: 10.1002/1520-6874(200007/08)42:4<445::AID-TIE6>3.0.CO;2-H

Hartley, J. (2004). What is a case study. In Cassell, C., & Symon, G. (Eds.), *Essential guide to qualitative methods in organizational research* (pp. 323–333). Sage. DOI: 10.4135/9781446280119.n26

Hussain, S., Khattak, J., Rizwan, A., & Latif, M. A. (2013). ANSOFF matrix, environment, and growth-an interactive triangle. *Management and Administrative Sciences Review*, 2(2), 196–206.

Johnson, G., Whittington, R., Scholes, K., Angwin, D., & Regner, P. (2017). *Exploring Corporate Strategy* (11th ed.). Pearson.

Kastenholz, E., Cunha, D., Eletxigerra, A., Carvalho, M., & Silva, I. (2022). The Experience Economy in a Wine Destination-Analysing Visitor Reviews. *Sustainability (Basel)*, 14(15), 9308. Advance online publication. DOI: 10.3390/su14159308

Liu, H., & Park, K.-S. (2024). Exploring the impact of metaverse tourism experiences on actual visit intentions: An integrated model of presence, the Technology Acceptance Model, and the Theory of Planned Behavior. *International Journal of Tourism Research*, 26(1), e2616. DOI: 10.1002/jtr.2616

Mahmoud, A. B., Fuxman, L., Asaad, Y., & Solakis, K. (2024). Exploring new realms or losing touch? Assessing public beliefs about tourism in the metaverse–a big-data approach. *International Journal of Contemporary Hospitality Management*. DOI: 10.1108/IJCHM-09-2023-1515

Martins, J., Gonçalves, R., Branco, F., Barbosa, L., Melo, M., & Bessa, M. (2017). A multisensory virtual experience model for thematic tourism: A Port wine tourism application proposal. *Journal of Destination Marketing & Management*, 6(2), 103–109. DOI: 10.1016/j.jdmm.2017.02.002

Maumon, N., & Bédé, D. (2023). Wine tourism next-gen: A case study of a virtual reality implementation in a wine cooperative in France. In *Technology advances and innovation in wine tourism: New managerial approaches and cases* (pp. 95–113). Springer. DOI: 10.1007/978-981-19-8277-4_7

McKinsey and Company. (2022). *Value Creation in the Metaverse*. McKinsey. https://www.mckinsey.com/capabilities/growth-marketing-and-sales/our-insights/value-creation-in-the-metaverse

Monaco, S., & Sacchi, G. (2023). Travelling the metaverse: Potential benefits and main challenges for tourism sectors and research applications. *Sustainability (Basel)*, 15(4), 3348. DOI: 10.3390/su15043348

Natarajan, T., Pragha, P., Dhalmahapatra, K., & Raghavan, D. R. V. (2024). Exploring tourist's metaverse experience using destination spatial presence quality & perceived augmentation: Metaverse exploration, physical expedition (MEPE). *Current Issues in Tourism*, 1–23. Advance online publication. DOI: 10.1080/13683500.2024.2372652

Pine, B. J., & Gilmore, J. H. (1998). Welcome to the experience economy. *Harvard Business Review*, 1998(July/August), 97–105. PMID: 10181589

Pine, B. J., & Gilmore, J. H. (2011). *The Experience Economy*. Harvard Business Press.

Quintal, V. A., Thomas, B., Phau, I., & Soldat, Z. (2022). Segmenting hedonic wine tourists using push–pull Winescape attributes. *Australasian Marketing Journal*, 30(3), 237–245. DOI: 10.1177/1839334921999478

Rather, R. A. (2023). Metaverse marketing and consumer research: Theoretical framework and future research agenda in tourism and hospitality industry. *Tourism Recreation Research*, 1–9. Advance online publication. DOI: 10.1080/02508281.2023.2216525

Sanchez-Amboage, E., Crespo-Pereira, V., Membiela-Pollan, M., & Faustino, J. P. J. (2024). Tourism marketing in the metaverse: A systematic literature review, building blocks, and future research directions. *PLoS One*, 19(5), e0300599. Advance online publication. DOI: 10.1371/journal.pone.0300599 PMID: 38728243

Sandeman. (2024a). *It all started in 1790…*. Sandeman. https://www.sandeman.com/history/

Sandeman. (2024b). *A true experience*. Sandeman. https://www.sandeman.com/visit-us/

Santos, V., Ramos, P., Sousa, B., & Valeri, M. (2022). Towards a framework for the global wine tourism system. *Journal of Organizational Change Management*, 35(2), 348–360. DOI: 10.1108/JOCM-11-2020-0362

Schmitt, B., Brakus, J. J., & Zarantonello, L. (2015). From experiential psychology to consumer experience. *Journal of Consumer Psychology*, 25(1), 166–171. DOI: 10.1016/j.jcps.2014.09.001

Shin, H., & Kang, J. (2024). How does the metaverse travel experience influence virtual and actual travel behaviors? Focusing on the role of telepresence and avatar identification. *Journal of Hospitality and Tourism Management*, 58, 174–183. DOI: 10.1016/j.jhtm.2023.12.009

Sousa, N., Alén, E., Losada, N., & Melo, M. (2024a). Influencing wine tourists' decision-making with VR: The impact of immersive experiences on their behavioural intentions. *Tourism Management Perspectives*, 51, 101235. Advance online publication. DOI: 10.1016/j.tmp.2024.101235

Sousa, N., Alén, E., Losada, N., & Melo, M. (2024b). Virtual reality in wine tourism: Immersive experiences for promoting travel destinations. *Journal of Vacation Marketing*, 13567667241267306. Advance online publication. DOI: 10.1177/13567667241267306

Spence, C. (2019). Multisensory experiential wine marketing. *Food Quality and Preference*, 71, 106–116. DOI: 10.1016/j.foodqual.2018.06.010

Thanh, T. V., & Kirova, V. (2018). Wine tourism experience: A netnography study. *Journal of Business Research*, 83, 30–37. DOI: 10.1016/j.jbusres.2017.10.008

Yin, R. K. (2003). Designing case studies. In Maruster, L. (Ed.), *Qualitative research methods* (Vol. 5, pp. 359–386).

Yin, R. K. (2009). How to do better case studies. In Bickman, L., & Rog, D. J. (Eds.), *The SAGE handbook of applied social research methods* (Vol. 2, pp. 254–282). DOI: 10.4135/9781483348858.n8

Yin, R. K. (2018). *Case Study Research and Applications* (6th ed.). Sage.

ADDITIONAL READING

Charters, S., & Ali-Knight, J. (2002). Who is the wine tourist? *Tourism Management*, 23(3), 311–319. DOI: 10.1016/S0261-5177(01)00079-6

Chen, Z. (2024). Beyond boundaries: Exploring the Metaverse in tourism. *International Journal of Contemporary Hospitality Management*. Advance online publication. DOI: 10.1108/IJCHM-06-2023-0900

Go, H., & Kang, M. (2023). Metaverse tourism for sustainable tourism development: Tourism agenda 2030. *Tourism Review*, 78(2), 381–394. DOI: 10.1108/TR-02-2022-0102

Hall, C. M., Johnson, G., Cambourne, B., Macionis, N., Mitchell, R., & Sharples, L. (2009). Wine tourism: an introduction. In *Wine tourism around the world* (pp. 1–23). Routledge. DOI: 10.4324/9780080521145-1

Ioannidis, S., & Kontis, A. P. (2023). Metaverse for tourists and tourism destinations. *Information Technology & Tourism*, 25(4), 483–506. DOI: 10.1007/s40558-023-00271-y

Koo, C., Kwon, J., Chung, N., & Kim, J. (2023). Metaverse tourism: Conceptual framework and research propositions. *Current Issues in Tourism*, 26(20), 3268–3274. DOI: 10.1080/13683500.2022.2122781

Mitchell, R., Hall, C. M., & McIntosh, A. (2009). Wine tourism and consumer behaviour. In *Wine tourism around the world* (pp. 115–135). Routledge. DOI: 10.4324/9780080521145-6

Yang, F. X., & Wang, Y. (2025). Rethinking metaverse tourism: A taxonomy and an agenda for future research. *Journal of Hospitality & Tourism Research (Washington, D.C.)*, 49(1), 3–12. DOI: 10.1177/10963480231163509

KEY TERMS AND DEFINITIONS

Augmented Reality (AR): A technology that overlays digital information and virtual elements onto the real world, enhancing users' perception and interaction with their physical environment through devices like smartphones, headsets, or VR glasses.

Digital Twin: A virtual replica of a physical object, system, or environment that enables real-time monitoring, analysis, and simulation. In tourism, digital twins can be used to allow travelers to explore destinations and attractions virtually, enhancing planning and accessibility while providing immersive previews of real-world experiences.

Metaverse: a virtual platform based on virtual reality and augmented reality technology that combines digital and physical reality, allowing immersive, interactive experiences.

Metaverse Tourism: The use of virtual environments to explore and experience travel destinations in an interactive and immersive way.

Millennials: The generation born approximately between 1981 and 1996, characterized by their adaptability to digital technology, strong preference for experiences over material goods, and emphasis on social and environmental responsibility.

Virtual Reality (VR): A technology that creates fully immersive, computer-generated environments where users can interact using specialized equipment, like VR headsets.

Wine Tourism: A type of tourism focused on wine experiences that involves traveling to vineyards, wineries, and wine regions, as well as participating in events and cultural activities related to wine.

Winescape: The unique landscape, environment, and cultural elements of a wine-producing region, encompassing vineyards, wineries, local traditions, and aesthetics that together create an immersive wine tourism experience.

Chapter 5
Use of Metaverse in Tourism and Hospitality Services

R. Velmurugan
https://orcid.org/0000-0002-7925-9757
Karpagam Academy of Higher Education, India

J. Sudarvel
https://orcid.org/0000-0001-6656-1992
Karpagam Academy of Higher Education, India

K. Jothi
https://orcid.org/0000-0002-8625-863X
KPR College of Arts, Science, and Research, India

Ravi Thirumalaisamy
https://orcid.org/0000-0002-5954-5940
Modern College of Business and Science, Oman

EXECUTIVE SUMMARY

The metaverse is revolutionizing the tourism and hospitality industries by offering immersive virtual experiences, enhancing customer engagement, and streamlining operations. Through virtual reality (VR) and augmented reality (AR), travelers can explore destinations, hotels, and attractions before booking, improving decision-making. Hotels and resorts leverage the metaverse for virtual concierge services, interactive guest experiences, and digital events. Travel agencies use it for virtual tours, reducing uncertainty and enhancing accessibility. Additionally, blockchain integration enables secure transactions and digital assets like NFTs for exclusive travel perks. While challenges such as high costs and technological adoption exist,

DOI: 10.4018/979-8-3693-7245-6.ch005

the metaverse presents a transformative shift, bridging the gap between physical and digital tourism, enhancing personalization, and fostering innovation in hospitality services.

INTRODUCTION

The digital frontier is expanding, and on the horizon lies the metaverse, a groundbreaking concept poised to reshape how we experience the world. Coined by Neal Stephenson in his 1992 novel *Snow Crash* (Stephenson, 1992), the metaverse is no longer confined to science fiction; it's rapidly evolving into a reality with profound implications for the tourism and hospitality industries. One of the most transformative aspects of the metaverse for tourism is its ability to create immersive experiences that transcend geographical and financial constraints. Imagine a traveler donning a virtual reality (VR) headset and instantly being transported to the bustling markets of Marrakech, navigating through narrow alleys and interacting with digital vendors. Such virtual tours not only replicate the sights and sounds but also enable users to engage with AI-guided avatars providing historical context and local insights.

Similarly, the metaverse can simulate visits to natural wonders like the Grand Canyon or cultural landmarks like the Great Wall of China, offering virtual explorations that are as educational as they are immersive. This democratization of travel experiences means that individuals with mobility limitations or financial constraints can access destinations and experiences that were once out of reach. As Buhalis and Sinarta (2019), Guttentag (2010), and Pritchard et al. (2011) suggest, these virtual environments foster real-time co-creation of experiences, enabling travelers to participate in cultural exchanges and engage with destinations remotely. Moreover, niche interests find a new avenue in the metaverse, where virtual tours of underwater coral reefs or expeditions to the International Space Station become feasible without physical risks. This not only expands the scope of travel but also encourages exploration of environments that are ecologically sensitive or inaccessible due to safety concerns. Research by Beck and Egger (2018) highlights how such technologies contribute to sustainable tourism by reducing the need for physical travel to sensitive ecosystems.

The hospitality sector is also poised to benefit significantly from metaverse technologies. Hotels and resorts can leverage VR to offer prospective guests virtual replicas of their accommodations, complete with detailed 360-degree views of rooms, facilities, and amenities. Potential guests can navigate through virtual lobbies, explore dining options, and even visualize event spaces before making reservations. This transparency enhances consumer confidence and allows for a more informed booking process, akin to "trying before buying," as discussed by Ivanov et al. (2020), Tung et al. (2020), and Li et al. (2020) in their studies on service automation and consumer decision-making in hospitality. Additionally, virtual events and conferences hosted in the metaverse present new opportunities for interactive and engaging experiences. Participants can attend seminars, networking sessions, and workshops in virtual environments that replicate physical venues with added digital enhancements. For instance, attending a business meeting in a virtual skyscraper or collaborating on a project in a virtual innovation hub offers novel ways to conduct professional activities while reducing travel costs and environmental impact. Pine and Gilmore (1998) argue that such experiential innovations redefine service delivery, emphasizing customization and engagement in the virtual domain.

Despite its transformative potential, the metaverse revolution faces several challenges that must be addressed to ensure ethical and sustainable adoption. Data privacy and security in virtual environments are paramount concerns, requiring robust safeguards to protect user information and ensure secure transactions. As highlighted by Gössling (2017), Tussyadiah (2020), and Yoo et al. (2021), maintaining ethical standards in digital interactions is crucial for building trust and credibility in virtual tourism and hospitality experiences. Furthermore, equitable access to metaverse technologies remains a critical issue. Disparities in internet connectivity, access to VR hardware, and digital literacy can exacerbate inequalities, limiting the benefits of virtual travel and hospitality experiences to privileged demographics. Bridging the digital divide through infrastructure investments and educational initiatives is essential to ensure that all individuals, regardless of background or location, can participate in and benefit from the metaverse's potential. According to Hanna et al. (2021), addressing digital inclusion is critical to ensuring the metaverse's role in equitable global development.

Moreover, the economic implications of the metaverse as a substitute for physical travel raise concerns about its impact on destinations reliant on tourism revenue. Balancing the benefits of virtual travel with the preservation of real-world cultural heritage and economic sustainability requires thoughtful planning and collaboration between stakeholders. As Urry and Larsen (2011), Reisinger and Mavondo (2005), and McKercher (2002) point out, tourism experiences are deeply tied to physical environments and local cultures, making it essential to integrate virtual and physical travel to maintain authenticity and sustainability.

Looking forward, the future of the metaverse in tourism and hospitality promises a convergence of virtual and physical experiences that enrich and redefine travel. As technology continues to evolve and metaverse platforms mature, we can anticipate a landscape where digital and physical realms seamlessly intertwine. Virtual voyages will offer not only convenience and accessibility but also authenticity and immersion, blurring the lines between physical travel and virtual exploration. Thus, the metaverse represents a transformative paradigm shift in how tourism and hospitality services are conceptualized, delivered, and experienced. By leveraging immersive technologies responsibly and addressing challenges proactively, industry stakeholders can unlock new frontiers of possibility and redefine the travel experience for a global audience. The present study has been carried out with the following objectives (i) To explore the transformative impact of the metaverse on tourism and hospitality services, focusing on virtual travel experiences, enhanced customer engagement, and immersive hospitality solutions, (ii) To analyze the challenges and opportunities associated with metaverse adoption, including technical infrastructure, data privacy, accessibility, and its implications for sustainable tourism and (iii) To identify strategic approaches for integrating metaverse technologies in tourism and hospitality, ensuring ethical, inclusive, and innovative applications that enhance customer satisfaction and industry growth.

LITERATURE REVIEW

Overview of Some Authors

Buhalis et al. (2021) Explored the transformative potential of the metaverse for immersive tourist experiences, emphasizing virtual tours and augmented reality applications in destination marketing. Guttentag (2010) Analyzed the impact of virtual reality technologies on tourism, laying the groundwork for understanding metaverse applications in creating realistic virtual environments. Dwivedi et al. (2021) Examined the role of artificial intelligence and the metaverse in enhancing personalized guest experiences and operational efficiencies in the hospitality sector. Lee et al. (2021) Discussed the concept of the metaverse and its integration into tourism, focusing on user engagement and creating virtual social spaces for travelers. Yung and Khoo-Lattimore (2019) Highlighted the adoption of immersive technologies like AR and VR in tourism to develop co-creation experiences within the metaverse. Tussyadiah (2020) Investigated how the metaverse could influence consumer behavior by offering gamified and interactive travel experiences. Chung et al. (2021) Explored the role of virtual reality and metaverse environments in facilitating virtual hotel visits and reservations to enhance customer decision-making. Neal Stephenson (1992) Introduced the concept of the metaverse in his novel *Snow Crash*, which inspired its application in various industries, including tourism and hospitality. Han et al. (2021) Studied the use of metaverse platforms to create virtual cultural heritage experiences, allowing global audiences to explore historical landmarks digitally. Huang et al. (2022) Explored how digital twins and metaverse technologies enhance sustainable tourism practices by reducing physical travel while providing immersive experiences. Park and Kim (2022) Focused on metaverse applications in event tourism, such as virtual conventions, trade shows, and hybrid tourism experiences. Wang et al. (2020) Analyzed the potential of the metaverse in fostering inclusivity by providing virtual travel opportunities for people with mobility constraints. Jeon et al. (2022) Discussed the development of smart tourism ecosystems, integrating metaverse technologies for seamless traveler engagement and satisfaction. Kim et al. (2023) Highlighted the role of NFTs and blockchain technologies in creating unique and monetizable virtual tourism experiences within the metaverse. Xiang et al. (2022) Examined the integration of metaverse technologies into destination marketing strategies, focusing on their effectiveness in creating memorable pre-trip experiences.

VIRTUAL TRAVEL EXPERIENCES

One of the most compelling applications of the metaverse in tourism is its ability to offer virtual travel experiences. Imagine exploring the ancient ruins of Machu Picchu or strolling through the bustling streets of Tokyo, all from the comfort of your home. Virtual tourism experiences provide accessibility to destinations that may be geographically distant or inaccessible due to travel restrictions or physical limitations. Platforms like Meta's Horizon Workrooms and VRChat facilitate immersive tours and simulations, allowing travelers to engage with destinations in ways previously unimaginable. Virtual tours not only cater to wanderlust but also promote cultural exchange and heritage preservation. Museums and historical sites can create virtual replicas of artifacts and exhibits, enabling global audiences to explore cultural treasures without physical constraints. This democratization of access to cultural and natural heritage fosters a deeper appreciation and understanding of diverse traditions and landscapes, as suggested by Peltier et al. (2019).

The integration of virtual reality (VR) into tourism can significantly enhance the visitor experience. According to Guttentag (2010), VR technology can offer a high level of interactivity and realism, providing users with a sense of presence in a virtual environment. This immersive experience can be particularly beneficial for educational tourism, where visitors can learn about historical events, architectural styles, and cultural practices in a more engaging and interactive manner. Moreover, virtual tourism can serve as a marketing tool for real-world travel. As noted by Beck et al. (2019), virtual tours can entice potential tourists by offering a preview of what they might experience in person. This “try before you buy” approach can help travelers make more informed decisions about their trips, potentially increasing their confidence and satisfaction with their travel plans, as highlighted by Leung et al. (2013).

Virtual tourism also addresses the growing concerns about overtourism and environmental sustainability. According to Goodwin (2017), the excessive influx of tourists to popular destinations can lead to environmental degradation, resource depletion, and the disruption of local communities. By providing an alternative to physical travel, virtual tourism can help mitigate these negative impacts. Travelers can enjoy the sights and sounds of a destination without contributing to its physical wear and tear, thus promoting more sustainable tourism practices, as discussed by Gössling et al. (2021). Additionally, virtual tourism can make travel experiences more inclusive. As Pritchard and Morgan (2010) highlight, traditional tourism often excludes individuals with disabilities, elderly travelers, and those with limited financial resources. Virtual reality offers an accessible alternative, allowing these groups to explore destinations and participate in cultural experiences that might otherwise be out of reach. This inclusivity aligns with the broader goals of social sustainability and equity in tourism, as noted by Fesenmaier et al. (2020).

The potential for virtual tourism to enhance customer engagement in the hospitality sector is also significant. For example, hotels and resorts can use VR to showcase their amenities and accommodations, providing prospective guests with a virtual tour of their facilities. This can enhance the booking experience and set realistic expectations, as noted by Tussyadiah et al. (2018). Furthermore, the use of VR in hospitality can extend beyond marketing; it can also be used for staff training, helping employees familiarize themselves with the property and service standards in a virtual environment before interacting with real guests, as suggested by Ivanov and Webster (2017). Thus, the metaverse offers transformative possibilities for the tourism and hospitality industry. Virtual travel experiences can make destinations more accessible, promote cultural exchange, support sustainable tourism practices, and enhance customer engagement. As VR technology continues to evolve, its integration into tourism and hospitality is likely to become increasingly sophisticated, providing even more immersive and enriching experiences for travelers around the world.

ENHANCED CUSTOMER ENGAGEMENT

In hospitality, the metaverse enhances customer engagement through personalized and immersive experiences. Hotels and resorts are leveraging virtual reality (VR) and augmented reality (AR) technologies to offer virtual room previews, allowing guests to visualize accommodations and amenities before making reservations. This virtual immersion goes beyond conventional booking platforms, providing a realistic preview of the guest experience and influencing travel decisions. One of the most significant benefits of VR in hospitality is its ability to offer an immersive and interactive experience that traditional 2D images or videos cannot match. As noted by Tussyadiah et al. (2018), VR provides a high level of engagement, making it easier for potential guests to form a connection with the property. By allowing guests to "walk through" rooms, explore facilities, and even check out the view from their window, hotels can significantly enhance the pre-booking experience. This can lead to higher conversion rates and increased customer satisfaction, as guests have a clear understanding of what to expect, as suggested by Egger and Buhalis (2020).

Moreover, virtual concierge services and digital assistants integrated into the metaverse enable seamless interactions between guests and hotel staff. These services can handle a wide range of tasks, from booking spa treatments to ordering room service, all through a virtual interface. According to Neuhofer et al. (2015), this integration of technology into customer service operations can streamline processes and improve efficiency, while still maintaining a personalized touch. For example, a guest can use a VR headset to interact with a virtual concierge, who can provide recommendations, answer questions, and assist with bookings, all in real time. These innovations are not just about convenience; they also play a crucial role in enhancing the overall guest experience. As described by Pine and Gilmore (1999) in their seminal work "The Experience Economy," creating memorable and engaging experiences is key to fostering customer loyalty and positive reviews. By incorporating VR and AR into their services, hotels can offer unique and memorable experiences that go beyond the standard expectations of hospitality, as pointed out by McCormick et al. (2021). This can lead to increased guest satisfaction and repeat business, as well as positive word-of-mouth and online reviews.

Furthermore, the use of VR and AR in hospitality can also support staff training and development. As highlighted by Wang et al. (2016), VR can be used to create realistic simulations for training purposes, allowing staff to practice their skills in a controlled environment. This can lead to improved performance and a higher level of service, as employees are better prepared to handle a wide range of scenarios, as noted by Guttentag (2010). The integration of VR and AR into the hospitality industry also aligns with broader trends towards digitalization and innovation. As noted by Buhalis and Leung (2018), the adoption of new technologies is essential for staying competitive in the rapidly evolving hospitality market. By embracing the metaverse, hotels can position themselves as forward-thinking and innovative, attracting tech-savvy guests who value cutting-edge experiences. Thus, the metaverse offers significant opportunities for enhancing customer engagement and operational efficiency in the hospitality industry. By leveraging VR and AR technologies, hotels can provide immersive and personalized experiences that enhance the pre-booking process, streamline customer service operations, and support staff training. These innovations not only improve guest satisfaction and loyalty but also position hotels as leaders in the digital age, as discussed by Ivanov and Webster (2017).

APPLICATIONS IN HOSPITALITY SERVICES

Beyond enhancing guest experiences, the metaverse revolutionizes internal operations and staff training within the hospitality industry. Virtual reality (VR) training modules simulate real-world scenarios, allowing staff to practice customer service interactions, emergency response protocols, and cultural sensitivity training in a safe and controlled environment. These simulations enhance employee competence and confidence, preparing them to deliver exceptional service in diverse situations. Virtual reality training is particularly beneficial for customer service training. According to Seyitoğlu and Ivanov (2020), VR can create realistic and immersive training environments that allow employees to practice handling various customer service scenarios, such as dealing with difficult guests or managing complaints. This hands-on approach helps staff develop the skills and confidence needed to provide high-quality service. For instance, a VR module might simulate a busy hotel lobby where employees must juggle multiple tasks, helping them improve their multitasking and problem-solving abilities, as also noted by Tussyadiah and Park (2018).

Emergency response training is another area where VR excels. As noted by Stansfield and Shawver (2016), VR can simulate emergency situations, such as fires or medical emergencies, allowing staff to practice their response protocols in a realistic yet safe environment. This type of training is crucial for ensuring that employees can react quickly and effectively in real-life emergencies, potentially saving lives and minimizing damage. Similarly, Guttentag (2010) emphasizes the importance of simulation-based training for enhancing preparedness, particularly in high-stress situations. Cultural sensitivity training is also greatly enhanced by VR. According to Kang and Gretzel (2012), VR can immerse employees in different cultural environments, helping them understand and appreciate cultural differences. This type of training is especially important in the hospitality industry, where staff frequently interact with guests from diverse backgrounds. By practicing cultural sensitivity in a VR setting, employees can learn how to provide more personalized and respectful service to all guests, an aspect also emphasized by McCartney et al. (2015).

Furthermore, virtual meetings and conferences hosted in the metaverse offer flexibility and cost-effectiveness for event planners and business travelers. Virtual event platforms can replicate physical conference settings, complete with interactive booths, networking opportunities, and keynote presentations. This digital transformation not only reduces the carbon footprint associated with travel but also expands accessibility to global audiences, democratizing participation in professional and cultural events. Virtual conferences and meetings can significantly reduce travel costs and logistical challenges. As pointed out by Bonetti et al. (2018), hosting events in the metaverse can eliminate the need for physical venues, catering, and transportation, leading to substantial cost savings. Additionally, virtual events can be more inclusive, allowing participants from around the world to join without the need for travel. This increased accessibility can lead to higher attendance and more diverse participation, enriching the overall experience, as also discussed by Yoo et al. (2018).

The environmental benefits of virtual events are also noteworthy. According to Gössling et al. (2010), travel-related carbon emissions are a significant contributor to climate change. By hosting events in the metaverse, the hospitality industry can reduce its carbon footprint and contribute to more sustainable practices. This shift is particularly relevant in the context of increasing awareness and concern about environmental issues, as highlighted by Lyu et al. (2021). Thus, the metaverse offers transformative potential for internal operations and staff training within the hospitality industry. VR training modules can enhance employee skills and confidence in customer service, emergency response, and cultural sensitivity. Virtual meetings and conferences provide flexible, cost-effective, and environmentally friendly alternatives to traditional events, expanding accessibility and democratizing participation. As the metaverse continues to evolve, its impact on the hospitality industry is likely to grow, driving innovation and efficiency across various aspects of operations, as noted by Ivanov and Webster (2017).

CHALLENGES AND CONSIDERATIONS

The adoption of metaverse technologies in tourism and hospitality services is not without challenges. Technical infrastructure requirements, such as high-speed internet connectivity and VR-compatible devices, pose significant barriers to widespread adoption. Addressing these infrastructure gaps is crucial to ensure equitable access and usability for all stakeholders, regardless of geographical location or economic status. High-speed internet connectivity is a fundamental requirement for accessing metaverse platforms. However, many regions, particularly in developing countries, lack the necessary infrastructure to support such high-bandwidth applications. According to Reiners et al. (2014), the digital divide between urban and rural areas can exacerbate inequalities in access to advanced technologies. To bridge this gap, substantial investments in telecommunications infrastructure are needed. Governments and private sector entities must collaborate to expand broadband coverage and enhance internet speeds, making the metaverse accessible to a broader audience. Furthermore, Castells (2010) emphasizes that expanding digital infrastructure in underserved regions is a key strategy for reducing inequality in the digital economy.

The cost of VR-compatible devices, such as headsets and controllers, also limits the adoption of metaverse technologies. As noted by Jung et al. (2020), the high price of these devices can be prohibitive for many potential users. To overcome this challenge, the industry needs to explore cost-effective solutions and consider subsidizing VR equipment for educational and public institutions. Additionally, advancements in technology should focus on developing affordable and user-friendly devices to encourage wider adoption. Similarly, Milgram et al. (1994) argue that technological advancements and economies of scale will eventually reduce the cost of VR devices, making them more accessible to a larger demographic. Moreover, concerns regarding data privacy and security in virtual environments necessitate robust safeguards and regulatory frameworks. Protecting personal information and ensuring user consent in metaverse interactions are paramount to building trust and maintaining integrity within the digital ecosystem. As highlighted by Kshetri (2014), the potential for data breaches and unauthorized access to personal information poses significant risks. To address these concerns, comprehensive cybersecurity measures must be implemented, including encryption, multi-factor authentication, and regular security audits.

Regulatory frameworks are essential to ensure that data privacy and security standards are upheld in the metaverse. Policymakers need to collaborate with industry leaders and technology developers to establish guidelines and regulations that protect users' rights. According to Zuboff (2015), regulatory oversight is critical in preventing the misuse of personal data and ensuring that users are informed about how their information is collected, stored, and used. Transparent data policies and user consent mechanisms should be mandatory for all metaverse platforms. Collaborative efforts between industry leaders, policymakers, and technology developers are essential to mitigate these risks and establish standards for ethical metaverse practices. As suggested by Cavusoglu et al. (2015), a multi-stakeholder approach can facilitate the development of best practices and encourage compliance with regulatory requirements. Industry associations and standards bodies should play a key role in defining ethical guidelines and promoting their adoption across the sector. Furthermore, Foucault (1977) warns of the surveillance potential in digital environments, urging stricter regulation to safeguard privacy rights.

Another challenge in adopting metaverse technologies is the potential for digital addiction and the negative impact on mental health. Prolonged use of VR environments can lead to issues such as cybersickness, eye strain, and psychological dependence. According to Riva et al. (2016), the immersive nature of VR can cause users to lose track of time and become overly absorbed in virtual experiences. To address these concerns, it is important to promote healthy usage habits and establish guidelines for safe and responsible use of metaverse technologies. Mental health professionals and researchers should work together to identify the risks and develop interventions to mitigate them. The integration of metaverse technologies in tourism and hospitality also raises questions about the impact on employment and the workforce. As automation and digitalization become more prevalent, there is a risk that certain jobs may become obsolete. However, as suggested by Frey and Osborne (2017), technological advancements can also create new job opportunities and transform existing roles. To navigate this transition, it is important to invest in workforce development and training programs that equip employees with the skills needed to thrive in a digital economy. This includes providing education on VR and AR technologies, digital marketing, and customer service in virtual environments. Similarly, Brynjolfsson and McAfee (2014) highlight that technology-induced job displacement is often coupled with the creation of new industries and roles in the evolving digital landscape.

Environmental concerns are another consideration in the adoption of metaverse technologies. While virtual tourism can reduce the carbon footprint associated with physical travel, the energy consumption of data centers and VR devices can contribute to environmental impact. According to Andrae and Edler (2015), the growing demand for data processing and storage requires significant energy resources. To address this issue, the industry should prioritize energy-efficient technologies and explore renewable energy sources to power data centers. Sustainable practices should be integrated into the design and operation of metaverse platforms to minimize their environmental impact. Likewise, Pagani (2013) suggests that the hospitality industry should adopt a circular economy model, focusing on sustainable consumption and reducing waste in digital ecosystems. Thus, while the metaverse offers transformative potential for the tourism and hospitality industry, its adoption is accompanied by several challenges. Technical infrastructure requirements, data privacy and security concerns, digital addiction, workforce implications, and environmental impact are key issues that need to be addressed. Collaborative efforts between industry leaders, policymakers, and technology developers are essential to overcome these challenges and establish ethical and sustainable metaverse practices. By addressing these issues, thc industry can unlock the full potential of the metaverse and create a more inclusive and innovative future for tourism and hospitality.

FUTURE OUTLOOK AND ADOPTION STRATEGIES

Looking ahead, the future of the metaverse in tourism and hospitality is promising, driven by continuous innovation and strategic partnerships. As technological advancements evolve, so too will the capabilities of virtual reality (VR), augmented reality (AR), and mixed reality (MR) experiences (Schwabe, 2020; Zengler, 2019). Industry stakeholders must embrace a proactive approach to integrating metaverse technologies into their business models, capitalizing on opportunities to enhance guest satisfaction, operational efficiency, and sustainability (Schwab, 2016; Matzler et al., 2020).

Investing in VR/AR Infrastructure

Investing in VR/AR infrastructure is a critical step for tourism and hospitality businesses looking to leverage the metaverse. According to Buhalis and Sinarta (2019), the integration of smart technologies in tourism is essential for creating immersive and personalized experiences. By investing in VR/AR, businesses can offer virtual tours, immersive marketing campaigns, and enhanced guest services. For instance, hotels can provide VR previews of rooms and amenities, allowing potential guests to explore the property before booking. Similarly, travel agencies can offer virtual tours of destinations, helping travelers make informed decisions. Moreover, AR can be used to enhance on-site experiences. Visitors can use AR apps to receive real-time information about historical sites, landmarks, and attractions, enriching their travel experience. The integration of AR into mobile apps can also offer personalized recommendations and navigation assistance, improving convenience and satisfaction for tourists. As noted by Guttentag (2015), these technological innovations can transform the way tourists interact with destinations, providing more interactive and engaging experiences. Additionally, the ability to create personalized virtual experiences, as discussed by Tussyadiah et al. (2018), is crucial in increasing customer satisfaction and loyalty in the competitive tourism market.

Fostering Digital Literacy

Fostering digital literacy among employees and guests is another crucial strategy for successful metaverse adoption. As highlighted by Gössling (2017), digital skills are increasingly important in the tourism industry, where technology is reshaping service delivery and customer interactions. Providing training programs for employees on how to use VR/AR technologies can enhance their ability to deliver innovative and engaging services. Employees equipped with digital skills can better assist guests, manage virtual interactions, and troubleshoot technical issues, ensuring a seamless experience. For guests, digital literacy initiatives can include tutorials and guides on how to use VR/AR applications and devices. Hotels and tourist attractions can offer workshops or informational sessions to help guests navigate the metaverse and make the most of the available technologies. By promoting digital literacy, businesses can ensure that both employees and guests are comfortable and confident in using VR/AR tools, enhancing overall satisfaction and engagement. Furthermore, as noted by Tussyadiah et al. (2017), digital literacy is essential not only for enhancing customer experience but also for driving the overall adoption of new technologies in the tourism industry. Similarly, Pizam and Shani (2020) emphasize that empowering employees with digital competencies can foster innovation in service delivery, further contributing to competitive advantage in the hospitality sector.

Cultivating Collaborative Ecosystems

Cultivating collaborative ecosystems for metaverse development is essential for fostering innovation and staying competitive. As noted by Dredge and Gyimóthy (2015), collaboration among industry stakeholders, including technology developers, academic institutions, and tourism businesses, can drive the creation of cutting-edge solutions. Partnerships with VR/AR technology providers can enable tourism and hospitality businesses to access the latest advancements and integrate them into their offerings. Collaborative ecosystems can also support the development of standardized practices and protocols for the metaverse. By working together, industry stakeholders can establish guidelines for data privacy, security, and ethical use of VR/AR technologies. This collective effort can help build trust among consumers and ensure that the adoption of the metaverse is aligned with best practices and regulatory requirements. As suggested by Wirtz et al. (2018), collaborative approaches not only enhance technological integration but also contribute to the development of more sustainable business practices in tourism. Furthermore, according to Sigala (2018), fostering partnerships between businesses and academic institutions can spur innovation and knowledge exchange, promoting the creation of more user-friendly and effective VR/AR applications in the tourism sector.

Enhancing Guest Satisfaction

The adoption of metaverse technologies can significantly enhance guest satisfaction by offering unique and immersive experiences. As stated by Pine and Gilmore (1998), the experience economy emphasizes the importance of creating memorable and engaging experiences for consumers. The metaverse allows tourism and hospitality businesses to offer such experiences by enabling virtual exploration, interactive storytelling, and personalized services. As noted by Tussyadiah et al. (2017), virtual experiences provide travelers with a sense of presence and immersion, enhancing emotional engagement and customer satisfaction. For example, theme parks can use VR to create virtual rides and attractions, allowing visitors to experience the excitement of the park from anywhere in the world. Hotels can offer virtual concierge services, where guests can interact with virtual assistants for recommendations and reservations. These innovative services can differentiate businesses in a competitive market and attract tech-savvy travelers seeking novel experiences. Furthermore, as highlighted by Buhalis and Law (2008), personalization of services through advanced technologies, such as AI and VR, enables businesses to cater more effectively to individual guest preferences, increasing loyalty and repeat visits.

Operational Efficiency and Sustainability

In addition to enhancing guest satisfaction, metaverse technologies can improve operational efficiency and sustainability. According to Ivanov et al. (2020), the use of automation and digitalization in tourism can streamline operations and reduce costs. VR training programs can prepare staff for various scenarios, improving their readiness and performance. Virtual meetings and conferences can reduce the need for business travel, lowering carbon footprints and contributing to sustainability goals. Furthermore, the metaverse can support sustainable tourism by promoting virtual tourism experiences. As noted by Gössling and Peeters (2015), reducing the environmental impact of tourism is critical for sustainable development. Virtual tourism allows people to explore destinations without the associated environmental costs of physical travel. By offering virtual tours and experiences, businesses can appeal to environmentally conscious travelers and promote sustainable practices. Additionally, as highlighted by Li and Xu (2020), immersive virtual experiences can reduce overtourism by providing alternative ways for people to engage with popular destinations. The future of the metaverse in tourism and hospitality is bright, with significant potential for enhancing guest satisfaction, operational efficiency, and sustainability. By investing in VR/AR infrastructure, fostering digital literacy, and cultivating collaborative ecosystems, industry stakeholders can position themselves as leaders in the digital age. Embracing metaverse technologies enables businesses to offer differentiated and memorable experiences that resonate with modern travelers seeking authenticity, convenience, and connection. As the metaverse continues to evolve, its integration into tourism and hospitality will drive innovation and transform the industry for years to come.

FUTURE RESEARCH DIRECTIONS

The integration of metaverse technologies in tourism and hospitality presents vast opportunities for further research, particularly in understanding user experience, engagement, and accessibility. Future studies can explore how different demographics interact with virtual travel experiences and the psychological impact of immersive tourism on user satisfaction. The role of AI-driven avatars in enhancing guest interactions and personalizing services also warrants deeper investigation. Additionally, research should focus on infrastructure challenges, including the availability of high-speed internet and cost-effective VR/AR devices, to ensure broader accessibility and inclusivity in metaverse tourism.

Sustainability and economic implications are also critical areas for further exploration. Virtual tourism has the potential to reduce carbon footprints and mitigate overtourism, yet the environmental impact of VR/AR technologies, such as high energy consumption, needs to be assessed. Research should also analyze new business models in metaverse tourism, including revenue streams from digital souvenirs, NFT-based experiences, and hybrid tourism offerings. Furthermore, understanding the long-term economic impact of virtual tourism on destinations that rely on traditional travel for revenue is essential to developing balanced strategies that support both physical and digital tourism.

Security, privacy, and ethical considerations remain pressing concerns in the adoption of metaverse technologies. Future research should focus on data privacy risks, cybersecurity challenges, and ethical guidelines for immersive tourism experiences. Issues such as the authenticity of virtual cultural heritage sites, deepfake tourism, and the psychological effects of prolonged virtual travel experiences need to be critically evaluated. Additionally, studies should explore the legal and regulatory frameworks governing virtual tourism businesses, particularly regarding digital property rights, transactions, and consumer protection in metaverse travel environments.

Lastly, technological advancements and future trends in metaverse tourism should be continuously explored. Research can focus on the role of artificial intelligence, blockchain, and mixed reality in shaping next-generation virtual tourism experiences. The potential of quantum computing in enhancing metaverse simulations, as well as the integration of augmented reality for hybrid travel experiences, are promising areas for future investigation. By addressing these research gaps, scholars and industry stakeholders can optimize metaverse technologies to create a more sustainable, inclusive, and engaging digital travel landscape.

CONCLUSION

In conclusion, the metaverse represents a paradigm shift in how tourism and hospitality services are conceptualized, delivered, and experienced. From virtual travel adventures to immersive hotel stays, the metaverse empowers industry stakeholders to transcend geographical boundaries and redefine customer engagement. While challenges persist, the transformative potential of metaverse technologies offers unprecedented opportunities for innovation, growth, and inclusivity within the global tourism and hospitality sectors. By embracing these technologies responsibly and strategically, businesses can navigate the evolving digital landscape and unlock new frontiers of possibility for the future of travel and hospitality. The metaverse redefines customer engagement by offering immersive and personalized experiences that bridge the gap between physical and virtual realms. As highlighted by Pine and Gilmore (1998), the experience economy values memorable and transformative encounters that resonate with consumers. Virtual tourism experiences, for instance, allow travelers to explore destinations and cultural landmarks in ways previously unimaginable, fostering a deeper connection to place and history. Hotels and resorts leverage VR/AR technologies to provide virtual room previews, interactive tours, and augmented reality guides, enhancing the guest experience and influencing travel decisions. Moreover, the metaverse enhances customer engagement through interactive storytelling and gamification. Virtual experiences can be tailored to individual preferences, offering personalized recommendations and activities that cater to diverse interests. For example, AR applications can overlay historical information onto physical surroundings, enriching sightseeing experiences with educational content and interactive challenges. Such innovations not only captivate guests but also encourage repeat visits and positive word-of-mouth, driving customer loyalty in a competitive market. While the adoption of metaverse technologies presents opportunities, it also entails challenges that must be addressed to realize its full potential in tourism and hospitality. Technical infrastructure requirements, such as high-speed internet connectivity and VR-compatible devices, pose barriers to widespread adoption, particularly in remote or underserved regions. Ivanov et al. (2020) emphasize the importance of investing in digital infrastructure to ensure equitable access and usability for all travelers and businesses. Furthermore, concerns related to data privacy, security, and ethical use of virtual environments necessitate robust safeguards and regulatory frameworks. Protecting personal information and ensuring transparent practices in data collection and usage are essential to building trust among consumers and maintaining the integrity of digital interactions. Collaborative efforts between industry stakeholders, policymakers, and technology developers are crucial for establishing standards and guidelines that promote responsible use of metaverse technologies. Despite challenges, the transformative potential of the metaverse fuels innovation and growth within the tourism and hospitality sectors. Virtual reality training programs, for instance, revolutionize staff development by simulating real-world scenarios and enhancing employee competence in customer service and crisis management. By reducing training costs and improving efficiency, VR-based simulations enable businesses to elevate service standards and adapt to evolving guest expectations. Moreover, the metaverse expands market reach and revenue streams through virtual events and digital experiences. Virtual conferences, trade shows, and cultural exhibitions hosted in the metaverse attract global audiences and foster international collaboration without the constraints of physical travel. This digital shift not only enhances event accessibility but also supports economic resilience by diversifying revenue sources and mitigating risks associated with fluctuating travel trends and geopolitical uncertainties. Inclusivity and accessibility lie at the heart of metaverse technologies' transformative impact on tourism and hospitality. Virtual tourism experiences democratize travel by offering equitable access to destinations and cultural heritage sites, regardless of physical ability or geographical location. Gössling (2017) argues that digital technologies can empower marginalized communities and promote social inclusion through virtual education, remote work opportunities, and accessible leisure experiences. Additionally, the metaverse enhances accessibility for individuals with disabilities by providing customizable settings and adaptive technologies that cater to diverse needs. Virtual environments can simulate barrier-free access to accommodations, attractions, and transportation options, ensuring that all guests can participate fully in travel experiences. By prioritizing inclusivity in metaverse development, tourism businesses uphold principles of diversity and equity, fostering a more accessible and inclusive global tourism landscape. To navigate the evolving digital landscape successfully, tourism and hospitality businesses must adopt metaverse technologies strategically and responsibly. This entails investing in robust digital infrastructure, cultivating digital literacy among employees and guests, and fostering collaborative partnerships for innovation. By embracing a forward-thinking approach, businesses can differentiate themselves in a competitive market, deliver exceptional guest experiences, and drive sustainable growth in a digital-first era. In conclusion, the metaverse heralds a new era of possibility and transformation for tourism and hospitality. By embracing innovative technologies and adapting strategically, industry stakeholders can reshape customer engagement, drive operational efficiency, and promote inclusivity within the global tourism landscape. As the metaverse continues to evolve, its integration promises to redefine industry standards, unlock new revenue streams, and elevate the travel experience for generations to come.

ACKNOWLEDGMENT

This research received no specific grant from any funding agency in the public, commercial, or not-for-profit sectors.

REFERENCES

Andrae, A. S. G., & Edler, T. (2015). On global electricity usage of communication technology: Trends to 2030. *Challenges*, 6(1), 117–157. DOI: 10.3390/challe6010117

Beck, J., & Egger, R. (2018). *Tourism and technology: An integrated framework for sustainable tourism development*. Springer.

Beck, J., Egger, R., & Buhalis, D. (2019). Virtual reality and the tourism experience: Innovation, disruption, and opportunities. *Journal of Tourism Futures*, 5(3), 300–318.

Bonetti, F. (2018). The role of virtual events in the metaverse and hospitality industry. *International Journal of Hospitality Management*, 69, 35–42.

Bonetti, F., Alvino, F., & Gatti, C. (2018). Virtual reality and its use in the hospitality industry: A review of current research and implications for future tourism. *Journal of Hospitality and Tourism Technology*, 9(4), 461–477.

Brynjolfsson, E., & McAfee, A. (2014). *The Second Machine Age: Work, Progress, and Prosperity in a Time of Brilliant Technologies*. W.W. Norton & Company.

Buhalis, D., & Law, R. (2008). Progress in information technology and tourism management: 20 years on and 10 years after the internet—the state of eTourism research. *Tourism Management*, 29(4), 609–623. DOI: 10.1016/j.tourman.2008.01.005

Buhalis, D., & Leung, R. (2018). Technology in hospitality: Digitalization and innovation. *International Journal of Contemporary Hospitality Management*, 30(12), 3367–3387.

Buhalis, D., Lin, M. S., & Leung, D. (2021). Metaverse as a driver for immersive tourism experiences: A transformative perspective. *Tourism Review*, 76(5), 1019–1033.

Buhalis, D., & Sinarta, Y. (2019). Real-time co-creation and experience in tourism and hospitality. *Journal of Travel Research*, 58(3), 271–282.

Castells, M. (2010). *The Rise of the Network Society* (2nd ed.). Wiley-Blackwell.

Cavusoglu, H., Hameed, S. M., & Iyer, B. (2015). Regulation of personal data in the digital age. *Journal of Information Privacy and Security*, 11(3), 23–44.

Chung, N., Han, H., & Lee, M. (2021). Virtual reality and the metaverse in hotel visits and reservations. *International Journal of Hospitality Management*, 97, 103–113.

Dredge, D., & Gyimóthy, S. (2015). The collaborative economy and the tourism industry: Critical perspectives, sound theoretical frameworks, and the need for new research. *Annals of Tourism Research*, 58, 61–70.

Dwivedi, Y. K., Rana, N. P., & Janssen, M. (2021). Artificial intelligence and the metaverse: Enhancing personalized experiences in hospitality services. *Journal of Hospitality and Tourism Technology*, 12(4), 389–410.

Egger, R., & Buhalis, D. (2020). Virtual and augmented reality applications in tourism and hospitality. *Journal of Tourism and Hospitality Technology*, 11(2), 235–245.

Fesenmaier, D. R. (2020). The role of virtual reality in tourism: Accessing the world through digital platforms. *Journal of Travel Research*, 59(4), 678–692.

Foucault, M. (1977). *Discipline and Punish: The Birth of the Prison*. Pantheon Books.

Frey, C. B., & Osborne, M. A. (2017). The future of employment: How susceptible are jobs to computerization? *Technological Forecasting and Social Change*, 114, 254–280. DOI: 10.1016/j.techfore.2016.08.019

Goodwin, H. (2017). Overtourism: What's the solution? *Journal of Tourism and Hospitality Management*, 18(2), 18–27.

Gössling, S. (2017). Digitalization in tourism: Implications for the future of the tourism industry. *Journal of Tourism Futures*, 3(3), 171–177.

Gössling, S. (2010). The environmental impact of tourism and travel: A sustainable future. *Journal of Sustainable Tourism*, 18(3), 239–253.

Gössling, S. (2021). The sustainable future of tourism: Virtual experiences and their role in managing overtourism. *Journal of Sustainable Tourism*, 29(7), 1–15.

Gössling, S., & Peeters, P. (2015). Assessing tourism's global environmental impact 1900-2050. *Journal of Sustainable Tourism*, 23(3), 477–493.

Guttentag, D. (2010). Virtual reality in tourism: A review of the applications, challenges, and opportunities. *Tourism Management*, 31(1), 39–49.

Guttentag, D. A. (2015). The role of augmented reality in tourism: A case study of tourism apps. *Journal of Tourism Studies*, 26(2), 36–50.

Han, C., Choi, S., & Koo, C. (2021). The use of metaverse in virtual cultural heritage experiences for global tourism. *International Journal of Heritage Studies*, 27(4), 287–301.

Hanna, S. (2021). Digital inclusion in the metaverse: Addressing barriers to access in virtual tourism. *Journal of Digital Tourism*, 1(2), 34–49.

Huang, R., Zhang, L., & Li, W. (2022). Sustainable tourism through metaverse technologies: Digital twins and virtual travel experiences. *Journal of Sustainable Tourism*, 30(1), 58–72.

Ivanov, S. (2020). Virtual reality and service automation in hospitality: The future of guest experiences. *Journal of Hospitality and Tourism Technology*, 11(3), 385–401.

Ivanov, S., & Webster, C. (2017). Virtual reality in hospitality: A tool for training and enhancing customer experience. *International Journal of Hospitality Management*, 61, 35–44.

Jeon, S., Kim, M., & Choi, H. (2022). Smart tourism ecosystems: Integration of metaverse for enhanced traveler engagement. *Tourism Review*, 77(2), 121–135.

Jung, T., tom Dieck, M. C., & Han, D. (2020). Virtual reality and augmented reality in tourism: A systematic review and implications for future research. *Journal of Travel Research*, 59(6), 1072–1090.

Kang, S. H., & Gretzel, U. (2012). The role of virtual reality in cultural sensitivity training. *Journal of Travel Research*, 51(3), 285–296.

Kim, J., Lee, H., & Choi, S. (2023). NFTs and blockchain in metaverse tourism: Creating unique virtual experiences. *Journal of Hospitality Innovation*, 15(1), 23–35.

Kshetri, N. (2014). Cybersecurity and international business. *Journal of International Business Studies*, 45(9), 1191–1212.

Lee, J., Kim, Y., & Lee, H. (2021). The metaverse in tourism: User engagement and virtual social spaces for travelers. *Tourism Management Perspectives*, 37, 100–110.

Leung, R. (2013). Marketing in virtual tourism: Using immersive technologies to attract customers. *JMR, Journal of Marketing Research*, 51(3), 257–268.

Li, X. (2020). Virtual reality as a tool for hospitality marketing: Exploring customer perceptions and behaviors. *International Journal of Contemporary Hospitality Management*, 32(2), 438–457.

Li, X., & Xu, H. (2020). The role of virtual reality in promoting sustainable tourism: A case study of China. *Journal of Sustainable Tourism*, 28(10), 1581–1599.

Lyu, J. (2021). Sustainable practices in virtual tourism and its environmental impact. *Journal of Sustainable Tourism*, 29(8), 1345–1361.

Matzler, K., Homburg, C., & Völckner, F. (2020). How to make your customers happy: Understanding the role of the metaverse in tourism and hospitality. *Journal of Business Research*, 113, 372–381.

Mc Cartney, G. (2015). Cultural awareness and virtual training in hospitality industries. *International Journal of Hospitality Management*, 47, 74–81.

Mc Cormick, B. (2021). Guest experience management through virtual technologies in hospitality. *Journal of Hospitality & Tourism Research (Washington, D.C.)*, 45(5), 874–893.

McKercher, B. (2002). The impact of virtual tourism on the real world. *Tourism Management*, 23(4), 395–409.

Milgram, P., Takemura, H., Utsumi, A., & Kishino, F. (1994). Augmented reality: A class of displays on the reality-virtuality continuum. *Proceedings of the Telemanipulator and Telepresence Technologies*, 282-292.

Neal Stephenson, N. (1992). *Snow crash*. Bantam Books.

Neuhofer, B. (2015). The role of technology in creating memorable guest experiences. *International Journal of Hospitality Management*, 47, 143–151.

Pagani, M. (2013). Digital transformation of business models in the hospitality industry. *Information & Management*, 50(8), 519–530.

Park, D., & Kim, S. (2022). Metaverse in event tourism: Virtual conventions, trade shows, and hybrid tourism experiences. *Event Management*, 26(3), 302–318.

Peltier, J. W. (2019). Virtual and augmented reality in tourism: The potential for new tourist experiences. *Tourism Management*, 71, 207–220.

Pine, B. J., & Gilmore, J. H. (1998). *The Experience Economy: Work is Theatre & Every Business a Stage*. Harvard Business Press.

Pizam, A., & Shani, A. (2020). Digital skills and the future of hospitality management: Implications for education and training. *Journal of Hospitality & Tourism Education*, 32(1), 21–35.

Pritchard, A. (2011). Experience and co-creation in tourism: Perspectives on innovation in tourism services. *Annals of Tourism Research*, 38(4), 1347–1366.

Pritchard, A., & Morgan, N. (2010). The experiences of virtual tourism and its social and cultural implications. *Journal of Tourism and Cultural Change*, 8(2), 147–165.

Reiners, T., Wood, C., & Tan, B. (2014). A digital divide for the metaverse: A global perspective. *Computers in Human Behavior*, 41, 423–430.

Reisinger, Y., & Mavondo, F. (2005). Travel and tourism services marketing: The impact of digitalization on the hospitality industry. *Journal of Travel & Tourism Marketing*, 17(4), 1–17.

Riva, G., Wiederhold, B. K., & Molinari, E. (2016). *Virtual reality in psychological treatment: Advances in research and applications*. Springer.

Schwab, K. (2016). *The Fourth Industrial Revolution*. Crown Publishing.

Schwabe, M. (2020). Virtual Reality and the Hospitality Industry: New Opportunities for Engagement and Innovation. *Tourism Management Perspectives*, 33.

Seyitoğlu, F., & Ivanov, S. (2020). Virtual reality as an innovative tool for hospitality training. *International Journal of Hospitality Management*, 89.

Sigala, M. (2018). Collaborative economy and sharing platforms in tourism: Innovation and opportunities for new business models. *Journal of Tourism Futures*, 4(3), 197–202.

Stansfield, M., & Shawver, M. (2016). Virtual reality simulations for emergency response training. *Journal of Safety Research*, 57, 27–35.

Stephenson, N. (1992). *Snow Crash*. Bantam Books.

Tung, V. W. S. (2020). Virtual reality in tourism: Exploring the future of travel in the metaverse. *Tourism Management Perspectives*, 35.

Tussyadiah, I. P. (2020). The role of gamification and interactivity in metaverse-based travel experiences. *Journal of Travel & Tourism Marketing*, 37(8), 925–940.

Tussyadiah, I. P. (2018). The role of virtual reality in tourism marketing and the guest experience. *Journal of Hospitality & Tourism Research (Washington, D.C.)*, 42(5), 788–812.

Tussyadiah, I. P., & Park, S. (2018). Consumer preferences for virtual reality in tourism. *Journal of Travel Research*, 57(7), 851–864.

Tussyadiah, I. P., Wang, D., & Jia, C. (2017). Exploring the role of digital literacy in tourism innovation. *Journal of Travel Research*, 56(7), 837–849.

Urry, J., & Larsen, J. (2011). *The tourist gaze 3.0*. Sage Publications. DOI: 10.4135/9781446251904

Wang, D. (2016). Training employees using virtual reality technology: Implications for service industries. *Journal of Service Research*, 19(2), 234–248.

Wang, Y., Liu, C., & Zhang, X. (2020). Metaverse technologies for inclusive tourism: Virtual travel for people with mobility constraints. *Journal of Inclusive Tourism*, 12(4), 115–130.

Wirtz, J., Zeithaml, V. A., & Gistri, G. (2018). Technology, service innovation, and the service experience: The role of business collaborations in developing customer-centric services. *Journal of the Academy of Marketing Science*, 46(3), 313–325.

Xiang, Z., Fesenmaier, D. R., & Wei, W. (2022). Metaverse and destination marketing: Virtual tourism experiences and their impact on travelers. *Tourism Management*, 83, 47–58.

Yoo, C. K. (2021). Ethical issues in virtual tourism: An exploration of privacy and security in the metaverse. *Journal of Travel Research*, 60(6), 1325–1341.

Yoo, K. H. (2018). The impact of virtual reality on the hospitality industry's business operations. *Journal of Hospitality Marketing & Management*, 27(3), 283–298.

Yung, R., & Khoo-Lattimore, C. (2019). Adoption of immersive technologies in tourism: Co-creation and virtual reality. *Journal of Travel Research*, 58(3), 315–331.

Zengler, T. (2019). Leveraging Augmented Reality and Virtual Reality in the Hospitality Industry. *Journal of Hospitality and Tourism Technology*, 10(4), 401–418.

Zuboff, S. (2015). *The Age of Surveillance Capitalism: The Fight for a Human Future at the New Frontier of Power*. Public Affairs.

KEY TERMS AND DEFINITIONS

Augmented Reality (AR): A technology that overlays digital information, such as images, texts, or animations, onto the real world, enhancing physical experiences. In hospitality, AR is used to provide interactive guides, real-time travel information, and virtual hotel previews.

Digital Concierge: An AI-powered virtual assistant that helps guests with inquiries, bookings, and personalized recommendations in a hotel or travel setting. It enhances customer engagement by offering seamless and interactive service experiences.

Digital Divide: The gap between individuals or communities with access to advanced digital technologies and those without. Limited internet connectivity, expensive VR hardware, and varying digital literacy levels create barriers to equitable participation in metaverse-based tourism experiences.

Immersive Experience: A digital engagement that creates a sense of presence and realism, making users feel as if they are physically in a different environment. The metaverse enables immersive tourism experiences, allowing travelers to visit places virtually without geographical constraints.

Metaverse: A virtual, immersive, and interconnected digital space where users can interact, explore, and engage with environments using virtual reality (VR), augmented reality (AR), and artificial intelligence (AI). It is increasingly shaping tourism and hospitality by enabling virtual travel experiences and digital customer interactions.

Sustainable Tourism: A concept focused on minimizing the environmental impact of travel by promoting eco-friendly practices. The metaverse supports sustainable tourism by reducing the need for physical travel, thus lowering carbon footprints and preserving natural and cultural heritage.

Virtual Events: Conferences, trade shows, or meetings conducted within digital environments, eliminating the need for physical venues. The metaverse facilitates virtual events with interactive networking spaces, keynote sessions, and digital collaboration tools.

Virtual Reality (VR): A simulated environment that users can experience through specialized headsets, allowing them to explore and interact with digital worlds. In tourism, VR facilitates immersive virtual tours of destinations, hotels, and attractions.

Chapter 6

Analysis of the Impact of Metaverse on the Retailer's Brand Perceptions:

The Example of Nike With Nikeland

Joaquim Monteiro Pratas
https://orcid.org/0000-0002-7432-9242
CEOS.PP, ISCAP, Polytechnic of Porto, Portugal

Gabriel Dias Moreira
University of Maia, Portugal

João Guilherme Garcez
https://orcid.org/0009-0005-9488-8171
University of Maia, Portugal

Ivan Simões
University of Maia, Portugal

Leonardo Roberto Neves Andrade
https://orcid.org/0009-0008-6116-534X
University of Maia, Portugal

João Miguel Da Silva Martins
https://orcid.org/0009-0006-1720-0414
University of Maia, Portugal

EXECUTIVE SUMMARY

Retailers are increasingly exploring new communication and sales channels, with the metaverse offering a promising opportunity. This study examines how Nike's presence in the metaverse, through Nikeland, impacts brand image and consumer expectations. Factors analyzed include respondent characteristics, metaverse knowledge and usage, valued Nike attributes, customer loyalty, and product quality perceptions. Data was collected with a survey of 401 respondents. Analysis using structural equation modeling revealed that most respondents view Nike's metaverse

DOI: 10.4018/979-8-3693-7245-6.ch006

presence as enhancing its innovative image, overall brand perception, brand awareness, and brand equity. Key consumer expectations for the metaverse store include attractive decoration, product quality, pleasant atmosphere, and a quality consumer experience. The study highlights the significant relationship between brand image and consumer expectations, providing strategic insights for retailers on target definition and refining metaverse experiences.

INTRODUCTION

Retailers are continuously on the lookout for innovative touchpoints to engage, communicate with, and sell to their customers. In the realm of omnichannel retail strategies, innovative touchpoints present a golden opportunity to foster more interactions between retailers and customers, ultimately driving sales through new customers and more frequent transactions. The touchpoints used by retailers span from physical stores, websites, mobile applications (Pratas & Brito, 2019), e-marketplaces, social media platforms, to innovative technologies like the metaverse and other spatial computing platforms.

Omnichannel retailing is all about seamlessly integration and management of multiple communication and sales touchpoints, ensuring a consistent and smooth buying journey for customers, no matter which touchpoint they choose (Rosenblum & Kilcourse, 2013). These strategies are intricately linked to challenges such as digitalization and the need to adapt retail strategies to evolving consumer behavior (Kotzab et al., 2016; Shi et al., 2020).

Today's consumers are "blended" forming a unified perception of brands and retailers across various touchpoints. They navigate these touchpoints fluidly, during their interactions with brands and retailers, without distinguishing rigid boundaries between online and offline experiences. This blending of channels creates a unified brand perception, and allows the showrooming and webrooming effects (Pratas & Amorim, 2022). Consequently, integrated touchpoints are crucial for achieving positive consumer experiences, significantly impacting customer satisfaction and brand loyalty (Bolton et al., 2022).

The metaverse represents a novel touchpoint and marketplace that brands and retailers can leverage to engage with consumers (Lopes et al., 2024). According to Gartner Inc. (2022), by 2026, 25% of the global population will spend at least one hour daily on metaverse platforms.

The metaverse is a dynamic, three-dimensional virtual world rooted in virtual reality, where users can live, socialize, work, and play. This immersive environment transcends the current two-dimensional cyberspace of websites, social media, and apps, creating a rich, avatar-populated landscape (Singh et al., 2024). Retailers must adopt this technology to stay ahead of the competition, avoiding the pitfall of marketing myopia (Jasrotia, 2023), leveraging the metaverse as an extension of their sales and communication channels, and offering a novel platform for immersive and interactive brand experiences. This virtual realm allows consumers to engage with products and services in captivating ways, such as through virtual stores and avatars, innovative consumer engagement, data insights, personalization, and significant business impacts (Pratas, 2023).

While numerous studies have underscored the benefits of a retailer's presence in new media, particularly in the metaverse, the impact of that presence on the retailer's brand image remains less explored.

This research aims to shed light on how opening a store in the metaverse can influence a retailer's global image, focusing on the evolution of consumer perceptions of the brand. It also intends to analyze different customer characteristics and behaviors that affect this brand image evolution. The methodology will be based on the analysis of Nike's brand image evolution due to the presence in the metaverse marketplace with Nikeland.

Thus, in the structure of this text, after this Introductory section, the Background section will highlight the general characterization of metaverse and its main technologies, potentialities for retail businesses utilization, impacts of metaverse on retailer's brand image and brand equity, and the strategy and latest actions of NIKE in metaverse as a brand's case-study. Additionally the conceptual model and research questions are presented. The Methodology section details the research design, the process of survey development, the sample selection, data collection strategies, and data analysis methods. Moving on to the Findings section, we describe the sample and highlight the relationships between variables using a structural equation model to assess reliability and estimate the model.

Finally, we suggest directions for future research and, in the Conclusions section, we underscore both the theoretical and managerial contributions of this work, along with its limitations.

BACKGROUND

Metaverse Characterization and Main Associated Technologies

Metaverse and augmented reality (AR) technologies are transforming several industries by crafting immersive and interactive shopping experiences. Although distinct, the Metaverse and AR are interconnected technologies. The Metaverse is a collective virtual shared space, born from the fusion of virtually enhanced physical reality and persistent virtual spaces, including virtual worlds, AR, and the internet.

This comprehensive digital environment allows users to interact with each other and digital objects in real-time (Shi et al., 2023). Accessing the Metaverse can be done in several ways: virtual reality (VR) headsets, such as the Oculus Rift, HTC Vive, and PlayStation VR, transport users into virtual worlds. Desktop and Mobile Applications, like Decentraland and Roblox, can be accessed through web browsers or dedicated apps on computers and smartphones. AR Glasses, such as Microsoft HoloLens and Magic Leap, enable users to interact with virtual elements overlaid on the real world.

The Metaverse represents a vast, immersive digital universe that integrates various technologies, including AR, to create a seamless blend of physical and virtual experiences. On the other hand, AR overlays digital information onto the real world, enhancing the user's perception of their environment. While AR can be a component of the Metaverse, it primarily focuses on enhancing the real world with digital elements rather than creating a fully immersive virtual environment. AR specifically enhances the real world with digital overlays, providing a more immediate and accessible form of interaction with digital content (Qamar et al., 2023).

Today accessing AR is easier than ever, thanks to a variety of devices and platforms. Smartphones and tablets, equipped with AR apps like IKEA Place and Pokémon GO, use their cameras and screens to overlay digital content onto the physical world, transforming everyday environments into interactive experiences. AR Glasses, such as Google Glass and the highly anticipated Apple Vision Pro, offer hands-free AR by projecting digital information directly into the user's field of view, making the experience seamless and immersive. Additionally, web-based AR allows users to dive into AR experiences directly through web browsers, without the need for additional apps, leveraging technologies like WebAR to bring digital enhancements to the real world effortlessly. QR codes if linked to products' packaging, shelf tag labels in stores and communication can also be seen as AR tools (Pratas & Oliveira, 2023).

Metaverse Potentialities for Retail

The integration of the Metaverse in retail is revolutionizing the shopping experience. Consumers can now explore virtual stores, interact with products in a 3D environment, and even try on items virtually, significantly enhancing their overall shopping experience (Kozinets, 2023). Retailers have also the option to develop stores specifically for the metaverse, or replicate their flagship stores in this digital realm creating one more channel to interact with their customers and sell (Pratas, 2023).

The presence of retailers in the metaverse offers a multitude of benefits, as highlighted by academic studies (Abumalloh et al., 2023; Bruni et al., 2023):

a) Sustainable Competitive Advantage: retailers can achieve a significant edge by innovating within the metaverse. This innovation stems from the immersive virtual environment, where interactions between users and digital objects closely mimic real-world experiences.
b) Tailored Shopping Experience: By leveraging customer data, metaverse retailers can craft highly personalized shopping journeys that cater to individual preferences and needs, ultimately boosting customer satisfaction and loyalty.
c) Collaborative Opportunities: The metaverse fosters collaboration not only between retailers and consumers but also among consumers themselves. It creates a sense of community and co-creation, breaking traditional retail boundaries.
d) Augmented Experiences: 3D virtual stores within the metaverse offer customers augmented experiences that go beyond standard online shopping, blurring the lines between physical and digital retail environments.
e) Market Expansion: By establishing virtual storefronts, retailers can reach a global audience without geographical limitations, significantly expanding their market presence.

A digital twin, a virtual replica of a physical system, is continually updated with real-time data about the system's performance, maintenance, and health status throughout its lifecycle (Madni et al., 2019). By incorporating precise analytics, digital twins aid in monitoring, comprehending, and optimizing the functions of all physical entities, enabling real-time decision-making capabilities (Fuller et al., 2020). The retail industry has greatly benefited from the use of digital twins, with applications ranging from optimizing store layout, planograms and inventory management to predictive maintenance and energy management, ultimately improving daily operations (Maizi and Bendavid, 2019). This innovative approach also introduces a new way for retailers to sell their products.

Metaverse stores, digital spaces, and digital twins are transforming the retail landscape, significantly boosting both profitability and operational efficiency. These innovations drive increased sales and market share, elevate the capital-to-labor ratio, and enhance promotional efforts. Retailers benefit from better inventory management, more efficient store layouts and planograms, and improved policies in predictive maintenance and energy management. Additionally, these technologies streamline supply chain efficiency and provide superior analysis and testing for new product development and marketing strategies (Pratas, 2023). In this way, several retailers are already taking advantage of metaverse, such as Walmart and IKEA, among others. Walmart has filed several patents related to the metaverse, including virtual shopping experiences and a digital currency for transactions. They are exploring how to integrate AR and VR technologies into their retail operations (Candelon et al. 2022). IKEA has developed a virtual reality app called "IKEA Place," which allows customers to visualize how furniture would look in their homes before making a purchase. They are also exploring other metaverse applications to enhance customer experience (De Vigan, 2022).

However, the metaverse isn't without its challenges. Key concerns surrounding its presence include (Statista, 2023):

a) Personal Data Safety: A significant number of users are anxious about the tracking and potential misuse of their personal information. The metaverse collects extensive personal data, including biometric data like gait, gaze, posture, and emotions. This raises concerns about how this data is used and who has access to it.
b) Data Protection and Cybersecurity: Ensuring robust defenses against cyber threats. Ensuring that users' identities are accurately verified and protected is essential to prevent identity theft and fraud. The metaverse is also susceptible to various cyber threats, including distributed denial-of-service attacks and theft of user identification information. Implementing comprehensive cybersecurity measures is necessary to mitigate these risks.
c) Illegal and Harmful Behaviors: Addressing and mitigating unlawful and damaging activities. Cyberbullying and harassment, fraud and scams, intellectual property violations, inclusivity and accessibility, among other aspects demand regulatory compliance.
d) Health Impacts: Particularly concerning for minors, the effects on health are a major worry. Psychological aspects (such as addiction, social isolation, and decreased physical activity), physical health (excessive use of VR headsets and other immersive technologies can cause physical discomfort, including eye strain, headaches, and motion sickness), and digital addition can affect metaverse regular users.
e) Accessibility and Inclusiveness: Overcoming barriers to ensure everyone can participate. Physical accessibility, digital literacy of potential users, affordability, inclusivity concerns and language barriers are some aspects that need to be addressed.
f) Energy consumption and sustainability issues: the use of metaverse technology and equipments enhances energy consumption.

Thus, the metaverse can transform how brands and retailers operate, offering numerous benefits but also raising concerns about potential negative consequences. Additionally, the influence of smart retailing initiatives, including a presence in the metaverse, intersects with considerations of brand leadership and market performance of retailers. The metaverse has also organizational challenges that must be addressed such as the potential for negative consumer experiences lowering retailer reputation levels, long term investment and maintenance costs, errors from inappropriate omnichannel integration, lack of internal processes synchronization, and potential of omniverse platform to generate anti-competitive practices benefiting leader worldwide retailers (Pratas et al., 2022). Lack of interoperability between different metaverse platforms can also hinder seamless user experiences and limit the potential for widespread adoption (Hennig-Thurau et al., 2023).

To date, due to its exploratory nature, it remains unclear how the presence of brands and retailers in the metaverse affects their image and brand equity in the minds of the public.

Retailer's Brand Image and Brand Equity

Brand image is a cornerstone for both academic research and practical branding efforts. Plumeyer et al.'s systematic review highlighted 12 essential methods for measuring brand image, based on an analysis of 224 high-quality articles published between 1991 and 2016. The seminal works of Aaker (1991) and Keller (1993) have profoundly shaped the field of brand management. In the realm of retail research, Jara and Cliquet (2012) expanded Keller's brand resonance pyramid by adding retailer-specific dimensions such as personality, service, and price image. Despite these enhancements, the framework missed a critical loyalty dimension, which is central to most brand equity models. Furthermore, the suggestion that the personality dimension should be retailer-specific limits the model's broader applicability across different retailers or sectors.

Arnett et al. (2003) introduced the retailer equity index, a notable model for applying the brand equity framework within a retail context. However, their focus on creating an overall retail equity scale using a single factor (comprising five items) did not allow for traditional testing of brand associations. The study of retailer image has a rich history, examining customer perceptions of both individual retail stores and entire chains (Martineau, 1958; Timmermans, 1993). Londoño et al. (2016) identified awareness, quality, and loyalty as key formative indicators of consumer-based brand-retailer-channel equity. In their investigation of retailer brand equity, Anselmsson et al. (2017) identified several dimensions, including awareness, image/associations, perceived quality, loyalty, personality, price image/value, and service quality, streamlining these dimensions into an efficient 17-item scale, enabling detailed retailer brand equity analysis in specific retail settings without the need for lengthy surveys. These studies provide an in-depth exploration of the progression of retailer brand equity and the myriad factors that have shaped its evolution over time.

Many scales that evaluate a retailer's image emphasize the quality of products sold, the level of service provided, the store's overall decoration, and the general store environment (Alic et al., 2017). These attributes are equally significant in the context of metaverse store environments.

Product quality stands out as a crucial factor that profoundly impacts a retailer's image. Superior product quality not only boosts customer satisfaction and loyalty but also enhances the retailer's reputation and brand image. Research underscores that product quality is intrinsically linked to brand image, store image, purchasing decisions, and repurchase intentions (Cuong, 2022).

Service quality is another pivotal element that shapes the retailer's image. Exceptional service quality elevates customer satisfaction, fosters loyalty, and strengthens the overall perception of the retailer. Studies highlight that aspects such as personal interactions, reliability, and problem-solving capabilities are essential components of service quality that directly influence customer satisfaction and loyalty (Kermanshachi et al., 2023).

Moreover, the overall store image, which encompasses service quality, plays a critical role in distinguishing retailers in a competitive market. Hence, prioritizing service quality is vital for retailers aiming to build a robust, positive image and maintain a competitive edge.

Attractive store decoration and a pleasant store atmosphere are also key attributes that significantly enhance a retailer's image. These elements create an inviting environment that positively influences customers' perceptions and shopping experiences. Research indicates that store atmospherics, including lighting, décor, and music, play a vital role in shaping customer satisfaction and loyalty (Waters, 2019). A thoughtfully crafted store atmosphere can stir positive emotions, encouraging customers to linger and spend more (Ndengane et al., 2021). Moreover, a delightful store environment enhances the overall store image, which is crucial for setting the retailer apart in a competitive market. Thus, investing in appealing store decor and maintaining a welcoming atmosphere are essential strategies for retailers striving to cultivate a strong, positive image. Metaverse stores, namely through digital twins, project their own image, and affect the global image of the retail brand. Additionally, consumers' metaverse store experiences provoke more positive emotions and increased perceived store attractiveness than traditional websites (Lin et al., 2021), but brands should apply a lens of cultural sensitivity and audience understanding to any activities where diversity representations are to occur within virtual environments (Ferraro et al., 2024).

NIKE Case-Study: Strategy and Latest Developments in Metaverse

Nike's journey began in 1964 under the name 'Blue Ribbon Sports,' initially importing Japanese running shoes to the U.S. In 1971, the company rebranded as Nike, Inc., drawing inspiration from the Greek goddess of victory. The iconic Nike Cortez was its first product. By 1984, the Air Jordan sneaker, developed in collaboration with Michael Jordan, propelled the brand to global fame. Today, Nike is recognized as the ninth most valuable brand worldwide (Interbrand, 2023).

Despite uncertainties surrounding the metaverse, Nike has boldly ventured into this new domain. Since 2021, Nikeland, a virtual world hosted on the Roblox platform, has served as both a promotional hub and an immersive brand experience. It democratizes brand access, allowing avatars to express themselves freely. Nikeland is a virtual space where fans can gather, socialize, and engage in various brand-related activities. Users can participate in promotions, play games, and even customize their avatars with Nike gear (Marr, 2022; Carter, 2023).

This 'micro metaverse' aims to create an immersive environment where sport knows no boundaries, and the future of sport is shaped by the users themselves. It uniquely blends gaming, social interaction, and brand engagement, reflecting Nike's innovative approach to digital experiences.

To drive more traffic to Nikeland, Nike leveraged cross-promotions on X (formerly known as Twitter) and Instagram, attracting millions of views with boosted video posts. Additionally, real-world activations through Snapchat at Nike's House of Innovation further enriched the overall brand experience for customers. In Nikeland, coveted sneakers, jerseys, and accessories are prominently featured, underscoring the metaverse's impact on digital identity. Items like LeBron James jerseys and futuristic hoverboards offer transferability, bridging virtual realms much like intertextuality in literature.

Nike's brand equity extends beyond the physical world, resonating throughout the metaverse. Nostalgic games come to life, and Lake Nike invites digital swimmers. Hidden Easter eggs in graffiti add an element of mystery, while skateboarding and whimsical pads bring joy. Nikeland's showroom subtly showcases virtual merchandise, and visitors participate in an immersive ad campaign by trying on holographic sneakers.

Nike's metaverse strategy also includes the 'Airphoria' experience in Fortnite from June 2022, promoting Air Max sneakers. Additionally, Nike's presence in '.Swoosh' offers exclusive access to real-life events and collaborative product creation using blockchain technology (Paspalj, 2022; Spatial Awareness by Kahris, 2022; Schulz, 2023). Nikeland has attracted over seven million visitors. Nike is also protecting its brands and logos by filing for trademarks for its virtual sneakers and logos in metaverse platforms.

Nike recognized the metaverse as a new channel for customer engagement and a source of new digital revenue streams, enhancing brand equity and solidifying its leadership position as an innovator.

While the exact impact on Nike's business remains indeterminable, this milestone highlights the success of Nike's venture into the metaverse and provides valuable insights for future metaverse commerce initiatives. Preliminary findings suggest that Nikeland has boosted brand recognition and leadership, while also influencing consumers' purchase intentions, thereby impacting sales and market share, despite the lack of precise statistical data (Fianto et al., 2022).

Conceptual Model and Research Questions

Nike has made a significant leap into the metaverse with its investment in platforms like Nikeland. Drawing from a comprehensive literature review, a conceptual model was developed to explore this venture. This model examines how various factors—such as consumer socio-demographical characteristics, the level of knowledge and use of the metaverse, the importance of attributes valued by its customers, customer loyalty behaviors, and perceptions of product quality in Nike's metaverse store—affect Nike's brand image and consumer expectations of metaverse stores.

The literature review reveals that socio-demographic characteristics significantly influence brand image and expectations (Parris & Guzmán, 2023). Moreover, knowledge about metaverse and its use have a profound impact on marketing and consumer behavior, transforming customer experiences and, consequently, brand image (Saridakis et al., 2024; Soliman et al., 2024).

Additionally, the attributes more important to Nike's customers can influence Nike's brand image. Plumeyer et al. (2019) provide an extensive review of techniques for measuring brand image, discussing how various attributes valued by customers shape their perception of a brand. Additionally, customer loyalty plays a crucial role in shaping brand image perceptions through emotional connections, consistency, trust, and enhanced perceived quality (Tu et al., 2013; Keller, 2020; Chen & Wu, 2022).

Perceptions of quality products in the metaverse can significantly influence the global image of retailers. Product innovation within the metaverse can also bolster a retailer's competitive advantage (Abumalloh et al., 2023). All these aspects can also affect the expectations about metaverse stores. These expectations can also be affected by Nike's brand image.

The global conceptual framework is highlighted in figure 1.

Figure 1. Conceptual framework

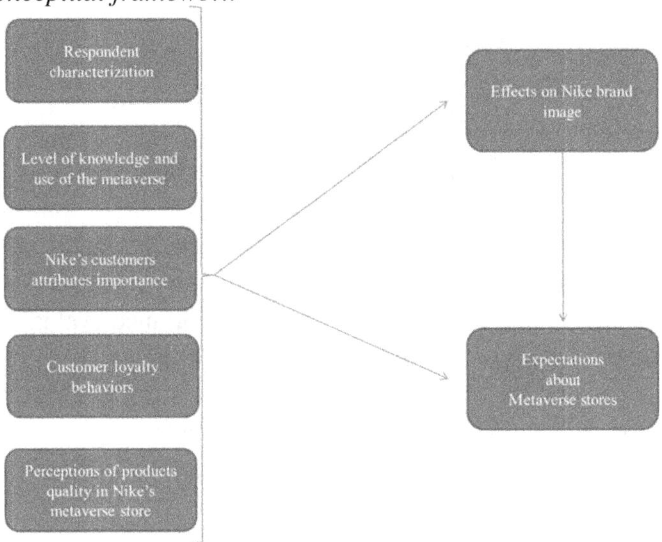

Thus, the following research questions are presented:

- Research question 1: How does Nike's presence in the metaverse, specifically through Nikeland, impact its brand image?
- Research question 2: What are consumers' expectations regarding Nike's metaverse stores?
- Research question 3: What is the relationship between the impact of Nike's metaverse presence on its brand image and consumer expectations of metaverse stores?
- Research question 4: Which factors - such as respondent characterization, metaverse knowledge and usage, the importance of Nike's customer attributes, customer loyalty behaviors, and perceptions of product quality in Nike's metaverse store - significantly influence Nike's brand image?
- Research question 5: Which factors - such as respondent characterization, metaverse knowledge and usage, the importance of Nike's customer attributes, customer loyalty behaviors, and perceptions of product quality in Nike's metaverse store - significantly affect consumer expectations of metaverse stores?

METHODOLOGY

Research Design and Survey Development

This study follows a quantitative approach. It delves into the collection and rigorous analysis of numerical data from a convenience sample employing a diverse array of statistical techniques to analyze the results.

The chosen instrument to data gathering was the questionnaire. It was divided into the following sections: respondent's characteristics, knowledge and use of metaverse platforms, Nike's customer attributes importance evaluation, customer loyalty behaviors, perceptions about the quality of Nike products offered in the metaverse, the perceptions regarding NIKE's presence in the metaverse with Nikeland and respective impacts in the brand's image, and expectations about Nike's metaverse stores. The questions posed are adapted from previous research works.

Table 1. Sections of the survey and respective topics/sentences/questions

Section	Topics / Sentences / Questions
Respondent characterization	- Age - Gender - Auto-characterization of the respondent as an innovative person -Main interests of the respondent
Level of knowledge and use of the metaverse and its main platforms	-Knowledge about the Metaverse -Use of metaverse platforms -Used specific metaverse platforms in the last year
Nike's customer attributes importance	- Brand reputation - Quality of the products - Customer service - Low prices - Trust and customer relationship
Customer loyalty behaviors	- I consider myself loyal to this brand - This brand is my first choice - Even when the products are not available, I wait until there is a restock
Quality of Nike products offered in the Metaverse	- Quality of Nike products offered in the Metaverse

continued on following page

Table 1. Continued

Section	Topics / Sentences / Questions
Analysis of perceptions about NIKE's presence in the metaverse and its impacts on the NIKE's brand	- Effects of metaverse presence for Nike's brand image: benefiting or harming, or both? - Perception of Nike as an innovative brand by opening a store in the Metaverse - Impact level likelihood on Nike Brand Equity - Impact on Nike's brand awareness
Expectations about Nike's metaverse stores	-High quality products -Kind and helpful employees -Good knowledge about the products of the employees -This store never disappoints me -Attractive store decor -Excellent store atmosphere

Sample, Data Collection and Data Analysis Methods

Data was harvested from a cohort of Portuguese and Brazilian consumers, united by their shared language, encompassing 401 individuals. The questionnaire found its way to respondents through the interconnected web of social media.

The analytical techniques used included statistical descriptive analysis, and structural equation modeling techniques. Structural Equation Modeling (SEM) is a powerful multivariate statistical analysis technique used to analyze structural relationships. This method combines factor analysis and multiple regression analysis, allowing researchers to examine complex relationships between observed and latent variables (also known as constructs). SEM is particularly useful in social sciences and behavioral sciences for testing theoretical models that involve multiple variables and their interrelationships. There are two main types of SEM: Covariance-Based SEM (CB-SEM) and Partial Least Squares SEM (PLS-SEM). CB-SEM is primarily used for theory testing and confirmation, while PLS-SEM is more prediction-oriented and is used when the research objective is to develop theories (Hair et al, 2021).

FINDINGS

Characterization of the Sample

The sample comprises Portuguese and Brazilian respondents, chosen for convenience due to the Portuguese language used in the online survey. The age distribution reveals that the majority of respondents, 25.2%, are between 35 and 44 years old. Notably, over 70% of the participants fall within the 18 to 44 age range. Gender representation is balanced, with an equal split between male and female respondents. Interestingly, when asked to self-identify as innovative, only about 40% of the sample agreed, while 41.3% remained neutral. The respondents' main interests span a variety of fields, including sports, fashion, music, arts, science, and food and gastronomy, with over 30% indicating these fields as their primary areas of interest.

Table 2. Respondents characterization

Respondents characterization	
Age	Less than 18 years old: 7,7%; Between 18 and 24 years old: 24,7%; Between 25 and 34 years old: 21,2%; Between 35 and 44 years old: 25,2%; Between 45 and 54 years old: 15,5%; More than 55 years old: 5,7%.
Gender	Masculine: 46,4%; Feminine: 47,6%; Other/Prefer not to say: 6,0%.
Auto-characterization of the respondent as an innovative person: "I'm an innovative person"	I totally disagree: 3,3%; I disagree: 14,1%; I neither agree or disagree: 41,3%; I agree: 31,5%; I totally agree: 9,8%.
Main interests of the respondent	Sports: 42,5%; Fashion: 40,7%; Music: 37,7%; Arts: 36,7%; Science: 35,7%; Food and Gastronomy: 33,7%; Playing games: 29,1%; Education: 24,4%.

When it comes to the respondents' familiarity and engagement with the metaverse, only about 15% claim to fully understand what the metaverse is. Meanwhile, around 35% are somewhat familiar but eager to learn more. This means that half of the respondents have some level of awareness about the metaverse, while the other half are still in the dark. This underscores the fact that the metaverse is still an emerging technology, with many yet to grasp its full potential. Moreover, only 52.5% of respondents have actually used metaverse platforms. Among these, Decentraland is the most popular, with 25.9% of users, followed by Second Life, Minecraft, Roblox, and VR Chat.

Table 3. Level of knowledge and use of the metaverse and its main platforms

Level of knowledge and use of the metaverse and its main platforms	
Knowledge about the Metaverse: "I know what metaverse is"	No: 9,2%; No, but I would like to know: 40,9%; Yes, but I would like to know more about it: 34,7%; Yes: 15,2%
Use of metaverse platforms	Yes: 52,5%; No: 47,5%
Used specific metaverse platforms in the last year.	Decentraland: 25,9%; Second Life: 18,5%; Minecraft: 18,0%; Roblox: 16,2%; VR Chat: 7,5%

When evaluating what matters most to Nike's customers, 50,2% focus on affordable prices, 50,1% prioritize product quality, 47,1% highlight the significance of brand reputation, 44,6% value excellent customer service, and 42,6% emphasize trust and strong customer relationships as very important or important attributes.

Table 4. Nike's customers attributes importance

Nike's customers attributes importance	
Brad reputation	Very important: 13,7% ; Important: 33,4%; Neutral: 24,4% ; Unimportant: 14,5%; Very unimportant: 3,0%; Don't know: 11,0%
Products' quality	Very important: 22,4%; Important: 27,7%; Neutral: 22,9%; Unimportant: 11,0%; Very unimportant: 3,0%; Don't know: 13,0%
Customer service	Very important: 14,7% ; Important: 29,9% ; Neutral: 28,2%; Unimportant: 11,7%; Very unimportant: 4,0%; Don't know: 11,5%
Low prices	Very important: 19,5%; Important: 30,7%; Neutral: 22,7%; Unimportant: 12,0%; Very unimportant: 4,5%; Don't know: 10,7%
Trust and customer relationship	Very important: 15,2%; Important: 27,4%; Neutral: 27,4%; Unimportant: 13,5%; Very unimportant: 5,7%; Don't know: 10,7%

When it comes to customer loyalty, 41.7% of respondents either agree or strongly agree that they are devoted to the Nike brand. Additionally, 39.7% consider Nike their top choice, and 40.9% are so committed that they prefer to wait for products to be restocked rather than switching to another brand. It seems that Nike has a loyal customer base, although it is possible to improve as less than 50% say are loyal customers. However only 17% disagree or totally disagree of being loyal to Nike.

Interestingly, more than 10% answers "Don't know", and about 30% says "Neither agree or disagree" in all the three questions. Thus about 40% of respondents have neutral answers about loyalty behaviors towards NIKE.

Table 5. Customer loyalty behaviors

Customer Loyalty Behaviors	
"I consider myself loyal to this brand".	Totally Agree: 12,5%; Agree: 29,2%; Neither agree or disagree: 28,2%; Disagree: 10,5%; Totally disagree: 6,5%; Don't know: 13,1%
"*This brand is my first choice*".	Totally Agree: 13,0%; Agree: 26,7%; Neither agree or disagree: 29,2%; Disagree: 15,7%; Totally disagree: 4,2%; Don't know: 11,2%
"*Even when products are not available, I wait until they are restocked*".	Totally Agree: 11,7%; Agree: 29,2%; Neither agree or disagree: 29,7%; Disagree: 14,5%; Totally disagree: 4,5%; Don't know: 10,5%

When it comes to the quality of Nike products in the metaverse, only 15.7% of people rate it as low or very low. On the other hand, around 75% of respondents believe the quality is either very high, high, or at least satisfactory/regular.

Table 6. Quality of Nike products offered in the metaverse

Quality of Nike products offered in the Metaverse	
Quality of Nike products offered in the Metaverse	Very high: 6,7%; High: 27,4%; Regular: 39,4%; Low: 10,5%; Very low: 5,2%; Don't know: 10,7%

When it comes to perceptions of Nike's brand image, the majority of respondents (66.8%) believe that the brand stands to benefit. A smaller group (13.5%) thinks it could be harmed, while 9.7% feel it could go either way. Interestingly, 10% are unsure about the effects. Moreover, a significant 68.1% of respondents feel that Nike's presence in the metaverse underscores its innovative edge, reinforcing its position as a brand leader. Nearly half (48%) believe that this metaverse presence is likely or very likely to enhance the brand's equity. Additionally, 52.4% say that Nike's brand awareness is on the rise thanks to its metaverse presence.

Table 7. Analysis of perceptions about NIKE's presence in the metaverse and its impacts on the NIKE's brand

Analysis of perceptions about NIKE's presence in the metaverse and its impacts on the NIKE's brand	
Effects of metaverse presence for Nike's brand image: benefiting or harming, or both?	The brand can be favored: 66,8% The brand can be harmed: 13,5% The brand can be simultaneously favored and harmed: 9,7% Don't know: 10,0%
Perception of Nike as an innovative brand by opening a store in the Metaverse	Yes: 68,1%; No: 17,2%; Don't know: 14,7%
Impact level likelihood on Nike Brand Equity	Very likely: 9,0%; Likely: 38,4%; Neutral: 24,0%; Unlikely: 15,4%; Very unlikely: 3,0%; Don't know: 10,2%
Impact on Nike's brand awareness	Brand awareness increases: 52,4%; Brand awareness stays the same: 25,5%; Decreases: 12,3%; Don't know: 9,8%

When it comes to expectations for metaverse stores, nearly half of the respondents (48,1%) anticipate high-quality products, while 47,4% look forward to excellent customer service. A notable 54,5% expect the stores to be attractively decorated, and 47,7% are hoping for a pleasant store atmosphere.

Interestingly, only a small fraction of respondents don't share these high expectations, saying that they disagree or totally disagree: 13% for product quality, 13,1% for customer service quality, 7,6% for attractive store decoration, and 7,9% for pleasant store atmosphere.

It appears that consumers have high expectations for the immersive environment of metaverse stores. They place a premium on attractive decoration and a pleasant store atmosphere, even more so than on product quality and customer service.

Table 8. Expectations about metaverse stores

Expectations about metaverse stores	
High quality products	Totally Agree: 10,7%; Agree: 37,4%; I neither agree or disagree: 28,2%; Disagree: 10,5%; Totally disagree: 2,5%; Don't know: 11,7%
Quality of customer service	Totally Agree: 10,5%; Agree: 36,9%; I neither agree or disagree: 27,5%; Disagree: 9,9%; Totally disagree: 3,2% ; Don't know: 12,0%
Attractive store decoration	Totally Agree: 14,8%; Agree: 39,7%; I neither agree or disagree: 25,7%; Disagree: 7,2%; Totally disagree: 0,4%; Don't know: 12,2%
Pleasant store atmosphere	Totally Agree: 13,0%; Agree: 34,7%; I neither agree or disagree: 30,2%; Disagree: 6,0%; Totally disagree: 1,9% ; Don't know: 14,2%

Relationships Between Variables: Structural Equation Modelling - Assessment of Reliability

A calculation with PLS-SEM algorithm was performed, using Smart PLS 4.0 software, with Path weighting scheme, and standardized type of results. A Bootstrapping analysis was also performed. Given the nature of formative constructs in our context, the assessment of Reliability Parameters encompassed Cronbach's Alpha, the revised Item-to-Construct Correlation (Rho_a), (Rho_c) and the calculation of average variance extracted (AVE).

Table 9. Reliability indicators

Item	Cronbach Alpha	Rho_a	Rho_c	AVE
Respondent Characterization	0,109	0,632	0,478	0,347
Level of knowledge and use of metaverse	0,152	0,152	0,702	0,541
Nike's_Customers attributes importance	0,910	0,912	0,933	0,763
Customer Loyalty Behavior	0,852	0,852	0,91	0,772
Effects on Nike's brand image	0,861	0,87	0,90	0,644
Expectations about metaverse stores	0,924	0,925	0,937	0,623

For a reliable measurement, Cronbach's Alpha values should ideally fall between 0.7 and 0.95. All constructs meet this criterion, except for "respondent characterization" and "Level of knowledge and use of the metaverse".

Additionally, to ensure robust reliability and internal consistency, Rho_a and Rho_C should exceed 0.7, and the Average Variance Extracted (AVE) should be above 0.5. Again, all constructs adhere to these guidelines, with the exception of "respondent characterization" and "Level of knowledge of the metaverse". In summary, all constructs demonstrate sufficient reliability, except "respondent characterization" and "level of knowledge and use of the metaverse".

PLS-SEM Model Estimation

To estimate the model, the PLS-SEM algorithm was used, and to access the goodness of fit was used the Bootstrapping calculation. The reference values generally accepted for T-Value, F^2, P-Value and R^2 that analyze the quality of model estimation are expressed in table 10.

Table 10. Reference values for the indicators used as criteria of goodness of fit.

Criteria	Reference value
T-Value	Above 1,96
F^2	More than 0,35 – Strong effect Between 0,15 and 0,34 – Moderate effect Between 0,02 and 0,14 – Small effect
P-Value	Below 0,05
R^2	More than 0,67 – Substantial Between 0,33 and 0,66 – Moderate Between 0,19 and 0,32 – Small

Based on the data of our model, the total effects and the values of T-Value, F^2, and P-Value are expressed in table 11. The indicators show that the relationship between "Perceptions of product quality in Nike's metaverse stores --> Expectations about metaverse stores" is not significant, because it doesn't comply the reference values. All the other relationships are significant. The greatest total effect is between Effects on Nike's brand image and expectations about metaverse stores with 0,507. The following is between in Perceptions of product quality in Nike's metaverse stores and Effects on Nike's brand image with a value of 0,358. The following total effects are between Customer loyalty behavior and Expectations about metaverse stores with 0,323, and between Nike's customers' attributes importance and Expectations about metaverse stores with 0,319.

Table 11. Total effects, T-Value, F^2 and P-Value of the coefficients of the model

	Total effects	T-Value	F^2	P-Value
Effects on Nike brand image → Expectation about metaverse stores	0,507	11,69	0,448	0,000
Respondent Characterization →Effects on Nike brand image	0,210	5,909	0,097	0,000
Respondent Characterization →Expectations about metaverse stores	0,203	3,057	0,032	0,002
Level of knowledge and use of metaverse →Effects on Nike brand image	0,133	4,883	0,041	0,000
Level of knowledge and use of metaverse →Expectations about metaverse stores	0,110	2,265	0,007	0,024
Nike's_Customers attributes importance → Effects on Nike brand image	0,276	3,057	0,131	0,002
Nike's_Customers attributes importance → Expectations about metaverse stores	0,319	4,904	0,085	0,000
Customer Loyalty Behavior → Effects on Nike brand image	0,125	2,886	0,026	0,004
Customer Loyalty Behavior → Expectations about metaverse stores	0,323	7,614	0,190	0,000
Perceptions of product quality in Nike's metaverse stores → Effects on Nike's brand image	0,358	9,787	0,207	0,000
Perceptions of product quality in Nike's metaverse stores → Expectations about metaverse stores	0,201	0,275	0,001	0,783

Note: Estimates using PLS-SEM algorithm and Bootstrapping for T-Values and P-Values.

The values of R^2 and Adjusted R^2 are higher than 0,67 for the regression of "Expectations about metaverse stores" indicating a substantial capability of the estimated model to reflect the data. For "Effects on Nike's brand image" the estimated model has a moderate capability to express the data, as the model has R^2 and Adjusted R^2 lower than 0,67.

Table 12. Quality criteria, using R^2 and Adjusted R^2

	R^2	R^2 Adjusted
Effects on Nike's brand image	0,617	0,612
Expectations about metaverse stores	0,78	0,776

The path coefficients of the estimated model are expressed in the table 13. Interestingly all the path coefficients are positive. The constructs "Respondent characterization", "level of knowledge and use of the metaverse", "Nike's customers attributes importance", and "Perceptions of product quality in Nike's metaverse stores" have higher path coefficients for "Effects on Nike's brand image" than in "Expectations about metaverse stores". The construct "Customer loyalty behavior" has higher path coefficient for "Expectations about metaverse stores". The relationship between "Effects on Nike's brand image" and "Expectations about metaverse stores" has the highest path coefficient with a value of 0,507.

Table 13. Path coefficients of estimated model.

	Path coefficients
Effects on Nike's brand image → Expectations about metaverse stores	0,507
Respondent Characterization → Effects on Nike brand image	0,210
Level of knowledge and use of metaverse → Effects on Nike brand image	0,133
Nike's_Customers attributes importance → Effects on Nike brand image	0,276
Customer Loyalty Behavior → Effects on Nike brand image	0,125
Perceptions of product quality in Nike's metaverse stores → Effects on Nike's brand image	0,358
Respondent Characterization → Expectations about metaverse stores	0,096
Level of knowledge and use of metaverse → Expectations about metaverse stores	0,042
Nike's_Customers attributes importance → Expectations about metaverse stores	0,179
Customer Loyalty Behavior → Expectations about metaverse stores	0,259
Perceptions of product quality in Nike's metaverse stores → Expectations about metaverse stores	0,019

Thus, in sum, it seems that the variables "Respondent Characterization" and "Level of Knowledge and use of metaverse" could be defined by more components than the ones used in this model (age, gender, auto-characterization of respondents as innovative persons and main interests for "Respondent characterization", and auto-perception about knowledge of metaverse, metaverse use and specific metaverse platforms for "Level of knowledge and use of the metaverse"). The measurement of these variables can be enhanced with other components and scales.

FUTURE RESEARCH DIRECTIONS

Building on the insights from this study, several future research directions emerge. These directions promise to deepen our understanding of how metaverse retailing shapes brand perception and can guide businesses in effectively leveraging this innovative technology, communication touchpoint, and sales channel. Future research could focus on longitudinal studies to examine how brand perception evolves over time as customers become more familiar with metaverse retailing, using brands like Nike and others as case studies. This approach will reveal the long-term effects and trends of virtual shopping environments. Cross-cultural comparisons could investigate how metaverse retailing impacts brand perception across different cultures and regions, uncovering valuable insights into cultural influences on consumer behavior within virtual environments. Conducting detailed segmentation analyses to understand how various customer segments, such as age groups, income levels, and tech-savviness, perceive brands in the metaverse would also be valuable. This can help in tailoring marketing strategies to specific audiences, benefiting brands like Nike and other retailers. Additionally, exploring how personalized and customized shopping experiences in the metaverse influence brand perception and customer satisfaction can offer strategies to enhance user engagement and loyalty. Delving into consumer trust and security, particularly by scrutinizing how data privacy and security concerns, within the metaverse affect brand perception, would be invaluable. This study would address consumer apprehensions and enhance trust. Examining how brands' sustainability and ethical practices in the metaverse affect consumer perception is another crucial area, as it helps brands position themselves as responsible and conscientious entities in virtual spaces. Investigating the impact of community and social interactions in the metaverse, such as virtual events, community engagement, and group shopping, on brand perception could inform strategies to foster a sense of belonging and community among consumers.

Finally, conducting a comparative analysis of metaverse retailing with physical retail and traditional websites would help identify unique advantages or challenges. Additionally, analyzing and comparing customer loyalty and retention rates across different sales channels could provide comprehensive insights into consumer behavior.

CONCLUSION

Theoretical Contributions

This study offers several significant contributions to the literature. It identifies the primary impacts on brand image associated with Nike's presence in the metaverse, particularly through Nikeland, and highlights consumers' expectations for Nike's stores. Nike's foray into the metaverse with Nikeland has reinforced its perception as an innovative pioneer, enhanced its brand image, increased brand awareness, and improved brand equity. Thus, other retailers could similarly benefit by establishing a presence in the metaverse, especially if they are early entrants in their respective categories.

Consumers' main expectations for metaverse stores include attractive store decoration, high-quality products, a pleasant store atmosphere, and excellent customer service. Therefore, it is crucial for retailers to invest in the quality of their metaverse stores and environments, including both décor and the provision of high-quality products, whether exclusive to the metaverse or not. Selecting the best store designs, such as flagship stores in the metaverse, with a well-displayed product assortment and opportunities for customization and personalization is fundamental. Notably, a significant number of consumers currently lack specific expectations due to the nascent stage of the metaverse. Consequently, retailers need to educate consumers, allowing them to experience metaverse stores to enhance their knowledge of this technology. The relationship between the perceived impact of Nike's metaverse presence on its brand image and consumer expectations for metaverse stores is very significant, indicating that changes in brand image due to metaverse presence affect consumer expectations for metaverse stores. As retailers aim to become fully omni-channel, the enhanced brand image due to metaverse presence will also influence expectations across all stores, including physical locations, traditional websites, and apps.

The factors affecting brand image include the perception of product quality in metaverse stores, the importance of Nike's customer attributes, respondent characterization, level of knowledge and use of the metaverse, and customer loyalty behavior. Retailers need to address all these variables, with particular emphasis on product quality in metaverse stores, as it has the highest impact. Additionally, the more demanding consumers are regarding attributes, the greater the impact on brand image.

Finally, the factors influencing consumers' expectations for metaverse stores, with the highest significance, are the effects on Nike's brand image, customer loyalty behavior, and the importance of Nike's customer attributes. Thus, consumer expectations for metaverse stores increase with changes in brand image due to metaverse presence, more loyal customers, and more demanding consumers regarding attributes. Table 14 specifically details the findings related to each formulated research question.

Table 14. Research questions and main findings summary

Research questions	Findings
Research question 1: How does Nike's presence in the metaverse, specifically through Nikeland, impact its brand image?	Most of respondents believe that brand improved its innovative character with the presence in the metaverse. Most of respondents believe that brand image can be favored, highlighting the innovative character of the brand. Most of respondents also believe that the brand awareness increases due to its presence on metaverse, and about a quarter of respondents believe it will stay the same. Almost, half of respondents believe that metaverse stores probably impacts Nike's brand equity.
Research question 2: What are consumers' expectations regarding Nike's metaverse stores?	The main expectations of consumers are regarding an attractive store decoration, followed by high quality products, pleasant store atmosphere and quality of customer experience respectively. It is also interesting the high number of respondents that don't know or don't have expectations about the store, being neutral.
Research question 3: What is the relationship between the impact of Nike's metaverse presence on its brand image and consumer expectations of metaverse stores?	The perceptions of impact in brand image caused by metaverse presence influence the consumers' expectations of metaverse stores. The model highlighted a very strong relationship between the constructs. The total effects coefficient was the highest in the model, with significant T-Values, P-values and F^2.

continued on following page

Table 14. Continued

Research questions	Findings
Research question 4: Which factors - such as respondent characterization, metaverse knowledge and usage, the importance of Nike's customer attributes, customer loyalty behaviors, and perceptions of product quality in Nike's metaverse store - significantly influence Nike's brand image?	The variables "respondent characterization" and "level of knowledge and use of metaverse were considered not reliable, and need some improvements in terms of the scales and questions used to measure them. Although this, all the factors were considered significant in terms of the total effects. The perception of product quality in metaverse stores was the variable with the highest coefficient, followed by Nike's customers' attributes importance, respondent characterization, level of knowledge and use of metaverse and customer loyalty behavior respectively.
Research question 5: Which factors - such as respondent characterization, metaverse knowledge and usage, the importance of Nike's customer attributes, customer loyalty behaviors, and perceptions of product quality in Nike's metaverse store - significantly affect consumer expectations of metaverse stores?	The variables "respondent characterization" and "level of knowledge and use of metaverse were considered not reliable, and need some improvements in terms of the scales and questions used to measure them. Although this, the factor "Effects on Nike brand image" had the biggest impact on customer expectations about Nike's metaverse stores, followed by "customer loyalty behavior", Nike's customers attributes importance, and respondent characterization and level of knowledge and use of the metaverse, respectively. The factor "Perceptions of product quality in Nike's metaverse stores" was considered not significant as it has a P-Value bigger than 0,05.

Managerial Contributions

This research sheds light on valuable insights for retailers aiming to establish their presence in the metaverse. Through the lens of the NIKE case study, retailers can either lay the groundwork for their ventures into the metaverse or enhance their current virtual storefronts.

The study provides a clear view of how a presence in the metaverse impacts a retailer's global brand image, also emphasizing the omni-channel value in retail.

Moreover, it reveals consumer expectations for retailers' metaverse presence, guiding the development of compelling and successful virtual strategies. The analysis of the relationship between brand image and consumer expectations uncovers crucial consequences of brand image effects stemming from metaverse retailing on consumer perceptions of the brand.

The research also underscores the importance of respondent characterization, metaverse knowledge and usage, key customer attributes of Nike, customer loyalty behaviors, and perceptions of product quality in Nike's metaverse store. These factors play a pivotal role in the evolution of brand image and customer expectations driven by metaverse presence. This information equips retail managers with strategic insights on target demographics and how to refine their metaverse experiences, spotlighting the opportunities, threats, and challenges posed by this innovative sales and communication channel.

Limitations

This research has several limitations that must be considered. The sample included only Portuguese and Brazilian respondents since the survey was in Portuguese language. Respondents from other countries could have different cultural aspects and levels of engagement with metaverse platforms, potentially influencing the results. Different studies have highlighted the importance of cultural aspects in metaverse adhesion and impacts (Trunfio & Rossi, 2022; Hennig-Thurau et al., 2023), that this work does not address.

Also the data collection was solely conducted using social media platforms, which may not provide a comprehensive representation of the broader population and could introduce biases related to the demographics and behaviors of social media users.

The methodology relied on data collected through surveys. Including focus groups and in-depth interviews could provide richer, qualitative insights.

Regarding the data obtained, the characterization of respondents and their level of knowledge and use of the metaverse are constructs that could be improved with new and complementary variables, as they do not align with the reference intervals for reliability indicators in structural equation modelling. Many respondents lacked significant knowledge and experience with the metaverse and its functionalities, which may have skewed the results.

A more informed sample could have a deeper understanding of the metaverse's impact on brand image.

Additionally, various models and scales that could have been used to assess brand image perception, such as the Retailer Equity Index, were not utilized.

The impact of each component of the metaverse store environment on the retailer's brand image was also not analyzed.

For Nike, this study was conducted over a specific period and did not analyze changes over time or the activities promoted by the retailer in its metaverse store. Furthermore, impacts on sales, market share, profitability, and cost-benefit analyses of retailers' presence in the metaverse were not examined.

The findings reported in this exploratory study are confined to the initiatives undertaken by Nike through this case study analysis to evaluate brand image impacts.

REFERENCES

Aaker, D. A. (1991). *Managing brand equity: Capitalizing on the value of a brand name*. Free Press.

Abumalloh, R. A., Nilashi, M., Ooi, K. B., Wei-Han, G., Cham, T. H., Dwivedi, Y. K., & Hughes, L. (2023). The adoption of metaverse in the retail industry and its impact on sustainable competitive advantage: Moderating impact of sustainability commitment. *Annals of Operations Research*, 342(1), 5–46. DOI: 10.1007/s10479-023-05608-8

Alic, A., Agic, E., & Činjarević, M. (2017). The Importance of Store Image and Retail Service Quality in Private Brand Image-Building. *Entrepreneurial Business and Economics Review*, 5(1), 27–42. DOI: 10.15678/EBER.2017.050102

Anselmsson, J., Burt, S., & Tunca, B. (2017). An integrated retailer image and brand equity framework: Re-examining, extending, and restructuring retailer brand equity. *Journal of Retailing and Consumer Services*, 38, 194–203. DOI: 10.1016/j.jretconser.2017.06.007

Bolton, R. N., Gustafsson, A., Tarasi, C. O., & Witell, L. (2022). Designing satisfying service encounters: Website versus store touchpoints. *Journal of the Academy of Marketing Science*, 50(1), 85–107. DOI: 10.1007/s11747-021-00808-9 PMID: 34608342

Bruni, R., Colamatteo, A., & Mladenović, D. (2023). How the metaverse influences marketing and competitive advantage of retailers: Predictions and key marketing research priorities. *Electronic Commerce Research*, 24(2), 965–982. DOI: 10.1007/s10660-023-09779-1

Candelon, F., Jacobides, M. G., Courtaux, M., & Nahas, G. (2022). How to take a strategic approach to investing in metaverses. 28th November. *World Economic Forum*. Retrieved 21th January 2024, from https://www.weforum.org/stories/2022/11/how-to-a-take-a-strategic-to-approach-to-investing-in-metaverses/

Carter, R. (2023). What is Nike's Metaverse? *An Introduction to Nikeland*. Retrieved 15th October 2024, from https://www.xrtoday.com/mixed-reality/what-is-nikes-metaverse-an-introduction-to-nikeland/

Chen, A. H., Wu, R.Y. (2022). Mediating Effect of Brand Image and Satisfaction on Loyalty through Experiential Marketing: A Case Study of a Sugar Heritage Destination. *Sustainability*, 14.

Cuong, D. T. (2022). The Relationship Between Product Quality, Brand Image, Purchase Decision, and Repurchase Intention. *Proceedings of International Conference on Emerging Technologies and Intelligent Systems. ICETIS 2021. Lecture Notes in Networks and Systems*, 299. DOI: 10.1007/978-3-030-82616-1_44

De Vigan, A. (2022). Stepping Into the Metaverse: How Retailers can Prepare. *Forbes Technology Council*. Retrieved 20th January 2025, from https://www.forbes.com/councils/forbestechcouncil/2022/11/16/stepping-into-the-metaverse-how-retailers-can-prepare/

Ferraro, C., Sands, S., Demsar, V., & Cohen, J. (2024). Diversity Representation in Virtual Environments: How Brand Motives Mediate Consumer Perceptions. *Australasian Marketing Journal*, 32(3), 239–249. DOI: 10.1177/14413582241244535

Fianto, A., Widyantara, H., & Baskara, D. (2022). Analisis Mediasi Brand Awareness dan Brand Trust dalam Hubungan Emotional Marketing dengan Purchase Intention. *Jurnal Manajemen dan Kewirausahaan*, 7(2), 47-59.

Fuller, A., Fan, Z., Day, C., & Barlow, C. (2020). Digital Twin: Enabling Technologies, Challenges and Open Research. *IEEE Access : Practical Innovations, Open Solutions*, 8, 108952–108971. DOI: 10.1109/ACCESS.2020.2998358

Gartner Inc. (2022). *Gartner predicts 25% of People Will Spend at least One Hour per Day in the Metaverse by 2026 -Metaverse Hype to Transition into New Business Models that Extend Digital Business*. Retrieved 15th August 2024, from https://www.gartner.com/en/newsroom/press-releases/2022-02-07-gartner-predicts-25-percent-of-people-will-spend-at-least-one-hour-per-day-in-the-metaverse-by-2026

Hair, J. F., Hult, G. T. M., Ringle, C. M., Sarstedt, M., Danks, N. P., & Ray, S. (2021). An Introduction to Structural Equation Modeling. In *Partial Least Squares Structural Equation Modeling (PLS-SEM) Using R. Classroom Companion: Business*. Springer. DOI: 10.1007/978-3-030-80519-7_1

Hennig-Thurau, T., Aliman, D. N., Herting, A. M., Cziehso, G. P., Linder, M., & Kubler, R. V. (2023). Social interactions in the Metaverse: Framework, initial evidence, and research roadmap. *Journal of the Academy of Marketing Science*, 51(4), 889–913. DOI: 10.1007/s11747-022-00908-0

Hübner, A. H., Kuhn, H., & Wollenburg, J. (2016). Last mile fulfilment and distribution in omni-channel grocery retailing: A strategic planning framework. *International Journal of Retail & Distribution Management*, 44(3). Advance online publication. DOI: 10.1108/IJRDM-11-2014-0154

Interbrand. (2023). *Best Global Brands 2023: How iconic brands Lead across Arenas*. Retrieved 20 August 2024 from https://interbrand.com/best-global-brands/

Jara, M., & Cliquet, G. (2012). Retail brand equity: Conceptualization and measurement. *Journal of Retailing and Consumer Services*, 19(1), 140–149. DOI: 10.1016/j.jretconser.2011.11.003

Jasrotia, S. S. (2023). Technological Innovations in Interactive Marketing: Enhancing Customer Experience at the New Retail Age. In Wang, C. L. (Ed.), *The Palgrave Handbook of Interactive Marketing*. Palgrave Macmillan. DOI: 10.1007/978-3-031-14961-0_8

Keller, K. L. (1993). Conceptualizing, measuring, and managing customer-based brand equity. *Journal of Marketing*, 57(1), 1–22. DOI: 10.1177/002224299305700101

Keller, K. L. (2020). Consumer Research Insights on Brands and Branding: A JCR Curation. *The Journal of Consumer Research*, 46(5), 995–1001. DOI: 10.1093/jcr/ucz058

Kermanshachi, S., Nipa, T. J., & Nadiri, H. (2023). Correction: Service quality assessment and enhancement using Kano model. *PLoS One*, 18(10), e0293766. DOI: 10.1371/journal.pone.0293766 PMID: 37883348

Kozinets, R. V. (2023). Immersive netnography: A novel method for service experience research in virtual reality, augmented reality and metaverse contexts. *Journal of Service Management*, 34(1), 100–125. DOI: 10.1108/JOSM-12-2021-0481

Lin, B., Kim, G., Moore, M., & Rothenberg, L. (2021). Consumer store experience through virtual reality: Its effect on emotional states and perceived store attractiveness. *Fashion and Textiles*, 8(19), 2–21.

Londoño, J. C., Elms, J., & Davies, K. (2016). Conceptualising and measuring consumer-based brand–retailer–channel equity. *Journal of Retailing and Consumer Services*, 29, 70–81. DOI: 10.1016/j.jretconser.2015.11.004

Lopes, T. S. A., Carreira, R., Carlos, V., Pereira, R., Alves, C., Pratas, J., & Santos, J. P. (2024). How Can Businesses, Low-Tech Businesses in Particular, Benefit from the Metaverse? A Delphi Perspective from Academics. In *Marketing and Smart Technologies. ICMarkTech 2023. Smart Innovation, Systems and Technologies* (vol. 386). Springer.

Madni, A., Madni, C., & Lucero, S. (2019). Leveraging digital twin technology in model-based systems engineering. *Systems*, 7(1), 7–19. DOI: 10.3390/systems7010007

Maizi, Y., & Bendavid, Y. (2019). Leveraging on the Digital Twin for improving retail store daily operations management. *Proceedings of the 18th International Conference on Modelling and Applied Simulation*, 92-100. DOI: 10.46354/i3m.2019.mas.013

Marr, B. (2022). *Nikeland, el espacio en el que Nike construye su metaverso en Roblox*. Retrieved 16th August 2024 from https://forbes.pe/negocios/2022-06-13/nikeland-el-espacio-en-el-que-nike-construye-su-metaverso-en-roblox

Martineau, P. (1958). The Personality of the Retail Store. *Harvard Business Review*, 36(1), 47–55.

Ndengane, R. M., Mason, R. B., & Mutize, M. (2021). The influence of Store Atmospherics on customers' satisfaction at selected South African retail outlets. *Innovative Marketing*, 17(1), 26–39. DOI: 10.21511/im.17(1).2021.03

Pantano, E., & Willems, K. (2022). *Introduction. Retail in a New World*. Emerald Publishing Limited.

Parris, D. L., & Guzmán, F. (2023). Evolving brand boundaries and expectations: Looking back on brand equity, brand loyalty, and brand image research to move forward. *Journal of Product and Brand Management*, 32(2), 191–234. DOI: 10.1108/JPBM-06-2021-3528

Paspalj, A. (2022). *Nike Ventures Into web3 With Exciting Metaverse Platform.* Swoosh. DesignRush, Retrieved 16th November 2024 from https://www.designrush.com/news/nike-swoosh-metaverse-platform

Plumeyer, A., Kottemann, P., Böger, D., & Decker, R. (2019). Measuring brand image: A systematic review, practical guidance, and future research directions. *Review of Managerial Science*, 13(2), 227–265. DOI: 10.1007/s11846-017-0251-2

Pratas, J. (2023). Metaverse and Digital Twins: An Opportunity to Increase Retailers' Profitability? An Exploratory Research Using Nike Case Study and Retail Managers' In-Depth Interviews. In *Management and Marketing for Improved Retail Competitiveness and Performance.* IGI Global Publisher.

Pratas, J., & Amorim, C. (2022). Consumer Research Shopping and Buying Behaviors in Sports Footwear Omni-Channel Retailing: A Conceptual Model. In Reis, J. L., Peter, M. K., Cayolla, R., & Bogdanović, Z. (Eds.), *Marketing and Smart Technologies. Smart Innovation, Systems and Technologies* (Vol. 280). Springer. DOI: 10.1007/978-981-16-9272-7_25

Pratas, J., Amorim, C., & Reis, J. L. (2022). Smart Retailing Technologies Impact in Brand Leadership and Market Performance: A Conceptual Model. In Reis, J. L., Peter, M. K., Cayolla, R., & Bogdanović, Z. (Eds.), *Marketing and Smart Technologies. Smart Innovation, Systems and Technologies* (Vol. 280). Springer. DOI: 10.1007/978-981-16-9272-7_26

Pratas, J., & Brito, P. (2019). *Distribuição - Gestão de pontos de venda e de retalho - Gestão eficiente do negócio*. Actual Editora.

Pratas, J., & Oliveira, Z. (2023). QR Codes Research in Marketing: A Bibliometric and Content Analysis. In Reis, J. L., Peter, M. K., Varela González, J. A., & Bogdanović, Z. (Eds.), *Marketing and Smart Technologies. Smart Innovation, Systems and Technologies* (Vol. 337). Springer. DOI: 10.1007/978-981-19-9099-1_19

Qamar, A., Anwar, Z., & Afzal, M. (2023). A systematic threat analysis and defense strategies for the Metaverse and extended reality systems. *Computers & Security*, 128(c), 103127. DOI: 10.1016/j.cose.2023.103127

Rosenblum, P., & Kilcourse, B. (2013). *Omni-channel 2013-the long road to adoption*. RSR Research.

Saridakis, G., Khan, Z., Knight, G., Idris, B., Mitra, J., & Khan, H. (2024). A Look into the Future: The Impact of Metaverse on Traditional Theories and Thinking in International Business. *MIR. Management International Review*, 64(4), 597–632. DOI: 10.1007/s11575-024-00550-8

Schulz, M. (2023). *Nike takes gaming to next level with metaverse space in Fortnite*. Vogue Business, Retrieved 20th June 2024 from https://www.voguebusiness.com/technology/nike-takes-gaming-to-next-level-with-metaverse-space-in-fortnite

Shi, F., Ning, H., Zhang, X., Li, R., Tian, Q., Zhang, S., Zheng, Y., Guo, Y., & Daneshmand, M. (2023). A new technology perspective of the Metaverse: Its essence, framework and challenges. *Digital Communications and Networks*.

Shi, S., Wang, Y., Chen, X., & Zhang, Q. (2020). Conceptualization of omnichannel customer experience and its impact on shopping intention: A mixed-method approach. *International Journal of Information Management*, 50, 325–336. DOI: 10.1016/j.ijinfomgt.2019.09.001

Singh, Y., Sujay, D., Shandilya, S. K., & Shandilya, S. (2024). The Metaverse: A Multidisciplinary Perspective on the Future of Human Interaction. In Jabbar, M. A., Tiwari, S., Ortiz-Rodríguez, F., Groppe, S., & Bano Rehman, T. (Eds.), *Applied Machine Learning and Data Analytics. AMLDA 2023. Communications in Computer and Information Science* (Vol. 2047). Springer. DOI: 10.1007/978-3-031-55486-5_3

Soliman, M. M., Ahmed, E., Darwish, A., & Hassanien, A. E. (2024). Artificial intelligence powered Metaverse: Analysis, challenges and future perspectives. *Artificial Intelligence Review*, 57(2), 36. DOI: 10.1007/s10462-023-10641-x

Spatial Awareness by Kharis. (2022). Just Do It. *An Overview of Nike's web3 strategy*. Retrieved 5th August from https://mirror.xyz/kahris.eth/eMIy5BgXnbEUcakM0EKYkgsbcTe6w8KJ8Aa65-eLogk

Statista. (2023). *Potential concerns in the metaverse according to internet users in the United States as of March 2022*. Retrieved 10th August from https://www.statista.com/statistics/1303391/us-adults-potential-metaverse-issues/

Timmermans, H. (1993). Retail Environments and Spatial Shopping Behavior. In Tommy, G., & Reginald, G. G. (Eds.), *Advances in Psychology* (Vol. 96, pp. 342–377). North-Holland.

Trunfio, M., & Rossi, S. (2022). Advances in Metaverse Investigation: Streams of Research and Future Agenda. *Virtual Worlds*, 1(2), 103–129. DOI: 10.3390/virtualworlds1020007

Tu, Y. T., Lin, S. Y., & Hsu, T. K. (2013). The Impact of Brand Image and Customer Commitment on Loyalty: An Empirical Study of Automobile Sector. *International Management and Business Review*, 5(4), 191–193.

Waters, S. (2019). *Why Store Atmosphere Matters to Your Customers*. Retrieved 11th August 2024 from https://www.liveabout.com/atmosphere-2890162

ADDITIONAL READING

Cheah, I., & Shimul, A. S. (2023). Marketing in the metaverse: Moving forward – What's next? *Journal of Global Scholars of Marketing Science*, 33(1), 1–10. DOI: 10.1080/21639159.2022.2163908

Hanji, S. V., Navalgund, N., Hanji, S. S., Jeyanthi, P. M., Raikar, R. V., & Pol, N. (2024). Immersive Experiences and Brand Recall in the Metaverse: A Comparative Analysis of Virtual Reality and 3D Interfaces. In Senjyu, T., So–, C., & Joshi, A. (Eds.), *Smart Trends in Computing and Communications. SmartCom 2024. Lecture Notes in Networks and Systems, 946*. Springer. DOI: 10.1007/978-981-97-1323-3_21

Ritterbusch, G. D., & Teichmann, M. (2023). Defining the Metaverse: A Systematic Literature Review. *IEEE Access : Practical Innovations, Open Solutions*, 11, 11. DOI: 10.1109/ACCESS.2023.3241809

Santoso, H. B., Windasari, N. A., & Wang, J. C. (2024). Avatar Manipulation in Metaverse: The Consequences on Customer-Brand Relationships in Tourism. In Rather, R. A. (Ed.), *Consumer Brand Relationships in Tourism. Tourism, Hospitality & Event Management*. Springer. DOI: 10.1007/978-3-031-59535-6_4

Sebastian, G. (2023). A Descriptive Study on Metaverse: Cybersecurity Risks, Controls, and Regulatory Framework. *International Journal of Security and Privacy in Pervasive Computing*, 15(1), 1–14.

Shen, J., Zhou, X., Wu, W., Wang, L., & Chen, Z. (2023). Worldwide Overview and Country Differences in Metaverse Research: A Bibliometric Analysis. *Sustainability (Basel)*, 15(4), 3541. DOI: 10.3390/su15043541

Soni, L., Kaur, A., & Sharma, A. (2023). A Review of Metaverse and Immersive Technologies. In *Third International Conference on Artificial Intelligence and Smart Energy (ICAIS)* (pp. 924-928). DOI: 10.1109/ICAIS56108.2023.10073666

Zhang, G., Cao, J., Liu, D., & Qi, J. (2022). Popularity of the metaverse: Embodied social presence theory perspective. *Frontiers in Psychology*, 13, 997751. DOI: 10.3389/fpsyg.2022.997751 PMID: 36248483

KEY TERMS AND DEFINITIONS

Augmented Reality: Is the real-time integration of digital information into a user's environment. Augmented reality overlays content onto the real world, enriching a user's perception of reality rather than replacing it. This can include 3D models, images or videos, blending digital and physical worlds seamlessly.

Brand Equity: Is the value and strength of a brand that results from consumer perception, experiences, and associations. It encompasses elements like brand loyalty, name recognition, perceived quality, and brand associations. Strong brand equity translates into significant competitive advantages, such as the ability to charge premium prices, customer loyalty, and greater market share. Essentially, it reflects the overall worth of a brand in the eyes of consumers.

Brand Image: Is the set of beliefs, ideas, and impressions that consumers hold about a brand. It is the overall perception that the public has towards a brand, formed through various interactions and experiences with the brand, including its marketing communications, customer service, product quality, and overall reputation. A strong brand image can lead to increased customer loyalty, trust, and a competitive advantage in the marketplace.

Metaverse: Is a collective virtual shared space, created by the convergence of virtually enhanced physical reality and physically persistent virtual space, including the sum of all virtual worlds, augmented reality, and the internet. The metaverse is a blend of various digital environments where users can interact, socialize, work, and play in immersive ways.

Metaverse Retailing: It defines the practice of selling products and services within a virtual, immersive environment created by the convergence of augmented reality (AR), virtual reality (VR), and the internet. This digital space allows businesses, namely retailers to create engaging, interactive experiences that mirror or enhance real-world retail scenarios, offering customers unique and personalized shopping experiences.

Nikeland: Is a "micro metaverse" built within the Roblox ecosystem designed by Nike. It offers a 3D space where users can explore a virtual environment inspired by Nike's real-world headquarters, try on virtual products, buy non-fungible tokens (NFTs), participate in mini-games, and earn rewards.

Omni-Channel Retailing: Is a strategy adopted by retailers that give to the customers a seamless and integrated shopping experience across various channels, both online and offline. It involves creating a cohesive and consistent brand presence across multiple platforms, such as physical stores, websites, mobile apps, and social media, and other stores such as metaverse stores allowing customers to interact, purchase, and receives services in a way that is convenient and personalized to their preferences.

Retailer Brand Image: Refers to the perception and mental impression that consumers hold about a retail brand. It encompasses various elements such as the quality of products, customer service, store environment, pricing, and overall shopping experience. A strong retailer brand image can influence consumer loyalty, trust, and their overall shopping behavior, often setting the retailer apart from its competitors in the market.

Chapter 7
Revolutionizing Retail: Enhancing Customer Experiences With the Metaverse

Muhammad Usman Tariq
https://orcid.org/0000-0002-7605-3040
Abu Dhabi University, UAE & University College Cork, Ireland

EXECUTIVE SUMMARY

This chapter investigates how the metaverse has affected the retail sector profoundly. It explores how immersive interactive experiences are being created from traditional shopping through the use of technologies like virtual reality (VR), augmented reality (AR), and extended reality (XR). Retailers can engage customers in novel and exciting ways, improving their overall experience by providing virtual stores and personalized environments. The chapter describes how the metaverse has developed in the retail industry and provides examples of creative business concepts and profitable endeavors. It also examines how customer behavior is evolving in virtual environments and emphasizes the advantages of incorporating metaverse components into traditional retail procedures. Furthermore, the chapter highlights the significance of calculating return on investment (ROI) for these endeavors and tackles significant ethical and privacy issues that retailers need to consider.

INTRODUCTION

The metaverse is the global augmented reality (AR) and virtual reality (VR) environment coupled with artificial digital interactions that could radically transform many industries and sectors, including the retail sector. It describes virtual environments where persons conduct operations in real time as well as interact with others. The emergence of the metaverse enables to introduce a new kind of

DOI: 10.4018/979-8-3693-7245-6.ch007

shopping experiences that cannot be discussed in the framework of e-commerce. Using technologies like AR and VR, retailers can create digital stores which can be browser, product can be tested, even the salesperson can be interacted from home as per the scenario depicted by Batat (2024), Dinh (2023). Metaverse technology has been implemented in the retailers' sales strategies, mainly because of its capability of enhancing and personalizing consumers' experiences. For example, some brands can come up with virtual replicas of tangible products, to make the customer understand how the items will appear in the real world. This approach helps customers to make better decisions, thereby increasing their satisfaction with the purchases that they have made (Rane, 2023). Besides, shopping can be made to be more like a game where people can attend a virtual event or the launch of a particular product in the metaverse, increasing engagement. Such interactivities are the inclusion of metaverse features that make the transition to the metaverse appealing for the future of retail (Park, Maddirala, & Eckert, 2023).

Apart from improving the entertainment value of the shop, the metaverse provides brand new ways of tracking customer activities. This information can be used to formulate marketing policies, include the rights offers and improve customer relations; all of which are critical success factors in the current retail business environment. In the virtual setup of the metaverse, retailers can obtain more data on how their customers engage with their products and services hence enhancing their advertising and customer retention (Singla, Shalender, & Singh, 2024). The chapter focuses on the various risks that retailers might face in while adopting metaverse technologies including the technical constraints which are increasingly becoming a major challenge, privacy and security issues, and the requirement of a huge capital investment in implementing the new technology (Koohang et al., 2023). To this end, through the integration of these innovations, the metaverse offers retailers an opportunity to redesign their business models to adapt the changing expectations of the contemporary consumers (Mehrotra et al., 2024). It is clearly important to outline the goals of the chapter as well as its scope in the sequence of the play (Tariq, 2025a).

Consumer Experience Improvement is the key area of the metaverse to be discussed in detail in this chapter to bring visibility to the retail business. It will categorize the different technologies that fuel the metaverse, which is AR/VR and evaluate the application of these technologies in the retail segment. In other words, the chapter will discuss how the metaverse can pose benefits and risks to retailers in the age of customer acquisition and retention in the digital environment which was predicted by Tavman in 2024. This chapter seeks to focus on the following research question; what strategies retailers can adopt to extend the metaverse to enhance customer relations and satisfaction. It will examine strategies from major industries that have implemented metaverse platforms in their value chains with special focus on advantages and challenges. The chapter will also include information on what challenges can metaverse respond to new customer expectations, including personalization, environmental and social issues (Kulova, Nikolova-Alexieva, & Paskalev, 2024). This chapter's content may also cover other aspects of metaverse application in retail, such as customer experience. Some of the areas that will be under discussion include the application of AR and VR in virtual stores, the elements of fun gaming, and social connection/motion that adds value to the shopping processes and combining the real and virtual shopping sphere (phygital). Additionally, this chapter will outline how metaverse technology is influencing retail marketing, advancing in details of using consumer behavior for targeted marketing (Buhalis, Leung & Lin, 2023).

Customer experience has now emerged as one of the key success factors that any retail firm ought to consider. As was highlighted earlier, competition in the retail business has increased and customer options are unlimited; therefore, it is imperative for the retailer to ensure that the customer's shopping experience is as beneficial and enjoyable as possible. Retailers get a chance in the metaverse to interact with their clients in a way that creates unique experiences that a competitor cannot copy (Chaudhuri, Titus, & Chaudhuri, 2024). Through digitalized environments that replicate actual shopping experiences, the retailers can therefore push the bar and meet the evolving expectations of the modern consumer who demands convenience, engagement and novelty in his/her shopping experience (Rane et al., 2023). There is therefore a need to improve the customer experience to help retailers transform for the new customer. The e-commerce market forced the consumer to get a single, unified window to shop at the physical store as well as online store and/or through an application. Thus, the metaverse helps the retailers to break down the division between real physical buying and virtual purchasing and offers the phygital interaction, which is a positive combination of both worlds (Batat, 2024). For example, customers can take products in a physical store, use them and then pay for them online, or vice versa. This integration offers a more flexible and convenient shopping experience of the products, and this has been considered paramount today which is characterized by rampant technological advancements. (Singha & Singha, 2024).

Lastly, with the help of the metaverse retailers can build better emotional relationship with customers. Trade is seen to be a more clinical social interface wherein, in most conventional different multichannel selling contexts, customers and retailers only come into contact when making a purchase. But in the metaverse, retailers can design the stores that represent themselves and their values, so customers would be able to feel themselves in the brand's universe. However, in the context of the metaverse, retailers are free to design spaces that align with their brand's principles and ethos, allowing customers to experience stores as they are a part of a brand's universe. For instance, for a fashion retailer, it can design an augmented/fashion show being held in the form of a virtual platform where customers can get a glimpse of the fashion designer's new collection and shop from there or a home decor retailer can create a virtual home tour where customers can see how products from the store will look like when placed in real homes (Golf-Papez et al., 2022). The above forms of immersion can result in greater customer identification with the brand and high levels of satisfaction (Khaliq & Manda, 2024).

The other essential advantage of improving the customer experience by adopting the metaverse is that customers can be reached at a personal level. Mobile shopping repertories elaborate the concept of metaverse technologies like AR and VR brings a social perspective towards customization of shopping characteristics as per the consumer's preferred behaviors. For example, they might be promoted similar products to those they've previously bought or even be led through a virtual shop (Ball, 2022). Such a level of personalization enhances the overall shopping experience while helping the retailers to foster long-term relationships with their customers through demonstrating that they need and are valued (Mehrotra et al., 2024)., the need to improve the customer experience cannot be overstated, as it is the key strength that can help retailers and brands attract and retain target and potential customers in an increasingly digital-focused environment. Thus, launching metaverse, retailers can stand out from the competition and form long term relationships with consumers (Kulova, Nikolova-Alexieva & Paskalev, 2024). Therefore, with time, it may be expected that customer experience will further dominate the metaverse retail environment further developing into a new norm that is supported by immersive and personalized experiences (Koohang et al., 2023). This means that retailers who can embrace these changes and use the metaverse effectively will be prepared for the future of retailing. The metaverse is a promising concept that can revolutionize the retail industry since it allows retailers to provide customers with better and individualized experiences. By adopting extended reality and other IT tools into its design, the metaverse helps retailers address the new generation's consumption expectations and collect additional information for enhancing marketing experiences and building better customer bonds. In view of the forthcoming changes in the structure of the retail business through the more efficient use of web-based technologies, the metaverse will be an essential component of future customer experience, how retailers can effectively compete for the consumer's patronage in the near-distant future (Batat, 2024; Rane, 2023).

BACKGROUND

The metaverse is a relatively new concept which includes AR/VR environments where people can collaborate and interact using blockchain and other elements of new digital technology. Users can communicate with other customers and digital products, and this communication can sometimes be instantaneous, creating a sense of people interacting with an object. Unlike conventional virtual environments that are typical for current Internet services, the metaverse is less distinct from the real world. In retail, the metaverse enables formation of virtual stores, an area where customers can browse through products, test the products, wear the products, among other things (Chaudhuri, Titus & Chaudhuri, 2024). Using immersive technologies, retailers are creating new ways of interacting with clients that will create new approaches to the conventional e-commerce model. The term metaverse is based on two important foundations, which include interaction and immersion. While it is normal for customers to go online and check out various products online, customers can go to virtual shops where they are able to move and 'walk' around the shops in a three-dimensional manner. For example, a clothing retailer is making it possible for users to have a fitting via avatars and see how they will look when wearing clothes in real-time (Singha & Singha, 2024). Personalised avatar where the clothes appear on the customer's figure as near to the real size as possible is an additional advantage (Tariq, 2024a).

This idea of how virtual environments is not limited to having individual products that are incorporated into the virtual space but how entire ecosystems become virtual, so that customer can attend virtual events or product launches and even be able to have meetings with virtual sales representatives from the comfort of their own homes (Mehrotra et al., 2024). Another feature which can be also discussed is the increase of the interactivity level compared to traditional online shopping, which is considered one of the main distinctive features of the metaverse. The changes in the metaverse in the retail business are related to developments in information technologies. The first attempt to implement digital environments in stores was aimed mainly at the provision of virtual stores through electronic commerce platforms. Retailers on the other hand have been reactive to the latest trends in technology including AR and VR. They help retailers interact with the customers in a more efficient way which includes for instance letting the customers feel how a particular product feels like before they buy it (Batat, 2024).

An area where brands have transitioned towards this way of operating is the furniture industry which has adopted AR applications that enable customers to see how a specific piece of furniture would look in their home, such as IKEA. Such experience is useful to make a transition between the store visits and the online shopping services to assist consumers to make the right decisions while purchasing items without necessarily visiting the physical stores (Rane, 2023). Besides, there is proof that blockchain technology has had an impact on the growth of the metaverse in retail. The advent of blockchain means the development of digital property, for example, non-fungible tokens, which can be bought, sold and traded within virtual spheres. As seen earlier, there are a lot of retailers who have incorporated NFTs

(Non-fungible token) in their strategies as a means of providing customers with unique digital goods. For instance, fashion companies have released digital wearable products which are made available for purchase and can be used as NFT such as a symbol of identity or self-actualization within the social media platform (Khaliq & Manda, 2024). The involvement of NFT and other blockchain-derived application in the metaverse also brings another layer of value for the customers, by being able to own distinctive digital assets that can further augment their online lives. Over time, more and more retailers are realizing the various benefits of the metaverse as part of their business models (Tariq, 2025b).

To this extent, the following is an evaluation of some of the advantages of implementing SCM (supply chain management) with reference to the offering of customized shopping experiences. The use of customer data allows the retailer to create shopping experiences in the metaverse that are aligned to the custom's preferences and behavior. For instance, virtual stores can be made to present those products to the customers that may interest them most, depending on how they have been shopping in the past (Mehrotra et al., 2024). Such a level of customization is impossible in the physical network and is usually constrained in conventional web-based stores. Due to the open environment of the metaverse, customers can have a closer look at products before purchasing any of them, hence increasing their chances of purchasing the products. Yet another advantage is the exposure that is accorded the retailers who can easily penetrate international markets and access customers from across the world. Physical stores are constrained by physical location while the metaverse is open for customers from anywhere in the world. This means that retailers can be established across the world without having purchased real shops in the different locations. Moreover, the metaverse provides retailers with the ability to interact with the clients any time a day making the processes of shopping round the clock as suggested by Rane, Choudhary, & Rane (2023). This constant accessibility is very important given that the time factor has now become so important in customers' satisfaction (Tariq, 2024b).

In addition, the use of the metaverse has new potential for retailers to nurture brand awareness and consumer relations. Customers are no longer limited to only the product and the company but are even able to engage with other customers. Some events that can be conducted are launching a new product through a virtual launch, fashion shows and or product promotion through actors, artists, or other famous personalities or influencers. Such events make the customers feel that they are in a common group thus are related to the specific brand (Singla, Shalender, & Singh, 2024). For instance, a luxury fashion apparel firm can organize an exclusive sales event for its loyal customers; the firm invites its customers to a virtual fashion event where they can preview certain products that will be in the market soon. Such exclusivity is good for the customer and increases his loyalty to the brand he buys or is associated with. Besides, the use of the metaverse will also provide the following advantages that will cut across cost-saving aspects for the retailers; Traditional physical stores for Perish's products will be highly costly to operate since they will be incurred costs such as rent, utility, and employees' salaries. However, the virtual stores, which existed in the metaverse, need limited amounts of investment, also in infrastructural terms (Koohang et al., 2023). It should be noted that there are always certain expenses regarding building and sustaining a virtual image, but such expenses are usually less than if a business had several physical storefronts. Hence, more resources can be invested into enhancing a customers' journey, for instance through creating unique virtual shops or providing services (Tariq, 2025c).

The metaverse panorama also offers retailers the opportunity to adapt and try out new approaches to actual selling. In the real world, operations such as changing store layouts or launching new product lines can sometimes take time and consume significant amounts of money. Peculiarly, this is not the case in the metaverse; retailers have an opportunity to experiment and make changes within a short period of time and, therefore, adapt ideas to customers' preferences (Park, Maddirala, & Eckert, 2023). For instance, a retail company can build a temporary store for a certain release and see how people respond to a certain product without making significant investments in its establishment. This agility assists retailers to have a competitive advantage over their counterparts and enables them to respond to emerging trends.

However, the use of the metaverse in retail has its own drawbacks which are listed below. One major challenge that adds great concern is the issue of capital investment in technology and other instruments. Hence, we need to ensure that their online tools are designed to present virtual realistic, high-quality shopping experiences. They should also consider the technical elements of incorporating metaverse with their existing e-commerce platforms and compliance with the security of the customers' data (Kulova, Nikolova-Alexieva, & Paskalev, 2024). Retailers need to be ready to teach their customers how to navigate virtual environments and maximize their digital shopping experience, since the metaverse is still a relatively new concept. Retailers can develop immersive, interactive experiences that engage customers in novel ways and promote enduring loyalty by implementing the metaverse (Batat, 2024). Nevertheless, cautious planning and technological investment will be needed for the metaverse to be successfully incorporated into retail strategies. The metaverse will probably become more significant in determining how retail develops in the future as digital environments continue to change (Koohang et al., 2023). Retailers who adopt this change will be well-positioned to satisfy contemporary consumers' needs and prosper in a dynamic environment (Tariq, 2024c).

Creating Immersive Customer Experiences

Through the creation of immersive and captivating shopping experiences, virtual reality (VR), augmented reality (AR), and extended reality (XR) are revolutionizing the way consumers interact with retail businesses. Customers may now examine things in ways that were previously impractical thanks to these technologies. With virtual reality (VR), consumers may visit a virtual store, navigate the aisles, and interact with the items exactly as they would in a real-world setting. A consumer may, for instance, enter a virtual clothes boutique, peruse the racks of apparel, and try on ensembles by tailoring their avatar to meet their body type (Chaudhuri, Titus, & Chaudhuri, 2024). In a similar vein, augmented reality (AR) improves the in-person purchasing experience by superimposing digital data on tangible items. Using a smartphone to display a 3D model of the sofa into their home room, a prospective furniture buyer may use augmented reality (AR) to view how the piece would appear there (Rane et al., 2023). The distinction between in-store and online buying is blurred by these technologies, adding to the process's dynamic and engaging nature. XR, which blends aspects of AR and VR, is especially effective in producing immersive shopping environments. Retailers may create hybrid venues where digital and physical areas coexist thanks to this technology. For example, XR technology may be used by a beauty firm to let customers try on cosmetic items in-store in real-time. The system would overlay several hues of lipstick or eyeshadow over the customer's reflection in a mirror (Singla, Shalender, & Singh, 2024). Customers may make better purchase selections when shopping with this type of interactive experience, which personalizes and engages the shopping experience. Retailers may provide distinctive and customized experiences that promote extended client interaction and strengthen bonds with the brand by using XR.

These technologies have been effectively embraced by several well-known retail firms to provide engaging virtual shop experiences. Gucci is one company that exemplifies this, having launched the Gucci Virtual 25, a virtual shoe that can be worn in both AR and virtual settings. Consumers can purchase these virtual footwear, which they can then flaunt on social networking sites like Snapchat or in the metaverse (Khaliq & Manda, 2024). Younger, tech-savvy consumers interested in digital fashion and self-expression may find this novel method appealing. Gucci's usage of augmented reality and the metaverse shows how companies may include digital-only items into their offerings to generate new value propositions. Nike is the subject of another case study as it embraces the metaverse through its online store, Nikeland. Users may explore Nike's newest items, personalize their avatars, and take part in virtual activities like games and fitness challenges by visiting Nikeland, a virtual environment (Batat, 2024). Through in-game interactions, the platform encourages clients to move more while offering them an enjoyable and dynamic method to connect with the Nike brand. Nike has expanded its brand presence beyond physical shops and internet platforms by developing an immersive virtual world that offers customers an unparalleled shopping and leisure experience. Using a range of strategies, retailers may improve consumer engagement and involvement in virtual environments. Customizing the purchasing experience according to the preferences of the client is one efficient strategy. Brands may use data analytics in virtual worlds to examine consumer behavior and suggest items based on their interests. A virtual fashion store may, for instance, make apparel recommendations based on a customer's browsing or past purchases, personalizing and contextualizing the experience (Mehrotra et al., 2024). Customization raises the possibility that a client will make a purchase in addition to making their shopping experience better.

Another tactic to increase consumer involvement in virtual environments is gamification. Retailers may enhance the fun and satisfaction of shopping by adding aspects of a game to the process. A store can, for example, grant virtual badges or awards to consumers who engage in virtual events or finish shopping objectives, including trying on a predetermined amount of clothes or discovering new product categories (Koohang et al., 2023). Customers are more likely to spend more time in the virtual shop and feel more accomplished because of these benefits, which raises their level of engagement with the company. Furthermore, chatbots and virtual sales assistants can improve consumer engagement in digital environments. Customers can communicate with AI-driven assistants in a virtual store that can provide product recommendations, respond to inquiries, and give tailored purchasing advice (Park, Maddirala, & Eckert, 2023). These virtual assistants provide a human element to the online shopping experience by taking on the duties of in-store staff. For instance, by providing recommendations based on consumers' design preferences and size details, a virtual sales assistant at a shoe store may aid customers in finding the ideal pair. Customers feel more supported during their shopping experience and an extra layer of ease is added because of this degree of engagement.

DEVELOPING NEW BUSINESS MODELS IN RETAIL

The emergence of the metaverse is bringing up previously unthinkable new and creative business models, which are revolutionizing the retail sector. More and more retailers are looking at how traditional methods of product sales might be enhanced or even replaced by digital and virtual places. The capacity for merchants to build fully virtual marketplaces where customers can connect, shop, and experience brands in immersive ways is one of the biggest advances brought about by the metaverse. The increasing need for digital experiences, customization, and the merging of the physical and virtual worlds is what is driving these new business models (Khaliq

& Manda, 2024). The development of virtual-only goods and experiences is one of the creative business models made possible by the metaverse. Under this approach, companies sell digital products that have no physical counterparts. Fashion labels such as Gucci and Balenciaga, for instance, have begun offering virtual apparel items for purchase that users may utilize on social media platforms or in virtual worlds. These digital products serve customers that appreciate the ability to express themselves in virtual worlds where virtual avatars are starting to take precedence over real-world appearances (Singla, Shalender, & Singh, 2024). With the help of this approach, businesses may access new consumer segments that are prepared to pay for virtual experiences that improve their online visibility, including gamers and digital natives. The idea of virtual real estate is another cutting-edge commercial strategy in the metaverse. Retailers can establish digital stores by buying or renting virtual areas within metaverse networks. Because these virtual locations are not limited by location or size like traditional stores are, marketers are able to develop highly personalized and engaging shopping environments. For example, high-end retailer Ralph Lauren debuted a virtual flagship shop on Roblox where users may browse and buy fashion-related virtual goods (Rane et al., 2023). The virtual shop offers distinctive experiences like avatar personalization and virtual fashion displays, all while maintaining the brand's physical image. With this strategy, businesses may continue to be present in virtual environments where younger customers spend a significant amount of their time.

The potential of these creative business models is demonstrated by successful retail endeavors in the metaverse. Nike's Nikeland, a virtual environment on the Roblox platform where users can play games, explore branded locations, and buy virtual Nike merchandise, is one of the best examples (Batat, 2024). Nike has expanded its reach beyond traditional retail into the metaverse, where it can engage with a younger, tech-savvy audience, by building an appealing virtual environment. Nikeland's success has demonstrated that virtual environments can be useful marketing tools for product promotion and brand engagement. Similarly, companies such as Decentral have made events and virtual real estate their business. Users may purchase, trade, and sell virtual land in Decentral and, which can be used to construct online shops, galleries, and even entertainment centers. Using this platform, several retail businesses have set up virtual stores where customers may peruse and buy virtual products. Retailers may now investigate new revenue streams outside of traditional commerce thanks to the robust ecosystem that has been generated by the capacity to own and monetize virtual property (Mehrotra et al., 2024). To further pique customer interest, this model also gives marketers the chance to work with digital artists and designers to produce limited-edition virtual goods.

Businesses are implementing several crucial tactics to incorporate metaverse aspects into conventional retail structures. Making hybrid experiences that incorporate both virtual and real-world components is one strategy. Retailers may, for instance, provide digital replicas of tangible goods that consumers can test out virtually before deciding to buy them in person. When purchasing a new automobile, a buyer may go to a virtual showroom from the comfort of their home, where they may personalize the car and take a virtual test drive (Koohang et al., 2023). With this kind of hybrid experience, firms can stay connected to their physical storefronts while providing customers with greater convenience and flexibility. Using the metaverse as a tool to improve consumer involvement and brand loyalty is another tactic. Virtual loyalty programs are being developed by several shops to incentivize consumers for their metaverse activities. For example, by taking part in a branded game or visiting a virtual fashion show, a consumer can earn virtual points or tokens that can be redeemed for real-world discounts or access to exclusive items (Chaudhuri, Titus, & Chaudhuri, 2024). This strategy encourages repeat business while fortifying the bond between digital and real experiences.

Before introducing new product lines to their actual locations, retailers are also employing metaverse platforms to test and develop them. Brands may measure consumer interest and get real-time feedback by launching digital-only versions of new products. This lowers the risk of investing in ideas that might not do well in the market. In addition to cutting expenses, this tactic enables companies to respond faster to market developments and consumer needs (Park, Maddirala, & Eckert, 2023).

Thus, a new generation of creative business models in the retail sector are made possible by the metaverse. Retailers are coming up with innovative methods to draw in customers and make money, from virtual-only goods to hybrid experiences that combine the digital and real worlds. The potential for expansion in this field is demonstrated by successful initiatives like Nikeland and virtual real estate platforms like Decentraland. Businesses may ensure their competitiveness in an increasingly digital environment by incorporating metaverse aspects into traditional retail models to provide more immersive, individualized, and engaging experiences for their consumers (Kulova, Nikolova-Alexiera, & Paskalev, 2024).

Understanding Consumer Behavior in the Metaverse

With the increasing accessibility and immersion of virtual settings, consumer behavior in the metaverse is changing quickly. Customers frequently connect with companies in completely new ways in the metaverse, combining social interaction, entertainment, and buying into a single, seamless experience. Retailers hoping to thrive in this digital environment need to understand the characteristics of their customers and how they behave online. In contrast to traditional retail, the desires of metaverse shoppers are frequently driven by a need for discovery, customization, and social engagement (Chaudhuri, Titus, & Chaudhuri, 2024). These customers, many of whom are younger and tech-savvy, are looking for opportunities to express themselves, interact with others, and discover new virtual worlds. Customers of the metaverse are known for having a strong need for personalization and self-expression. Users in virtual worlds can select digital attire, make avatars, and take part in activities that represent who they are. Fashion labels like Gucci and Balenciaga, for instance, have capitalized on this trend by providing customers with the option to buy virtual-exclusive apparel for their avatars (Singla, Shalender, & Singh, 2024). With the help of these digital items, customers may express their own style and personality in settings where tangible things are not required. Gen Z and Millennials find these experiences particularly appealing as they are used to living in digital environments and like to stand out in online groups.

The tastes and purchase decisions of consumers are significantly influenced by the metaverse. When shopping in virtual settings, people are more likely to base their choices on immersive experiences and strong emotional bonds than on functional requirements. Customers could, for example, buy virtual commodities like digital art or collectibles because they symbolize status or a sense of belonging in a virtual community rather than because they are useful (Mehrotra et al., 2024). Due to this change in customer behavior, companies are now re-evaluating their product marketing strategies and concentrating on developing compelling stories and experiences that emotionally connect with consumers. Case studies provide more insight into the ways in which the metaverse is changing consumer behavior. Nike's Nikeland on Roblox is a noteworthy instance, where users may explore virtual environments, engage in branded activities, and buy virtual Nike merchandise (Batat, 2024). A sense of community and belonging is fostered by this virtual world, where people interact with the brand through enjoyable and interactive activities. Consequently, Nike has witnessed a rise in interaction from younger customers who may not have been contacted through conventional retail methods. Thus, new avenues for social contact, emotional connection, and self-expression are being opened up by the metaverse, which is changing consumer behavior. In this changing digital market, brands that recognize these trends and address the distinct needs of virtual customers will have a greater chance of success. Businesses may encourage long-term loyalty and deeper involvement among metaverse users by providing individualized, immersive experiences (Park, Maddirala, & Eckert, 2023).

Enhancing Communication and Brand Interaction

Advertising in the metaverse is an effective way of interacting with consumers since it changes conventional approaches to marketing. In this digital domain, brands cannot afford to convey fixed or one- off messages to the audiences. They can design rich and engaging experiences, at the same time, encouraging real time conversations with the consumers. Brands get to engage with customers in novel ways by producing content in the virtual environment customers exist in. For instance, brands can organize virtual events, or staged product demonstrations, brands' avatars can provide customer services in real time; making communication more engrossing and impactful (Chaudhuri; Titus; & Chaudhuri, 2024).

In terms of networking, one of the most effective forms of communication in metaverse is by use of virtual events or substantially engaging experiences. Customers can be invited to Launching ceremonies, Fashion shows or Product exhibition where they can touch and feel the products and buy them live. One such case is the virtual concerts where artists such as Travis Scott performed, and millions of fans could watch, and the brands could easily place their products and advertisements within the concerts (Singla, Shalender, & Singh 2024). It not only develops an effective brand experience among the consumers, but the brands can also reach a wide group of interested people. Promoting brand communities within the metaverse is also a meaningful endeavor for improving communication and increasing loyalty. It is very social and collaborative and since consumers connect online, virtual spaces are a perfect ground for such interaction. Companies can bring customers together in social networks where they can share experiences, keeping them engaged with the brand. For instance, a premium clothing line can make a separate virtual parlor only for the loyal customers of the brand where they can interact with other fashion lovers, get to know the new collections first and attend some virtual parties and shows (Mehrotra et al., 2024). Thus, by developing such environments brands not only affect customer experience but also lead to brand loyalty since positive social connections are linked to brands.

There is also a possibility of developing a loyal base using the virtual platforms, this is through the provision of bonuses and incentives towards further participation. Customers are entertained using gaming features hence the increase in the use of the metaverse by many brands. They give incentives related to events, challenges, or any form of engagement that is related to the brand to their customers such as virtual goods, NFTs, or piece of content. For example, Adidas has employed the concept of metaverse to give its loyal customer sets of exclusive digital accessories that can be used by their avatars in virtual space (Batat, 2024). This type of engagement helps to enhance the customer loyalty since customers get to experience new added-value services not limited to purchasing alone. Many companies have effectively interacted with consumer in the metaverse which illustrates some real-life examples for learning on how these virtual environments add value to consumption. One of the examples is Gucci that developed the digital copy of its flagship store and placed it in Roblox. Here, the consumers could walk around the virtual store naked, trying on clothes and accessories, and buying some of them personal avatars on the grounds of the Gucci universe. Through providing such an impressive and detailed experience, people, especially the young generation who prefers to spend much time on the internet, could better associate Gucci with themselves, hence they increased their awareness and engagement with the brand (Park et al., 2023). Another current trend that is associated with the metaverse is also actively developing by Coca-Cola, which has released tokens and organizes meetings with supporters in the digital space. In conclusion, the metaverse introduces a new way of communication between the brands and customers and gives a chance to create engaging experiences. Using virtual events, building brand communities, and effective adoption of gamification, brands companies can improve their communication effort and the relationship between the company and the consumer. As much as the brands of Gucci, Coca-Cola, and Adidas have proved iconic in the metaverse, it will be logical to agree with Chaudhuri, Titus, and Chaudhuri (2024) that virtual platforms are essential to future marketing and hence the metaverse must be embraced.

MEASURING ROI (RETURN ON INVESTMENT) IN THE METAVERSE

Evaluating ROI in the metaverse is an essential move for companies that seek to understand whether the time and resources they invest in this virtual space are providing the intended returns. Recalling brands become involved in generating immersive virtual experiences, it becomes critical to monitor and evaluate its effects with the help of KPI. Unfortunately, in ROI for metaverse, simple profit making relating to sales figures is not well applicable; instead, many factors such as, customer interfaces, brand recognition and community development cooperates to make profit in the long run. So, through the usage of right parameters, tools, and approaches, it is possible to measure the results of investment decisions and tailor relevant strategies (Singla, Shalender, & Singh, 2024). Engagement is one of the best ways to measure the ROI on metaverse investment since the metaverse may not be popular at first glance. This can be gauged by the amount of time spent on a brand's virtual world, the number of times an individual interface within the brand's virtual space within the same session, the frequency of the latter within the space of one session. The users who spend more time interacting with the brand and its online representations will appreciate the value of the virtual experience, be more loyal to the brand and more likely to make repeat purchases. Further, the click-through rates, product trials, and shares on social media within the metaverse are valuable in determining if the virtual environment is inspiring the consumers to engage with brand offerings (Mehrotra et al., 2024).

Another valued parameter is the conversion rate. It means, that how many users who interact with metaverse experience of specific brand then continue their purchasing and buy various goods, both, offline and online. The conversion rate is useful to track so that the organization can determine the extent to which the virtual environment affects the purchase behavior brands that deal in digital products, such as music or art, or products that are sold in the form of NFTs, then the sales made from these products can evidently contribute to the company's revenues, and therefore, ROI. For example, Nike has been selling air Jordan sneakers in the metaverse; the effectiveness of such ventures runs a tally by the number of units of items sold and the amount of money made (Park et al., 2023). Brand recognition and perception are also important factors while assessing or calculating the ROI in the context of the metaverse. The metaverse is advantageous to brands because it helps them present their products to new clienteles and leave the best impressions. Thus, businesses can follow social media mentions, shares, and analyze sentiment to know how the metaverse is being received by users. Positive brand attitude has an impact on brand trust which results in future purchase intentions and customer advocacy. For instance, when Coca-Cola introduced the virtual collectibles, it elicited favorable discussions in the social media platforms which increased the visibility of the brand and more focus which in turn improved the overall ROI of the exercise as noted by Chaudhuri, Titus, & Chaudhuri, 2024). To track these metrics effectively there are various tools and techniques that organizations employ for the purpose of analyzing performance in relation to the metaverse. One of them is analytics tools which can identify and measure user activities in the VE (virtual environment) including number of visitors, the time spent and touch points. These data are useful for business to know how their customers interact with the virtual environment and which aspects they find the most stimulating. Platforms such as Roblox or Decentral already contain intuitions that can be used for the measurement of effectiveness in real-time, where brands would leverage (Batat, 2024). Customer feedback surveys are another method used to measure ROI. This was said because it allows those in business, particularly those who deal with people, to get direct feedback from customers about their experiences. Surveys can be done through the points of contact within the metaverse or follow up emails or through social media engagements. Customer feedback is especially useful for the quantifiable matrix since the qualitative aspects regarding the return on investment from consumers' point of view are difficult to measure (Chaudhuri, Titus, & Chaudhuri, 2024).

Some of the presented examples pertain to metaverse retail and demonstrate effective measurement of ROI. A good example is the Gucci virtual experience on Roblox where the brand was able to develop a virtual store through which users were able to shop for exclusive Virtual items. Following the frequency and amount of engagement, including the number of users who entered the store, the amount of time spent in the virtual environment, and the volume of the Gucci's digital products sold, the company was able to quantify the economic and brand results of the initiative. The project was considered a success as it not only sold virtual products and made actual money, but it also was famous among the people especially those from the generation Y (Singla, Shalender, & Singh, 2024). Another example is Nike which recently initiated its voyage in the metaverse through Nikeland. Nike monitored overall traffic through its virtual site and actual sales of virtual commodities, for instance, digital sneakers that could be bought for an avatar. Social media awareness and conversation analysis were also used to track the overall footprint of the firm's metaverse involvement and brand perception. This was proved by the success of Nikeland moving up a proposal that brands have applied high ROI by combining both virtual and physical concepts of retailing. Thus, it is useful to conclude that there are no clear means to calculate the ROI in the metaverse, which should be done using reference to multiple types of quantitative indicators. This includes factors such as the level of interaction of the users, the conversion rates of the business, the identification of the brand, as well as the sentiment of the users towards the metaverse projects of the business. Customer feedback surveys and analytics tools offer insight that indicates how brands can enhance their strategies and results at the virtual interface. Nike and Gucci and more have outrightly shown that an investment in the metaverse yields both profit and a high impact Return on Investment (ROI) (Batat, 2024).

ADDRESSING ETHICAL AND PRIVACY CONSIDERATIONS

With the advent of the metaverse, there are new fronts for retailers to consider but several ethical and privacy issues are most notably, the data of consumers. It has also been found that users of virtual environments disclose considerably more information about themselves than in conventional Web locations, ranging from their preferences to intricate behavior patterns. Such a broad collection of data causes doubts about how the businesses operate and manage such data. Based on an analysis of the literature, the issues of ethics in the metaverse are exemplified by consumer privacy, the existence of vulnerabilities existing in the metaverse that can be exploited by brands, as well as proper disclosure of data usage by the brands (Batat, 2024). Business entities must be very sensitive to users' data privacy and act correctly to ensure that their data is protected in the right way as a way of encouraging users to trust the companies.

A lot of ethical concerns regarding metaverse are associated with the acquisition and utilization of consumer data without the proper consent. Most of the metaverse platforms solicit users' personal information for personalization purposes but such information may be used to place advertisements or resold with the user's consent. Some of these practices can be considered as rather unethical, because the consumers may not be very conscious of what they are getting into when they are accessing the virtual environments. In this regard, therefore, companies must come up with clear policies with regards to data collection. Transparency in terms of what data is being collected as well as the purpose for which it is being collected is critical in gaining consumers' trust. Furthermore, letting the user pause data collection can even go a long way in showing that an organization is ethical and cares about the privacy of its consumers (Mehrotra et al., 2024). A few other points of concern in the Metaverse are that of data vulnerability. Due to the large amount of personal information, in many cases residents' information, contained within these environments, they are vulnerable to hackers. The responsibility to protect customers' information lies with the retailers and the platform developers, which means that they must go out of their way to guard the data they obtain. Other measures which may include encryption, frequent security assessment, and adherence to global data privacy laws including GDPR are important in protecting the consumers' data. Adopting good measures helps in safeguarding consumers also and can also improve the image of the brand because of being ethical (Chaudhuri et al., 2024). Another aspect of trust in the metaverse is the need to follow the recommended procedures when collecting and storing consumers' data. One such technique is the decentralized data management technique which can be realized by using blockchain technology. It gives users more control over their personal information, reducing the likelihood that third parties will access and use it. In this way, brands allow the user to know that their data is safe and that any activity within this virtual world, such as buying/selling, meetings, etc.-, is not vulnerable to hackers (Park, Maddirala, & Eckert, 2023). As such, it not only secures data, but also helps to meet all the ethical practices required to ensure that consumers feel safe when interacting with brands in the metaverse. Another important area that must be well regulated about privacy rights is the question of consent. In most virtual environments, the users sometimes have no idea of how their data is being used or even shared with other third parties. As a result, brands should develop and clearly explain to the consumers their consent procedures before data are harvested. The provisions concerning consent must be specific on the kind of data to be collected and for what purposes that will be collected as well as who will have access to it. As part of the best practices when it comes to data ethics, one should make sure that the details provided to the users allow them to give their informed consent before they can interact with a given brand in the metaverse (Singla et al., 2024).

Some brands have already adopted several best practices for ethical marketing in the metaverse, and many can become their role models. For example, luxury fashion brand Gucci, which has already participated in the use of the metaverse using platforms such as Roblox, has been launched to integrate privacy-first marketing approaches. One of Gucci's safeguards to ensure that its virtual occasion and item drops adequately consider consent is transparency, which in turn helps to build trust with the virtual crowd. Thus, the brand has developed strict policies regarding the collection of data: it has limited users' personal data and made all interactions with them explicit and consensual. Moreover, this approach is consistent with ethical marketing values and contributes to the recognition of Gucci as a company that does not only has respect for people's rights but also is oriented towards the future (Mehrotra et al., 2024). Another example of best practices of the metaverse is known as 'Coca-Colonization'. Virtual worlds have enhanced Coca-Cola ability to capture consumers' attention, entertain them and at the same time follow the highest standards of consumer privacy. In this way, Coca-Cola has been able to create experiences that do not require the collection of large amounts of data from users, but instead provide delightful, augmented reality and virtual reality experiences. Still, the focus on privacy and thus no temporary collection of data has made the brand appreciate ethical ways of creating the metaverse' marketing experiences (Chaudhuri, Titus, & Chaudhuri, 2024).

Another issue that relates to ethic regarding metaverse is the issue of equal representation of all people to the metaverse. Apparently, retailers must make efforts to ensure that virtual spaces of stores are accessible to people with disabilities or members of other vulnerable groups. This may involve offering tools for creating or selecting personal representations in avatars or interactions which can represent certain user's identity and other parameters of his/her personal world and, finally, making virtual environment accessible for users with different kinds of disabilities. As with any other real-life industry, brands have the corporate social responsibility to engage the metaverse with more inclusiveness (Batat, 2024). Therefore, it is crucial for Companies' expectations to consider ethical and privacy issues in the metaverse to gain the consumers' confidence and form long term relationships with them. It is also suggested that brands should be smart and cautious about the methods of data collection, security and the ways of asking the user's consent to respect the user's privacy. Also, it is possible to mention that by following the principles of ethical marketing, companies of Gucci and Coca-Cola, for example, create an effective marketing mix that will allow them to target consumers without violating their ethical obligations. Hence, as the metaverse environment grows and expands, it will be paramount to keep the ethical/as ethical and the privacy interdependent as a means of guaranteeing a safe, secure, and effective virtual space.

CHALLENGES AND FUTURE DIRECTIONS

Retailers willing to join the metaverse have numerous issues to solve, even though they comprehend the opportunity of revolutionizing customers' experiences here. The most frequent problem is that some neoclassical assumptions are prohibitive to implement. Creating convincing and realistic AV environments involves immense capital in sophisticated tools and applications, including VR, AR and XR and the supporting systems. The following financial impacts are the reasons why many, if not most retailers especially the small ones find it challenging to fully adopt the metaverse; In addition, the requirement of some specialized technical competencies to develop and manage those venues is also a challenge. Some of these companies may not possess the necessary skills to design wonderful Virtual Environments, thus they might have to hire third-party developers who may be very costly (Chaudhuri, Titus, & Chaudhuri, 2024).

One of the other main issues retailers must address regarding the integration of metaverse solutions is how to get more clients to use them. The metaverse is popular now, but for most of the shoppers, this format is unordinary and unfamiliar, they may not feel confident in virtual environment, don't have VR and AR devices. This can reduce the extensiveness and effectiveness of metaverse based retail marketing. Furthermore, there are questions regarding inclusiveness, for not all customers have the right hardware or the proper internet connection to become an active participant in such arrangements. This is a concern for retailers as everything that can be sold online has to be put online hence many consumers are shut out, they must find ways to ensure that everything they offer online is accessible to everyone (Batat, 2024). However, the futuristic model of metaverse retail has been deemed to have a steady and optimistic outlook. As one of the trends it is possible to credit the further application of artificial intelligence to increase the level of personalization in virtual shopping. Advanced techniques of artificial intelligence could enable organizations gather customer characteristics and tendencies in detail and in the process, real-time interventions could be implemented for personalized recommendations of products and services as well as the prices inside the virtual stores. Another innovation is increased production of VR/AR devices, their improvement in terms of quality and the efforts to make products key-oriented. This may make it easier for consumers and retailers to enter the market, allowing metaverse technologies to be adopted more widely (Singla, Shalender, & Singh, 2024).

Additionally, it is anticipated that blockchain technology will be crucial to the development of metaverse retail. The decentralized and transparent transactions enabled by blockchain technology give customers a safe platform to purchase, sell, and exchange virtual items. This innovation is especially important given the expanding market for digital assets, such non-fungible tokens (NFTs), which are already becoming popular in online retail environments. Blockchain technology may enable new business models centered on the ownership and trade of digital goods as the metaverse develops, providing shops with even more options (Park, Maddirala, & Eckert, 2023). Several suggestions can assist shops wishing to enter the metaverse in overcoming these obstacles. Initially, businesses must start small, concentrating on developing a single, well-thought-out virtual experience instead of attempting to introduce a complete metaverse presence at once. This enables trial and error prior to significant investments. Working with IT partners who are knowledgeable in blockchain, VR, and AR may also assist in getting over technical obstacles and guarantee a more seamless deployment process. Lastly, when creating their virtual environments, businesses should give accessibility and diversity priority. Companies may make sure that their investments have the greatest potential impact by opening their metaverse experiences to a larger audience, including people who might not have access to pricey technology (Mehrotra et al., 2024).

Thus, there are several obstacles associated with the metaverse in addition to the great prospects it offers the retail industry. Significant obstacles that merchants must overcome include high costs, technological restrictions, and the requirement for customer adoption. Nonetheless, advancements like blockchain, artificial intelligence, and more widely available virtual reality technologies hold great promise for metaverse retail's future. Retailers that want to thrive in the metaverse should adopt a methodical, inclusive strategy, making sure to solve the issues

CONCLUSION

This chapter has looked at the revolutionary role of the metaverse in changing the retail landscape. The metaverse offers a new opportunity for shops to create immersive, digital shopping experiences via the use of virtual reality (VR), augmented reality (AR), and extended reality (XR). The metaverse holds enormous promise for the retail sector, enabling new business models and improving customer engagement. We began by explaining what the metaverse is, looking at how it has developed in the retail industry, and emphasizing the advantages that shops may have by implementing this technology. Gaining access to new revenue sources via digital assets and virtual storefronts, enhanced consumer interaction, and individualized shopping experiences are some of these advantages. The chapter then went into detail about the importance of using VR, AR, and XR technology to create immersive customer experiences. Brands that have already started to offer virtual shopping experiences were the subject of case studies, demonstrating how early adopters are benefiting from metaverse integration. The potential for stronger brand-customer relationships in digital contexts was demonstrated by the techniques for improving consumer contact and engagement in these virtual areas that were also covered. These immersive experiences provide new and engaging ways for customers to connect with products, not only increasing sales but also fostering lasting brand loyalty.

Next, we looked at how new business models are emerging in the metaverse. The need for personalised, frictionless, and interactive shopping experiences is being driven by customers' shifting expectations and tastes as they get more accustomed to traversing digital places. Case studies illustrate how customer behavior is being transformed by metaverse experiences, highlighting the increasing significance of virtual environments in the retail sector. We also spoke about how merchants may strengthen their brand communities and improve communication by using the metaverse. Brands may encourage consumer involvement and loyalty by using virtual platforms to create engaging interactive experiences. There were examples of businesses that have successfully interacted with customers in the metaverse, showcasing the ability of these digital channels to build deep relationships with clients. We also looked at the difficulties in calculating the return on investment (ROI) of metaverse projects. Key performance indicators for evaluating these initiatives were determined, and case studies provided useful illustrations of ROI evaluation in retail metaverse initiatives. Retailers now have a useful framework to assess the return on their metaverse investments. The ethical and privacy issues that merchants face while joining the metaverse were covered at the chapter's conclusion. Techniques for guaranteeing customer security and trust were addressed as worries about consumer data and privacy became more significant. The article emphasized ethical marketing best practices in the metaverse to give merchants a direction on how to do business properly in this new digital environment. In conclusion, the retail industry has a revolutionary potential thanks to the metaverse, which allows businesses to develop cutting-edge, immersive experiences that increase consumer engagement and loyalty. Although there are certain difficulties with metaverse integration, such as high implementation costs, technological hurdles, and consumer adoption, the possible advantages much exceed these difficulties. As blockchain, VR, and AR technology advance, new avenues for virtual stores, digital asset trading, and customized purchasing experiences will become possible. In a market that is evolving quickly, retailers who use these technologies will have a competitive advantage. Retailers have a clear call to action: the moment has come to investigate metaverse technology. Retailers may be at the vanguard of this digital transformation by implementing VR, AR, and blockchain into their business models through small steps.

Early adoption can help companies not only now, but also in the future as the retail industry changes. The metaverse gives retailers a strong tool for future development and innovation, whether via blockchain-powered transactions, individualized digital experiences, or virtual shops.

REFERENCES

AR, S., Katiravan, D. J., & Kumar, K. M. (2024). *METACOMMERCE360 pioneering the future of e-commerce in the boundless metaverse landscape.*

Ball, M. (2022). *The metaverse: And how it will revolutionize everything*. Liveright Publishing. DOI: 10.15358/9783800669400

Batat, W. (2024). Phygital customer experience in the metaverse: A study of consumer sensory perception of sight, touch, sound, scent, and taste. *Journal of Retailing and Consumer Services*, 78, 103786. DOI: 10.1016/j.jretconser.2024.103786

Bathla, D., & Singh, A. (Eds.). (2022). *Applying metalytics to measure customer experience in the metaverse*. IGI Global. DOI: 10.4018/978-1-6684-6133-4

Buhalis, D., Leung, D., & Lin, M. (2023). Metaverse as a disruptive technology revolutionising tourism management and marketing. *Tourism Management*, 97, 104724. DOI: 10.1016/j.tourman.2023.104724

Castenetto, C. (2022). Redefining fashion ecommerce: A comprehensive study on the transformative impact of technologies on user experience.

Chakraborty, U., & Biswal, S. K. (2024). Diffusion of innovation in direct-to-avatar (D2A): A study of immersive communication and branding in the metaverse. *Computers in Human Behavior*, 158, 108318. DOI: 10.1016/j.chb.2024.108318

Chaudhuri, A., Titus, R., & Chaudhuri, A. (2024). Impact of technology on customer experience in the metaverse era. *Journal of Management and Public Policy*, 15(4), 28–47.

Dinh, T. L. H. (2023). Customer behaviors toward metaverse/metaverse as a stimulus for customer experience: Implications for marketing.

Dwivedi, Y. K., Hughes, L., Baabdullah, A. M., Ribeiro-Navarrete, S., Giannakis, M., Al-Debei, M. M., Dennehy, D., Metri, B., Buhalis, D., Cheung, C. M. K., Conboy, K., Doyle, R., Dubey, R., Dutot, V., Felix, R., Goyal, D. P., Gustafsson, A., Hinsch, C., Jebabli, I., & Wamba, S. F. (2022). Metaverse beyond the hype: Multidisciplinary perspectives on emerging challenges, opportunities, and agenda for research, practice and policy. *International Journal of Information Management*, 66, 102542. DOI: 10.1016/j.ijinfomgt.2022.102542

Gadekallu, T. R., Wang, W., Yenduri, G., Ranaweera, P., Pham, Q. V., da Costa, D. B., & Liyanage, M. (2023). Blockchain for the metaverse: A review. *Future Generation Computer Systems*, 143, 401–419. DOI: 10.1016/j.future.2023.02.008

Golf-Papez, M., Heller, J., Hilken, T., Chylinski, M., de Ruyter, K., Keeling, D. I., & Mahr, D. (2022). Embracing falsity through the metaverse: The case of synthetic customer experiences. *Business Horizons*, 65(6), 739–749. DOI: 10.1016/j.bushor.2022.07.007

Habil, S. G. M., El-Deeb, S., & El-Bassiouny, N. (2024). The metaverse era: Leveraging augmented reality in the creation of novel customer experience. *Management & Sustainability: An Arab Review*, 3(1), 1–15. DOI: 10.1108/MSAR-10-2022-0051

Hoyer, W. D., Kroschke, M., Schmitt, B., Kraume, K., & Shankar, V. (2020). Transforming the customer experience through new technologies. *Journal of Interactive Marketing*, 51(1), 57–71. DOI: 10.1016/j.intmar.2020.04.001

Khaliq, L. N., & Manda, V. K. (2024). Customer experience in the Web 3.0 era: The meeting of blockchain and the metaverse. In *The rise of blockchain applications in customer experience* (pp. 258–274). IGI Global.

Köksal, C. G. (2024). Where is digital retailing evolving? An evaluation from the perspective of digital retailing technologies. In *Navigating the shifting landscape of consumer behavior* (pp. 139–173). IGI Global. DOI: 10.4018/979-8-3693-1594-1.ch006

Koohang, A., Nord, J. H., Ooi, K. B., Tan, G. W. H., Al-Emran, M., Aw, E. C. X., Baabdullah, A. M., Buhalis, D., Cham, T.-H., Dennis, C., Dutot, V., Dwivedi, Y. K., Hughes, L., Mogaji, E., Pandey, N., Phau, I., Raman, R., Sharma, A., Sigala, M., & Wong, L. W. (2023). Shaping the metaverse into reality: A holistic multidisciplinary understanding of opportunities, challenges, and avenues for future investigation. *Journal of Computer Information Systems*, 63(3), 735–765. DOI: 10.1080/08874417.2023.2165197

Kulova, I., Nikolova-Alexieva, V., & Paskalev, R. (2024). The metaverse and sustainability as drivers revolutionizing customer experience in the food industry. In *BIO Web of Conferences* (Vol. 102, p. 04009). EDP Sciences. DOI: 10.1051/bioconf/202410204009

Machalický, J. (2023). The impact of COVID-19 on the development and application of new technologies in assisted retail in the Czech Republic. *Ad Alta: Journal of Interdisciplinary Research, 13*(1).

Mehrotra, A., Agarwal, R., Khalil, A., Alzeiby, E. A., & Agarwal, V. (2024). Nitty-gritties of customer experience in metaverse retailing. *Journal of Retailing and Consumer Services*, 79, 103876. DOI: 10.1016/j.jretconser.2024.103876

Park, E., Maddirala, S., & Eckert, P. (2023). A new era for technology: How the metaverse will transform retail. *Journal of Student Research*, 12(3). Advance online publication. DOI: 10.47611/jsrhs.v12i3.5104

Rane, N. (2023). Metaverse marketing strategies: Enhancing customer experience and analysing consumer behaviour through leading-edge metaverse technologies, platforms, and models. *Available atSSRN*. DOI: 10.2139/ssrn.4624199

Rane, N., Choudhary, S., & Rane, J. (2023). *Metaverse for enhancing customer loyalty: Effective strategies to improve customer relationship, service, engagement, satisfaction, and experience.*

Seth, S., & Seth, S. (2022). A critical investigation in measuring the impact of the metaverse in revolutionising the future of financial services. In *Applying metalytics to measure customer experience in the metaverse* (pp. 1–8). IGI Global. DOI: 10.4018/978-1-6684-6133-4.ch001

Singha, R., & Singha, S. (2024). Building capabilities and workforce for metaverse-driven retail formats. In *Creator's economy in metaverse platforms: Empowering stakeholders through omnichannel approach* (pp. 111–131). IGI Global. DOI: 10.4018/979-8-3693-3358-7.ch007

Singla, B., Shalender, K., & Singh, N. (Eds.). (2024). *Omnichannel approach to co-creating customer experiences through metaverse platforms*. IGI Global. DOI: 10.4018/979-8-3693-1866-9

Tariq, M. U. (2024a). Smart Transportation Systems: Paving the Way for Sustainable Urban Mobility. In Munuhwa, S. (Ed.), *Contemporary Solutions for Sustainable Transportation Practices* (pp. 254–283). IGI Global. DOI: 10.4018/979-8-3693-3755-4.ch010

Tariq, M. U. (2024b). Leading Smart Technologies and Innovations for E-Business 5.0: Applications and Management Frameworks. In Popkova, E. (Ed.), *Smart Technologies and Innovations in E-Business* (pp. 25–46). IGI Global. DOI: 10.4018/978-1-6684-7840-0.ch002

Tariq, M. U. (2024c). The role of emerging technologies in shaping the global digital government landscape. In Guo, Y. (Ed.), *Emerging developments and technologies in digital government* (pp. 160–180). IGI Global. DOI: 10.4018/979-8-3693-2363-2.ch009

Tariq, M. U. (2025a). Innovating Education and Entrepreneurship Through Computational Thinking: New Pathways for Economic Development. In Tunio, M. (Ed.), *Entrepreneurial Ecosystems Driving Economic Transformation and Job Creation* (pp. 1–28). IGI Global Scientific Publishing. DOI: 10.4018/979-8-3693-9486-1.ch001

Tariq, M. U. (2025b). Navigating the Ethical Frontier-Human Oversight in AI-Driven Decision-Making System. In Hai-Jew, S. (Ed.), *Enhancing Automated Decision-Making Through AI* (pp. 425–448). IGI Global Scientific Publishing.,DOI: 10.4018/979-8-3693-6230-3.ch013

Tariq, M. U. (2025c). Navigating the Landscape of Qualitative Research in Doctoral Studies: Methodologies, Design, and Implementation. In R. Throne (Ed.), *Qualitative Research Methods for Dissertation Research* (pp. 1-24). IGI Global Scientific Publishing. DOI: 10.4018/979-8-3693-3069-2.ch001

Tavman, E. B. (2024). Metaverse retailing: Opportunities and challenges. *PressAcademia Procedia*, 19(1), 10–15.

Xi, N., Chen, J., Gama, F., Korkeila, H., & Hamari, J. (2024). Acceptance of the metaverse: A laboratory experiment on augmented and virtual reality shopping. *Internet Research*, 34(7), 82–117. DOI: 10.1108/INTR-05-2022-0334

ADDITIONAL READING

Raimi, L., Kah, J. M., & Tariq, M. U. (2022). The discourse of blue economy definitions, measurements, and theories: Implications for strengthening academic research and industry practice. In Raimi, L., & Kah, J. (Eds.), *Implications for entrepreneurship and enterprise development in the blue economy* (pp. 1–17). IGI Global. DOI: 10.4018/978-1-6684-3393-5.ch001

Raimi, L., Tariq, M. U., & Kah, J. M. (2022). Diversity, equity, and inclusion as the future workplace ethics: Theoretical review. In Raimi, L., & Kah, J. (Eds.), *Mainstreaming diversity, equity, and inclusion as future workplace ethics* (pp. 1–27). IGI Global. DOI: 10.4018/978-1-6684-3657-8.ch001

Tariq, M. U. (2025). *AI-Driven Learning and Engagement in Higher Education.* IGI Global. DOI: 10.4018/979-8-3693-4074-5

Tariq, M. U., & Sergio, R. P. (Eds.). (2025). *Cases on AI-Driven Solutions to Environmental Challenges.* IGI Global. DOI: 10.4018/979-8-3693-7483-2

KEY TERMS AND DEFINITIONS

Augmented Reality (AR): A technology that overlays digital content onto the physical world, enhancing real-world environments with virtual elements in retail, such as virtual try-ons or product displays.

Extended Reality (XR): An umbrella term that encompasses VR, AR, and other immersive technologies used to create dynamic customer experiences in retail.

Metaverse: A virtual, interconnected space where users can interact, shop, and engage through digital avatars, merging physical and digital retail experiences.

Return on Investment (ROI): A measure used to evaluate the profitability of metaverse-related investments in retail.

Virtual Reality (VR): A fully immersive technology that creates a simulated environment where users can interact, used in retail for creating virtual stores and shopping experiences.

Chapter 8
Metaverse Healthcare in Advancing Patient Care Through Digital Realms

Rajaprabakaran Rajendran
https://orcid.org/0009-0005-9272-5475
CMS Business School, Jain University, India

Yavana Rani S.
https://orcid.org/0000-0001-7870-8007
CMS Business School, Jain University, India

Senthilnathan Dhanasekaran
https://orcid.org/0009-0006-1601-1478
JP Morgan, USA

EXECUTIVE SUMMARY

The metaverse is an emerging technology that has the potential to transform many fields in the future. It is the outcome of the fusion of numerous innovative technologies, such as artificial intelligence, robotics, blockchain, quantum computing, augmented reality, virtual reality, and the internet of medical devices (IoMT), to list some of them. Medical science could undergo a major upheaval owing to the rapidly developing concept of the MEDverse. By incorporating the metaverse into medicine, there are even more opportunities to improve patient outcomes, access to care, and professional collaboration among healthcare providers as telemedicine and other remote care technologies such as telehealth continue to gain popularity in the healthcare sector. The triangulation method is employed to gather relevant information from numerous sources. The primary objective is to understand the metaverse technology, the convergence of metaverse and healthcare, and its impact

DOI: 10.4018/979-8-3693-7245-6.ch008

on the healthcare professional's competency and patient outcomes.

INTRODUCTION

The metaverse is an emerging technology that has the potential to transform many fields in the future. The metaverse is a virtual world that is being developed to allow people to interact with each other and with digital objects in a more immersive way than is currently possible through traditional screens and interfaces. It can be seen as a part of Web 3.0, in which we move to a decentralized web using technologies such as blockchain and artificial intelligence (AI). In the gaming world, the metaverse is already present in, for example, gaming platforms such as Second Life, Minecraft and Roblox or Massively Multiplayer Online Role-playing Games (MMORPGs) such as RuneScape or World of Warcraft. Other areas and industries are following the gaming world in setting up presence in the metaverse, such as tourism, marketing, transportation and banking. Healthcare is now following this metaverse trend as well, although some of its applications are still in their infancy (Hulsen, 2024).

The continual improvement of the physical, social, and psychological well-being of the global population has been proven to depend on the accessibility of healthcare offerings (Salloum & Tekli, 2021). The significance of healthcare services is highlighted by their potential to minimise the adverse consequences of injuries, diseases, and sickness and foster longevity and well-being. The healthcare industry has experienced a swift and dynamic transformation regardless of its long history of development, primarily as a result of its integration with state-of-the-art developments in technology (Chengoden et al., 2023) – a recent development that has the potential to improve the future of the field is known as the Metaverse. The high prevalence of chronic illnesses, the lack of state-of-the-art technology in community hospitals, patients not having enough knowledge of numerous medical services, and the lack of understanding of advanced technologies are some of the important issues and challenges the healthcare sector is currently facing (Lu et al., 2022). Considering these major challenges, it is imperative to provide healthcare services to people at their doorsteps (Alshamrani, 2022; Kapoor et al., 2020).

The COVID-19 epidemic, which has made circumstances more serious, has been the primary driver of dramatic shifts in the healthcare environment. It has forced all stakeholders to reconsider how they approach this industry, and implementing cutting-edge technologies has become essential for staying up with the swiftly evolving industry (Shakeel et al., 2023). In this scenario, the Metaverse could be a game-changer. It is the outcome of the fusion of numerous innovative technologies, such as artificial intelligence, robotics, blockchain, quantum computing, augmented reality, virtual reality, and the Internet of Medical Devices (IoMT), to list some of them. Taking advantage of these state-of-the-art technologies presents exciting opportunities to research new strategies for delivering outstanding health services and care. The potential of the Metaverse is to offer patients and healthcare providers realistic experiences that present exciting possibilities for improving healthcare outcomes (Ullah et al., 2023).

Research Method

The triangulation method is employed to gather relevant information from numerous sources (Wilson V, 2014). The primary goal of this study was to find earlier and more recently published articles that discussed or were connected to the topic of interest. Four steps were taken to complete the book chapter. The first step was to find all pertinent studies. A number of databases were checked to make sure the majority of the identified articles were appropriate. PubMed, Google Scholar, Science Direct, and JSTOR were among the databases used. Furthermore, the authors used the Google search engine to find related publications.

The next step was the identification of keywords. The authors employed keywords to make it simpler as well as easier for readers to find their work when publishing their findings (Demiris et al., 2018). As a result, keywords are crucial while performing searches on databases. The following search terms were incorporated into this article - "HEALTHCARE AND METAVERSE OR 3D ENVIRONMENT " OR " Virtual Immersive Experience " OR "Cutting Edge Technology " AND " Metaverse of Medical Technology". The subsequent step was to review all the abstracts and articles gathered to ensure that the papers selected were related to this work. Finally, the outcomes and results were compiled and developed from the chosen articles (Ferrari R, 2015).

Objectives

The objectives of this book chapter are

- To understand the metaverse technology, components of metaverse and metaverse enabling technologies
- To explore the convergence of mestaverse and healthcare
- To comprehend the practical application of metaverse in healthcare and its impact on the healthcare professional's consultation and patient outcomes
- To discover the impact of MV, AR, AI and ML in improving healthcare professionals' competency towards enhanced patient care

A CONCISE OVERVIEW OF THE METAVERSE

The Metaverse is a technologically advanced virtual reality simulation that offers a fully immersive 3D world that perfectly mimics real-world settings and experiences, above the capabilities of traditional 2D platforms (Lippert et al., 2021). Alternatively, it is referred to as a "virtual world," mimicking the geographical and physical characteristics of the actual world and creating a virtual scenario where people are portrayed by avatars The components that comprise the metaverse are as follows: the environment, which represents the world users are in; the interface, which represents how you communicate with the world; the interaction itself; and the safety, which ensures everything is maintained safely (Ullah et al., 2023). Figure 1 illustrates these components.

Figure 1. Components of the metaverse. Adapted from (Ullah et al., 2023)

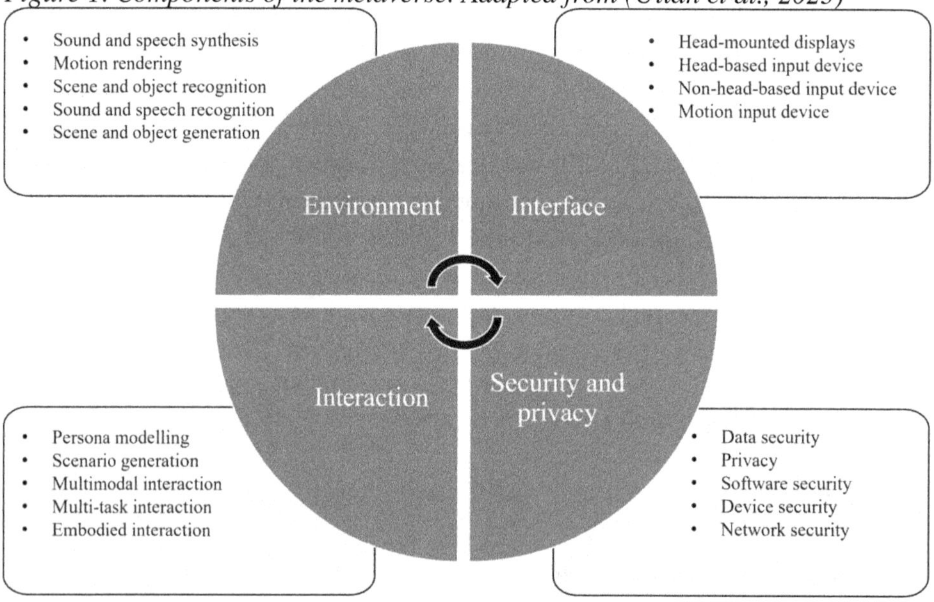

Note. The Metaverse consists of components like interface, privacy, security, and interactivity.

Metaverse-Enhancing Technologies

Specifically, artificial intelligence (AI), and internetworking/telecommunication, blockchain, digital twinning, augmented reality (AR), virtual reality (VR), are the six core technologies that enhance the advancement of the Metaverse. The seamless operation of the Metaverse is the responsibility of several subsystems, which are depicted in Figure 2. The diagram shows the components that work together to maintain the networked and immersive virtual world that is called the Metaverse. The below diagram highlights the interrelated relationships across various subsystems and offers a comprehensive understanding of the fundamental framework required to facilitate Metaverse functions (Ullah et al., 2023).

Figure 2. Technologies that enable the metaverse. Adapted from (Ullah et al., 2023)

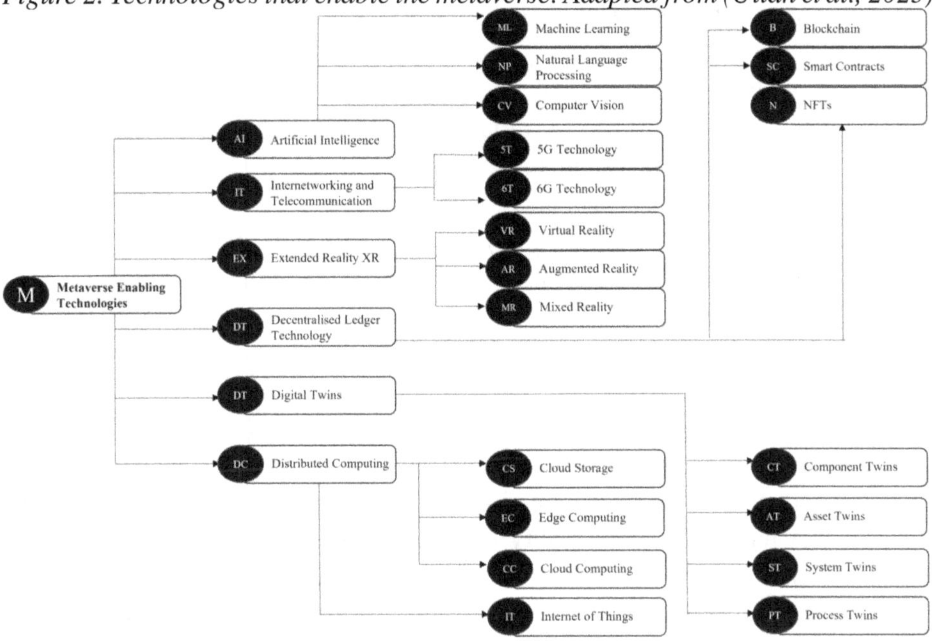

Note. The numerous subsystems that enable the Metaverse and make it work smoothly.

Artificial Intelligence (AI)

Referring to a machine's ability to simulate human intelligence, which enables it to display cognitive capacities and execute tasks with human-like proficiency (Russell & Norvig, 2016). Natural language processing (NLP), computer vision (CV), and machine learning (ML) are just a few of the subsets that make up artificial intelligence. The metaverse provides a seamless user experience with Natural Language Processing (NLP) technology. NLP transforms natural language into computer-readable formats, which are then processed and analysed to provide the desired result. It takes the integration of multiple AI technologies, including NLP, neural networks, and deep learning, to achieve the best possible accuracy in speech recognition. This technology facilitates worldwide user engagement and allows avatars to speak in a natural language, both of which are beneficial to the metaverse. A metaverse of medical technology and AI (MeTAI) includes the essential components such as virtual comparative scanning, raw data sharing, augmented regulatory science, and metaverse medical intervention. MeTAI can help with the development, evaluation, regulation, and improvement of AI-based medical practice (Wang et al., 2022).

Telecommunication/Inter-Networking

Data networking technologies, including the Internet of Things (IoT), Software-Defined Networks (SDN), and Sixth Generation Internet (6G), are essential for facilitating the instantaneous and smooth transfer of data between the virtual and physical worlds, as well as between various sub-metaverses within the metaverse. The metaverse can become more widely available and significantly more interconnected by utilising these technologies, which will make user interactions easier and more coherent (Du et al., 2022).

Extended Reality (XR)

A completely immersive, multi-sensory experience with real-time interaction between users, their avatars, and the virtual environment is made possible by technologies that integrate virtual reality (VR), augmented reality (AR), and mixed reality (MR). Technologies like front-projected holographic displays, advanced brain-computer interface (BCI) methods, and large-scale 3D modelling provide this unmatched experience (Jaynes et al., 2003). Even though these technologies fall under the general category of XR, it is crucial to clarify these basic concepts because they have different meanings (Çöltekin et al., 2020).

Augmented Reality (AR)

This cutting-edge technology has the potential to change how we see and engage with our surroundings. AR can improve our sensory experience by fusing virtual items with our physical surroundings in a seamless manner. This allows us to interact with digital information in real-time with amazing accuracy. The capacity of augmented reality (AR) to create a harmonic merger of the digital and physical worlds by achieving precise and seamless 3D registration of virtual and real things is critical to its success. Among the benefits AR can provide are face recognition, object identification, plane detection, and movement monitoring (Musamih et al., 2022).

Virtual Reality (VR)

VR is distinguished by its exceptional ability to create a state of profound immersion (Steffen et al., 2019). This experience is the consequence of the sophisticated technological capabilities of its hardware and software, which enable it to successfully duplicate reality within the user's sensory surroundings (Parong et al., 2020). Head-mounted displays (HMDs) are the basis for modern VR, which offers unmatched degrees of presence and immersion. This makes it feasible for virtual environments to possibly affect users' cognitive, behavioural, and emotional states in ways that were previously unthinkable (Hershfield et al., 2011; Spence et al., 2017).

Augmented Virtuality (AV)

This technology offers a distinctive method of interacting with virtual worlds. Actual-time object captures and integration into virtual settings is achieved by Augmented Virtuality (AV) in contrast to Augmented Reality (AR), which superimposes virtual items on the actual world. Because of this, users get a more immersive experience and feel more completely embodied in the virtual world (Wang et al., 2022).

Mixed Reality (MR)

The amalgamation of AR and VR characteristics yields a distinct perceptual landscape that facilitates the coexistence and real-time interaction of digital and physical elements. Blending virtual and real-world elements into one display is known as a Mixed Reality (MR) environment. The fundamental function of MR technology is to allow users to view both virtual and real items simultaneously (Wang et al., 2022).

Decentralised Ledger Technology: Blockchain

In general, blockchain refers to a distributed digital ledger that uses cryptography to record assets and transactions inside a safe network (Gadekallu et al., 2021). This ledger guarantees quick, global, and transparent data that is stored in an unchangeable, impenetrable structure that only authorised network users may access. Within the metaverse, vast quantities of data, such as e-books and virtual reality videos, are routinely moved and kept in data centres that do not give enough priority to security protocols, making them vulnerable to malevolent cyberattacks. However, data privacy issues inside the metaverse can be efficiently minimised with the introduction of blockchain technology, which has unmatched properties like immutability and cryptographic security protocols (Cannavo & Lamberti, 2020).

Digital Twins (DT)

The notion of digital twins is centred on developing a comprehensive digital rendering of physical entities and systems (Chu et al., 2023); it makes it possible to create digital copies of real-world physical objects (Yaqoob et al., 2020), which makes it easier to predict and optimise their virtual counterparts. The utilisation of cutting-edge artificial intelligence technology facilitates the creation of realistic simulations of complex physical processes, which offers substantial advantages for the creation and display of expansive metaverse landscapes. The digital twin of the metaverse is a reflection of reality that acts as a gateway for users to interact and explore virtual world offerings (Al-Zyoud et al., 2022).

Cloud Storage and Computing

Cloud storage and computing, more commonly known as "the cloud," is an advanced system that offers a wide range of technologies for computing, encompassing storage of data, archives of data, networking facilities software tools, hosting, analytics for data, and intelligence, through the Internet. This approach has proven especially advantageous since it can offer economies of scale, resource flexibility, and faster invention. By enabling users to simply monitor and assess enormous amounts of information without fretting about device storage restrictions, cloud-based computing may advance metaverse technology (Song & Qin, 2022).

THE CONVERGENCE OF HEALTHCARE AND THE METAVERSE

The healthcare sector has constantly recognised how important it is to engage with patients physically on a regular basis in order to assess their mental and physical wellbeing. Nevertheless, this process has been blatantly interrupted by the COVID-19 pandemic, leaving medical professionals unable to come up with any other ideas. In order to provide healthcare services from a distance, the industry is increasingly turning to remote care technologies like telehealth (Song & Qin, 2022). Telehealth makes use of digital information and communication technology. According to a study (Thomason, 2021), just 43% of US healthcare facilities were set up to provide telehealth services before to the COVID-19 outbreak; by 2020, that number had risen to 95% (Elhence et al., 2022).

Medical science could undergo a major upheaval owing to the rapidly developing concept of the "MEDverse." By incorporating the metaverse into medicine, there are even more opportunities to improve patient outcomes, access to care, and professional collaboration among healthcare providers as telemedicine and other remote care technologies such as telehealth continue to gain popularity in the healthcare sector (Cerasa et al., 2022; Zeng et al., 2022). Especially in the post-COVID-19 era, the development of virtual healthcare settings allows medical professionals possibilities to collaborate, exchange knowledge, and progress the field of medicine in addition to providing a safe and convenient platform for patients (Chamola et al., 2020).

Stages in the Development of the Medical Metaverse

An overview of the use of metaverse in medicine has been provided by Yang et al. (2022). The research recommends broadening the scope of consideration while building the holographic world by incorporating holistic perception into the holographic development process. Furthermore, it suggests incorporating intelligent processing into holographic simulation to enable more complex simulations. The report also recommends extending quality control and human-machine connection into the integration of virtual and actual settings. By applying cutting-edge methods and technology, the aim is to raise the standard and efficacy of Metaverse in Medicine. The general steps involved in creating a metaverse in the medical field are shown in Figure 3.

Figure 3. Four stages involved in creating a medical metaverse. Adapted from (Yang et al., 2022)

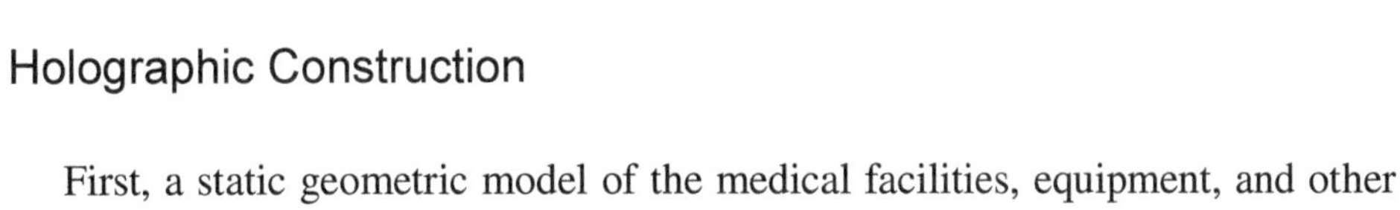

Note. An overview of the four stages involved in implementing the Medical Metaverse

Holographic Construction

First, a static geometric model of the medical facilities, equipment, and other objects in the virtual environment would be constructed. Three main categories can be used to group the objects: people, scenes, and events. Typically, the "scene" in a surgical setting is the interior space and medical equipment, and the "people" are the patients and healthcare providers. Things that have to do with the data and kinetic information that come from the interactions happen with other people, with the environment, or between people. It is possible that holographic construction will improve medical practice (Yang et al., 2022).

Holographic Simulation

The application of holographic simulation in medicine seems promising, especially when paired with sophisticated processing. Improving training and teaching effectiveness is the main goal of the enlarged Metaverse in medicine. Immersion learning opportunities are provided via holographic simulations, such as learning about the connection between smoking and lung cancer. They also support the teaching of intricate medical procedures like endoscopic surgery. Additionally, integrating artificial intelligence technology makes intelligent diagnosis and therapy possible while addressing clinical difficulties (Ullah et al., 2023).

Fusion of Real and Virtual Worlds

The advancement of digital technology will enhance the realism of the virtual medical environment through computer simulation. As a result, it will be harder to distinguish between the virtual and actual worlds, especially when creating a mixed reality (MR) environment for therapeutic purposes. For instance, a physician can speak with a patient using an XR device in an outpatient situation. The ability to recognise, track, and communicate information instantly will make it possible to get patient data. This data can then be presented as augmented reality, creating a new kind of interaction with the existing natural environment (Ullah et al., 2023).

Real-Virtual Linkages

The development of computer simulation technology, artificial intelligence (AI), brain computer interfaces (BCI), and other technologies will result in the establishment of new medical facilities, tools, and procedures. The real-world methods of performing medical procedures will evolve along with technology. According to Ullah et al. (2023), these modifications will progressively increase the intersections between medical interventions in the physical and virtual realms, which will ultimately result in the emergence of new concepts and methods.

Metaverse for Specific Medical Specialties

The utilisation of metaverse services in the healthcare sector is shown in a meta-analysis in Table 1. With descriptions and author details provided for each, the study pinpoints 11 distinct domains in which these services are used. The majority of the examined studies took place in the last year or two (Ullah et al., 2023).

Table 1. An overview of metaverse technology and its uses in several medical domains. Adapted from (Ullah et al., 2023)

Operational sphere	Description	Authors
Senior care	Addressing issues and providing senior citizens with chances for social engagement	(Cho, 2022; Nugroho et al., 2022)
Vascular system fitness	Applications of metaverse technology in relation to heart health	(Mesko, 2022; Skalidis et al., 2023)
Prolonged and chronic diseases	Managing chronic disease	(Sun et al., 2022; Southworth et al., 2020)
Dentistry	Exploring the potential uses of a metaverse in dentistry	(Duman et al., 2022; Afrashtehfar & Abu-Fanas, 2022)
Gynaecology	Metaverse technology applications in gynaecology and foetus health	(Noben et al., 2021; Werneet al., 2022) (Noben et al., 2021; Sridhar et al., 2020)
Oncology	Potential applications of the metaverse for cancer therapy	(Zeng et al., 2022; Dzimitrowicz & Armstrong, 2022; McWilliam & Scarfe, 2022)
Ophthalmology	Opportunities and challenges for vision care	(Tan et al., 2022)
Mental health	Prospective applications of metaverse for mental wellness	(Almarzouqi et al., 2022; Turbyne, 2022; Usmani et al., 2022)
Physical Health	Possible applications of the metaverse to physical health	(Smith et al., 2020)
Medical education and training	Instruments that support clinical simulation, information exchange, and the delivery of healthcare	(Holloway, 2012; Wu & Ho, 2023; Parsons, 2012) (Román-Belmonte et al., 2023; Mesko, 2022) (Bansal et al., 2022; Pottle, 2019) (Pottle, 2019; Jones et al., 2021; Jones et al., 2019) (Wu & Ho, 2023; Almousa et al., 2019; Zikas et al., 2021)
Emergency	Metaverse applications in emergency medicine	(Wu & Ho, 2023)

Note. A meta-analysis evaluating the application of metaverse services in the medical field.

Practical Applications of Metaverse in Medicine and Healthcare

In the field of healthcare, the Metaverse presents a plethora of opportunities, from physical examinations and research to diagnosis and clinical treatment. Medical procedures can then be performed in a virtual environment using VR equipment (Figure 3) (Hou et al., 2022).

Figure 4. Applying virtual reality technology for surgical training (Image by raw-pixel.com on Freepik)

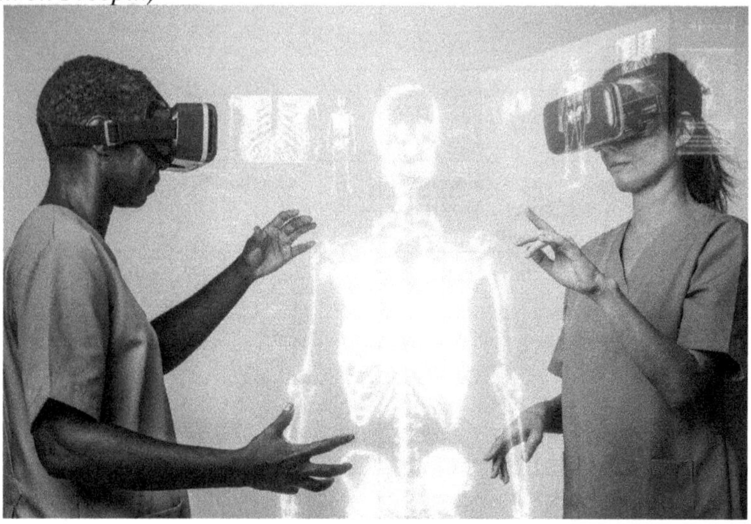

Note. Doctors exploring the human anatomy using VR

We will now examine a few particular applications that Metaverse can provide for the healthcare field.

Virtual Medical Consultations

Virtual consultations, in which the doctor can talk to the patient using video conferencing technology such as Skype, Teams or Facetime, already exist for many years. However, when using these technologies, the patient might feel distant to the doctor. With VR, this distance feels smaller because it's a much more immersive experience, enabling more personal discussions. Mixed reality (MR) software is used for virtual consultations and other purposes, in which physical and virtual objects may co-exist and interact in real time. Software like these could be part of a larger metaverse, allowing patients to receive medical advice and guidance without having to leave their homes. Applications of the metaverse in medicine and healthcare could be integrated with DT, enabling the patient and the doctor to see a digital representation of the patient while discussing the patient's health, improving the patient's understanding of the disease (Hulsen, 2024).

Medical Education and Training

The metaverse could be used to provide healthcare providers with virtual training and simulation experiences, allowing them to practice and improve their skills without putting patients at risk. Surgical simulations using VR were already proposed in the previous century. Currently, several systems exist that make training and simulation in

VR possible. For example, the Precision VR platform of Surgical Theatre creates patient-specific 360°VR models from volumetric scans (e.g., CT, MRI) that can be manipulated and viewed from any angle using a touchscreen monitor or VR headset with controllers. The MetaMedicsVR platform provides VR training for any kind of healthcare professional, such as nurses, surgeons and other medical specialists (Hulsen, 2024).

Patient Education

The metaverse could be used to provide patients with virtual educational resources on topics such as healthy living and disease prevention. They could also help the patient to get an impression of what their operation could look like, or what research has been carried out in the laboratory. "Preoperative patient counselling services" aim to dispel patients' fears by disclosing information related to anaesthesia, surgical procedure, and post-surgical complications and by familiarizing them with the environment in which the operation will take place. Advantages of virtual counselling over verbal counselling include: reduced effect of a possible language barrier; reduced time for the doctor and no need for physically disabled patients to leave their home. The company HealthBlocks launched a blockchain based app to assist users with getting active and staying healthy, and Healthify developed a sports and health metaverse based on blockchain technology. DTs could be used to improve the understanding of a patient's disease by showing a digital representation of the patient with the disease (Hulsen, 2024).

Medical Research

The metaverse could be used to simulate medical procedures and treatments, allowing researchers to test and refine new treatments and interventions. This is especially useful for treating mental disorders such as Attention Deficit Hyperactivity Disorder (ADHD), Alzheimer's disease (AD) or diseases causing a reduced mobility, such as Parkinson's disease (PD). In the latter case, VR interventions were carried out in the form of immersive games with individualized training programs, stimulating patients to work on their mobility as well as their autobiographical memory. Clinical trials could be sped up significantly by using the metaverse, breaking down physical and geographical barriers between clinicians and patients enrolled in a trial. Blockchain can also be used to improve the security of Electronic Health Records (EHRs), making sure that researchers can use information from these medical records with reduced security risks. DTs can be used to simulate patients and medical devices, enabling researchers to perform studies without directly interfering with the patient (Hulsen, 2024).

Drug Development

The metaverse can enable the creation of virtual environments where drug developers can simulate the effects of drugs on the human body. These simulations can help researchers identify potential safety and efficacy issues with new drugs before they are tested in human clinical trials, potentially reducing the time and cost required for drug development. In drug design, VR can be used not only to visualize and interact with (DTs of the) molecules, but also to interact with molecular dynamics simulations 'on the fly' (also named "interactive molecular dynamics in VR" or "IMD-VR"). Examples of drug development software that support VR are UCSF ChimeraX and YASARA, through which docking, the virtual simulation of molecular interactions, can take place. An example of IMD-VR software is Narupa iMD, which enables users to collaborate in a single virtual reality space and interact with real-time molecular simulations (Hulsen, 2024).

Therapy and Support

Patients suffering from certain phobias (e.g., agoraphobia, acrophobia, fear of flying) or disorders such as posttraumatic stress disorder (PTSD) can be helped by applying 'exposure therapy', in which they are exposed to situations that gives them an anxiety attack. Normally this would be done 'in vivo', in which the patient has to face his/her fear in real life, but it can also be done by providing a VR virtual environment which simulates the 'dangerous' situation. This VR exposure therapy (VRET) is more safe, convenient, controllable and cost-effective than its 'in vivo' counterpart. Recent developments in this field focus on making the VR experience more realistic, in order to create an 'embodiment illusion' using multisensory integrations in which patients feel as if they are really living in their virtual body (or 'avatar'). This kind of 'immersive virtual reality' (IVR) shows promising results in people with mild to borderline intellectual disability (MBID). The metaverse could facilitate remote rehabilitation and physical therapy as well. Patients could use VR exercises to improve their mobility and coordination from the comfort of their own home (Hulsen, 2024).

Expanding Metaverse and Augmented & Virtual Reality to the Healthcare System

Medicine has always involved direct, in-person interaction between people. But with the introduction of more advanced technologies, this is quickly evolving. It's true that AR and VR technologies have revolutionised the gaming and entertainment sectors, but they also have a great deal of potential to change the healthcare sector because they can alter many traditional healthcare branches and operations, such as radiology, oncology, training, and more (Bapatla et al., 2021).

In the therapeutic domain, AR/VR has shown to be especially advantageous. When a patient is receiving aversion therapy—a controlled, secure setting where their interactions are continuously monitored—psychologists and psychiatrists use it to customise settings for each patient (Marr, 2022). Early Metaverse uses will include surgical simulations, diagnostic imaging, patient care management, rehabilitative therapies, and healthcare administration. Utilising this technology, patients can gain more knowledge about their conditions and available treatment options. Point-of-care nursing teams can benefit from AR/VR in a clinical setting. When AR is combined with radiology, doctors can more clearly study internal anatomy by superimposing medical images—like those from a CT scan—directly onto patients and arranging them to fit their bodies, even when they are moving. It is evident that the Metaverse has the ability to connect both virtual and physical objects as well as real-time locations and objects used in the provision of medical services. Instead of displacing current medical service delivery, the main objective of the medical IoT is to enhance it (Mesko, 2022).

Intelligent Healthcare leveraging the Metaverse and AI

MeTAI, or the metaverse of "medical technology and AI," can help with the creation, testing, assessment, control, interpretation, and improvement of AI-based medicine, particularly imaging-guided diagnosis and treatment.

MeTAI Applications

Four significant applications—virtual comparative scanning, raw data sharing, augmented regulatory science, and metaversed medical intervention—that best represent MeTAI are highlighted, with a focus on medical imaging, given the revolutionary role that the metaverse can play in the healthcare arena. These applications have precedents, but what makes them fascinating are their original features in terms of depth, scope, scale, and integration mechanisms (Wang et al., 2022).

Virtual Comparative Scanning

Digital twin computing, which combines data from real and virtual things, is the result of ongoing efforts to create sophisticated computer models of the human body and the devices that scan it. Build vendor-specific virtual tomographic scanners, customised computational avatars with anatomical attributes that the scanners can resolve, and AI-enabled graphical tools to add, remove, and alter diseases in these avatars if we want to further capitalise on these advancements for medical imaging. Every sort of virtual CT scanner can be used to scan potential pathologies within the patient's avatar if they are referred for a CT scan due to a cardiac condition (Wang et al., 2022).

Raw Data Sharing

Medical tomographic scanners, which provide copious amounts of multi-dimensional measurements that are sophisticated algorithms used to reconstruct into images, are the primary source of medical imaging data. Researcher access to tomographic raw data, such as CT sinograms, has long been a challenge, and in the age of AI-based medical imaging, this issue is becoming increasingly serious. When tomographic image reconstruction occurs, not all of the information included in raw data may be retained. This is why raw data are necessary for algorithmic optimisation, as was realised decades ago. In addition, a number of labs have lately worked on what is known as the "end-to-end deep learning workflow"—also known as "rawdiomics"—which requires access to raw data in order to produce diagnostic conclusions (Wang et al., 2022).

Augmented Regulatory Science

AI has significantly improved medical imaging, particularly deep learning, pushing the boundaries of regulatory science used in the pre-market evaluation of such AI-enabled medical products. Deep neural networks are known to frequently suffer from generalizability problems and are susceptible to adversarial attacks. To maximise the advantages and safety, these difficulties must be resolved. An action plan to strengthen the regulation of AI-powered software as medical devices (SaMDs) was released by the Food and Drug Administration (FDA) last year. The proposal highlights the use of "regulatory science methods related to algorithm bias and robustness" as one activity. To optimise the entire workflow, from data gathering to picture reconstruction and analysis to diagnostic finding, a wide range of high-quality, reasonably priced huge datasets are required. Acquiring huge clinical datasets is expensive in practice. Here, the virtual and emulated scans discussed before will be extremely helpful (Wang et al., 2022).

Metaversed Medical Intervention

MeTAI will have a significant influence on how doctors and people use tools and medical data to comprehend conditions, choose treatments, and carry out interventions. We can arrange complicated surgical and therapeutic scenarios, for instance, in such a virtual environment. Procedures can be repeatedly practiced through virtual practice using the trial-and-error method. The current surgical technologies, like da Vinci (https://www.davincisurgery.com), which let a surgeon to work from a nearby room or from across the world via high-speed internet, work well with this. Surgeons in MeTAI have the option to try various techniques on avatars, such as plastic surgery. Another example is radiotherapy. MeTAI would extend the routine optimisation of treatment plans using patient-specific computer simulations to all medical interventions. Before and during a course of therapy, biological reactions to radiation delivery could also be simulated in order to optimise the treatment response based on the patient's genetic information and response data from prior patients. Because of computational constraints and biological model errors, this approach is currently not practicable for routine treatment planning. Future radiation therapy injury to at-risk organs could be significantly minimised by utilising simulator and clinical information libraries that are instantly usable due to their metaverse integration (Wang et al., 2022).

The Power of Machine Learning in Modern Healthcare

Machine learning, or ML, is one of the most intriguing applications of AI, and numerous organisations are exploring ways to implement it. There is a growing need for ML. It utilises algorithms to facilitate the learning based on the data and may be applied in various categories, such as medical care and business. The healthcare sector continually evolves as a result of novel concepts and technologies emerging so swiftly. Medical professionals may find applications for machine learning in some of these new scenarios. With the advantage of this new plethora of ML-powered intelligence, medical professionals and administrators are able to make prompt, decisions that are informed about treatment of patients and operational endeavours that have implications for millions of lives (Li et al., 2020; Rahane et al., 2018; Ahmed et al., 2020).

Numerous articles have discussed the potential advantages of machine learning and its versatility for the healthcare sector. Figure 4 examines the many quality components and enablers that provide care and support for healthcare facilities.

The renowned machine learning concepts comprise several highly established quality pillars, such as the ability to predict outbreaks of disease, regulate actions, preserve patient information, and even more. By offering healthcare services, the notion significantly broadens its contribution to society. (Emanet et al., 2014; Healy & Walsh, 2017).

Figure 5. The key components of machine learning for healthcare services, adapted from (Javaid et al., 2022)

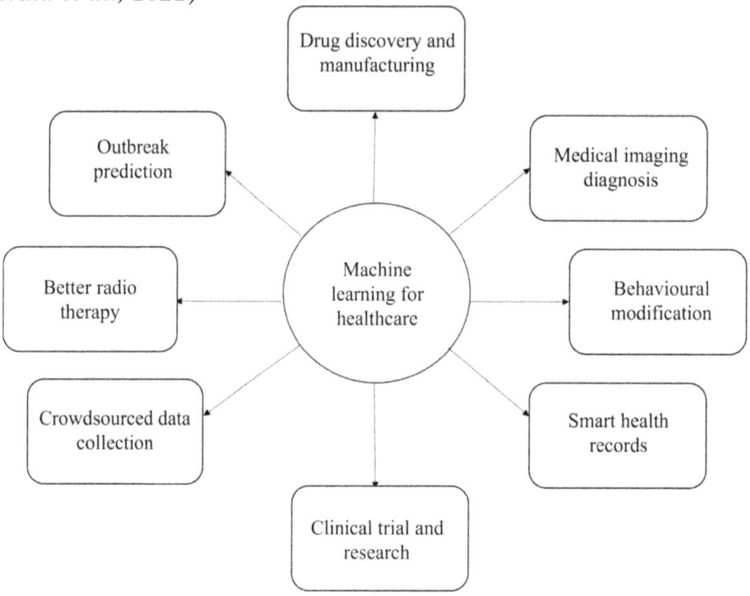

Note. Various machine learning enablers and quality pillars for supporting and maintaining healthcare facilities.

ML plays a critical role in diagnosing the patient's medical health issues, tracking his health, and suggesting the appropriate preventative measures. It might encompass all that from minor illnesses to serious diseases like cancer that are difficult to identify in the beginning stages. The application of machine learning to healthcare includes the identification and prognosis of mental illness issues globally or within specific population groups. By analysing biological function, digestion, distribution, metabolism, and elimination characteristics, it can select compounds with the required physicochemical qualities and biological function (Sathya et al., 2020; Gartner & Padman, 2020; Pitoglou, 2020).

By offering tailored treatment recommendations, ML may aid in shifting the emphasis on medical care from an emergency response to a proactive technique. It can assist doctors in providing incredibly customised care in healthcare applications by taking considering the unique traits and symptoms of each patient. As a result, the likelihood of people experiencing negative drug responses from prescribed medications will be minimised. ML algorithms can help the healthcare sector with the observation and forecasting of disease outbreaks. Furthermore, ML can decrease the adverse outcomes of epidemics (Zhu et al., 2020; Kraft et al., 2020).

Drug research and clinical trials could be streamlined and optimised by machine learning. Pharmaceutical companies operating in this sector encounter numerous challenges. Clinical trial execution always requires an abundance of effort and time because of the numerous factors that need to be considered. For this purpose, in order to obtain reliable results, potential participants in clinical trials must be thoroughly screened utilising an extensive list of criteria. This continuously tracks and assesses a substantial amount of data to ensure the safety and efficacy of the medications (Souri, et al., 2020; Sarkar, et al., 2020).

PROBABLE HURDLES IN THE HEALTHCARE METAVERSE

Although the metaverse has enormous potential for the future, there are certain difficulties and challenges that require to be addressed before it can be effectively implemented, particularly in the healthcare industry. Figure 5 summarises the probable issues and challenges in the healthcare metaverse.

Figure 6. Probable hurdles in the healthcare metaverse, adapted from (Athar et al., 2023)

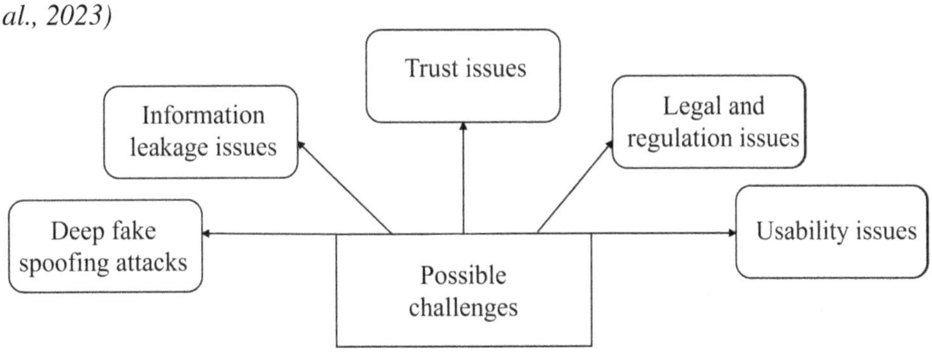

Note. probable issues and challenges in the metaverse of healthcare.

Spoofing Threats through Deepfakes Technique

The metaverse is plagued with deepfakes, which has emphasised the need for data distinctness. It is essential to comprehend the significance of genuine data, which reveals if the information was taken from a genuine patient or whether another person attempted to provide a different perspective after stealing or getting access to the same information. Spoofing attacks have a direct impact on the distinctiveness of clinical records. Nonetheless, it is essential to present the real data in the metaverse since it is crucial for the patient and makes it harder for the doctor to differentiate between the information being presented. It has an immediate effect on both the diagnosing process and the reliability of information regarding patients. Any misunderstanding in its detection could have a major detrimental influence on the efficacy of the medication because diagnosis is an essential stage in determining the type of illness and the appropriate treatments to be delivered (Wang, et al., 2022).

Challenges with Leakage of Information

Various digital organisations acquire information about patients through various strategies. For the purpose of delivering treatments in a more effective manner, healthcare professionals adopt a metaverse virtual setting (Wang, et al., 2022). Recent studies on virtual reality and augmented reality suggest that the metaverse may be applied more successfully for diagnoses and surgeries, as well as for the treatment of stroke, cancer, pain, anxiety, depression, fear, and several other ailments (Petrigna, & Musumeci, 2022). When patients and clinicians communicate through the metaverse and virtual reality (VR), in which they exchange information, patients are seriously endangered since they do not have data security. However, personal data could be hacked at any time by hackers or other cyber criminals, which might result in negative consequences if individuals use the metaverse domain for health services (Wang et al., 2022).

Building Trust Amongst Stakeholders

While ensuring a quick, reliable, and efficient cross-platform experience is essential, anyone wishing to access medical services should also be concerned about how their stakeholders will communicate with them—whether in person or virtually. When using other online services, users typically don't give the service much thought or disclose personal information to any facility. However, when receiving medical services—particularly in a metaverse setting—they require a reliable medical service provider organisation to guarantee that their data is secure. But data that are not secure and that are accessible to any other entity or individual have the ability to alter information. The inability to correctly diagnose the illness if any component of the data changes could have an impact on the service provider (Athar et al., 2023).

Legal and Regulatory Concerns

Patients can acquire their prescription and diagnosis promptly in a metaverse setting for the healthcare domain because the majority of people prefer using time-saving services that are easily accessible because of advancements in technology. The swift development of the metaverse in the healthcare sector poses challenges for regulators as pharmaceuticals, healthcare providers, and insurance can provide patients with efficient services. There are no domain-specific regulations or laws in the Metaverse that provide autonomy to all stakeholders engaged. They must ensure that the appropriate policies are established and upheld in order to curtail any illegal conduct in a virtual environment (Chengoden et al., 2023).

Utilisation in the Visually Challenged Population

Recent years have seen an upsurge in the adoption of metaverse technologies, however, this presents an obstacle for the visually challenged patients in the medical settings because it can be extremely challenging for them to access the metaverse's medical services or acquire any advantage from it (Thase et al., 2020).

FUTURE DIRECTIONS

The Metaverse has the potential to significantly transform the healthcare industry with its entirely comprehensive healthcare offerings. The provision of a broad range of medical services, such as preventing diseases, medical diagnosis, and medical care as well as the application of online communication among professionals and end-users, can accomplish this. Additionally, there are still specific challenges that should be resolved over time in order to improve the Metaverse's practicality for utilisation in the field of healthcare (Ullah et al., 2023).

Blockchain: An Optimistic Prospect for Health Record Incorporation and Depository

In the field of medical documentation in particular, blockchain technology shows significant potential for the healthcare sector as it could boost personal control, eliminate fragmented infrastructure, and enhance data storage capacity. Advantages like enhanced security, simpler accessibility, and the ability to allow access to doctors from anywhere in the globe are made possible by decentralisation of blockchain, which facilitates the safe storage of records in personal blockchain accounts. Furthermore, blockchain technology can facilitate professional collaboration, which will eventually lead to the implementation of an improved assimilated medical system, assisting in addressing the complexity of multiple health conditions. With the potential to revolutionise the industry, enhance outcomes for patients, and subdue current obstacles, the adoption of blockchain in the healthcare sector thus offers itself as a significant and intriguing way for further investigation in the domains of metaverse, healthcare, and blockchain (Ullah et al., 2023).

Tackling Privacy Concerns associated with Medical Technologies in the realm of Metaverse

The Metaverse boosts user experiences by integrating the virtual and real worlds through communication and technology. It is capable of tracking physiological responses and capturing patients' personal information, however, there are security and privacy concerns. "Private copy" and "clone clouds" are two innovative approaches for minimising breaches of information and malicious manipulation. A significant emphasis on privacy protections is essential for establishing Metaverse-based medical solutions that consider interactive, behavioural, and sensory components. Additional studies in this domain could be significant. The metaverse in the medical field can transform healthcare. When Metaverse combines software, wearables, and hardware in digital settings, the safety and integrity of sensitive data become paramount. Tackling hurdles demands developing robust communication channels and effective strategies for data integration (Ullah et al., 2023).

Assessing the Framework of an Integrated Edge-Cloud Metaverse

The conventional server-centric network architecture utilised in the Metaverse has two primary challenges that ultimately deteriorate user experience: high latency and data loss. To solve this issue and realise the full value of Metaverse technology in the healthcare industry, it is vital to look into a future research pathway that focusses on the development of an integrated edge-cloud Metaverse framework. This novel approach entails the dynamic distribution of processing and communication across multiple network nodes. Adopting such a framework could significantly improve the user experience and quality of service for applications related to healthcare (Ullah et al., 2023).

CONCLUSION

The healthcare industry encounters challenge due to financial scarcity, shortages of resources, and geographic limitations that impede the accessibility of care. The healthcare industry can curtail expenditures by leveraging the endless possibilities of the Metaverse and reallocating resources to areas such as enhanced diagnostic technological devices. The global Metaverse healthcare market is projected to reach 71.97 billion USD by 2030, demonstrating an enormous opportunity for progress (Chengoden et al., 2023). This provides an opportunity to completely reshape the healthcare field by enhancing accessibility, affordability, and patient care. In pursuit of this goal, the research that was performed presents an extensive evaluation of professional discussions and studies related to the Metaverse, the healthcare industry, and cutting-edge technologies.

The growing demand for telemedicine and the influence of electronic gaming on youngsters are two prominent instances showing how the mindset is shifting to adapt the widening utilisation of technology in healthcare. As we strive towards proactive healthcare, numerous technologies are transforming the healthcare sector, which includes virtual reality (VR), blockchain, and digital twins. Assessing and managing the impact on human beings is equally important when implementing technologies into health services. The interoperability challenges, the legal ramifications of data ownership and distribution, and ethical and pragmatic obstacles around the privacy and security of data should all be handled with caution. By actively tackling these obstacles, we can ensure that the implementation of Metaverse technologies adheres to the regulations of safety for patients and excellent care.

With a patient-focused approach and a careful consideration of both the benefits and risks, we may maximise the optimal application of the Metaverse in the healthcare industry. Technology should be employed as a facilitator instead of an impediment in this approach, which calls for meticulous planning and process. This approach enables us to maximise the advantages of the metaverse for improved healthcare outcomes while protecting the well-being and interests of patients.

LIMITATION AND FUTURE INVESTIGATION

Due to the extensive nature of the study topic, this review synthesised and summarised the conclusions and findings of the publications that were chosen, and it includes the brief assessments of the area of study. Selection bias is another potential restriction. While conducting database searches with predetermined keywords, the authors of this paper tried to minimise selection bias. Furthermore, the search was conducted across several databases (Google, Google Scholar, JSTOR, Science Direct, and PubMed).

The authors evaluated a number of prospective publications before deciding whether or not to include any particular papers in this study. As a result of the rapid development of metaverse in healthcare industry, this analysis concentrated on shifts and developments of metaverse technology in healthcare industry. Therefore, the results cannot be extrapolated and applied to different sectors. Lack of time is another barrier. There may have been more articles published during the time that this study's search was being done and articles were being found. Thus, the literature evaluation and search could be carried on for additional research in the future. Future studies are needed to examine improvements and trends in metaverse healthcare.

REFERENCES

Afrashtehfar, K. I., & Abu-Fanas, A. S. (2022). Metaverse, crypto, and NFTs in dentistry. *Education Sciences*, 12(8), 538. DOI: 10.3390/educsci12080538

Ahmed, Z., Mohamed, K., Zeeshan, S., & Dong, X. (2020). Artificial intelligence with multi-functional machine learning platform development for better healthcare and precision medicine. *Database : The Journal of Biological Databases and Curation*, 2020, baaa010. DOI: 10.1093/database/baaa010 PMID: 32185396

Al-Zyoud, I., Laamarti, F., Ma, X., Tobón, D., & El Saddik, A. (2022). Towards a machine learning-based digital twin for non-invasive human bio-signal fusion. *Sensors (Basel)*, 22(24), 9747. DOI: 10.3390/s22249747 PMID: 36560115

Almarzouqi, A., Aburayya, A., & Salloum, S. A. (2022). Prediction of user's intention to use metaverse system in medical education: A hybrid SEM-ML learning approach. *IEEE Access : Practical Innovations, Open Solutions*, 10, 43421–43434. DOI: 10.1109/ACCESS.2022.3169285

Almousa, O., Prates, J., Yeslam, N., Mac Gregor, D., Zhang, J., Phan, V., Nielsen, M., Smith, R., & Qayumi, K. (2019). Virtual reality simulation technology for cardiopulmonary resuscitation training: An innovative hybrid system with haptic feedback. *Simulation & Gaming*, 50(1), 6–22. DOI: 10.1177/1046878118820905

Alshamrani, M. (2022). IoT and artificial intelligence implementations for remote healthcare monitoring systems: A survey. *Journal of King Saud University. Computer and Information Sciences*, 34(8), 4687–4701. DOI: 10.1016/j.jksuci.2021.06.005

Anwer, A., Jamil, Y., & Bilal, M. (2022). Provision of surgical pre-operative patient counseling services through the metaverse technology. *International Journal of Surgery*, 104, 106792. DOI: 10.1016/j.ijsu.2022.106792 PMID: 35918004

Bansal, G., Rajgopal, K., Chamola, V., Xiong, Z., & Niyato, D. (2022). Healthcare in metaverse: A survey on current metaverse applications in healthcare. *IEEE Access : Practical Innovations, Open Solutions*, 10, 119914–119946. DOI: 10.1109/ACCESS.2022.3219845

Bapatla, N., Fine, L., & Rajput, V. (2021). The future role of augmented reality and virtual reality simulation in clinical skills assessment. *Indian Journal of Medical Specialities*, 12(3), 113–115. DOI: 10.4103/injms.injms_41_21

Bhugaonkar, K., Bhugaonkar, R., & Masne, N. (2022). The trend of metaverse and augmented & virtual reality extending to the healthcare system. *Cureus*, 14(9). Advance online publication. DOI: 10.7759/cureus.29071 PMID: 36258985

Cannavo, A., & Lamberti, F. (2020). How blockchain, virtual reality, and augmented reality are converging, and why. *IEEE Consumer Electronics Magazine*, 10(5), 6–13. DOI: 10.1109/MCE.2020.3025753

Chamola, V., Hassija, V., Gupta, S., Goyal, A., Guizani, M., & Sikdar, B. (2020). Disaster and pandemic management using machine learning: A survey. *IEEE Internet of Things Journal*, 8(21), 16047–16071. DOI: 10.1109/JIOT.2020.3044966 PMID: 35782181

Chengoden, R., Victor, N., Huynh-The, T., Yenduri, G., Jhaveri, R. H., Alazab, M., Bhattacharya, S., Hegde, P., Maddikunta, P. K. R., & Gadekallu, T. R. (2023). Metaverse for healthcare: A survey on potential applications, challenges and future directions. *IEEE Access : Practical Innovations, Open Solutions*, 11, 12765–12795. DOI: 10.1109/ACCESS.2023.3241628

Cho, M. G. (2022). A study on smart aging system for the elderly based on metaverse. *Journal of Digital Convergence*, 20(2), 261–268.

Chu, N. H., Hoang, D. T., Nguyen, D. N., Phan, K. T., Dutkiewicz, E., Niyato, D., & Shu, T. (2023). Metaslicing: A novel resource allocation framework for metaverse. *IEEE Transactions on Mobile Computing*, 23(5), 4145–4162. DOI: 10.1109/TMC.2023.3288085

Çöltekin, A., Lochhead, I., Madden, M., Christophe, S., Devaux, A., Pettit, C., Lock, O., Shukla, S., Herman, L., Stachoň, Z., Kubíček, P., Snopková, D., Bernardes, S., & Hedley, N. (2020). Extended reality in spatial sciences: A review of research challenges and future directions. *ISPRS International Journal of Geo-Information*, 9(7), 439. DOI: 10.3390/ijgi9070439

Demiris, G., Oliver, D. P., & Washington, K. T. (2018). *Behavioral intervention research in hospice and palliative care: Building an evidence base*. Academic press.

Du, H., Niyato, D., Miao, C., Kang, J., & Kim, D. I. (2022, December). Optimal targeted advertising strategy for secure wireless edge metaverse. In *GLOBECOM 2022-2022 IEEE Global Communications Conference* (pp. 4346-4351). IEEE. DOI: 10.1109/GLOBECOM48099.2022.10001331

Duman, S., Çelik Özen, D., & Duman, Ş. B. (2022). Metaverse in paediatric dentistry. *European Archives of Paediatric Dentistry; Official Journal of the European Academy of Paediatric Dentistry*, 23(4), 655–656. DOI: 10.1007/s40368-022-00733-7 PMID: 35821383

Dzimitrowicz, H. E., & Armstrong, A. J. (2022). Triplet Therapy: Entering the Metaverse of Metastatic Hormone-sensitive Prostate Cancer Treatment. *European Urology*, 82(6), S0302–S2838. DOI: 10.1016/j.eururo.2022.08.031 PMID: 36114081

Elhence, A., Kohli, V., Chamola, V., & Sikdar, B. (2022). Enabling cost-effective and secure minor medical teleconsultation using artificial intelligence and blockchain. *IEEE Internet of Things Magazine*, 5(1), 80–84. DOI: 10.1109/IOTM.001.2100142

Emanet, N., Öz, H. R., Bayram, N., & Delen, D. (2014). A comparative analysis of machine learning methods for classification type decision problems in healthcare. *Decision Analysis*, 1, 1–20.

Ferrari, R. (2015). Writing narrative style literature reviews. *Medical Writing*, 24(4), 230–235. DOI: 10.1179/2047480615Z.000000000329

Gadekallu, T. R., Pham, Q. V., Nguyen, D. C., Maddikunta, P. K. R., Deepa, N., Prabadevi, B., Pathirana, P. N., Zhao, J., & Hwang, W. J. (2021). Blockchain for edge of things: Applications, opportunities, and challenges. *IEEE Internet of Things Journal*, 9(2), 964–988. DOI: 10.1109/JIOT.2021.3119639

Gartner, D., & Padman, R. (2020). Machine learning for healthcare behavioural OR: Addressing waiting time perceptions in emergency care. *The Journal of the Operational Research Society*, 71(7), 1087–1101. DOI: 10.1080/01605682.2019.1571005

Gerup, J., Soerensen, C. B., & Dieckmann, P. (2020). Augmented reality and mixed reality for healthcare education beyond surgery: An integrative review. *International Journal of Medical Education*, 11, 1–18. DOI: 10.5116/ijme.5e01.eb1a PMID: 31955150

Hajesmaeel-Gohari, S., Sarpourian, F., & Shafiei, E. (2021). Virtual reality applications to assist pregnant women: A scoping review. *BMC Pregnancy and Childbirth*, 21(1), 1–8. DOI: 10.1186/s12884-021-03725-5 PMID: 33765969

Healy, M., & Walsh, P. (2017, November). Detecting demeanor for healthcare with machine learning. In *2017 IEEE international conference on bioinformatics and biomedicine (BIBM)* (pp. 2015-2019). IEEE. DOI: 10.1109/BIBM.2017.8217970

Hershfield, H. E., Goldstein, D. G., Sharpe, W. F., Fox, J., Yeykelis, L., Carstensen, L. L., & Bailenson, J. N. (2011). Increasing saving behavior through age-progressed renderings of the future self. *Journal of marketing research, 48*(SPL), S23-S37.

Holloway, D. (2012). Virtual worlds and health: Healthcare delivery and simulation opportunities. In *Virtual worlds and metaverse platforms: New communication and identity paradigms* (pp. 251–270). IGI Global. DOI: 10.4018/978-1-60960-854-5.ch017

Hooper, J., Tsiridis, E., Feng, J. E., Schwarzkopf, R., Waren, D., Long, W. J., Poultsides, L., Macaulay, W., Papagiannakis, G., Kenanidis, E., Rodriguez, E. D., Slover, J., Egol, K. A., Phillips, D. P., Friedlander, S., & Collins, M. (2019). Virtual reality simulation facilitates resident training in total hip arthroplasty: A randomized controlled trial. *The Journal of Arthroplasty*, 34(10), 2278–2283. DOI: 10.1016/j.arth.2019.04.002 PMID: 31056442

Jaynes, C., Seales, W. B., Calvert, K., Fei, Z., & Griffioen, J. (2003, May). The Metaverse: a networked collection of inexpensive, self-configuring, immersive environments. In *Proceedings of the workshop on Virtual environments 2003* (pp. 115-124). DOI: 10.1145/769953.769967

Jones, D., Hazelton, M., Evans, D. J., Pento, V., See, Z. S., Van Leugenhaege, L., & Fealy, S. (2021). The road to birth: Using digital technology to visualise pregnancy anatomy. In *Digital Anatomy: Applications of Virtual, Mixed and Augmented Reality* (pp. 325–342). Springer International Publishing. DOI: 10.1007/978-3-030-61905-3_17

Kapoor, A., Guha, S., Das, M. K., Goswami, K. C., & Yadav, R. (2020). Digital healthcare: The only solution for better healthcare during COVID-19 pandemic? *Indian Heart Journal*, 72(2), 61–64. DOI: 10.1016/j.ihj.2020.04.001 PMID: 32534691

Kraft, S. A. (2020). Respect and trustworthiness in the patient-provider-machine relationship: Applying a relational lens to machine learning healthcare applications. *The American Journal of Bioethics*, 20(11), 51–53. DOI: 10.1080/15265161.2020.1820108 PMID: 33103984

Li, J. P., Haq, A. U., Din, S. U., Khan, J., Khan, A., & Saboor, A. (2020). Heart disease identification method using machine learning classification in e-healthcare. *IEEE Access : Practical Innovations, Open Solutions*, 8, 107562–107582. DOI: 10.1109/ACCESS.2020.3001149

Lippert, K., Khan, M. N. R., Rabbi, M. M., Dutta, A., & Cloutier, R. (2021, December). A framework of metaverse for systems engineering. In *2021 IEEE International Conference on Signal Processing, Information, Communication & Systems (SPICSCON)* (pp. 50-54). IEEE. DOI: 10.1109/SPICSCON54707.2021.9885722

Lu, Y., Yang, D., Yang, Y., & Bai, C. (2022). MIoT integrates health, MM benefits humans: Funding conference for International Association and Alliance of Metaverse in Medicine successfully held. *Clinical eHealth, 5*, 17-18.

Marr, B. (2022). The amazing possibilities of healthcare in the metaverse. *Forbes*.

McWilliam, A., & Scarfe, P. (2022). The metaverse and oncology.

Mesko, B. (2022). The promise of the metaverse in cardiovascular health.

Musamih, A., Yaqoob, I., Salah, K., Jayaraman, R., Al-Hammadi, Y., Omar, M., & Ellahham, S. (2022). Metaverse in healthcare: Applications, challenges, and future directions. *IEEE Consumer Electronics Magazine*.

Noben, L., Goossens, S. M. T. A., Truijens, S. E. M., Van Berckel, M. M. G., Perquin, C. W., Slooter, G. D., & Van Rooijen, S. J. (2019). A virtual reality video to improve information provision and reduce anxiety before cesarean delivery: Randomized controlled trial. *JMIR Mental Health*, 6(12), e15872. DOI: 10.2196/15872 PMID: 31850850

Nugroho, R. A., Prakoso, S. G., Hidayati, K. N., Rahmawati, A. D., Kartinawanty, A. T., & Santoso, S. A. (2022, October). Challenges of The Metaverse Adoption for the Health of the Elderly: Case in Surakarta. In *2022 IEEE International Conference of Computer Science and Information Technology (ICOSNIKOM)* (pp. 1-6). IEEE. DOI: 10.1109/ICOSNIKOM56551.2022.10034914

Parong, J., Pollard, K. A., Files, B. T., Oiknine, A. H., Sinatra, A. M., Moss, J. D., Passaro, A., & Khooshabeh, P. (2020). The mediating role of presence differs across types of spatial learning in immersive technologies. *Computers in Human Behavior*, 107, 106290. DOI: 10.1016/j.chb.2020.106290

Parsons, T. D. (2012). Virtual simulations and the second life metaverse: paradigm shift in neuropsychological assessment. In *Virtual worlds and metaverse platforms: New communication and identity paradigms* (pp. 234–250). IGI Global. DOI: 10.4018/978-1-60960-854-5.ch016

Petrigna, L., & Musumeci, G. (2022). The metaverse: A new challenge for the healthcare system: A scoping review. *Journal of Functional Morphology and Kinesiology*, 7(3), 63. DOI: 10.3390/jfmk7030063 PMID: 36135421

Pitoglou, S. (2020). Machine learning in healthcare: introduction and real-world application considerations. In *Quality Assurance in the Era of Individualized Medicine* (pp. 92–109). IGI Global. DOI: 10.4018/978-1-7998-2390-2.ch004

Pottle, J. (2019). Virtual reality and the transformation of medical education. *Future Healthcare Journal*, 6(3), 181–185. DOI: 10.7861/fhj.2019-0036 PMID: 31660522

Rahane, W., Dalvi, H., Magar, Y., Kalane, A., & Jondhale, S. (2018, March). Lung cancer detection using image processing and machine learning healthcare. In *2018 International Conference on Current Trends towards Converging Technologies (ICCTCT)* (pp. 1-5). IEEE. DOI: 10.1109/ICCTCT.2018.8551008

Román-Belmonte, J. M., Rodríguez-Merchán, E. C., & De la Corte-Rodríguez, H. (2023). Metaverse applied to musculoskeletal pathology: Orthoverse and Rehabverse. *Postgraduate Medicine*, 135(5), 440–448. DOI: 10.1080/00325481.2023.2180953 PMID: 36786393

Russell, S. J., & Norvig, P. (2016). *Artificial intelligence: a modern approach*. Pearson.

Salloum, G., & Tekli, J. (2021). Automated and personalized nutrition health assessment, recommendation, and progress evaluation using fuzzy reasoning. *International Journal of Human-Computer Studies*, 151, 102610. DOI: 10.1016/j.ijhcs.2021.102610

Sarkar, S. K., Roy, S., Alsentzer, E., McDermott, M. B., Falck, F., Bica, I., & Hyland, S. L. (2020, November). Machine learning for health (ML4H) 2020: Advancing healthcare for all. In *Machine Learning for Health* (pp. 1–11). PMLR.

Sathya, D., Sudha, V., & Jagadeesan, D. (2020). Application of machine learning techniques in healthcare. In *Handbook of Research on Applications and Implementations of Machine Learning Techniques* (pp. 289–304). IGI Global. DOI: 10.4018/978-1-5225-9902-9.ch015

Shakeel, T., Habib, S., Boulila, W., Koubaa, A., Javed, A. R., Rizwan, M., Gadekallu, T. R., & Sufiyan, M. (2023). A survey on COVID-19 impact in the healthcare domain: Worldwide market implementation, applications, security and privacy issues, challenges and future prospects. *Complex & Intelligent Systems*, 9(1), 1027–1058. DOI: 10.1007/s40747-022-00767-w PMID: 35668731

Skalidis, I., Muller, O., & Fournier, S. (2023). CardioVerse: The cardiovascular medicine in the era of Metaverse. *Trends in Cardiovascular Medicine*, 33(8), 471–476. DOI: 10.1016/j.tcm.2022.05.004 PMID: 35568263

Smith, V., Warty, R. R., Sursas, J. A., Payne, O., Nair, A., Krishnan, S., da Silva Costa, F., Wallace, E. M., & Vollenhoven, B. (2020). The effectiveness of virtual reality in managing acute pain and anxiety for medical inpatients: Systematic review. *Journal of Medical Internet Research*, 22(11), e17980. DOI: 10.2196/17980 PMID: 33136055

Song, Y. T., & Qin, J. (2022). Metaverse and personal healthcare. *Procedia Computer Science*, 210, 189–197. DOI: 10.1016/j.procs.2022.10.136

Souri, A., Ghafour, M. Y., Ahmed, A. M., Safara, F., Yamini, A., & Hoseyninezhad, M. (2020). A new machine learning-based healthcare monitoring model for student's condition diagnosis in Internet of Things environment. *Soft Computing*, 24(22), 17111–17121. DOI: 10.1007/s00500-020-05003-6

Southworth, M. K., Silva, J. R., & Silva, J. N. A. (2020). Use of extended realities in cardiology. *Trends in Cardiovascular Medicine*, 30(3), 143–148. DOI: 10.1016/j.tcm.2019.04.005 PMID: 31076168

Spence, C., Obrist, M., Velasco, C., & Ranasinghe, N. (2017). Digitizing the chemical senses: Possibilities & pitfalls. *International Journal of Human-Computer Studies*, 107, 62–74. DOI: 10.1016/j.ijhcs.2017.06.003

Sridhar, A., Shiliang, Z., Woodson, R., & Kwan, L. (2020). Non-pharmacological anxiety reduction with immersive virtual reality for first-trimester dilation and curettage: A pilot study. *The European Journal of Contraception & Reproductive Health Care*, 25(6), 480–483. DOI: 10.1080/13625187.2020.1836146 PMID: 33140989

Steffen, J. H., Gaskin, J. E., Meservy, T. O., Jenkins, J. L., & Wolman, I. (2019). Framework of affordances for virtual reality and augmented reality. *Journal of Management Information Systems*, 36(3), 683–729. DOI: 10.1080/07421222.2019.1628877

Sun, M., Xie, L., Liu, Y., Li, K., Jiang, B., Lu, Y., ... Yang, D. (2022). The metaverse in current digital medicine. *Clinical eHealth, 5*, 52-57.

Tan, T. F., Li, Y., Lim, J. S., Gunasekeran, D. V., Teo, Z. L., Ng, W. Y., & Ting, D. S. (2022). Metaverse and virtual health care in ophthalmology: Opportunities and challenges. *Asia-Pacific Journal of Ophthalmology*, 11(3), 237–246. DOI: 10.1097/APO.0000000000000537 PMID: 35772084

Thase, M. E., McCrone, P., Barrett, M. S., Eells, T. D., Wisniewski, S. R., Balasubramani, G. K., Brown, G. K., & Wright, J. H. (2020). Improving cost-effectiveness and access to cognitive behavior therapy for depression: Providing remote-ready, computer-assisted psychotherapy in times of crisis and beyond. *Psychotherapy and Psychosomatics*, 89(5), 307–313. DOI: 10.1159/000508143 PMID: 32396917

Thomason, J. (2021). Metahealth-how will the metaverse change health care? *Journal of Metaverse*, 1(1), 13–16.

Turbyne, C. A. (2022). Virtuality technologies in mental healthcare: The medical metaverse of tomorrow.

Ullah, H., Manickam, S., Obaidat, M., Laghari, S. U. A., & Uddin, M. (2023). Exploring the potential of metaverse technology in healthcare: Applications, challenges, and future directions. *IEEE Access : Practical Innovations, Open Solutions*, 11, 69686–69707. DOI: 10.1109/ACCESS.2023.3286696

Usmani, S. S., Sharath, M., & Mehendale, M. (2022). Future of mental health in the metaverse. *General Psychiatry*, 35(4), e100825. DOI: 10.1136/gpsych-2022-100825 PMID: 36189180 van Leeuwen, F. W., & van der Hage, J. A. (2022). Where robotic surgery meets the metaverse. *Cancers (Basel)*, 14(24), 6161. DOI: 10.3390/cancers14246161 PMID: 36551645

Wang, G., Badal, A., Jia, X., Maltz, J. S., Mueller, K., Myers, K. J., Niu, C., Vannier, M., Yan, P., Yu, Z., & Zeng, R. (2022). Development of metaverse for intelligent healthcare. *Nature Machine Intelligence*, 4(11), 922–929. DOI: 10.1038/s42256-022-00549-6 PMID: 36935774

Wang, Y., Su, Z., Zhang, N., Xing, R., Liu, D., Luan, T. H., & Shen, X. (2022). A survey on metaverse: Fundamentals, security, and privacy. *IEEE Communications Surveys and Tutorials*, 25(1), 319–352. DOI: 10.1109/COMST.2022.3202047

Werner, H., Ribeiro, G., Arcoverde, V., Lopes, J., & Velho, L. (2022). The use of metaverse in fetal medicine and gynecology. *European Journal of Radiology*, 150, 150. DOI: 10.1016/j.ejrad.2022.110241 PMID: 35299111

Wilson, V. (2014). Research methods: triangulation.

Wu, T. C., & Ho, C. T. B. (2023). A scoping review of metaverse in emergency medicine. *Australasian Emergency Care (Online)*, 26(1), 75–83. DOI: 10.1016/j.auec.2022.08.002 PMID: 35953392

Yang, D., Zhou, J., Song, Y., Sun, M., & Bai, C. (2022). Metaverse in medicine. *Clinical eHealth, 5*, 39-43.

Yaqoob, I., Salah, K., Uddin, M., Jayaraman, R., Omar, M., & Imran, M. (2020). Blockchain for digital twins: Recent advances and future research challenges. *IEEE Network*, 34(5), 290–298. DOI: 10.1109/MNET.001.1900661

Zeng, Y., Zeng, L., Zhang, C., & Cheng, A. S. (2022). The metaverse in cancer care: Applications and challenges. *Asia-Pacific Journal of Oncology Nursing*, 9(12), 100111. DOI: 10.1016/j.apjon.2022.100111 PMID: 36276879

Zhu, J., Ren, Z., & Lee, C. (2020). Toward healthcare diagnoses by machine-learning-enabled volatile organic compound identification. *ACS Nano*, 15(1), 894–903. DOI: 10.1021/acsnano.0c07464 PMID: 33307692

Zikas, P., Kamarianakis, M., Kartsonaki, I., Lydatakis, N., Kateros, S., Kentros, M., . . . Papagiannakis, G. (2021). Covid-19-VR strikes back: innovative medical VR training. In *ACM SIGGRAPH 2021 Immersive Pavilion* (pp. 1-2). DOI: 10.1145/3450615.3464546

ADDITIONAL READING

Al Kuwaiti, A., Nazer, K., Al-Reedy, A., Al-Shehri, S., Al-Muhanna, A., Subbarayalu, A. V., Al Muhanna, D., & Al-Muhanna, F. A. (2023). A review of the role of artificial intelligence in healthcare. *Journal of Personalized Medicine*, 13(6), 951. DOI: 10.3390/jpm13060951 PMID: 37373940

Danish, S., Khan, A., Dang, L. M., Alonazi, M., Alanazi, S., Song, H.-K., & Moon, H. (2024). Metaverse Applications in Bioinformatics: A Machine Learning Framework for the Discrimination of Anti-Cancer Peptides. *Information, 15*(1), 48. DOI: 10.3390/info15010048

Gurusamy, A., & Mohamed, I. A. (2021). The Role of AI and Machine Learning in Full Stack Development for Healthcare Applications. *Journal of Knowledge Learning and Science Technology ISSN: 2959-6386 (online), 1*(1), 116-123.

Hou, Y., Song, J., & Wang, L. (2022, October). P-2.6: Based on the status quo of virtual reality and prospects for future development. In *SID Symposium. Digest of Technical Papers*, 53(S1, No. S1), 640–642. DOI: 10.1002/sdtp.16049

Keshmiri Neghab, H., Jamshidi, M., & Keshmiri Neghab, H. (2022). Digital Twin of a Magnetic Medical Microrobot with Stochastic Model Predictive Controller Boosted by Machine Learning in Cyber-Physical Healthcare Systems. *Information, 13*(7), 321. DOI: 10.3390/info13070321

Mah, E. (2023). Metaverse, AR, machine learning & AI in Orthopaedics? *Journal of Orthopaedic Surgery (Hong Kong)*, 31(1). DOI: 10.1177/10225536231165362 PMID: 36932039

Moztarzadeh, O., Jamshidi, M., Sargolzaei, S., Jamshidi, A., Baghalipour, N., Malekzadeh Moghani, M., & Hauer, L. (2023). Metaverse and healthcare: Machine learning-enabled digital twins of cancer. *Bioengineering (Basel, Switzerland)*, 10(4), 455. DOI: 10.3390/bioengineering10040455 PMID: 37106642

Mozumder, M. A. I., Armand, T. P. T., Imtiyaj Uddin, S. M., Athar, A., Sumon, R. I., Hussain, A., & Kim, H. C. (2023). Metaverse for digital anti-aging healthcare: An overview of potential use cases based on artificial intelligence, blockchain, IoT technologies, its challenges, and future directions. *Applied Sciences (Basel, Switzerland)*, 13(8), 5127. DOI: 10.3390/app13085127

KEY TERMS AND DEFINITIONS

6G: Sixth Generation Internet.
AI: Artificial Intelligence.
AR: Augmented Reality.
CV: Computer Vision.
DT: Digital Twins.
FDA: Food and Drug Administration.
IoT: Internet of Things.
MeTAI: Metaverse of medical technology and AI.
ML: Machine Learning.
MR: Mixed Reality.
NLP: Natural language processing.
SaMDs: Software as Medical Devices.
SDN: Software-Defined Networks.
VR: Virtual Reality.
VRET: VR Exposure Therapy.
XR: Extended Reality.

Chapter 9
Metaverse Mastery: Elevating Consumer Experience in the Virtual Era

S. Sekarini
https://orcid.org/0009-0006-6168-8920
SASTRA University, India

S. Selvabaskar
SASTRA University, India

EXECUTIVE SUMMARY

This chapter explores the growing impact of the metaverse on customer experiences in today's digital landscape. The metaverse is defined as a persistent, immersive, virtual environment that blends physical and digital realities through the use of technologies like virtual reality (VR), augmented reality (AR), artificial intelligence (AI), and blockchain. It highlights the importance of these technologies in transforming various sectors, including retail, education, entertainment, and professional training. The metaverse enables rich, interactive experiences that enhance user engagement by providing personalized, customizable, real-time interactions within digital spaces. Furthermore, the economic potential of the metaverse is discussed, emphasizing opportunities such as virtual real estate and NFTs, which create new avenues for businesses to monetize digital assets. The chapter also addresses the role of AI and machine learning in providing adaptive and intelligent user experiences, while blockchain ensures secure ownership and transactions of digital goods.

DOI: 10.4018/979-8-3693-7245-6.ch009

INTRODUCTION

Understanding Metaverse: Definition and Its Application

The Metaverse is a perpetual and persistent multiuser environment that combines physical reality with digital virtuality. It is built on the convergence of technologies that allow for multimodal interactions with virtual environments, digital items, and people, such as virtual reality (VR) and augmented reality (AR). As a result, the Metaverse is a linked web of social, networked immersive environments hosted by permanent multiuser platforms. It enables smooth real-time embodied user communication as well as dynamic interactions with digital artifacts. Its earliest iteration was a network of virtual worlds in which avatars could teleport between them. The Metaverse as it exists now includes social, immersive VR systems that are compatible with huge multiplayer online video games, open game worlds, and augmented reality collaboration spaces. The metaverse allows for social activities such as discussion, collaboration, gaming, and problem-solving (Bourlakis, 2009); (Jovanović, 2022) & (Park, 2022). In the metaverse, lovers or companions can be actual or virtual characters. In the metaverse, economic activity, political events, and natural disasters can occur similarly to the actual world (Davis, 2009). In such a virtual environment, the only restriction is people's creativity. Furthermore, using the lifelogging function, the specifics of life in the metaverse can be completely recorded (Thawonmas, 2011, July).

Metaverse applications have been reported globally, particularly by computer game businesses and social networks like Facebook (Egliston, 2021); (Jeong, 2022) & (Wiederhold, 2022). (Cipresso, 2018) suggest that wearable devices and other emerging technologies could be used in the metaverse. Mark Zuckerberg, CEO of Meta Platforms, describes Oculus as a "social computing platform" (Egliston, 2021). Scholars predict that advancements in brain-computer interfaces (BCI) will aid in the acceptance of the metaverse, alongside VR and AR (Mystakidis, 2024). The metaverse's concerns and applications have received a great deal of attention in recent years. Several institutes and papers propose that the metaverse has numerous applications. The most frequently suggested use is digital gaming (Park S. M., 2022). AR and VR are widely used in healthcare to train students in medical and nursing skills (Huang, 2023). AR and VR have been utilized to promote new items and provide virtual experiences (Bourlakis M. P., Electronic commerce research). It is crucial to understand that AI plays a significant role in the metaverse. AI technologies are required to ensure that the metaverse's "world" operates in accordance with the rules specified by its creator. When there are problems among metaverse users, the AI module performs "arbitration" as one of its functions.

Importance of the Metaverse in Today's Digital Landscape

The metaverse represents a pivotal shift in the digital landscape, integrating various technologies to create immersive, interactive environments that blend physical and virtual experiences. This evolving digital realm has significant implications across multiple sectors, including social interaction, commerce, entertainment, and education.

Technological Integration and User Engagement

To deliver rich and immersive experience, metaverse leverages augmented reality, virtual reality and block chain technologies. The environment of the Virtual Reality in metaverse has enhanced the user engagement by giving more interactive and realistic experiences when compared to traditional digital platforms. In facilitating secure transactions and ownership of digital assets, block chain technology has played a crucial role (Tapscott, 2016)

Economic Impact

The metaverse has opened new avenues for economic activity. Virtual real estate, for instance, is a burgeoning market where digital land is bought, sold, and developed. It is also highlighted that the economic potential of virtual real estate and its role in the broader digital economy. Additionally, the rise of NFTs (non-fungible tokens) within the metaverse has introduced innovative ways for creators to monetize digital content (Kugler, 2020)

Educational and Professional Applications

The metaverse also transforms education and professional training. Virtual classrooms and simulations offer interactive learning experiences that can enhance comprehension and retention. Moreover, VR-based training programs are increasingly used for skill development and professional education (Hancock, 2021).

Social and Cultural Impact

Social interactions within the metaverse are reshaping how people connect and engage. Virtual spaces enable users to meet, collaborate, and participate in events irrespective of geographical constraints. This has implications for global connectivity and cultural exchange (Schroeder, 2020)

DIGITAL FRONTIER: METAVERSE AND IT'S ELEMENTS

Metaverse

The evolving nature of the Metaverse has resulted in variations in how the term is used and understood (Barrera, 2023); (Dwivedi, 2023). Although both industry leaders and academic scholars have proposed different frameworks for conceptualizing the Metaverse, there is a general acknowledgment that a universally accepted definition has yet to emerge (Ball, 2022). For instance, (Ryskeldiev, 2018) describe the Metaverse as a "persistent and continually evolving collection of mixed reality environments linked to various physical locations". In contrast, (Ball, 2022) defines it as "a large-scale, interoperable network of real-time rendered 3D virtual worlds and environments, experienced synchronously and persistently by an unlimited number of users with an individualized sense of presence, ensuring data continuity like identity, history, and transactions". This diversity in definitions highlights the ongoing development and complexity of the Metaverse concept.

Five Elements

Synthesizing these perspectives, we define the Metaverse as a network of digital environments that fully immerse users in shared, interactive experiences in real-time. This conceptualization (as depicted in Figure 1) hinges on five core characteristics: it is (1) digitally mediated, (2) spatial, (3) immersive, (4) shared, and (5) real-time. Together, these features distinguish the Metaverse as a unique platform. While individual elements like digitally mediated communication or immersive gaming experiences can be found in existing platforms (e.g., video conferencing tools enable real-time digital interaction, and many modern video games offer immersive virtual worlds), it is the fusion of all five elements that forms the Metaverse's distinct identity. The interplay of these components creates an environment where users not only engage with virtual spaces but also interact meaningfully with others in a shared, continuous experience. Next, we will explore each of these components individually and discuss how their combination may shape consumer behaviour and experiences within the Metaverse.

Figure 1. Elements of metaverse

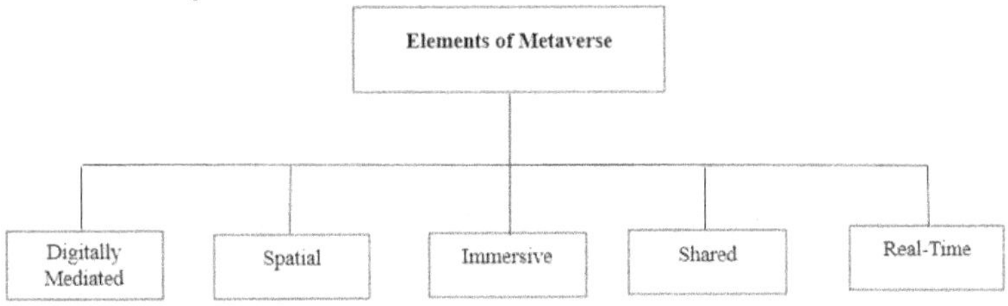

Digitally Mediated

Consumer experiences within the Metaverse are facilitated through digital technologies, which serve as both the medium for interaction and the content itself. This mediation allows consumers to engage with both the platform as a tool for interacting with others and with the digital content presented (Hoffman, 1996). The technologies employed in these experiences, ranging from hardware to software, vary widely. For example, highly detailed 3D computer graphics are frequently used to render Metaverse environments (Ball, 2022). Although not always necessary, many Metaversal experiences incorporate extended reality (XR) technologies, such as virtual reality (VR) and augmented reality (AR), to enhance the immersive nature of digital spaces (Zhao, 2022). VR achieves immersion by placing users in a fully synthetic environment, isolating them from the physical world (Sadowski, 2002), whereas AR overlays digital elements onto the real world, enabling simultaneous interaction with both (Bimber, 2005). These experiences can be accessed via various devices, from flat screens (e.g., desktops, laptops, or smartphones) to more immersive options like VR headsets and AR glasses. In all scenarios, digital technology plays a critical role as both the creator and facilitator of consumer experiences.

A significant feature of Metaversal experiences is that they are not bound by the laws of the physical world. While some Metaverse spaces mirror real-world locations E.g., "digital twins"; others are completely imaginative. For instance, Ariana Grande's Fortnite concert provided attendees with experiences such as racing along a rainbow track, battling a demonic boss, and flying alongside a giant avatar of the singer (Hatmaker, 2021). Consumers may also choose avatars that either resemble their real-life selves or take on fantastical forms, allowing them to interact with digital objects that defy conventional norms, such as teleportation devices. Although digital mediation fosters limitless creativity, it also introduces the concept of dematerialization (Belk, 2013). Unlike the physical world, where products can be physically handled, in the Metaverse, products exist solely as digital representations.

Even though consumers can purchase virtual items such as clothing, these items are merely digital versions of their real-world counterparts.

Spatial

The Metaverse is a network of digitally interconnected spaces where users interact within three-dimensional virtual worlds, unlike traditional social media platforms that primarily rely on static profiles, pages, and feeds (Peters, 2013). These virtual environments share characteristics with physical spaces, as interactions within the Metaverse are often constrained to individuals and objects present within a user's immediate virtual environment. Just like in real-world settings, the user's attention is shaped by what they can perceive—typically those within visual or auditory range of the Metaversal space. However, unlike physical spaces, users are not constrained by geography but only by their position within the digital environment at any given moment (Gursoy, 2022).

Spatial and geo-locational concepts, such as proximity and distance, influence how behaviour is structured in the Metaverse. A clear example of this is the expanding virtual real estate market, which mirrors physical real estate dynamics where properties with high visitor traffic hold more value (Frank, 2022). Additionally, transportation plays a key role in these spaces. While users can navigate by walking through virtual environments, they can also acquire vehicles or use public transportation options, including airplanes. Notably, the human brain often reacts similarly to virtual and physical experiences, allowing environmental cues in the Metaverse to impact consumer behaviour just as they do in real-world environments (Spence, 2014). Given these dynamics, the Metaverse is poised to become a hub for innovation in fields such as urban planning, architecture, landscape design, and interior design, as users can explore and experiment with new designs in immersive, digital spaces, offering valuable insights into their potential social impacts.

Immersive

In the Metaverse, users are not just accessing the internet but are essentially "within" it. This unique attribute of the Metaverse distinguishes it through the immersive experiences it offers. Immersion, though inconsistently defined across various disciplines (Nilsson, 2016), can be understood here following Slater and Wilbur's definition as the user's sense of being present in a digital environment (Cummings, 2016). The more immersive the experience, the stronger the feeling of presence. Studies on virtual environments and gaming have highlighted factors that contribute to immersion. A system is considered more immersive if it engages multiple sensory modalities with high-quality inputs. Visual elements, such as image resolution, depth perception, and panoramic views, play a crucial role in this, as vision is often mediated by devices like screens or headsets. Similarly, auditory inputs enhance immersion, particularly when spatial audio replicates real-world sound dynamics (Zotkin, 2004)

In addition to visual and auditory modalities, tactile feedback, or haptic technology, has gained attention for increasing immersion. Haptic devices such as gloves, sneakers, and vests allow users to experience sensations like touch in the Metaverse. Emerging technologies even experiment with olfactory feedback, enhancing the multisensory nature of the Metaverse. Immersion is further amplified through avatars—anthropomorphic digital representations of users within the virtual space. These avatars act as mediators of interaction and can blur the distinction between the user and their digital self (Bartle, 2004). When an avatar's movements mirror the user's real-world gestures, the sense of immersion deepens, making the virtual environment feel even more realist. By engaging multiple senses and embodying users through avatars, the Metaverse creates an immersive experience where users feel as though they are truly present in the digital world.

Shared

The Metaverse is inherently a shared space, where user interactions shape collective experiences. Unlike traditional social platforms, the Metaverse offers real-time, immersive, co-created experiences. Users, through their avatars, engage in social interactions that resemble physical-world behaviours like collaborating, trading, and forming communities (Zwass, 2010). However, questions arise about whether these avatar-driven interactions evoke the same social emotions—such as trust, empathy, and belonging—as in face-to-face encounters. Early studies on computer-mediated communication (CMC) suggested reduced social presence compared to in-person interactions, often resulting in diminished empathy and cooperation (Walther, 1996). This was largely due to the lack of true co-location and limited sensory cues, such as body language and tone. The immersive nature of the Metaverse, however, could bridge this gap by simulating the sensations of co-location more effectively. Several studies indicate that avatars enhance social presence through behavioural realism, eye contact, voice recognition, and even haptic feedback. Advanced devices like VR headsets with eye and face tracking further deepen this sense of presence by mimicking real-world non-verbal cues. For instance, virtual eye contact and human-like voice interactions increase the authenticity of social exchanges (Bente, 2008). Haptic peripherals that simulate touch (e.g., high fives or handshakes) amplify the feeling of being physically present with others. As Metaversal platforms evolve, these sensory-rich interactions help foster social bonds and create a sense of community, increasingly resembling real-world social presence, despite the digital medium. The real-time nature of the Metaverse further strengthens these social illusions, blurring the line between virtual and physical interactions.

Real–Time

The final distinctive feature of the Metaverse is its real-time operation, comprising two key components: temporal synchronicity and temporal persistence. Temporal synchronicity refers to users experiencing the flow of time simultaneously and consistently across the Metaverse, ensuring shared, collective experiences (Hoffman, 1996). This creates a unified event structure, where activities like walking or talking are rendered synchronously for all users present. Such synchronicity heightens social presence, allowing users to feel more connected and engaged, much like in live-streamed content (Duani, 2018). Users can interact instantly, boosting responsiveness, connection, and trust. On the other hand, temporal persistence reflects the one-way flow of time, where events and interactions are fleeting, much like in the physical world (Kivetz, 2017). This sense of ephemerality enhances immersion, as users feel more present in the moment. Experiences are dynamic and transient, compelling users to process events more deeply, similar to the effect observed on platforms like Twitch (Barnea, 2023). The Metaverse uniquely combines this temporal dynamism with a spatially structured and immersive environment, setting it apart from other digital platforms.

The shift from Physical to Virtual Experiences

The transition from physical to virtual experiences represents a profound transformation in how consumers interact with brands and services. Historically, physical environments offered tangible touchpoints—retail stores, event venues, and face-to-face interactions—that fostered personal engagement and sensory connections. However, the rise of digital technologies and the advent of the Metaverse have catalysed a shift towards immersive virtual experiences. This transition is driven by advancements in Virtual Reality (VR) and Augmented Reality (AR), which enable users to experience environments and interactions that were once confined to the physical realm. Virtual experiences offer unparalleled convenience, accessibility, and personalization. Users can now explore virtual storefronts, attend events, and engage with brands from the comfort of their homes, transcending geographical and physical limitations. This shift also allows for enhanced interactivity, with real-time modifications and customizations that cater to individual preferences. As brands embrace this new frontier, they must adapt their strategies to ensure that virtual experiences match or exceed the quality and impact of their physical counterparts, ensuring seamless and engaging interactions for their digital audiences.

UNDERSTANDING CONSUMER EXPERIENCE

Customer experiences encompass a multifaceted framework that focuses on how consumers respond to marketing stimuli across various dimensions: behavioural, cognitive, affective, sensory, and social. The behavioural aspect involves actions, physical experiences, and interactions with brands. Auditory stimuli, for instance, impact consumers' emotions and feelings, influencing their mood and behaviour, thus enhancing their comfort and convenience during the purchasing process when exposed to sound or music in a retail setting. Cognitive experiences can be categorized into two types: Type One, where a product is acquired based on its functional features, and Type Two, where the purchase is driven by the product's price and perceived value. Products that provide affective experiences are chosen to fulfil emotional needs. Cultivating an emotional connection with a product or service can attract new customers and help retain existing ones. Sensory experiences, involving the five senses, are crucial in human life. Engaging sensory stimuli like music, lighting, and product displays can positively affect consumers' purchase intentions.

Metaverse, Virtual Reality, and Augmented Reality

Virtual and augmented reality concepts have been around for over twenty years, playing a significant role in advancing and challenging the study of interfaces and human-computer interaction. From its inception, virtual reality (VR) has faced considerable obstacles, including the development of compatible software and hardware, addressing human factors, and the need for high-speed networks (Zheng, 1998). Today, VR delivers immersive three-dimensional experiences within a virtual environment through advanced computer technologies. It relies on devices such as headsets, gloves, and other controllers that enable users to experience and visualize virtual reality (Kardong-Edgren, 2019).

Augmented reality (AR), in contrast, is often viewed as an extension of VR because it allows users to perceive the real world while overlaying digital elements. Unlike VR, which immerses users in a fully digital world (Azuma, 1997), AR integrates digital objects into the real-world environment in real-time, enhancing the user experience. The fusion of AR and VR is referred to as mixed reality, which facilitates real-time interactions and enriches user experiences and perceptions (Bekele, 2018). The metaverse aims to create a fully immersive 3D environment, where interactions occur through avatars, closely mimicking real-life interactions such as visual contact and object manipulation. This space will encompass areas for commerce, art, and education, as highlighted in existing studies. However, there remain critical issues to address, including data privacy, security, and legal regulations, all of which impact real-life scenarios (Ball, 2022). Additionally, assessing experiences within the metaverse presents its own set of challenges, particularly in developing standardized evaluation methods.

Extended Virtual, Augmented, and Mixed Reality

Extended Reality (XR), also known as Cross Reality, encompasses a range of immersive technologies, including Virtual Reality (VR), Augmented Reality (AR), and Mixed Reality (MR) (Milgram, 1995). XR represents digital environments where data are visualized and projected, allowing users to interact within fully or partially synthetic spaces created by technology. VR creates a completely separate, digitally generated artificial environment where users feel as if they are immersed in a different world, functioning similarly to physical surroundings (Slater, 2016). Specialized multisensory equipment, such as VR headsets, immersion helmets, and omnidirectional treadmills, enhance this experience by engaging multiple senses, including sight, sound, touch, and movement.

In contrast, AR integrates digital elements into the real world to enhance physical spaces (Ibáñez, 2018). It merges virtual and physical environments, creating a layer of digital artifacts visible through devices such as smartphones, tablets, glasses, or contact lenses. AR can also be implemented in VR headsets with pass-through mode, utilizing integrated camera sensors to display the real world. MR is a more intricate concept, evolving with technological advancements and shifting linguistic definitions (Speicher, 2019). Often viewed as an advanced form of AR, MR allows real-time interaction between the physical environment and digital data. For example, an MR game might feature a non-player character that interacts with physical objects, such as hiding behind furniture. MR typically requires special glasses and is considered a blend of AR and VR, along with variations like augmented virtuality. Milgram and Kishino's reality-virtuality continuum provides a framework for understanding these immersive technologies (Milgram P. T., 1995). This continuum ranges from the physical environment on one end to the fully artificial virtual environment on the other, with AR positioned closer to the physical end and VR at the opposite end. MR encompasses elements of both.

Multimodal Metaverse Interactions

The Metaverse relies on technologies that facilitate multisensory interactions with virtual environments, digital objects, and people. XR systems achieve representational fidelity through stereoscopic displays that create depth perception by providing separate, slightly varied images for each eye (El Beheiry, 2019). High-resolution XR displays offer a broad field of view, ranging from 90 to 180 degrees, and advanced auditory experiences with 3D, spatial, or binaural audio, which enhances immersion and allows users to locate sound sources effectively (Hong, 2017). Beyond passive sensory inputs, XR systems enable active interaction with virtual elements via motion controllers. These handheld devices with grips, buttons, triggers, and thumb sticks allow users to touch, grab, and manipulate virtual objects (Maereg, 2017). Ongoing developments aim to improve user interfaces through full hand tracking and wearable devices like haptic suits and gloves that simulate touch (Maereg, 2017). Research is also exploring the digitalization and simulation of smell (Cheok, 2018). XR environments support dynamic user movements, transferring physical actions into virtual spaces through positional and rotational tracking (Atsikpasi, 2022). Movement can be tracked using external cameras (outside-in) or built-in sensors in standalone headsets (inside-out). Modern headsets offer advanced tracking with six degrees of freedom (DoF), including lateral body movements along the x, y, and z axes (Atsikpasi, 2022). One innovative approach in VR involves unidirectional treadmills for continuous movement in occluded spaces.

METAVERSE CONTEMPORARY DEVELOPMENT

Source in Literary Tradition

The concept of the Metaverse was introduced in Neal Stephenson's 1992 science fiction novel *Snow Crash* (Mystakidis S. P., 2021). In this work, the Metaverse is depicted as a parallel virtual reality universe constructed from computer graphics, accessible globally through goggles and earphones. Its core is a protocol known as the Street, which connects various virtual neighbourhoods and locations, analogous to the information superhighway. Within the Metaverse, users appear as customizable digital avatars. Despite its digital and synthetic nature, experiences within the Metaverse can significantly affect the physical self. A literary forerunner to the Metaverse is William Gibson's VR cyberspace called Matrix, featured in his 1984 novel *Neuromancer* (Dionisio, 2013).

A contemporary literary embodiment of the Metaverse is the OASIS, presented in Ernest Cline's 2011 novel *Ready Player One* (Slater M. G.-L.-C., 2020). OASIS is a vast multiplayer online VR game that has become the leading platform for work, education, and entertainment. It is an expansive virtual realm composed of numerous planets. Users access OASIS using headsets, haptic gloves, and suits. In terms of education, OASIS surpasses a traditional public library by offering a techno-utopian vision of virtual learning. It includes hundreds of luxurious public-school campuses on a planet dedicated solely to K-12 education. These online classes, akin to holodecks, allow teachers to take students on virtual field trips to historical sites, foreign locations, prestigious museums, other planets, and even inside the human body, leading to increased student engagement and interest.

Implementations of Metaverse

In the realm of VR, the Metaverse was envisioned as the 3D Internet or Web 3.0 (Kapp, 2009). Its initial iteration was imagined as a network of interconnected virtual worlds, where avatars could seamlessly travel between them. This concept materialized in Opensim's Hypergrid (Dionisio, 2013). The Hypergrid network enables access to various social and stand-alone virtual worlds built on the open-source software Open simulator, allowing the transfer of digital agents and their inventories across different platforms via hyperlinks. Despite its innovation, Hypergrid remains incompatible with popular proprietary virtual worlds like Second Life.

At present, the second iteration of the Metaverse is being developed, focusing on integrating social, immersive VR platforms with massive multiplayer online games, open-world games, and AR collaborative environments. In this new vision, users can gather, interact, and socialize without barriers in embodied forms, such as 3D holograms or avatars, within both physical and virtual environments. Although currently possible within the same platform, there are still limitations. The next step is achieving cross-platform and cross-technology interactions, where some users engage in VR and others in AR settings. Fundamental principles of the Metaverse involve software interconnectivity and user teleportation between virtual worlds. This requires interoperability for avatar customization and the portability of accessories, props, and inventory based on shared standards.

The "seven rules of the Metaverse" serve as a high-level framework, outlining a vision for future development that draws upon past experiences with the Internet and the World Wide Web [58]. According to these principles, there should be only one Metaverse (rule #1) and not multiple Metaverses or Multiverses, representing the next iteration of the Internet (rule #7). The Metaverse should be inclusive (#2), open to all (#4), hardware-neutral (#5), networked (#6), and collectively managed (#3)

Challenges in Metaverse

The Metaverse encounters several challenges stemming from the underlying AR and VR technologies. Both AR and VR have the power to affect users' cognition, emotions, and behaviours (Slater M. G.-L.-C., 2020) . One significant hurdle is the high cost of equipment, which hampers widespread adoption but is expected to be reduced over time. Risks associated with AR can be categorized into four main areas: (i) physical well-being, health, and safety, (ii) psychological effects, (iii) moral and ethical concerns, and (iv) data privacy (Christopoulos, 2021). Physically, users of location-based AR applications may suffer from accidents caused by distraction. Psychologically, information overload poses a challenge that must be addressed. Moral issues include unauthorized augmentation and manipulation of facts, which can lead to biased perspectives. Data privacy is a major concern, with risks including unauthorized data collection and sharing, potential cybersecurity threats, and spatial doxing, which can infringe on privacy. Additionally, Metaverse participants might compile biometric psychographic profiles based on emotional data, potentially leading to unintended behavioural inferences and algorithmic biases (Heller, 2020).

In the realm of VR, commonly reported health issues include motion sickness, nausea, and dizziness (Pellas, 2021). The weight of VR headsets can cause head and neck fatigue during extended use. Prolonged VR engagement may also result in addiction, social isolation, and neglect of physical health (Slater M. G.-L.-C., 2020). Open social VR environments can foster toxic behaviour such as griefing, cyberbullying, and harassment (Chesney, 2009). High-fidelity VR environments and violent content can induce traumatic experiences. Moreover, data ethics concerns arise with the use of AI algorithms and deep learning to create VR deep fake avatars and facilitate identity theft.

Innovative Immersive Metaverse Applications

In the Metaverse, immersive technologies are poised to make significant strides in areas such as Spatial Computing and Brain-Computer Interfaces (Yuste, 2017). Spatial Computing facilitates the control of computing devices using natural gestures and voice commands (Delmerico, 2022). Brain-Computer Interfaces, on the other hand, enable interaction with devices through brain activity alone (Kim, 2021), allowing users to control synthetic limbs or assist individuals with paralysis in operating computers. Additionally, the integration of blockchain-based cryptocurrencies (e.g., Bitcoin) and non-fungible tokens (NFTs) supports the development of new virtual economy models and transaction systems. On a larger scale, technologies related to the Metaverse are anticipated to intersect and evolve with other exponential technologies, such as wireless broadband, cloud computing, robotics, artificial intelligence, and 3D printing. These advancements signal a shift towards the fourth industrial revolution. Consequently, the Metaverse is expected to play a crucial role in Education 4.0, representing the evolution of education within the industry 4.0 framework (Salmon, 2019).

Technologies Enabling the Metaverse

Virtual Reality and Augmented Reality

Virtual Reality (VR) and Augmented Reality (AR) are foundational technologies for the Metaverse. VR immerses users in a fully digital environment, using headsets, gloves, and treadmills to create a sensation of being in a different world. This immersion is achieved through multisensory experiences, including vision, sound, and touch. AR, on the other hand, overlays digital information onto the real world, enhancing physical surroundings with virtual elements visible through devices like smartphones or AR glasses (Azuma, 1997). Together, VR and AR create immersive and interactive experiences that are essential for Metaverse environments, allowing users to interact with both digital and physical worlds in novel ways. These technologies enable the creation of rich, interactive virtual spaces where users can explore, socialize, and engage in various activities, marking a significant shift from traditional online interactions to more engaging and immersive experiences. (Milgram P. H., 1995)

Blockchain and Decentralization

Blockchain technology and decentralization are pivotal to the Metaverse, underpinning its structure and operations. Blockchain provides a secure, transparent way to record transactions and manage digital assets, such as cryptocurrencies and non-fungible tokens (NFTs). It enables decentralized ownership and control, reducing reliance on central authorities and intermediaries (Tapscott, 2016). In the Metaverse, blockchain supports the creation and exchange of virtual assets, ensuring authenticity and ownership through immutable records. Decentralization enhances user control and privacy while fostering a more democratic and open virtual space. By integrating blockchain technology, the Metaverse can facilitate trust less transactions, secure digital ownership, and innovative economic models, shaping the future of virtual interactions and commerce.

AI and Machine Learning in the Metaverse

Artificial Intelligence (AI) and Machine Learning (ML) play crucial roles in the Metaverse, enhancing user experiences and interactions. AI algorithms power virtual assistants, chatbots, and automated systems that assist users within the Metaverse (Russell, 2016). Machine Learning helps analyse user data, personalize experiences, and improve interactions based on behavioural patterns. AI-driven content creation tools generate realistic avatars, environments, and scenarios, contributing to more immersive and dynamic virtual worlds. Furthermore, AI enhances security by detecting and preventing malicious activities. In the Metaverse, AI and ML are integral for creating responsive, adaptive, and intelligent systems that enrich user engagement and streamline operations, paving the way for sophisticated virtual experiences.

Interoperability and Digital Identity

Interoperability and digital identity are key components of the Metaverse's functionality. Interoperability refers to the ability of different virtual worlds and platforms to work together seamlessly, allowing users to transfer assets and identities across various environments. This requires standardized protocols and systems that facilitate smooth interactions between diverse virtual spaces. Digital identity involves creating and managing a user's presence and reputation within the Metaverse. It encompasses avatars, personal data, and digital assets that define a user's virtual persona. Effective interoperability and robust digital identity management are essential for a cohesive Metaverse experience, enabling users to maintain consistent identities and access multiple platforms without barriers. (KÖLÜŞ, 2020)

METAVERSE PLATFORMS AND VIRTUAL WORLDS

Overview of Leading Metaverse Platforms

Leading Metaverse platforms like Decentraland, Roblox, and Meta offer diverse virtual worlds where users can interact, create, and explore. Decentraland is a decentralized virtual reality platform built on the Ethereum blockchain, where users can buy, develop, and monetize virtual land. Roblox, a popular online platform, allows users to create and play games in a user-generated virtual world, fostering a vibrant community of developers and players (Goanta, 2020). Meta (formerly Facebook) is developing its own Metaverse through Horizon Workrooms and other initiatives, aiming to create immersive social and professional environments. Each platform provides unique features and experiences, contributing to the growing landscape of the Metaverse and offering users various ways to engage with virtual spaces (Milgram P., 1994) & (Azuma, 1997).

Customization and Individualization in Metaverse Platforms

Customization and personalization are integral to the Metaverse experience, allowing users to tailor their virtual environments and avatars to reflect their preferences and identities. In platforms like Decentraland and Roblox, users can customize avatars with a wide range of clothing, accessories, and other digital assets. Personalization extends to virtual spaces, where users can design and modify their properties, create unique experiences, and establish personal brands. This level of customization enhances user engagement by enabling individuals to express themselves creatively and interact in environments that resonate with their personal tastes. As the Metaverse evolves, advanced customization options and personalized experiences will continue to play a crucial role in shaping user satisfaction and retention (Lu, 2022)

MARKETING AND BRANDING IN THE METAVERSE

Virtual Advertising and Product Placement

Virtual advertising and product placement are emerging strategies in the Metaverse, offering innovative ways for brands to reach audiences. In virtual worlds like Decentraland and Roblox, brands can place advertisements within the environment, such as virtual billboards or branded objects that users encounter during their activities. Product placement involves integrating brand products into the virtual experience, such as featuring virtual fashion items or in-game assets tied to real-world brands. These approaches provide immersive advertising opportunities that engage users in a contextually relevant manner, blending marketing seamlessly with the virtual experience. As the Metaverse expands, virtual advertising will become a key tool for brands to enhance visibility and connect with consumers in novel ways

Influencer Marketing in Virtual Spaces

Influencer marketing in virtual spaces leverages popular figures within the Metaverse to promote products and brands. Virtual influencers, or avatars controlled by real individuals, can collaborate with brands to create engaging content and drive user interaction. For example, influencers in platforms like Roblox and Decentraland can host virtual events, showcase branded items, or participate in interactive campaigns. This form of marketing capitalizes on the influencers' established audiences and their ability to create authentic, relatable content within the virtual environment. By partnering with virtual influencers, brands can enhance their reach and impact in the Metaverse, tapping into new channels for consumer engagement and brand promotion.

Creating and Managing Virtual Brand Assets

Creating and managing virtual brand assets involves developing and maintaining digital elements that represent a brand within the Metaverse. This includes designing virtual products, spaces, and experiences that align with the brand's identity and values. Brands can create virtual storefronts, interactive environments, and digital collectibles to engage users and drive brand loyalty. Effective management of these assets requires ongoing updates and maintenance to ensure they remain relevant and functional within the evolving virtual landscape. By strategically developing and managing virtual brand assets, businesses can establish a strong presence in the Metaverse and foster meaningful connections with their audience

RETAIL IN THE METAVERSE: A NEW FRONTIER

Virtual Shopping Experiences

Virtual shopping experiences in the Metaverse offer a novel way for consumers to engage with brands and make purchases. Users can visit virtual stores, explore digital products, and make transactions using cryptocurrencies or virtual currencies. These experiences often include interactive features such as virtual fitting rooms, product demonstrations, and immersive environments that replicate real-world shopping. Virtual shopping allows for a more engaging and personalized experience compared to traditional online retail, providing opportunities for brands to showcase their products in creative and interactive ways. As technology advances, virtual shopping will continue to evolve, offering new possibilities for consumer engagement and retail innovation.

NFT-Based Products and Services

NFT-based products and services are transforming the retail landscape within the Metaverse. Non-fungible tokens (NFTs) represent unique digital assets that can be bought, sold, and traded within virtual environments. Retailers can create and offer limited-edition virtual items, collectibles, and exclusive experiences as NFTs, providing customers with digital ownership and scarcity. NFTs enable brands to offer innovative products and services, such as virtual fashion items, digital art, and access to exclusive virtual events. The integration of NFTs into retail strategies opens up new revenue streams and enhances customer engagement by offering unique and verifiable digital assets.

Omnichannel Strategies in the Metaverse

Omnichannel strategies in the Metaverse involve integrating virtual and physical retail experiences to create a seamless customer journey. Brands can combine their virtual storefronts with physical locations, allowing customers to interact with both environments. For example, customers might explore virtual product previews and make purchases online, with the option to pick up items at a physical store. Omnichannel approaches also include synchronized promotions and loyalty programs that bridge virtual and real-world interactions. By adopting omnichannel strategies, retailers can enhance customer convenience, drive engagement across multiple touchpoints, and create a cohesive brand experience that spans both physical and virtual realms.

HOW METAVERSE ELEVATES CONSUMER EXPERIENCE IN VIRTUAL SPACES?

The Metaverse, a digital universe combining virtual reality (VR), augmented reality (AR), and the Internet, is revolutionizing how brands engage with consumers. This immersive virtual world creates new ways to enhance customer experience, offering personalization, interactivity, and deeper engagement, all of which are crucial to modern consumer satisfaction

Immersive and Interactive Engagement

One of the key ways the Metaverse elevates customer experience is by providing immersive, interactive environments where users can fully engage with products and services. Virtual spaces offer consumers the ability to explore digital replicas of stores, try on products using AR technology, and even attend virtual events, all from the comfort of their homes. These experiences create a sense of presence, where consumers feel as though they are physically interacting with a product, leading to a more meaningful connection between brands and customers. Research suggests that immersive experiences in virtual spaces are perceived as more engaging and emotionally impactful compared to traditional online interactions (Flavián, 2019). By leveraging technologies like VR and AR, companies can deliver more compelling and personalized experiences, transforming passive online shopping into active, experiential engagement. For example, luxury fashion brands like Gucci and Balenciaga have launched virtual showrooms and events in the Metaverse, allowing customers to explore their collections in fully immersive environments (Park & Yoo, 2021).

Personalization and Customization

The Metaverse also allows for enhanced personalization of customer experiences. Through data collection and AI-driven insights, companies can offer tailored experiences to individual users based on their preferences and past behaviours. Customizable avatars and digital identities give users the freedom to express themselves in virtual environments, leading to a sense of ownership and attachment to the experience. Brands like Nike have used the Metaverse to offer customizable virtual products, allowing users to design their own sneakers or apparel in a 3D environment. This type of customization increases engagement and gives customers a deeper sense of satisfaction, as they feel more connected to the products, they help create (Rogers, 2021). The use of AI in these virtual spaces also enables brands to anticipate customer needs, offering recommendations and guiding users through personalized journeys that closely match their preferences (Pantano, 2017).

Social Interaction and Community Building

Another powerful feature of the Metaverse is its capacity for social interaction. In contrast to traditional e-commerce, where transactions are typically solitary, virtual spaces in the Metaverse allow users to interact with friends, family, and even brand representatives in real-time. Social interaction in the Metaverse often takes the form of shared experiences, such as virtual shopping trips, events, or games, which enhances the emotional bond between the consumer and the brand. Community building is a critical aspect of customer engagement in virtual worlds. Brands can create virtual spaces where users come together to discuss products, share experiences, and even co-create content. These communities foster a sense of belonging, which in turn strengthens brand loyalty. For instance, platforms like Roblox and Decentraland have thriving virtual communities where users can interact not only with each other but also with brands that host virtual events and experiences (Serrano, 2020).

Seamless Omnichannel Integration

The Metaverse is also poised to elevate customer experience through its integration with omnichannel strategies. By bridging the gap between physical and virtual shopping experiences, brands can create seamless transitions between different retail environments. For example, a customer might try on a virtual product in the Metaverse and then purchase it in a physical store, or vice versa. This interconnectedness of the virtual and physical worlds offers unprecedented convenience and flexibility, enhancing the overall shopping experience. The integration of blockchain technology within the Metaverse also enables the ownership of digital assets, such as NFTs (non-fungible tokens), which can represent unique virtual goods or even real-world assets. These digital assets can enhance the customer experience by providing exclusive products or memberships that are tied to the Metaverse. For example, companies like Adidas have used NFTs to offer limited-edition virtual apparel that can also be redeemed for physical products (Rejeb, 2023).

Overcoming Challenges and Ethical Considerations

While the Metaverse holds immense potential for elevating customer experiences, it also poses challenges related to accessibility, privacy, and security. The cost of VR and AR equipment can limit access for certain demographics, and data privacy concerns remain significant, as companies in the Metaverse collect vast amounts of user data to provide personalized experiences (Dwivedi Y. K., 2022). Ethical considerations must also be addressed, as the line between virtual and physical realities blurs. Brands must ensure that their practices within the Metaverse do not exploit users or manipulate their behaviour through hyper-targeted marketing strategies. Transparency in data collection and usage will be key to maintaining customer trust and ensuring positive experiences in the Metaverse (Xu, 2022).

CASE STUDIES: BRANDS THAT HAVE SUCCESSFULLY USED THE "THE METAVERSE FOR THEIR CAMPAIGNS"

The Metaverse offers brands a dynamic platform to craft immersive and interactive experiences, enabling unique engagement opportunities with customers. Leading global brands have successfully utilized this technology to run impactful campaigns. By examining these case studies, we can uncover valuable strategies for harnessing the potential of the Metaverse in marketing efforts. This approach showcases how brands can effectively create memorable campaigns that drive customer engagement and boost sales, offering new ways to interact with audiences in digital spaces

Wendy's

Challenge: Strengthening Distinction and Brand Identity in a Competitive Market

Wendy's has the particular difficulty of setting itself apart in the fast-food sector, particularly since younger consumers frequently had short-term brand loyalty. In order to overcome this, Wendy's looked for a distinctive method to communicate their dedication to quality—more especially, their use of fresh, never-frozen beef—in a market full with comparable claims. Younger audiences were drawn to Fortnite and other gaming platforms, which made it the perfect chance for Wendy's to engage with them directly and reaffirm its brand message.

Wendy's made a bold entry into the Metaverse by launching a playful "Food Fight" game mode on Fortnite. This interactive experience revolved around a fun battle between frozen beef and fresh beef, aligning with Wendy's commitment to serving never-frozen ingredients. The campaign's design aimed to engage younger audiences, using Fortnite's immense popularity to promote Wendy's message in an engaging, memorable way.

Results:

- 1.5 million Minutes Watched on Twitch: The campaign's visibility sky-rocketed, as players and viewers flocked to watch the game unfold.
- 119% Increase in Mentions on social media: Wendy's successfully sparked conversations, gaining widespread social media attention and boosting their brand recognition among younger demographics.

Gucci

Reimagining the Brand Experience in the Digital Age: Taking on a New Generation of High-end customers luxury firms have found that traditional marketing methods are less efficient as they try to reach younger, digitally native audiences. Gucci has to balance attracting young customers on platforms where they spend a lot of time with retaining its upscale appeal. The brand transformed its iconic style into an interactive virtual experience that combined art, fashion and technology by developing the "Gucci Garden" on Roblox. This gave Gucci the opportunity to establish itself as a pioneer while offering the upcoming generation of luxury connoisseurs an engaging entrance point.

Gucci created a unique, immersive experience with the "Gucci Garden" on Roblox, mirroring its famous Gucci Garden in Florence. The virtual environment allowed players to explore art installations, attend digital fashion shows, and even purchase exclusive digital wearables for their avatars. This experience blended fashion with the digital world, enabling Gucci to connect with younger, tech-savvy audiences.

Results:

- Reached over 4.5 million Roblox users in the first week: The campaign quickly gained traction, attracting millions of users within just days of its launch.
- Total visits exceeded 20 million in the first month: Gucci's presence in the virtual world continued to grow rapidly, with a significant number of users engaging with the virtual space.

- The average visit time was over 29 minutes: Users were highly engaged, spending considerable time exploring the virtual garden and interacting with the content.
- Sold over $1.2 million worth of limited-edition virtual items: The campaign's success translated into strong sales of digital Gucci wearables, highlighting the potential of virtual goods in the fashion industry.

Nike

The challenge of establishing a presence in the Web3 space Establishing Yourself as a pioneer in the digital fashion industry, Nike saw thar digital wearables and NFTs were becoming increasingly important as extensions of contemporary fashion and lifestyle. The brand has to gain reputation in the Web 3.0 and Metaverse domains fast in order to seize this new market and interact with tech-savvy customers. Nike made a calculated decision to establish itself as a leader in digital fashion by purchasing RTFKT and introducing the "CloneX" collection. This allowed the company to access the NFT market and strengthened its reputation for innovation in both the real and virtual worlds.

Nike made waves in the Metaverse by acquiring RTFKT, a top NFT footwear brand, and launching the "CloneX" collection. This innovative project featured 20,000 unique digital sneakers with customizable traits, captivating both the crypto and fashion communities. By blending cutting-edge technology with sneaker culture, Nike established itself as a leader in Web3 innovation. The "CloneX" collection marked a pivotal moment in virtual fashion, with RTFKT solidifying its position at the forefront of this growing trend.

Results:

- Nike's move into the NFT space generated significant buzz in the digital and fashion industries, solidifying its position as a pioneer in virtual and Web3 experiences.
- The collaboration with RTFKT expanded Nike's influence into virtual wearables and digital collections, a rapidly growing sector driven by the Metaverse.

Rexona

Using virtual movement to encourage inclusivity redefining accessibility in digital experience is a challenge. In the metaverse, where inclusivity isn't always valued, Rexona sought to apply its principle of enabling everyone to roam freely. As online spaces develop, the brand identified a need for virtual events that accommodate individuals of all abilities. Rexona was able to offer an inclusive experience for all participants, including those who depend on adaptive wearables, by organising the "Degree Metathon" in Decentraland. By demonstrating Rexona's commitment to inclusively and engaging an audience that is enthusiastic about diversity and empowerment, this event brought the company's mission and digital presence into harmony.

Rexona (also known as Degree) launched the world's first Metaverse marathon, the Degree Metathon in Decentraland, a groundbreaking virtual event that allowed participants to run a 26.2-mile marathon without physical limitations. This event was designed to be inclusive, providing adaptive wearables such as wheelchairs and running blades, ensuring that people of all abilities could join the race. Participants created avatars that mirrored their identities, celebrating diversity and inclusion in an immersive virtual landscape. This unique event underlined the brand's commitment to empowering individuals to move without barriers, both in the real world and the digital realm.

Results:

- First-of-its-kind inclusive Metaverse event, amplifying Rexona's dedication to accessibility.
- Promoted body positivity and inclusivity, engaging diverse communities through customizable avatars and wearables.
- Showcased brand innovation in merging fitness and virtual experiences, appealing to both athletes and digital enthusiasts

Coca–Cola

Using virtual tasting Experience to increase Engagement: The challenge is to bridge the gap between virtual interaction and physical products. Coca-Cola saw the launch of Coca-Cola Zero Sugar Byte as a chance to generate awareness about a new product in a fresh way, but in a crowded beverage industry, traditional advertising was insufficient to draw in consumers. The company viewed Fortnite's "Pixel Point" as an engaging platform that connected virtual and real-world flavours, enabling players to interact with the Coca-Cola brand in a fun and memorable way. Through this effort, Coca-Cola was able to reach gamers Worldwide, increasing brand awareness, obtaining data on virtual space interaction, and solidifying its reputation as an innovator.

Revolutionized the virtual experience with "Pixel Point" in Fortnite. This engaging feature enabled players to join mini-games and try various flavours of Coca-Cola Zero Sugar Byte, which debuted in the metaverse

Results:

- High Engagement: The campaign saw significant player participation with extensive time spent on "Pixel Point" and its mini-games.
- Increased Brand Visibility: Coca-Cola Zero Sugar Byte achieved notable visibility and awareness in the metaverse, boosting its brand presence in Fortnite.
- Positive Brand Perception: The innovative virtual product launch fostered a positive view of Coca-Cola as a cutting-edge brand.
- Data and Insights: The campaign offered valuable insights into consumer preferences and behaviours in virtual environments for future marketing strategies

LEGAL AND ETHICAL ASPECTS OF METAVERSE

Data Privacy

Challenge: The Metaverse collects vast amounts of personal and biometric data through virtual reality (VR) and augmented reality (AR) devices, making users' data highly vulnerable. Legal Aspect: Regulations like GDPR or CCPA offer frameworks for data protection, but new policies are needed to address immersive and real-time data usage. Ethical Concern: The constant collection and processing of data raise issues about surveillance, consent, and potential misuse by corporations.

Identity and Psychological Impact

Challenge: Users often create avatars that may differ vastly from their real-world identities, impacting self-perception and mental health. Legal Aspect: Identity theft and impersonation can become more complex in virtual settings, necessitating laws that address avatar-related rights and responsibilities. Ethical Concern: The anonymity and disconnect between real and virtual identities may encourage harmful behaviour, such as cyberbullying, leading to ethical debates about the responsibility of platform providers.

Intellectual Property (IP) Rights

Challenge: The Metaverse allows for the creation and trade of digital assets, but questions arise about who owns virtual content and creations. Legal Aspect: Current IP laws struggle to apply to virtual goods, and new frameworks may be required for NFT ownership and digital art. Ethical Concern: Users who invest in creating virtual assets may face exploitation without clear ownership rights, leading to a need for fair use and compensation guidelines.

CONCLUSION

The metaverse represents a significant shift in the digital landscape, offering immersive and interactive experiences that redefine how consumers engage with brands and services. By integrating emerging technologies like VR, AR, blockchain, and AI, the metaverse provides opportunities for customization, social interaction, and seamless integration between physical and virtual worlds. This convergence is poised to elevate customer experiences by offering personalized and engaging environments, transcending geographical barriers, and fostering deeper emotional connections between consumers and brands. However, the widespread adoption of the metaverse faces challenges related to accessibility, privacy, and ethical considerations, which need to be addressed to ensure equitable and safe user experiences. Brands that successfully adapt to this new frontier will benefit from enhanced customer engagement and loyalty, as demonstrated by early adopters like Gucci and Nike. The metaverse, though still evolving, has the potential to reshape the future of commerce, education, entertainment, and social interaction.

REFERENCES

Atsikpasi, P., & Fokides, E. (2022). A scoping review of the educational uses of 6DoF HMDs. *Virtual Reality (Waltham Cross)*, 26(1), 205–222. DOI: 10.1007/s10055-021-00556-9

Azuma, R. T. (1997). A Survey of Augmented Reality. Presence. *Teleoperators and Virtual Environments.*

Barnea, U. M. (2023). The effects of content ephemerality on information processing. *ournal of Marketing Research*, 60(4), 750-766.

Barrera, K. G. (2023). Marketing in the Metaverse: Conceptual understanding, framework, and research agenda. *Journal of Business Research*, 155, 113420. DOI: 10.1016/j.jbusres.2022.113420

Bartle, R. A. (2004). *Designing virtual worlds*. New Riders.

Belk, R. W. (2013). Extended self in a digital world. *The Journal of Consumer Research*, 40(3), 477–500. DOI: 10.1086/671052

Bente, G. R., Rüggenberg, S., Krämer, N. C., & Eschenburg, F. (2008). Avatar-mediated networking: Increasing social presence and interpersonal trust in net-based collaborations. *Human Communication Research*, 34(2), 287–318. DOI: 10.1111/j.1468-2958.2008.00322.x

Bimber, O. (2005). *Spatial augmented reality: merging real and virtual worlds*. AK Peters. DOI: 10.1201/b10624

Bourlakis, M. P. (2009). *Retail spatial evolution: paving the way from traditional to metaverse retailing*.

Bourlakis, M. P., Papagiannidis, S., & Li, F. (2009). Retail spatial evolution: Paving the way from traditional to metaverse retailing. *Electronic Commerce Research*, 9(1-2), 135–148. DOI: 10.1007/s10660-009-9030-8

Cheok, A. D. (2018). Virtual taste and smell technologies for multisensory internet and virtual reality. Springer.

Chesney, T. C., Coyne, I., Logan, B., & Madden, N. (2009). Griefing in virtual worlds: Causes, casualties and coping strategies. *Information Systems Journal*, 19(6), 525–548. DOI: 10.1111/j.1365-2575.2009.00330.x

Christopoulos, A. M., Mystakidis, S., Pellas, N., & Laakso, M.-J. (2021). ARLEAN: An augmented reality learning analytics ethical framework. *Computers*, 10(8), 92. DOI: 10.3390/computers10080092

Cipresso, P. G., Giglioli, I. A. C., Raya, M. A., & Riva, G. (2018). The past, present, and future of virtual and augmented reality research: A network and cluster analysis of the literature. *Frontiers in Psychology*, 9, 2086. DOI: 10.3389/fpsyg.2018.02086 PMID: 30459681

Cummings, J. J., & Bailenson, J. N. (2016). How immersive is enough? A meta-analysis of the effect of immersive technology on user presence. *Media Psychology*, 19(2), 272–309. DOI: 10.1080/15213269.2015.1015740

Davis, A. M., Murphy, J., Owens, D., Khazanchi, D., & Zigurs, I. (2009). Avatars, people, and virtual worlds: Foundations for research in metaverses. *Journal of the Association for Information Systems*, 10(2), 1. DOI: 10.17705/1jais.00183

Delmerico, J. P., Poranne, R., Bogo, F., Oleynikova, H., Vollenweider, E., Coros, S., Nieto, J., & Pollefeys, M. (2022). Spatial computing and intuitive interaction: Bringing mixed reality and robotics together. *IEEE Robotics & Automation Magazine*, 29(1), 45–57. DOI: 10.1109/MRA.2021.3138384

Dionisio, J. D. (2013). 3D virtual worlds and the metaverse: Current status and future possibilities. *ACM Computing Surveys*, 45(3), 1-38.

Duani, N. B. (2018). *"Brought to you live": On the consumption experience of live social media streams*. ACR North American Advances.

Dwivedi, Y. K., Hughes, L., Wang, Y., Alalwan, A. A., Ahn, S. J. G., Balakrishnan, J., Barta, S., Belk, R., Buhalis, D., Dutot, V., Felix, R., Filieri, R., Flavián, C., Gustafsson, A., Hinsch, C., Hollensen, S., Jain, V., Kim, J., Krishen, A. S., & Wirtz, J. (2023). Metaverse marketing: How the metaverse will shape the future of consumer research and practice. *Psychology and Marketing*, 40(4), 750–776. DOI: 10.1002/mar.21767

Egliston, B., & Carter, M. (2021). Critical questions for Facebook's virtual reality: Data, power and the metaverse. *Internet Policy Review*, 10(4). Advance online publication. DOI: 10.14763/2021.4.1610

El Beheiry, M. D., Doutreligne, S., Caporal, C., Ostertag, C., Dahan, M., & Masson, J.-B. (2019). Virtual reality: Beyond visualization. *Journal of Molecular Biology*, 431(7), 1315–1321. DOI: 10.1016/j.jmb.2019.01.033 PMID: 30738026

Farjami, S. e. (2011). Multilingual problem based learning in metaverse. In *Knowledge-Based and Intelligent Information and Engineering Systems. 5th International Conference, KES 2011* (pp. pp. 499-509). Springer Berlin Heidelberg.

Frank, R. (2022). Metaverse real estate sales top $500 million, MetaMetric solutions says.

Goanta, C. (2020). Selling LAND in Decentraland: The regime of non-fungible tokens on the Ethereum blockchain under the digital content directive. *Disruptive technology, legal innovation, and the future of real estate*, 139-154.

Gursoy, D. M., Malodia, S., & Dhir, A. (2022). The metaverse in the hospitality and tourism industry: An overview of current trends and future research directions. *Journal of Hospitality Marketing & Management*, 31(5), 527–534. DOI: 10.1080/19368623.2022.2072504

Hancock, J. T., & Bailenson, J. N. (2021). The social impact of deepfakes. *Cyberpsychology, Behavior, and Social Networking*, 24(3), 149–152. DOI: 10.1089/cyber.2021.29208.jth PMID: 33760669

Hatmaker, T. (2021). *Fortnite's Ariana Grande concert offers a taste of music in the metaverse*. Tech Crunch.

Heller, B. (2020). Watching androids dream of electric sheep: Immersive technology, biometric psychography, and the law. *Vand. J. Ent. & Tech. L*, 23, 1.

Hoffman, D. L., & Novak, T. P. (1996). Marketing in hypermedia computer-mediated environments: Conceptual foundation. *Journal of Marketing*, 60(3), 50–68. DOI: 10.1177/002224299606000304

Hong, J. Y., He, J., Lam, B., Gupta, R., & Gan, W.-S. (2017). Spatial audio for soundscape design: Recording and reproduction. *Applied Sciences (Basel, Switzerland)*, 7(6), 627. DOI: 10.3390/app7060627

Huang, H. H., Hwang, G.-J., & Chang, S.-C. (2023). Facilitating decision making in authentic contexts: An SVVR-based experiential flipped learning approach for professional training. *Interactive Learning Environments*, 31(8), 5219–5235. DOI: 10.1080/10494820.2021.2000435

Ibáñez, M. B.-K., & Delgado-Kloos, C. (2018). Augmented reality for STEM learning: A systematic review. *Computers & Education*, 123, 109–123. DOI: 10.1016/j.compedu.2018.05.002

Jeong, H. Y. (2022). An innovative e-commerce platform incorporating metaverse to live commerce. *International Journal of Innovative Computing, Information, & Control*, 18(1), 221–229.

Jovanović, A., & Milosavljević, A. (2022). VoRtex Metaverse platform for gamified collaborative learning. *Electronics (Basel)*, 11(3), 317. DOI: 10.3390/electronics11030317

Kardong-Edgren, S. S., Farra, S. L., Alinier, G., & Young, H. M. (2019). A call to unify definitions of virtual reality. *Clinical Simulation in Nursing*, 31, 28–34. DOI: 10.1016/j.ecns.2019.02.006

Kim, S. L., Lee, S., Kang, H., Kim, S., & Ahn, M. (2021). P300 brain–computer interface-based drone control in virtual and augmented reality. *Sensors (Basel)*, 21(17), 5765. DOI: 10.3390/s21175765 PMID: 34502655

Kivetz, R. (2017). *Being in the moment: The effects of ephemeral communication in social media*. Marketing Science Institute.

Kölüş, Ç. (2020). Blockchain based digital identity management. *Euroasia Journal of Mathematics, Engineering, Natural &Medical Science*, 7(8), 202–209.

Kugler, T. Y., Ye, B., Motro, D., & Noussair, C. N. (2020). On trust and disgust: Evidence from face reading and virtual reality. *Social Psychological & Personality Science*, 11(3), 317–325. DOI: 10.1177/1948550619856302

Kye, B. H., Han, N., Kim, E., Park, Y., & Jo, S. (2021). Educational applications of metaverse: Possibilities and limitations. *Journal of Educational Evaluation for Health Professions*, 18, 18. DOI: 10.3352/jeehp.2021.18.32 PMID: 34897242

Lu, J. L., Liu, R., Zhang, Y., Zhang, X., Zheng, L., Zhang, C., Zhang, K., Li, S., & Lu, Y. (2022). Development and application of a detection platform for colorectal cancer tumor sprouting pathological characteristics based on artificial intelligence. *Intelligent Medicine*, 2(02), 82–87. DOI: 10.1016/j.imed.2021.08.003

Maereg, A. T., Nagar, A., Reid, D., & Secco, E. L. (2017). Wearable vibrotactile haptic device for stiffness discrimination during virtual interactions. *Frontiers in Robotics and AI*, 4, 42. DOI: 10.3389/frobt.2017.00042

Mattila, V. (2024). *Metaverse Dynamics: Economics*. Operations, and Investment.

Milgram, P. (1994). taxonomy of mixed reality visual displays. *IEICE Transactions on Information and Systems*, 77(12), 1321–1329.

Milgram, P. H. (1995). Augmented reality: A class of displays on the reality-virtuality continuum. In *Telemanipulator and telepresence technologies* (Vol. 2351, pp. 282–292). Spie. DOI: 10.1117/12.197321

Milgram, P. T. (1995). Augmented reality: A class of displays on the reality-virtuality continuum. *In Telemanipulator and Telepresence Technologies, 2351*, 282-292.

Mystakidis, S. P. (2021). Virtual reality escape rooms for STEM education in industry 4.0: Greek teachers perspectives. In *2021 6th South-East Europe Design Automation, Computer Engineering, Computer Networks and Social Media Conference (SEEDA-CECNSM)* (pp. 1-5). IEEE.

Mystakidis, S. T.-G. (2024). Virtual Museum Gamification for Discovery-Based Online Learning in the Metaverse. *CSEDU*, 711-719.

Nilsson, N. C., Nordahl, R., & Serafin, S. (2016). Immersion revisited: A review of existing definitions of immersion and their relation to different theories of presence. *Human Technology*, 12(2), 108–134. DOI: 10.17011/ht/urn.201611174652

Pantano, E. P. (2017). The role of AI in retailing: Enhancing customer experience with intelligent systems. *International Journal of Retail & Distribution Management,* 45(7/8), 698-713.

Park, S. M., & Kim, Y.-G. (2022). A metaverse: Taxonomy, components, applications, and open challenges. *IEEE Access : Practical Innovations, Open Solutions*, 10, 4209–4251. DOI: 10.1109/ACCESS.2021.3140175

Pellas, N. M., Mystakidis, S., & Kazanidis, I. (2021). Immersive Virtual Reality in K-12 and Higher Education: A systematic review of the last decade scientific literature. *Virtual Reality (Waltham Cross)*, 25(3), 835–861. DOI: 10.1007/s10055-020-00489-9

Peters, K. C., Chen, Y., Kaplan, A. M., Ognibeni, B., & Pauwels, K. (2013). Social media metrics—A framework and guidelines for managing social media. *Journal of Interactive Marketing*, 27(4), 281–298. DOI: 10.1016/j.intmar.2013.09.007

Rejeb, A. R., Rejeb, K., & Treiblmaier, H. (2023). Mapping metaverse research: Identifying future research areas based on bibliometric and topic modeling techniques. *Information (Basel)*, 14(7), 356. DOI: 10.3390/info14070356

Russell, S. J. (2016). *Artificial intelligence: a modern approach*. Pearson.

Ryskeldiev, B. O. (2018). Distributed metaverse: creating decentralized blockchain-based model for peer-to-peer sharing of virtual spaces for mixed reality applications. In *Proceedings of the 9th augmented human international conference* (pp. 1-3).

Sadowski, W. (2002). Presence in virtual environments. *Handbook of virtual environments*, 831-846.

Salmon, G. (2019). May the fourth be with you: Creating education 4.0. *Journal of Learning for Development*, 6(2), 95–115. DOI: 10.56059/jl4d.v6i2.352

Serrano, J. S. (2020). Virtual world marketing strategies: A study of Roblox and Decentraland. *Journal of Virtual Economies*, 12(3), 189–205.

Slater, M. G.-L.-C., Gonzalez-Liencres, C., Haggard, P., Vinkers, C., Gregory-Clarke, R., Jelley, S., Watson, Z., Breen, G., Schwarz, R., Steptoe, W., Szostak, D., Halan, S., Fox, D., & Silver, J. (2020). he ethics of realism in virtual and augmented reality. *Frontiers in Virtual Reality*, 1, 512449. DOI: 10.3389/frvir.2020.00001

Slater, M. V., & Sanchez-Vives, M. V. (2016). Enhancing our lives with immersive virtual reality. *Frontiers in Robotics and AI*, 3, 74. DOI: 10.3389/frobt.2016.00074

Speicher, M. H. (2019). What is mixed reality? In *Proceedings of the 2019 CHI conference on human factors in computing systems* (pp. 1-15).

Spence, C. P., Puccinelli, N. M., Grewal, D., & Roggeveen, A. L. (2014). Store atmospherics: A multisensory perspective. *Psychology and Marketing*, 31(7), 472–488. DOI: 10.1002/mar.20709

Thawonmas, R. &. (2011, July). Frame extraction based on displacement amount for automatic comic generation from metaverse museum visit log. In *Intelligent Interactive MultimediaSystems and Services: Proceedings of the 4th International Conference on Intelligent Interactive Multimedia Systems and Services (IIMSS 2011)* (pp. 153-162). Springer Berlin Heidelberg. DOI: 10.1007/978-3-642-22158-3_16

Walther, J. B. (1996). Computer-mediated communication: Impersonal, interpersonal, and hyperpersonal interaction. *Communication Research*, 23(1), 3–43. DOI: 10.1177/009365096023001001

Wiederhold, B. K. (2022). Ready (or Not) player one: Initial musings on the metaverse. *Cyberpsychology, Behavior, and Social Networking*, 25(1), 1–2. DOI: 10.1089/cyber.2021.29234.editorial PMID: 34964667

Xu, F. K. (2022). Ethical considerations in the development of Metaverse experiences: Balancing innovation and privacy. *Journal of Business Ethics*, 179(2).

Zhao, Y. J., Jiang, J., Chen, Y., Liu, R., Yang, Y., Xue, X., & Chen, S. (2022). Metaverse: Perspectives from graphics, interactions and visualization. *Visual Informatics*, 6(1), 56–67. DOI: 10.1016/j.visinf.2022.03.002

Zheng, J. M., Chan, K. W., & Gibson, I. (1998). Virtual reality. *IEEE Potentials*, 17(2), 20–23. DOI: 10.1109/45.666641

Zotkin, D. N., Duraiswami, R., & Davis, L. S. (2004). Rendering localized spatial audio in a virtual auditory space. *IEEE Transactions on Multimedia*, 6(4), 553–564. DOI: 10.1109/TMM.2004.827516

Zwass, V. (2010). Co-creation: Toward a taxonomy and an integrated research perspective. *International Journal of Electronic Commerce*, *15*(1), 11-48.

ADDITIONAL READINGS

Ball, M. (2022). *The metaverse: and how it will revolutionize everything*. Liveright Publishing. DOI: 10.15358/9783800669400

Bekele, M. K., Pierdicca, R., Frontoni, E., Malinverni, E. S., & Gain, J. (2018). A survey of augmented, virtual, and mixed reality for cultural heritage. *Journal on Computing and Cultural Heritage*, 11(2), 1–36. DOI: 10.1145/3145534

Dwivedi, Y. K. (2022). rtificial intelligence (AI): Multidisciplinary perspectives on emerging challenges, opportunities, and agenda for research, practice and policy. *International Journal of Information Management*, 57, 102272.

Flavián, C. I.-S., Ibáñez-Sánchez, S., & Orús, C. (2019). The impact of virtual, augmented and mixed reality technologies onthe customer experience. *Journal of Business Research*, 00, 547–560. DOI: 10.1016/j.jbusres.2018.10.050

Kapp, K. M. (2009). *Learning in 3D: Adding a new dimension to enterprise learning and collaboration*. John Wiley & Sons.

Park, S. M., & Kim, Y.-G. (2022). A metaverse: Taxonomy, components, applications, and open challenges. *IEEE Access : Practical Innovations, Open Solutions*, 10, 4209–4251. DOI: 10.1109/ACCESS.2021.3140175

Rogers, K. (2021). Nike and the Metaverse: A case study on personalization in virtual spaces. *Journal of Interactive Marketing*, 55, 120–134.

Schroeder, A. G. (2020). Infinite walking in three dimensions in virtual reality: A shopping mall simulator game. In *Extended Abstracts of the 2020 Annual Symposium on Computer Human Interaction in Play* (pp. 76-79).

Yuste, R. G., Goering, S., Arcas, B. A., Bi, G., Carmena, J. M., Carter, A., Fins, J. J., Friesen, P., Gallant, J., Huggins, J. E., Illes, J., Kellmeyer, P., Klein, E., Marblestone, A., Mitchell, C., Parens, E., Pham, M., Rubel, A., Sadato, N., & Wolpaw, J. (2017). Four ethical priorities for neurotechnologies and AI. *Nature*, 551(7679), 159–163. DOI: 10.1038/551159a PMID: 29120438

KEY TERMS AND DEFINITIONS

Augmented Reality: It is a technique or technology that allow users to interact with both physical and virtual components.

Blockchain: A technology that is decentralised and secured with digital ledger to enable recording of transactions across multiple computers and it is often used for NFT and digital assets in the metaverse.

Digital Identity: The online presence of an users including the profile name, profile data, avatars, virtual assets etc. represents them in the environment of metaverse.

Extended Reality (XR): Combined term of all immersive technologies such as Mixed Reality, Augmented Reality and Virtual Reality.

Immersive Technology: These are often used as digital tool or platforms often used in Virtual and Augmented Reality in apps or in store to create highly engaging and interactive experiences by simulating real world sensations.

Metaverse: A collective virtual space where users can interact with each other in both physical and digital world through immersive technologies.

Spatial Computing: Use of digital technologies and immersive technologies to interact with physical world in three-dimensional space.

Chapter 10
Corporate Metaverse Adoption:
A Case Study of Accenture's Nth Floor Virtual Onboarding and Training Platform

Sahil Kohli
https://orcid.org/0000-0002-3792-988X
Chandigarh University, India

EXECUTIVE SUMMARY

This chapter examines Accenture's implementation of the Nth Floor, a pioneering enterprise metaverse platform that has transformed corporate training and onboarding processes. Through detailed analysis of quantitative and qualitative outcomes, the chapter explores how Accenture successfully deployed virtual reality technology across its global workforce of 700,000 employees, resulting in the onboarding of 150,000 new hires and deployment of 60,000 VR headsets. The study investigates the strategic planning, technical architecture, and change management approaches that contributed to achieving a 33% improvement in learning retention and a 4.7/5 employee satisfaction rating. The chapter provides comprehensive insights into implementation challenges, success factors, and best practices for organizations considering similar digital transformation initiatives. Additionally, the research examines the platform's impact on global collaboration, organizational culture, and operational efficiency, while identifying future implications and research directions for enterprise metaverse adoption.

DOI: 10.4018/979-8-3693-7245-6.ch010

INTRODUCTION

The global workplace is still experiencing dramatic changes in this recent technological advancement due to the speedy improvement in technologies and changes in expectations of the workforce. Thinking all these dynamics, the enterprise metaverse has emerged as a revolutionizing approach to corporate training, onboarding, and collaboration. One such shift is the exemplary work done by Accenture, which had started with the Nth Floor, a nearly fully-developmental environment transforming paradigms in employee motivation and professional training (Kumar & Shankar, 2024).

The environment for the corporate training has been revolutionized in the last decade. Face-to-face classroom learning is less common, and more solutions are moving to the virtual space as global companies are pouring a lot of money into virtual learning solutions. The enterprise metaverse market had risen from $60.7 billion in 2023 to $258.3 billion by 2031, showing that while companies have slowly integrated immersive technology into the workplace (Kumar & Shankar, 2024).

Several factors explain for this condition; First, virtual and augmented reality technologies have come of age and it is possible to implement them at the enterprise level. Two, when a hybrid work model is implemented around the world, it becomes even more important to have more effective tools for virtual collaboration. Third, the increasing complexity of the training necessary for corporate persons in the technologically advanced sectors is also giving a call for an enhanced training environment (Bag et al., 2023).

With this background, then, Accenture's implementation of the Nth Floor was very pioneering in the enterprise metaverse adoption approach. Not only were it virtual meetings and content execution, but it became a complete ecosystem of employee development, collaboration, and engagement. In the first wave of implementation, the objectives were on building a scalable one which should be capable of handling the global workforce while ensuring equivalent training quality and cultural cohesion over geography.

These applications of immersive technologies combined with enterprise needs create potential for organizations to redesign new operational paradigms. In particular, metaverses ensure an effective solution to the issues of hybrid work environments in terms of training, motivating, and building corporate culture (Bag et al., 2023). Accenture demonstrates impressive consistency in its case study on the enterprise adoption through the Nth Floor. The company has managed to implement onboarding for over 150000 employees and distributed 60000 VR headsets for its 700000 people strong workforce.

Problem Statement

There has been a lot of progress in realising the full potential of metaverse technologies for organisational use, but the deployment and scaling of organisational solutions remain challenging. Technical requirements are one of the main issues affecting the implementation of such solutions, alongside with the user's acceptance and the ability to find affordable ROI indicators (Kuo & Choi, 2024). These challenges are addressed in this case study because the author goes deeper into the details of Accenture's Nth Floor implementation to give a rich source of information on how enterprise metaverse can be implemented effectively.

The challenges that surround implementation are numerous as well as complex. At the infrastructure level, organisations require very high technical specifications including high bandwidth connectivity, high level security, and interfaces to other enterprise systems. The case of Accenture reveals that such systems require strong technological investment in their implementation, as well as consideration of the system architecture to accommodate globalisation (Kuo & Choi, 2024).

Some other significant issues are associated with security and privacy issues. Virtual environments are getting tonnes of user data and organisation compliance for such a wide range of international regulations must be ensured. Furthermore, this is highly critical as such training scenario comprises discussion of various business practises and information belonging to the organisation most of the time (Yazıcı et al., 2024).

The human side of implementation also results in similar critical issues. Low acceptance of new technologies is caused by the resistance of the employees, as well as the differing levels of expertise across the company. Such immersive environments have to address organisational concerns of virtual environment fatigue, problems of access and challenges of boundary management.

There are cultural transformation requirements, which makes it slightly more complicated. The management of organisations must find ways of transforming changes from traditional to virtual and maintain the team cohesiveness and corporate culture. It is most difficult especially in multinational organisations where the working culture or the working environment in the regions is quite distinct (Chaves et al., 2024).

Research Objectives

This chapter aims to:

- Analyse the strategic framework and implementation methodology of Accenture's Nth Floor platform

- Evaluate the effectiveness of virtual onboarding and training programmes in large-scale enterprise environments
- Assess the impact of immersive technologies on employee engagement and learning outcomes
- Identify key success factors and potential barriers in enterprise metaverse adoption
- Develop a comprehensive framework for organisations considering similar implementations

The chapter is structured to provide a systematic analysis of Accenture's metaverse implementation. Beginning with a comprehensive literature review, it examines the evolution of corporate virtual environments and enterprise metaverse platforms. The case implementation section details the strategic planning, technical architecture, and change management approaches employed by Accenture. The analysis section evaluates both quantitative metrics and qualitative outcomes, including the documented 33% improvement in learning retention compared to traditional methods. The chapter concludes with future implications and recommendations for organisations considering similar initiatives.

Significance of Study

This research contributes significantly to the emerging body of knowledge surrounding enterprise metaverse adoption in several ways. Firstly, it provides empirical evidence of successful large-scale implementation, addressing a critical gap in current literature (Yazıcı et al., 2024). The documented success metrics, including the 4.7/5 employee satisfaction rating and substantial improvements in learning retention, offer valuable benchmarks for organisations considering similar initiatives.

As noted by Accenture's CTO Paul Daugherty, "We see the metaverse as a continuum that spans the spectrum of digitally enhanced worlds, realities and business models. It applies across all aspects of business, from consumer to worker and across the entire enterprise." This perspective underscores the broader implications of this case study for corporate digital transformation strategies.

The research also addresses practical implementation challenges, including the integration of virtual environments with existing enterprise systems, the development of digital twins for offices in Bangalore, Madrid, and San Francisco, and the successful deployment of VR technology at scale. These insights are particularly valuable given the accelerated adoption of virtual solutions during the recent global shift to remote work (Chaves et al., 2024).

Furthermore, the study contributes to the theoretical understanding of virtual learning environments and their impact on employee engagement. The documented success in facilitating global collaboration and creating immersive learning experiences provides a framework for understanding how organisations can leverage metaverse technologies to enhance corporate training and development programmes (Zille et al., 2024).

LITERATURE REVIEW

Evolution of Corporate Virtual Environments

The evolution of corporate virtual environments has marked a transformative journey in organizational learning and collaboration approaches. Early virtual corporate environments emerged during the late 2000s, initially manifesting as basic video conferencing and learning management systems. Bag et al. (2023) have documented that the transition from traditional to virtual corporate spaces was primarily driven by two factors: the increasing need for cost-effective training solutions and the growing demand for global collaboration capabilities.

This developmental trajectory has progressed through several distinct phases. The initial phase, spanning from 2008 to 2015, focused primarily on enabling remote meetings and basic knowledge sharing through digital platforms. During this period, organizations experimented with rudimentary virtual training environments, though these were limited by technological constraints and user acceptance barriers. The second phase, from 2015 to 2019, introduced more sophisticated interactive elements, including preliminary 3D environments and enhanced virtual training capabilities. The third phase, accelerated by technological advancements and global workplace transformations post-2020, has witnessed the emergence of fully immersive corporate environments integrated with enterprise systems.

Contemporary corporate virtual environments have evolved into sophisticated ecosystems that fundamentally reshape organizational learning and collaboration. Kuo and Choi (2024) emphasize that current implementations focus on creating seamless, immersive experiences that effectively bridge the gap between physical and digital workspaces. These modern environments incorporate advanced technologies, including virtual reality, augmented reality, and artificial intelligence, fundamentally transforming corporate training and collaboration paradigms.

The present landscape demonstrates remarkable sophistication in several key areas. Organizations now implement immersive learning environments that support both structured training programs and spontaneous knowledge exchange opportunities. Advanced visualization capabilities enable complex scenario simulations, particularly valuable in high-risk or high-cost training situations. Real-time collaboration tools have evolved to support nuanced global team interactions, while adaptive learning systems now deliver personalized training experiences based on individual learning patterns and organizational requirements.

The trajectory of corporate virtual environments points towards increasingly sophisticated and integrated solutions. Yazıcı et al. (2024) identify several emerging trends that are reshaping the future landscape. Artificial intelligence integration is expected to revolutionize personalized learning experiences, adapting content and delivery methods in real-time based on user responses and learning patterns. The emphasis on social and emotional aspects of virtual interaction continues to grow, with developments in haptic feedback systems promising more realistic and engaging training scenarios.

Research by Chaves et al. (2024) predicts the emergence of "hybrid experience spaces" - environments that seamlessly blend physical and digital interactions. These spaces will support natural interactions through advanced spatial computing, enhanced collaborative capabilities, and improved environmental awareness. The evolution of these environments has significant implications for organizational learning and development strategies.

Several critical factors continue to drive this evolution. Technological capabilities in graphics processing and network infrastructure are advancing rapidly, enabling more sophisticated virtual experiences. Workforce expectations regarding flexible work arrangements have fundamentally shifted, creating demand for more immersive remote collaboration tools. Organizations increasingly emphasize sustainable business practices, recognizing virtual environments' role in reducing carbon footprints associated with traditional training and collaboration methods.

Additionally, the growing need for scalable global training solutions drives innovation in virtual environment capabilities. Organizations face increasing pressure to deliver consistent, high-quality training experiences across geographically dispersed teams while maintaining cultural sensitivity and local relevance. The rise of data-driven decision-making in corporate learning has led to enhanced analytics capabilities within virtual environments, enabling organizations to measure and optimize learning outcomes more effectively.

Enterprise Metaverse Platforms

The enterprise metaverse technology landscape has evolved into a sophisticated ecosystem of interconnected platforms and solutions. Current technological implementations encompass a broad spectrum of innovations, ranging from immersive virtual reality environments to advanced artificial intelligence integration. Alshurideh et al. (2023) have documented that successful enterprise metaverse deployments require a robust technological foundation incorporating multiple layers of infrastructure, security, and user interaction systems.

The hardware infrastructure supporting enterprise metaverse platforms has matured significantly. Large-scale implementations, such as Accenture's deployment of 60,000 VR headsets, demonstrate the feasibility of enterprise-wide adoption. Chengoden et al. (2023) emphasize that modern enterprise platforms must support various access methods, from high-end VR headsets to mobile devices, ensuring accessibility across diverse workforce demographics. This technological democratization has proven crucial for widespread adoption and engagement.

The software architecture of contemporary enterprise metaverse platforms exhibits increasing sophistication. Digital twin technologies, exemplified by Accenture's recreation of offices in Bangalore, Madrid, and San Francisco, represent a significant advancement in spatial computing capabilities. These implementations leverage advanced rendering engines, real-time collaboration tools, and sophisticated data analytics systems to create immersive, interactive environments. Kim et al. (2023) note that the integration of AI-driven features has enhanced personalization capabilities, enabling adaptive learning experiences and intelligent environment responses.

The implementation of enterprise metaverse platforms demands structured approaches that address both technical and organizational considerations. Koohang et al. (2023) have developed a comprehensive framework that emphasizes the importance of phased deployment strategies. Their research indicates that successful implementations typically progress through distinct stages: infrastructure assessment, pilot deployment, scaled rollout, and continuous optimization.

Organizations must consider multiple dimensions when implementing enterprise metaverse solutions. Technical architecture considerations include network capacity, data security protocols, and integration with existing enterprise systems. Rutitis and Aksjonenko (2022) emphasize that successful implementations require robust governance frameworks that address data privacy, security compliance, and user authentication. Their research demonstrates that organizations must establish clear protocols for managing virtual assets, protecting intellectual property, and ensuring regulatory compliance across different jurisdictions.

Change management plays a crucial role in implementation success. Denisova and Lopatnikov (2022) argue that organizations must develop comprehensive stakeholder engagement strategies to ensure adoption and sustained usage. Their framework incorporates elements of cultural transformation, skills development, and resistance management. The research indicates that successful implementations often establish centers of excellence to guide deployment, manage best practices, and facilitate knowledge transfer across the organization.

The evaluation of enterprise metaverse platforms requires sophisticated measurement frameworks that capture both quantitative and qualitative outcomes. Sui and Yao (2023) have developed a comprehensive metrics framework that encompasses multiple dimensions of success. Their research indicates that organizations must track technical performance indicators, user engagement metrics, and business impact measures to fully understand platform effectiveness.

Quantitative metrics have evolved beyond basic usage statistics to include sophisticated measures of engagement quality and learning outcomes. Accenture's documented achievement of a 4.7/5 satisfaction rating and 33% improvement in learning retention demonstrates the potential impact of well-implemented platforms. Zanon et al. (2021) emphasizes the importance of measuring both immediate and long-term impacts, including improved operational efficiency, enhanced collaboration effectiveness, and reduced training costs.

Recent research has highlighted the importance of measuring cultural and organizational impact. Nemashkalo et al. (2024) propose a framework for evaluating how enterprise metaverse platforms influence organizational culture, employee engagement, and global team effectiveness. Their findings suggest that successful implementations generate measurable improvements in cross-cultural collaboration, knowledge sharing, and innovation capacity.

The longitudinal assessment of enterprise metaverse implementations has revealed several critical success indicators. Pinnington and Ayoko (2021) have identified that successful platforms demonstrate progressive improvement across three key dimensions: user adoption rates, learning effectiveness, and operational efficiency. Their research indicates that organizations achieving high performance in these areas typically experience cascading benefits in employee retention, innovation capability, and global collaboration effectiveness.

Standardization of success metrics remains an evolving challenge. Poppe et al. (2017) argue that organizations must develop context-specific measurement frameworks while maintaining alignment with industry benchmarks. Their research demonstrates that successful measurement approaches balance quantitative performance indicators with qualitative assessments of user experience and organizational impact. This balanced approach enables organizations to make data-driven decisions about platform evolution while maintaining focus on user needs and business objectives.

Virtual Training and Development

The transformation from traditional to virtual training methodologies represents a fundamental shift in corporate learning paradigms. Contemporary organizations have witnessed a significant evolution in how knowledge transfer and skill development are approached. Minter et al. (2024) have documented that virtual training environments offer distinct advantages over traditional methods, particularly in scalability, consistency, and personalization capabilities.

Traditional training approaches, characterized by classroom-based instruction and physical simulations, have historically faced limitations in scalability and global reach. The transition to virtual training environments has addressed these constraints while introducing new possibilities for learning engagement. Varshney (2022) reports that effective Virtual Employee Onboarding (VEO) programs enhance inclusivity and engagement by leveraging advanced technologies. Accenture's implementation of the Nth Floor demonstrates this evolution, achieving a 33% improvement in learning retention compared to traditional methods.

The comparison between traditional and virtual approaches extends beyond delivery mechanisms. Torres et al. (2019) emphasize that virtual environments enable more sophisticated tracking of learning progression, immediate feedback mechanisms, and adaptive content delivery. Their research indicates that virtual reality and augmented reality technologies in onboarding processes significantly enhance cultural assimilation and task familiarization rates.

Contemporary virtual training platforms have necessitated the development of new engagement models that account for the unique characteristics of digital learning environments. Carlos and Muralles (2021) highlight that remote onboarding success depends on structured best practices that maintain continuity while fostering engagement. Their research demonstrates that virtual environments must actively promote social connection and community building to achieve optimal learning outcomes.

The evolution of engagement models in virtual training environments reflects a deeper understanding of digital learning dynamics. Holliday et al. (2022) demonstrate the feasibility and effectiveness of online curricula for virtual onboarding, particularly in professional education contexts. Their findings indicate that well-organized virtual training programs can effectively support learning goals while maintaining high levels of participant engagement. This is evidenced by Accenture's achievement of a 4.7/5 employee satisfaction rating in their virtual training programs.

Virtual engagement models have also evolved to address the challenges of maintaining attention and motivation in digital environments. Recent implementations incorporate gamification elements, social learning components, and interactive scenarios to enhance engagement. The success of these approaches is demonstrated through Accenture's ability to effectively onboard 150,000 new hires through their metaverse platform, maintaining high engagement levels throughout the process.

The measurement of learning effectiveness in virtual training environments requires sophisticated evaluation frameworks that capture both immediate and long-term outcomes. Minter et al. (2024) have developed comprehensive assessment methodologies that evaluate various dimensions of virtual learning effectiveness, including knowledge retention, skill application, and behavioural change. Their research indicates that virtual training environments can maintain high satisfaction rates while reducing appointment times compared to traditional approaches.

Learning effectiveness in virtual environments manifests through multiple dimensions of measurement. Holliday et al. (2022) emphasize the importance of establishing comprehensive evaluation frameworks that assess both technical proficiency and soft skill development. Their research demonstrates that virtual training environments can effectively support complex learning objectives when properly structured and monitored. This is particularly evident in Accenture's documented success, where virtual training initiatives have demonstrated measurable improvements in both learning outcomes and employee engagement metrics.

The evolution of effectiveness measures has led to the development of more sophisticated assessment tools. Varshney (2022) argues that traditional success metrics must be adapted and expanded for virtual environments to capture the unique advantages of digital learning platforms. These advanced measurement systems incorporate real-time analytics, behavioral indicators, and longitudinal performance tracking to provide a comprehensive view of learning effectiveness.

The landscape of virtual training and development continues to evolve, driven by technological advancements and changing organizational needs. Carlos and Muralles (2021) identify several emerging trends that are reshaping virtual learning effectiveness:

The integration of artificial intelligence and machine learning has enabled more personalized learning experiences, adapting content delivery based on individual progress and learning styles. Organizations have begun implementing predictive analytics to identify potential learning challenges before they impact performance. This proactive approach to learning management represents a significant advancement over traditional reactive methods.

Furthermore, the development of hybrid learning models has emerged as a promising direction for future training initiatives. Torres et al. (2019) note that successful organizations are increasingly adopting blended approaches that combine the benefits of virtual immersion with selective physical interactions. This hybrid methodology maximizes the advantages of both virtual and traditional learning environments while minimizing their respective limitations.

Corporate Digital Transformation

The implementation of enterprise metaverse platforms represents a significant organizational transformation requiring robust change management approaches. Rutitis and Aksjonenko (2022) emphasize that successful digital transformation initiatives must address both technological and human aspects of change. Their research demonstrates that organizations achieving successful transformations typically employ comprehensive change management frameworks that encompass leadership alignment, stakeholder engagement, and cultural adaptation.

Strategic change management in the context of metaverse adoption requires careful consideration of organizational readiness and capability development. Denisova and Lopatnikov (2022) have identified that effective change strategies must balance technological innovation with organizational capacity for absorption. Their findings indicate that successful transformations often progress through distinct phases, each requiring specific change management approaches and interventions.

The role of leadership in driving digital transformation has emerged as a critical success factor. Cui et al. (2023) demonstrate that organizations with strong leadership support for digital initiatives achieve significantly higher adoption rates and better outcomes. This is evidenced in Accenture's implementation, where executive sponsorship and clear communication of the metaverse vision have contributed to widespread adoption across their global workforce.

The adoption of enterprise metaverse technologies follows distinct patterns that reflect both organizational and individual acceptance processes. Sui and Yao (2023) have documented that successful adoption typically progresses through multiple stages, from initial awareness and experimentation to full integration and optimization. Their research indicates that organizations must carefully manage each stage to ensure sustainable adoption and value realization.

Technology adoption patterns in enterprise metaverse implementations reveal interesting dynamics between different user groups and use cases. Zanon et al. (2021) observe that early adopters often emerge from specific organizational functions, particularly those involved in training, collaboration, and innovation activities. These early adoption patterns create momentum for broader organizational acceptance and help identify optimization opportunities for subsequent deployment phases.

Organizational readiness for metaverse adoption encompasses multiple dimensions of capability and preparedness. Nemashkalo et al. (2024) argue that successful digital transformation requires a comprehensive assessment of technical infrastructure, workforce capabilities, and cultural readiness. Their research demonstrates that organizations must develop specific competencies across multiple domains to support effective metaverse implementation.

Infrastructure readiness represents a foundational element of successful transformation. Organizations must ensure their technical architecture can support the demanding requirements of immersive virtual environments. Chengoden et al. (2023) emphasize that network capacity, data security protocols, and integration capabilities form critical prerequisites for successful implementation. Accenture's successful deployment of digital twins across multiple global locations exemplifies the importance of robust infrastructure preparation.

Cultural readiness plays an equally important role in transformation success. Koohang et al. (2023) identify that organizations must cultivate a digital-first mindset while maintaining focus on human-centric values. Their research indicates that successful transformations balance technological advancement with organizational culture preservation, ensuring that digital innovations enhance rather than disrupt existing social structures.

The trajectory of corporate digital transformation through metaverse technologies suggests significant implications for organizational development and sustainability. Alshurideh et al. (2023) predict that organizations successfully implementing metaverse platforms will experience fundamental shifts in operational models, collaboration patterns, and innovation capabilities. Their analysis indicates that early adopters gain significant competitive advantages through enhanced operational efficiency and improved employee engagement.

Sustainability considerations have emerged as a critical factor in digital transformation strategies. The implementation of virtual environments demonstrates potential for significant environmental impact reduction through decreased physical travel and resource consumption. Kim et al. (2023) note that organizations leveraging metaverse technologies for training and collaboration report substantial reductions in carbon footprint while maintaining or improving operational effectiveness.

Long-term sustainability of digital transformation initiatives requires continuous evolution and adaptation. Organizations must develop mechanisms for ongoing assessment and refinement of their metaverse implementations. The documented success of Accenture's Nth Floor, with its 93% favorability rating and successful onboarding of 150,000 new hires, demonstrates the potential for sustainable transformation when properly executed and maintained.

CASE IMPLEMENTATION

The implementation of Accenture's Nth Floor represents one of the most comprehensive and successful enterprise metaverse deployments documented in recent organizational studies (Alshurideh et al., 2023). This section examines the systematic approach taken by Accenture in conceptualizing, developing, and scaling their virtual environment across a global workforce of 700,000 employees. Recent research by Koohang et al. (2023) emphasizes that successful metaverse implementations require careful consideration of multiple organizational dimensions, which this case study explores through four key areas: strategic planning, technical architecture, implementation processes, and change management strategies.

The significance of this implementation extends beyond its scale, demonstrating innovative approaches to virtual onboarding and training. Shitole et al. (2024) have documented that large-scale virtual implementations require robust frameworks for measuring success and impact. Accenture's achievement in onboarding over 150,000 new hires through their metaverse platform while maintaining a 4.7/5 employee satisfaction rating provides empirical evidence of successful enterprise-scale adoption (Chengoden et al., 2023). This aligns with recent findings by Yazıcı et al. (2024) regarding the effectiveness of immersive technologies in corporate training environments.

The implementation journey, initiated before the pandemic and accelerated during global workplace transformations, offers valuable insights into both planned and adaptive approaches to large-scale digital transformation (Kim et al., 2023). Research by Rutitis and Aksjonenko (2022) suggests that successful digital transformations require careful attention to both technological and cultural elements. Accenture's creation of digital twins for offices in Bangalore, Madrid, and San Francisco demonstrates this balanced approach, addressing both technical capabilities and cultural nuances in global deployment.

Strategic Planning Phase

Accenture's strategic planning for the Nth Floor implementation began with a comprehensive vision-setting exercise that aligned metaverse adoption with broader organizational objectives. Koohang et al. (2023) emphasize that successful enterprise metaverse implementations require clear strategic alignment between technological innovation and business outcomes. Accenture's approach focused on three primary objectives: enhancing global workforce connectivity, standardizing training quality, and reducing environmental impact through virtual collaboration.

The initial vision, as articulated by Accenture's CTO Paul Daugherty, positioned the metaverse as "a continuum that spans the spectrum of digitally enhanced worlds, realities and business models" (Alshurideh et al., 2023). This perspective shaped the development of specific, measurable objectives for the Nth Floor implementation. Sui and Yao (2023) note that organizations achieving successful digital transformations typically establish clear metrics for success early in their planning phase. Accenture's strategic objectives included onboarding 150,000 new hires through the platform, maintaining employee satisfaction scores above 4.5/5, and achieving a 30% improvement in learning retention rates.

The stakeholder engagement strategy adopted by Accenture demonstrated a sophisticated understanding of change management principles in digital transformation initiatives. Rutitis and Aksjonenko (2022) argue that early and consistent stakeholder engagement significantly influences implementation success. Accenture's approach involved systematic identification and engagement of key stakeholder groups, including senior leadership, regional managers, training facilitators, and end users across different geographical locations.

Senior leadership engagement proved particularly crucial in establishing implementation momentum. Research by Denisova and Lopatnikov (2022) indicates that visible executive sponsorship significantly impacts adoption rates in enterprise-wide digital transformations. Accenture's success in engaging 150 managing directors in virtual strategy sessions demonstrated the effectiveness of their stakeholder engagement approach. The organization established feedback mechanisms that enabled continuous refinement of the implementation strategy based on stakeholder input and experiences.

The resource allocation strategy for the Nth Floor implementation reflected a comprehensive understanding of enterprise metaverse requirements. Chengoden et al. (2023) emphasize that successful metaverse implementations require careful consideration of both technological and human resource investments. Accenture's deployment of 60,000 VR headsets represented a significant capital investment, supported by substantial allocations for infrastructure development, content creation, and training support.

Human resource allocation focused on building internal capabilities while leveraging external expertise where necessary. Kim et al. (2023) note that organizations must develop specific competencies to support enterprise metaverse implementations effectively. Accenture's approach included the establishment of dedicated teams for platform development, content creation, and user support. The resource allocation strategy also incorporated flexibility to accommodate regional variations in implementation requirements and user needs.

The financial planning framework developed for the Nth Floor implementation emphasized long-term sustainability while acknowledging short-term investment requirements. Yazıcı et al. (2024) argue that successful digital transformation initiatives require balanced investment approaches that consider both immediate implementation needs and ongoing operational requirements. Accenture's investment strategy included provisions for platform development, hardware procurement, and continuous improvement initiatives, with clear alignment between resource allocation and expected business outcomes.

Technical Architecture

The selection of appropriate technological platforms for Accenture's Nth Floor implementation represented a critical decision point in the project's architecture. Koohang et al. (2023) emphasize that enterprise metaverse platform selection must consider scalability, integration capabilities, and user experience requirements. Accenture's partnership with Microsoft using AltspaceVR demonstrated a strategic approach to platform selection, prioritizing enterprise-grade capabilities and global accessibility.

The platform selection process incorporated multiple technical and operational criteria. According to Chengoden et al. (2023), successful enterprise metaverse implementations require platforms that support both synchronous and asynchronous interactions while maintaining high performance standards. Accenture's evaluation framework assessed platforms based on their ability to support digital twin creation, as evidenced by the successful replication of offices in Bangalore, Madrid, and San Francisco. The selected platform architecture needed to accommodate diverse use cases, from large-scale virtual events hosting 150 managing directors to intimate training sessions.

The development of supporting infrastructure for the Nth Floor initiative required careful consideration of global deployment requirements. Kim et al. (2023) note that enterprise metaverse implementations demand robust technical infrastructure capable of supporting immersive experiences across diverse geographical locations. Accenture's infrastructure development strategy focused on creating a resilient, scalable foundation capable of supporting 60,000 VR headsets while maintaining consistent performance standards.

Network architecture played a crucial role in infrastructure development. Sui and Yao (2023) emphasize that successful metaverse implementations require sophisticated network designs that minimize latency while maximizing reliability. Accenture's approach included the deployment of edge computing solutions and content delivery networks to ensure optimal performance across global locations. The infrastructure development process also incorporated provisions for future scaling, anticipating growing demand for virtual collaboration and training capabilities.

Security architecture represented a fundamental component of the Nth Floor implementation. Alshurideh et al. (2023) highlight that enterprise metaverse security must address both traditional cybersecurity concerns and unique challenges posed by immersive environments. Accenture's security framework incorporated multiple layers of protection, from user authentication and authorization to data encryption and privacy controls.

The security architecture extended beyond technical controls to encompass governance and compliance requirements. Recent research by Yazıcı et al. (2024) indicates that enterprise metaverse implementations must address regulatory compliance across multiple jurisdictions while maintaining operational efficiency. Accenture's approach included the development of comprehensive security policies, regular security assessments, and continuous monitoring capabilities to ensure platform integrity and data protection.

Integration security posed particular challenges in the implementation. Rutitis and Aksjonenko (2022) argue that security considerations must extend to all integration points between metaverse platforms and existing enterprise systems. Accenture's security architecture incorporated specific controls for protecting sensitive corporate information while enabling necessary data flows between the Nth Floor platform and other enterprise systems. This balanced approach enabled the achievement of both security objectives and operational requirements.

Implementation Process

The implementation of Accenture's Nth Floor began with strategically designed pilot programs to validate the approach and gather early feedback. According to Accenture's Technology Vision 2022 report, the initial pilot phase focused on testing both technical capabilities and user acceptance across different geographical locations (Accenture, 2022). This approach aligns with research by Bag et al. (2023) suggesting that pilot implementations play a crucial role in enterprise metaverse adoption.

The pilot programs were structured to evaluate multiple aspects of the platform's effectiveness. HRD Connect's (2023) analysis of Accenture's implementation reveals that early pilots included controlled groups of new hires across different regions, allowing for comparative analysis of virtual versus traditional onboarding approaches. These pilot initiatives demonstrated a 33% improvement in learning retention compared to traditional methods, providing crucial validation for broader deployment.

Following successful pilot programs, Accenture executed a phased global rollout strategy. The Enterprise Metaverse Consulting Services documentation indicates that the rollout prioritized regions based on technological readiness and business criticality (Accenture, 2023). This systematic approach enabled the successful deployment of 60,000 VR headsets and the creation of digital twins for offices in Bangalore, Madrid, and San Francisco.

The global implementation strategy incorporated lessons learned from initial deployments. Pangea.ai's (2024) analysis of Accenture's metaverse initiatives highlights how the organization adapted its rollout approach based on early adoption patterns and user feedback. The phased deployment strategy proved particularly effective, with the platform achieving a 93% favourability rating among participants while successfully onboarding over 150,000 new hires.

The training component of the implementation process represented a crucial success factor. Business Wire's (2022) coverage of Accenture's Technology Vision emphasizes the organization's comprehensive approach to employee preparation and support. The training strategy encompassed both technical skills development and cultural adaptation to virtual environments.

Training methodologies evolved throughout the implementation process. According to i4cp's (2023) analysis, Accenture developed a multi-tiered training approach that addressed different user proficiency levels and use cases. This approach proved particularly effective in supporting the platform's adoption across diverse user groups, contributing to the documented 4.7/5 employee satisfaction rating.

The implementation of training programs demonstrated careful attention to cultural nuances and regional requirements. Accenture's internal documentation reveals that training materials and approaches were customized for different regions while maintaining consistent core learning objectives. This balanced approach to localization and standardization supported the successful scaling of the platform across Accenture's global workforce of 700,000 employees.

Change Management

Accenture's change management approach for the Nth Floor implementation cantered on a comprehensive communication framework. According to Accenture's Technology Vision 2022 report, the organization developed a multi-channel communication strategy that emphasized both the technological and cultural aspects of the transformation (Accenture, 2022). This approach aligned with Paul Daugherty's vision of the metaverse as "a continuum that spans the spectrum of digitally enhanced worlds, realities and business models."

The communication strategy incorporated multiple layers of engagement. HRD Connect's (2023) analysis reveals that Accenture implemented a cascading communication model, ensuring consistent messaging while allowing for regional customization. This approach proved particularly effective in achieving the documented 94% favourability rating from post-onboarding surveys, demonstrating successful stakeholder engagement across different organizational levels.

The change management initiative included specialized training programs designed to support different user groups through the transition. Business Wire (2022) reports that Accenture's approach focused on building both technical competency and cultural readiness. The training framework encompassed multiple elements:

The implementation team developed role-specific training modules that addressed varying levels of technical proficiency. According to i4cp (2023), the successful onboarding of 45,000 new hires across 29 countries demonstrated the effectiveness of this differentiated approach. The training programs particularly emphasized the development of virtual collaboration skills and immersive learning capabilities.

Accenture implemented a sophisticated framework for measuring and tracking adoption across the organization. The Metaverse Enterprise Consulting Services documentation (Accenture, 2023) outlines how the organization monitored both quantitative and qualitative indicators of adoption success. Key metrics included:

- Platform engagement rates across different user groups
- Training completion and effectiveness measures
- User satisfaction scores, achieving a consistent 4.7/5 rating
- Learning retention improvements, documented at 33% above traditional methods
- Virtual collaboration effectiveness indicators

The cultural dimension of change management received particular attention in the implementation strategy. Pangea.ai's (2024) analysis highlights how Accenture focused on creating an inclusive virtual environment that respected diverse cultural perspectives while maintaining organizational cohesion. This approach was particularly evident in the successful creation and integration of digital twins for offices in Bangalore, Madrid, and San Francisco, each reflecting local cultural nuances while maintaining consistent organizational values.

ANALYSIS AND IMPACT

The comprehensive analysis of Accenture's Nth Floor implementation reveals significant impacts across multiple organizational dimensions. This section examines both quantitative and qualitative outcomes of the enterprise metaverse adoption, providing detailed insights into the initiative's effectiveness and business value. As noted in Accenture's Technology Vision report (2022), the implementation has demonstrated measurable improvements in training effectiveness, employee engagement, and operational efficiency.

The analysis framework incorporates multiple evaluation dimensions to provide a holistic understanding of the implementation's impact. According to HRD Connect's (2023) detailed case study, Accenture's metaverse initiative has achieved remarkable success metrics, including a 93% favorability rating and significant improvements in learning outcomes. Business Wire (2022) further emphasizes that the platform's impact extends beyond traditional training metrics to influence broader organizational dynamics and cultural transformation.

The evaluation approach considers both immediate operational impacts and longer-term strategic benefits. Pangea.ai's (2024) analysis of Accenture's metaverse implementation highlights how the organization has leveraged data analytics to measure and validate the platform's effectiveness.

Quantitative Metrics

The analysis of training completion rates through the Nth Floor platform demonstrates significant improvements in learning efficiency and engagement. According to Accenture's Metaverse Enterprise Consulting Services documentation (2023), the platform successfully facilitated the onboarding of over 150,000 new hires, achieving completion rates notably higher than traditional training methods. This scale of implementation provides robust data for analyzing the platform's effectiveness in delivering consistent training outcomes across a global workforce.

The platform's ability to track and measure completion rates with granular detail has provided valuable insights into learning patterns. Business Wire's (2022) analysis reveals that the digital tracking capabilities of the Nth Floor enabled real-time monitoring of progress and immediate intervention when needed. The data indicates a 33% improvement in learning retention compared to traditional methods, with particularly strong performance in technical and soft skill development areas.

Employee satisfaction metrics have emerged as a key indicator of the platform's success. HRD Connect's (2023) detailed case analysis documents an impressive 4.7/5 employee satisfaction rating, demonstrating strong user acceptance of the virtual training environment. This high satisfaction score is particularly noteworthy given the scale of implementation across Accenture's 700,000-person global workforce.

Detailed satisfaction surveys, as reported by i4cp (2023), reveal several contributing factors to these high scores:

- Intuitive interface design and accessibility
- Flexibility in learning pace and schedule
- Enhanced interaction capabilities
- Consistent experience across global locations
- Immediate access to resources and support

Platform usage statistics provide compelling evidence of successful adoption and engagement. According to Pangea.ai's (2024) analysis, the deployment of 60,000 VR headsets has resulted in significant platform utilization across various use cases.

Usage patterns indicate strong engagement across different organizational levels, from new hire orientation to senior leadership meetings.

- The metrics demonstrate particularly strong adoption in specific areas:
- Virtual team meetings and collaboration sessions
- Training and development programs
- Global leadership gatherings, including the successful coordination of 150 managing directors across 25 locations
- Informal networking and mentoring sessions

Usage data analysis, as documented in Accenture's Technology Vision report (2022), indicates sustained engagement levels post-initial implementation. The platform has maintained consistent daily active user rates, with peak usage during global events and training sessions. These statistics support the platform's effectiveness in supporting both structured learning activities and spontaneous collaboration.

Qualitative Outcomes

The qualitative analysis of employee feedback provides rich insights into the transformative impact of the Nth Floor platform. According to Accenture's Technology Vision report (2022), employee testimonials consistently highlight the platform's effectiveness in creating immersive and engaging learning experiences. These narrative accounts offer valuable perspectives on how virtual environments have enhanced professional development and workplace connectivity.

Employee feedback particularly emphasizes the platform's role in fostering authentic connections across geographical boundaries. HRD Connect's (2023) analysis reveals that participants frequently commend the platform's ability to create natural interactions despite physical distances. The testimonials demonstrate how the digital twins of offices in Bangalore, Madrid, and San Francisco have enabled employees to develop a stronger sense of organizational culture and belonging, even in remote work settings.

The implementation of the Nth Floor has precipitated significant cultural transformation within Accenture. Business Wire's (2022) comprehensive analysis documents how the platform has influenced organizational dynamics, communication patterns, and collaborative behaviors. The creation of a shared virtual environment has fostered a more inclusive and connected organizational culture, transcending traditional geographical and hierarchical boundaries.

The cultural impact extends beyond immediate workplace interactions. According to i4cp's (2023) research, the platform has fundamentally altered how employees perceive and engage with virtual work environments. The synthesis of physical and digital workspaces has created new norms for professional interaction and collaboration. This cultural evolution is particularly evident in the high engagement levels observed during global leadership meetings, where 150 managing directors successfully collaborated across 25 locations.

The qualitative assessment of collaboration effectiveness reveals substantial improvements in cross-functional and global teamwork. Pangea.ai's (2024) analysis demonstrates that the Nth Floor has enabled more sophisticated forms of virtual collaboration, supporting both structured and spontaneous interactions. The platform's ability to facilitate natural conversation flows and non-verbal communication has enhanced the quality of virtual meetings and training sessions.

The effectiveness of collaborative activities is particularly evident in complex training scenarios. Accenture's Enterprise Consulting Services documentation (2023) highlights how the platform enables simultaneous collaboration across multiple time zones while maintaining high levels of engagement and participation. The qualitative data indicates that virtual collaboration through the Nth Floor has become increasingly intuitive and effective, supporting complex decision-making processes and creative problem-solving activities.

ROI Analysis

The financial impact analysis of Accenture's Nth Floor implementation reveals significant cost efficiencies across multiple operational dimensions. According to Accenture's Enterprise Consulting Services documentation (2023), the transition to virtual training and collaboration has generated substantial reductions in traditional training expenses, including travel costs, physical infrastructure requirements, and material production. The deployment of 60,000 VR headsets, while representing a significant initial investment, has demonstrated compelling long-term cost advantages compared to traditional training and collaboration methods.

Travel cost reduction emerges as a particularly significant area of savings. Business Wire's (2022) analysis indicates that the platform's ability to facilitate high-quality virtual interactions has substantially reduced the need for physical travel, especially for training and onboarding purposes. The successful virtual onboarding of 150,000 new hires represents a notable achievement in cost optimization while maintaining high satisfaction rates, as evidenced by the 4.7/5 employee satisfaction score.

Operational efficiency improvements constitute a crucial component of the platform's ROI profile. HRD Connect's (2023) detailed case analysis documents significant gains in training delivery efficiency, with the 33% improvement in learning retention rates translating into reduced training time and accelerated skill acquisition. The platform's ability to scale training delivery across multiple time zones and geographical locations has enabled more efficient resource utilization and improved program delivery timelines.

Process optimization through virtual implementation has yielded measurable productivity benefits. Pangea.ai's (2024) evaluation demonstrates how the Nth Floor has streamlined various organizational processes, from new hire orientation to leadership development programs. The ability to simultaneously engage multiple stakeholders across different locations, as evidenced by the successful coordination of 150 managing directors across 25 locations, illustrates the platform's capacity to enhance operational efficiency at scale.

The analysis of resource utilization patterns reveals sophisticated optimization opportunities enabled by the virtual platform. i4cp's (2023) research highlights how the Nth Floor has facilitated more efficient allocation of training resources and expertise across the organization. The creation of digital twins for offices in Bangalore, Madrid, and San Francisco has enabled better utilization of physical and virtual assets while maintaining consistent quality standards across global operations.

Human capital optimization represents another significant area of return on investment. Accenture's Technology Vision report (2022) emphasizes how the platform has enhanced the organization's ability to leverage internal expertise more effectively. The virtual environment enables subject matter experts to engage with larger audiences more efficiently, while the improved learning retention rates suggest more effective knowledge transfer and skill development outcomes.

FUTURE IMPLICATIONS

The implementation of Accenture's Nth Floor metaverse platform provides valuable insights into the future trajectory of enterprise virtual environments. As organizations increasingly embrace immersive technologies, the lessons learned from this implementation offer crucial guidance for future deployments. According to Accenture's Technology Vision report (2022), the metaverse represents not merely a technological shift but a fundamental transformation in how organizations approach workforce development and collaboration.

The implications of this transformation extend beyond immediate operational benefits to shape long-term strategic considerations. Business Wire's (2022) analysis suggests that enterprise metaverse implementations will continue to evolve, influenced by technological advancements and changing workforce expectations. This evolution demands careful consideration of emerging trends, best practices, and future research directions to ensure sustainable value creation.

Industry Trends

The enterprise metaverse landscape is experiencing rapid technological advancement. HRD Connect's (2023) analysis indicates that improvements in virtual reality hardware, particularly in areas of user comfort and interface design, are driving increased adoption rates. Accenture's successful deployment of 60,000 VR headsets demonstrates the growing maturity of enterprise-grade immersive technologies and suggests a trajectory toward more sophisticated hardware solutions.

The market for enterprise metaverse solutions continues to expand and mature. According to Pangea.ai's (2024) research, organizations are increasingly recognizing the strategic value of immersive platforms for training and collaboration. This trend is evidenced by Accenture's achievement of a 33% improvement in learning retention rates, establishing new benchmarks for virtual learning effectiveness.

The competitive landscape for enterprise metaverse solutions is evolving rapidly. i4cp's (2023) industry analysis reveals increasing competition among technology providers and implementation partners. Accenture's partnership with Microsoft using AltspaceVR exemplifies the strategic alliances forming within the industry, suggesting a trend toward integrated solution offerings that combine platform capabilities with implementation expertise.

The emergence of new market entrants and solutions is reshaping implementation approaches. Accenture's Enterprise Consulting Services documentation (2023) emphasizes the importance of platform flexibility and scalability in supporting evolving business requirements. The successful creation of digital twins for offices in Bangalore, Madrid, and San Francisco demonstrates the growing sophistication of enterprise metaverse capabilities and suggests future trends in spatial computing and virtual environment design.

Best Practices

The analysis of Accenture's Nth Floor implementation reveals several critical best practices for enterprise metaverse adoption. These insights, derived from both successful outcomes and implementation challenges, provide valuable guidance for organizations contemplating similar initiatives. As noted in Accenture's Technology Vision report (2022), successful enterprise metaverse implementations require a comprehensive approach that balances technological capabilities with organizational readiness.

Strategic alignment emerges as a fundamental best practice in enterprise metaverse implementation. Business Wire's (2022) analysis emphasizes that organizations must ensure clear alignment between metaverse initiatives and broader business objectives. This alignment is evidenced in Accenture's approach, where the platform's deployment supported multiple strategic goals, including enhanced global collaboration, standardized training delivery, and improved operational efficiency. The achievement of a 4.7/5 employee satisfaction rating demonstrates the effectiveness of this aligned approach.

Change management practices play a crucial role in successful implementation. HRD Connect's (2023) case analysis reveals that effective stakeholder engagement and comprehensive communication strategies significantly impact adoption rates. Accenture's success in onboarding 150,000 new hires through the platform underscores the importance of well-structured change management approaches. The organization's emphasis on continuous feedback and adaptation has enabled sustained engagement and platform optimization.

Technical implementation best practices focus on scalability and user experience. According to i4cp's (2023) research, successful implementations require robust technical architectures that support global deployment while maintaining consistent performance standards. Accenture's deployment of 60,000 VR headsets demonstrates the importance of careful hardware selection and infrastructure planning. The creation of digital twins for offices in multiple locations highlights the need for standardized technical approaches that accommodate local requirements.

Risk mitigation strategies represent another critical area of best practice development. Pangea.ai's (2024) analysis identifies several key risk management approaches, including phased implementation strategies, comprehensive security protocols, and regular performance monitoring. These practices have enabled Accenture to achieve significant improvements in learning outcomes, including a 33% increase in retention rates, while maintaining robust platform security and reliability.

Implementation Guidelines

The successful deployment of enterprise metaverse platforms requires comprehensive implementation guidelines derived from practical experience and empirical evidence. Accenture's Technology Vision report (2022) emphasizes that effective implementation guidelines must address three fundamental dimensions: strategic planning, technical execution, and organizational adaptation. These guidelines emerge from the documented experience of implementing the Nth Floor across Accenture's global operations.

Strategic implementation guidelines focus on establishing clear organizational foundations. According to Business Wire's (2022) analysis, organizations must develop detailed implementation roadmaps that incorporate both short-term milestones and long-term objectives. Accenture's experience demonstrates the importance of establishing clear success metrics early in the implementation process, as evidenced by their ability to track and validate improvements in learning retention and employee satisfaction rates.

Technical implementation considerations demand careful attention to infrastructure requirements and integration capabilities. HRD Connect's (2023) case analysis reveals that successful implementations require robust technical frameworks that support scalable deployment while maintaining performance standards. The guidelines derived from Accenture's experience emphasize the importance of comprehensive testing protocols, particularly when deploying sophisticated hardware solutions like their 60,000 VR headsets across diverse geographical locations.

Organizational preparedness guidelines address the human aspects of implementation. i4cp's (2023) research highlights the critical importance of developing comprehensive readiness assessment frameworks. These frameworks should evaluate multiple organizational dimensions, including technical capabilities, cultural readiness, and change management capacity. Accenture's success in maintaining a 93% favorability rating demonstrates the effectiveness of their preparedness approach.

Integration guidelines focus on ensuring seamless connectivity between metaverse platforms and existing enterprise systems. Pangea.ai's (2024) analysis emphasizes the importance of developing clear integration protocols that maintain data security while enabling efficient information flow. The successful creation of digital twins for offices in Bangalore, Madrid, and San Francisco illustrates the significance of establishing standardized integration approaches that accommodate local requirements while maintaining global consistency.

Future Research Directions

The evolution of enterprise metaverse implementations reveals significant opportunities for future research and theoretical development. Accenture's Technology Vision report (2022) identifies several critical knowledge gaps that warrant further investigation, particularly in understanding the long-term impacts of immersive technologies on organizational effectiveness and employee development. The successful implementation of the Nth Floor provides a foundation for exploring these emerging research directions.

Longitudinal impact assessment emerges as a primary area requiring further investigation. According to Business Wire's (2022) analysis, while initial metrics such as Accenture's 33% improvement in learning retention are promising, understanding the sustained impact of metaverse platforms on organizational performance requires more extensive longitudinal studies. This includes examining how virtual environments influence career progression, knowledge retention, and organizational culture over extended periods.

Cross-cultural dynamics in virtual environments present another significant research opportunity. HRD Connect's (2023) case analysis of Accenture's global implementation, particularly their success in operating across diverse cultural contexts, highlights the need for deeper understanding of cultural adaptation in virtual spaces. The creation of digital twins for offices in Bangalore, Madrid, and San Francisco raises important questions about cultural representation and adaptation in virtual environments.

Technical evolution and its organizational implications demand continued research attention. i4cp's (2023) research suggests that as metaverse technologies advance, understanding the relationship between technological sophistication and organizational value creation becomes increasingly important. Accenture's experience with deploying 60,000 VR headsets provides valuable insights, but questions remain about optimal technology adoption patterns and integration strategies.

Theoretical framework development represents another crucial research direction. Pangea.ai's (2024) analysis indicates that existing organizational theories may require adaptation to fully account for the unique characteristics of enterprise metaverse environments. The documented success of Accenture's implementation, achieving a 4.7/5 employee satisfaction rating, suggests the need for new theoretical frameworks that better explain virtual environment effectiveness and adoption patterns.

CONCLUSION

The implementation of Accenture's Nth Floor represents a significant milestone in enterprise metaverse adoption, offering valuable insights for organizations contemplating similar digital transformation initiatives. This comprehensive analysis demonstrates how large-scale virtual environments can fundamentally transform organizational learning, collaboration, and employee engagement. As evidenced by the successful onboarding of 150,000 new hires and deployment of 60,000 VR headsets, the initiative validates the feasibility and effectiveness of enterprise-scale metaverse implementations.

Key Findings

The analysis reveals several critical success factors in enterprise metaverse implementation. As documented in Accenture's Technology Vision report (2022), the achievement of a 4.7/5 employee satisfaction rating demonstrates the platform's effectiveness in meeting user needs while supporting organizational objectives. The documented 33% improvement in learning retention compared to traditional methods provides compelling evidence of the platform's impact on training effectiveness.

The implementation success extends beyond quantitative metrics to encompass significant qualitative improvements in organizational dynamics. Business Wire's (2022) analysis highlights how the creation of digital twins for offices in Bangalore, Madrid, and San Francisco has enhanced global collaboration and cultural integration. These achievements underscore the platform's role in fostering a more connected and engaged global workforce.

Recommendations

Based on Accenture's experience, several key recommendations emerge for organizations considering enterprise metaverse implementations. HRD Connect's (2023) case analysis emphasizes the importance of comprehensive change management strategies and robust technical infrastructure. Organizations should prioritize:

The development of clear implementation roadmaps that align technological capabilities with organizational objectives remains crucial. According to i4cp's (2023) research, successful implementations require careful attention to both technical and cultural considerations, supported by comprehensive stakeholder engagement strategies.

Research Contributions

This case study makes significant contributions to both theoretical understanding and practical implementation of enterprise metaverse platforms. Pangea.ai's (2024) analysis of Accenture's implementation provides valuable insights into the scalability and effectiveness of virtual environments in global organizations. The documented success metrics and implementation approaches offer a framework for future research and practical application.

The research advances understanding of how large organizations can effectively leverage immersive technologies for training and collaboration. These insights contribute to the growing body of knowledge regarding enterprise metaverse implementation, while highlighting areas requiring further investigation and theoretical development.

REFERENCES

Accenture. (2022). Metaverse masters? Expect the unexpected. https://www.accenture.com/content/dam/accenture/final/accenture-com/document/Accenture-Growth-Markets-Metaverse-POV-June2.pdf

Accenture. (2023). Metaverse Enterprise Consulting Services & Solutions. https://www.accenture.com/in-en/services/metaverse

Alshurideh, M. T., Alzoubi, H. M., Akour, I. A., Al Kurdi, B., & Hamadneh, S. (2023). Impact of metaverse and marketing innovation on digital transformation. *IEEE ICBATS*, 2023, 1–5. Advance online publication. DOI: 10.1109/ICBATS57792.2023.10111241

Bag, S., Shrivastav, S. K., Rahman, M. S., & Srivastava, G. (2023). Unveiling metaverse potential in supply chain management and overcoming implementation challenges: An empirical study. *Benchmarking*, 32(11), 79–108. Advance online publication. DOI: 10.1108/BIJ-05-2023-0314

Business Wire. (2022). Accenture Technology Vision 2022: "Metaverse Continuum" Redefining How the World Works, Operates and Interacts. https://www.businesswire.com/news/home/20220315006355/en/

Carlos, A. R., & Muralles, D. C. (2021). Onboarding in the age of COVID-19. *IFLA Journal*. Advance online publication. DOI: 10.1177/03400352211035413

Chaves, M. Z., Frio, R. S., Pereira, E. F. Z.Jr, & Lunardi, G. L. (2024). *Metaverse and its commercial applications: Opportunities and challenges for companies*. Revista e-TECH. DOI: 10.18624/etech.v17i1.1304

Chengoden, R., Maddikunta, P. K. R., Jhaveri, R. H., & Gadekallu, T. R. (2023). *Metaverse for healthcare: A survey on potential applications, challenges, and future directions*. IEEE. DOI: 10.1109/ACCESS.2023.3241628

Connect, H. R. D. (2023). How Accenture's enterprise metaverse has elevated employee onboarding. https://www.hrdconnect.com/casestudy/how-accentures-enterprise-metaverse-has-elevated-employee-onboarding/

Cui, J., Yin, M., Wang, P., & Kuang, T. (2023). Impact of digital transformation on corporate innovation: Empirical evidence from public companies. SHS Web of Conferences. DOI: 10.1051/shsconf/202316901046

Denisova, A. L., & Lopatnikov, A. N. (2022). Digital transformation and corporate strategy. Management (Russia). DOI: 10.26425/2309-3633-2022-10-2-71-79

Holliday, S., Essandoh, M., Start, A. R., Clinchot, D., & Barbee, J. (2022). The feasibility and effectiveness of an online curriculum for virtual onboarding of graduate medical education learners. *Advances in Medical Education and Practice*. Advance online publication. DOI: 10.2147/AMEP.S386286 PMID: 36411750

i4cp. (2023). How Accenture Uses Virtual Reality to Onboard Employees and More. https://www.i4cp.com/productivity-blog/how-accenture-uses-virtual-reality-to-onboard-employees-and-more

Kim, K., Yang, H., Lee, J., & Lee, W. G. (2023). Metaverse wearables for immersive digital healthcare: A review. *Advancement of Science*, 10(31), 2303234. Advance online publication. DOI: 10.1002/advs.202303234 PMID: 37740417

Koohang, A., Cham, T.-H., Ueno, A., & Buhalis, D. (2023). Shaping the metaverse into reality: A multidisciplinary understanding of opportunities, challenges, and avenues for future investigation. *Journal of Computer Information Systems*, 63(3), 735–765. Advance online publication. DOI: 10.1080/08874417.2023.2165197

Koohang, A., Cham, T.-H., Ueno, A., & Buhalis, D. (2023). Shaping the metaverse into reality: A multidisciplinary understanding. *Journal of Computer Information Systems*. Advance online publication. DOI: 10.1080/08874417.2023.2165197

Kumar, A., & Shankar, A. (2024). Building a sustainable future with enterprise metaverse in a data-driven era: A TOE perspective. *Journal of Retailing and Consumer Services*. Advance online publication. DOI: 10.1016/j.jretconser.2024.103986

Kuo, H. T., & Choi, T. M. (2024). Metaverse in transportation and logistics operations: An AI-supported digital technological framework. *Transportation Research Part E, Logistics and Transportation Review*, 185, 103496. Advance online publication. DOI: 10.1016/j.tre.2024.103496

Minter, S., Hainy, C., Swift, M., Yee, C., Meyers, J., Nos, A., & Breeher, L. (2024). Quality assessment of a virtual post-offer placement assessment in employee occupational health services. *Journal of Occupational and Environmental Medicine*, 66(9), e435–e439. Advance online publication. DOI: 10.1097/JOM.0000000000003177 PMID: 38955800

Nemashkalo, K., Maliuk, O., & Ostrikov, V. (2024). Управління організаційними трансформаціями в процесі розвитку підприємства. Actual Problems of Innovative Economy and Law. DOI: 10.36887/2524-0455-2024-4-1

Pangea.ai. (2024). The Accenture Metaverse — New Frontiers in Work. https://pangea.ai/resources/the-accenture-metaverse-new-frontiers-in-work

Pinnington, A. H., & Ayoko, O. B. (2021). Managing physical and virtual work environments during the COVID-19 pandemic. *Journal of Management & Organization*, 27(6), 993–1002. Advance online publication. DOI: 10.1017/jmo.2022.2

Poppe, E., Brown, R., Recker, J., Johnson, D., & Vanderfeesten, I. (2017). Design and evaluation of virtual environments mechanisms to support remote collaboration. *Information Systems*, 66, 59–81. Advance online publication. DOI: 10.1016/j.is.2017.01.004

Rutitis, D., & Aksjonenko, E. (2022). The impact of digital transformation on corporate identity management. *Proceedings of AHFE 2022 Conference*. DOI: 10.54941/ahfe1002802

Shitole, P. T., Chogule, O., Jadhav, G., Gurav, P., & Lad, S. (2024). Virtual digital metaverse healthcare assistant. International Journal of Advanced Research in Science. *Tongxin Jishu*, 284–287. Advance online publication. DOI: 10.48175/IJARSCT-18443

Sui, B., & Yao, L. (2023). *The impact of digital transformation on corporate financialization: The mediating effect of green technology innovation*. Innovation and Green Development. DOI: 10.1016/j.igd.2022.100032

Sui, B., & Yao, L. (2023). *The impact of digital transformation on corporate financialization*. Innovation and Green Development. DOI: 10.1016/j.igd.2022.100032

Torres, M., Correia, T., Carneiro, A., & Meirinhos, V. (2019). *Virtual reality and augmented reality in onboarding of new employees*. Independent Research on Human Resources. DOI: 10.1234/vrar-2019

Varshney, D. (2022). Understanding virtual employee onboarding (VEO): The new normal and beyond. Emirati Journal of Business, Economics, &. *Social Studies*, 1(1), 55–72. Advance online publication. DOI: 10.54878/jhhm2y12

Yazıcı, A. M., Özkan, A., & Özkan, H. (2024). Meta: XR-AR-MR and Mirror World Technologies Business Impact of Metaverse. Journal of Metaverse. DOI: 10.57019/jmv.1344489

Zanon, G. N., Szejka, A. L., & Loures, E. D. F. R. (2021). *Towards an integrated MCDM and BSC method to support the digital transformation strategy in railway companies*. Advances in Transdisciplinary Engineering. DOI: 10.3233/ATDE210109

Zille, M. C., Frio, R. S., Pereira, E. F. Z.Junior, & Lunardi, G. L. (2024). *Metaverse and its commercial applications: Opportunities and challenges for companies*. Revista e-TECH. DOI: 10.18624/etech.v17i1.1304

KEY TERMS AND DEFINITIONS

Enterprise Metaverse: A continuum spanning digitally enhanced worlds, realities, and business models applied across all aspects of business, from consumer to worker and across the entire enterprise, as demonstrated by Accenture's Nth Floor implementation.

Hybrid Experience Spaces: Environments that seamlessly blend physical and digital interactions, supporting natural interactions through advanced spatial computing, enhanced collaborative capabilities, and improved environmental awareness.

Nth Floor: A pioneering enterprise metaverse platform developed by Accenture that serves as a complete ecosystem for employee development, collaboration, and engagement, successfully implementing onboarding for over 150,000 employees.

Organizational Digital Transformation: The systematic process of leveraging immersive technologies and virtual environments to fundamentally change how organizations approach workforce development, training, and collaboration.

Technical Architecture: The foundational infrastructure required for enterprise metaverse implementation, encompassing high bandwidth connectivity, security protocols, and interfaces to other enterprise systems.

Virtual Collaboration: The use of immersive technologies for remote teamwork and communication, enabling global teams to interact effectively across geographical boundaries while maintaining cultural cohesion.

Virtual Onboarding: A comprehensive digital approach to employee integration utilizing immersive technologies, resulting in documented improvements in learning retention and engagement compared to traditional methods.

Virtual Training Environment: An immersive digital space designed for corporate learning and development, incorporating advanced visualization capabilities and adaptive learning systems to deliver personalized training experiences.

Chapter 11
Metaverse Marketing:
Unleashing the Potential of Virtual Influencers

Anadi Trikha
https://orcid.org/0000-0003-0792-0195
Manipal University Jaipur, India

Madhu Bala Kaushik
https://orcid.org/0000-0002-3336-6717
Manipal University Jaipur, India

EXECUTIVE SUMMARY

The chapter explores the rise of virtual influencers within the Metaverse and their significant impact on marketing's future. The Metaverse, blending augmented and virtual reality with the real world, is a new frontier for brands to engage the digital generation innovatively. Virtual influencers, created through CGI with scripted personalities, have gained immense popularity and influence. The research examines the concept, origins, and psychological factors driving these digital avatars' impact on consumers. It looks at how they reshape marketing strategies through sponsored content, product placements, and brand collaborations, driving consumer engagement and purchase behaviour. The study also highlights their impact on traditional advertising and potential for hyper-personalized experiences using data analytics and AI. Finally, it addresses ethical considerations, including transparency, authenticity, potential exploitation of vulnerable consumers, and the need for responsible practices in this emerging field.

DOI: 10.4018/979-8-3693-7245-6.ch011

INTRODUCTION

The digital landscape is rapidly evolving, and the metaverse concept has emerged as a captivating territory with immense potential for marketers and brands. Metaverse is a union of augmented reality, virtual reality, and the real world, creating an immersive digital space for people to interact, create and explore new dimensions. With a blend of physical and virtual experiences, Metaverse has become a platform for making strategies that enable brands to connect to consumers innovatively. Metaverse is challenging traditional ways of marketing by creating immersive and hyper-personalised experiences.

What Is Metaverse?

The Metaverse is a spatial computing platform providing immersive digital experiences replicating or enhancing the real world. It integrates essential societal elements such as social interactions, currency, trade, economy, and property ownership, all grounded in blockchain technology.

Drawing parallels to the internet's early development in the 1970s and 1980s, the Metaverse is nascent, and its full potential and practical applications are yet to be understood. However, its market is projected to grow significantly, reaching an estimated $800 billion by 2024, with major technology companies like Facebook, Microsoft, Apple, and Google heavily investing in its realisation.

Functionally, the Metaverse comprises interconnected 3D virtual spaces accessible via browsers, mobile apps, or headsets, enabling real-time interactions across vast distances. It is envisioned as a vast ecosystem where physical and digital realms merge, impacting essential facets of everyday life(Basu Mallick, 2022).

REVIEW OF LITERATURE

The Metaverse's appeal lies in its potential to revolutionise how individuals socialise, work, and engage in commerce. As it matures, it is expected to become a large-scale, dynamically optimised system that fosters collaboration among creators across diverse fields, paving the way for innovative virtual reality applications and integrated online experiences(Basu Mallick, 2022).

Metaverse provides fertile ground for creating experiences where brands can craft virtual environments, avatars, and interactive narratives that resonate with their target audiences. Regardless of geographical boundaries, metaverse helps brands reach global audiences, fostering brand awareness and loyalty across borders. It also offers unparalleled opportunities for brands to tap into the power of storytelling.

The metaverse allows marketers to generate lasting impressions through interactive games, virtual events, or a personalised virtual environment. (Diwivedi, 2022).

Additionally, Metaverse empowers consumers to participate actively in brand experiences, enabling co-creation and collaboration. Brands can involve consumers in designing and developing virtual products, solicit feedback, and integrate their ideas into future offerings. This approach will foster a sense of ownership and loyalty and provide valuable insights into consumer preferences. (Leighton, 2022).

With the expansion of Metaverse, traversing from virtual news to virtual influencers, AI(Artificial intelligence) humans are boldly stepping into roles earlier reserved for their human counterparts, often surpassing expectations and excelling with unparalleled finesse ("The Metaverse in Asia: Strategies for Accelerating Economic Impact," 2023). Studies have found that the engagement rate of virtual influencers is three times more than real influencers. Millennials and Generation Z, born and brought up in the Internet age, have a unique appetite for virtual influencers and do not realise that these are just masterful creations of codes and pixels. (Frolov, 2021).

Virtual influencers have emerged in the last few years, but they are becoming the next big thing in influencer marketing, which is set to grow to $ 2.1 billion by 2023 (Geyser, 2023). Technology has enabled advertisers to create virtual influencers with compelling personalities that share their lives and try to connect with real people. (Arora, 2022). Brands believe these avatars are way more customisable than real influencers. Brands use influencer marketing to bridge the gap between a brand and its audience. (Frolov, 2021). Studies also demonstrated that the human-like appearance of virtual influencers shows higher message credibility than anime-like virtual influencers. (Kim, 2023). These cost-effective influencers are controllable and have a lower risk to a brand's reputation. They are scripted and controlled by the creators, which appears to be the safest option for any brand.

The after-effects of the global pandemic have transformed the global economy from reality to virtual reality. Ways of dealing with currency have changed. The emergence of AI significantly impacts various sectors like marketing, education, tourism, and healthcare. (Dwivedi, 2022). This rapidly evolving digital landscape thus gave birth to a new kind of influencer: virtual influencers, computer-generated imagery (CGI) or animated characters that exist only on the internet. These characters purposefully have human-like personalities, features, and voices. This allows their followers to create a bond of trust and influence their purchasing habits. (Bringé, Forbes, 2022).

A recent survey on virtual influencers conducted by Influencer Marketing Factory with American respondents provides deep insights into the impact of these Virtual Influencers on the youth today. The main findings were that 58% of the respondents at least follow one VI. 35-44-year-old users found Virtual Influencers relatable.

Thirty-five per cent of people have bought one product that Virtual Influencers advertised(*Virtual Influencers Survey + INFOGRAPHIC*, 2023).

Another study proposed that virtual influencers could be an alternative to human influencers. One benefit of utilising VIs is the reduction of human error in advertising. Virtual influencers do not experience anxiety or isolation in the face of uncertainty, which allows them to post frequently. (Appel, 2020).

OVERVIEW OF METAVERSE IN VARIOUS SECTORS

1. Applications of the Metaverse and Education in the World

Stanoevska-Slabeva (2022) highlights the revolutionary potential of the Metaverse in the educational setting. Students who participated in learning activities based on the Metaverse exhibited a greater sense of presence than those who participated in traditional video-based environments. They also got higher scores in knowledge evaluations. According to users, the use of the Metaverse spans specialist sectors such as obstetrics and fetal care. Users reported enhanced social presence and understanding in these areas while resolving medical difficulties in a virtual setting. Despite this, there are still challenges that prevent widespread use, such as the difficulty of acquiring the necessary resources, credentials, and precise hardware specs.

In their 2021 study, Park, Kim, and Whang investigated the individualised learning experiences that may be had through virtual avatars in the Metaverse. Their findings showed that avatars resembling the participants' facial traits significantly boosted familiarity, attractiveness, and audience engagement. Heo and Kim (2021) described a climbing training system based on augmented reality. This system demonstrated comparable efficacy to traditional instruction methods, giving pupils increased flexibility and autonomy.

2. Developments in both Agricultural and Industrial Technology

Cheng (2023) highlights the significance of technological breakthroughs such as the Internet, artificial intelligence, virtual reality, and augmented reality in the progression of the Metaverse. Some of the most prominent technological companies in the world, including Facebook and Roblox, are making significant investments in this sector due to the disruptive potential it brings. An Internet-centric future inspired by the Metaverse is made possible by the decentralised structure of the Metaverse, which provides individuals complete autonomy over their data and experiences.

The authors Wang et al. (2023) provide a multi-technology paradigm for the Metaverse, highlighting the social, immersive, and hyper-spatio-temporal characteristics of the Metaverse experience. Individuals can interact with one another within three-dimensional places within the Metaverse, which functions as a virtual social world that transcends the boundaries of time and space. In 2023, Rawat and colleagues investigated the standards, architecture, difficulties, and breakthroughs required to construct the Metaverse. They also investigate the transformative influence that the Metaverse has on digital ecosystems.

Lik-Hang Lee and colleagues (2021) investigated the advancements in the Metaverse ecosystem. They proposed a research agenda on user-centric concerns like trust, responsibility, security, privacy, and virtual economics. In the years to come, new technologies, including digital twins, are projected to revolutionise virtual settings.

3. Implications for Society and Culture to Consider

Narin (2021) investigates the socio-cultural and psychological effects of incorporating the Metaverse into ordinary life. Creating and interacting with three-dimensional avatars inside a digital environment helps maintain and strengthen one's identity. This modification creates new study domains and expands existing ones, with the enormous data generated within the Metaverse serving as a supporting factor.

Villalba (2016) evaluated Second Life (SL) as a precursor to Metaverse environments. The author highlighted several challenges, such as decreased user involvement due to feelings of alienation, a lack of story, and societal flaws mirrored on thc platform. Despite these limitations, the research predicted that user interaction paradigms would need to be rethought to address these concerns.

4. Creativity and Participation in Collaborative Endeavours

Using the Avatar Orchestra as a case study, Martín (2018) investigated virtual environments' impact on communities' creative output. By eliminating obstacles such as age, race, and geographical variance in face-to-face interactions, the Metaverse encourages the development of symbolic ties between individuals, stimulating creative thinking.

5. Applications in the Fields of Healthcare and Wellness

Stanoevska-Slabeva (2022) and Thomason et al. (2022) investigated the possible applications of the Metaverse in healthcare, namely in the areas of gamification, education, and the management of non-communicable diseases such as obesity. By combining reward-based systems and virtual settings, the Metaverse presents the possibility of innovative methods for diagnostic, preventative, and therapeutic procedures.

6. Implications for the Marketing and Business Strategy of the Corporation

A study by Dwivedi and colleagues (2023) investigated the potential of the corporate Metaverse to impact future customer research and marketing approaches. With widespread adoption, the Metaverse has the potential to revolutionise how businesses connect with their customers by facilitating immersive and engaging experiences, hence increasing customer satisfaction and loyalty to the brand over time.

In terms of theological and philosophical considerations Jun (2020) investigated the role that the Metaverse plays in religious rites, drawing attention to the proliferation of virtual reality churches that fulfill traditional functions within digital surroundings. Although these advancements broaden the scope of ministry, they concurrently stimulate theological issues concerning the fundamental nature of worship and fellowship within virtual environments.

Bolger (2021) analysed the Metaverse from contextual theology and cultural integration perspectives. He then proposed various methods for communication and production within these digital worlds. The study establishes a connection between traditional religious frameworks and the rapid development of the digital environment.

7. Interoperability and Adherence to Standards

The authors Buchholz, Oppermann, and Prinz (2022) emphasised the importance of establishing open standards in XR systems to promote the smooth sharing of data, enhanced security, and integrated systems. They drew parallels between the rapid adoption of remote communication technology during the outbreak and the endorsement of equivalent frameworks to enable the spread of the Metaverse. In the material that was reviewed, the revolutionary potential of the Metaverse was highlighted in a variety of fields, such as education, healthcare, corporate operations, and cultural interactions. Although significant progress has been made, many difficulties still need to be handled before the potential of the Metaverse can be fully exploited. These issues include resource allocation, hardware specifications, and interoperability standards. Subsequent research ought to concentrate on these challenges in order to construct virtual worlds that are inclusive, secure, and sustainable.

METHODOLOGY

This study adopts a mixed-method approach, combining qualitative and quantitative techniques to analyse virtual influencers in the Metaverse comprehensively. The methodology is divided into two phases: historical review and content analysis.

1. **Historical Review**
    - o Archival research was conducted to review the evolution of traditional to virtual influencers from the 1990s to the present.
    - o Sources included academic journals, industry reports, and digital media archives.
    - o Key milestones and technological advancements were identified and documented.
2. **Content Analysis**
    - o Social media platforms (e.g., Instagram, TikTok) and Metaverse environments (e.g., Decentraland, Roblox) were analysed to study the activity and impact of contemporary virtual influencers.
    - o Six prominent virtual influencers were selected based on their engagement metrics, platform presence, and brand collaborations. Future trends and virtual influencers' evolving role in the Metaverse are discussed.

Virtual Influencers in the Metaverse: Evolution and Current Scenario

Virtual influencers have undergone significant transformation over the decades, emerging as a key component of the digital ecosystem and now playing an integral role in the Metaverse. These computer-generated personas, often powered by artificial intelligence, have evolved from simple avatars to highly sophisticated entities capable of engaging audiences, promoting brands, and influencing public opinion in ways comparable to human influencers. An 'influencer' is a decades-old advertising archetype that perhaps never owned the impact that it does now. (Bringé, 2022). Virtual influencers are fundamentally synonyms with virtual idols, originating from Japan's anime and idol culture, dating to the 1980s (Eisenbeis, 2012). Different generations have called them different names, from the era of Cynthia, the "Gaba Girl", to Kyra, India's latest virtual influencer who joined YouTube in March 2022. However, all of them were created to influence mass audiences (Rasmussen, 2022).

Cynthia: The Gaba Girl(1930-1950s)

This was a mannequin created by Lester Gaba in 1930. The unusual and human-looking mannequin caught attention quickly. It was invited to many shows, operas, and weddings and featured in Life magazine. This was one reason for using mannequins in retail sales marketing. Brands like Cartier and Tiffany sent her jewellery.

Figure 1. Old Photo of Cynthia at a Party. Source: virtualhumans.org

Accessed on 13 June 2024

Alvin and the Chipmunks(1950s-Present)

These andromorphic characters with fun personalities represented 2D characters, three singing chipmunks with their storylines. They were a massive hit at that time, which continues as movies and songs are still made today. (Rasmussen, 2022).

Figure 2. Poster of Chipmunk. Source: virtualhumans.org

Accessed on 13 June 2024

Archies(1968-Present)

Like Chipmunks, this popular comic series became a popular sitcom called The Archie Show. Even recently, Netflix announced its new movie, which will soon be released, an adaptation of Archie Comics featuring Indian actors. (Ramachandran, 2023).

Figure 3. Poster of The Archie Show. Source: Wikipedia.

Accessed on 19 June 2024

Max Headroom (1980s)

Max Headroom, the first computer-generated TV personality, was a fictional AI whose distinctive brand of comedy parodied news anchors and chat show hosts. Matt Frewer wore special effects makeup for his computer-generated appearance. (Rasmussen, 2022).

Figure 4. Poster of Max Headroom. Source: Virtualhumans.org Accessed on 19th June 2024

Hatsune Miku(2000s)

It is a vocal software voice bank developed by Crypton Future Media. The official mascot was a 16-year-old animated character with two long ponytails. It slowly became the virtual idol, performing via animated projection at various live virtual concerts. (Wikipedia).

Figure 5. Cover of Vocaloid Miku. Source: Wikipedia Accessed on 22 June 2024

Ami Yamato (2010s)

Ami Yamato is a Japanese virtual YouTube vlogger. Her vlogs are light-hearted and deal with various trending topics. She has produced a series of parodies named "Mash-Ins", depicting herself as a famous actor in movies and TV shows with a comical twist. (Wikipedia). She claims to come from Japan and is currently living in London.

Figure 6. Poster of Ami Yamato. Source: Wikipedia

Accessed on 22 June 2024

- ⇒ **Extended Reach and Global Appeal**: Virtual influencers have the potential to reach audiences globally without the limitations of physical presence or language barriers. They can connect with diverse audiences and expand brand visibility across regions, cultures, and languages (Rob, 2023).
- ⇒ **Authenticity and Creative Storytelling**: Virtual influencers allow brands to create compelling narratives and stories that resonate with their target audience. Brands can develop unique personalities, backstories, and character arcs for virtual influencers, resulting in creative and engaging content that captures consumers' attention ((*The Rise of Virtual Influencers and What It Means for Brands*, 2022)
- ⇒ **Flexibility and Cost-effectiveness**: Unlike human influencers, virtual influencers do not require physical appearances, travel, or personal needs. They are available 24/7 and can generate content more frequently, making them more flexible for brand campaigns. Additionally, working with virtual influencers can be cost-effective compared to traditional influencer marketing campaigns that involve contracts, negotiations, and higher fees(Rob, 2023).
- ⇒ **Controlling Brand Image**: Brands have greater control over the virtual influencers' actions, messaging, and brand representation. They can carefully craft the virtual influencer's personality to align with their brand values and ensure consistent brand messaging, mitigating the risks associated with human influencers who may deviate from the brand's image (*The Pros and Cons of Virtual Influencers*, n.d.).

⇒ **Enhanced Creativity and Innovation**: Virtual influencers push the boundaries of creativity and innovation in content creation. Brands can experiment with different visual styles, aesthetics, and storytelling formats to captivate their audience and differentiate themselves from competitors. This opens up new avenues for creative marketing campaigns that leverage the virtual influencer's digital nature.

⇒ **Data-driven Insights**: Virtual influencers generate data and analytics that provide valuable insights into audience demographics, engagement metrics, and content preferences. Brands can leverage this data to refine their marketing strategies, optimise content, and target specific consumer segments (Williams, 2024).

⇒ **Integration with Technology**: Virtual influencers often embrace emerging technologies such as augmented reality (AR), virtual reality (VR), and artificial intelligence (AI). This integration allows brands to explore immersive and interactive marketing experiences, leveraging cutting-edge technology to engage with consumers uniquely and uniquely (Shuttleworth, 2024).

ETHICAL CONSIDERATION AND RESPONSIBLE PRACTICES

While virtual influencers present exciting brand opportunities, it is essential to balance authenticity and transparency. Consumers are becoming more discerning and aware of virtual influencers, and maintaining trust and credibility should remain a priority for successful marketing campaigns in this evolving landscape. Key ethical aspects that creators and brands must consider:

Transparency and Disclosure

Brands must disclose the virtual nature of influencers to their audiences. As VIs have flawless appearances, which can perpetuate unrealistic beauty standards, disclosing that the influencer is a computer-generated character can prevent followers from being misled or confused. This transparency develops trust and upholds ethical practice. Brands must avoid misinterpreting VIs as real individuals and promoting deceptive or misleading content (Wikipedia Contributors, 2024).

Responsible Content Creation

Virtual influencers should create content that adheres to ethical standards and avoids promoting harmful, offensive, or discriminatory messages. It is crucial to consider the potential impact of the content on the audience and ensure that it promotes positive values and responsible behaviour(Kasumovic, 2024).

Privacy and Data Protection

Virtual influencers may collect and process user data as they interact with their audience. It is essential to handle user data responsibly, respect privacy rights, and adhere to relevant data protection regulations. Clear privacy policies and consent mechanisms should be in place to protect user information(Wikipedia contributors, 2024).

Responsibility and Accountability

Influencers must ensure that ethical values and brand reputation are aligned when collaborating with brands. VI and Brand must ensure they share similar objectives and ethical business practices. These VI will not only influence but also define social norms. To be viewed favourably, virtual influencers must promote diversity, inclusion, etc. Brands must help identify and address potential ethical concerns to reduce unintended consequences(Wikipedia contributors, 2024).

Adhering to ethical considerations and responsible practices, brands and creators will create a positive, safe space for these digital citizens of the metaverse, whom users can trust and resonate with.

RESHAPING MARKETING LANDSCAPE: THE CONSUMER METAVERSE (*HOW THE METAVERSE IS SHAPING CONSUMER BEHAVIOR - IEEE METAVERSE,* N.D.)

The Consumer Metaverse is an innovative concept integrating diverse technologies to create an immersive, interconnected virtual realm where individuals can engage with products, services, and experiences. This digital ecosystem dissolves the lines between physical and virtual realities, fostering dynamic interactions and participation in a shared persistent space.

Core Components of the Consumer Metaverse

1. **Virtual Reality (VR):** VR immerses users in simulated environments, offering a heightened sense of presence and enabling realistic interactions.
2. **Augmented Reality (AR):** AR enriches the real world by overlaying digital elements and blending physical and virtual experiences.
3. **Digital Avatars:** Users design customisable avatars to navigate and interact within the metaverse.
4. **Virtual Worlds:** Persistent, shared digital environments mimic or reinvent physical spaces for exploration and interaction.
5. **Social Connectivity:** The metaverse fosters communication, collaboration, and social interaction in virtual settings.

This concept is evolving rapidly, spurred by technological advancements and consumer demand for engaging, immersive experiences. VR and AR, as they become more accessible and refined, are pivotal to its growth.

Enhancing Customer Engagement

The Consumer Metaverse presents unparalleled opportunities for brands to connect with consumers. Immersive experiences like virtual product launches or collaborative design sessions enable deeper engagement and foster brand loyalty. Interactive campaigns and co-creation opportunities allow consumers to participate directly in branding.

However, this innovation faces challenges such as ensuring inclusivity, addressing privacy and security issues, and navigating digital ownership complexities. Bridging the gap between existing technological capabilities and metaverse aspirations is critical for broader adoption and success.

Technological Pillars of the Consumer Metaverse

The Consumer Metaverse is underpinned by cutting-edge technologies that make its immersive environments possible:

- **AR and VR Integration:** AR enriches real-world settings with virtual elements, while VR immerses users in wholly virtual spaces, offering realistic interactions.
- **Blockchain Technology:** Decentralized and secure, blockchain supports digital ownership and asset trading, creating new economic opportunities in the metaverse.

- **Artificial Intelligence (AI):** AI personalises experiences, generates dynamic content, and facilitates intelligent interactions. Machine learning further optimises virtual environments and user engagement.
- **5G Networks:** With their high speed and low latency, 5G enables real-time data transmission, enhancing the quality of interactive experiences.
- **Advanced Graphics and Spatial Computing:** High-fidelity visuals and spatial technologies provide intuitive interactions, making virtual environments more engaging.

As these technologies evolve, they will enable more realistic, interactive, and personalised experiences, pushing the boundaries of what the metaverse can achieve.

Economic and Business Impacts

The Consumer Metaverse reshapes industries, creating new opportunities in e-commerce, marketing, and advertising while influencing consumer behaviours.

- **E-Commerce:** Virtual shopping experiences allow consumers to explore products in 3D, try items virtually, and attend interactive events, enhancing engagement and driving sales.
- **Marketing and Advertising:** Branded virtual spaces, influencer avatars, and immersive campaigns redefine how businesses connect with their audiences.
- **Challenges:** The transition to the metaverse demands significant investment in infrastructure, talent, and technology. Companies must also navigate legal and ethical complexities surrounding digital ownership and intellectual property.

Immersive experiences deepen emotional connections with brands, fostering consumer loyalty and influencing purchasing decisions.

Top Virtual Influencers on the Internet

Lu of Magalu: Lu is a Brazilian influencer with over 6 million Instagram followers. Brazilian retail giant Magazine Luiza created this VI. She promotes brands and interacts with followers on social media using her energetic appearance and on-trend style. She posts content inspired by her daily life as an influencer. She has collaborated with brands like Adidas, Burberry, Heinz, and Apple to produce engaging content.

Nobody Sausage: This Instagram influencer has over 6 million followers and has a unique sense of style and light-hearted demeanour enchanted by his aesthetic of whimsy and colour. He has collaborated with GUESS, Justin Bieber, and Marvel to advertise their merchandise.

CB of Cases Bahia: CB, an abbreviation for "Casas Bahia", is a well-known Brazilian Virtual Influencer. With over 4 million fans following, he promotes brands like Samsung, Motorola, and Xbox. He keeps posting his thoughts on lifestyle, product evaluation, etc.

Miquela Sousa(Lil Miquela): She is a trailblazer in the VI space with over 2.8 million followers on Instagram. With her natural appearance and fashion-forward style, she has amassed a global audience of her followers. Lil Miquela has collaborated with renowned brands, such as Dior, Apple, and Best Buy, that support social causes and created content that blurs the boundaries between reality and virtuality.

Good Counsel Cupcake: Sound Counsel Cupcake is a prominent online influencer known for her motivational and uplifting content. With her adorable cupcake-like appearance, this character shares motivational quotations, self-care advice, and messages of empowerment. Good Counsel Cupcake has amassed a devoted fan base by disseminating cheerful and elevating messages across numerous social media platforms.

Kyra: Kyra or Kyraonig is a fictitious Indian woman invented by Himanshu Goel. She was introduced as an Instagram profile in January 2022. This account is the first Virtual Influencer in India. She is becoming increasingly popular among Indian youth. She is collaborating with companies such as L'Oreal, American Tourister, Budweiser, Boat, Amazon Prime, Sunfeast, and MG Vehicles to leverage this new trend. She has over 1 Lakh subscribers on YouTube, wherein one of the shorts she is with Titan EyeX 2.0; she can be seen donning smart glasses with a fitness tracker, open-ear speakers and Bluetooth.

Figure 7. Top virtual influencers on the internet. Source: Google for thumbnail Images. Accessed on 25th July 2024.

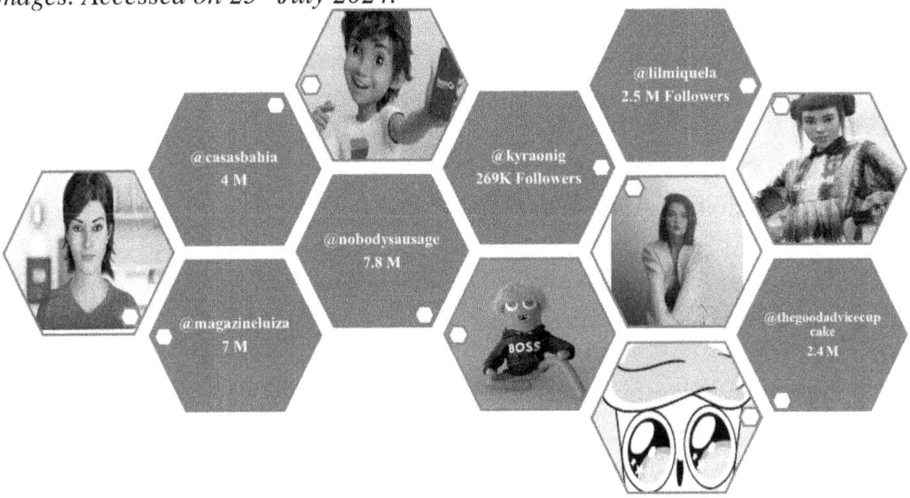

These virtual influencers have effectively used their digital personas to engage audiences, promote brands, and establish meaningful connections. Each contributes a distinct style and personality to the virtual influencer landscape, captivating followers and contributing to the rising influence of internet personalities. In many ways, virtual influencers are reshaping today's marketing scenario. Earlier marketers used to hunt the top real influencers/celebrities and tempt them with deals to promote sponsored content. However, when virtual influencers entered this market, everything changed. These virtual avatars use innovative and immersive ways to engage customers with brands. They are programmed to generate hype about the product's features in the market and create impressions. (Saha, 2023)

REGULATORY AND ETHICAL CONSIDERATIONS

The Consumer Metaverse introduces unique challenges that require robust frameworks to address digital rights, privacy, and ethical AI deployment.

1. **Digital Ownership:** Clear policies are needed to regulate the virtual asset ownership, transfer, and intellectual property.
2. **Privacy Protections:** Safeguarding user data through transparent measures is critical to building trust.
3. **Ethical AI Use:** Responsible deployment of AI is essential to prevent manipulation and ensure user autonomy.

4. **Content Moderation:** Effective mechanisms must balance freedom of expression with maintaining safe and inclusive virtual spaces.

Collaboration between policymakers, industry leaders, and stakeholders is vital to creating a regulatory environment that supports innovation while protecting users.

FUTURE TRENDS AND EVOLUTION

The Consumer Metaverse is poised to transform industries, from retail to education, with key trends including:

- **Industry Integration:** Retailers may offer virtual showrooms, educators might create interactive learning spaces, and entertainment could feature virtual concerts and immersive storytelling.
- **Improved Accessibility:** Advances in affordable VR/AR devices and intuitive interfaces will make the metaverse more user-friendly.
- **AI Advancements:** AI-driven personalisation and dynamic content will enhance user experiences.
- **Blockchain Integration:** Decentralized platforms will support secure transactions and digital identity control, fostering user trust.

As immersive experiences become the norm, businesses must adapt to meet consumer expectations for interactive and engaging product and service exploration.

CONCLUSION

The research investigated the emerging landscape of metaverse marketing and its potential for utilising virtual influencers. As technology advances, the distinction between reality and the virtual interface becomes less distinct. This Metaverse journey appears to have just begun and has a long way to go with future generations. Metaverse citizens provide new opportunities for creative storytelling, global reach, and increased consumer engagement. In an era where voice assistants Alexa and Siri are becoming household names, we may soon discover our best companions among these influencers.

Critical aspects of virtual influencers, such as unparalleled flexibility and cost-effectiveness, the availability of virtual influencers to produce content 24 hours a day, seven days a week, the ability to experiment to demonstrate the product's features, etc., make metaverse marketing a thrilling opportunity that every marketer would love to exploit. This study awakens the various societal stakeholders who have yet to acknowledge and embrace virtual reality. In addition, the study urges policymakers to consider its legal implications.

The Metaverse, a convergence of augmented and virtual reality with the real world, has emerged as a dynamic platform where brands can innovately engage the digital generation. Designed through computer-generated imagery (CGI) with meticulously scripted personalities, virtual influencers have gained substantial popularity and influence. These digital avatars offer a novel way for brands to connect with consumers, leveraging their flexibility, availability, and ability to produce content around the clock.

The research delves into the origins and psychological factors contributing to the growing influence of virtual influencers. These digital personas are not limited by human constraints, enabling them to experiment freely and demonstrate product features in engaging and imaginative ways. This capability, combined with their cost-effectiveness, positions virtual influencers as a valuable asset for marketers aiming to reach a global audience.

As the Metaverse continues to evolve, it offers new opportunities for creative storytelling and enhanced consumer engagement. Brands can utilise virtual influencers to create immersive experiences, blending reality with the virtual world. This integration not only captures the attention of the digital generation but also fosters deeper connections with consumers.

However, the study also highlights the need for ethical considerations in this emerging field. Transparency and authenticity are crucial to maintaining consumer trust. The potential for exploiting vulnerable consumers, particularly impressionable youth, raises concerns that must be addressed. Responsible practices and clear guidelines are essential to ensure virtual influencers operate within ethical boundaries.

Furthermore, the research underscores the importance of hyper-personalized advertising experiences. Utilising data analytics and artificial intelligence (AI), brands can tailor content to individual preferences, enhancing the relevance and impact of their marketing efforts. This approach boosts consumer engagement and drives purchase behaviour more effectively.

The study also examines the impact of virtual influencers on traditional advertising channels. As these digital avatars gain traction, they challenge conventional advertising methods, prompting a shift towards more innovative and interactive strategies. Brands embracing this transformation benefit from increased visibility and consumer loyalty.

In conclusion, the rise of virtual influencers within the Metaverse represents a significant shift in the marketing landscape. Their ability to engage consumers around the clock and their cost-effectiveness and creative potential make them a valuable brand asset. However, ethical considerations and responsible practices must be prioritised to ensure the sustainable growth of this emerging field. As technology continues to blur the lines between reality and the virtual world, the Metaverse offers exciting possibilities for the future of marketing. Policymakers and societal stakeholders must recognise and embrace these opportunities while addressing the associated challenges.

REFERENCES

Arora, M. (2022, November 21). The rise of virtual influencers: Another level of branding. *The Times of India Blogs*. Retrieved May 27, 2023, from https://timesofindia.indiatimes.com/blogs/voices/the-rise-of-virtual-influencers-another-level-of-branding/?source=app&frmapp=yes

Bojic, L. (2022). Metaverse through the prism of power and addiction: What will happen when the virtual world becomes more attractive than reality? *European Journal of Futures Research*, 10(1), 22. Advance online publication. DOI: 10.1186/s40309-022-00208-4

Bolger, R. K. (2021). Finding wholes in the metaverse: Posthuman mystics as agents of evolutionary contextualization. *Religions*, 12(9), 768. DOI: 10.3390/rel12090768

Bringé, A. (2022, October 18). The rise of virtual influencers and what it means for brands. *Forbes*. Retrieved from https://www.forbes.com/sites/forbescommunicationscouncil/2022/10/18/the-rise-of-virtual-influencers-and-what-it-means-for-brands/?sh=629fceaa6b56

Buchholz, F., Oppermann, L., & Prinz, W. (2022). There's more than one metaverse. *i-com, 21*(3), 313–324.

Cheng, S. (2023). Metaverse. In *Metaverse: Concept, Content and Context* (pp. 1–23). Springer Nature Switzerland.

Deloitte. (2023, April). *The Metaverse in Asia: Strategies for accelerating economic impact*. Deloitte. Retrieved June 1, 2023, from https://www2.deloitte.com/content/dam/Deloitte/sg/Documents/center-for-the-edge/sg-metaverse-in-asia-deloitte-center-for-the-edge-apr2023.pdf

Dwivedi, Y. K., Hughes, L., Baabdullah, A. M., Ribeiro-Navarrete, S., Giannakis, M., Al-Debei, M. M., Dennehy, D., Metri, B., Buhalis, D., Cheung, C. M. K., Conboy, K., Doyle, R., Dubey, R., Dutot, V., Felix, R., Goyal, D. P., Gustafsson, A., Hinsch, C., Jebabli, I., & Wamba, S. F. (2022). Metaverse beyond the hype: Multidisciplinary perspectives on emerging challenges, opportunities, and agenda for research, practice, and policy. *International Journal of Information Management*, 66, 102542. Advance online publication. DOI: 10.1016/j.ijinfomgt.2022.102542

Eisenbeis, R. (2012, September 7). The fictional (yet amazingly popular) singers of Japan. Retrieved June 5, 2023, from https://kotaku.com/the-fictional-yet-amazingly-popular-singers-of-japan-5940894

Frolov, A. (2021, April 27). Virtual influencers – Are they all they're cracked up to be? Retrieved May 25, 2023, from https://marketech-apac.com/virtual-influencers-are-they-all-theyre-cracked-up-to-be/

Geyser, W. (2023). *The state of influencer marketing 2023: Benchmark report.* Retrieved June 3, 2023, from https://influencermarketinghub.com/influencer-marketing-benchmark-report/

Heo, M. H., & Kim, D. (2021). Effect of augmented reality affordance on motor performance: In the sport climbing. *Human-Centric Computing and Information Sciences, 11.* How the metaverse is shaping consumer behavior. *IEEE Metaverse.* Retrieved from https://metaversereality.ieee.org/publications/articles/how-the-metaverse-is-shaping-consumer-behavior

Jun, G. (2020). Virtual reality church as a new mission frontier in the metaverse: Exploring theological controversies and missional potential of virtual reality church. *Transformation (Durban)*, 37(4), 297–305. DOI: 10.1177/0265378820963155

Kasumovic, D. (2024, October 24). Influencer marketing sustainability and ethics. *Influencer Marketing Hub.* Retrieved from https://influencermarketinghub.com/influencer-marketing-sustainability-and-ethics

Kim, E. A., Kim, D., e, Z., & Shoenberger, H. (2023). The next hype in social media advertising: Examining virtual influencers' brand endorsement effectiveness. *Frontiers in Psychology*, 14, 1089051. Advance online publication. DOI: 10.3389/fpsyg.2023.1089051 PMID: 36949930

Lee, L.-H. (2021). All one needs to know about the metaverse: A complete survey on technological singularity, virtual ecosystem, and research agenda. *arXiv Preprint.* Retrieved from http://arxiv.org/abs/2110.05352

Leighton, E. E. (2022). *From microverse to metaverse: Modelling the future through today's virtual worlds.* Emerald Publishing Limited.

Martín, G. F. (2018). Social and psychological impact of musical collective creative processes in virtual environments: The Avatar Orchestra Metaverse in Second Life. *Musica/Tecnologia Music/Technology, 75.*

Narin, N. G. (2021). A content analysis of the metaverse articles. *Journal of Metaverse*, 1(1), 17–24.

Park, S., Kim, S. P., & Whang, M. (2021). Individual's social perception of virtual avatars embodied with their habitual facial expressions and facial appearance. *Sensors (Basel)*, 21(17), 5986. DOI: 10.3390/s21175986 PMID: 34502877

Rasmussen, M. (2022, January 27). Virtual humans. Retrieved from https://www.virtualhumans.org/article/who-was-the-first-virtual-influencer

Rawat, D. B., & El Alami, H. (2023). Metaverse: Requirements, architecture, standards, status, challenges, and perspectives. *IEEE Internet of Things Magazine*, 6(1), 14–18. DOI: 10.1109/IOTM.001.2200258

Rob. (2023, December 19). Virtual influencers: The pros, cons & controversies. *Hoopla Marketing*. Retrieved from https://www.hoopla-marketing.com/virtual-influencers-pros-cons-and-controversies/

Saha, G. (2023, June 13). How AI influencers are changing the marketing landscape. Retrieved June 22, 2023, from *AdLift:*https://www.adlift.com/in/blog/how-ai-influencers-are-changing-the-marketing-landscape/

Shuttleworth, L. (2024, June 14). A virtual influencer: What are they and why you need them for your brand. *P2P Marketing*. Retrieved from https://peertopeermarketing.co/virtual-influencer

Stanoevska-Slabeva, K. (2022). Opportunities and challenges of metaverse for education: A literature review. *Edulearn22 Proceedings,* 10401–10410.

The Influencer Marketing Factory. (2022, March). *Virtual influencers survey infographic*. Retrieved from https://theinfluencermarketingfactory.com/virtual-influencers-survey-infographic/

The pros and cons of virtual influencers. (n.d.). *Emplifi | Customer Experience & Social Media Marketing Software*. Retrieved from https://emplifi.io/resources/blog/virtual-influencers-pros-and-cons

Thomason, J. (2022). Metaverse, token economies, and non-communicable diseases. *Global Health Journal (Amsterdam, Netherlands)*, 6(3), 164–167. DOI: 10.1016/j.glohj.2022.07.001

Tlili, A. (2023). Smart learning environments. DOI: 10.1186/s40561-023-00237-x

Villalba, E. R. (2016). *Cultural simulation through virtual worlds: The case of Second Life*. Musica/Tecnologia Music/Technology.

Wang, H., Ning, H., Lin, Y., Wang, W., Dhelim, S., Farha, F., Ding, J., & Daneshmand, M. (2023). A survey on the metaverse: The state-of-the-art, technologies, applications, and challenges. *IEEE Internet of Things Journal*, 10(16), 14671–14688. DOI: 10.1109/JIOT.2023.3278329

Wikipedia contributors. (2024, December 3). Influencer marketing. Retrieved from *Wikipedia:*https://en.wikipedia.org/wiki/Influencer_marketing

Wikipedia contributors. (n.d.-a). *Ami Yamato*. Retrieved from https://en.wikipedia.org/wiki/Ami_Yamato

Wikipedia contributors. (n.d.-b). *Hatsune Miku*. Retrieved from https://en.wikipedia.org/wiki/Hatsune_Miku

Williams, J. (2024, August 23). The rise of virtual influencers: Are they here to stay? *Sprout Social*. Retrieved from https://sproutsocial.com/insights/virtual-influencers

Yang, S. J. (2021). Precision education: A new challenge for AI in education. *Journal of Educational Technology & Society*, 24(1), 105–108. https://link.gale.com/apps/doc/A657722701/AONE?u=anon~b693f685&sid=googleScholar&xid=e057ad51

ADDITIONAL READING

Cascio Rizzo, G. L., Berger, J., & Villarroel, F. (2023). *What drives virtual influencer's impact?arXiv preprint arXiv:2301.09874*. Retrieved from https://arxiv.org/abs/2301.09874

Haikel-Elsabeh, M. (2023). Virtual Influencers versus Real Influencers Advertising in the Metaverse, Understanding the Perceptions, and Interactions with Users. *Journal of Current Issues and Research in Advertising*, 44(3), 252–273. DOI: 10.1080/10641734.2023.2218420

Joshi, N. (2024, December 27). Virtual influencers: The future of brand storytelling in India? *Campaign India*. https://www.campaignindia.in/article/virtual-influencers-the-future-of-brand-storytelling-in-india/500045

Kim, D., & Wang, Z. (2023). The ethics of virtuality: Navigating the complexities of human-like virtual influencers in the social media marketing realm. *Frontiers in Communication*, 8, 1205610. Advance online publication. DOI: 10.3389/fcomm.2023.1205610

KEY TERMS AND DEFINITIONS

Artificial Intelligence (AI): The simulation of human intelligence by machines to perform tasks such as learning, reasoning, and problem-solving, enabling virtual influencers to act autonomously.

Augmented Reality (AR): A technology that overlays digital elements onto the real world, often used in the metaverse to enhance interactive marketing campaigns.

Brand Engagement: The emotional or intellectual connection a consumer has with a brand, influenced by activities such as interactions with virtual influencers.

Digital Identity: A persona created online that represents an individual, group, or brand in the virtual environment, including avatars and virtual influencers.

Immersive Experience: A deeply engaging user experience achieved through technologies like AR, VR, or the metaverse, fostering more profound consumer interactions with brands.

Metaverse: A virtual, interconnected network of 3D spaces where users interact with digital environments and entities, including virtual influencers, for work, play, and commerce.

Virtual Influencers: Computer-generated characters designed to perform influencer roles, creating content, engaging audiences, and promoting brands within the metaverse and other digital platforms.

Virtual Reality (VR): A fully simulated digital environment that users can explore and interact with, often used in metaverse marketing to create immersive consumer experiences.

Chapter 12
Unstrapping AI and ML in the Ethical and Legal Implications of E-Business Transformation:
Projecting Consumer Privacy – Security Concerns in Era of Digital Disruption

Bhupinder Singh
https://orcid.org/0009-0006-4779-2553
Sharda University, India

Kittisak Wongmahesak
https://orcid.org/0000-0003-3245-8705
North Bangkok University, Thailand

Saurabh Chandra
https://orcid.org/0000-0003-4172-9968
Bennett University, India

EXECUTIVE SUMMARY

E-business is changing quickly, pushed by artificial intelligence (AI) and machine learning (ML), enabling new efficiencies and growth. With this evolution, however, comes lingering ethical and legal vulnerabilities specifically at the level of consumer privacy and security. As personalised experiences are developed, AI and ML algorithms must focus on breaking down silos, which will inadvertently expose greater amounts of sensitive information that is susceptible to cyberattacks or pathway

DOI: 10.4018/979-8-3693-7245-6.ch012

into a data breach or fraud. This chapter comprehensively explores the concerns of consumer privacy-security in era of digital disruption with AI and ML in the ethical and legal implications of e-business transformation.

1. INTRODUCTION AND BACKGROUND

Trust and transparency has to be inculcated specially now in the times of digital disruption. Questions of ethics, data ownership, consent and the equilibrium between business innovation and individual privacy are raised. Laws like the General Data Protection Regulation (GDPR) and California Consumer Privacy Act (CCPA) have been enacted to protect consumers, but compliance mechanisms tend not to keep up with the complexity of AI-driven systems. Reconciling innovation with ethical standards can only be done through a proactive approach in which companies follow strict privacy compliance, implement strong security techniques and make sure AI decision-making is transparent. Addressing these issues is essential to the development of the digital economy as e-business continues to mature (Hussain, & Alaya, 2024).

Data is the new oil in an e-business landscape where companies are focusing on AI and ML technologies to help them take advantage of this information for better decision-making processes across all channels - from personalized customer experiences at scale down even through overall operational efficiency. Within evolving frameworks, businesses have to be conscious of the ethical and legal considerations that come with those technologies - using them in a responsible way. Being able to effectively incorporate the AI and ML into e-business strategies requires a close eye on the innovation of tomorrow, but also protecting consumer trust in privacy-related principles.

This digital disruption resulted in the creation of entirely new business models, including e-commerce platform providers such as Shopify and Magento; online marketplaces like Amazon Marketplace; subscription-based services (SaaS) for businesses and consumers. Even in the e-business landscape, AI and ML have a long way to go. It is with the help of these technologies only, businesses have been able to better utilize data for smarter decisions, automate routine tasks and make their product offerings as unique to each end customer. The world can be very intimidating because of how quickly information and communication technology (ICT) has evolved in the past two decades. The advent of the information technology era in early 1990s allowed different forms of application to be conducted using internets (or better known as World Wide Web) and it is now well embedded across all domains, one prominent form being e-business that allows electronic transactions over digitally enabled network resources, by organisation with other business entities.

The biggest developments in global business is how e-business enterprises changed traditional models (Jagirdar, & Gupta, 2024). Nowadays, companies harnessing the nations on a worldwide scale to streamline their operations and improve customer engagement. So that when these are combined with all the e-business platforms along with customer reading habits or social interactions, AI and ML algorithms can analyze this quotient amount of data captured to learn about consumer nuances. This digital disruption resulted in the creation of entirely new business models, including e-commerce platform providers such as Shopify and Magento; online marketplaces like Amazon Marketplace; subscription-based services (SaaS) for businesses and consumers.

The use of AI/ML in e-business has brought up modern personalization, represent one but recommended systems that can predict what an individual customer may want based on his or her history and behavior. E-commerce platforms, online streaming services and social media using these systems to improve customer engagement in boosting sales scale. In addition, AI and ML have also been incorporated to streamline e-business operations with solutions like supply chain management, inventory optimization and pricing strategies AI and ML algorithms provide more data insights by comparing historical data and market trends, producing smarter outcomes to allow better predictions for businesses that minimize expenses affiliated with the process as well.

1.1 Objective of the Chapter

The chapter has the following main objectives to:

- give an overview of the journey from e-business to digital transformation and how AI & ML has played a major role in this modern-day form of trade.
- highlighting consumer data security and privacy issues and of expansive Use of AI/ML in e-Business.
- analyse the challenges and opportunities from AI & ML in e-business, the risks businesses can face if they do not implement it properly plus strategies on how companies might go about doing so.
- stress the importance of responsible and ethical use of AI and ML in e-business as well growing need for strong regulatory frameworks,
- study the industry standards that safeguarding consumer rights in addition to fair & transparent practices.

2. AI AND ML IN E-BUSINESS

Artificial Intelligence (AI) and Machine learning (ML), have become game changers in e-business across all industries, changing the way companies do business interact with their customers to make strategic decisions. With digital transformation in full flight, companies are looking to deploy a broader range of AI and ML technologies to improve productivity and customer experiences that ultimately keep them ahead of the competition as markets continue growing ever more competitive. AI is a host of technologies that allow machines to do things previously only done by humans. Natural Language Understanding, Image Pattern recognition, Decision making on large data and Problem Solving. There are mainly two types of AI: narrow intelligence which is designed to perform a particular task (such as language translation or image recognition), and general intelligence which seek to recreate human cognitive faculties on broad categories.

Though hypothetical, General AI has seen enormous usage in numerous fields including e-business where narrow AI are being utilized. AI is a discipline in computer science that focuses on creating software agents able to accomplish things which would require human intellect, Machine learning (ML) commonly considered as the subset of AI field but not exactly. It focusses more around development and phenomena of building algorithms for predictive modeling approaches using dataset pieces. ML Algorithms instead of being explicitly programmed to do so, learns from the data patterns that they identify which allow them further up in their task performance. This is essential when it comes to e-businesses where your company generates massive amounts of data through its customer interactions, transactions and other.

The combination of AI and ML technologies have resulted into more advanced tools, applications that are radically changed the aspect for e-business. For example, AI-driven chatbots and virtual assistants are automating customer service for immediate help with personalized suggestions. These are the tools that use natural language processing (NLP) to understand the questions customers have and respond at scale in real time, which means an enhanced experience for all. AI and ML are already being applied beyond customer service to data analytics, business intelligence etc. Through historical data analysis and pattern recognition, organizations can inform their strategic plans for inventory management, marketing strategies as well as product development. Predictive analytics, which is driven by complex machine learning algorithms provides companies with the ability to predict customer behavior and tailor their services accordingly. Among the biggest benefits of AI and ML in e-commerce is their capability to personalized user experiences. Businesses can, for example, analyze customer data such as browsing history or purchase behavior and demographic information to better target marketing campaigns and product recommendations. This level of customization not just helps increase the satisfaction rate amongst customers but in addition boosts conversion rates along with increases brand loyalty (Lo, & Zhang, 2024).

With the evolution of e-business, AI and ML technologies will be increasingly leveraged in this field. More companies are putting these technologies to the test where they can automate processes, streamline operations, and build smarter decision-making capabilities. AI-driven pricing algorithms are able to interpret these conditions, which alongside historical data from market-behavior within the firm sector and stronger competitors allows the business to better understand their price-sensitivity in real-time, equipping businesses with all they need not for only achieving revenue-based welfares but also tactical advantages. On the other hand, embedding AI/ML into e-business also has legal ethical issues. Consumer Privacy - Businesses gather unfathomable data about their customers and analysing them that raised alarms on the privacy issues, as this report reveals personal insights into customer minutiae which is directly helpful in context specific marketing. Businesses that rely on AI and ML technologies must comply with data protection regulations, like the General Data Protection Regulation (GDPR) in Europe. Leveraging such technologies tactically, companies have a chance to convene new vistas for expansion and digital transformation (Kabir, et al., 2024).

3. AI AND ML APPLICATIONS IN E-BUSINESS

There is no question that Artificial Intelligence (AI) and Machine Learning (ML) are being deployed incredibly fast in all types of e-business transformation, often into consumer-oriented services with real ramifications on individual privacy & even personal security. To operate these technologies in a way that is consistent with ethical principles and respects user data, companies face myriad regulations like the EU AI Act (proposed) or California Consumer Privacy Act (CCPA). These include not to be vulnerable from bias and discrimination, keeping the transparency and accountability high as well as respect for privacy or personal autonomy. In addition, businesses have to fulfil data privacy laws and deploy different techniques of preserving online user privacy while maintaining transparency on their part regarding the collection and usage pattern.

Guarding against the prevalence of biased AI systems, earning consumer trust and ensuring legal compliance all require a proactive strategy that is both holistic in nature. This requires @Companies to establish their AI ethics principles and data sets, more aware not only with diversity/inclusion but also automated privacy policy enforcement or PPMl. Ensure ethical and legal guidelines for businesses to harnessing the true power of AI and ML technology while enhancing consumer privacy & security in leveraging digital disruption era.

Figure 1. Shows the points of AI and ML applications in E-Business (Source- Original)

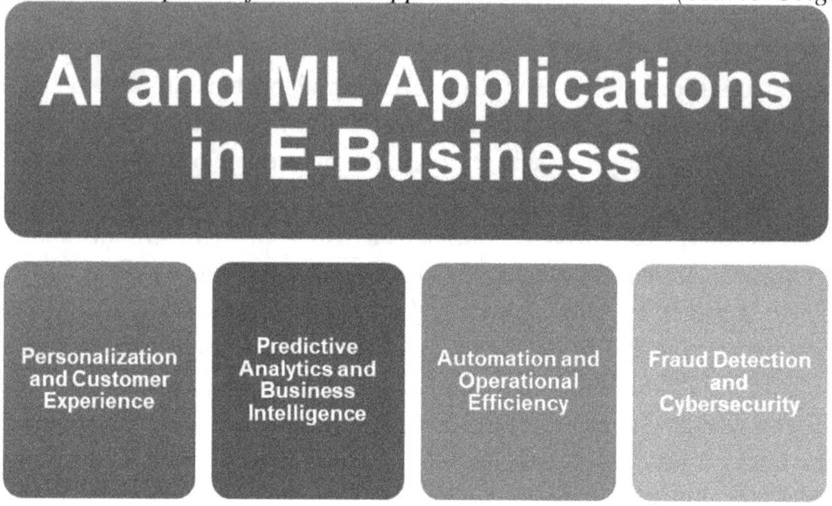

3.1 Personalization and Customer Experience

Customer experience today is all about how you communicate with your user and its the era of Artificial Intelligence (AI) driven customer experiences. With the help of AI-driven personalization, businesses can drive personalized experiences that are customized to fit perfectly into every individual customer. AI personalization, it turns out; enhances customer satisfaction. By analyzing large data sets of customer information, AI uncovers patterns and provides insights that allow businesses to offer tailored recommendations, relevant content and seamless engagement. This kind of customization keeps customers feeling supportive and sensation understood which leads to more involvement, retention as well as lifetime worth. Not to mention, AI-powered personalization is very scalable which means that companies can provide personalized experiences on a large scale compared to manual efforts. AI such as natural language processing, predictive analytics or audience segmentation skills help businesses to predict the future customer needs and provide leading-proactive one:one experiences. Using AI, together with human intelligence and creative juices will create a harmony between data driven personalization and the emotional quotient of creating real customer relationships. All of this ultimately combines to create an experience that is not just tailored, but also lasting and meaningful for a customer.

AI-powered personalization is one of the strategic imperatives that businesses looking to flourish in a customer-centric modern marketplace must adopt. As we continue into an ever-changing digital generation, AI powered nexus pillar will be more important as companies aspire for exceptional experiences with their customers.

3.2 Predictive Analytics and Business Intelligence

Predictive analytics and business intelligence (BI) are very close, but their differences make each of them better suited for different tasks that help organizations to make informed decisions based on data, and they give an upper hand over the competition. While BI concentrates on analyzing historical as well as current data to know the performance of past, predictive analytics moves forward from it by making use of advanced statistical models and machine learning algorithms for forecasting future trends & outcomes. It is nothing more than a means of capturing, organizing and delivering data pertaining to your business in the most meaningful way. They empower businesses to find trends, monitor KPIs and make fact-based decisions. BI is really a excellent tool for process optimization, discovering places that need improvement and communication of strategies to the stakeholders. Predictive analytics, on the other hand utilises data as well albeit to predict what may happen in future. Predictive models can be used to find hidden patterns, relationships and trends in large amounts of data coming from a wide variety of sources. This enables businesses to predict what customers want, mitigate risk before it arises and make more strategic decisions faster that result in growth and improved profitability. Organizations can leverage both tools to get an overall view of their business, new predictions with high accuracy and act upon those decisions made. As data grows and expands, the integration of these two fields is important for organisations who are trying to remain ahead in a fast-moving business world.

3.3 Automation and Operational Efficiency

Predictive analytics and business intelligence (BI) are very close, but their differences make each of them better suited for different tasks that help organizations to make informed decisions based on data, and they give an upper hand over the competition. While BI concentrates on analyzing historical as well as current data to know the performance of past, predictive analytics moves forward from it by making use of advanced statistical models and machine learning algorithms for forecasting future trends & outcomes. It is nothing more than a means of capturing, organizing and delivering data pertaining to your business in the most meaningful way. They empower businesses to find trends, monitor KPIs and make fact-based decisions. BI is really a excellent tool for process optimization, discovering places that need improvement and communication of strategies to the stakeholders. Predictive analytics, on the other hand utilises data as well albeit to predict what may happen in future. Predictive models can be used to find hidden patterns, relationships and trends in large amounts of data coming from a wide variety of sources. This enables businesses to predict what customers want, mitigate risk before it arises and make more strategic decisions faster that result in growth and improved profitability. Organizations can leverage both tools to get an overall view of their business, new predictions with high accuracy and act upon those decisions made. As data grows and expands, the integration of these two fields is important for organisations who are trying to remain ahead in a fast-moving business world.

3.4 Fraud Detection and Cybersecurity

With the myriads of security threats businesses are facing from malicious actors, in this digital era fraud detection and cybersecurity become more important than ever. By incorporating advanced analytics and machine learning capabilities, companies can create superior fraud detection systems that capture unusual behaviors or patterns as they happen to prevent huge financial loss and reputational harm. These fraud detection solutions, driven by AI and machine learning principles sift through tons of data such as transaction history, customer activity and global threat intelligence. This in turn enables them to identify and flag potential cases of fraud with a high degree of accuracy, which ensures that businesses can respond as soon as possible. Machine learning algorithms, on the other hand, can learn and evolve their ability to identify fraudulent activity much better than even sophisticated heuristics - adapting more quickly compared with rule-based systems as fraud tactics change. Cybersecurity next to fraud detection is one of the main concerns for businesses operating in a digital landscape The use of AI and machine learning can greatly improve cyber security defenses by automating threat detection, incident response as well as vulnerability management. These technologies can scan the network traffic, user behavior & security logs to detect and mitigate timely and effective manner the cyber threats like Malware, Phishing attack etc.). Organizations can boost their defense against various financial and digital threats by incorporating AI and machine learning to fraud detection as well as cybersecurity solutions. This end-to-end assurance does more than just protect vital assets and data - it creates trust with customers, partners and investors that the business is a reliable and credible member of their digital ecosystem.

4. BENEFITS OF AI AND ML IN E-BUSINESS

The AI/ML enables e-business to grow and become more efficient in terms of improving the customer experience, making better decisions faster, increasing productivity with security.

Enhanced Customer Engagement

The e-commerce landscape has witnessed a revolution in the way businesses interact with customers and it is all thanks to artificial intelligence (AI) and machine learning that have played an indispensable role. These powerful technologies allow companies to create personalized experiences tailored to the tastes and desires of an individual customer. AI-enabled chatbots and virtual assistants can come to the rescue of customers providing immediate support, guidance making sure that information they are looking is provided even beyond office hours. Additionally, ML algorithms are able to look through massive customer data sets and identify behavioral trends that enable businesses to provide specific recommendations, personalized content delivery e seamless interactions. This degree of personalization not only improves consumer satisfaction but also generates brand loyalty and advocacy. With the ongoing changes in the digital space, leveraging AI and ML for e-commerce strategies is an essential entity to ace up their sleeves when it comes to enhancing user experience so your business can differentiate itself from competitors while building relationships with customers that last.

Improved Decision-Making Processes

Because this is the world of e-commerce, one which moves fast and for a business to survive it needs to make decisions that are informed. AI/ML as a technology can help and assist in decision-making process, with better insights backed up by data crunching capabilities which are way beyond human anticipations today. These technologies bring the most value in analyzing data from numerous sources and linkages between, e.g., customer behavior with market demand or business performance metrics to identify hidden patterns as well as risks and even forecast future events. This data aids organizations to take informed decisions, optimize their blueprints and rephrase resources where they work best. By adopting AI-driven demand forecasting applications, companies will be able to predict the demands of their customer and forecast stock requirement accurately. Real-Time Fraud Detection ML algorithms can pick up on fraudulent activities and security threats, enabling businesses to respond proactively to curb the risks of exposure or collateral damage. There is a tremendous data explosion happening worldwide and it will soon become mandatory for AI/ ML, to be integrated into decision-making workflows otherwise e-commerce businesses would not be able to adapt themselves fast enough thereby making them risk falling behind the competition.

Increased Operational Efficiency

In the digital era, operational efficiency becomes one of most important priority for an e-commerce business to sustain or expand its operations. A big part of this is the automation or asariarizarion a tilements. With the help of advanced technologies like AI, ML and others that businesses already use they can automate order management; supply chain workflows, inventory tracking etc. This eliminates the potential for human error and empowers team members to spend their time elsewhere-specifically, on higher-level strategic activities that contribute more meaningfully to business success. Another important part of improving operational efficiency is optimizing organizational structures. AI and predictive analytics can offer precious intelligence which helps in faster decision-making, better operational flow. For example, predicting future market trends and consumer behavior as well as supply chain dynamics can allow the organizations to anticipate these shifts in landscape & adapt their operation accordingly so that they remain agile. Visibility and Tracking throughout the supply chain level is critical. Technological advances like real-time tracking and monitoring (e.g., geocoding) have made it possible for companies to keep a close watch on their operations so they can deliver items as soon as promised. An e-commerce organization can reach the operational visibility through these solutions making it a comprehensive package for all channels.

Better Risk Management

Understanding the importance of risk management is part and parcel with e-commerce, given a higher digital-first emphasis that we see in businesses today. One of the primary strategic goals is to perform a complete risk assessment, which means that you need to find out what may be at risk and decide on how likely it is. It takes an in-depth look at risk analysis, both internally and externally (ie - operational risks, financial-hazards or reputational hazards) and continue to revise these analyses as the business landscape changes over time. Another key element of risk management is to build resilience and redundancy. Putting backup systems in place, spreading supply chains and distribution networks around more than one geographic location or provider as appropriate and creating contingency plans can all help protect your business against disruption. Innovative technologies like artificial intelligence and machine learning are a boon to boost risk detection, response capabilities, helping enterprises take swift action against the risks. Manage risk on an ongoing basis

- This includes continuous monitoring and real-time evaluation of measures being used to manage risks. Businesses that monitor the most important metrics and stay alert, constantly updating their strategy based on what is happening behind them are those who ultimately function best over time. Developing a risk-aware and risk accountable organization culture is also important to effective risk management. In turn, e-commerce businesses' risk management processes can grow stronger through collaboration and partnerships. Integrating with industry experts, consultants and participating in groups are some of the ways by which organizations can gather latest information on outlook sowie risk evolution. Having strategic partners with whom you can share learnings, resources and risk management strategies will also keep your business in the fast lane. By adopting these solutions, the businesses in e-commerce would be able to improvise upon their operational efficiency by poorly handling risks and creating opportunities for itself eventually from technology advancements trends.

The other important ethical consideration is the respect for consumer privacy. It is Reputation that will matter and it goes without saying, if consumer data must be collected and maintained, it needs to be done securely because you never know when a major leap employee may jump ship with the mother-lode of digital gold. They must also adhere to the relevant data collection laws (for ex: GDPR or CCPA) and store the collected data safely, protecting it from unauthorized access. These include the adoption of strong security measures to prevent data leakage or abuse.

Figure 2. Displays the benefits of AI and ML in E-Business (Source- Original)

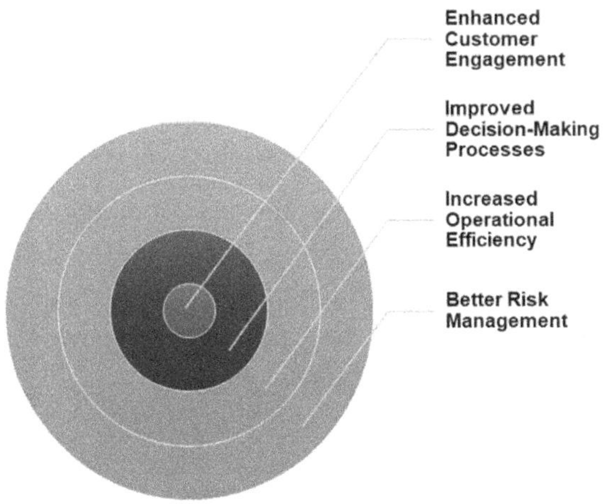

5. ETHICAL IMPLICATIONS

Ethical data privacy requires adherence to the law, established ethical principles as well as considering societal and environmental elements. It also protects the privacy of our data and makes doing business more ethically. Ideally, businesses should not collect too much information that they cannot utilise to serve the consumer better. Taking an ethical standpoint would allow businesses to create a model code of practice upholding all persons in the organisation responsible for safeguarding critical data.

5.1 Consumer Privacy Concerns

The important ethical consideration is the respect for consumer privacy. It is Reputation that will matter and if consumer data must be collected and maintained, it needs to be done securely because you never know when a major leap employee may jump ship with the mother-lode of digital gold. They must also adhere to the relevant data collection laws (for ex: GDPR or CCPA) and store the collected data safely, protecting it from unauthorized access. These include the adoption of strong security measures to prevent data leakage or abuse. But achieving this balance while maintaining transparent, responsible third-party data use remains critical for businesses that want to access and capitalize on consumer data responsibly. This means that if the data is used, it should be predominantly to serve the consumer and where businesses are behaving as transparently as possible while also being respectful of consumer privacy. Businesses need to be able to strike this balance, otherwise they could lose the trust of consumers or find themselves breaking the law in at least some jurisdictions when it comes to data collection practices.

Data Collection and Usage Practices

Data collected should serve a purpose in supporting the business's marketing efforts and not intrude on consumer privacy. Data collected should increase to the quality as well, data is being fed and incorrect data can rule out any digital marketing campaign. All businesses should strive to collect good quality data that informs decision-making, and enhances marketing strategies.

Consent and Transparency Issues

Consumers must be given the opportunity to opt out, or in some cases have their data erased altogether. This process allows consumers to delete or opt out of receiving tracking information, and creates confidence in the fact that they are dealing with a company which is respectul of their data. Offering these choices will allow companies to show their commitment in consumer privacy and make sure that consumers are the ones who own, socialize or handle information.

5.2 Security Anxieties

Artificial Intelligence (AI) and Machine Learning(Ml): The growing implementation of Artificial intelligence & ML in e-business has created a serious state of insecurity among the pursuers. These fears often originate from the susceptibility that is naturally intrinsic to AI and ML systems, as well as businesses becoming increasingly vulnerable due to cyber attacks.

Vulnerabilities in AI and ML Systems

AI and ML systems need plenty of data in their training to build these models, upon which they base decisions. Yet, this data is also open to various biases and errors in the real world that can result in spurious or even harmful outputs. E.g. if training data for a facial recognition system is biased towards certain demographics, the system might behave discriminatively Moreover, the complexity of AI and ML algorithms makes them low on interpretation audits which in turn create issues related to transparency and accountability. These security gaps may be leveraged by threat actors for bypassing defenses or influencing the system's evaluations.

Cyber Threats and Malicious Attacks

E-business has seen a huge increase in our dependence on digital technologies, and the use of internet-based tools for commerce is vulnerable to any number of attacks including malware, phishing or distributed denial-of-service (DDoS) attacks. These attacks can lead to data breaches, loss of money and even destroy organizational reputation which in turn increases consumer woes. The main issues of such vulnerabilities are in fact malware, with more and more advanced malwares being created by cybercriminals to take advantage over these vulnerable software design or system. One such type of malware, known a ransomware has stirred up considerable amount of disruption and financial damage to businesses across the globe.

Mitigation Strategies and Best Practices

Businesses can tackle this anxiety by combining technological solutions with robust security practices and clear communication aound the measures being taken to ensure data is secure. This includes:

- This includes doing so by encrypting data, controlled access to documents and regular backups against loss of information caused due to online breaches or possible cyber crimes.
- Creating AI and ML systems with an emphasis on fairness, transparency, and accountability that are both unbiased and audit-able for security vulnerabilities.
- Cybersecurity tools and technologies, including firewalls, intrusion detection systems (IDS), behavioural analytics software for advanced threat detection
- Ensuring that employees have the proper security awareness to identify and respond accordingly when under attack, for example phishing emails or socially engineered attacks.
- Open, transparent communications with consumers about the security controls in place and what is being done to protect their data or if there was a breach
- When businesses address these security fears, it boosts consumer confidence and improves the company reputation as a reliable player in today's era of digital disruption

5.3 Bias and Discrimination

Algorithmic Bias and Fairness

In other words, if AI systems produce results that are systematically skewed towards certain groups or individuals - we refer to it as algorithmic bias. This may occur due to biased training data, algorithmic process or model development assumptions. This includes facial recognition algorithms not being able to correctly identify people of color, or voice recognition systems that have a hard time understanding certain accents. Lack Of Fairness: This is amongst the biggest biases in AI and ML systems, which if corrected can help a lot of these problems go away. Fair: The process of designing algorithms that will provide fair predictions with respect to various demographic groups. That's only possible using techniques such as disparate impact analysis, equal opportunity and counterfactual fairness. In the two diagrams above we have seen mechanisms to evaluate fairness and check for biases on data/models.

Ethical Considerations in AI and ML Model Training

In the field of AI and ML model training, efforts have to been made during model design for instance in prescriptive analytics, New era application development architecture etc. where Ethical considerations taken being Fairness, transparency and accountable models This requires sampling rich representative data, auditing your own and the models for biases, identifying fairness metrics beyond mere accuracy to be incorporated in decision making using human insights and last but not least - transparent algorithms that can flag themselves as biased. It is also important that diverse development teams are built because people from different backgrounds help in identifying and suppressing these biases. We need not only to monitor and adjust but also continuously update the detection algorithms of AI systems for them to be fair by design over time. Failure to consider these ethical concerns could result in serious societal inequalities being perpetuated by discriminatory AI systems against minority groups. If companies can tackle these challenges and must protect against the potential risks of AI by putting fairness and transparency first, responsible development will lead to a healthier future.

Ensuring Diversity and Inclusion in Technology

This makes promoting diversity and inclusion in technology more critical than ever to ensure that AI systems are created fairly and without bias. This requires using data from a wide variety of sources to ensure that the examples used for training are representative, creating development teams that reflect the diversity in society as a whole and maintaining transparency around how AI models develop. Gathering broad data allows businesses to avoid narrowing down the intelligence of an AI model, programmed with bias. Machine learning models and data that trains the model can have inherent biases, but diverse teams of developers - those from different backgrounds with maybe even a wider range of experiences- will be able to spot potential issues during both development and deployment.

5.4 Accountability and Responsibility

Transparency, accountability and responsibility are key concepts in the deployment of AI/ML models so Model Card is a good way to provide information about these properties. The important things to define while defining accountability for AI and ML deployment -

Legal Frameworks and Regulatory Guidelines

There are not yet explicit requirements for which kinds of AI models will comply, but there is a legal landscape that naturally predisposes over how AIs can be used such as data privacy and security regulations. The GDPR is an example of this, which mandates requirements to protect data and security; on the other hand are China's Interim Measures for the Management of Generative AI Services that compelling developers engaged in generating content with AI making it positive or healthy. The EU is also developing its AI Act, which would outlaw specific applications of artificial intelligence and set reliability as well as data protection rules. There are also increasing steps in the U.S. to lay down guidelines -- such as the Blueprint for an AI Bill of Rights, aimed at protecting people from abuses by artificial intelligence systems. The regulations for AI are still a work in progress, and as they evolve rapidly businesses must stay updated to determine how it alters their practices.

Ethical Decision-Making in AI and ML

When building and operating AI/ML systems, ethical decision-making is key. This includes transparency and explainability, bias in the machine learning model /AI system by guaranteeing fairness/not discriminating any community or region, respect for human rights it acquires; if task purely depends on AI), accountability of user interaction with the assistance of a human # onboarded to supervise methods deployed (human oversight) making sure action does not deviate from outlined scope initially recognised set-to achieve, monitoring regularly so that effectiveness can be evaluated & adjusting eventually support more clear desired goal accomplishment. One way to make the ML models understandable is by using techniques like interpretable models and expla-, methods. Ethical considerations should take account of these principles, such as respect for human rights (including data subject participation), fairness, transparency, accountability and privacy. By making use of regular audits and monitoring ensuring that AI continues to obey the quick regime of changing regulatory constrains / ethical standards. Prioritizing ethical decision-making, and ensuring that businesses understand what is required by the legal frameworks in place globally will enable us to harness AI for good without fallout on trust, responsibility or regulatory compliance.

6. LEGAL INFERENCES

Fast developing technology, particularly in Artificial Intelligence (AI) and Machine Learning (ML), has also resulted into some most influential legal and regulatory questions. Businesses are turning to these technologies more than ever for innovation but also creating a minefield of data protection laws and ethical considerations At the top of this landscape are kings like European Union's General Data Protection Regulation (GDPR) which went live in 2018. The GDPR sanctions the storage, processing and collection of individual data only under strict circumstances accompanied by stringent penalties (for example fines amounting up to €20 Million or 4%

of global annual turnover in case a business is found non-compliant). Organizations must now acquire informed consent, clearly communicate their data use practices and ensure the implementation of security measures to safeguard sensitive information.

6.1 Current Regulatory Landscape

In the US, they have a similar intent with laws such as the California Consumer Privacy Act (CCPA) and potentially something like the American Data Privacy and Protection Act some day. Introduced in 2020, the CCPA gives Californians the right to find out what information is being collected on them and remove it if desired as well as opt-out of having their data sold. A national standard for data privacy and security, the ADPPAICYMI would set lawmakers on a “collision course” with big tech Major data protection regulations also include China's Personal Information Protection Law (PIPL), Brazil's General Data Protection Law (LGPD) and the Indian Personal Data Protection Bill that is likely to be in place soon. While the requirements differ in some respects among these regulations, all are focused on protecting individual privacy and promoting good data practices.

Overview of Global Data Protection Laws (e.g., GDPR, CCPA)

Over and above shielding data, the legal and regulatory landscape is also troubled with ethical consequences of AI and ML. Algorithmic bias, transparency and accountability concerns have spurred the creation of a number of ethical frameworks such as the EU's Ethics Guidelines for Trustworthy AI, or OECD Principles on Artificial Intelligence. They seek to foster the development and deployment of AI technologies for social good by ensuring that these are rights-respecting, non-discriminatory, responsible in allowing human oversight and control. With the changing legal and regulatory environment, businesses need to remain updated with these changes and comply accordingly. Ensuring compliance with data protection legislation and ethical AI principles is not just a legal obligation: it also helps maintain consumer confidence in the use of data at an individual level, while ensuring trust across the wider digital economy.

AI and ML-Specific Regulations

With the rise of AI and ML technologies in e-businesses, there are certain rules already formulated for their development (and sometimes deployment). The re-drafting of the proposed regulations aims to ensure AI is developed and applied in an ethical, transparent, accountable way. The most prominent among dedicated AI regulations is the EU's proposed Artificial Intelligence Act. The package lays down a coordinated approach to creating rules on AI development, marketing and use in the EU. The AI Act categorizes AI systems based on the level of risk with which it is associated -- higher-risk applications will be held to more stringent requirements and can have genuine effects on people's lives. This includes AI systems that are used in a way that could significantly impact society at large, or an entire group of people. The provision also covers other uses of high-risk artificial intelligence such as during critical infrastructure there is maintenance and operation; for educational or vocational training purposes; assessing eligibility to recognize employment circumstances including recruitment processes as well it concerns granted access to vital private and public services whether due the scarcity nature (unforeseen failure cum hacking) communal goods issuance requirements goals. High-risk AI systems will need to comply with game-specific provisions on data quality, human oversight, robustness and accuracy as well as security requirements set out in the Articles of EU`s Artificial Intelligence Act. These systems providers have to meet risk management and keep a lot of documentation and other things, they even need to go through a conformity assessment before these are put in place. In addition, the regulation specifies that AI systems must be designed so their behaviour can be easily understood and users informed as to why a decision was reached. Although there is no federal AI regulation in the United States, several agencies have issued guidance related to specific aspects of AI and ML. This includes guidelines on AI use in advertising and marketing, such as from the Federal Trade Commission (FTC), which reminds that heresies conducted with hocus pocus algorithms are still deceptive practices - you know the usual stuff: thou shalt not be unfair or deviate unduly. The National Institute of Standards and Technology (NIST), meanwhile, has developed a framework for managing the risks that AI poses to privacy, security and ethical alignment.

Compliance Requirements for E-Businesses

Many regulations cover data privacy, security and consumer protection that e-businesses must comply to. Although these are not AI and ML specific regulations, they will highly affect the use of these technologies for e-commerce. Other critical compliance that e-businesses must follow is the Data privacy laws like GDPR in EU, and CCPA in US. These laws define very strict regulations for the collection, storage and processing of personal data like consent requirements, transparency obligations or rights to information access etc. E-businesses are also subject to laws related to consumer protection, such as the Federal Trade Commission Act in the USA. This act is something most business operators using e-commerce should be aware of (this means all businesses), but it`s important not only focuses on large enterprises catching up with technology and safety for clients who may never purchase anything but ends like "flicker". For example, making sure that AI recommendations or pricing mechanism are transparent and fair. Businesses that operate electronically must also comply with industry-specific regulations, such as the Payment Card Industry Data Security Standard (PCI DSS) if they handle credit card transactions. Typically, such laws include provisions regarding data security and incident response planning. Compliance with said regulations should be secure by e-businesses implementing a sound data governance structure, and regular risk assessments being carried out in order to fine tune such implementation as well as training the staff on what is needed for making effective security processes. It is also important to work closely with legal and compliance teams, so that these professionals are aware of changes in law or regulation.

6.2 Legal Challenges in AI and ML Implementation

One of the repercussions, however, under increasing litigation are the legal challenges brought on by emerging technologies like artificial intelligence (AI) and machine learning (ML). It includes issues across a wide range of areas like data privacy, intellectual property rights, liability and algorithmic bias. Data protection is one of the other biggest issues that we have today with meeting compliance requirements around GDPR in EU and also consumer privacy act like CCPA in USA. Machine learning systems of AI are extremely data-hungry, with personal and sensitive details leading to worries around user permissioning, information security concerns as well about privacy rights. Conglomerates need to provide impenetrable data governance mechanisms and also require an express consent from individuals in order to capture, hold or trade their personal information. More challenging still is the problem of what, if any, are Intellectual Property Rights in works generated by AI. With AI advancing to the stage where it could potentially create original works, like art pieces or even music and published literature as we will see - who gets the copyright for making? Unfortunately, given the status of our current intellectual property laws regarding copyrighting software programs described above - this would be a bit of an open question. When AI systems cause harm or become erroneous, other complicated issue arises like liability attribution. Which party is liable. The developer, the user or AI entity itself: Clarification of who will be held accountable in instances such as these can help lay down legal frameworks to handle it.

There is another problem called the algorithmic bias, in which human biases from training data are reflected posited and augmented by AI systems. The result, especially for high-impact areas like employment, lending and law enforcement can be quite discriminatory. Business always has to ensure that their AI systems are fair and not biased, they should also conduct regular audits for finding bias (Saltık, 2024). These legal barriers have no easy solution for compliance, so a multi-pronged approach is required. To design a legal framework that responds to AI innovation, collaboration between technologists and the law is crucial (Silver, 2024). To tackle these legal risks, businesses need to be aware of new laws and regulations as they develop, conduct AI ethics reviews on a consistent basis and follow transparent processes while using AI (Raja & MESSAOUDI, 2024). Given the ongoing march of AI and ML into industry and everyday life, solving these legal problems will be vital to control deployment in a responsible manner.

Intellectual Property Rights and AI-Generated Content

When AI systems start creating works of art, music and literature, this raises complex legal issues in the field of intellectual property rights at issue (Ni, 2024). Most copyright laws assume that human creators are behind the works to which authorial rights attach, raising questions as to whether AI-generated outputs can attain any form of proprietary status.

Control over the copyright in AI-generated content is another area of concern. Should the AI developer, the user that caused an AI to repeat it or even more directly should a specific utterance/trace of reused output can be considered copyrighted under similar principles (Cervellati, et al., 2024). Bottom line if the AI system in question could create an original work, does it constitute as law under copyright law or is to simply just credited towards humans who created and use this new technology (Zhu, et al., 2024). These issues raise political challenges to the conventional notion of creativity and authorship, long associated historically with expressive individualism.

However, the fact that AI can produce content as easily raises concerns over potential copyright issues (Cervellati, et al., 2024). This is a common problem because the output of AI systems may reproduce copyrighted material, intentionally or not; users might pretend that their derived-from-AI works are more original than they actually are (Othman, 2024). Creating established guidelines for using or transforming AI-generated content is pertinent; such as examples in fair use and how to create derivative (Saltik, et al., 2024). Established regulations need to be made around the domain of copyrighted works created by an artificial intelligence. Addressing these intellectual property problems necessitates a fair balance between promoting AI innovation and securing the interests of creators (Dimitriadou, 2024). Possible approaches could include creating new legal concepts dedicated uniquely to AI-created works e.g., the granting of subsidiary rights or hobbling them while reinterpreting traditional exceptions and limitations on a zoomed-in basis like fair uses with automatic attribution elements, as well as thinking outside copyright, such as by looking into collective management organizations' models for enforcement (Shukla, et al., 2024).

The rapid progress in content creation using AI highlights the importance of policymakers sitting down with legal practitioners and technology developers to create a common framework that enables creativity, innovation and is also respects other people's rights. With AI breaking new ground in the creative arts, it is clear that this evolution will continue to challenge existing legal frameworks and necessitate a balanced system between all parties (Abdullah, et al., 2024).

Liability and Risk Management

Liability has been a key concern as AI and ML systems are increasingly used in an array of industries (Ncube, et al., 2024). For any harm or loss that results from decisions made by an AI system, this question raises issues for the creation of legal frameworks to cover these circumstances and investigate liability on the part of developers who created such a service; users and also considering whether culpability can be squarely placed on what is essentially software developed in some respects with concepts quite parallel to those applied when laws develop guidelines about responsibility.

A method to minimize risk of liability is through the enhancement of overall enterprise wide operational-risk management (Talbi, et al., 2024). Before implementing AI/ML systems into businesses, they must conduct comprehensive risk assessments to avert all possible risks and have necessary controls in place. This includes for example verifying that the data used to train models is accurate, representative and unbiased; monitoring performance of the system as well are results on a regular basis (Su & Deng, 2024). Moreover, companies ought to have effective Error Handling Procedures which includes the procedures for error notification to related parties, rollback of changes and Root Cause Analysis (Ahmed, et al., 2024). Peripherals can be an easy target for attackers, so make sure to continuously audit and test the device or system being used. Developers of AI and ML systems should focus on developing interpretable models that can provide explanations to their outputs. That could come down to features importance analysis, partial dependence plots, SHAP values - essentially any method that helps us dig deeper into what factors our system thinks the most about while making its decisions (Persakis, & Koutoupis, 2024).

Cross-Border Data Transfer and Jurisdictional Issues

The international borders are no match for the global reach of AI and ML system- but then we have an entire other can to worms- ethereal nature brings cross border data transfer a jurisdictional concern. Businesses falling under the directive must manage a complex system of data protection laws and regulations that come into effect when personal information starts being collected, processed or stored across

European state borders (Vidani, 2024). The key challenges is to secure compliance, with requirements like GDPR in Europe or CCPA in California just a few examples from diversity/increasing patchwork of data protection regulation. These are the laws that demand explicit consent of individuals to collect, store and process their personal data making it mandatory for a company to be clear about its use from time-to-time (Manahov, 2024).

Another thing that businesses need to think about is data localization laws, concerned with the requirement of saving a certain type of consumer or other subject-associated facts within the country where its subject(s) resides. AI, ML Systems with Multiple Data Sources and Jurisdictions Face Challenges. While these risks cannot be eliminated, businesses can manage the risk by rolling-out end-to-end data governance frameworks that involve cross-border data flows and jurisdictional challenges (Vukovic, et al., 2024). Such responsibilities should include practising appropriate protection measures for data security, to obtain approvals and consents where necessary, as well as processing the protected personal information in accordance with laws (Brini & Lenz, 2024). For building lawful systems that will change alongside the quick development of AI, it is important to combine efforts on part from technologists with legal and policy experts (Afifah et al., 2024). The good news is more solutions are emerging, Marsh says, and the industry will sort out how to discern AI truth from fiction once organizations that follow these approaches to help with liability risk management - as illustrated by what China has done regarding cross-border data transfers thus far (Nia, et al., 2024).

Figure 3. Illuminates the legal inferences (Source- Original)

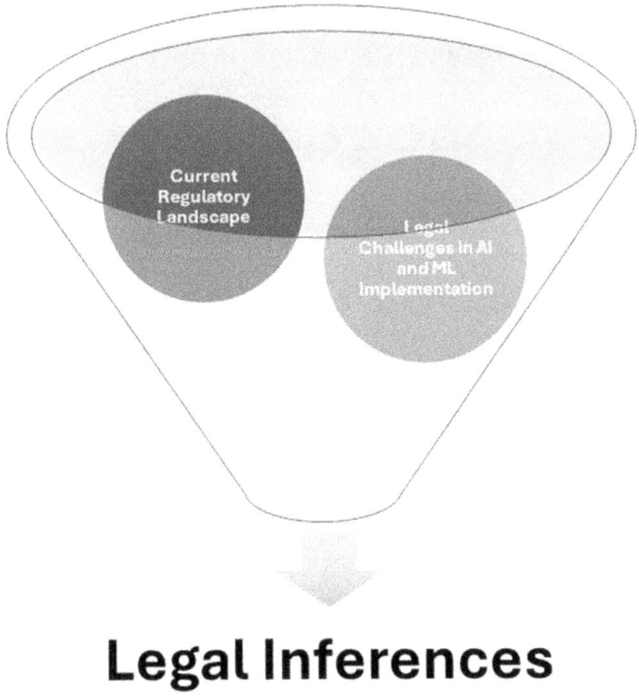

7. CONCLUSION AND FUTURE SCOPE

The rapid progression of artificial intelligence and machine learning technologies has led to a transformation in the way business is conducted, mainly in the e-commerce domain. The innovative approach of integrating emerging technologies has allowed for a better level of customer service, decision-making, efficiency, and risk management. The integration of AI and ML also gives rise to serious legal and ethical concerns which need to be overcome to ensure the responsible and sustainable introduction of the technology. With new legislations and regulations emerging, companies should also consider staying informed about data protection, intellectual property rights and their regulation, accountability, and algorithmic bias. In terms of the technological aspects, it is essential to develop a regulatory sandbox for companies that are developing new products, help companies adopt it, and aid associations to embrace this innovative attitude. It is critical to investigate the feasibility of the idea of a data trusteeship. Even more main changes will be provided through more refined, more precise, and more novel use cases as the technology matures. The ability to reach a more engaging market, use a more reliable and efficient delivery system, and properly analyze the market, among other things, will improve in very creative respects.

REFERENCES

Abdullah, M., Sulong, Z., & Chowdhury, M. A. F. (2024). Explainable deep learning model for stock price forecasting using textual analysis. *Expert Systems with Applications*, 249, 123740. DOI: 10.1016/j.eswa.2024.123740

Afifah, N., Nugraha, N., Purnamasari, I., Supriatna, Y., Rahayu, A., & Wibowo, L. A. (2024, June). Strategic Role of Climate Finance: A Bibliometric Analysis. In *8th Global Conference on Business, Management, and Entrepreneurship (GCBME 2023)* (pp. 141-146). Atlantis Press. DOI: 10.2991/978-94-6463-443-3_21

Ahmed, M. S., El-Masry, A. A., Al-Maghyereh, A. I., & Kumar, S. (2024). Cryptocurrency Volatility: A Review, Synthesis, and Research Agenda. *Research in International Business and Finance*, 71, 102472. DOI: 10.1016/j.ribaf.2024.102472

Brini, A., & Lenz, J. (2024). A comparison of cryptocurrency volatility-benchmarking new and mature asset classes. *Financial Innovation*, 10(1), 122. DOI: 10.1186/s40854-024-00646-y

Cervellati, E. M., Angelini, N., & Stella, G. P. (2024). Behavioral finance and wealth management: Market anomalies, investors' behavior and the role of financial advisors.

Cervellati, E. M., Angelini, N., & Stella, G. P. (2024). Behavioral finance and wealth management: Market anomalies, investors' behavior and the role of financial advisors.

Dimitriadou, A. (2024). *The influence of news and investor sentiment on exchange rate determination: new evidence using panel data in the banking sector* (Doctoral dissertation, College of Business, Law and Social Sciences, University of Derby).

Hussain, S. M., & Alaya, A. (2024). Investor response to financial news in the digital transformation era: The impact of accounting disclosures and herding behavior as indirect effect. *Journal of Financial Reporting and Accounting*, 22(2), 254–273. DOI: 10.1108/JFRA-05-2023-0287

Jagirdar, S. S., & Gupta, P. K. (2024). *Charting the financial odyssey: a literature review on history and evolution of investment strategies in the stock market (1900–2022)*. China Accounting and Finance Review.

Kabir, A. I., Vyas, S., Mitra, S., Uddin, M. M., & Jakowan, J. (2024, March). Evaluating the machine learning based momentum stock trading strategies with back-testing: An emerging market perspective. In *AIP Conference Proceedings* (Vol. 2919, No. 1). AIP Publishing.

Lo, A. W., & Zhang, R. (2024). *The Adaptive Markets Hypothesis: An Evolutionary Approach to Understanding Financial System Dynamics*. Oxford University Press. DOI: 10.1093/oso/9780199681143.001.0001

Manahov, V. (2024). The great crypto crash in September 2018: Why did the cryptocurrency market collapse? *Annals of Operations Research*, 332(1), 579–616. DOI: 10.1007/s10479-023-05575-0

Ncube, M., Sibanda, M., & Matenda, F. R. (2024). Application of Explainable Artificial Intelligence to model the influence of firm-specific factors on stock performance in sub-Saharan Africa during *COVID* 19.

Ni, Y. (2024). Navigating Energy and Financial Markets: A Review of Technical Analysis Used and Further Investigation from Various Perspectives. *Energies*, 17(12), 2942. DOI: 10.3390/en17122942

Nia, V. M., Siregar, H., Sembel, R., & Zulbainarmi, N. (2024). Behavioral Finance in Psycho-Social Approaches: A Literature Review. In *International Conference on Business and Technology* (pp. 311-329). Springer. DOI: 10.1007/978-3-031-53998-5_27

Othman, N. N. (2024). Mind Games in the Market: Unraveling the Impact of Psychological Biases on Your Stock Portfolio. *Available atSSRN* 4844961. DOI: 10.2139/ssrn.4844961

Persakis, A., & Koutoupis, A. (2024). Synchronicity and Sentiment: Decoding Earnings Quality and Market Returns in EU under Economic Policy Uncertainty. *Journal of Behavioral Finance*, 1–21. DOI: 10.1080/15427560.2024.2345342

Raja, E. L., & Messaoudi, A. (2024). Behavioral biases influencing investment decision making in emergent markets: A systematic literature review. *International Journal of Accounting, Finance, Auditing. Management and Economics*, 5(6), 18–39.

Saltık, Ö. (2024). Navigating the Stock Market: Modeling Wealth Exchange and Network Interaction with Loss Aversion, Disposition Effect and Anchoring and Adjustment Bias. *Ekonomi Politika ve Finans Araştırmaları Dergisi*, 9(1), 88–122. DOI: 10.30784/epfad.1435009

Saltik, O., Jalil, F., & Degirmen, S. (2024). Viral decisions: Unmasking the impact of COVID-19 info and behavioral quirks on investment choices. *Humanities & Social Sciences Communications*, 11(1), 1–20.

Shukla, A., Dadhich, M., & Dipesh Vaya, A. G. (2024). Impact of Behavioral Biases on Investors' Stock Trading Decisions: A Comparehensive Quantitative Analysis. *Indian Journal of Science and Technology*, 17(8), 670–678. DOI: 10.17485/IJST/v17i8.2845

Silver, S. D. (2024). Agent expectations and news sentiment in the dynamics of price in a financial market. *Review of Behavioral Finance*, 16(5), 836–859. DOI: 10.1108/RBF-09-2023-0237

Singh, D., Malik, G., Jain, P., & Abouraia, M. (2024). A systematic review and research agenda on the causes and consequences of financial overconfidence. *Cogent Economics & Finance*, 12(1), 2348543. DOI: 10.1080/23322039.2024.2348543

Su, Q., & Deng, Y. (2024). Tax Avoidance News, Investor Behavior, and Stock Market Performance. *Finance Research Letters*, 67, 105834. DOI: 10.1016/j.frl.2024.105834

Talbi, M., Ferchichi, M., Ismaalia, F., & Samil, S. (2024). Resilience Amidst Turbulence: Unraveling COVID-19's Impact on Financial Stability through Price Dynamics and Investor Behavior in GCC Markets. *International Journal of Economics and Finance*, 16(4), 22. DOI: 10.5539/ijef.v16n4p22

Vidani, J. (2024). Why 90% of Stock Market Traders are in Loss? *Available atSSRN* 4849875.

Vukovic, D. B., Kurbonov, O. O., Maiti, M., Özer, M., & Radovanovic, M. (2024). Outperforming the market: A comparison of Star and NonStar analysts' investment strategies and recommendations. *Humanities & Social Sciences Communications*, 11(1), 1–15. DOI: 10.1057/s41599-023-02527-8

Zhu, X., Li, S., Srinivasan, K., & Lash, M. T. (2024). Impact of the COVID-19 pandemic on the stock market and investor online word of mouth. *Decision Support Systems*, 176, 114074. DOI: 10.1016/j.dss.2023.114074

ADDITIONAL READING

Abdullah, M., Sulong, Z., & Chowdhury, M. A. F. (2024). Explainable deep learning model for stock price forecasting using textual analysis. *Expert Systems with Applications*, 249, 123740. DOI: 10.1016/j.eswa.2024.123740

Ahmed, M. S., El-Masry, A. A., Al-Maghyereh, A. I., & Kumar, S. (2024). Cryptocurrency Volatility: A Review, Synthesis, and Research Agenda. *Research in International Business and Finance*, 71, 102472. DOI: 10.1016/j.ribaf.2024.102472

Cervellati, E. M., Angelini, N., & Stella, G. P. (2024). Behavioral finance and wealth management: Market anomalies, investors' behavior and the role of financial advisors.

Ni, Y. (2024). Navigating Energy and Financial Markets: A Review of Technical Analysis Used and Further Investigation from Various Perspectives. *Energies*, 17(12), 2942. DOI: 10.3390/en17122942

Othman, N. N. (2024). Mind Games in the Market: Unraveling the Impact of Psychological Biases on Your Stock Portfolio. *Available atSSRN* 4844961. DOI: 10.2139/ssrn.4844961

Saltik, O., Jalil, F., & Degirmen, S. (2024). Viral decisions: Unmasking the impact of COVID-19 info and behavioral quirks on investment choices. *Humanities & Social Sciences Communications*, 11(1), 1–20.

Shukla, A., Dadhich, M., & Dipesh Vaya, A. G. (2024). Impact of Behavioral Biases on Investors' Stock Trading Decisions: A Comparehensive Quantitative Analysis. *Indian Journal of Science and Technology*, 17(8), 670–678. DOI: 10.17485/IJST/v17i8.2845

Su, Q., & Deng, Y. (2024). Tax Avoidance News, Investor Behavior, and Stock Market Performance. *Finance Research Letters*, 67, 105834. DOI: 10.1016/j.frl.2024.105834

Talbi, M., Ferchichi, M., Ismaalia, F., & Samil, S. (2024). Resilience Amidst Turbulence: Unraveling COVID-19's Impact on Financial Stability through Price Dynamics and Investor Behavior in GCC Markets. *International Journal of Economics and Finance*, 16(4), 22. DOI: 10.5539/ijef.v16n4p22

Zhu, X., Li, S., Srinivasan, K., & Lash, M. T. (2024). Impact of the COVID-19 pandemic on the stock market and investor online word of mouth. *Decision Support Systems*, 176, 114074. DOI: 10.1016/j.dss.2023.114074

Compilation of References

Aaker, D. A. (1991). *Managing brand equity: Capitalizing on the value of a brand name*. Free Press.

Abdullah, M., Sulong, Z., & Chowdhury, M. A. F. (2024). Explainable deep learning model for stock price forecasting using textual analysis. *Expert Systems with Applications*, 249, 123740. DOI: 10.1016/j.eswa.2024.123740

Abovitz, R., Banerjee, S., Gilliland, G., Liu, C., Sackey, E., Timashkov, A., & Trollinger, R. (2022). How the Metaverse Will Remake Your Strategy. Boston Consulting Group. https://mkt-bcg-com-public-pdfs.s3.amazonaws.com/prod/impact-of-metaverse-on-business.pdf

Abrash, M. (2021). Creating the Future: Augmented Reality, the next Human-Machine Interface. *IEEE International Electron Devices Meeting*.

Abumalloh, R. A., Nilashi, M., Ooi, K. B., Wei-Han, G., Cham, T. H., Dwivedi, Y. K., & Hughes, L. (2023). The adoption of metaverse in the retail industry and its impact on sustainable competitive advantage: Moderating impact of sustainability commitment. *Annals of Operations Research*, 342(1), 5–46. DOI: 10.1007/s10479-023-05608-8

Accenture. (2022). Metaverse masters? Expect the unexpected. https://www.accenture.com/content/dam/accenture/final/accenture-com/document/Accenture-Growth-Markets-Metaverse-POV-June2.pdf

Accenture. (2023). Metaverse Enterprise Consulting Services & Solutions. https://www.accenture.com/in-en/services/metaverse

Afifah, N., Nugraha, N., Purnamasari, I., Supriatna, Y., Rahayu, A., & Wibowo, L. A. (2024, June). Strategic Role of Climate Finance: A Bibliometric Analysis. In *8th Global Conference on Business, Management, and Entrepreneurship (GCBME 2023)* (pp. 141-146). Atlantis Press. DOI: 10.2991/978-94-6463-443-3_21

Afrashtehfar, K. I., & Abu-Fanas, A. S. (2022). Metaverse, crypto, and NFTs in dentistry. *Education Sciences*, 12(8), 538. DOI: 10.3390/educsci12080538

Ahmed, M. S., El-Masry, A. A., Al-Maghyereh, A. I., & Kumar, S. (2024). Cryptocurrency Volatility: A Review, Synthesis, and Research Agenda. *Research in International Business and Finance*, 71, 102472. DOI: 10.1016/j.ribaf.2024.102472

Ahmed, Z., Mohamed, K., Zeeshan, S., & Dong, X. (2020). Artificial intelligence with multi-functional machine learning platform development for better healthcare and precision medicine. *Database : The Journal of Biological Databases and Curation*, 2020, baaa010. DOI: 10.1093/database/baaa010 PMID: 32185396

Akyürek, S., Genç, G., Çalık, İ., & Şengel, Ü. (2024). Metaverse in tourism education: A mixed method on vision, challenges and extended technology acceptance model. *Journal of Hospitality, Leisure, Sport and Tourism Education, 35*. DOI: 10.1016/j.jhlste.2024.100503

Alfaisal, R., Hashim, H., & Azizan, U. H. (2022). Metaverse system adoption in education: a systematic literature review. In *Journal of Computers in Education* (Issue 0123456789). Springer Berlin Heidelberg. DOI: 10.1007/s40692-022-00256-6

Alfaisal, R., Hashim, H., & Azizan, U. H. (2024). *Empowering the Metaverse in Education: ChatGPT's Role in Transforming Learning Experiences* (pp. 13–31). DOI: 10.1007/978-3-031-65996-6_2

Al-Ghaili, A. M., Kasim, H., Al-Hada, N. M., Hassan, Z. B., Othman, M., Tharik, J. H., Kasmani, R. M., & Shayea, I. (2022). A review of Metaverse's definitions, architecture, applications, challenges, issues, solutions, and future trends. *IEEE Access : Practical Innovations, Open Solutions*, 10, 125835–125866. DOI: 10.1109/ACCESS.2022.3225638

Alic, A., Agic, E., & Činjarević, M. (2017). The Importance of Store Image and Retail Service Quality in Private Brand Image-Building. *Entrepreneurial Business and Economics Review*, 5(1), 27–42. DOI: 10.15678/EBER.2017.050102

Almarzouqi, A., Aburayya, A., & Salloum, S. A. (2022). Prediction of user's intention to use metaverse system in medical education: A hybrid SEM-ML learning approach. *IEEE Access : Practical Innovations, Open Solutions*, 10, 43421–43434. DOI: 10.1109/ACCESS.2022.3169285

Almousa, O., Prates, J., Yeslam, N., Mac Gregor, D., Zhang, J., Phan, V., Nielsen, M., Smith, R., & Qayumi, K. (2019). Virtual reality simulation technology for cardiopulmonary resuscitation training: An innovative hybrid system with haptic feedback. *Simulation & Gaming*, 50(1), 6–22. DOI: 10.1177/1046878118820905

Alshamrani, M. (2022). IoT and artificial intelligence implementations for remote healthcare monitoring systems: A survey. *Journal of King Saud University. Computer and Information Sciences*, 34(8), 4687–4701. DOI: 10.1016/j.jksuci.2021.06.005

Alshurideh, M. T., Alzoubi, H. M., Akour, I. A., Al Kurdi, B., & Hamadneh, S. (2023). Impact of metaverse and marketing innovation on digital transformation. *IEEE ICBATS*, 2023, 1–5. Advance online publication. DOI: 10.1109/ICBATS57792.2023.10111241

Al-Zyoud, I., Laamarti, F., Ma, X., Tobón, D., & El Saddik, A. (2022). Towards a machine learning-based digital twin for non-invasive human bio-signal fusion. *Sensors (Basel)*, 22(24), 9747. DOI: 10.3390/s22249747 PMID: 36560115

Ampountolas, A., Menconi, G., & Shaw, G. (2024). Metaverse research propositions: Online intermediaries. *Tourism Economics*, 30(1), 255–261. DOI: 10.1177/13548166231159520

Andrae, A. S. G., & Edler, T. (2015). On global electricity usage of communication technology: Trends to 2030. *Challenges*, 6(1), 117–157. DOI: 10.3390/challe6010117

Anselmsson, J., Burt, S., & Tunca, B. (2017). An integrated retailer image and brand equity framework: Re-examining, extending, and restructuring retailer brand equity. *Journal of Retailing and Consumer Services*, 38, 194–203. DOI: 10.1016/j.jretconser.2017.06.007

Ante, L. (2022). The Non-Fungible Token (NFT) Market and Its Relationship with Bitcoin and Ethereum. MDPI. https://www.mdpi.com/2674-1032/1/3/17

Anwer, A., Jamil, Y., & Bilal, M. (2022). Provision of surgical pre-operative patient counseling services through the metaverse technology. *International Journal of Surgery*, 104, 106792. DOI: 10.1016/j.ijsu.2022.106792 PMID: 35918004

AR, S., Katiravan, D. J., & Kumar, K. M. (2024). *METACOMMERCE360 pioneering the future of e-commerce in the boundless metaverse landscape*.

Arantes, J. (2024). Digital twins and the terminology of "personalization" or "personalized learning" in educational policy: A discussion paper. *Policy Futures in Education*, 22(4), 524–543. DOI: 10.1177/14782103231176357

Arora, M. (2022, November 21). The rise of virtual influencers: Another level of branding. *The Times of India Blogs*. Retrieved May 27, 2023, from https://timesofindia.indiatimes.com/blogs/voices/the-rise-of-virtual-influencers-another-level-of-branding/?source=app&frmapp=yes

Atsikpasi, P., & Fokides, E. (2022). A scoping review of the educational uses of 6DoF HMDs. *Virtual Reality (Waltham Cross)*, 26(1), 205–222. DOI: 10.1007/s10055-021-00556-9

Avara, H. (2023). *The art of teaching English in the 21st century settings.*

Aziz, O., Farooq, M. S., Khelifi, A., & Shoaib, M. (2024). Archaeometa: Leveraging blockchain for secure and scalable virtual museums in the Metaverse. *Heritage Science*, 12(1), 308. DOI: 10.1186/s40494-024-01416-w

Azuma, R. T. (1997). A Survey of Augmented Reality. Presence. *Teleoperators and Virtual Environments.*

Azuma, R., Baillot, Y., Behringer, R., Feiner, S., Julier, S., & MacIntyre, B. (2001). Recent advances in augmented reality. *IEEE Computer Graphics and Applications*, 21(6), 34–47. DOI: 10.1109/38.963459

Bag, S., Shrivastav, S. K., Rahman, M. S., & Srivastava, G. (2023). Unveiling metaverse potential in supply chain management and overcoming implementation challenges: An empirical study. *Benchmarking*, 32(11), 79–108. Advance online publication. DOI: 10.1108/BIJ-05-2023-0314

Bálint, K. (2024). The Possibility of Creating an NFT (Non-Fungible Token) Based University Diploma. https://ieeexplore.ieee.org/stamp/stamp.jsp?tp=&arnumber=10432827

Ball, M. (2022). *The Metaverse: And How it Will Revolutionize Everything*. WW Norton. https://books.google.pt/books?id=fPyqzgEACAAJ

Ball, M. (2022). *The metaverse: And how it will revolutionize everything*. Liveright Publishing. DOI: 10.15358/9783800669400

Bansal, G., Rajgopal, K., Chamola, V., Xiong, Z., & Niyato, D. (2022). Healthcare in metaverse: A survey on current metaverse applications in healthcare. *IEEE Access : Practical Innovations, Open Solutions*, 10, 119914–119946. DOI: 10.1109/ACCESS.2022.3219845

Bapatla, N., Fine, L., & Rajput, V. (2021). The future role of augmented reality and virtual reality simulation in clinical skills assessment. *Indian Journal of Medical Specialities*, 12(3), 113–115. DOI: 10.4103/injms.injms_41_21

Bar-El, D., & Ringland, E., K. (2020). Crafting Game-Based Learning: An Analysis of Lessons for Minecraft Education Edition. *International Conference on the Foundations of Digital Games*, 1–4. DOI: 10.1145/3402942.3409788

Barnea, U. M. (2023). The effects of content ephemerality on information processing. *ournal of Marketing Research*, 60(4), 750-766.

Barrera, K. G. (2023). Marketing in the Metaverse: Conceptual understanding, framework, and research agenda. *Journal of Business Research*, 155, 113420. DOI: 10.1016/j.jbusres.2022.113420

Bartle, R. A. (2004). *Designing virtual worlds*. New Riders.

Bartolotta, S., Gaggioli, A., & Riva, G. (2023). The META-Learning Project: Design and Evaluation of an Experiential-Learning Intervention in the Metaverse for Soft Skills Improvement. *Cyberpsychology, Behavior, and Social Networking*, 26(3), 221–224. DOI: 10.1089/cyber.2023.29268.ceu PMID: 36827312

Basyoni, L., Tabassum, A., Shaban, K., Elmahjub, E., Halabi, O., & Qadir, J. (2024). Navigating Privacy Challenges in the Metaverse: A Comprehensive Examination of Current Technologies and Platforms. *IEEE Internet of Things Magazine*, 7(4), 144–152. DOI: 10.1109/IOTM.001.2300197

Batat, W. (2024). Phygital customer experience in the metaverse: A study of consumer sensory perception of sight, touch, sound, scent, and taste. *Journal of Retailing and Consumer Services*, 78, 103786. DOI: 10.1016/j.jretconser.2024.103786

Bathla, D., & Singh, A. (Eds.). (2022). *Applying metalytics to measure customer experience in the metaverse*. IGI Global. DOI: 10.4018/978-1-6684-6133-4

Baxter, G., & Hainey, T. (2024). Using immersive technologies to enhance the student learning experience. *Interactive Technology and Smart Education*, 21(3), 403–425. DOI: 10.1108/ITSE-05-2023-0078

Beck, J., & Egger, R. (2018). *Tourism and technology: An integrated framework for sustainable tourism development*. Springer.

Beck, J., Egger, R., & Buhalis, D. (2019). Virtual reality and the tourism experience: Innovation, disruption, and opportunities. *Journal of Tourism Futures*, 5(3), 300–318.

Belk, R. W. (2013). Extended self in a digital world. *The Journal of Consumer Research*, 40(3), 477–500. DOI: 10.1086/671052

Bente, G. R., Rüggenberg, S., Krämer, N. C., & Eschenburg, F. (2008). Avatar-mediated networking: Increasing social presence and interpersonal trust in net-based collaborations. *Human Communication Research*, 34(2), 287–318. DOI: 10.1111/j.1468-2958.2008.00322.x

Berndtsson, I., Dahlborg, E., & Pennbrant, S. (2020). Work-integrated learning as a pedagogical tool to integrate theory and practice in nursing education – An integrative literature review. *Nurse Education in Practice*, 42, 102685. DOI: 10.1016/j.nepr.2019.102685 PMID: 31841809

Bhandari, P. (2023). What Is Qualitative Research? | Methods & Examples. https://www.scribbr.com/methodology/qualitative-research/

Bhattacharya, P., Saraswat, D., Savaliya, D., Sanghavi, S., Verma, A., Sakariya, V., Tanwar, S., Sharma, R., Raboaca, M. S., & Manea, D. L. (2023). Towards Future Internet: The Metaverse Perspective for Diverse Industrial Applications. *Mathematics*, 11(4), 941. Advance online publication. DOI: 10.3390/math11040941

Bhugaonkar, K., Bhugaonkar, R., & Masne, N. (2022). The trend of metaverse and augmented & virtual reality extending to the healthcare system. *Cureus*, 14(9). Advance online publication. DOI: 10.7759/cureus.29071 PMID: 36258985

Bimber, O. (2005). *Spatial augmented reality: merging real and virtual worlds*. AK Peters. DOI: 10.1201/b10624

Boffi, P., Clerici, M., Gallace, A., & Lanzi, P. L. (2023). An educational experience in ancient Rome to evaluate the impact of virtual reality on human learning processes. *Computers & Education: X Reality, 2*, 100014. DOI: 10.1016/j.cexr.2023.100014

Bojic, L. (2022). Metaverse through the prism of power and addiction: What will happen when the virtual world becomes more attractive than reality? *European Journal of Futures Research*, 10(1), 22. Advance online publication. DOI: 10.1186/s40309-022-00208-4

Bolger, R. K. (2021). Finding wholes in the metaverse: Posthuman mystics as agents of evolutionary contextualization. *Religions*, 12(9), 768. DOI: 10.3390/rel12090768

Bolton, R. N., Gustafsson, A., Tarasi, C. O., & Witell, L. (2022). Designing satisfying service encounters: Website versus store touchpoints. *Journal of the Academy of Marketing Science*, 50(1), 85–107. DOI: 10.1007/s11747-021-00808-9 PMID: 34608342

Bonetti, F. (2018). The role of virtual events in the metaverse and hospitality industry. *International Journal of Hospitality Management*, 69, 35–42.

Bonetti, F., Alvino, F., & Gatti, C. (2018). Virtual reality and its use in the hospitality industry: A review of current research and implications for future tourism. *Journal of Hospitality and Tourism Technology*, 9(4), 461–477.

Bonetti, F., Warnaby, G., & Quinn, L. (2018). Augmented Reality and Virtual Reality in Physical and Online Retailing: A Review, Synthesis and Research Agenda. In Jung, T., & tom Dieck, M. C. (Eds.), *Augmented Reality and Virtual Reality: Empowering Human, Place and Business* (pp. 119–132). Springer International Publishing. DOI: 10.1007/978-3-319-64027-3_9

Botezatu, U. E., & Ciupercă, E. M. (2023). Expanding the virtual learning horizons: the case of Galileo and Copernicus space-based technologies and services. *Proceedings of the International Conference on Virtual Learning - Virtual Learning - Virtual Reality (18th Edition)*, 27–42. DOI: 10.58503/icvl-v18y202302

Bourlakis, M. P. (2009). *Retail spatial evolution: paving the way from traditional to metaverse retailing.*

Bourlakis, M. P., Papagiannidis, S., & Li, F. (2009). Retail spatial evolution: Paving the way from traditional to metaverse retailing. *Electronic Commerce Research*, 9(1-2), 135–148. DOI: 10.1007/s10660-009-9030-8

Bowman, D. A., & McMahan, R. P. (2007). Virtual Reality: How Much Immersion Is Enough? *Computer*, 40(7), 36–43. DOI: 10.1109/MC.2007.257

Bringé, A. (2022, October 18). The rise of virtual influencers and what it means for brands. *Forbes*. Retrieved from https://www.forbes.com/sites/forbescommunicationscouncil/2022/10/18/the-rise-of-virtual-influencers-and-what-it-means-for-brands/?sh=629fceaa6b56

Brini, A., & Lenz, J. (2024). A comparison of cryptocurrency volatility-benchmarking new and mature asset classes. *Financial Innovation*, 10(1), 122. DOI: 10.1186/s40854-024-00646-y

Brochado, A., Stoleriu, O., & Lupu, C. (2021). Wine tourism: A multisensory experience. *Current Issues in Tourism*, 24(5), 597–615. DOI: 10.1080/13683500.2019.1649373

Bruni, R., Colamatteo, A., & Mladenović, D. (2023). How the metaverse influences marketing and competitive advantage of retailers: Predictions and key marketing research priorities. *Electronic Commerce Research*, 24(2), 965–982. DOI: 10.1007/s10660-023-09779-1

Bruwer, J., & Rueger-Muck, E. (2019). Wine tourism and hedonic experience: A motivation-based experiential view. *Tourism and Hospitality Research*, 19(4), 488–502. DOI: 10.1177/1467358418781444

Brynjolfsson, E., & McAfee, A. (2014). *The Second Machine Age: Work, Progress, and Prosperity in a Time of Brilliant Technologies*. W.W. Norton & Company.

Buchholz, F., Oppermann, L., & Prinz, W. (2022). There's more than one metaverse. *i-com, 21*(3), 313–324.

Buhalis, D., & Law, R. (2008). Progress in information technology and tourism management: 20 years on and 10 years after the internet—the state of eTourism research. *Tourism Management*, 29(4), 609–623. DOI: 10.1016/j.tourman.2008.01.005

Buhalis, D., Leung, D., & Lin, M. C. (2023). Metaverse as a disruptive technology revolutionising tourism management and marketing. *Tourism Management*, 97, 104724. Advance online publication. DOI: 10.1016/j.tourman.2023.104724

Buhalis, D., & Leung, R. (2018). Technology in hospitality: Digitalization and innovation. *International Journal of Contemporary Hospitality Management*, 30(12), 3367–3387.

Buhalis, D., Lin, M. S., & Leung, D. (2021). Metaverse as a driver for immersive tourism experiences: A transformative perspective. *Tourism Review*, 76(5), 1019–1033.

Buhalis, D., & Sinarta, Y. (2019). Real-time co-creation and experience in tourism and hospitality. *Journal of Travel Research*, 58(3), 271–282.

Business Wire. (2022). Accenture Technology Vision 2022: "Metaverse Continuum" Redefining How the World Works, Operates and Interacts. https://www.businesswire.com/news/home/20220315006355/en/

Canavarro, A., & Moreira, B. (2024). *Metaverso no Marketing, nas Marcas e nos Negócios*. Grupo LIDEL.

Candelon, F., Jacobides, M. G., Courtaux, M., & Nahas, G. (2022). How to take a strategic approach to investing in metaverses. 28th November. *World Economic Forum*. Retrieved 21th January 2024, from https://www.weforum.org/stories/2022/11/how-to-a-take-a-strategic-to-approach-to-investing-in-metaverses/

Cannavo, A., & Lamberti, F. (2020). How blockchain, virtual reality, and augmented reality are converging, and why. *IEEE Consumer Electronics Magazine*, 10(5), 6–13. DOI: 10.1109/MCE.2020.3025753

Cao, Y. (2023). Microsoft's Layout in the Gaming Industry and Metaverse: Starting from Blizzard. *Advances in Economics. Management and Political Sciences*, 36(1), 99–103. DOI: 10.54254/2754-1169/36/20231791

Carlos, A. R., & Muralles, D. C. (2021). Onboarding in the age of COVID-19. *IFLA Journal*. Advance online publication. DOI: 10.1177/03400352211035413

Carter, R. (2023). What is Nike's Metaverse? *An Introduction to Nikeland.* Retrieved 15th October 2024, from https://www.xrtoday.com/mixed-reality/what-is-nikes-metaverse-an-introduction-to-nikeland/

Castells, M. (2010). *The Rise of the Network Society* (2nd ed.). Wiley-Blackwell.

Castenetto, C. (2022). Redefining fashion ecommerce: A comprehensive study on the transformative impact of technologies on user experience.

Cavusoglu, H., Hameed, S. M., & Iyer, B. (2015). Regulation of personal data in the digital age. *Journal of Information Privacy and Security*, 11(3), 23–44.

Cervellati, E. M., Angelini, N., & Stella, G. P. (2024). Behavioral finance and wealth management: Market anomalies, investors' behavior and the role of financial advisors.

Chakraborty, U., & Biswal, S. K. (2024). Diffusion of innovation in direct-to-avatar (D2A): A study of immersive communication and branding in the metaverse. *Computers in Human Behavior*, 158, 108318. DOI: 10.1016/j.chb.2024.108318

Chamola, V., Hassija, V., Gupta, S., Goyal, A., Guizani, M., & Sikdar, B. (2020). Disaster and pandemic management using machine learning: A survey. *IEEE Internet of Things Journal*, 8(21), 16047–16071. DOI: 10.1109/JIOT.2020.3044966 PMID: 35782181

Chan, K. (2023). *Metaverse: What are the economic benefits?* World Economic Forum. https://www.weforum.org/stories/2023/06/what-will-be-the-economic-benefits-of-the-metaverse/

Chanda, R. S., Pabalkar, V., & Sharma, S. (2024). Attitude and behavioral intention for using metaverse in education: Learner's perspective. *Journal of Applied Research in Higher Education*, 16(5), 2168–2184. Advance online publication. DOI: 10.1108/JARHE-07-2023-0307

Chandra, Y. (2022). Non-fungible token-enabled entrepreneurship: A conceptual Framework. Elsevier. https://www.sciencedirect.com/science/article/pii/S235267342200021X?via%3Dihub

Charters, S., & Ali-Knight, J. (2002). Who is the wine tourist? *Tourism Management*, 23(3), 311–319. DOI: 10.1016/S0261-5177(01)00079-6

Chaudhuri, A., Titus, R., & Chaudhuri, A. (2024). Impact of technology on customer experience in the metaverse era. *Journal of Management and Public Policy*, 15(4), 28–47.

Chaves, M. Z., Frio, R. S., Pereira, E. F. Z.Jr, & Lunardi, G. L. (2024). *Metaverse and its commercial applications: Opportunities and challenges for companies.* Revista e-TECH. DOI: 10.18624/etech.v17i1.1304

Chen, A. H., Wu, R.Y. (2022). Mediating Effect of Brand Image and Satisfaction on Loyalty through Experiential Marketing: A Case Study of a Sugar Heritage Destination. *Sustainability*, 14.

Chen, A., Mari, S., Grech, S., & Levitt, J. (2020). What We Know About Massively Multiplayer Online Role-Playing Games. *Harvard Review of Psychiatry*, 28(2), 107–112. DOI: 10.1097/HRP.0000000000000247 PMID: 32134835

Chengoden, R., Victor, N., Huynh-The, T., Yenduri, G., Jhaveri, R. H., Alazab, M., Bhattacharya, S., Hegde, P., Maddikunta, P. K. R., & Gadekallu, T. R. (2023). Metaverse for healthcare: A survey on potential applications, challenges and future directions. *IEEE Access : Practical Innovations, Open Solutions*, 11, 12765–12795. DOI: 10.1109/ACCESS.2023.3241628

Cheng, S. (2023). Metaverse. In *Metaverse: Concept, Content and Context* (pp. 1–23). Springer Nature Switzerland.

Chen, X., Zhong, Z., & Wu, D. (2023). Metaverse for Education: Technical Framework and Design Criteria. *IEEE Transactions on Learning Technologies*, 16(6), 1034–1044. DOI: 10.1109/TLT.2023.3276760

Chen, X., Zou, D., Xie, H., & Wang, F. L. (2023). Metaverse in Education: Contributors, Cooperations, and Research Themes. *IEEE Transactions on Learning Technologies*, 16(6), 1111–1129. DOI: 10.1109/TLT.2023.3277952

Chen, Y., & Cheng, H. (2022). *The economics of the metaverse: A comparison with the real economy*. Metaverse.

Cheok, A. D. (2018). Virtual taste and smell technologies for multisensory internet and virtual reality. Springer.

Cheremnykh, P. (2024). *Gaming the Metaverse: user experience analysis and insights from Fortnite* Metropolia University of Applied Sciences]. https://www.theseus.fi/handle/10024/850495

Chesney, T. C., Coyne, I., Logan, B., & Madden, N. (2009). Griefing in virtual worlds: Causes, casualties and coping strategies. *Information Systems Journal*, 19(6), 525–548. DOI: 10.1111/j.1365-2575.2009.00330.x

Chiu, T. K. F., Sun, J. C.-Y., & Ismailov, M. (2022). Investigating the relationship of technology learning support to digital literacy from the perspective of self-determination theory. *Educational Psychology*, 42(10), 1263–1282. DOI: 10.1080/01443410.2022.2074966

Chohan, U. W. (2024). Non-Fungible Tokens (NFTs): Early Thoughts & A Research Agenda. *SSRN.*

Cho, M. G. (2022). A study on smart aging system for the elderly based on metaverse. *Journal of Digital Convergence*, 20(2), 261–268.

Chowdhury, R. (2023). The Metaverse Will Transform Existing Brand Marketing Strategies. O https://www.prweb.com/releases/the-metaverse-will-transform-existing-brand-marketing-strategies-raj-chowdhury-894680040.html

Christensen, L., & Robinson, A. (2022). *The potential global economic impact of the metaverse.* Analysis Group. https://www.analysisgroup.com/globalassets/insights/publishing/2022-the-potential-global-economic-impact-of-the-metaverse.pdf

Christopoulos, A. M., Mystakidis, S., Pellas, N., & Laakso, M.-J. (2021). ARLEAN: An augmented reality learning analytics ethical framework. *Computers*, 10(8), 92. DOI: 10.3390/computers10080092

Chu, N. H., Hoang, D. T., Nguyen, D. N., Phan, K. T., Dutkiewicz, E., Niyato, D., & Shu, T. (2023). Metaslicing: A novel resource allocation framework for metaverse. *IEEE Transactions on Mobile Computing*, 23(5), 4145–4162. DOI: 10.1109/TMC.2023.3288085

Chung, N., Han, H., & Lee, M. (2021). Virtual reality and the metaverse in hotel visits and reservations. *International Journal of Hospitality Management*, 97, 103–113.

Cipresso, P. G., Giglioli, I. A. C., Raya, M. A., & Riva, G. (2018). The past, present, and future of virtual and augmented reality research: A network and cluster analysis of the literature. *Frontiers in Psychology*, 9, 2086. DOI: 10.3389/fpsyg.2018.02086 PMID: 30459681

Clark, T., Foster, L., Bryman, A., & Sloan, L. (2021). *Bryman's social research methods.* Oxford University Press.

Clement, J. (2024). *Registered users of Fortnite worldwide from August 2017 to March 2023.* Statista. Retrieved 22 September 2024 from https://www.statista.com/statistics/746230/fortnite-players/

Çöltekin, A., Lochhead, I., Madden, M., Christophe, S., Devaux, A., Pettit, C., Lock, O., Shukla, S., Herman, L., Stachoň, Z., Kubíček, P., Snopková, D., Bernardes, S., & Hedley, N. (2020). Extended reality in spatial sciences: A review of research challenges and future directions. *ISPRS International Journal of Geo-Information*, 9(7), 439. DOI: 10.3390/ijgi9070439

Connect, H. R. D. (2023). How Accenture's enterprise metaverse has elevated employee onboarding. https://www.hrdconnect.com/casestudy/how-accentures-enterprise-metaverse-has-elevated-employee-onboarding/

Constantin, M., Genovese, G., Munawar, K., & Stone, R. (2023). *Tourism in the metaverse: Can travel go virtual?* McKinsey & Company. https://www.mckinsey.com/industries/travel-logistics-and-infrastructure/our-insights/tourism-in-the-metaverse-can-travel-go-virtual

Coulter, J. (2023). Using E-Textiles to Challenge Gender Perceptions in STEM, Design and Career Aspirations of Secondary School Students. *Journal of Textile Design Research and Practice*, 11(1–2), 168–193. DOI: 10.1080/20511787.2023.2209960

Crespo-Pereira, V., Sánchez-Amboage, E., & Membiela-Pollán, M. (2023). Facing the challenges of metaverse: a systematic literature review from Social Sciences and Marketing and Communication. Profesional de la informació́n. https://revista.profesionaldelainformacion.com/index.php/EPI/article/view/87104/63308

Crespo-Pereira, V., Sánchez-Amboage, E., & Membiela-Pollán, M. (2023). Facing the challenges of metaverse: a systematic literature review from Social Sciences and Marketing and Communication. Profesional de la informació́n/Information Professional, 32(1). DOI: 10.3145/epi.2023.ene.02

Crews, T., Goodwin, C., Rowe, S., & Olmeta-Schult, F. (2023). The Quest to Support Community Resilience in the Face of Coastal Hazards and Natural Disasters. *Current: The Journal of Marine Education*, 37(2), 3–7. DOI: 10.5334/cjme.81

Cui, J., Yin, M., Wang, P., & Kuang, T. (2023). Impact of digital transformation on corporate innovation: Empirical evidence from public companies. SHS Web of Conferences. DOI: 10.1051/shsconf/202316901046

Cui, Y., & van Esch, P. (2024). A sip in the Metaverse: How to implement a multisensory vineyard. *Journal of Wine Research*, 35(2), 160–178. DOI: 10.1080/09571264.2023.2254248

Cummings, J. J., & Bailenson, J. N. (2016). How immersive is enough? A meta-analysis of the effect of immersive technology on user presence. *Media Psychology*, 19(2), 272–309. DOI: 10.1080/15213269.2015.1015740

Cuong, D. T. (2022). The Relationship Between Product Quality, Brand Image, Purchase Decision, and Repurchase Intention. *Proceedings of International Conference on Emerging Technologies and Intelligent Systems. ICETIS 2021. Lecture Notes in Networks and Systems*, 299. DOI: 10.1007/978-3-030-82616-1_44

Damar, M. (2021). Metaverse Shape of Your Life for Future: A bibliometric snapshot. *Journal of Metaverse*, 1(1), 1–8.

Davis, A. M., Murphy, J., Owens, D., Khazanchi, D., & Zigurs, I. (2009). Avatars, people, and virtual worlds: Foundations for research in metaverses. *Journal of the Association for Information Systems*, 10(2), 1. DOI: 10.17705/1jais.00183

De Vigan, A. (2022). Stepping Into the Metaverse: How Retailers can Prepare. *Forbes Technology Council*. Retrieved 20th January 2025, from https://www.forbes.com/councils/forbestechcouncil/2022/11/16/stepping-into-the-metaverse-how-retailers-can-prepare/

Deavours, D. (2023). Virtual Allies: Why Allyship is Critical to Diversification of Virtual Reality Gaming? *Games and Culture*, 0(0), 15554120231208406. Advance online publication. DOI: 10.1177/15554120231208406

Delmerico, J. P., Poranne, R., Bogo, F., Oleynikova, H., Vollenweider, E., Coros, S., Nieto, J., & Pollefeys, M. (2022). Spatial computing and intuitive interaction: Bringing mixed reality and robotics together. *IEEE Robotics & Automation Magazine*, 29(1), 45–57. DOI: 10.1109/MRA.2021.3138384

Deloitte. (2023, April). *The Metaverse in Asia: Strategies for accelerating economic impact*. Deloitte. Retrieved June 1, 2023, from https://www2.deloitte.com/content/dam/Deloitte/sg/Documents/center-for-the-edge/sg-metaverse-in-asia-deloitte-center-for-the-edge-apr2023.pdf

Demiris, G., Oliver, D. P., & Washington, K. T. (2018). *Behavioral intervention research in hospice and palliative care: Building an evidence base*. Academic press.

Denisova, A. L., & Lopatnikov, A. N. (2022). Digital transformation and corporate strategy. Management (Russia). DOI: 10.26425/2309-3633-2022-10-2-71-79

Di Paolo, F., Bettiga, D., & Lamberti, L. (2025). Leveraging social capital for destination promotion in the metaverse: The Enoverse case. *Tourism Management*, 107, 105072. DOI: 10.1016/j.tourman.2024.105072

Digest, H. (2022). The Metaverse Will Transform Existing Brand Marketing Strategies: Raj Chowdhury. CISION PRWeb. https://www.prweb.com/releases/the-metaverse-will-transform-existing-brand-marketing-strategies-raj-chowdhury-894680040.html

Dimitriadou, A. (2024). *The influence of news and investor sentiment on exchange rate determination: new evidence using panel data in the banking sector* (Doctoral dissertation, College of Business, Law and Social Sciences, University of Derby).

Dinh, T. L. H. (2023). Customer behaviors toward metaverse/metaverse as a stimulus for customer experience: Implications for marketing.

Diogo, J., & Veiga, P. M. (2022). Metaverse applications in business: A systematic literature review and integrative framework. Implementing Automation Initiatives in Companies to Create Better-Connected Experiences, 110-136. DOI: 10.4018/978-1-6684-5538-8.ch006

Dionisio, J. D. (2013). 3D virtual worlds and the metaverse: Current status and future possibilities. *ACM Computing Surveys*, 45(3), 1-38.

Dionisio, J. D. N., III, W. G. B., & Gilbert, R. (2013). 3D Virtual worlds and the Metaverse. *ACM Computing Surveys, 45*(3), 1–38. DOI: 10.1145/2480741.2480751

Dionisio, J. D. N., Iii, W. G. B., & Gilbert, R. (2013). 3D virtual worlds and the metaverse: Current status and future possibilities. ACM computing surveys (CSUR), 45(3), 1-38. https://dl.acm.org/doi/abs/10.1145/2480741.2480751

Dixie, M. A. (2020). Investigação Qualitativa. Politécnico de Leiria. https://iconline.ipleiria.pt/bitstream/10400.8/5250/1/Manual%20de%20apoio_Investiga%c3%a7%c3%a3o%20II_Qualitativa_Silvia_silva_FINAL_alunos_29.09.2020.pdf

Donvito, R., Acuti, D., & Song, S. (2024). Fashion and the metaverse: Implications for consumers and firms. *Journal of Global Fashion Marketing*, 15(1), 1–5. DOI: 10.1080/20932685.2023.2293290

Dreamson, N., & Park, G. (2023). Metaverse-Based Learning Through Children's School Space Design. *International Journal of Art & Design Education*, 42(1), 125–138. DOI: 10.1111/jade.12449

Dredge, D., & Gyimóthy, S. (2015). The collaborative economy and the tourism industry: Critical perspectives, sound theoretical frameworks, and the need for new research. *Annals of Tourism Research*, 58, 61–70.

Du, H., Niyato, D., Miao, C., Kang, J., & Kim, D. I. (2022, December). Optimal targeted advertising strategy for secure wireless edge metaverse. In *GLOBECOM 2022-2022 IEEE Global Communications Conference* (pp. 4346-4351). IEEE. DOI: 10.1109/GLOBECOM48099.2022.10001331

Duani, N. B. (2018). *"Brought to you live": On the consumption experience of live social media streams*. ACR North American Advances.

Duman, S., Çelik Özen, D., & Duman, Ş. B. (2022). Metaverse in paediatric dentistry. *European Archives of Paediatric Dentistry; Official Journal of the European Academy of Paediatric Dentistry*, 23(4), 655–656. DOI: 10.1007/s40368-022-00733-7 PMID: 35821383

Dwivedi, Y., Hughes, L., Baabdullah, A., Ribeiro-Navarrete, S., Giannakis, M., Al-Debei, M., Dennehy, D., Metri, B., Buhalis, D., Cheung, C., Conboy, K., Doyle, R., Dubey, R., Dutot, V., Felix, R., Goyal, G., Gustafsson, A., Hinsch, C., Jebabli, I., Janssen, M., Kim, Y., Kim, J., Koos, S., Kreps, D., Kshetri, N., Kumar, V., Ooi, K., Papagiannidis, S., Pappas, I., Polyviou, A., Park, S., Pandey, N., Queiroz, M., Raman, R., Rauschnabek, P., Shirish, A., Sigala, M., Spanaki, K., Tan, G., Tiwari, M., Viglia, G., Wamba, S. (2022). Metaverse beyond the hype: Multidisciplinary perspectives on emerging challenges, opportunities, and agenda for research, practice and policy. International Journal of Information Management

Dwivedi, Y. K., Hughes, L., Baabdullah, A. M., Ribeiro-Navarrete, S., Giannakis, M., Al-Debei, M. M., Dennehy, D., Metri, B., Buhalis, D., Cheung, C. M. K., Conboy, K., Doyle, R., Dubey, R., Dutot, V., Felix, R., Goyal, D. P., Gustafsson, A., Hinsch, C., Jebabli, I., & Wamba, S. F. (2022). Metaverse beyond the hype: Multidisciplinary perspectives on emerging challenges, opportunities, and agenda for research, practice and policy. *International Journal of Information Management*, 66, 102542. Advance online publication. DOI: 10.1016/j.ijinfomgt.2022.102542

Dwivedi, Y. K., Hughes, L., Wang, Y., Alalwan, A. A., Ahn, S. J. G., Balakrishnan, J., Barta, S., Belk, R., Buhalis, D., Dutot, V., Felix, R., Filieri, R., Flavián, C., Gustafsson, A., Hinsch, C., Hollensen, S., Jain, V., Kim, J., Krishen, A. S., & Wirtz, J. (2023). Metaverse marketing: How the metaverse will shape the future of consumer research and practice. *Psychology and Marketing*, 40(4), 750–776. DOI: 10.1002/mar.21767

Dwivedi, Y. K., Rana, N. P., & Janssen, M. (2021). Artificial intelligence and the metaverse: Enhancing personalized experiences in hospitality services. *Journal of Hospitality and Tourism Technology*, 12(4), 389–410.

Dzimitrowicz, H. E., & Armstrong, A. J. (2022). Triplet Therapy: Entering the Metaverse of Metastatic Hormone-sensitive Prostate Cancer Treatment. *European Urology*, 82(6), S0302–S2838. DOI: 10.1016/j.eururo.2022.08.031 PMID: 36114081

Egger, R., & Buhalis, D. (2020). Virtual and augmented reality applications in tourism and hospitality. *Journal of Tourism and Hospitality Technology*, 11(2), 235–245.

Egliston, B., & Carter, M. (2021). Critical questions for Facebook's virtual reality: Data, power and the metaverse. *Internet Policy Review*, 10(4). Advance online publication. DOI: 10.14763/2021.4.1610

Egliston, B., Carter, M., & Clark, K. (2024). Who will govern the metaverse? Examining governance initiatives for extended reality (XR) technologies. *New Media & Society*. Advance online publication. DOI: 10.1177/14614448231226172

Eisenbeis, R. (2012, September 7). The fictional (yet amazingly popular) singers of Japan. Retrieved June 5, 2023, from https://kotaku.com/the-fictional-yet-amazingly-popular-singers-of-japan-5940894

El Beheiry, M. D., Doutreligne, S., Caporal, C., Ostertag, C., Dahan, M., & Masson, J.-B. (2019). Virtual reality: Beyond visualization. *Journal of Molecular Biology*, 431(7), 1315–1321. DOI: 10.1016/j.jmb.2019.01.033 PMID: 30738026

Elhence, A., Kohli, V., Chamola, V., & Sikdar, B. (2022). Enabling cost-effective and secure minor medical teleconsultation using artificial intelligence and blockchain. *IEEE Internet of Things Magazine*, 5(1), 80–84. DOI: 10.1109/IOTM.001.2100142

Emanet, N., Öz, H. R., Bayram, N., & Delen, D. (2014). A comparative analysis of machine learning methods for classification type decision problems in healthcare. *Decision Analysis*, 1, 1–20.

EpicGames. (2022). *Sony and KIRKBI Invest in Epic Games to Build the Future of Digital Entertainment*. Epic Games. Retrieved 10 September 2024 from https://www.epicgames.com/site/en-US/news/sony-and-kirkbi-invest-in-epic-games-to-build-the-future-of-digital-entertainment

Escueta, M., Nickow, A. J., Oreopoulos, P., & Quan, V. (2020). Upgrading Education with Technology: Insights from Experimental Research. *Journal of Economic Literature*, 58(4), 897–996. DOI: 10.1257/jel.20191507

Fakhar, H., Lamrabet, M., Echantoufi, N., khattabi, K. E., & Ajana, L. (2024). Towards a New Artificial Intelligence-based Framework for Teachers' Online Continuous Professional Development Programs: Systematic Review. *International Journal of Advanced Computer Science and Applications*, 15(4). Advance online publication. DOI: 10.14569/IJACSA.2024.0150450

Farjami, S. e. (2011). Multilingual problem based learning in metaverse. In *Knowledge-Based and Intelligent Information and Engineering Systems. 5th International Conference, KES 2011* (pp. pp. 499-509). Springer Berlin Heidelberg.

Farrant, T. (2022). *Fancy a virtual hot air balloon trip over Saudi Arabia's ancient tombs? Now, you can.* Euronews. https://www.euronews.com/culture/2023/02/22/fancy-a-virtual-hot-air-balloon-trip-over-saudi-arabias-ancient-tombs-now-you-can

Fegert, J. (2023). *Virtual realities, real participation: Challenges and opportunities of public participation in the metaverse.* Project Immersive Democracy. Retrieved 17 September 2024 from https://www.metaverse-forschung.de/en/2023/11/13/virtual-realities-real-participation-challenges-and-opportunities-of-public-participation-in-the-metaverse/

Feng, J., Spence, I., & Pratt, J. (2007). Playing an action video game reduces gender differences in spatial cognition. *Psychological Science*, 18(10), 850–855. DOI: 10.1111/j.1467-9280.2007.01990.x PMID: 17894600

Feng, Z., González, V. A., Amor, R., Lovreglio, R., & Cabrera-Guerrero, G. (2018). Immersive virtual reality serious games for evacuation training and research: A systematic literature review. *Computers & Education*, 127, 252–266. DOI: 10.1016/j.compedu.2018.09.002

Ferrari, F., & McKelvey, F. (2023). Hyperproduction: A social theory of deep generative models. *Distinktion : Scandinavian Journal of Social Theory*, 24(2), 338–360. DOI: 10.1080/1600910X.2022.2137546

Ferrari, R. (2015). Writing narrative style literature reviews. *Medical Writing*, 24(4), 230–235. DOI: 10.1179/2047480615Z.000000000329

Ferraro, C., Sands, S., Demsar, V., & Cohen, J. (2024). Diversity Representation in Virtual Environments: How Brand Motives Mediate Consumer Perceptions. *Australasian Marketing Journal*, 32(3), 239–249. DOI: 10.1177/14413582241244535

Fesenmaier, D. R. (2020). The role of virtual reality in tourism: Accessing the world through digital platforms. *Journal of Travel Research*, 59(4), 678–692.

Fianto, A., Widyantara, H., & Baskara, D. (2022). Analisis Mediasi Brand Awareness dan Brand Trust dalam Hubungan Emotional Marketing dengan Purchase Intention. *Jurnal Manajemen dan Kewirausahaan*, 7(2), 47-59.

Flavián, C., Ibáñez-Sánchez, S., & Orús, C. (2021). Impacts of technological embodiment through virtual reality on potential guests' emotions and engagement. *Journal of Hospitality Marketing & Management*, 30(1), 1–20. DOI: 10.1080/19368623.2020.1770146

Foucault, M. (1977). *Discipline and Punish: The Birth of the Prison.* Pantheon Books.

Frank, R. (2022). Metaverse real estate sales top $500 million, MetaMetric solutions says.

Frey, C. B., & Osborne, M. A. (2017). The future of employment: How susceptible are jobs to computerization? *Technological Forecasting and Social Change*, 114, 254–280. DOI: 10.1016/j.techfore.2016.08.019

Frolov, A. (2021, April 27). Virtual influencers – Are they all they're cracked up to be? Retrieved May 25, 2023, from https://marketech-apac.com/virtual-influencers-are-they-all-theyre-cracked-up-to-be/

Fuller, A., Fan, Z., Day, C., & Barlow, C. (2020). Digital Twin: Enabling Technologies, Challenges and Open Research. *IEEE Access : Practical Innovations, Open Solutions*, 8, 108952–108971. DOI: 10.1109/ACCESS.2020.2998358

Gadekallu, T. R., Pham, Q. V., Nguyen, D. C., Maddikunta, P. K. R., Deepa, N., Prabadevi, B., Pathirana, P. N., Zhao, J., & Hwang, W. J. (2021). Blockchain for edge of things: Applications, opportunities, and challenges. *IEEE Internet of Things Journal*, 9(2), 964–988. DOI: 10.1109/JIOT.2021.3119639

Gaetjens, A., Corsi, A. M., & Plewa, C. (2023). Customer engagement in domestic wine tourism: The role of motivations. *Journal of Destination Marketing & Management*, 27, 100761. DOI: 10.1016/j.jdmm.2022.100761

Garcia, G., & Jung, I. (2020). Understanding immersion in 2D platform-based online collaborative learning environments. *Australasian Journal of Educational Technology*, 57–67. DOI: 10.14742/ajet.6106

Gartner Inc. (2022). *Gartner predicts 25% of People Will Spend at least One Hour per Day in the Metaverse by 2026 -Metaverse Hype to Transition into New Business Models that Extend Digital Business*. Retrieved 15th August 2024, from https://www.gartner.com/en/newsroom/press-releases/2022-02-07-gartner-predicts-25-percent-of-people-will-spend-at-least-one-hour-per-day-in-the-metaverse-by-2026

Gartner, D., & Padman, R. (2020). Machine learning for healthcare behavioural OR: Addressing waiting time perceptions in emergency care. *The Journal of the Operational Research Society*, 71(7), 1087–1101. DOI: 10.1080/01605682.2019.1571005

Gerup, J., Soerensen, C. B., & Dieckmann, P. (2020). Augmented reality and mixed reality for healthcare education beyond surgery: An integrative review. *International Journal of Medical Education*, 11, 1–18. DOI: 10.5116/ijme.5e01.eb1a PMID: 31955150

Geyser, W. (2023). *The state of influencer marketing 2023: Benchmark report*. Retrieved June 3, 2023, from https://influencermarketinghub.com/influencer-marketing-benchmark-report/

Goanta, C. (2020). Selling LAND in Decentraland: The regime of non-fungible tokens on the Ethereum blockchain under the digital content directive. *Disruptive technology, legal innovation, and the future of real estate*, 139-154.

Golam, M., Ara Tuli, E., Naufal Alief, R., Kim, D.-S., & Lee, J.-M. (2024). Meta-Learning: A Digital Learning Management Framework Using Blockchain for Metaverses. *IEEE Access : Practical Innovations, Open Solutions*, 12, 92774–92786. DOI: 10.1109/ACCESS.2024.3408878

Golf-Papez, M., Heller, J., Hilken, T., Chylinski, M., de Ruyter, K., Keeling, D. I., & Mahr, D. (2022). Embracing falsity through the metaverse: The case of synthetic customer experiences. *Business Horizons*, 65(6), 739–749. DOI: 10.1016/j.bushor.2022.07.007

Gomathi, C., & Rajamani, V. (2018). Skill-based education through fuzzy knowledge modeling for e-learning. *Computer Applications in Engineering Education*, 26(2), 393–404. DOI: 10.1002/cae.21892

Gomes, R. S. (2024). *Portugal dá passos tímidos no metaverso*. Jornal Expresso. https://expresso.pt/premio-nacional-turismo/2024-04-18-portugal-da-passos-timidos-no-metaverso-babd3116

Gómez-Carmona, D., Paramio, A., Cruces-Montes, S., Marín-Dueñas, P. P., Montero, A. A., & Romero-Moreno, A. (2023). The effect of the wine tourism experience. *Journal of Destination Marketing & Management*, 29, 100793. Advance online publication. DOI: 10.1016/j.jdmm.2023.100793

Gonzalez-Romo, N. I., Mignucci-Jiménez, G., Hanalioglu, S., Gurses, M. E., Bahadir, S., Xu, Y., Koskay, G., Lawton, M. T., & Preul, M. C. (2023). Virtual neurosurgery anatomy laboratory: A collaborative and remote education experience in the Metaverse. *Surgical Neurology International*, 14, 90. DOI: 10.25259/SNI_162_2023 PMID: 37025523

Goodwin, H. (2017). Overtourism: What's the solution? *Journal of Tourism and Hospitality Management*, 18(2), 18–27.

Google. (2024). *Google AR & VR*. Google. Retrieved 23 September 2024 from https://arvr.google.com/

Gössling, S. (2010). The environmental impact of tourism and travel: A sustainable future. *Journal of Sustainable Tourism*, 18(3), 239–253.

Gössling, S. (2017). Digitalization in tourism: Implications for the future of the tourism industry. *Journal of Tourism Futures*, 3(3), 171–177.

Gössling, S. (2021). The sustainable future of tourism: Virtual experiences and their role in managing overtourism. *Journal of Sustainable Tourism*, 29(7), 1–15.

Gössling, S., & Peeters, P. (2015). Assessing tourism's global environmental impact 1900-2050. *Journal of Sustainable Tourism*, 23(3), 477–493.

Grand View Research. (2024). *Wine tourism market size & trends*. Grand View Research. https://www.grandviewresearch.com/industry-analysis/wine-tourism-market-report

Gupta, R., Aggarwal, A., Sable, D., Chahar, P., Sharma, A., Kumari, A., & Maji, R. (2022). Covid-19 Pandemic and Online Education: Impact on Students, Parents and Teachers. *Journal of Human Behavior in the Social Environment*, 32(4), 426–449. DOI: 10.1080/10911359.2021.1909518

Gursoy, D. M., Malodia, S., & Dhir, A. (2022). The metaverse in the hospitality and tourism industry: An overview of current trends and future research directions. *Journal of Hospitality Marketing & Management*, 31(5), 527–534. DOI: 10.1080/19368623.2022.2072504

Guttentag, D. (2010). Virtual reality in tourism: A review of the applications, challenges, and opportunities. *Tourism Management*, 31(1), 39–49.

Guttentag, D. A. (2015). The role of augmented reality in tourism: A case study of tourism apps. *Journal of Tourism Studies*, 26(2), 36–50.

Habil, S. G. M., El-Deeb, S., & El-Bassiouny, N. (2024). The metaverse era: Leveraging augmented reality in the creation of novel customer experience. *Management & Sustainability: An Arab Review*, 3(1), 1–15. DOI: 10.1108/MSAR-10-2022-0051

Hair, J. F., Hult, G. T. M., Ringle, C. M., Sarstedt, M., Danks, N. P., & Ray, S. (2021). An Introduction to Structural Equation Modeling. In *Partial Least Squares Structural Equation Modeling (PLS-SEM) Using R. Classroom Companion: Business*. Springer. DOI: 10.1007/978-3-030-80519-7_1

Hajesmaeel-Gohari, S., Sarpourian, F., & Shafiei, E. (2021). Virtual reality applications to assist pregnant women: A scoping review. *BMC Pregnancy and Childbirth*, 21(1), 1–8. DOI: 10.1186/s12884-021-03725-5 PMID: 33765969

Hall, C. M., & Mitchell, R. (2000). Wine tourism in the Mediterranean: A tool for restructuring and development. *Thunderbird International Business Review*, 42(4), 445–465. DOI: 10.1002/1520-6874(200007/08)42:4<445::AID-TIE6>3.0.CO;2-H

Han, C., Choi, S., & Koo, C. (2021). The use of metaverse in virtual cultural heritage experiences for global tourism. *International Journal of Heritage Studies*, 27(4), 287–301.

Hancock, J. T., & Bailenson, J. N. (2021). The social impact of deepfakes. *Cyberpsychology, Behavior, and Social Networking*, 24(3), 149–152. DOI: 10.1089/cyber.2021.29208.jth PMID: 33760669

Han, J., Liu, G., & Gao, Y. (2023). Learners in the Metaverse: A Systematic Review on the Use of Roblox in Learning. *Education Sciences*, 13(3), 296. DOI: 10.3390/educsci13030296

Hanna, S. (2021). Digital inclusion in the metaverse: Addressing barriers to access in virtual tourism. *Journal of Digital Tourism*, 1(2), 34–49.

Han, S., & Noh, Y. (2021). Analyzing Higher Education Instructors' perception on Metaverse-based Education. *Journal of Digital Contents Society*, 22(11), 1793–1806. DOI: 10.9728/dcs.2021.22.11.1793

Hardy, W., Paliński, M., & Rożynek, S. (2022). *Roblox and the digital market for virtual experiences* (3). DELab.

Harley, D. (2022). "This would be sweet in VR": On the discursive newness of virtual reality. *New Media & Society*, 17. Advance online publication. DOI: 10.1177/14614448221084655

Hartley, J. (2004). What is a case study. In Cassell, C., & Symon, G. (Eds.), *Essential guide to qualitative methods in organizational research* (pp. 323–333). Sage. DOI: 10.4135/9781446280119.n26

Hasan, H. R., Madine, M., Musamih, A., Jayaraman, R., Salah, K., Yaqoob, I., & Omar, M. (2024). Non-fungible tokens (NFTs) for digital twins in the industrial metaverse: Overview, use cases, and open challenges. *Computers & Industrial Engineering*, 193, 110315. DOI: 10.1016/j.cie.2024.110315

Hassan, M. A., Habiba, U., Majeed, F., & Shoaib, M. (2021). Adaptive gamification in e-learning based on students' learning styles. *Interactive Learning Environments*, 29(4), 545–565. DOI: 10.1080/10494820.2019.1588745

Hatmaker, T. (2021). *Fortnite's Ariana Grande concert offers a taste of music in the metaverse*. Tech Crunch.

Healy, M., & Walsh, P. (2017, November). Detecting demeanor for healthcare with machine learning. In *2017 IEEE international conference on bioinformatics and biomedicine (BIBM)* (pp. 2015-2019). IEEE. DOI: 10.1109/BIBM.2017.8217970

Healy, P., & Standiford, H. (2023). Enter the Paraverse: Challenging Assumptions of Live Music in the Metaverse. *European Conference on Games Based Learning, 17*, 251-259. https://doi.org/DOI: 10.34190/ecgbl.17.1.1634

Hedrick, E., Harper, M., Oliver, E., & Hatch, D. (2022). Teaching & Learning in Virtual Reality: Metaverse Classroom Exploration. *2022 Intermountain EngineeringTechnology and Computing*, 1–5, 1–5. Advance online publication. DOI: 10.1109/IETC54973.2022.9796765

Heller, B. (2020). Watching androids dream of electric sheep: Immersive technology, biometric psychography, and the law. *Vand. J. Ent. & Tech. L*, 23, 1.

Hennig-Thurau, T., Aliman, D. N., Herting, A. M., Cziehso, G. P., Linder, M., & Kubler, R. V. (2023). Social interactions in the Metaverse: Framework, initial evidence, and research roadmap. *Journal of the Academy of Marketing Science*, 51(4), 889–913. DOI: 10.1007/s11747-022-00908-0

Heo, M. H., & Kim, D. (2021). Effect of augmented reality affordance on motor performance: In the sport climbing. *Human-Centric Computing and Information Sciences, 11*. How the metaverse is shaping consumer behavior. *IEEE Metaverse*. Retrieved from https://metaversereality.ieee.org/publications/articles/how-the-metaverse-is-shaping-consumer-behavior

Hershfield, H. E., Goldstein, D. G., Sharpe, W. F., Fox, J., Yeykelis, L., Carstensen, L. L., & Bailenson, J. N. (2011). Increasing saving behavior through age-progressed renderings of the future self. *Journal of marketing research, 48*(SPL), S23-S37.

Hoffman, D. L., & Novak, T. P. (1996). Marketing in hypermedia computer-mediated environments: Conceptual foundation. *Journal of Marketing*, 60(3), 50–68. DOI: 10.1177/002224299606000304

Holliday, S., Essandoh, M., Start, A. R., Clinchot, D., & Barbee, J. (2022). The feasibility and effectiveness of an online curriculum for virtual onboarding of graduate medical education learners. *Advances in Medical Education and Practice*. Advance online publication. DOI: 10.2147/AMEP.S386286 PMID: 36411750

Holloway, D. (2012). Virtual worlds and health: Healthcare delivery and simulation opportunities. In *Virtual worlds and metaverse platforms: New communication and identity paradigms* (pp. 251–270). IGI Global. DOI: 10.4018/978-1-60960-854-5.ch017

Hollweck, T. (2016). Yin Review. Canadian Journal of Program Evaluation. https://www.researchgate.net/publication/308385754_Robert_K_Yin_2014_Case_Study_Research_Design_and_Methods_5th_ed_Thousand_Oaks_CA_Sage_282_pages

Holt, S. (2023). Virtual reality, augmented reality and mixed reality: For astronaut mental health; and space tourism, education and outreach. *Acta Astronautica*, 203, 436–446. DOI: 10.1016/j.actaastro.2022.12.016

Hong, J. Y., He, J., Lam, B., Gupta, R., & Gan, W.-S. (2017). Spatial audio for soundscape design: Recording and reproduction. *Applied Sciences (Basel, Switzerland)*, 7(6), 627. DOI: 10.3390/app7060627

Hooper, J., Tsiridis, E., Feng, J. E., Schwarzkopf, R., Waren, D., Long, W. J., Poultsides, L., Macaulay, W., Papagiannakis, G., Kenanidis, E., Rodriguez, E. D., Slover, J., Egol, K. A., Phillips, D. P., Friedlander, S., & Collins, M. (2019). Virtual reality simulation facilitates resident training in total hip arthroplasty: A randomized controlled trial. *The Journal of Arthroplasty*, 34(10), 2278–2283. DOI: 10.1016/j.arth.2019.04.002 PMID: 31056442

Hoyer, W. D., Kroschke, M., Schmitt, B., Kraume, K., & Shankar, V. (2020). Transforming the customer experience through new technologies. *Journal of Interactive Marketing*, 51(1), 57–71. DOI: 10.1016/j.intmar.2020.04.001

Huang, H. H., Hwang, G.-J., & Chang, S.-C. (2023). Facilitating decision making in authentic contexts: An SVVR-based experiential flipped learning approach for professional training. *Interactive Learning Environments*, 31(8), 5219–5235. DOI: 10.1080/10494820.2021.2000435

Huang, R., Zhang, L., & Li, W. (2022). Sustainable tourism through metaverse technologies: Digital twins and virtual travel experiences. *Journal of Sustainable Tourism*, 30(1), 58–72.

Hübner, A. H., Kuhn, H., & Wollenburg, J. (2016). Last mile fulfilment and distribution in omni-channel grocery retailing: A strategic planning framework. *International Journal of Retail & Distribution Management*, 44(3). Advance online publication. DOI: 10.1108/IJRDM-11-2014-0154

Hussain, S. (2023). Metaverse for education – Virtual or real? *Frontiers in Education*, 8, 1177429. Advance online publication. DOI: 10.3389/feduc.2023.1177429

Hussain, S. M., & Alaya, A. (2024). Investor response to financial news in the digital transformation era: The impact of accounting disclosures and herding behavior as indirect effect. *Journal of Financial Reporting and Accounting*, 22(2), 254–273. DOI: 10.1108/JFRA-05-2023-0287

Hussain, S., Khattak, J., Rizwan, A., & Latif, M. A. (2013). ANSOFF matrix, environment, and growth-an interactive triangle. *Management and Administrative Sciences Review*, 2(2), 196–206.

Huynh-The, T., Gadekallu, T. R., Wang, W. Z., Yenduri, G., Ranaweera, P., Pham, Q. V., da Costa, D. B., & Liyanage, M. (2023). Blockchain for the metaverse: A Review [Review]. *Future Generation Computer Systems*, 143, 401–419. DOI: 10.1016/j.future.2023.02.008

i4cp. (2023). How Accenture Uses Virtual Reality to Onboard Employees and More. https://www.i4cp.com/productivity-blog/how-accenture-uses-virtual-reality-to-onboard-employees-and-more

Ibáñez, M. B.-K., & Delgado-Kloos, C. (2018). Augmented reality for STEM learning: A systematic review. *Computers & Education*, 123, 109–123. DOI: 10.1016/j.compedu.2018.05.002

Interbrand. (2023). *Best Global Brands 2023: How iconic brands Lead across Arenas*. Retrieved 20 August 2024 from https://interbrand.com/best-global-brands/

Ivanov, S. (2020). Virtual reality and service automation in hospitality: The future of guest experiences. *Journal of Hospitality and Tourism Technology*, 11(3), 385–401.

Ivanov, S., & Webster, C. (2017). Virtual reality in hospitality: A tool for training and enhancing customer experience. *International Journal of Hospitality Management*, 61, 35–44.

Jagirdar, S. S., & Gupta, P. K. (2024). *Charting the financial odyssey: a literature review on history and evolution of investment strategies in the stock market (1900–2022)*. China Accounting and Finance Review.

Jara, M., & Cliquet, G. (2012). Retail brand equity: Conceptualization and measurement. *Journal of Retailing and Consumer Services*, 19(1), 140–149. DOI: 10.1016/j.jretconser.2011.11.003

Jasrotia, S. S. (2023). Technological Innovations in Interactive Marketing: Enhancing Customer Experience at the New Retail Age. In Wang, C. L. (Ed.), *The Palgrave Handbook of Interactive Marketing*. Palgrave Macmillan. DOI: 10.1007/978-3-031-14961-0_8

Jaynes, C., Seales, W. B., Calvert, K., Fei, Z., & Griffioen, J. (2003, May). The Metaverse: a networked collection of inexpensive, self-configuring, immersive environments. In *Proceedings of the workshop on Virtual environments 2003* (pp. 115-124). DOI: 10.1145/769953.769967

Jeong, H. Y. (2022). An innovative e-commerce platform incorporating metaverse to live commerce. *International Journal of Innovative Computing, Information, & Control*, 18(1), 221–229.

Jeon, S., Kim, M., & Choi, H. (2022). Smart tourism ecosystems: Integration of metaverse for enhanced traveler engagement. *Tourism Review*, 77(2), 121–135.

Jingen Liang, L., & Elliot, S. (2021). A systematic review of augmented reality tourism research: What is now and what is next? *Tourism and Hospitality Research*, 21(1), 15–30. DOI: 10.1177/1467358420941913

Johnson, G., Whittington, R., Scholes, K., Angwin, D., & Regner, P. (2017). *Exploring Corporate Strategy* (11th ed.). Pearson.

Jones, S. E. (2008). *The Meaning of Video Games: Gaming and Textual Strategies* (1st ed. ed.). Routledge. https://doi.org/https://doi.org/10.4324/9780203929926

Jones, D., Hazelton, M., Evans, D. J., Pento, V., See, Z. S., Van Leugenhaege, L., & Fealy, S. (2021). The road to birth: Using digital technology to visualise pregnancy anatomy. In *Digital Anatomy: Applications of Virtual, Mixed and Augmented Reality* (pp. 325–342). Springer International Publishing. DOI: 10.1007/978-3-030-61905-3_17

Joshi, R., Pandey, K., & Kumari, S. (2024). A Metaverse: Significance and Dimensions in Various Sectors. 2024 11th International Conference on Computing for Sustainable Global Development (INDIACom). https://doi.org/https://doi.org/10.1177/20563051221107641

Joshua, J. (2017). Information Bodies: Computational Anxiety in Neal Stephenson's Snow Crash. *Interdisciplinary Literary Studies*, 19(1), 17–47. DOI: 10.5325/intelitestud.19.1.0017

Jovanović, A., & Milosavljević, A. (2022). VoRtex Metaverse Platform for Gamified Collaborative Learning. *Electronics (Basel)*, 11(3), 317. DOI: 10.3390/electronics11030317

Jun, G. (2020). Virtual reality church as a new mission frontier in the metaverse: Exploring theological controversies and missional potential of virtual reality church. *Transformation (Durban)*, 37(4), 297–305. DOI: 10.1177/0265378820963155

Jung, T., tom Dieck, M. C., & Han, D. (2020). Virtual reality and augmented reality in tourism: A systematic review and implications for future research. *Journal of Travel Research*, 59(6), 1072–1090.

Júnior, A. F. B., & Júnior, N. F. (2011). A utilização da técnica da entrevista em trabalhos científicos. Revista Evidência. https://ojs.uniaraxa.edu.br/index.php/evidencia/article/view/200/186

Kabir, A. I., Vyas, S., Mitra, S., Uddin, M. M., & Jakowan, J. (2024, March). Evaluating the machine learning based momentum stock trading strategies with back-testing: An emerging market perspective. In *AIP Conference Proceedings* (Vol. 2919, No. 1). AIP Publishing.

Kadaruddin, K. (2023). Empowering Education through Generative AI: Innovative Instructional Strategies for Tomorrow's Learners. *International Journal of Business, Law, and Education*, 4(2), 618–625. DOI: 10.56442/ijble.v4i2.215

Kaddoura, S., & Al Husseiny, F. (2023). The rising trend of Metaverse in education: Challenges, opportunities, and ethical considerations. *PeerJ. Computer Science*, 9, e1252. DOI: 10.7717/peerj-cs.1252 PMID: 37346578

Kalning, K. (2008). *The anatomy of the first video game*. NBC News. Retrieved 10 September 2024 from https://www.nbcnews.com/id/wbna27328345

Kalyvaki, M. (2023). Navigating the Metaverse Business and Legal Challenges: Intellectual Property, Privacy, and Jurisdiction. *Journal of Metaverse*. .DOI: 10.57019/jmv.1238344

Kang, S. H., & Gretzel, U. (2012). The role of virtual reality in cultural sensitivity training. *Journal of Travel Research*, 51(3), 285–296.

Kapoor, A., Guha, S., Das, M. K., Goswami, K. C., & Yadav, R. (2020). Digital healthcare: The only solution for better healthcare during COVID-19 pandemic? *Indian Heart Journal*, 72(2), 61–64. DOI: 10.1016/j.ihj.2020.04.001 PMID: 32534691

Kardong-Edgren, S. S., Farra, S. L., Alinier, G., & Young, H. M. (2019). A call to unify definitions of virtual reality. *Clinical Simulation in Nursing*, 31, 28–34. DOI: 10.1016/j.ecns.2019.02.006

Kastenholz, E., Cunha, D., Eletxigerra, A., Carvalho, M., & Silva, I. (2022). The Experience Economy in a Wine Destination-Analysing Visitor Reviews. *Sustainability (Basel)*, 14(15), 9308. Advance online publication. DOI: 10.3390/su14159308

Kasumovic, D. (2024, October 24). Influencer marketing sustainability and ethics. *Influencer Marketing Hub*. Retrieved from https://influencermarketinghub.com/influencer-marketing-sustainability-and-ethics

Kaur, G., Pande, R., Mohan, R., Vij, S., Agrawal, P., Shobhane, P., Pinjarkar, L., Maheshwari, S., & Bagane, P. (2024). A Comprehensive Review of Metaverse: Taxonomy, Impact, and the Hype around It. *Engineering Proceedings*, 62(1).

Keller, K. L. (1993). Conceptualizing, measuring, and managing customer-based brand equity. *Journal of Marketing*, 57(1), 1–22. DOI: 10.1177/002224299305700101

Keller, K. L. (2020). Consumer Research Insights on Brands and Branding: A JCR Curation. *The Journal of Consumer Research*, 46(5), 995–1001. DOI: 10.1093/jcr/ucz058

Kermanshachi, S., Nipa, T. J., & Nadiri, H. (2023). Correction: Service quality assessment and enhancement using Kano model. *PLoS One*, 18(10), e0293766. DOI: 10.1371/journal.pone.0293766 PMID: 37883348

Khaliq, L. N., & Manda, V. K. (2024). Customer experience in the Web 3.0 era: The meeting of blockchain and the metaverse. In *The rise of blockchain applications in customer experience* (pp. 258–274). IGI Global.

Kılıçarslan, Ö., & Yozukmaz, N. Albayrak, T. & Buhalis, D. (2024). The impacts of Metaverse on tourist behavior and marketing implications. *Current Issues in Tourism*. Advance online publication. DOI: 10.1080/13683500.2024.2326989

Kim, E. A., Kim, D., e, Z., & Shoenberger, H. (2023). The next hype in social media advertising: Examining virtual influencers' brand endorsement effectiveness. *Frontiers in Psychology*, 14, 1089051. Advance online publication. DOI: 10.3389/fpsyg.2023.1089051 PMID: 36949930

Kim, J., Lee, H., & Choi, S. (2023). NFTs and blockchain in metaverse tourism: Creating unique virtual experiences. *Journal of Hospitality Innovation*, 15(1), 23–35.

Kim, K., Yang, H., Lee, J., & Lee, W. G. (2023). Metaverse wearables for immersive digital healthcare: A review. *Advancement of Science*, 10(31), 2303234. Advance online publication. DOI: 10.1002/advs.202303234 PMID: 37740417

Kim, S. L., Lee, S., Kang, H., Kim, S., & Ahn, M. (2021). P300 brain–computer interface-based drone control in virtual and augmented reality. *Sensors (Basel)*, 21(17), 5765. DOI: 10.3390/s21175765 PMID: 34502655

Kim, Y.-J., & Lee, S.-H. (2021). The Relationships among Quality of Online Education, Learning Immersion, Learning Satisfaction, and Academic Achievement in Cooking-Practice Subject. *Sustainability (Basel)*, 13(21), 12152. DOI: 10.3390/su132112152

Kivetz, R. (2017). *Being in the moment: The effects of ephemeral communication in social media*. Marketing Science Institute.

Knox, J. (2022). The metaverse, or the serious business of tech frontiers. Postdigital Science and Education, 4(2), 207-215. DOI: 10.1007/s42438-022-00300-9

Köksal, C. G. (2024). Where is digital retailing evolving? An evaluation from the perspective of digital retailing technologies. In *Navigating the shifting landscape of consumer behavior* (pp. 139–173). IGI Global. DOI: 10.4018/979-8-3693-1594-1.ch006

Kölüş, Ç. (2020). Blockchain based digital identity management. *Euroasia Journal of Mathematics, Engineering, Natural &Medical Science*, 7(8), 202–209.

Koohang, A., Nord, J. H., Ooi, K.-B., Tan, G. W.-H., Al-Emran, M., Aw, E. C.-X., Baabdullah, A. M., Buhalis, D., Cham, T.-H., Dennis, C., Dutot, V., Dwivedi, Y. K., Hughes, L., Mogaji, E., Pandey, N., Phau, I., Raman, R., Sharma, A., Sigala, M., & Wong, L.-W. (2023). Shaping the Metaverse into Reality: A Holistic Multidisciplinary Understanding of Opportunities, Challenges, and Avenues for Future Investigation. *Journal of Computer Information Systems*, 63(3), 735–765. DOI: 10.1080/08874417.2023.2165197

Korkmaz, B. (2023). *Shaping the Future of Spatial Computing with Apple's Vision Pro*. Medium. Retrieved 23 September 2024 from https://barankorkmaz.medium.com/shaping-the-future-of-spatial-computing-with-apples-vision-pro-e70448cb21d9

Kozinets, R. V. (2023). Immersive netnography: A novel method for service experience research in virtual reality, augmented reality and metaverse contexts. *Journal of Service Management*, 34(1), 100–125. DOI: 10.1108/JOSM-12-2021-0481

Kraft, S. A. (2020). Respect and trustworthiness in the patient-provider-machine relationship: Applying a relational lens to machine learning healthcare applications. *The American Journal of Bioethics*, 20(11), 51–53. DOI: 10.1080/15265161.2020.1820108 PMID: 33103984

Kshetri, N. (2014). Cybersecurity and international business. *Journal of International Business Studies*, 45(9), 1191–1212.

Kugler, T. Y., Ye, B., Motro, D., & Noussair, C. N. (2020). On trust and disgust: Evidence from face reading and virtual reality. *Social Psychological & Personality Science*, 11(3), 317–325. DOI: 10.1177/1948550619856302

Kulova, I., Nikolova-Alexieva, V., & Paskalev, R. (2024). The metaverse and sustainability as drivers revolutionizing customer experience in the food industry. In *BIO Web of Conferences* (Vol. 102, p. 04009). EDP Sciences. DOI: 10.1051/bioconf/202410204009

Kumar, A., & Shankar, A. (2024). Building a sustainable future with enterprise metaverse in a data-driven era: A TOE perspective. *Journal of Retailing and Consumer Services*. Advance online publication. DOI: 10.1016/j.jretconser.2024.103986

Kuo, H. T., & Choi, T. M. (2024). Metaverse in transportation and logistics operations: An AI-supported digital technological framework. *Transportation Research Part E, Logistics and Transportation Review*, 185, 103496. Advance online publication. DOI: 10.1016/j.tre.2024.103496

Kye, B., Han, N., Kim, E., Park, Y., & Jo, S. (2021). Educational applications of Metaverse: Possibilities and limitations. *Journal of Educational Evaluation for Health Professions*, 18, 32. DOI: 10.3352/jeehp.2021.18.32 PMID: 34897242

Lampropoulos, G., Fernández-Arias, P., Antón-Sancho, Á., & Vergara, D. (2024). Affective Computing in Augmented Reality, Virtual Reality, and Immersive Learning Environments. *Electronics (Basel)*, 13(15), 2917. DOI: 10.3390/electronics13152917

Latino, M. E., De Lorenzi, M. C., Corallo, A., & Petruzzelli, A. M. (2024). The impact of metaverse for business model innovation: A review, novel insights and research directions. *Technological Forecasting and Social Change*, 206, 123571. DOI: 10.1016/j.techfore.2024.123571

Lbmsolutions, B. (2024). *Who Are the Top Investors in the Metaverse and How Is It Used in Real Life?* Medium. Retrieved 21 September 2024 from https://medium.com/@bhavya21.lbmsolutions/who-are-the-top-investors-in-the-metaverse-and-how-is-it-used-in-real-life-751df6d292ef

Lee, L., Braud, T., Zhou, P., Wang, L., Xu, D., Lin, Z., Kumar, A., Bermejo, C., & Hui, P. (2021). All One Needs to Know about Metaverse: A Complete Survey on Technological Singularity, Virtual Ecosystem, and Research Agenda. Journal of Latex Class Files, 14(8).

Lee, C. T., Ho, T. Y., & Xie, H. H. (2023). Building brand engagement in metaverse commerce: The role of branded non-fungible toekns (BNFTs). *Electronic Commerce Research and Applications*, 58, 101248. Advance online publication. DOI: 10.1016/j.elerap.2023.101248

Lee, J., Kim, Y., & Lee, H. (2021). The metaverse in tourism: User engagement and virtual social spaces for travelers. *Tourism Management Perspectives*, 37, 100–110.

Lee, J., & Min, H. (2022). *Review of legal protection measures against security threats related to Metaverse*. Korean Association of Public Safety and Criminal Justice. DOI: 10.21181/KJPC.2022.31.3.321

Lee, L.-H. (2021). All one needs to know about the metaverse: A complete survey on technological singularity, virtual ecosystem, and research agenda. *arXiv Preprint*. Retrieved from http://arxiv.org/abs/2110.05352

Lee, L.-H., Braud, T., Zhou, P., Wang, L., Xu, D., Lin, Z., Kumar, A., Bermejo, C., & Hui, P. (2021). All One Needs to Know about Metaverse: A Complete Survey on Technological Singularity, Virtual Ecosystem, and Research Agenda, 14(8), 1–66. http://arxiv.org/abs/2110.05352

Lee, S.-M. (2023). Second Language Learning Through an Emergent Narrative in a Narrative-Rich Customizable Metaverse Platform. *IEEE Transactions on Learning Technologies*, 16(6), 1071–1081. DOI: 10.1109/TLT.2023.3267563

Leighton, E. E. (2022). *From microverse to metaverse: Modelling the future through today's virtual worlds*. Emerald Publishing Limited.

Leung, R. (2013). Marketing in virtual tourism: Using immersive technologies to attract customers. *JMR, Journal of Marketing Research*, 51(3), 257–268.

Li, J. P., Haq, A. U., Din, S. U., Khan, J., Khan, A., & Saboor, A. (2020). Heart disease identification method using machine learning classification in e-healthcare. *IEEE Access : Practical Innovations, Open Solutions*, 8, 107562–107582. DOI: 10.1109/ACCESS.2020.3001149

Lin, B., Kim, G., Moore, M., & Rothenberg, L. (2021). Consumer store experience through virtual reality: Its effect on emotional states and perceived store attractiveness. *Fashion and Textiles*, 8(19), 2–21.

Lin, H., Wan, S., Gan, W., Chen, J., & Chao, H.-C. (2022). Metaverse in Education: Vision, Opportunities, and Challenges. *2022 IEEE International Conference on Big Data (Big Data)*, 2857–2866. DOI: 10.1109/BigData55660.2022.10021004

Lippert, K., Khan, M. N. R., Rabbi, M. M., Dutta, A., & Cloutier, R. (2021, December). A framework of metaverse for systems engineering. In *2021 IEEE International Conference on Signal Processing, Information, Communication & Systems (SPICSCON)* (pp. 50-54). IEEE. DOI: 10.1109/SPICSCON54707.2021.9885722

Liu, H., & Park, K.-S. (2024). Exploring the impact of metaverse tourism experiences on actual visit intentions: An integrated model of presence, the Technology Acceptance Model, and the Theory of Planned Behavior. *International Journal of Tourism Research*, 26(1), e2616. DOI: 10.1002/jtr.2616

Li, X. (2020). Virtual reality as a tool for hospitality marketing: Exploring customer perceptions and behaviors. *International Journal of Contemporary Hospitality Management*, 32(2), 438–457.

Li, X., & Xu, H. (2020). The role of virtual reality in promoting sustainable tourism: A case study of China. *Journal of Sustainable Tourism*, 28(10), 1581–1599.

Lnenicka, M., Rizun, N., Alexopoulos, C., & Janssen, M. (2024). Government in the Metaverse: Requirements and suitability for providing digital public services. *Technological Forecasting and Social Change*, 203, 123346. DOI: 10.1016/j.techfore.2024.123346

Lo, A. W., & Zhang, R. (2024). *The Adaptive Markets Hypothesis: An Evolutionary Approach to Understanding Financial System Dynamics*. Oxford University Press. DOI: 10.1093/oso/9780199681143.001.0001

Londoño, J. C., Elms, J., & Davies, K. (2016). Conceptualising and measuring consumer-based brand–retailer–channel equity. *Journal of Retailing and Consumer Services*, 29, 70–81. DOI: 10.1016/j.jretconser.2015.11.004

Lopes, T. S. A., Carreira, R., Carlos, V., Pereira, R., Alves, C., Pratas, J., & Santos, J. P. (2024). How Can Businesses, Low-Tech Businesses in Particular, Benefit from the Metaverse? A Delphi Perspective from Academics. In *Marketing and Smart Technologies. ICMarkTech 2023. Smart Innovation, Systems and Technologies* (vol. 386). Springer.

Lu, Y., Yang, D., Yang, Y., & Bai, C. (2022). MIoT integrates health, MM benefits humans: Funding conference for International Association and Alliance of Metaverse in Medicine successfully held. *Clinical eHealth, 5*, 17-18.

Lu, J. L., Liu, R., Zhang, Y., Zhang, X., Zheng, L., Zhang, C., Zhang, K., Li, S., & Lu, Y. (2022). Development and application of a detection platform for colorectal cancer tumor sprouting pathological characteristics based on artificial intelligence. *Intelligent Medicine*, 2(02), 82–87. DOI: 10.1016/j.imed.2021.08.003

Lyu, J. (2021). Sustainable practices in virtual tourism and its environmental impact. *Journal of Sustainable Tourism*, 29(8), 1345–1361.

Machalický, J. (2023). The impact of COVID-19 on the development and application of new technologies in assisted retail in the Czech Republic. *Ad Alta: Journal of Interdisciplinary Research, 13*(1).

Madni, A., Madni, C., & Lucero, S. (2019). Leveraging digital twin technology in model-based systems engineering. *Systems*, 7(1), 7–19. DOI: 10.3390/systems7010007

Maereg, A. T., Nagar, A., Reid, D., & Secco, E. L. (2017). Wearable vibrotactile haptic device for stiffness discrimination during virtual interactions. *Frontiers in Robotics and AI*, 4, 42. DOI: 10.3389/frobt.2017.00042

Mahmoud, A. B., Fuxman, L., Asaad, Y., & Solakis, K. (2024). Exploring new realms or losing touch? Assessing public beliefs about tourism in the metaverse–a big-data approach. *International Journal of Contemporary Hospitality Management.* DOI: 10.1108/IJCHM-09-2023-1515

Maizi, Y., & Bendavid, Y. (2019). Leveraging on the Digital Twin for improving retail store daily operations management. *Proceedings of the 18th International Conference on Modelling and Applied Simulation*, 92-100. DOI: 10.46354/i3m.2019.mas.013

Manahov, V. (2024). The great crypto crash in September 2018: Why did the cryptocurrency market collapse? *Annals of Operations Research*, 332(1), 579–616. DOI: 10.1007/s10479-023-05575-0

Marr, B. (2022). *Nikeland, el espacio en el que Nike construye su metaverso en Roblox*. Retrieved 16th August 2024 from https://forbes.pe/negocios/2022-06-13/nikeland-el-espacio-en-el-que-nike-construye-su-metaverso-en-roblox

Marr, B. (2022). The amazing possibilities of healthcare in the metaverse. *Forbes.*

Martín, G. F. (2018). Social and psychological impact of musical collective creative processes in virtual environments: The Avatar Orchestra Metaverse in Second Life. *Musica/Tecnologia Music/Technology, 75.*

Martineau, P. (1958). The Personality of the Retail Store. *Harvard Business Review*, 36(1), 47–55.

Martins, H. T. S. (2004). Metodologia Qualitativa de Pesquisa. Universidade de São Paulo. http://educa.fcc.org.br/pdf/ep/v30n02/v30n02a07.pdf

Martins, J., Gonçalves, R., Branco, F., Barbosa, L., Melo, M., & Bessa, M. (2017). A multisensory virtual experience model for thematic tourism: A Port wine tourism application proposal. *Journal of Destination Marketing & Management*, 6(2), 103–109. DOI: 10.1016/j.jdmm.2017.02.002

Massaro, M. (2023). Digital transformation in the healthcare sector through blockchain technology. Insights from academic research and business developments. *Technovation*, 120, 102386. Advance online publication. DOI: 10.1016/j.technovation.2021.102386

Mattila, V. (2024). *Metaverse Dynamics: Economics*. Operations, and Investment.

Matzler, K., Homburg, C., & Völckner, F. (2020). How to make your customers happy: Understanding the role of the metaverse in tourism and hospitality. *Journal of Business Research*, 113, 372–381.

Maumon, N., & Bédé, D. (2023). Wine tourism next-gen: A case study of a virtual reality implementation in a wine cooperative in France. In *Technology advances and innovation in wine tourism: New managerial approaches and cases* (pp. 95–113). Springer. DOI: 10.1007/978-981-19-8277-4_7

Mc Cartney, G. (2015). Cultural awareness and virtual training in hospitality industries. *International Journal of Hospitality Management*, 47, 74–81.

Mc Cormick, B. (2021). Guest experience management through virtual technologies in hospitality. *Journal of Hospitality & Tourism Research (Washington, D.C.)*, 45(5), 874–893.

McKercher, B. (2002). The impact of virtual tourism on the real world. *Tourism Management*, 23(4), 395–409.

McKinsey & Company. (2022). Value creation in the metaverse. https://www.mckinsey.com/~/media/mckinsey/business%20functions/marketing%20and%20sales/our%20insights/value%20creation%20in%20the%20metaverse/Value-creation-in-the-metaverse.pdf

McKinsey & Company. (2022). What is the metaverse? https://www.mckinsey.com/featured-insights/mckinsey-explainers/what-is-the-metaverse

McKinsey and Company. (2022). *Value Creation in the Metaverse*. McKinsey. https://www.mckinsey.com/capabilities/growth-marketing-and-sales/our-insights/value-creation-in-the-metaverse

McWilliam, A., & Scarfe, P. (2022). The metaverse and oncology.

Mehrotra, A., Agarwal, R., Khalil, A., Alzeiby, E. A., & Agarwal, V. (2024). Nitty-gritties of customer experience in metaverse retailing. *Journal of Retailing and Consumer Services*, 79, 103876. DOI: 10.1016/j.jretconser.2024.103876

Mesko, B. (2022). The promise of the metaverse in cardiovascular health.

Metuarau, T. (2023). *A History of Video Games (Version 2)*. Te Herenga Waka—Victoria University of Wellington.

Milgram, P. T. (1995). Augmented reality: A class of displays on the reality-virtuality continuum. *In Telemanipulator and Telepresence Technologies, 2351*, 282-292.

Milgram, P. (1994). taxonomy of mixed reality visual displays. *IEICE Transactions on Information and Systems*, 77(12), 1321–1329.

Milgram, P. H. (1995). Augmented reality: A class of displays on the reality-virtuality continuum. In *Telemanipulator and telepresence technologies* (Vol. 2351, pp. 282–292). Spie. DOI: 10.1117/12.197321

Milgram, P., Takemura, H., Utsumi, A., & Kishino, F. (1994). Augmented reality: A class of displays on the reality-virtuality continuum. *Proceedings of the Telemanipulator and Telepresence Technologies*, 282-292.

Minter, S., Hainy, C., Swift, M., Yee, C., Meyers, J., Nos, A., & Breeher, L. (2024). Quality assessment of a virtual post-offer placement assessment in employee occupational health services. *Journal of Occupational and Environmental Medicine*, 66(9), e435–e439. Advance online publication. DOI: 10.1097/JOM.0000000000003177 PMID: 38955800

Mitra, S. (2023). Metaverse: A Potential Virtual-Physical Ecosystem for Innovative Blended Education and Training. *Journal of Metaverse*, 3(1), 66–72. DOI: 10.57019/jmv.1168056

Monaco, S., & Sacchi, G. (2023). Travelling the metaverse: Potential benefits and main challenges for tourism sectors and research applications. *Sustainability (Basel)*, 15(4), 3348. DOI: 10.3390/su15043348

Mosco, V. (2023). Into the Metaverse: Technical Challenges, Social Problems, Utopian Visions, and Policy Principles. *Javnost - The Public*, 30, 161 - 173. .DOI: 10.1080/13183222.2023.2200688

Musamih, A., Yaqoob, I., Salah, K., Jayaraman, R., Al-Hammadi, Y., Omar, M., & Ellahham, S. (2022). Metaverse in healthcare: Applications, challenges, and future directions. *IEEE Consumer Electronics Magazine*.

Mystakidis, S. (2022). Metaverse. Encyclopedia, 2(1), 486-497. https://www.mdpi.com/2673-8392/2/1/31

Mystakidis, S. P. (2021). Virtual reality escape rooms for STEM education in industry 4.0: Greek teachers perspectives. In *2021 6th South-East Europe Design Automation, Computer Engineering, Computer Networks and Social Media Conference (SEEDA-CECNSM)* (pp. 1-5). IEEE.

Mystakidis, S. T.-G. (2024). Virtual Museum Gamification for Discovery-Based Online Learning in the Metaverse. *CSEDU*, 711-719.

Mystakidis, S. (2022). Metaverse. *Encyclopedia*, 2(1), 486–497. DOI: 10.3390/encyclopedia2010031

Narin, N. G. (2021). A content analysis of the metaverse articles. *Journal of Metaverse*, 1(1), 17–24.

Natarajan, T., Pragha, P., Dhalmahapatra, K., & Raghavan, D. R. V. (2024). Exploring tourist's metaverse experience using destination spatial presence quality & perceived augmentation: Metaverse exploration, physical expedition (MEPE). *Current Issues in Tourism*, 1–23. Advance online publication. DOI: 10.1080/13683500.2024.2372652

Navarro, C., Arias-Calderón, M., Henríquez, C. A., & Riquelme, P. (2024). Assessment of Student and Teacher Perceptions on the Use of Virtual Simulation in Cell Biology Laboratory Education. *Education Sciences*, 14(3), 243. DOI: 10.3390/educsci14030243

Ncube, M., Sibanda, M., & Matenda, F. R. (2024). Application of Explainable Artificial Intelligence to model the influence of firm-specific factors on stock performance in sub-Saharan Africa during *COVID* 19.

Ndengane, R. M., Mason, R. B., & Mutize, M. (2021). The influence of Store Atmospherics on customers' satisfaction at selected South African retail outlets. *Innovative Marketing*, 17(1), 26–39. DOI: 10.21511/im.17(1).2021.03

Neal Stephenson, N. (1992). *Snow crash*. Bantam Books.

Nemashkalo, K., Maliuk, O., & Ostrikov, V. (2024). Управління організаційними трансформаціями в процесі розвитку підприємства. Actual Problems of Innovative Economy and Law. DOI: 10.36887/2524-0455-2024-4-1

Neuhofer, B. (2015). The role of technology in creating memorable guest experiences. *International Journal of Hospitality Management*, 47, 143–151.

Neves, J., Bacalhau, L. M., & Santos, V. (2024). *A Systematic Review on the Customer Journey Between Two Worlds: Reality and Immersive World*. Marketing and Smart Technologies.

Ng, D. T. K. (2022). What is the Metaverse? Definitions, technologies and the community of inquiry. *Australasian Journal of Educational Technology*, 38(4), 190–205. DOI: 10.14742/ajet.7945

Ng, L. L., & Chew, S. Y. (2022). Factors Influencing ESL Players' Use of Vocabulary Learning Strategies in Massively Multiplayer Online Role-Playing Games (MMORPG). *The Asia-Pacific Education Researcher*, 31(4), 369–381. DOI: 10.1007/s40299-021-00578-6

Nguyen, H., & Voznak, M. (2024). A Bibliometric Analysis of Technology in Digital Health: Exploring Health Metaverse and Visualizing Emerging Healthcare Management Trends, in IEEE Access, 12, 23887-23913. DOI: 10.3389/fpsyg.2022.851753

Nia, V. M., Siregar, H., Sembel, R., & Zulbainarmi, N. (2024). Behavioral Finance in Psycho-Social Approaches: A Literature Review. In *International Conference on Business and Technology* (pp. 311-329). Springer. DOI: 10.1007/978-3-031-53998-5_27

Nilsson, N. C., Nordahl, R., & Serafin, S. (2016). Immersion Revisited: A review of existing definitions of immersion and their relation to different theories of presence. *Human Technology*, 12(2), 108–134. DOI: 10.17011/ht/urn.201611174652

Ni, Y. (2024). Navigating Energy and Financial Markets: A Review of Technical Analysis Used and Further Investigation from Various Perspectives. *Energies*, 17(12), 2942. DOI: 10.3390/en17122942

Noben, L., Goossens, S. M. T. A., Truijens, S. E. M., Van Berckel, M. M. G., Perquin, C. W., Slooter, G. D., & Van Rooijen, S. J. (2019). A virtual reality video to improve information provision and reduce anxiety before cesarean delivery: Randomized controlled trial. *JMIR Mental Health*, 6(12), e15872. DOI: 10.2196/15872 PMID: 31850850

Nugroho, R. A., Prakoso, S. G., Hidayati, K. N., Rahmawati, A. D., Kartinawanty, A. T., & Santoso, S. A. (2022, October). Challenges of The Metaverse Adoption for the Health of the Elderly: Case in Surakarta. In *2022 IEEE International Conference of Computer Science and Information Technology (ICOSNIKOM)* (pp. 1-6). IEEE. DOI: 10.1109/ICOSNIKOM56551.2022.10034914

Oliveira, J. I. V. R. (2022). Gestão da Presença da Marca no Metaverso - O caso da marca de moda Fly London [Unpublished master's thesis]. ISAG.

Onu, P., Pradhan, A., & Mbohwa, C. (2024). Potential to use Metaverse for future teaching and learning. *Education and Information Technologies*, 29(7), 8893–8924. DOI: 10.1007/s10639-023-12167-9

Othman, N. N. (2024). Mind Games in the Market: Unraveling the Impact of Psychological Biases on Your Stock Portfolio. *Available atSSRN* 4844961. DOI: 10.2139/ssrn.4844961

Pagani, M. (2013). Digital transformation of business models in the hospitality industry. *Information & Management*, 50(8), 519–530.

Pakinee, A., & Puritat, K. (2021). Designing a gamified e-learning environment for teaching undergraduate ERP course based on big five personality traits. *Education and Information Technologies*, 26(4), 4049–4067. DOI: 10.1007/s10639-021-10456-9 PMID: 33613080

Pangea.ai. (2024). The Accenture Metaverse — New Frontiers in Work. https://pangea.ai/resources/the-accenture-metaverse-new-frontiers-in-work

Pantano, E. P. (2017). The role of AI in retailing: Enhancing customer experience with intelligent systems. *International Journal of Retail & Distribution Management,* 45(7/8), 698-713.

Pantano, E., & Willems, K. (2022). *Introduction. Retail in a New World.* Emerald Publishing Limited.

Parham, A., & Breitinger, C. (2022). Non-fungible Tokens: Promise or Peril? https://arxiv.org/pdf/2202.06354

Park, D., & Kim, S. (2022). Metaverse in event tourism: Virtual conventions, trade shows, and hybrid tourism experiences. *Event Management*, 26(3), 302–318.

Park, E., Maddirala, S., & Eckert, P. (2023). A new era for technology: How the metaverse will transform retail. *Journal of Student Research*, 12(3). Advance online publication. DOI: 10.47611/jsrhs.v12i3.5104

Park, S. M., & Kim, Y.-G. (2022). A metaverse: Taxonomy, components, applications, and open challenges. *IEEE Access : Practical Innovations, Open Solutions*, 10, 4209–4251. DOI: 10.1109/ACCESS.2021.3140175

Park, S., Kim, S. P., & Whang, M. (2021). Individual's social perception of virtual avatars embodied with their habitual facial expressions and facial appearance. *Sensors (Basel)*, 21(17), 5986. DOI: 10.3390/s21175986 PMID: 34502877

Parong, J., Pollard, K. A., Files, B. T., Oiknine, A. H., Sinatra, A. M., Moss, J. D., Passaro, A., & Khooshabeh, P. (2020). The mediating role of presence differs across types of spatial learning in immersive technologies. *Computers in Human Behavior*, 107, 106290. DOI: 10.1016/j.chb.2020.106290

Parris, D. L., & Guzmán, F. (2023). Evolving brand boundaries and expectations: Looking back on brand equity, brand loyalty, and brand image research to move forward. *Journal of Product and Brand Management*, 32(2), 191–234. DOI: 10.1108/JPBM-06-2021-3528

Paspalj, A. (2022). *Nike Ventures Into web3 With Exciting Metaverse Platform.* Swoosh. DesignRush, Retrieved 16th November 2024 from https://www.designrush.com/news/nike-swoosh-metaverse-platform

Pellas, N. M., Mystakidis, S., & Kazanidis, I. (2021). Immersive Virtual Reality in K-12 and Higher Education: A systematic review of the last decade scientific literature. *Virtual Reality (Waltham Cross)*, 25(3), 835–861. DOI: 10.1007/s10055-020-00489-9

Peltier, J. W. (2019). Virtual and augmented reality in tourism: The potential for new tourist experiences. *Tourism Management*, 71, 207–220.

Persakis, A., & Koutoupis, A. (2024). Synchronicity and Sentiment: Decoding Earnings Quality and Market Returns in EU under Economic Policy Uncertainty. *Journal of Behavioral Finance*, 1–21. DOI: 10.1080/15427560.2024.2345342

Peters, K. C., Chen, Y., Kaplan, A. M., Ognibeni, B., & Pauwels, K. (2013). Social media metrics—A framework and guidelines for managing social media. *Journal of Interactive Marketing*, 27(4), 281–298. DOI: 10.1016/j.intmar.2013.09.007

Petrigna, L., & Musumeci, G. (2022). The metaverse: A new challenge for the healthcare system: A scoping review. *Journal of Functional Morphology and Kinesiology*, 7(3), 63. DOI: 10.3390/jfmk7030063 PMID: 36135421

Pham, L., Williamson, S., & Berry, R. (2018). Student Perceptions of E-Learning Service Quality, E-Satisfaction, and E-Loyalty. *International Journal of Enterprise Information Systems*, 14(3), 19–40. DOI: 10.4018/IJEIS.2018070102

Pine, B. J., & Gilmore, J. H. (1998). *The Experience Economy: Work is Theatre & Every Business a Stage*. Harvard Business Press.

Pine, B. J., & Gilmore, J. H. (1998). Welcome to the experience economy. *Harvard Business Review*, 1998(July/August), 97–105. PMID: 10181589

Pine, B. J., & Gilmore, J. H. (2011). *The Experience Economy*. Harvard Business Press.

Pinnington, A. H., & Ayoko, O. B. (2021). Managing physical and virtual work environments during the COVID-19 pandemic. *Journal of Management & Organization*, 27(6), 993–1002. Advance online publication. DOI: 10.1017/jmo.2022.2

Pinto-Gutiérrez, C., Gaitán, S., Jaramillo, D., Velasquez, S. (2022) The NFT Hype: What Draws Attention to Non-Fungible Tokens? DOI: 10.3390/math10030335

Pitoglou, S. (2020). Machine learning in healthcare: introduction and real-world application considerations. In *Quality Assurance in the Era of Individualized Medicine* (pp. 92–109). IGI Global. DOI: 10.4018/978-1-7998-2390-2.ch004

Pizam, A., & Shani, A. (2020). Digital skills and the future of hospitality management: Implications for education and training. *Journal of Hospitality & Tourism Education*, 32(1), 21–35.

Plumeyer, A., Kottemann, P., Böger, D., & Decker, R. (2019). Measuring brand image: A systematic review, practical guidance, and future research directions. *Review of Managerial Science*, 13(2), 227–265. DOI: 10.1007/s11846-017-0251-2

Poppe, E., Brown, R., Recker, J., Johnson, D., & Vanderfeesten, I. (2017). Design and evaluation of virtual environments mechanisms to support remote collaboration. *Information Systems*, 66, 59–81. Advance online publication. DOI: 10.1016/j.is.2017.01.004

Pottle, J. (2019). Virtual reality and the transformation of medical education. *Future Healthcare Journal*, 6(3), 181–185. DOI: 10.7861/fhj.2019-0036 PMID: 31660522

Pratas, J. (2023). Metaverse and Digital Twins: An Opportunity to Increase Retailers' Profitability? An Exploratory Research Using Nike Case Study and Retail Managers' In-Depth Interviews. In *Management and Marketing for Improved Retail Competitiveness and Performance*. IGI Global Publisher.

Pratas, J. M. (2023). Metaverse and Digital Twins: An Opportunity to Increase Retailers’ Profitability? An Exploratory Research Using Nike Case Study and Retail Managers’ In-Depth Interviews. In *Management and Marketing for Improved Retail Competitiveness and Performance* (pp. 217–235). IGI Global., DOI: 10.4018/978-1-6684-8574-3.ch011

Pratas, J., & Amorim, C. (2022). Consumer Research Shopping and Buying Behaviors in Sports Footwear Omni-Channel Retailing: A Conceptual Model. In Reis, J. L., Peter, M. K., Cayolla, R., & Bogdanović, Z. (Eds.), *Marketing and Smart Technologies. Smart Innovation, Systems and Technologies* (Vol. 280). Springer. DOI: 10.1007/978-981-16-9272-7_25

Pratas, J., & Brito, P. (2019). *Distribuição - Gestão de pontos de venda e de retalho - Gestão eficiente do negócio*. Actual Editora.

Pritchard, A. (2011). Experience and co-creation in tourism: Perspectives on innovation in tourism services. *Annals of Tourism Research*, 38(4), 1347–1366.

Pritchard, A., & Morgan, N. (2010). The experiences of virtual tourism and its social and cultural implications. *Journal of Tourism and Cultural Change*, 8(2), 147–165.

Qadir, A. M.-A., & Alwardat, R. B. Z. (2023). Get Real in the Virtual World: Branding in the Metaverse Demystified. *Tuijin Jishu/Journal of Propulsion Technology, 44*(3), 163-170. https://doi.org/DOI: 10.52783/tjjpt.v44.i3.254

Qamar, A., Anwar, Z., & Afzal, M. (2023). A systematic threat analysis and defense strategies for the Metaverse and extended reality systems. *Computers & Security*, 128(c), 103127. DOI: 10.1016/j.cose.2023.103127

Quintal, V. A., Thomas, B., Phau, I., & Soldat, Z. (2022). Segmenting hedonic wine tourists using push–pull Winescape attributes. *Australasian Marketing Journal*, 30(3), 237–245. DOI: 10.1177/1839334921999478

Radanliev, P., De Roure, D., Novitzky, P., & Sluganovic, I. (2024). Accessibility and inclusiveness of new information and communication technologies for disabled users and content creators in the Metaverse. *Disability and Rehabilitation. Assistive Technology*, 19(5), 1849–1863. DOI: 10.1080/17483107.2023.2241882 PMID: 37585705

Rahane, W., Dalvi, H., Magar, Y., Kalane, A., & Jondhale, S. (2018, March). Lung cancer detection using image processing and machine learning healthcare. In *2018 International Conference on Current Trends towards Converging Technologies (ICCTCT)* (pp. 1-5). IEEE. DOI: 10.1109/ICCTCT.2018.8551008

Raja, E. L., & Messaoudi, A. (2024). Behavioral biases influencing investment decision making in emergent markets: A systematic literature review. *International Journal of Accounting, Finance, Auditing. Management and Economics*, 5(6), 18–39.

Ramezani, D., Jaferian, G., & Wagner, M. (2024). An investigation into the educational possibilities of metaverse in the context of educational gaming. *RE:view*, 5120–5129. DOI: 10.21125/inted.2024.1326

Rane, N., Choudhary, S., & Rane, J. (2023). *Metaverse for enhancing customer loyalty: Effective strategies to improve customer relationship, service, engagement, satisfaction, and experience.*

Rane, N. (2023). Metaverse marketing strategies: Enhancing customer experience and analysing consumer behaviour through leading-edge metaverse technologies, platforms, and models. *Available atSSRN*. DOI: 10.2139/ssrn.4624199

Rane, N., Choudhary, S., & Rane, J. (2024). Leading-edge Metaverse in education: Framework, applications, challenges, and future development. *TESOL and Technology Studies*, 5(2). Advance online publication. DOI: 10.48185/tts.v5i2.1002

Rasmussen, M. (2022, January 27). Virtual humans. Retrieved from https://www.virtualhumans.org/article/who-was-the-first-virtual-influencer

Rather, R. A. (2023). Metaverse marketing and consumer research: Theoretical framework and future research agenda in tourism and hospitality industry. *Tourism Recreation Research*, 1–9. Advance online publication. DOI: 10.1080/02508281.2023.2216525

Rawat, D. B., & El Alami, H. (2023). Metaverse: Requirements, architecture, standards, status, challenges, and perspectives. *IEEE Internet of Things Magazine*, 6(1), 14–18. DOI: 10.1109/IOTM.001.2200258

Reeves, S. M., & Crippen, K. J. (2021). Virtual Laboratories in Undergraduate Science and Engineering Courses: A Systematic Review, 2009–2019. *Journal of Science Education and Technology*, 30(1), 16–30. DOI: 10.1007/s10956-020-09866-0

Regner, F., Urbach, N., & Schweizer, A. (2019). NFTs in Practice – Non-Fungible Tokens as Core Component of a Blockchain-based Event Ticketing Application. *Fortieth International Conference on Information Systems*

Reiners, T., Wood, C., & Tan, B. (2014). A digital divide for the metaverse: A global perspective. *Computers in Human Behavior*, 41, 423–430.

Reis, I. W., Peruchini, M., Ulbricht, V. R., & Teixeira, J. M. (2024). The Dilemma of Teacher Training for the Use of the Metaverse and Other Immersive Technologies in Teaching and Learning Processes. *Communications in Computer and Information Science*, 2130, 105–123. DOI: 10.1007/978-3-031-63235-8_7

Reisinger, Y., & Mavondo, F. (2005). Travel and tourism services marketing: The impact of digitalization on the hospitality industry. *Journal of Travel & Tourism Marketing*, 17(4), 1–17.

Rejeb, A. R., Rejeb, K., & Treiblmaier, H. (2023). Mapping metaverse research: Identifying future research areas based on bibliometric and topic modeling techniques. *Information (Basel)*, 14(7), 356. DOI: 10.3390/info14070356

Ritterbusch, G. D., & Teichmann, M. R. (2023). Defining the Metaverse: A Systematic Literature Review. *IEEE Access : Practical Innovations, Open Solutions*, 11(January), 12368–12377. DOI: 10.1109/ACCESS.2023.3241809

Riva, G., & Wiederhold, B. K. (2022). What the metaverse is (really) and why we need to know about it. *Cyberpsychology, Behavior, and Social Networking*, 25(6), 355–359. DOI: 10.1089/cyber.2022.0124 PMID: 35696299

Riva, G., Wiederhold, B. K., & Molinari, E. (2016). *Virtual reality in psychological treatment: Advances in research and applications*. Springer.

Rob. (2023, December 19). Virtual influencers: The pros, cons & controversies. *Hoopla Marketing.* Retrieved from https://www.hoopla-marketing.com/virtual-influencers-pros-cons-and-controversies/

Román-Belmonte, J. M., Rodríguez-Merchán, E. C., & De la Corte-Rodríguez, H. (2023). Metaverse applied to musculoskeletal pathology: Orthoverse and Rehabverse. *Postgraduate Medicine*, 135(5), 440–448. DOI: 10.1080/00325481.2023.2180953 PMID: 36786393

Roman, M., Kosiński, R., Bhatta, K., Niedziółka, A., & Krasnodębski, A. (2022). Virtual and Space Tourism as New Trends in Travelling at the Time of the COVID-19 Pandemic. *Sustainability (Basel)*, 14(2), 628. DOI: 10.3390/su14020628

Rosário, A., Lopes, P., & Rosário, F. (2023). Metaverse in Marketing: Challenges and Opportunities. In IGI Global Handbook of Research on AI-Based Technologies and Applications in the Era of the Metaverse. DOI: 10.4018/978-1-6684-8851-5.ch003

Rosenblum, P., & Kilcourse, B. (2013). *Omni-channel 2013-the long road to adoption*. RSR Research.

Rostami, S., & Maier, M. (2022). The Metaverse and Beyond: Implementing Advanced Multiverse Realms With Smart Wearables. *IEEE Access : Practical Innovations, Open Solutions*, 10, 110796–110806. DOI: 10.1109/ACCESS.2022.3215736

Russell, S. J., & Norvig, P. (2016). *Artificial intelligence: a modern approach*. Pearson.

Ruthberg, J. S., Tingle, G., Tan, L., Ulrey, L., Simonson-Shick, S., Enterline, R., Eastman, H., Mlakar, J., Gotschall, R., Henninger, E., Griswold, M. A., & Wish-Baratz, S. (2020). Mixed reality as a time-efficient alternative to cadaveric dissection. *Medical Teacher*, 42(8), 896–901. DOI: 10.1080/0142159X.2020.1762032 PMID: 32401090

Rutitis, D., & Aksjonenko, E. (2022). The impact of digital transformation on corporate identity management. *Proceedings of AHFE 2022 Conference*. DOI: 10.54941/ahfe1002802

Ryskeldiev, B. O. (2018). Distributed metaverse: creating decentralized blockchain-based model for peer-to-peer sharing of virtual spaces for mixed reality applications. In *Proceedings of the 9th augmented human international conference* (pp. 1-3).

Sadowski, W. (2002). Presence in virtual environments. *Handbook of virtual environments*, 831-846.

Safian-Demers, E. (2022). The metaverse glossary. Obtido a partir de https://www.vml.com/insight/the-metaverse-glossary

Saha, G. (2023, June 13). How AI influencers are changing the marketing landscape. Retrieved June 22, 2023, from *AdLift:*https://www.adlift.com/in/blog/how-ai-influencers-are-changing-the-marketing-landscape/

Saleh, M. I. (2024). From tourism in the Darkverse to tourism with digital detox: Designing responsible Metaverse tourism experiences. *Current Issues in Tourism*, 1–21. DOI: 10.1080/13683500.2024.2322694

Salloum, G., & Tekli, J. (2021). Automated and personalized nutrition health assessment, recommendation, and progress evaluation using fuzzy reasoning. *International Journal of Human-Computer Studies*, 151, 102610. DOI: 10.1016/j.ijhcs.2021.102610

Salmon, G. (2019). May the fourth be with you: Creating education 4.0. *Journal of Learning for Development*, 6(2), 95–115. DOI: 10.56059/jl4d.v6i2.352

Saltık, Ö. (2024). Navigating the Stock Market: Modeling Wealth Exchange and Network Interaction with Loss Aversion, Disposition Effect and Anchoring and Adjustment Bias. *Ekonomi Politika ve Finans Araştırmaları Dergisi*, 9(1), 88–122. DOI: 10.30784/epfad.1435009

Saltik, O., Jalil, F., & Degirmen, S. (2024). Viral decisions: Unmasking the impact of COVID-19 info and behavioral quirks on investment choices. *Humanities & Social Sciences Communications*, 11(1), 1–20.

Sanchez-Amboage, E., Crespo-Pereira, V., Membiela-Pollan, M., & Faustino, J. P. J. (2024). Tourism marketing in the metaverse: A systematic literature review, building blocks, and future research directions. *PLoS One*, 19(5), e0300599. Advance online publication. DOI: 10.1371/journal.pone.0300599 PMID: 38728243

Sandeman. (2024a). *It all started in 1790…*. Sandeman. https://www.sandeman.com/history/

Sandeman. (2024b). *A true experience*. Sandeman. https://www.sandeman.com/visit-us/

Santos, V., Ramos, P., Sousa, B., & Valeri, M. (2022). Towards a framework for the global wine tourism system. *Journal of Organizational Change Management*, 35(2), 348–360. DOI: 10.1108/JOCM-11-2020-0362

Sá, P., Costa, A. P., & Moreira, A. (2021). *Reflexões em torno de Metodologias de Investigação: recolha de dados*. Universidade de Aveiro.

Saridakis, G., Khan, Z., Knight, G., Idris, B., Mitra, J., & Khan, H. (2024). A Look into the Future: The Impact of Metaverse on Traditional Theories and Thinking in International Business. *MIR. Management International Review*, 64(4), 597–632. DOI: 10.1007/s11575-024-00550-8

Sarkar, S. K., Roy, S., Alsentzer, E., McDermott, M. B., Falck, F., Bica, I., & Hyland, S. L. (2020, November). Machine learning for health (ML4H) 2020: Advancing healthcare for all. In *Machine Learning for Health* (pp. 1–11). PMLR.

Sathya, D., Sudha, V., & Jagadeesan, D. (2020). Application of machine learning techniques in healthcare. In *Handbook of Research on Applications and Implementations of Machine Learning Techniques* (pp. 289–304). IGI Global. DOI: 10.4018/978-1-5225-9902-9.ch015

Savin-Baden, M., & Burden, D. (2024). The Metaverse for Learning and Education. In *The Metaverse for Learning and Education* (pp. 4–16). Chapman and Hall/CRC. DOI: 10.1201/9781003413875-2

Scavarelli, A., Arya, A., & Teather, R. J. (2021). Virtual reality and augmented reality in social learning spaces: A literature review. *Virtual Reality (Waltham Cross)*, 25(1), 257–277. DOI: 10.1007/s10055-020-00444-8

Schmitt, B., Brakus, J. J., & Zarantonello, L. (2015). From experiential psychology to consumer experience. *Journal of Consumer Psychology*, 25(1), 166–171. DOI: 10.1016/j.jcps.2014.09.001

Schulz, M. (2023). *Nike takes gaming to next level with metaverse space in Fortnite*. Vogue Business, Retrieved 20th June 2024 from https://www.voguebusiness.com/technology/nike-takes-gaming-to-next-level-with-metaverse-space-in-fortnite

Schwabe, M. (2020). Virtual Reality and the Hospitality Industry: New Opportunities for Engagement and Innovation. *Tourism Management Perspectives*, 33.

Schwab, K. (2016). *The Fourth Industrial Revolution*. Crown Publishing.

Sebastian, G. (2023). A Descriptive Study on Metaverse: Cybersecurity Risks, Controls, and Regulatory Framework. *International Journal of Security and Privacy in Pervasive Computing*, 15(1), 1–14. DOI: 10.4018/IJSPPC.315591

Serrano, J. S. (2020). Virtual world marketing strategies: A study of Roblox and Decentraland. *Journal of Virtual Economies*, 12(3), 189–205.

Seyitoğlu, F., & Ivanov, S. (2020). Virtual reality as an innovative tool for hospitality training. *International Journal of Hospitality Management*, 89.

Shakeel, T., Habib, S., Boulila, W., Koubaa, A., Javed, A. R., Rizwan, M., Gadekallu, T. R., & Sufiyan, M. (2023). A survey on COVID-19 impact in the healthcare domain: Worldwide market implementation, applications, security and privacy issues, challenges and future prospects. *Complex & Intelligent Systems*, 9(1), 1027–1058. DOI: 10.1007/s40747-022-00767-w PMID: 35668731

Shi, F., Ning, H., Zhang, X., Li, R., Tian, Q., Zhang, S., Zheng, Y., Guo, Y., & Daneshmand, M. (2023). A new technology perspective of the Metaverse: Its essence, framework and challenges. *Digital Communications and Networks*.

Shin, H., & Kang, J. (2024). How does the metaverse travel experience influence virtual and actual travel behaviors? Focusing on the role of telepresence and avatar identification. *Journal of Hospitality and Tourism Management*, 58, 174–183. DOI: 10.1016/j.jhtm.2023.12.009

Shi, S., Wang, Y., Chen, X., & Zhang, Q. (2020). Conceptualization of omnichannel customer experience and its impact on shopping intention: A mixed-method approach. *International Journal of Information Management*, 50, 325–336. DOI: 10.1016/j.ijinfomgt.2019.09.001

Shitole, P. T., Chogule, O., Jadhav, G., Gurav, P., & Lad, S. (2024). Virtual digital metaverse healthcare assistant. International Journal of Advanced Research in Science. *Tongxin Jishu*, 284–287. Advance online publication. DOI: 10.48175/IJARSCT-18443

Shukla, P., & Taneja, B. (2024). Navigating the Metaverse in Business and Commerce: Opportunities, Challenges, and Ethical Consideration in the Virtual World. *Advances in Social Networking and Online Communities Research, Innovation, and Industry Impacts of the Metaverse*, 183-196. https://doi.org/https://doi.org/10.4018/979-8-3693-2607-7.ch011

Shukla, A., Dadhich, M., & Dipesh Vaya, A. G. (2024). Impact of Behavioral Biases on Investors' Stock Trading Decisions: A Comparehensive Quantitative Analysis. *Indian Journal of Science and Technology*, 17(8), 670–678. DOI: 10.17485/IJST/v17i8.2845

Shuttleworth, L. (2024, June 14). A virtual influencer: What are they and why you need them for your brand. *P2P Marketing*. Retrieved from https://peertopeermarketing.co/virtual-influencer

Sigala, M. (2018). Collaborative economy and sharing platforms in tourism: Innovation and opportunities for new business models. *Journal of Tourism Futures*, 4(3), 197–202.

Silver, S. D. (2024). Agent expectations and news sentiment in the dynamics of price in a financial market. *Review of Behavioral Finance*, 16(5), 836–859. DOI: 10.1108/RBF-09-2023-0237

Singha, R., & Singha, S. (2024). Building capabilities and workforce for metaverse-driven retail formats. In *Creator's economy in metaverse platforms: Empowering stakeholders through omnichannel approach* (pp. 111–131). IGI Global. DOI: 10.4018/979-8-3693-3358-7.ch007

Singh, D., Malik, G., Jain, P., & Abouraia, M. (2024). A systematic review and research agenda on the causes and consequences of financial overconfidence. *Cogent Economics & Finance*, 12(1), 2348543. DOI: 10.1080/23322039.2024.2348543

Singh, Y., Sujay, D., Shandilya, S. K., & Shandilya, S. (2024). The Metaverse: A Multidisciplinary Perspective on the Future of Human Interaction. In Jabbar, M. A., Tiwari, S., Ortiz-Rodríguez, F., Groppe, S., & Bano Rehman, T. (Eds.), *Applied Machine Learning and Data Analytics. AMLDA 2023. Communications in Computer and Information Science* (Vol. 2047). Springer. DOI: 10.1007/978-3-031-55486-5_3

Singla, B., Shalender, K., & Singh, N. (Eds.). (2024). *Omnichannel approach to co-creating customer experiences through metaverse platforms*. IGI Global. DOI: 10.4018/979-8-3693-1866-9

Sinha, E. (2023). 'Co-creating' experiential learning in the Metaverse- extending the Kolb's learning cycle and identifying potential challenges. *International Journal of Management Education*, 21(3), 100875. DOI: 10.1016/j.ijme.2023.100875

Skalidis, I., Muller, O., & Fournier, S. (2023). CardioVerse: The cardiovascular medicine in the era of Metaverse. *Trends in Cardiovascular Medicine*, 33(8), 471–476. DOI: 10.1016/j.tcm.2022.05.004 PMID: 35568263

Slater, M. G.-L.-C., Gonzalez-Liencres, C., Haggard, P., Vinkers, C., Gregory-Clarke, R., Jelley, S., Watson, Z., Breen, G., Schwarz, R., Steptoe, W., Szostak, D., Halan, S., Fox, D., & Silver, J. (2020). he ethics of realism in virtual and augmented reality. *Frontiers in Virtual Reality*, 1, 512449. DOI: 10.3389/frvir.2020.00001

Slater, M. V., & Sanchez-Vives, M. V. (2016). Enhancing our lives with immersive virtual reality. *Frontiers in Robotics and AI*, 3, 74. DOI: 10.3389/frobt.2016.00074

Smith, V., Warty, R. R., Sursas, J. A., Payne, O., Nair, A., Krishnan, S., da Silva Costa, F., Wallace, E. M., & Vollenhoven, B. (2020). The effectiveness of virtual reality in managing acute pain and anxiety for medical inpatients: Systematic review. *Journal of Medical Internet Research*, 22(11), e17980. DOI: 10.2196/17980 PMID: 33136055

Soliman, M. M., Ahmed, E., Darwish, A., & Hassanien, A. E. (2024). Artificial intelligence powered Metaverse: Analysis, challenges and future perspectives. *Artificial Intelligence Review*, 57(2), 36. DOI: 10.1007/s10462-023-10641-x

Song, Y. T., & Qin, J. (2022). Metaverse and personal healthcare. *Procedia Computer Science*, 210, 189–197. DOI: 10.1016/j.procs.2022.10.136

Song, Y., Cao, J., Wu, K., Yu, P. L. H., & Lee, J. C.-K. (2023). Developing "Learningverse"—A 3-D Metaverse Platform to Support Teaching, Social, and Cognitive Presences. *IEEE Transactions on Learning Technologies*, 16(6), 1165–1178. DOI: 10.1109/TLT.2023.3276574

Sopher, H., & Lescop, L. (2023). Learning in Metaverse: The immersive atelier model of the architecture studio. *Archnet-IJAR: International Journal of Architectural Research*, 17(3), 536–553. DOI: 10.1108/ARCH-10-2022-0213

Souri, A., Ghafour, M. Y., Ahmed, A. M., Safara, F., Yamini, A., & Hoseyninezhad, M. (2020). A new machine learning-based healthcare monitoring model for student's condition diagnosis in Internet of Things environment. *Soft Computing*, 24(22), 17111–17121. DOI: 10.1007/s00500-020-05003-6

Sousa, N., Alén, E., Losada, N., & Melo, M. (2024a). Influencing wine tourists' decision-making with VR: The impact of immersive experiences on their behavioural intentions. *Tourism Management Perspectives*, 51, 101235. Advance online publication. DOI: 10.1016/j.tmp.2024.101235

Sousa, N., Alén, E., Losada, N., & Melo, M. (2024b). Virtual reality in wine tourism: Immersive experiences for promoting travel destinations. *Journal of Vacation Marketing*, 13567667241267306. Advance online publication. DOI: 10.1177/13567667241267306

Southworth, M. K., Silva, J. R., & Silva, J. N. A. (2020). Use of extended realities in cardiology. *Trends in Cardiovascular Medicine*, 30(3), 143–148. DOI: 10.1016/j.tcm.2019.04.005 PMID: 31076168

Spatial Awareness by Kharis. (2022). Just Do It. *An Overview of Nike's web3 strategy*. Retrieved 5th August from https://mirror.xyz/kahris.eth/eMIy5BgXnbEUcakM0EKYkgsbcTe6w8KJ8Aa65-eLogk

Speicher, M. H. (2019). What is mixed reality? In *Proceedings of the 2019 CHI conference on human factors in computing systems* (pp. 1-15).

Spence, C. (2019). Multisensory experiential wine marketing. *Food Quality and Preference*, 71, 106–116. DOI: 10.1016/j.foodqual.2018.06.010

Spence, C. P., Puccinelli, N. M., Grewal, D., & Roggeveen, A. L. (2014). Store atmospherics: A multisensory perspective. *Psychology and Marketing*, 31(7), 472–488. DOI: 10.1002/mar.20709

Spence, C., Obrist, M., Velasco, C., & Ranasinghe, N. (2017). Digitizing the chemical senses: Possibilities & pitfalls. *International Journal of Human-Computer Studies*, 107, 62–74. DOI: 10.1016/j.ijhcs.2017.06.003

Sridhar, A., Shiliang, Z., Woodson, R., & Kwan, L. (2020). Non-pharmacological anxiety reduction with immersive virtual reality for first-trimester dilation and curettage: A pilot study. *The European Journal of Contraception & Reproductive Health Care*, 25(6), 480–483. DOI: 10.1080/13625187.2020.1836146 PMID: 33140989

Stanoevska-Slabeva, K. (2022). Opportunities and challenges of metaverse for education: A literature review. *Edulearn22 Proceedings,* 10401–10410.

Stansfield, M., & Shawver, M. (2016). Virtual reality simulations for emergency response training. *Journal of Safety Research*, 57, 27–35.

Statista Market Insights. (2024). Metaverse – Worldwide. Accessed through https://www.statista.com/outlook/amo/metaverse/worldwide#market-size

Statista. (2023). *Potential concerns in the metaverse according to internet users in the United States as of March 2022*. Retrieved 10th August from https://www.statista.com/statistics/1303391/us-adults-potential-metaverse-issues/

Statista. (2024). *Metaverse Gaming - Worldwide*. Statista. Retrieved 22 September 2024 from https://www.statista.com/outlook/amo/metaverse/metaverse-gaming/worldwide

Steffen, J. H., Gaskin, J. E., Meservy, T. O., Jenkins, J. L., & Wolman, I. (2019). Framework of affordances for virtual reality and augmented reality. *Journal of Management Information Systems*, 36(3), 683–729. DOI: 10.1080/07421222.2019.1628877

Stephenson, N. (1992). *Snow Crash*. Bantam Books.

Suh, W., & Ahn, S. (2022). Utilizing the Metaverse for Learner-Centered Constructivist Education in the Post-Pandemic Era: An Analysis of Elementary School Students. *Journal of Intelligence*, 10(1), 17. DOI: 10.3390/jintelligence10010017 PMID: 35324573

Sui, B., & Yao, L. (2023). *The impact of digital transformation on corporate financialization: The mediating effect of green technology innovation*. Innovation and Green Development. DOI: 10.1016/j.igd.2022.100032

Sun, M., Xie, L., Liu, Y., Li, K., Jiang, B., Lu, Y., ... Yang, D. (2022). The metaverse in current digital medicine. *Clinical eHealth, 5*, 52-57.

Sung, E., Kwon, O., & Sohn, K. (2023). NFT luxury brand marketing in the metaverse: Leveraging blockchain-certified NFTs to drive consumer behavior [Article]. *Psychology and Marketing*, 40(11), 2306–2325. DOI: 10.1002/mar.21854

Sun, Z., Zhu, M., Shan, X., & Lee, C. (2022). Augmented tactile-perception and haptic-feedback rings as human-machine interfaces aiming for immersive interactions. *Nature Communications*, 13(1), 5224. DOI: 10.1038/s41467-022-32745-8 PMID: 36064838

Su, Q., & Deng, Y. (2024). Tax Avoidance News, Investor Behavior, and Stock Market Performance. *Finance Research Letters*, 67, 105834. DOI: 10.1016/j.frl.2024.105834

Taçgın, Z., & Dalgarno, B. (2021). Building an Instructional Design Model for Immersive Virtual Reality Learning Environments. In *Designing* (pp. 20–47). Deploying, and Evaluating Virtual and Augmented Reality in Education. DOI: 10.4018/978-1-7998-5043-4.ch002

Taghizadeh, M., & Ejtehadi, A. (2023). Investigating pre-service EFL teachers' and teacher educators' experience and attitudes towards online interaction tools. *Computer Assisted Language Learning*, 36(8), 1633–1667. DOI: 10.1080/09588221.2021.2011322

Talbi, M., Ferchichi, M., Ismaalia, F., & Samil, S. (2024). Resilience Amidst Turbulence: Unraveling COVID-19's Impact on Financial Stability through Price Dynamics and Investor Behavior in GCC Markets. *International Journal of Economics and Finance*, 16(4), 22. DOI: 10.5539/ijef.v16n4p22

Tamimi, R., & Toth, C. (2023). Comparison of iPhone 13 pro's camera and lidar sensor to uas photogrammetric model of the great Pyramid of Giza. *The International Archives of the Photogrammetry, Remote Sensing and Spatial Information Sciences,* 3, 299–306. DOI: 10.5194/isprs-archives-XLVIII-M-3-2023-299-2023

Tan, T. F., Li, Y., Lim, J. S., Gunasekeran, D. V., Teo, Z. L., Ng, W. Y., & Ting, D. S. (2022). Metaverse and virtual health care in ophthalmology: Opportunities and challenges. *Asia-Pacific Journal of Ophthalmology*, 11(3), 237–246. DOI: 10.1097/APO.0000000000000537 PMID: 35772084

Tan, Y., Xu, W., Li, S., & Chen, K. (2022). Augmented and Virtual Reality (AR/VR) for Education and Training in the AEC Industry: A Systematic Review of Research and Applications. *Buildings (Basel, Switzerland)*, 12(10), 1529. DOI: 10.3390/buildings12101529

Tariq, M. U. (2025c). Navigating the Landscape of Qualitative Research in Doctoral Studies: Methodologies, Design, and Implementation. In R. Throne (Ed.), *Qualitative Research Methods for Dissertation Research* (pp. 1-24). IGI Global Scientific Publishing. DOI: 10.4018/979-8-3693-3069-2.ch001

Tariq, M. U. (2024a). Smart Transportation Systems: Paving the Way for Sustainable Urban Mobility. In Munuhwa, S. (Ed.), *Contemporary Solutions for Sustainable Transportation Practices* (pp. 254–283). IGI Global. DOI: 10.4018/979-8-3693-3755-4.ch010

Tariq, M. U. (2024b). Leading Smart Technologies and Innovations for E-Business 5.0: Applications and Management Frameworks. In Popkova, E. (Ed.), *Smart Technologies and Innovations in E-Business* (pp. 25–46). IGI Global. DOI: 10.4018/978-1-6684-7840-0.ch002

Tariq, M. U. (2024c). The role of emerging technologies in shaping the global digital government landscape. In Guo, Y. (Ed.), *Emerging developments and technologies in digital government* (pp. 160–180). IGI Global. DOI: 10.4018/979-8-3693-2363-2.ch009

Tariq, M. U. (2025a). Innovating Education and Entrepreneurship Through Computational Thinking: New Pathways for Economic Development. In Tunio, M. (Ed.), *Entrepreneurial Ecosystems Driving Economic Transformation and Job Creation* (pp. 1–28). IGI Global Scientific Publishing. DOI: 10.4018/979-8-3693-9486-1.ch001

Tariq, M. U. (2025b). Navigating the Ethical Frontier-Human Oversight in AI-Driven Decision-Making System. In Hai-Jew, S. (Ed.), *Enhancing Automated Decision-Making Through AI* (pp. 425–448). IGI Global Scientific Publishing.,DOI: 10.4018/979-8-3693-6230-3.ch013

Tavman, E. B. (2024). Metaverse retailing: Opportunities and challenges. *PressAcademia Procedia*, 19(1), 10–15.

Thanh, T. V., & Kirova, V. (2018). Wine tourism experience: A netnography study. *Journal of Business Research*, 83, 30–37. DOI: 10.1016/j.jbusres.2017.10.008

Thase, M. E., McCrone, P., Barrett, M. S., Eells, T. D., Wisniewski, S. R., Balasubramani, G. K., Brown, G. K., & Wright, J. H. (2020). Improving cost-effectiveness and access to cognitive behavior therapy for depression: Providing remote-ready, computer-assisted psychotherapy in times of crisis and beyond. *Psychotherapy and Psychosomatics*, 89(5), 307–313. DOI: 10.1159/000508143 PMID: 32396917

Thawonmas, R. &. (2011, July). Frame extraction based on displacement amount for automatic comic generation from metaverse museum visit log. In *Intelligent Interactive MultimediaSystems and Services: Proceedings of the 4th International Conference on Intelligent Interactive Multimedia Systems and Services (IIMSS 2011)* (pp. 153-162). Springer Berlin Heidelberg. DOI: 10.1007/978-3-642-22158-3_16

The Influencer Marketing Factory. (2022, March). *Virtual influencers survey infographic.* Retrieved from https://theinfluencermarketingfactory.com/virtual-influencers-survey-infographic/

The pros and cons of virtual influencers. (n.d.). *Emplifi | Customer Experience & Social Media Marketing Software.* Retrieved from https://emplifi.io/resources/blog/virtual-influencers-pros-and-cons

Thomason, J. (2021). Metahealth-how will the metaverse change health care? *Journal of Metaverse*, 1(1), 13–16.

Thomason, J. (2022). Metaverse, token economies, and non-communicable diseases. *Global Health Journal (Amsterdam, Netherlands)*, 6(3), 164–167. DOI: 10.1016/j.glohj.2022.07.001

Timmermans, H. (1993). Retail Environments and Spatial Shopping Behavior. In Tommy, G., & Reginald, G. G. (Eds.), *Advances in Psychology* (Vol. 96, pp. 342–377). North-Holland.

Tlili, A. (2023). Smart learning environments. DOI: 10.1186/s40561-023-00237-x

Tlili, A., Huang, R., Shehata, B., Liu, D., Zhao, J., Metwally, A. H. S., Wang, H., Denden, M., Bozkurt, A., Lee, L.-H., Beyoglu, D., Altinay, F., Sharma, R. C., Altinay, Z., Li, Z., Liu, J., Ahmad, F., Hu, Y., Salha, S., & Burgos, D. (2022). Is Metaverse in education a blessing or a curse: A combined content and bibliometric analysis. *Smart Learning Environments*, 9(1), 24. DOI: 10.1186/s40561-022-00205-x

Torres, M., Correia, T., Carneiro, A., & Meirinhos, V. (2019). *Virtual reality and augmented reality in onboarding of new employees*. Independent Research on Human Resources. DOI: 10.1234/vrar-2019

Trunfio, M., & Rossi, S. (2022). Advances in Metaverse Investigation: Streams of Research and Future Agenda. *Virtual Worlds*, 1(2), 103–129. DOI: 10.3390/virtualworlds1020007

Tsappi, E., Deliyannis, I., & Papageorgiou, G. N. (2024). Developing a Performance Evaluation Framework Structural Model for Educational Metaverse. *Technologies*, 12(4), 53. DOI: 10.3390/technologies12040053

Tsirulnikov, D., Suart, C., Abdullah, R., Vulcu, F., & Mullarkey, C. E. (2023). Game on: Immersive virtual laboratory simulation improves student learning outcomes & motivation. *FEBS Open Bio*, 13(3), 396–407. DOI: 10.1002/2211-5463.13567 PMID: 36723273

Tung, V. W. S. (2020). Virtual reality in tourism: Exploring the future of travel in the metaverse. *Tourism Management Perspectives*, 35.

Turbyne, C. A. (2022). Virtuality technologies in mental healthcare: The medical metaverse of tomorrow.

Türkmen, N., & Sürmeli, D. (2024). *The Metaverse Virtual Economy: A Comprehensive Overview*. MANAS Sosyal Araştırmalar Dergisi. DOI: 10.33206/mjss.1350087

Tussyadiah, I. P. (2018). The role of virtual reality in tourism marketing and the guest experience. *Journal of Hospitality & Tourism Research (Washington, D.C.)*, 42(5), 788–812.

Tussyadiah, I. P. (2020). The role of gamification and interactivity in metaverse-based travel experiences. *Journal of Travel & Tourism Marketing*, 37(8), 925–940.

Tussyadiah, I. P., & Park, S. (2018). Consumer preferences for virtual reality in tourism. *Journal of Travel Research*, 57(7), 851–864.

Tussyadiah, I. P., Wang, D., & Jia, C. (2017). Exploring the role of digital literacy in tourism innovation. *Journal of Travel Research*, 56(7), 837–849.

Tu, Y. T., Lin, S. Y., & Hsu, T. K. (2013). The Impact of Brand Image and Customer Commitment on Loyalty: An Empirical Study of Automobile Sector. *International Management and Business Review*, 5(4), 191–193.

Ullah, H., Manickam, S., Obaidat, M., Laghari, S. U. A., & Uddin, M. (2023). Exploring the potential of metaverse technology in healthcare: Applications, challenges, and future directions. *IEEE Access : Practical Innovations, Open Solutions*, 11, 69686–69707. DOI: 10.1109/ACCESS.2023.3286696

UnrealEngine. (2023). *Real-Time round-up: the state of interactive 3D*. Epic Games. Retrieved 22 September 2024 from https://www.unrealengine.com/en-US/blog/real-time-round-up-the-state-of-interactive-3d

Urry, J., & Larsen, J. (2011). *The tourist gaze 3.0*. Sage Publications. DOI: 10.4135/9781446251904

Usmani, S. S., Sharath, M., & Mehendale, M. (2022). Future of mental health in the metaverse. *General Psychiatry*, 35(4), e100825. DOI: 10.1136/gpsych-2022-100825 PMID: 36189180 van Leeuwen, F. W., & van der Hage, J. A. (2022). Where robotic surgery meets the metaverse. *Cancers (Basel)*, 14(24), 6161. DOI: 10.3390/cancers14246161 PMID: 36551645

Varshney, D. (2022). Understanding virtual employee onboarding (VEO): The new normal and beyond. Emirati Journal of Business, Economics, &. *Social Studies*, 1(1), 55–72. Advance online publication. DOI: 10.54878/jhhm2y12

Vidal-Tomás, D. (2023). The illusion of the metaverse and meta-economy. *International Review of Financial Analysis*, 86, 102560. Advance online publication. DOI: 10.1016/j.irfa.2023.102560

Vidani, J. (2024). Why 90% of Stock Market Traders are in Loss? *Available atSSRN* 4849875.

Vieira, C. A. (2023). Case study as a qualitative research methodology. Performance Improvement, 62(4).

Villalba, E. R. (2016). *Cultural simulation through virtual worlds: The case of Second Life*. Musica/Tecnologia Music/Technology.

Vukovic, D. B., Kurbonov, O. O., Maiti, M., Özer, M., & Radovanovic, M. (2024). Outperforming the market: A comparison of Star and NonStar analysts' investment strategies and recommendations. *Humanities & Social Sciences Communications*, 11(1), 1–15. DOI: 10.1057/s41599-023-02527-8

Walther, J. B. (1996). Computer-mediated communication: Impersonal, interpersonal, and hyperpersonal interaction. *Communication Research*, 23(1), 3–43. DOI: 10.1177/009365096023001001

Wang, D., Yan, X., & Zhou, Y. (2021). Research on Metaverse: Concept, development and standard system. https://ieeexplore.ieee.org/stamp/stamp.jsp?arnumber =9741935

Wang, Q., Li, R., Wang, Q., & Chen, S. (2021). Non-Fungible Token (NFT): Overview, Evaluation, Opportunities and Challenges. https://arxiv.org/pdf/2105.07447

Wang, Y., Lee, L.-H., Braud, T., & Hui, P. (2022). Re-shaping Post-COVID-19 Teaching and Learning: A Blueprint of Virtual-Physical Blended Classrooms in the Metaverse Era. *2022 IEEE 42nd International Conference on Distributed Computing Systems Workshops*, 241–247. DOI: 10.1109/ICDCSW56584.2022.00053

Wang, D. (2016). Training employees using virtual reality technology: Implications for service industries. *Journal of Service Research*, 19(2), 234–248.

Wang, G., Badal, A., Jia, X., Maltz, J. S., Mueller, K., Myers, K. J., Niu, C., Vannier, M., Yan, P., Yu, Z., & Zeng, R. (2022). Development of metaverse for intelligent healthcare. *Nature Machine Intelligence*, 4(11), 922–929. DOI: 10.1038/s42256-022-00549-6 PMID: 36935774

Wang, H., Ning, H., Lin, Y., Wang, W., Dhelim, S., Farha, F., Ding, J., & Daneshmand, M. (2023). A Survey on the Metaverse: The State-of-the-Art, Technologies, Applications, and Challenges. *IEEE Internet of Things Journal*, 10(16), 14671–14688. DOI: 10.1109/JIOT.2023.3278329

Wang, M., Yu, H., Bell, Z., & Chu, X. (2022). Constructing an Edu-Metaverse Ecosystem: A New and Innovative Framework. *IEEE Transactions on Learning Technologies*, 15(6), 685–696. DOI: 10.1109/TLT.2022.3210828

Wang, Y., Liu, C., & Zhang, X. (2020). Metaverse technologies for inclusive tourism: Virtual travel for people with mobility constraints. *Journal of Inclusive Tourism*, 12(4), 115–130.

Wang, Y., Su, Z., Zhang, N., Xing, R., Liu, D., Luan, T. H., & Shen, X. (2022). A survey on metaverse: Fundamentals, security, and privacy. *IEEE Communications Surveys and Tutorials*, 25(1), 319–352. DOI: 10.1109/COMST.2022.3202047

Waquar, A., Sujood, , Kareem, S., Yasmeen, N., & Hussain, S. (2024, July 26). Sujood, Kareem, S., Yasmeen, N., & Hussain, S. (2024). From traditional to virtual classrooms: Unravelling themes and shaping the future of Metaverse education. *Interactive Technology and Smart Education*. Advance online publication. DOI: 10.1108/ITSE-02-2024-0032

Waters, S. (2019). *Why Store Atmosphere Matters to Your Customers*. Retrieved 11th August 2024 from https://www.liveabout.com/atmosphere-2890162

Werner, H., Ribeiro, G., Arcoverde, V., Lopes, J., & Velho, L. (2022). The use of metaverse in fetal medicine and gynecology. *European Journal of Radiology*, 150, 150. DOI: 10.1016/j.ejrad.2022.110241 PMID: 35299111

Wiederhold, B. K. (2022). Ready (or Not) player one: Initial musings on the metaverse. *Cyberpsychology, Behavior, and Social Networking*, 25(1), 1–2. DOI: 10.1089/cyber.2021.29234.editorial PMID: 34964667

Wikipedia contributors. (2024, December 3). Influencer marketing. Retrieved from *Wikipedia:*https://en.wikipedia.org/wiki/Influencer_marketing

Wikipedia contributors. (n.d.-a). *Ami Yamato*. Retrieved from https://en.wikipedia.org/wiki/Ami_Yamato

Wikipedia contributors. (n.d.-b). *Hatsune Miku*. Retrieved from https://en.wikipedia.org/wiki/Hatsune_Miku

Williams, J. (2024, August 23). The rise of virtual influencers: Are they here to stay? *Sprout Social*. Retrieved from https://sproutsocial.com/insights/virtual-influencers

Wilson, V. (2014). Research methods: triangulation.

Wilson, K. B., Karg, A., & Ghaderi, H. (2022). *Prospecting non-fungible tokens in the digital economy: Stakeholders and ecosystem, risk and opportunity*. Elsevier.

Wirtz, J., Zeithaml, V. A., & Gistri, G. (2018). Technology, service innovation, and the service experience: The role of business collaborations in developing customer-centric services. *Journal of the Academy of Marketing Science*, 46(3), 313–325.

Wohlgenannt, I., Simons, A., & Stieglitz, S. (2020). Virtual Reality. *Business & Information Systems Engineering*, 62(5), 455–461. DOI: 10.1007/s12599-020-00658-9

Wu, C. H., & Liu, C. Y. (2023). Educational Applications of Non-Fungible Tokens (NFT). *Sustainability (Basel)*, 15(1), 7. Advance online publication. DOI: 10.3390/su15010007

Wunderman Thompson Intelligence. (2021). *Into the Metaverse* (2021 Edition). Wunderman Thompson Intelligence.

Wunderman Thompson Intelligence. (2022). *New realities Into the Metaverse and beyond* (2022 Edition). Wunderman Thompson Intelligence.

Wu, P., Chen, D., & Zhang, R. (2024). Topic prevalence and trends of metaverse in healthcare: A bibliometric analysis. *Data Science and Management*, 7(2), 129–143. DOI: 10.1016/j.dsm.2023.12.003

Wu, S., Xu, L., Dai, Z., & Pan, Y. (2023). Factors Affecting Avatar Customization Behavior in Virtual Environments. *Electronics (Basel)*, 12(10), 2286. DOI: 10.3390/electronics12102286

Wu, T. C., & Ho, C. T. B. (2023). A scoping review of metaverse in emergency medicine. *Australasian Emergency Care (Online)*, 26(1), 75–83. DOI: 10.1016/j.auec.2022.08.002 PMID: 35953392

Xiang, Z., Fesenmaier, D. R., & Wei, W. (2022). Metaverse and destination marketing: Virtual tourism experiences and their impact on travelers. *Tourism Management*, 83, 47–58.

Xi, N., Chen, J., Gama, F., Korkeila, H., & Hamari, J. (2024). Acceptance of the metaverse: A laboratory experiment on augmented and virtual reality shopping. *Internet Research*, 34(7), 82–117. DOI: 10.1108/INTR-05-2022-0334

Xu, F. K. (2022). Ethical considerations in the development of Metaverse experiences: Balancing innovation and privacy. *Journal of Business Ethics*, 179(2).

Yadav, S., Pandey, S.K. & Sharma, D. (2024). Marketing beyond reality: a systematic literature review on metaverse, Management Research Review. DOI: 10.1108/MRR-06-2023-0456

Yang, D., Zhou, J., Song, Y., Sun, M., & Bai, C. (2022). Metaverse in medicine. *Clinical eHealth, 5*, 39-43.

Yang, Q., Zhao, Y., Huang, H., Xiong, Z., Kang, J., & Zheng, Z. (2022). Fusing Blockchain and AI With Metaverse: A Survey. *IEEE Open Journal of the Computer Society*, 3, 122–136. DOI: 10.1109/OJCS.2022.3188249

Yang, R. (2022). Multimodal Fusion Blended Teaching Under the New Era of "Internet+. *Lecture Notes of the Institute for Computer Sciences, Social Informatics and Telecommunications Engineering*, 439, 686–698. DOI: 10.1007/978-3-031-04245-4_61

Yang, S. J. (2021). Precision education: A new challenge for AI in education. *Journal of Educational Technology & Society*, 24(1), 105–108. https://link.gale.com/apps/doc/A657722701/AONE?u=anon~b693f685&sid=googleScholar&xid=e057ad51

Yaqoob, I., Salah, K., Uddin, M., Jayaraman, R., Omar, M., & Imran, M. (2020). Blockchain for digital twins: Recent advances and future research challenges. *IEEE Network*, 34(5), 290–298. DOI: 10.1109/MNET.001.1900661

Yasar, A. G., Thomas, A., Barr, K., & Eben, M. (2023). Gaming without Frontiers: Copyright and Competition in the Changing Video Game Sector.

Yazıcı, A. M., Özkan, A., & Özkan, H. (2024). Meta: XR-AR-MR and Mirror World Technologies Business Impact of Metaverse. Journal of Metaverse. DOI: 10.57019/jmv.1344489

Yin, R. K. (n.d.). How to do Better Case Studies (Chapter 8). https://books.google.com.br/books?hl=pt-PT&lr=&id=9_bUtEp-bGUC&oi=fnd&pg=PA254&dq=yin+case+study+research&ots=-xO67LJMXN&sig=IUg2rTfPCO9JPGFeIbIXr7WVwdc#v=onepage&q=yin%20case%20study%20research&f=false

Yin, R. K. (2003). Designing case studies. In Maruster, L. (Ed.), *Qualitative research methods* (Vol. 5, pp. 359–386).

Yin, R. K. (2009). *Case Study Research: Design and Methods* (4th ed.). Bookman.

Yin, R. K. (2009). How to do better case studies. In Bickman, L., & Rog, D. J. (Eds.), *The SAGE handbook of applied social research methods* (Vol. 2, pp. 254–282). DOI: 10.4135/9781483348858.n8

Yin, R. K. (2013). Validity and generalization in future case study evaluations. *Evaluation*, 19(3), 321–332. DOI: 10.1177/1356389013497081

Yin, R. K. (2018). *Case Study Research and Applications* (6th ed.). Sage.

Yoo, C. K. (2021). Ethical issues in virtual tourism: An exploration of privacy and security in the metaverse. *Journal of Travel Research*, 60(6), 1325–1341.

Yoo, K. H. (2018). The impact of virtual reality on the hospitality industry's business operations. *Journal of Hospitality Marketing & Management*, 27(3), 283–298.

Yuan, Y., & Yang, Y. (2022). *Embracing the Metaverse: Mechanism and logic of a new digital economy*. Metaverse. DOI: 10.54517/met.v3i2.1814

Yu, H., Wen, G., Gan, J., Zheng, W., & Lei, C. (2020). Self-paced Learning for K-means Clustering Algorithm. *Pattern Recognition Letters*, 132, 69–75. DOI: 10.1016/j.patrec.2018.08.028

Yung, R., & Khoo-Lattimore, C. (2019). Adoption of immersive technologies in tourism: Co-creation and virtual reality. *Journal of Travel Research*, 58(3), 315–331.

Zabel, C., O'Brien, D., & Natzel, J. (2023). Sensing the Metaverse: The microfoundations of complementor firms' dynamic sensing capabilities in emerging-technology ecosystems. *Technological Forecasting and Social Change*, 192, 122562. DOI: 10.1016/j.techfore.2023.122562

Zanon, G. N., Szejka, A. L., & Loures, E. D. F. R. (2021). *Towards an integrated MCDM and BSC method to support the digital transformation strategy in railway companies*. Advances in Transdisciplinary Engineering. DOI: 10.3233/ATDE210109

Zengler, T. (2019). Leveraging Augmented Reality and Virtual Reality in the Hospitality Industry. *Journal of Hospitality and Tourism Technology*, 10(4), 401–418.

Zeng, Y., Zeng, L., Zhang, C., & Cheng, A. S. (2022). The metaverse in cancer care: Applications and challenges. *Asia-Pacific Journal of Oncology Nursing*, 9(12), 100111. DOI: 10.1016/j.apjon.2022.100111 PMID: 36276879

Zhang, C. (2020). The Why, What, and How of Immersive Experience. *IEEE Access : Practical Innovations, Open Solutions*, 8, 90878–90888. DOI: 10.1109/ACCESS.2020.2993646

Zhang, X., Chen, Y., Hu, L., & Wang, Y. (2022). The Metaverse in education: Definition, framework, features, potential applications, challenges, and future research topics. *Frontiers in Psychology*, 13, 1016300. Advance online publication. DOI: 10.3389/fpsyg.2022.1016300 PMID: 36304866

Zhao, Y. J., Jiang, J., Chen, Y., Liu, R., Yang, Y., Xue, X., & Chen, S. (2022). Metaverse: Perspectives from graphics, interactions and visualization. *Visual Informatics*, 6(1), 56–67. DOI: 10.1016/j.visinf.2022.03.002

Zhao, Z., Zhao, B., Ji, Z., & Liang, Z. (2022). On the Personalized Learning Space in Educational Metaverse Based on Heart Rate Signal. *International Journal of Information and Communication Technology Education*, 18(2), 1–12. DOI: 10.4018/ijicte.314565

Zheng, J. M., Chan, K. W., & Gibson, I. (1998). Virtual reality. *IEEE Potentials*, 17(2), 20–23. DOI: 10.1109/45.666641

Zhu, J., Ren, Z., & Lee, C. (2020). Toward healthcare diagnoses by machine-learning-enabled volatile organic compound identification. *ACS Nano*, 15(1), 894–903. DOI: 10.1021/acsnano.0c07464 PMID: 33307692

Zhu, X., Li, S., Srinivasan, K., & Lash, M. T. (2024). Impact of the COVID-19 pandemic on the stock market and investor online word of mouth. *Decision Support Systems*, 176, 114074. DOI: 10.1016/j.dss.2023.114074

Zikas, P., Kamarianakis, M., Kartsonaki, I., Lydatakis, N., Kateros, S., Kentros, M., . . . Papagiannakis, G. (2021). Covid-19-VR strikes back: innovative medical VR training. In *ACM SIGGRAPH 2021 Immersive Pavilion* (pp. 1-2). DOI: 10.1145/3450615.3464546

Zotkin, D. N., Duraiswami, R., & Davis, L. S. (2004). Rendering localized spatial audio in a virtual auditory space. *IEEE Transactions on Multimedia*, 6(4), 553–564. DOI: 10.1109/TMM.2004.827516

Zuboff, S. (2015). *The Age of Surveillance Capitalism: The Fight for a Human Future at the New Frontier of Power*. Public Affairs.

Zwass, V. (2010). Co-creation: Toward a taxonomy and an integrated research perspective. *International Journal of Electronic Commerce*, *15*(1), 11-48.

About the Contributors

Maria Antónia Rodrigues has a PhD in Communication/Marketing from the University of Vigo a Master's Degree in Marketing from the University of Porto, and two Bachelor Degrees, one in Marketing and one in International Trade, both from Business School (ISCAP) of the Polytechnic of Porto. She is a researcher at CEOS. PP and a Senior Lecturer at ISCAP, where she is also a member of the Scientific and Consulting Boards, and the Director of the Bachelor Degree in Marketing. She has published several papers and 3 books indexed in SCOPUS and WoS. She has received two awards, and works in Social Sciences with an emphasis on business, services, consumer behavior, and Marketing. Additionally, she has supervised several MSc dissertations, and organizes and participates in several scientific events, seminars, and workshops.

Maria Amélia Carvalho (Ph.D.) is an invited adjunct professor at the Business School of Polytechnic of Porto. She has published papers in the Journal of Marketing Theory and Practice, the International Journal of Tourism Cities, and the Tourism Recreation Research Journal, among others.

Joaquim Monteiro Pratas has a PhD in Business and Management Studies (with a specialization in Marketing and Strategy) from Faculdade de Economia do Porto - University of Porto. Currently, he is an Adjunct Professor at Instituto Superior de Contabilidade e Administração - Instituto Politécnico do Porto (ISCAP - IPP), and invited lecturer in Porto Business School - University of Porto. He is a researcher at Centro de Estudos Organizacionais e Sociais do Politécnico do Porto (CEOS.PP), and at Governance, Competitiveness and Public Policy (GOVCOPP) unit research from Universidade de Aveiro. His main interests involve Retail, Marketing, Management, Sales and Tourism, and has published academic papers and book chapters in these topics.

***

Leonardo Andrade has a degree in Marketing Management from the University of Maia and stands out for his entrepreneurial spirit and passion for personal development. He believes that practical experience and constant challenges are fundamental to professional growth, and he continually strives to expand his horizons and improve his skills. Throughout his academic career, she has always shown an active search for new challenges and experiences. In the second year of his degree, he joined the WEL(L)COME I UMAIA project as a Mentor, where he actively contributed to promoting a culture of peer mentoring at the University of Maia. In his third year, he collaborated in the development of RISE UP // UMAIA Junior Enterprise, where he took part in the organization of events such as ChallANJE 2023, UMAIA RHsummit 2023 and others. This experience has also allowed his to take part in various entrepreneurship and innovation events. He also took part in two international projects under the Erasmus+ program, Blended Mobility, in which he acted as Marketing Manager, and the project D - PBL, where he acted as Project and Marketing Manager. Alongside his studies, he worked at the Grupo Jorge Anjos as a waiter, which allowed him to further develop his sense of responsibility and commitment. With all this experience, Leonardo Andrade has consolidated a strong interest and skills in the areas of Marketing Management, Project Management, Entrepreneurship, Innovation, Market Research, Sales and Communication.

Belem Barbosa received her PhD in Business and Management Studies – Specialisation in Marketing and Strategy from the University of Porto, Portugal. She is Assistant Professor at the School of Economics and Management of the University of Porto. She is full researcher at cef.up Center for Economics and Finance at the University of Porto. Her research interests lie primarily in the areas of digital marketing and consumer behavior.

Camila Carvalho holds a Master's degree in Food Science and Technology from the University of Porto. She is involved in the local coordination of projects in the wine and wine tourism sectors at the University of Porto. Her main research interest is on wine tourism.

Saurabh Chandra is an accomplished legal scholar and currently serves as an Associate Professor at the School of Law, Bennett University, India. With a robust academic foundation, he earned his Bachelor of Arts and Bachelor of Laws (B.A. LL.B.) from the prestigious Aligarh Muslim University (AMU). He further specialized in Business Laws, completing his Master of Laws (LL.M.) at the renowned National Law School of India University (NLSIU), Bangalore. Dr. Chandra's academic journey culminated in a Doctorate in Law (Ph.D.) from the esteemed National Law University. In addition to his impressive legal education from some of India's most prestigious institutions, Dr. Saurabh Chandra also holds a master's degree in Management with specialization in Human Resources in Management and another in Journalism and Mass Communication. With 16 years of teaching experience, he has established himself as an expert in Business and Corporate Laws, with numerous publications to his credit. Dr. Saurabh Chandra is a distinguished expert in Business and Corporate Laws, with a profound understanding of the intricate legal frameworks that govern the business world. His expertise is complemented by a robust portfolio of scholarly publications, which underscores his commitment to advancing knowledge in his field. Throughout his career, Dr. Chandra has consistently produced high-impact research that addresses critical issues in business and corporate law. His publications are widely recognized for their depth of analysis, innovative perspectives, and practical relevance. He has contributed extensively to leading journals, where his work has often set new standards for legal scholarship. His publications not only reflect his scholarly rigor but also his dedication to addressing contemporary challenges faced by businesses and policymakers. By bridging the gap between theoretical insights and real-world applications, Dr. Chandra's work serves as a valuable resource for academics, legal practitioners, and industry professionals alike. Dr. Chandra brings a wealth of experience in Academic Administration, having successfully held various key administrative positions. His diverse qualifications and extensive experience make him a distinguished figure in the academic and legal communities.

Kittisak Wongmahesak lectures at North Bangkok University's Faculty of Political Science and directs the Association of Legal & Political Studies. He is also a Research Fellow at Shinawatra University in Thailand and Universiti Sultan Zainal Abidin in Malaysia. His academic influence also extends to Indonesia, where he holds roles such as Adjunct Professor at Sekolah Tinggi Ilmu Administrasi Abdul Haris and various other Indonesian universities, including Universitas Muhammadiyah Sinjai, Makassar, and Sidenreng Rappang. He has served as a Full Professor of Public Administration at Huanghe Business School, Henan University of Economics and Law in China, and University of City Island, Cyprus. Furthermore, he was an Adjunct Researcher at Vietnam's Ton Duc Thang University and Duy Tan University. He holds a Ph.D. in Social Sciences alongside his M.A. and B.A. in Political Science from Kasetsart University, and obtained an M.B.A. and M.P.A. from Ramkhamhaeng University, alongside a B.Pol.Sc. in International Relations from Sukhothai Thammathirat Open University. His expertise covers Political Science, Public and Private Management, International Political Economy, and Social Research. He is an editor for several renowned journals like Sustainability, Frontiers in Psychology, and PLOS One. Recognized among the top 2% of scientists globally by Stanford University since 2020, he holds an impressive record of over

450 indexed publications with an h-index of 57 and more than 10,000 citations, showcasing his substantial contributions to the academic field.

Jothi K. is working as an Associate Professor and Head, Department of Commerce with E Commerce at KPR College of Arts, Science and Research, Coimbatore. She produced more than 10 Ph.D. Scholars and published more than 10 articles in Scopus Indexed Journals and more than 50 articles in International journals. She is also acting as a subject expert in Board of Studies at various colleges.

Amit Kakkar is an Associate Professor at Mittal School of Business, Lovely Professional University. He has a total experience of 21 years, with industry experience of more than 11 years and teaching experience of more than 10 years. He has completed his PhD from the Lovely Professional University in the consumption enhancement of VoD services. He has presented papers at more than fourteen international conferences in 10 years. He has also published more than ten papers in journals of repute. His areas of interest are strategic management, brand management, and consumer behaviour. He got the best paper awards in NICOM in 2018 and IIM Jammu in 2023.

Ruchi Kakkar is currently an Associate Professor at Mittal School of Business, Lovely Professional University. She completed her PhD from Lovely Professional University in the Management domain. She completed her MFC and MBA from Punjabi University, Patiala. She has presented papers in International and National conferences.

Madhu Bala Kaushik is a distinguished academic with over 17 years of experience in Human Resource Management (HRM) and Entrepreneurship. A certified mentor from the Micro, Small, & Medium Enterprises (MSME) sector, she has authored more than 20 research papers in reputed journals, holds two patents and two copyrights, and is a reviewer for many Scopus-indexed journals. Her innovative research and dedication to mentoring emerging entrepreneurs have made her a respected figure in academia. Dr. Kaushik's work continues to bridge theory and practice, shaping future leaders in HRM and entrepreneurship.

Sahil Kohli is an Assistant Professor at Chandigarh University and the visionary Program Lead for the MBA - Data Science & AI, in collaboration with SAS. With over 15 years of robust experience in Digital Marketing and Project Management across Web and Mobile Applications, Sahil brings a wealth of industry knowledge to his academic role. He is currently completing his PhD in Business Management, with research focused on Webrooming Behaviours affecting Consumer Purchase Intentions for EV Cars, integrating Consumer Behaviour with Digital Marketing

Strategies. An authoritative voice in Digital Marketing and Data Science, Sahil has authored Five Specialized Books that serve as significant academic resources in these fields. These publications, along with his Seven Scopus-Indexed Articles that span Journal Papers, Book Chapters, and Conference Papers, underscore his prolific contribution to scholarly literature and his commitment to bridging theoretical knowledge with practical applications. Sahil's notable academic achievements include the development and leadership of several pioneering programs at Chandigarh University. He was instrumental in establishing the BBA in Digital Marketing, MBA in Digital Marketing, and the recent BBA in Strategic HR, alongside the MBA in Data Science & AI. These programs reflect his forward-thinking approach and his dedication to enriching the academic landscape with an industry-relevant curriculum. Before transitioning to academia, Sahil's extensive industry tenure involved leading numerous high-stake projects, which not only honed his expertise in strategic and operational aspects of business but also enriched his teaching, making him a pivotal figure in educational advancement and student success.

João Miguel Da Silva Martins is a Marketing Management student at the University of Maia (UMAIA), with a strong interest in Digital Marketing, Branding, and Marketing Strategy. Currently, he works as a Content Creator & Marketing Manager at Quinta da Rabiana, where he develops brand communication and digital content strategies. He previously completed a curricular internship at 5D Denim Development & Production, focusing on launching the company's digital marketing strategy. Additionally, he gained experience in sales while working at Sebastião & Martins SA, first as a Quality Control Analyst and later as a Sales Technician. His main interests include Digital Marketing, Brand Management, and Business Strategy. Passionate about continuous learning, he aims to further specialize in marketing, potentially through international education and professional experiences.

Gabriel Dias Moreira has a degree in Marketing Management from Universidade da Maia and a postgraduate degree in Project Management from Porto Business School. Currently, he is an Export Manager at Fruut, where he applies his expertise in strategic marketing, problem-solving, and management. His main interests involve Strategic Marketing, Problem-Solving, and Management. Throughout his career, he has developed strong skills in international business and market expansion, contributing to the growth and positioning of brands in global markets.

Senthil Nathan is a finance and technology professional who is a respected payments specialist and researcher in the banking industry with 24+ years of experience in delivering innovative payments platform on cutting edge technology for multinational banks across Asia Pacific, Europe and Americas.

Velmurugan R. is presently working as an Associate Professor in Commerce, Karpagam Academy of Higher Education, Coimbatore. He started his career as a Project Fellow under UGC Sponsored Major Research Project at NGM College, Pollachi. He has 18 years of teaching experience has 15 years of research experience. To his credit he produced 22 Ph.D. Scholars and 5 M.Phil. Scholars. At present 1 scholar submitter his thesis, 6 Ph.D. Scholars are under his guidance. Moreover, to his credit he published 163 articles in various International Journals, of which 54 articles are published in Scopus Indexed Journals and 15 articles in Web of Science and 76 articles in edited volumes. He also participates and presented 27 papers in various International Seminar / Conference and 54 National Seminar / Conference. He acted as an external examiner for various M.Phil. and Ph.D. Viva voce examinations. He acted as a Vice Chancellor nominee for Doctoral Committee Expert at Bharathiar University, Coimbatore and Periyar University, Salem. He acted as a Chairperson at various National Level Conferences. He also acted as an Expert for Syllabus Scrutiny Committee, Question Paper Scrutiny Committee and Expert members for Board of Studies at various reputed Colleges. Considering his meritorious contribution, he received awards like Best Paper Presenter, Best Research Supervisor and Best Faculty Awards from various research foundations and councils. He too acted as a resource person for 27 Guest Lectures, 30 Workshops and 10 faculty development programmes.

Rajaprabakaran Rajendran is an incisive medical communication professional with over 23 years of experience in CME/CPD, medico-marketing/ medical communication, client servicing, and KOL management; managing medcom programmes for healthcare professionals in Asia Pacific and the Middle East and North Africa regions. He has extensive experience in the planning and delivery of key innovative medcom programmes through multi-channel platforms for leading pharmaceutical companies in order to facilitate effective engagement with their target audiences across medical specialties. Raja is mainly responsible for designing medical communication/education strategies and delivering high quality medical communication/education programmes in collaboration with national and international medical associations, universities and hospitals, and key opinion leaders across medical specialties. Now he is a research scholar at CMS Business School, Jain Deemed To-Be University, Bengaluru, India.

Manpreet Kaur Riyat, Doctoral Candidate at Mittal School of Business, Lovely Professional University, Phagwara, Punjab, India, specializes in marketing with

Masters in Business Administration in International Business and Marketing. Her research focuses on the impact of gamification marketing activities on marketing outcomes in education technology, aiming to bridge the gap between traditional marketing approaches and the digital landscape. With a keen interest in gamification, the metaverse, consumer behaviour, education technology, and technology adoption, she is committed to advancing knowledge in these cutting-edge fields and exploring their implications for marketing strategies.

Bhupinder Singh is working as Professor at Sharda University, India. Also, Honorary Professor in University of South Wales UK and Santo Tomas University Tunja, Colombia. His areas of publications as Smart Healthcare, Medicines, fuzzy logics, artificial intelligence, robotics, machine learning, deep learning, federated learning, IoT, PV Glasses, metaverse and many more. He has 3 books, 139 paper publications, 163 paper presentations in international/national conferences and seminars, participated in more than 40 workshops/FDP's/QIP's, 25 courses from international universities of repute, organized more than 59 events with international and national academicians and industry people's, editor-in-chief and co-editor in journals, developed new courses. He has given talks at international universities, resource person in international conferences such as in Nanyang Technological University Singapore, Tashkent State University of Law Uzbekistan; KIMEP University Kazakhstan, All'ah meh Tabatabi University Iran, the Iranian Association of International Criminal law, Iran and Hague Center for International Law and Investment, The Netherlands, Northumbria University Newcastle UK.

Shalini Singh earned her Master's in Wine Tourism from the Rovira i Virgili University. She is an expert in wine tourism management, marketing, and communication. As a junior researcher, her main research interests are related to wine consumption and wine tourism.

Yavana Rani Subramanian has devoted her career to Research and Teaching. She also has a Master's degree in Structural Engineering. She is the University rank holder in MBA. She has 18 years of teaching experience. Dr. Rani has received Young Scientist Fellowship Award from Tamilnadu State Council for Science and Technology (TNSCST). She has completed her fellowship from Indian Institute of Science (IISc), Bangalore. She is the life time member in Indian Society for Technical Education (ISTE). Dr. Yavana Rani has done two research projects sponsored by Indian Council for Social Science and Research (ICSSR). She has published more than 10 research articles in Scopus indexed and Springer journals. She has presented papers in National and International conferences in India and abroad. She is the editor for many reputed journals. She has delivered key note address in countries like Egypt, Malaysia. Prof. Rani holds many administrative roles such as Dean Student Affairs, Director Coordination for various activities. She has been project Director for Entrepreneurship Cell (EDC) sponsored by Department of Science and Technology (DST). She also coordinated many programmes. Professor has got funding for conducting conferences, International visit from various funding agencies like DST and ICSSR.

Muhammad Usman Tariq has more than 16+ year's experience in industry and academia. He has authored more than 200+ research articles, 110+ case studies, 95+ book chapters and several books other than 4 patents. He is founder and CEO of The Case HQ, a unique repository for courses, narrative and video case studies. He has been working as a consultant and trainer for industries representing six sigma, quality, health and safety, environmental systems, project management, and information security standards. His work has encompassed sectors in aviation, manufacturing, food, hospitality, education, finance, research, software and transportation. He has diverse and significant experience working with accreditation agencies of ABET, ACBSP, AACSB, WASC, CAA, EFQM and NCEAC. Additionally, Dr. Tariq has operational experience in incubators, research labs, government research projects, private sector startups, program creation and management at various industrial and academic levels. He is Certified Higher Education Teacher from Harvard University, USA, Certified Online Educator from HMBSU, Certified Six Sigma Master Black Belt and has been awarded PFHEA, SMIEEE, and CMBE.

Ravi Thirumalaisamy is working as an Assistant Professor, Department of Business and Economics, Modern College of Business and Science. To his credit, he published more than 10 articles in Scopus indexed journals.

Anadi Trikha is currently working as an Assistant Professor and Course Coordinator at the Centre for Distance and Online Education, Manipal University Jaipur. Her area of specialization is Marketing. She has over 8 years of experience in academics and teaches subjects like Consumer Behaviour, Digital Marketing, Sales, and Brand Management.

Tuğçe Yetik is a student of Management and Psychology at Sabanci University. As a junior researcher, her main interests include corporate strategy and sustainability.

Index

Symbols

A

B

C

D

E

G

H

I

M

O

P

R

S

T

U

V

W

www.ingramcontent.com/pod-product-compliance
Lightning Source LLC
LaVergne TN
LVHW080344011026
849161LV00009B/2189
* 9 7 9 8 3 6 9 3 7 2 4 5 6 *